LEGAL PATH SERIES™

CONSTITUTIONAL LAW

Keyed To

Chemerinsky
2nd Edition

ALSO AVAILABLE IN THIS SERIES:

Civil Procedure keyed to: Friedenthal, 9th Ed
Contracts keyed to: Farnsworth, 6th Ed
Contracts keyed to: Fuller, 7th Ed
Criminal Law keyed to: Johnson, 7th Ed
Criminal Law keyed to: Kadish, 7th Ed
Criminal Law keyed to: Dressler, 3rd Ed
Criminal Procedure keyed to: Kamisar, 11th Ed
Criminal Procedure keyed to: Saltzburg, 7th Ed
Constitutional Law keyed to: Stone, 5th Ed
Constitutional Law keyed to: Sullivan, 15th Ed
Constitutional Law keyed to: Chemerinsky, 2nd Ed
Corporations keyed to: Hamilton, 9th Ed
Corporations keyed to: Eisenberg, 9th Ed
Evidence keyed to: Waltz & Park, 10th Ed
Evidence keyed to: Mueller & Kirkpatrick, 5th Ed
Property keyed to: Dukeminier, 5th Ed
Torts keyed to Epstein, 8th Ed
Torts keyed to Prosser, 11th Ed
Legal Path MBE Bar Review

LEGAL PATH SERIES™

CONSTITUTIONAL LAW

First Edition

Megan Connolly, Esq.

Albany Law School

Mclaren Legal Publishers LLC

New York

ISBN 0-9779855-1-2

Published by
Mclaren Legal Publishers LLC
136 West 21 Street, 8th Floor
New York, NY 10011

www.mclarenpublishing.com
Email: contact@mclarenpublishing.com

Printed in the United States of America

HOW TO USE THIS BOOK

This law school study aid is a "keyed" book. It summarizes all of the major cases in the text book to which it is linked and in the order those cases are presented. The cases are presented in the IRAC format (Issue, Rule, Analysis and Conclusion); and each case uses a text symbol preceding the Issue, Rule, Analysis and Conclusion of the case referenced. The material that follows provides additional detail.

"Repetition is the Mother of Learning"

Throughout each case, many of the key Black Letter law and/or Issues are repeated. You may see the same legal conclusion repeated in the Issue, Rule, Analysis and/or Conclusion. This was done intentionally. All too often, the most important concepts in law school are mentioned only once by a law professor in a lecture hall. However, more often than not, what is mentioned the least is what is tested the most. We feel the more you see (and read) exactly what is important, the more likely you will be to remember it. Recalling key legal points quickly is the key to the successful application of those same rules on an exam. This **is** the difference between an "A" and a "C" for the course.

"All of what you need, none of what you don't"

Our law school study guides give you exactly what you need to understand the key principles of the case, including the sometimes elusive Black Letter law. We are not a replacement for an in depth legal analysis of the subject matter covered; however, we do present what is absolutely critical in a very concise format.

"Do it right in the beginning; it'll be easier in the end"

You may notice that the issues for each case are very specific. They are presented to you as accurately as we can print them. However, be mindful that there may be slight variations in their interpretation from lecture hall to lecture hall. With that in mind, our experience has taught us that if you do the labor-intensive, hard work in the beginning of the course and parse out the specific issue(s), rule(s) and conclusion, the analysis will be easier to formulate and write. It is the analysis of a case that separates the A, B and C grades on an exam (trust me).

"Who's the Plaintiff, who's the Defendant?"

You may notice that in some cases, a case title lists the plaintiff v. defendant in one order but the facts list the parties in the reverse or may refer to the plaintiff/ defendant as the petitioner/ respondent/ appellant/ appellee. This is usually seen, for example, when one party is appealing to a higher court or where various counterclaims and cross-claims are asserted by the parties. When you see the parties change in the facts, keep the procedural history (and the parties) of the case organized in your mind and don't get confused.

Abbreviations used in this book

I This symbol "I" stands for "Issue" using the IRAC method of case analysis. What follows is the issue of the case.

R This symbol "R" stands for "Rule" using the IRAC method of case analysis. What follows is the rule or black letter law of the case.

A This symbol "A" stands for "Analysis" using the IRAC method of case analysis. What follows is the Analysis of the case.

C This symbol "C" stands for "Conclusion" using the IRAC method of case analysis. What follows is the conclusion of the case.

* Use of the word "his" in this book is gender neutral and is meant to encompass both "his" and "her."

ALPHABETICAL TABLE OF CASES

Marbury v. Madison

1 Cranch (5 U.S.) 137 (1803)

FACTS

Under the administrations of Washington and his successor, John Adams, only members of the ruling Federalist Party were appointed to the bench, and under the terms of the Constitution, they held office for life during "good behavior." Thus, when the opposing Republicans won the election of 1800 (Thomas Jefferson was now the incoming president) the "Jeffersonians" found that while they controlled the presidency and Congress, the Federalists still dominated the judiciary. One of the first acts of the new administration was to repeal the Judiciary Act of 1800, which had created a number of new judgeships. Although President Adams had attempted to fill the vacancies prior to the end of his term, a number of commissions had not been delivered, and one of the appointees, William Marbury, sued Secretary of State James Madison to force him to deliver his commission as a justice of the peace. The new chief justice, John Marshall, understood that if the Court awarded Marbury a writ of mandamus (an order to force Madison to deliver the commission) the Jefferson administration would ignore it, and thus significantly weaken the authority of the courts. On the other hand, if the Court denied the writ, it might well appear that the justices had acted out of fear. Either case would be a denial of the basic principle of the supremacy of the law.

I

(1) Does Marbury (P) have a right to the commission? (2) If he has a right, and that right has been violated, do the laws of his country afford him a remedy? (3) Is a writ of mandamus issued by the Supreme Court proper to that end?

R

When the U.S. Constitution conflicts with laws enacted by Congress, the U.S. Supreme Court may nullify such laws and declare them unconstitutional, as interpreted by the Court.

A

Plaintiff Marbury has a right to the commission. The discretion of the executive is to be exercised until the appointment has been made. But having once made the appointment, his power over the office is terminated in all cases, where, by law, the officer is not removable by him. The right to the office is then in the person appointed, and he has the absolute, unconditional, power of accepting or rejecting it. Mr. Marbury, then, since his commission was signed by the President, and sealed by the secretary of state, was appointed; and as the law creating the office, gave the officer a right to hold for five years, independent of the executive, the appointment was not revocable; but vested in the officer legal rights, which are protected by the laws of his country. To withhold his commission, therefore, is an act deemed by the court not warranted by law, but violative of a vested legal right. Since Plaintiff Marbury has a right to the commission, he has a legal remedy for a violation of that right. The very essence of civil liberty certainly consists in the right of every individual to claim the protection of the laws, whenever he receives an injury. One of the first duties of government is to afford that protection. The government of the United States has been emphatically termed a government of laws, and not of men. It will certainly cease to deserve this high appellation, if the laws furnish no remedy for the violation of a vested legal right. By the constitution of the United States, the President is invested with certain important political powers, in the exercise of which he is to use his own discretion, and is accountable only to his country in his political character, and to his own conscience. To aid him in the performance of these duties, he is authorized to appoint certain officers, who act by his authority and in conformity with his orders. But where a duty is assigned to the head of the department by the Legislature, and individual rights depend on performance of that duty, an individual who is injured has a right to a remedy. Turning to the last issue, we are called upon to decide whether the writ was a proper remedy for a violation of his right to the commission. The answer to this question depends on the nature of the writ and whether the Supreme Court has the power to issue, or deny, the writ in the first place. While the mandamus is a proper remedy in this case, it must be denied. The Secretary of State was directed by law to perform an act and the writ of mandamus is the only appropriate remedy for violation of these rights. The Supreme Court is vested with the power to issue writs of mandamus by the Judiciary Act of 1789. However, this statute conflicts with Article III of the Constitution, which does not grant original jurisdiction to the Supreme Court over cases involving executive officers. Where such a conflict exists, it is the duty of the judiciary to say what the law is; and if two laws conflict, the Court must decide the case such that it is in conformity with the Constitution. The Supremacy Clause of Article IV of the Constitution mentions the Constitution first and the laws of the land that are granted by Congress are made pursuant to it.

C Writ of mandamus denied.

United States v. Emerson

270 F.3d 203 (5th Cir. 2001), *cert. denied,* 536 U.S. 907 (2002)

FACTS

Defendant-appellee Dr. Timothy Joe Emerson was indicted for violating 18 U.S.C. §922(g)(8) which made it illegal for a person under a restraining order to possess a firearm. Defendant's wife served him with the restraining order during state divorce proceedings. To issue the order, the judge was not required to find that defendant had committed any wrongful act or was like to in the future. The judge issued the indictment but on appeal, the district court dismissed it. The United States thereafter appealed to the 5th Circuit.

I

Does the Second Amendment create a right for individuals to possess firearms?

R

A federal statute that made it illegal for a person to possess a firearm while under a state restraining order not based on particular findings violated the Second Amendment right of individuals to bear arms.

A

The Government steadfastly maintains that the Supreme Court's decision in *United States v. Miller* (1939) mandated acceptance of the collective rights models and rejection of the individual rights or standard model as a basis for the construction of the Second Amendment. We disagree. Only in *Miller* has the Supreme Court rendered any holding respecting the Second Amendment as applied to the federal government. We believe that the Court decided Miller on the basis of the government's argument that a "shotgun having a barrel of less than 18 inches in length" as stated in the National Firearms Act is not one of the "Arms" which the Second Amendment prohibits infringement of the right of the people to keep and bear – and NOT on the basis of the government's argument that the Second Amendment protect the right of the people to keep and bear no character of "arms" when not borne in actual, active service in the militia or some other military organization provided for y law. We conclude that *Miller* does not support the government's collective rights or sophisticated collective rights approach to the Second Amendment. We hold, consistent with Miller, that it protects the rights of individuals, including those not then actually a member of any militia or engaged in active military service. However, because of our holding that §922(g)(8), as applied to Emerson, does not infringe his individual rights under the Second Amendment we will not here further elaborate as to the exact scope of all Second Amendment rights. Although, as we have held, the Second Amendment DOES protect individual rights, that does not mean that those rights may never be made subject to any limited, narrowly-tailored specific exceptions or restrictions. For the reasons stated above, we reverse the district court's order granting the motion to dismiss the indictment under the Fifth Amendment.

C

District court's order granting the motion to dismiss is Reversed.

Silveira v. Lockyer

312 F.3d 1052 (9th Cir. 2002), cert. denied, 540 U.S. 1046 (2003)

FACTS

In 1999, the State of California enacted amendments to its gun control laws that significantly strengthened the state's restrictions on the possession, use and transportation of the semi-automatic weapons popularly known as "assault weapons." Plaintiffs, California residents who either own assault weapons, seek to acquire them or both, brought challenge to the gun control statute, asserting the law, as amended, violates the Second Amendment.

I Does the Second Amendment confer an individual right to own or possess arms such that California's gun control law is unconstitutional?

R The Second Amendment does not confer an individual right to own or possess arms such that California's gun control law is constitutional.

A Because the Second Amendment does not confer an individual right to own or possess arms, we affirm dismissal of all claims brought pursuant to constitutional provision. There are three principal schools of thought that form the basis for the debate. The first, which we will refer to as the "traditional individual rights" model, holds that the Second Amendment guarantees to individual private citizens a fundamental right to possess firearms for any purpose at all, subject only to limited governmental regulation. The second view, a variant of the first, we will refer to as the "limited individual rights" model. Under this view, individuals maintain a constitutional right to possess firearms insofar as such possession bears a reasonable relationship to militia service. The third, a wholly contrary view, commonly called the "collective rights" model, asserts that the Second Amendment right to "Bear Arms" guarantees the right of the people to maintain effective state militias, but does not provide any type of individual rights to own or possess weapons. Under this theory, federal and state governments have full authority to enact prohibitions and restrictions on the use and possession of firearms, subject only to generally applicable constitutional constraints, such as due process, equal protection and the like. This has long been the dominant view of the Second Amendment, and widely accepted by the federal courts. After conducting a full analysis of the Amendment, its history, and its purpose, we reaffirm that it is this collective rights model which provides the best interpretation of the Second Amendment.

C Affirmed.

Ex Parte McCardle

74 U.S. 506 (1868)

FACTS

Congress imposed military government on many former Confederate States under the post-Civil War Reconstruction Acts. Plaintiff William McCardle was arrested by federal authorities in 1867 for writing and publishing a series of editorials in his Mississippi newspaper. The editorials were sharply critical of Reconstruction. McCardle sought a writ of habeas corpus on the ground that the Reconstruction Acts under which he was arrested were unconstitutional. McCardle appealed to the Supreme Court under an 1867 Congressional statute that conferred jurisdiction on appeal to the High Court. After hearing arguments in the case, but prior to announcing a decision, the Congress withdrew its 1867 act conferring jurisdiction.

I

May the Congress withdraw appellate jurisdiction from the High Court after that jurisdiction has been given?

R

Congress may withdraw appellate jurisdiction from the Supreme Court even though such jurisdiction is derived from the Constitution and not from acts of Congress; nevertheless, jurisdiction is conferred "with such exceptions and under such regulations as Congress shall make."

A

Appellate jurisdiction for this Court is not derived from acts of Congress, but, strictly speaking, from the language of the Constitution. But it is conferred "with such exceptions and under such regulations as Congress shall make." On September 24, 1789, the first Congress acted in its first session to establish the judicial courts of the United States. Congressional withdrawal of the Court's jurisdiction is validated by the exceptions clause of Article III Section 2. However, the 1868 statute repealing jurisdiction "does not affect the jurisdiction which was previously exercised." The exception to the appellate case before us, however, is not an inference from the affirmation of other appellate jurisdiction. The provision of 1867 affirming the appellate jurisdiction in cases of habeas corpus is repealed. We cannot inquire into the motives of the Legislature. We only examine its power under the Constitution, and the power to make exceptions was expressly given. Without jurisdiction, the Court cannot proceed with in any cause nor pronounce judgment in this case.

C

Appeal dismissed for lack of jurisdiction.

United States v. Klein

80 U.S. 128 (1871)

FACTS

Congress passed a law in 1863 following the Civil War that allowed individuals to sue the federal government in the Court of Claims to recover property seized during the war. Proof that the claimant had not offered to give comfort to the emery was requires to prevail on such a suit. The U.S. Supreme Court rules that a Presidential pardon could be used as proof in these types of cases. Congress reacted by passing a bill which required that, absent an explicit statement of innocence, pardons would have the effect of proving the pardoned individual had aided the enemy. Plaintiff Klein sued for recovery of property seized during the war and won. The pardon in issue had been granted to an intestate to whom plaintiff was the heir with regard to the property in question. The case was appealed to the U.S. Supreme Court.

I Did Congress violate the separation of powers and usurp Constitutional authority when it enacted a law dismissing federal court jurisdiction on claims against the government?

R Congress violated the separation of powers and usurped Constitutional authority when it enacted a law rescinding the Supreme Court's appellate jurisdiction in claims supported by a presidential pardon on claims against the government.

A Congress' bill violates the separation of powers. The law exceeds congressional authority to create exceptions and regulations to the Supreme Court's appellate jurisdiction. Additionally, the law interferes with the Executive branch's power to pardon, a power granted without limit by the U.S. Constitution. If Congress had decided to deny appeals of all Court of Claims, it could have done so – here, however, the language of the statute shows that the intent of Congress was to nullify the effects of presidential pardons.

C See above.

Plaut v. Spendthrift Farm Inc.

514 U.S. 211 (1995)

FACTS

In a 1987 civil action, petitioners alleged that in 1983 and 1984 respondents committed fraud and deceit in the sale of stock in violation of 10(b) of the Securities Exchange Act of 1934 and Rule 10b-5 of the Securities and Exchange Commission. The District Court dismissed the action with prejudice following this Court's decision in *Lampf, Pleva, Lipkind, Prupis & Petigrow v. Gilbertson*, which required that suits such as petitioners' be commenced within one year after the discovery of the facts constituting the violation and within three years after such violation. After the judgment became final, Congress enacted 27A(b) of the 1934 Act, which provides for reinstatement on motion of any action commenced pre-*Lampf* but dismissed thereafter as time barred, if the action would have been timely filed under applicable pre-*Lampf* state law. Although finding that the statute's terms required that petitioners' ensuing 27A(b) motion be granted, the District Court denied the motion on the ground that 27A(b) is unconstitutional. The Court of Appeals affirmed.

I

Is the separation of powers doctrine violated by legislation that requires the federal courts to reopen cases upon which the courts have rendered a final decision?

R

The separation of powers doctrine is violated constitutionally by legislation that requires the federal courts to reopen cases upon which the courts have rendered a final decision.

A

Section 27A(b) contravenes the Constitution's separation of powers to the extent that it requires federal courts to reopen final judgments entered before its enactment. Despite respondents' arguments to the contrary, there is no reasonable construction on which 27A(b) does not require federal courts to reopen final judgments in suits dismissed with prejudice by virtue of *Lampf*. Article III establishes a "judicial department" with the "province and duty . . . to say what the law is" in particular cases and controversies. The Framers crafted this charter with an expressed understanding that it gives Page II the Federal Judiciary the power, not merely to rule on cases, but to decide them conclusively, subject to review only by superior courts in the Article III hierarchy. Thus, the Constitution forbids the Legislature to interfere with courts' final judgments. Section 27A(b) effects a clear violation of the foregoing principle by retroactively commanding the federal courts to reopen final judgments. This Court's decisions have uniformly provided fair warning that retroactive legislation such as 27A(b) exceeds congressional powers. Petitioners are correct that when a new law makes clear that it is retroactive, an appellate court must apply it in reviewing judgments still on appeal, and must alter the outcome accordingly. However, once a judgment has achieved finality in the highest court in the hierarchy, the decision becomes the last word of the judicial department with regard to the particular case or controversy, and Congress may not declare by retroactive legislation that the law applicable to that case was in fact something other than it was. It is irrelevant that 27A(b) reopens (or directs the reopening of) final judgments in a whole class of cases rather than in a particular suit, and that the final judgments so reopened rested on the bar of a statute of limitations rather than on some other ground. Apart from 27A(b), the Court knows of no instance in which Congress has attempted to set aside the final judgment of an Article III court by retroactive legislation. Congress's prolonged reticence would be amazing if such interference were not understood to be constitutionally proscribed by the Constitution's separation of powers. The Court rejects the suggestion that 27A(b) might be constitutional if it exhibited prospectivity or a greater degree of general applicability.

C Affirmed.

Allen v. Wright

468 U.S. 737 (1984)

FACTS

The Internal Revenue Service (IRS) denies tax-exempt status under the Internal Revenue Code - and hence eligibility to receive charitable contributions deductible from income taxes under the Code - to racially discriminatory private schools, and has established guidelines and procedures for determining whether a particular school is in fact racially nondiscriminatory. Respondents, parents of black children who were attending public schools in seven States in school districts undergoing desegregation, brought a nationwide class action in Federal District Court against petitioner Government officials (petitioner Allen, the head of a private school identified in the complaint, intervened as a defendant), alleging that the IRS has not adopted sufficient standards and procedures to fulfill its obligation to deny tax-exempt status to racially discriminatory private schools and has thereby harmed respondents directly and interfered with their children's opportunity to receive an education in desegregated public schools. Respondents also alleged that many racially segregated private schools were created or expanded in their communities at the time the public schools were undergoing desegregation, and had received tax exemptions despite the IRS policy and guidelines; and that these unlawful tax exemptions harmed respondents in that they constituted tangible financial aid for racially segregated educational institutions and encouraged the organization and expansion of institutions that provided segregated educational opportunities for white students avoiding attendance in the public schools. Respondents did not allege that their children had ever applied or would ever apply for admission to any private school. They sought declaratory and injunctive relief. The District Court dismissed the complaint on the ground that respondents lacked standing to bring the suit. The Court of Appeals reversed.

I

Does a plaintiff have standing to bring suit when he has not alleged personal injury?

R

Art. III doctrine of "standing" has a core constitutional component that a plaintiff must allege personal injury fairly traceable to the defendant's allegedly unlawful conduct and likely to be redressed by the requested relief.

A

Respondents do not have standing to bring this suit. The "case or controversy" requirement of Art. III of the Constitution defines with respect to the Judicial Branch the idea of separation of powers on which the Federal Government is founded, and the Art. III doctrine of "standing" has a core constitutional component that a plaintiff must allege personal injury fairly traceable to the defendant's allegedly unlawful conduct and likely to be redressed by the requested relief. The concepts of standing doctrine present questions that must be answered by reference to the Art. III notion that federal courts may exercise power only in the last resort and as a necessity, and only when adjudication is consistent with a system of separated powers and the dispute is one traditionally thought to be capable of resolution through the judicial process. Respondents' claim that they are harmed directly by the mere fact of Government financial aid to discriminatory private schools fails because it does not constitute judicially cognizable injury. Insofar as the claim may be interpreted as one simply to have the Government avoid the alleged violation of law in granting the tax exemptions, an asserted right to have the Government act in accordance with law is not sufficient, standing alone, to confer jurisdiction on a federal court. Nor do respondents have standing to litigate their claim based on the stigmatizing injury often caused by racial discrimination. Such injury accords a basis for standing only to those persons who are personally denied equal treatment by the challenged discriminatory conduct, and respondents do not allege a stigmatic injury suffered as a direct result of having personally been denied equal treatment. Respondents' claim of injury as to their children's diminished ability to receive an education in a racially integrated school because of the federal tax exemptions granted to some racially discriminatory private schools - though a judicially cognizable injury - fails because the alleged injury is not fairly traceable to the Government conduct that is challenged as unlawful. Respondents have not alleged that there were enough racially discriminatory private schools receiving tax exemptions in respondents' communities for withdrawal of those exemptions to make an appreciable difference in public school integration. Moreover, it is entirely speculative whether withdrawal of a particular school's tax exemption would lead the school to change its policies; whether any given parent of a child attending such a private school would decide to transfer the child to public school as a result of any changes in policy of a private school threatened with loss of tax-exempt status; or whether, in a particular community, a large enough number of school officials and parents would reach decisions that collectively would have a significant impact on the racial composition of the public schools. To recognize respondents' standing to seek a restructuring of the apparatus established by the Executive Branch to fulfill its legal duties would run afoul of the idea of separation of powers that underlies standing doctrine. The Constitution assigns to the Executive Branch, not to the Judicial Branch, the duty to take care that the laws be faithfully executed. None of the cases relied on by the Court of Appeals and by respondents to establish standing requires a finding of standing here.

C

Reversed.

Singleton v. Wulff

428 U.S. 106 (1976)

FACTS

Respondents, two Missouri-licensed physicians, brought this action for injunctive relief and a declaration of the unconstitutionality of a Missouri statute that excludes abortions that are not "medically indicated" from the purposes for which Medicaid benefits are available to needy persons. In response to petitioner's pre-answer motion to dismiss, each respondent averred that he had provided, and anticipated providing, abortions to needy patients, and that petitioner, the responsible state official, acting in reliance on the challenged statute, had refused all Medicaid applications filed in connection with such abortions. A three-judge District Court dismissed the relevant count of the complaint for lack of standing, having concluded that no logical nexus existed between the status asserted by respondents and the claim that they sought to have adjudicated. The Court of Appeals reversed, finding that respondents had alleged sufficient "injury in fact" and also an interest "arguably within the zone of interests to be protected" That court then considered the case on the merits and found a violation of the Equal Protection Clause.

I

Do doctors who performed abortions have standing to challenge a Medicaid statute that excludes abortions that are not "medically indicated" thus barring any compensation owed to the physicians for such procedures?

R

Persons have standing and may invoke a third party's right(s) only when the relationship between the parties is such that the person suing may advocate effectively for the right and there are no genuine obstacles to the third party asserting the right in court.

A

Respondents had standing to maintain this suit. Respondents alleged "injury in fact," - a sufficiently concrete interest in the outcome of their suit to make it a case or controversy subject to the District Court's Art. III jurisdiction. If respondent physicians prevail in their suit to remove the statutory limitation on reimbursable abortions, they will benefit by receiving payment for the abortions and the State will be out of pocket by the amount of the payments. The Court of Appeals should not have proceeded to resolve the merits of this case, since petitioner, who has not filed an answer or other pleading addressed to the merits, has not had the opportunity to present evidence or legal arguments in defense of the statute. As a prudential matter, respondents are proper proponents of the particular rights on which they base their suit. A woman cannot safely secure an abortion without a physician's aid, and an impecunious woman cannot easily secure an abortion without the physician being paid by the State. Aside from the woman herself, the physician is uniquely qualified, by virtue of his confidential, professional relationship with her, to litigate the constitutionality of the State's interference with, or discrimination against, the abortion decision. Moreover, there are obstacles to the woman's assertion of her own rights, in that the desire to protect her privacy may deter her from herself bringing suit, and her claim will soon become at least technically moot if she is forced to forgo the abortion.

C

Reversed and remanded.

Elk Grove Unified School Dist. v. Newdow

124 S. Ct. 2301 (2004)

FACTS

Petitioner school district requires each elementary school class to recite daily the Pledge of Allegiance. Respondent Newdow's daughter participates in this exercise. Newdow, an atheist, filed suit alleging that, because the Pledge contains the words "under God," it constitutes religious indoctrination of his child in violation of the Establishment and Free Exercise Clauses. He also alleged that he had standing to sue on his own behalf and on behalf of his daughter as "next friend." The Magistrate Judge concluded that the Pledge is constitutional, and the District Court agreed and dismissed the complaint. The Ninth Circuit reversed, holding that Newdow has standing as a parent to challenge a practice that interferes with his right to direct his daughter's religious education, and that the school district's policy violates the Establishment Clause. Sandra Banning, the child's mother, then filed a motion to intervene or dismiss, declaring, *inter alia*, that she had exclusive legal custody under a state-court order and that, as her daughter's sole legal custodian, she felt it was not in the child's interest to be a party to Newdow's suit. Concluding that Banning's sole legal custody did not deprive Newdow, as a non-custodial parent, of Article III standing to object to unconstitutional government action affecting his child, the Ninth Circuit held that, under California law, Newdow retains the right to expose his child to his particular religious views even if they contradict her mother's, as well as the right to seek redress for an alleged injury to his own parental interests.

I Can a non-custodial parent sue on behalf of his daughter as "next fiend" to challenge the recitation of the daily the Pledge of Allegiance as constituting religious indoctrination in violation of the Establishment and Free Exercise Clauses because the Pledge contains the words "under God?"

R A non-custodial parent can not sue on behalf of his daughter as "next fiend" when a state law defines the non-custodial parent's rights and relationship to his child in such as way as to limit them thus depriving the litigant of the status necessary to confer standing.

A Because California law deprives Newdow of the right to sue as next friend, he lacks prudential standing to challenge the school district's policy in federal court. The standing requirement derives from the constitutional and prudential limits to the powers of an unelected, unrepresentative judiciary. The Court's prudential standing jurisprudence encompasses, *inter alia*, "the general prohibition on a litigant's raising another person's legal rights," and the Court generally declines to intervene in domestic relations, a traditional subject of state law. The extent of the standing problem raised by the domestic relations issues in this case was not apparent until Banning filed her motion to intervene or dismiss, declaring that the family court order gave her "*sole* legal custody" and authorized her to "exercise legal control " over her daughter. Newdow's argument that he nevertheless retains an unrestricted right to inculcate in his daughter his beliefs fails because his rights cannot be viewed in isolation. This case also concerns Banning's rights under the custody orders and, most important, their daughter's interests upon finding herself at the center of a highly public debate. Newdow's standing derives entirely from his relationship with his daughter, but he lacks the right to litigate as her next friend. Their interests are not parallel and, indeed, are potentially in conflict. Newdow's parental status is defined by state law, and this Court customarily defers to the state-law interpretations of the regional federal court. Here, the Ninth Circuit relied on intermediate state appellate cases recognizing the right of each parent, whether custodial or non-custodial, to impart to the child his or her religious perspective. Nothing that Banning or the school board has done, however, impairs Newdow's right to instruct his daughter in his religious views. Instead, he requests the more ambitious relief of forestalling his daughter's exposure to religious ideas endorsed by her mother, who wields a form of veto power, and to use his parental status to challenge the influences to which his daughter may be exposed in school when he and Banning disagree. The California cases simply do not stand for the proposition that Newdow has a right to reach outside the private parent-child sphere to dictate to others what they may and may not say to his child respecting religion. A next friend surely could exercise such a right, but the family court's order has deprived Newdow of that status.

C

Reversed.

United States v. Richardson

418 U.S. 166 (1974)

FACTS

Respondent, as a federal taxpayer, brought this suit for the purpose of obtaining a declaration of unconstitutionality of the Central Intelligence Agency Act, which permits the CIA to account for its expenditures "solely on the certificate of the Director . . ." 50 U.S.C. 403j (b). The complaint alleged that the Act violated Art. I, 9, cl. 7, of the Constitution insofar as that clause requires a regular statement and account of public funds. The District Court's dismissal of the complaint for, inter alia, respondent's lack of standing under *Flast v. Cohen*, was reversed by the Court of Appeals. That court held that respondent had standing as a taxpayer on the ground that he satisfied *Flast's* requirements that the allegations (1) challenge an enactment under the Taxing and Spending Clause of Art I, 8, and show (2) a "nexus" between the plaintiff's status and a specific constitutional limitation on the taxing and spending power.

I

Does an individual's status as a taxpayer give him standing to challenge the constitutionality of a statute regulating the CIA's financial accounting and reporting?

R

An individual's status as a taxpayer alone, without more, does NOT give him standing to challenge the constitutionality of a statute regulating the CIA's financial accounting and reporting.

A

Respondent lacks standing to maintain this suit. *Flast*, which stressed the need for meeting the requirements of Art. III, did not "undermine the salutary principle . . . established by *Frothingham* [*v. Mellon*] . . . that a taxpayer may not `employ a federal court as a forum in which to air his generalized grievances about the conduct of government or the allocation of power in the Federal System.'" Respondent's challenge, not being addressed to the taxing or spending power but to the statutes regulating the CIA's accounting and reporting procedures, provides no "logical nexus" between his status as "taxpayer" and the asserted failure of Congress to require more detailed reports of expenditures of the CIA. Respondent's claim that without detailed information on the CIA's expenditures he cannot properly follow legislative or executive action and thereby fulfill his obligations as a voter is a generalized grievance insufficient under *Frothingham* or *Flast* to show that "he has sustained or is immediately in danger of sustaining a direct injury as the result" of such action.

C

Reversed.

Flast v. Cohen

392 U.S. 83 (1968)

FACTS

Appellant taxpayers allege that federal funds have been disbursed by appellee federal officials under the Elementary and Secondary Education Act of 1965 to finance instruction and the purchase of educational materials for use in religious and sectarian schools, in violation of the Establishment and Free Exercise Clauses of the First Amendment. Appellants sought a declaration that the expenditures were not authorized by the Act or, in the alternative, that the Act is to that extent unconstitutional, and requested the convening of a three-judge court. A three-judge court ruled, on the authority of *Frothingham v. Mellon*, that appellants lacked standing to maintain the action.

I

Does taxpayer status confer standing to challenge congressional expenditures in violation of the First Amendment Establishment and Free Exercise clauses?

R

An individual's status as a taxpayer is sufficient to confer standing to challenge congressional expenditures in violation of the First Amendment Establishment and Free Exercise clauses.

A

The three-judge court was properly convened, as the constitutional attack, even though focused on the program's operations in New York City, would if successful affect the entire regulatory scheme of the statute, and the complaint alleged a constitutional ground for relief, albeit one coupled with an alternative non-constitutional ground. There is no absolute bar in Art. III of the Constitution to suits by federal taxpayers challenging allegedly unconstitutional federal taxing and spending programs since the taxpayers may or may not have the requisite personal stake in the outcome. To maintain an action challenging the constitutionality of a federal spending program, individuals must demonstrate the necessary stake as taxpayers in the outcome of the litigation to satisfy Art. III requirements. Taxpayers must establish a logical link between that status and the type of legislative enactment attacked, as it will not be sufficient to allege an incidental expenditure of tax funds in the administration of an essentially regulatory statute. Taxpayers must also establish a nexus between that status and the precise nature of the constitutional infringement alleged. They must show that the statute exceeds specific constitutional limitations on the exercise of the taxing and spending power and not simply that the enactment is generally beyond the powers delegated to Congress by Art. I, 8. The taxpayer-appellants here have standing consistent with Art. III to invoke federal judicial power since they have alleged that tax money is being spent in violation of a specific constitutional protection against the abuse of legislative power, i. e., the Establishment Clause of the First Amendment.

C

Reversed.

Valley Forge Christian College v. Americans United for Separation of Church and State Inc., et al.

454 U.S. 464 (1982)

FACTS

Pursuant to its authority under the Property Clause, Congress enacted the Federal Property and Administrative Services Act of 1949 to provide an economical and efficient system for the disposal of surplus Federal Government property. Under the statute, property that has outlived its usefulness to the Government is declared "surplus" and may be transferred to private or other public entities. The Act authorizes the Secretary of Health, Education, and Welfare (HEW) (now the Secretary of Education) to assume responsibility for disposing of surplus real property for educational use, and he may sell such property to nonprofit, tax-exempt educational institutions for consideration that takes into account any benefit which has accrued or may accrue to the United States from the transferee's use of the property. Property formerly used as a military hospital was declared to be "surplus property" under the Act and was conveyed by the Department of HEW to petitioner church-related college. The appraised value of the property, $577,500, was discounted by the Secretary of HEW's computation of a 100% public benefit allowance, thus permitting petitioner to acquire the property without making any financial payment. Respondents, an organization dedicated to the separation of church and State and several of its employees, brought suit in Federal District Court, challenging the conveyance on the ground that it violated the Establishment Clause of the First Amendment, and alleging that each member of respondent organization "would be deprived of the fair and constitutional use of his (her) tax dollars." The District Court dismissed the complaint on the ground that respondents lacked standing to sue as taxpayers under *Flast v. Cohen*, and failed to allege any actual injury beyond a generalized grievance common to all taxpayers. The Court of Appeals reversed, holding that although respondents lacked standing as taxpayers to challenge the conveyance, they had standing merely as "citizens," claiming "`injury in fact' to their shared individuated right to a government that `shall make no law respecting the establishment of religion,'" which standing was sufficient to satisfy the "case or controversy" requirement of Art. III.

I

Does status as a taxpayer(s) confer standing to challenge to bring suit in federal court alleging that a transfer of surplus government real property to religious college violated the Establishment Clause?

R

Taxpayer status does not confer standing to challenge to bring suit in federal court alleging that a transfer of surplus government real property to religious college violated the Establishment Clause.

A

Respondents do not have standing, either in their capacity as taxpayers or as citizens, to challenge the conveyance in question. The exercise of judicial power under Art. III is restricted to litigants who can show "injury in fact" resulting from the action that they seek to have the court adjudicate. Respondents are without standing to sue as taxpayers, because the source of their complaint is not a congressional action but a decision by HEW to transfer a parcel of federal property and because the conveyance in question was not an exercise of Congress' authority conferred by the Taxing and Spending Clause but by the Property Clause. or have respondents sufficiently alleged any other basis for standing to bring suit. Although they claim that the Constitution has been violated, they claim nothing else. They fail to identify any personal injury suffered as a consequence of the alleged constitutional error, other than the psychological consequence presumably produced by observation of conduct with which one disagrees. That is not injury sufficient to confer standing under Art. III. While respondents are firmly committed to the constitutional principle of separation of church and State, standing is not measured by the intensity of the litigant's interest or the fervor of his advocacy. Enforcement of the Establishment Clause does not justify special exceptions from the standing requirements of Art. III. There is no place in our constitutional scheme for the philosophy that the business of the federal courts is correcting constitutional errors and that "cases and controversies" are at best merely convenient vehicles for doing so and at worst nuisances that may be dispensed with when they become obstacles to that transcendent endeavor. And such philosophy does not become more palatable when the underlying merits concern the Establishment Clause.

C

Reversed.

Poe v. Ullamn

367 U.S. 497 (1961)

FACTS

These are appeals from a decision of the Supreme Court of Errors of Connecticut affirming dismissals of complaints in three cases in which the plaintiffs sued for declaratory judgments that certain Connecticut statutes which prohibit the use of contraceptive devices and the giving of medical advice on their use violate the Fourteenth Amendment by depriving the plaintiffs of life and property without due process of law. The complaints alleged that two plaintiffs who were married women needed medical advice on the use of such devices for the protection of their health but that a physician, who was the plaintiff in the third case, was deterred from giving such advice because the State's Attorney intended to prosecute offenses against the State's laws and he claimed that the giving of such advice and the use of such devices were forbidden by state statutes. However, it appeared that the statutes in question had been enacted in 1879 and that no one ever had been prosecuted thereunder except two doctors and a nurse, who were charged with operating a birth-control clinic, and that the information against them had been dismissed after the State Supreme Court had sustained the legislation in 1940 on an appeal from a demurrer to the information.

I

Does a declaratory judgment in a state court make the issue of a state criminal statute's constitutionality ripe for federal court determination when the individuals in question have not been prosecuted under the statute?

R

The declaratory judgment of a state court upholding a statute on the books does not make the issue of a state criminal statute's constitutionality ripe for federal court determination when the individuals in question have not been prosecuted under the statute.

A

The appeals are dismissed, because the records in these cases do not present controversies justifying the adjudication of a constitutional issue. These appeals challenge the constitutionality, under the Fourteenth Amendment, of Connecticut statutes which, as authoritatively construed by the Connecticut Supreme Court of Errors, prohibit the use of contraceptive devices and the giving of medical advice in the use of such devices. In proceedings seeking declarations of law, not on review of convictions for violation of the statutes, that court has ruled that these statutes would be applicable in the case of married couples and even under claim that conception would constitute a serious threat to the health or life of the female spouse. Appellants' complaints in these declaratory judgment proceedings do not clearly, and certainly do not in terms, allege that appellee Ullman threatens to prosecute them for use of, or for giving advice concerning, contraceptive devices. The allegations are merely that, in the course of his public duty, he intends to prosecute any offenses against Connecticut law, and that he claims that use of and advice concerning contraceptives would constitute offenses. The lack of immediacy of the threat described by these allegations might alone raise serious questions of non-justiciability of appellants' claims. But even were we to read the allegations to convey a clear threat of imminent prosecutions, we are not bound to accept as true all that is alleged on the face of the complaint and admitted, technically, by demurrer, any more than the Court is bound by stipulation of the parties. Formal agreement between parties that collides with plausibility is too fragile a foundation for indulging in constitutional adjudication. Justiciability is of course not a legal concept with a fixed content or susceptible of scientific verification. Its utilization is the resultant of many subtle pressures, including the appropriateness of the issues for decision by this Court and the actual hardship to the litigants of denying them the relief sought. Both these factors justify withholding adjudication of the constitutional issue raised under the circumstances and in the manner in which they are now before the Court.

C Dismissed.

Abbott Laboratories v. Gardner

387 U.S. 136 (1967)

FACTS

The Commissioner of Food and Drugs, exercising authority delegated to him by the Secretary of Health, Education, and Welfare, issued regulations requiring that labels and advertisements for prescription drugs which bear proprietary names for the drugs or the ingredients carry the corresponding "established name" (designated by the Secretary) every time the proprietary or trade name is used. These regulations were designed to implement the 1962 amendment to 502(e)(1)(B) of the Federal Food, Drug, and Cosmetic Act. Petitioners, drug manufacturers and a manufacturers' association, challenged the regulations on the ground that the Commissioner exceeded his authority under the statute. The District Court granted the declaratory and injunctive relief sought, finding that the scope of the statute was not as broad as that of the regulations. The Court of Appeals reversed without reaching the merits, holding that pre-enforcement review of the regulations was unauthorized and beyond the jurisdiction of the District Court, and that no "actual case or controversy" existed.

I

Is a case ripe for federal court determination prior to an enforcement action when it presents legal issues and the parties may suffer injury if the court fails to hear the case?

R

A case is considered "ripe" for federal court resolution when the issues presented are appropriate for a judicial decision and the parties would face hardship if the court declined to hear the action.

A

Pre-enforcement review of these regulations is not prohibited by the Federal Food, Drug, and Cosmetic Act. The courts should restrict access to judicial review only upon a showing of "clear and convincing evidence" of a contrary legislative intent. The statutory scheme in the food and drug area does not exclude pre-enforcement judicial review. The special-review provisions of 701(f) of the Act, applying to regulations embodying technical factual determinations, were simply intended to assure adequate judicial review of such agency decisions and manifest no congressional purpose to eliminate review of other kinds of agency action. The saving clause of 701(f)(6) which states that the "remedies provided for in this subsection shall be in addition to and not in substitution for any other remedies provided by law," does not foreclose pre-enforcement judicial review and should be read in harmony with the policy favoring judicial review expressed in the Administrative Procedure Act and court decisions. This case presents a controversy "ripe" for judicial resolution. The issue of statutory construction is purely legal, and the regulations are "final agency action" within 10 of the Administrative Procedure Act. The impact of the regulations upon petitioners is sufficiently direct and immediate as to render the issue appropriate for judicial review. Here, the pre-enforcement challenge is not calculated to delay or impede effective enforcement of the Act.

C

Reversed and remanded.

Friends of the Earth Inc. v. Laidlaw Environ. Services

528 U.S. 167 (2000)

FACTS

Defendant-respondent Laidlaw Environmental Services (TOC), Inc., bought a facility in Roebuck, South Carolina, that included a wastewater treatment plant. Shortly thereafter, the South Carolina Department of Health and Environmental Control (DHEC), acting under the Clean Water Act (Act), 33 U. S. C. §1342(a)(1), granted Laidlaw a National Pollutant Discharge Elimination System (NPDES) permit. The permit authorized Laidlaw to discharge treated water into the North Tyger River, but limited, among other things, the discharge of pollutants into the waterway. Laidlaw began to discharge various pollutants into the waterway; these discharges, particularly of mercury, an extremely toxic pollutant, repeatedly exceeded the limits set by the permit. On April 10, 1992, plaintiff-petitioners Friends of the Earth and Citizens Local Environmental Action Network, Inc. (referred to collectively here, along with later joined plaintiff-petitioner Sierra Club, as "FOE"), notified Laidlaw of their intention to file a citizen suit against it under the Act, 33 U. S. C. §1365(a), after the expiration of the requisite 60-day notice period. DHEC acceded to Laidlaw's request to file a lawsuit against the company. On the last day before FOE's 60-day notice period expired, DHEC and Laidlaw reached a settlement requiring Laidlaw to pay $100,000 in civil penalties and to make "every effort" to comply with its permit obligations. On June 12, 1992, FOE filed this citizen suit against Laidlaw, alleging noncompliance with the NPDES permit and seeking declaratory and injunctive relief and an award of civil penalties. Laidlaw moved for summary judgment on the ground that FOE lacked Article III standing to bring the lawsuit. After examining affidavits and deposition testimony from members of the plaintiff organizations, the District Court denied the motion, finding that the plaintiffs had standing. The District Court also denied Laidlaw's motion to dismiss on the ground that the citizen suit was barred under §1365(b)(1)(B) by DHEC's prior action against the company. After FOE initiated this suit, but before the District Court rendered judgment on January 22, 1997, Laidlaw violated the mercury discharge limitation in its permit 13 times and committed 13 monitoring and 10 reporting violations. In issuing its judgment, the District Court found that Laidlaw had gained a total economic benefit of $1,092,581 as a result of its extended period of noncompliance with the permit's mercury discharge limit; nevertheless, the court concluded that a civil penalty of $405,800 was appropriate. In particular, the District Court found that the judgment's "total deterrent effect" would be adequate to forestall future violations, given that Laidlaw would have to reimburse the plaintiffs for a significant amount of legal fees and had itself incurred significant legal expenses. The court declined to order injunctive relief because Laidlaw, after the lawsuit began, had achieved substantial compliance with the terms of its permit. FOE appealed as to the amount of the District Court's civil penalty judgment, but did not appeal the denial of declaratory or injunctive relief. The Fourth Circuit vacated the District Court's order and remanded with instructions to dismiss the action. Assuming, *arguendo*, that FOE initially had standing, the appellate court held that the case had become moot once Laidlaw complied with the terms of its permit and the plaintiffs failed to appeal the denial of equitable relief. The court reasoned that the only remedy currently available to FOE, civil penalties payable to the Government, would not redress any injury.

I Does the defendant's voluntary compliance and plant closure make moot a citizen suit alleging violations of the Clean Water Act?

Friends of the Earth Inc. v. Laidlaw Environ. Services

528 U.S. 167 (2000)

R

The defendant's voluntary compliance and plant closure does not make moot a citizen suit alleging violations of the defendant's NPDES permit.

A

The Fourth Circuit erred in concluding that a citizen suitor's claim for civil penalties must be dismissed as moot when the defendant, after commencement of the litigation, has come into compliance with its NPDES permit. The Constitution's case-or-controversy limitation on federal judicial authority, Art. III, §2, underpins both standing and mootness doctrine, but the two inquiries differ in crucial respects. Because the Fourth Circuit was persuaded that the case had become moot, it simply assumed that FOE had initial standing. But because this Court concludes that the Court of Appeals erred as to mootness, this Court has an obligation to assure itself that FOE had Article III standing at the outset of the litigation. FOE had Article III standing to bring this action. This Court has held that to satisfy Article III's standing requirements, a plaintiff must show "injury in fact," causation, and redressability. An association has standing to bring suit on behalf of its members when its members would have standing to sue in their own right, the interests at stake are germane to the organization's purpose, and neither the claim asserted nor the relief requested requires individual members' participation in the lawsuit. The relevant showing for Article III standing is not injury to the environment but injury to the plaintiff. To insist on the former rather than the latter is to raise the standing hurdle higher than the necessary showing for success on the merits in a citizen's NPDES permit enforcement suit. Here, injury in fact was adequately documented by the affidavits and testimony of FOE members asserting that Laidlaw's pollutant discharges, and the affiants' reasonable concerns about the effects of those discharges, directly affected those affiants' recreational, aesthetic, and economic interests. These submissions present dispositively more than the mere "general averments" and "conclusory allegations" found inadequate in *Lujan* v. *National Wildlife Federation.*

C

Reversed and remanded.

Baker v. Carr

369 U.S. 186 (1962)

FACTS

Plaintiff-appellants are persons allegedly qualified to vote for members of the General Assembly of Tennessee representing the counties in which they reside. They brought suit in a Federal District Court in Tennessee under 42 U.S.C. 1983, on behalf of themselves and others similarly situated, to redress the alleged deprivation of their federal constitutional rights by legislation classifying voters with respect to representation in the General Assembly. They alleged that, by means of a 1901 statute of Tennessee arbitrarily and capriciously apportioning the seats in the General Assembly among the State's 95 counties, and a failure to reapportion them subsequently notwithstanding substantial growth and redistribution of the State's population, they suffer a "debasement of their votes" and were thereby denied the equal protection of the laws guaranteed them by the Fourteenth Amendment. They sought, *inter alia*, a declaratory judgment that the 1901 statute is unconstitutional and an injunction restraining certain state officers from conducting any further elections under it. The District Court dismissed the complaint on the grounds that it lacked jurisdiction of the subject matter and that no claim was stated upon which relief could be granted.

I

Does an equal protection claim alleging a misrepresentation of a state assembly constitute a nonjusticiable political question, precluding redress by the federal courts?

R

The Guaranty Clause may not be used to invalidate a state action, but an equal protection claim may be used where it does not implicate a political question.

A

The District Court had jurisdiction of the subject matter of the federal constitutional claim asserted in the complaint. Appellants had standing to maintain this suit. The complaint's allegations of a denial of equal protection presented a justiciable constitutional cause of action upon which appellants are entitled to a trial and a decision. The District Court was uncertain whether our cases withholding federal judicial relief rested upon a lack of federal jurisdiction or upon the inappropriateness of the subject matter for judicial consideration - what we have designated "nonjusticiability." The distinction between the two grounds is significant. In the instance of nonjusticiability, consideration of the cause is not wholly and immediately foreclosed; rather, the Court's inquiry necessarily proceeds to the point of deciding whether the duty asserted can be judicially identified and its breach judicially determined, and whether protection for the right asserted can be judicially molded. In the instance of lack of jurisdiction the cause either does not "arise under" the Federal Constitution, laws or treaties (or fall within one of the other enumerated categories of Art. III, 2), or is not a "case or controversy" within the meaning of that section; or the cause is not one described by any jurisdictional statute. Our conclusion that this cause presents no nonjusticiable "political question" settles the only possible doubt that it is a case or controversy. Under the present heading of "Jurisdiction of the Subject Matter" we hold only that the matter set forth in the complaint does arise under the Constitution and is within 28 U.S.C. 1343. Article III, 2, of the Federal Constitution provides that "The judicial Power shall extend to all Cases, in Law and Equity, arising under this Constitution, the Laws of the United States, and Treaties made, or which shall be made, under their Authority . . ." It is clear that the cause of action is one which "arises under" the Federal Constitution. Since the complaint plainly sets forth a case arising under the Constitution, the subject matter is within the federal judicial power defined in Art. III, sec. 2, and so within the power of Congress to assign to the jurisdiction of the District Courts. Congress has exercised that power in 28 U.S.C. 1343(3). We hold that the District Court has jurisdiction of the subject matter of the federal constitutional claim asserted in the complaint. With regard to the issue of standing we hold that a federal court cannot "pronounce any statute, either of a State or of the United States, void, because irreconcilable with the Constitution, except as it is called upon to adjudge the legal rights of litigants in actual controversies." Have the appellants alleged such a personal stake in the outcome of the controversy as to assure that concrete adverseness which sharpens the presentation of issues upon which the court so largely depends for illumination of difficult constitutional questions? This is the gist of the question of standing. It is, of course, a question of federal law. We hold that the appellants do have standing to maintain this suit. Our decisions plainly support this conclusion. It would not be necessary to decide whether appellants' allegations of impairment of their votes by the 1901 apportionment will, ultimately, entitle them to any relief, in order to hold that they have standing to seek it. If such impairment does produce a legally cognizable injury, they are among those who have sustained it. They are entitled to a hearing and to the District Court's decision on their claims. "The very essence of civil liberty certainly consists in the right of every individual to claim the protection of the laws, whenever he receives an injury." *Marbury v. Madison.* Turning to the issue of justiciability, we find the district court's decision was erroneous. In holding that the subject matter of this suit was not justiciable, the District Court relied on *Colegrove v. Green* and subsequent cases. We understand the District Court to have read the cited cases as compelling the conclusion that since the appellants sought to have a legislative apportionment held unconstitutional, their suit presented a "political question" and was therefore nonjusticiable. We hold that this challenge to an apportionment presents no nonjusticiable "political question." The cited cases do not hold the contrary. Of course the mere fact that the suit seeks protection of a political right does not mean it presents a political question. We hold that the claim pleaded here neither rests upon nor implicates the Guaranty Clause and that its justiciability is therefore not foreclosed by our decisions of cases involving that clause. The District Court misinterpreted *Colegrove v. Green* and other decisions of this Court on which it relied. Appellants' claim that they are being denied equal protection is justiciable, and if "discrimination is sufficiently shown, the right to relief under the equal protection clause is not diminished by the fact that the discrimination relates to political rights." But just because a Guaranty Clause approach could not have succeeded does not mean that the voters cannot have their case heard on the equal protection claim.

C

Reversed and remanded.

Vieth v. Jubelirer

541 U.S. 267 (2004)

FACTS

After Pennsylvania's General Assembly adopted a congressional redistricting plan, plaintiffs-appellants sued to enjoin the plan's implementation, alleging, *inter alia,* that it constituted a political gerrymander in violation of Article I and the Fourteenth Amendment's Equal Protection Clause. The three-judge District Court dismissed the gerrymandering claim, and the plaintiffs appealed.

I

Are political gerrymandering claims justiciable?

R

Political gerrymandering claims are nonjusticiable because no judicially discernible and manageable standards for adjudicating such claims exist.

A

Justice *Scalia*, joined by *The Chief Justice*, *Justice O'Connor,* and *Justice Thomas,* concluded that political gerrymandering claims are nonjusticiable because no judicially discernible and manageable standards for adjudicating such claims exist. They would therefore overrule *Davis* v. *Bandemer,* in which this Court held that political gerrymandering claims are justiciable, but could not agree upon a standard for assessing political gerrymandering claims. Political gerrymanders existed in colonial times and continued through the framing. The Framers provided a remedy for the problem: the Constitution gives state legislatures the initial power to draw federal-election districts, but authorizes Congress to "make or alter" those districts. U. S. Const., Art. I, §4. In *Bandemer,* the Court held that the Equal Protection Clause also grants judges the power--and duty--to control that practice. Neither Art. I, §2 or §4, nor the Equal Protection Clause, provides a judicially enforceable limit on the political considerations that the States and Congress may take into account when districting. Among the tests for determining the existence of a "nonjusticiable" or "political" question is a lack of judicially discoverable and manageable standards for resolving the question. Because the *Bandemer* Court was "not persuaded" that there are no such standards for deciding political gerrymandering cases, such cases *were* justiciable. However, the six-Justice majority in *Bandemer* could not discern what the standards might be. For the past 18 years, the lower courts have simply applied the *Bandemer* plurality's standard, almost invariably producing the same result as would have obtained had the question been nonjusticiable: judicial intervention has been refused. Eighteen years of judicial effort with virtually nothing to show for it justifies revisiting whether the standard promised by *Bandemer* exists. The *Bandemer* plurality's standard - that a political gerrymandering claim can succeed only where the plaintiffs show "both intentional discrimination against an identifiable political group and an actual discriminatory effect on that group," - has proved unmanageable in application. Because that standard was misguided when proposed, has not been improved in subsequent application, and is not even defended by the appellants in this Court, it should not be affirmed as a constitutional requirement. Appellants' proposed two-pronged standard based on Art. I, §2, and the Equal Protection Clause is neither discernible nor manageable. Appellants are mistaken when they contend that their intent prong ("predominant intent") is no different from that which this Court has applied in racial gerrymandering cases. In those cases, the predominant intent test is applied to the challenged district in which the plaintiffs voted, whereas here appellants assert that their test is satisfied only when partisan advantage was the predominant motivation *behind the entire statewide plan.* Vague as a predominant-motivation test might be when used to evaluate single districts, it all but evaporates when applied statewide. For this and other reasons, the racial gerrymandering cases provide no comfort. The effects prong of appellants' proposal requires (1) that the plaintiffs show that the rival party's voters are systematically "packed" or "cracked"; and (2) that the court be persuaded from the totality of the circumstances that the map can thwart the plaintiffs' ability to translate a majority of votes into a majority of seats. This standard is not discernible because the Constitution provides no right to proportional representation. Even if the standard was discernible, it is not judicially manageable. There is no effective way to ascertain a party's majority status, and, in any event, majority status in statewide races does not establish majority status for particular district contests. Moreover, even if a majority party could be identified, it would be impossible to assure that it won a majority of seats unless the States' traditional election structures were radically revised. For many of the same reasons, Justice Powell's *Bandemer* standard - a totality-of-the-circumstances analysis that evaluates districts with an eye to ascertaining whether the particular gerrymander is not "fair" - must also be rejected. "Fairness" is not a judicially manageable standard. Some criterion more solid and more demonstrably met than that is necessary to enable state legislatures to discern the limits of their districting discretion, to meaningfully constrain the courts' discretion, and to win public acceptance for the courts' intrusion into a process that is the very foundation of democratic decisionmaking. Writing separately in dissent, *Justices Stevens, Souter,* and *Breyer* each propose a different standard for adjudicating political gerrymandering claims. These proposed standards each have their own deficiencies, but additionally fail for reasons identified with respect to the standards proposed by appellants and those proposed in *Bandemer*. *Justice Kennedy* concurs in the judgment, recognizing that there are no existing manageable standards for measuring whether a political gerrymander burdens the representational rights of a party's voters. *Justice Kennedy,* while agreeing that appellants' complaint must be dismissed, concluded that all possibility of judicial relief should not be foreclosed in cases such as this because a limited and precise rationale may yet be found to correct an established constitutional violation.

C

The judgment is affirmed.

Powell v. McCormack

395 U.S. 486 (1969)

FACTS

Petitioner Powell, who had been duly elected to serve in the House of Representatives for the 90th Congress, was denied his seat by the adoption of House Resolution No. 278 which the Speaker had ruled was on the issue of excluding Powell and could be decided by majority vote. The House's action followed charges that Powell had misappropriated public funds and abused the process of the New York courts. Powell and certain voters of his congressional district thereafter brought suit in the District Court for injunctive, mandatory, and declaratory relief against respondents, certain named House members, the Speaker, Clerk, Sergeant at Arms, and Doorkeeper of the House, alleging that the Resolution barring his seating violated Art. I, 2, cl. 1, of the Constitution as contrary to the mandate that House members be elected by the people of each State and cl. 2 which sets forth the qualifications for membership of age, citizenship, and residence (all concededly met by Powell), which they claimed were exclusive. The complaint alleged that the House Clerk threatened to refuse to perform the service to which Powell as a duly elected Congressman was entitled; that the Sergeant at Arms refused to pay Powell's salary; and that the Doorkeeper threatened to deny Powell admission to the House chamber. The District Court granted respondents' motion to dismiss the complaint "for want of jurisdiction of the subject matter." The Court of Appeals affirmed on somewhat different grounds. While the case was pending in this Court, the 90th Congress ended and Powell was elected to and seated by the 91st Congress. Respondents contend that (1) the case is moot; (2) the Speech or Debate Clause (Art. I, 6) forecloses judicial review; (3) the decision to exclude Powell is supported by the expulsion power in Art. I, 5, under which the House, which "shall be the Judge of the . . . Qualifications of its own Members," can by a two-thirds vote (exceeded here) expel a member for any reason at all; (4) the Court lacks subject matter jurisdiction over this litigation, or, alternatively, (5) the litigation is not justiciable under general criteria or because it involves a political question.

I

Are federal courts barred from deciding political questions: that is, the question of whether Congress, by majority vote, has the discretionary authority to deny a member-elect membership?

R

Federal courts are not bar red from deciding a case concerning whether Congress, by majority vote, has the discretionary authority to deny a member-elect membership when the text of the Constitution does not specifically commit the issue in the case to Congressional resolution.

A

The case has not been mooted by Powell's seating in the 91st Congress, since his claim for back salary remains a viable issue. Powell's averments as to declaratory relief are sufficient. The mootness of Powell's claim to a seat in the 90th Congress does not affect the viability of his back salary claim with respect to the term for which he was excluded. Although the Speech or Debate Clause bars action against respondent Congressmen, it does not bar action against the other respondents, who are legislative employees charged with unconstitutional activity, *Kilbourn v. Thompson*; *Dombrowski v. Eastland*, and the fact that House employees are acting pursuant to express orders of the House does not preclude judicial review of the constitutionality of the underlying legislative decision. House Resolution No. 278 was an exclusion proceeding and cannot be treated as an expulsion proceeding (which House members have viewed as not applying to pre-election misconduct). This Court will not speculate whether the House would have voted to expel Powell had it been faced with that question. The Court has subject matter jurisdiction over petitioners' action. The case is one "arising under" the Constitution within the meaning of Art. III, since petitioners' claims "will be sustained if the Constitution . . . [is] given one construction and will be defeated if it [is] given another." *Bell v. Hood.* The district courts are given a broad grant of jurisdiction by 28 U.S.C. 1331 (a), over "all civil actions wherein the matter in controversy . . . arises under the Constitution . . ." and while that grant is not entirely co-extensive with Art. III, there is no indication that 1331 (a) was intended to foreclose federal courts from entertaining suits involving the seating of Congressmen. This litigation is justiciable because the claim presented and the relief sought can be judicially resolved. Petitioners' claim does not lack justiciability on the ground that the House's duty cannot be judicially determined, since if petitioners are correct the House had a duty to seat Powell once it determined that he met the standing qualifications set forth in the Constitution. The relief sought is susceptible of judicial resolution, since regardless of the appropriateness of a coercive remedy against House personnel (an issue not here decided) declaratory relief is independently available. The case does not involve a "political question," which under the separation-of-powers doctrine would not be justiciable. The Court's examination of relevant historical materials shows at most that Congress' power under Art. I, 5, to judge the "Qualifications of its Members" is a "textually demonstrable constitutional commitment . . . to [that] co-ordinate political department of government" (*Baker v. Carr*) to judge only standing qualifications which are expressly set forth in the Constitution; hence, the House has no power to exclude a member-elect who meets the Constitution's membership requirements. The case does not present a political question in the sense, also urged by respondents, that it would entail a "potentially embarrassing confrontation between coordinate branches" of the Government, since our system of government requires federal courts on occasion to interpret the Constitution differently from other branches. In judging the qualifications of its members under Art. I, 5, Congress is limited to the standing qualifications expressly prescribed by the Constitution.

C

Affirmed in part, reversed in part, and remanded to the District Court for entry of a declaratory judgment and for further proceedings.

Goldwater v. Carter

444 U.S. 996 (1979)

FACTS

In the late 1970, President Jimmy Carter terminated the United States treaty with Taiwan in conjunction with actions recognizing the People's Republic of China. The Senate debated a resolution which would have stated that Senate approval was required in the termination of this treaty, but it never came to a vote. Some members of Congress, led by Senator Barry Goldwater sued, claiming that the President's actions were unconstitutional because Art. II, sec. 2 ate to ratify treaties.

I

May federal courts resolve conflicts involving the Senate's role in the termination of treaties?

R

The Senate's role in the termination of treaties is a nonjusticiable political question which may not be resolved by the federal courts.

A

The petition for a writ of certiorari is granted. The judgment of the Court of Appeals is vacated and the case is remanded to the District Court with directions to dismiss the complaint. This Court has recognized that an issue should not be decided if it is not ripe for judicial review. Prudential considerations persuade me that a dispute between Congress and the President is not ready for judicial review unless and until each branch has taken action asserting its constitutional authority. Differences between the President and the Congress are commonplace under our system. The differences should, and almost invariably do, turn on political rather than legal considerations. The Judicial Branch should not decide issues affecting the allocation of power between the President and Congress until the political branches reach a constitutional impasse. Otherwise, we would encourage small groups or even individual Members of Congress to seek judicial resolution of issues before the normal political process has the opportunity to resolve the conflict.

C

Vacated and remanded.

Nixon v. United States

506 U.S. 224 (1993)

FACTS

After Plaintiff-petitioner Nixon, the Chief Judge of a Federal District Court, was convicted of federal crimes and sentenced to prison, the House of Representatives adopted articles of impeachment against him and presented them to the Senate. Following proceedings pursuant to Senate Rule XI - which allows a committee of Senators to hear evidence against an impeached individual and to report that evidence to the full Senate - the Senate voted to convict Nixon, and the presiding officer entered judgment removing him from his judgeship. He then commenced the present suit for a declaratory judgment and reinstatement of his judicial salary and privileges, arguing that, because Senate Rule XI prohibits the whole Senate from taking part in the evidentiary hearings, it violates the first sentence of the Constitution's Impeachment Trial Clause, Art. I, 3, cl. 6, which provides that the "Senate shall have the sole Power to try all Impeachments." The District Court held that his claim was nonjusticiable, i.e., involved a political question that could not be resolved by the courts. The Court of Appeals affirmed.

I

Can the Judicial Branch review impeachment proceedings?

R

The federal judiciary may not review impeachment proceedings which are within the realm of the Legislative Branch.

A

Nixon's claim that Senate Rule XI violates the Impeachment Trial Clause is nonjusticiable. A controversy is nonjusticiable where there is "a textually demonstrable constitutional commitment of the issue to a coordinate political department; or a lack of judicially discoverable and manageable standards for resolving it. . . ." These two concepts are not completely separate; the lack of judicially manageable standards may strengthen the conclusion that there is a textually demonstrable commitment to a coordinate branch. The language and structure of Art. I, 3, cl. 6, demonstrate a textual commitment of impeachment to the Senate. Nixon's argument that the use of the word "try" in the Clause's first sentence impliedly requires a judicial-style trial by the full Senate that is subject to judicial review is rejected. The conclusion that "try" lacks sufficient precision to afford any judicially manageable standard of review is compelled by older and modern dictionary definitions, and is fortified by the existence of the three very specific requirements that the Clause's second and third sentences do impose - that the Senate's Members must be under oath or affirmation, that a two-thirds vote is required to convict, and that the Chief Justice presides when the President is tried - the precise nature of which suggests that the Framers did not intend to impose additional limitations on the form of the Senate proceedings. The Clause's first sentence must instead be read as a grant of authority to the Senate to determine whether an individual should be acquitted or convicted, and the commonsense and dictionary meanings of the word "sole" indicate that this authority is reposed in the Senate alone. Nixon's attempts to negate the significance of "sole" are unavailing, while his alternative reading of the word as requiring impeachment only by the full Senate is unnatural, and would impose on the Senate additional procedural requirements that would be inconsistent with the three express limitations that the Clause sets out. A review of the Constitutional Convention's history and the contemporary commentary supports a reading of the constitutional language as deliberately placing the impeachment power in the Legislature, with no judicial involvement, even for the limited purpose of judicial review. Justiciability is also refuted by (1) the lack of finality inherent in exposing the country's political life - particularly if the President were impeached - to months, or perhaps years, of chaos during judicial review of Senate impeachment proceedings, or during any retrial that a differently constituted Senate might conduct if its first judgment of conviction were invalidated, and by (2) the difficulty of fashioning judicial relief other than simply setting aside the Senate's judgment of conviction. A holding of nonjusticiability is consistent with this Court's opinion in *Powell v. McCormack*. Unlike the situation in that case, there is no separate constitutional provision which could be defeated by allowing the Senate final authority to determine the meaning of the word "try" in Art. I, 3, cl. 6. While courts possess power to review legislative action that transgresses identifiable textual limits, the word "try" does not provide such a limit on the authority committed to the Senate.

C

Affirmed.

McCulloch v. Maryland

17 U.S. (4 Wheat) 316 (1819)

FACTS

Congress chartered the Second Bank of the United States in 1816. The bank soon established branches in many states. In 1918, the Maryland Legislature enacted a law requiring all banks not chartered by the State to pay an annual tax of $15,000 in advance; and provided for penalties for violators, including a forfeit of $500 per officer (President, Vice President, cashier etc.) per offence. John James, on behalf of himself and the State of Maryland, sued Plaintiff-in-error James McCulloch (actually the defendant), the cashier of the Baltimore branch of the Bank of the United States. McCulloch admitted that he had issued bank notes without complying with the Maryland law, thus refusing to pay the tax. The case was decided against McCulloch and in the Maryland Court of Appeals affirmed. The case was taken by writ of error to the Supreme Court.

I

1) Does Congress have the power to incorporate a bank? 2) May Maryland, or any other State for that matter, tax a branch of the Bank of the United States without violating the Constitution?

R

Congress has the power to incorporate a bank and the states may not tax a branch of the United States; that is, encumber federal laws whose power is derived from the Constitution.

A

Congress is vested with certain powers; and within the scope of these powers, it is sovereign. Even without the aid of the general clause in the Constitution, empowering Congress to pass all necessary and proper laws for carrying its powers into execution, the grant of powers itself necessarily implies the grant of all usual and suitable means for the execution of the powers granted. A bank is a proper and suitable instrument to assist the operations of the government, in the collection and disbursement of the revenue; in the occasional anticipations of taxes and imposts; and in the regulation of the actual currency, as being a part of the trade and exchange between the states. It is not for this court to decide whether a bank be the best possible means to aid these purposes of government. Such topics must be left to the two houses of Congress. Here, the only question is, whether a bank, in its known and ordinary operations, is capable of being so connected with the finances and revenues of the government, as to be fairly within the discretion of Congress, when selecting means and instruments to execute its powers and perform its duties. A bank is no less the proper subject for the choice of Congress nor less Constitutional because it requires a charter of incorporation. It is not, of itself, unconstitutional for Congress to create a corporation. Corporations are but means. They are not ends and objects of government. They are institutions established to effect certain beneficial purposes; and, as means, take their character generally from purpose. Congress has duties to perform and powers to execute. It has a right to the means by which these duties can be properly and most usefully performed, and these powers executed. Among other means, it has established a bank; and before the act establishing it can be pronounced unconstitutional and void, it must be shown, that a bank has no fair connection with the execution of any power or duty of the national government, and that its creation is consequently a manifest usurpation. The second question we address is whether the state governments have power to tax the bank. The people of the United States have seen fit to divide sovereignty, and to establish a complex system. They have conferred certain powers on the state governments, and certain other powers on the national government. The Constitution, therefore, declares, that the Constitution itself, and the laws passed in pursuance of its provisions, shall be the supreme law of the land, and shall control all state legislation and state constitutions, which may be incompatible therewith; and it confides to this court the ultimate power of deciding all questions arising under the constitution and laws of the United States. The laws of the United States, then, made in pursuance of the constitution, are to be the supreme law of the land, anything in the laws of any state to the contrary notwithstanding. The only inquiry, therefore, in this case is whether the law of the State of Maryland imposing this tax is consistent with the free operation of the law establishing the bank, and the full enjoyment of the privileges conferred by it? If the states may tax the bank, to what extent shall they tax it, and where shall they stop? An unlimited power to tax involves, necessarily, a power to destroy; because there is a limit beyond which no institution and no property can bear taxation. A question of constitutional power can hardly be made to depend on a question of more or less. If the states may tax, they have no limit but their discretion; and the bank, therefore, must depend on the discretion of the state governments for its existence. This consequence is inevitable. The Government of the United States has itself a great pecuniary interest in this corporation. The United States has, and must have, property locally existing in all the states; and may the states impose on this property, whether real or personal, such taxes as they please? We think not. It is a direct imposition on the power, privilege or franchise of the corporation. The act purports, also, to restrain the circulation of the paper of the bank to bills of certain descriptions. It narrows and abridges the powers of the bank in a manner which, it would seem, even Congress could not do. This law of Maryland cannot be sustained, but upon principles and reasoning which would subject every important measure of the national government to the revision and control of the state legislatures. By the charter, the bank is authorized to issue bills of any denomination above five dollars. The act of Maryland purports to restrain and limit their powers in this respect. The charter, as well as the laws of the United States, makes it the duty of all collectors and receivers to receive the notes of the bank in payment of all debts due the government. The act of Maryland makes it penal, both on the person paying and the person receiving such bills, until stamped by the authority of Maryland. This is a direct interference with the revenue. This is either an attempt to expel the bank from the state; or it is an attempt to raise revenue for state purposes, by an imposition on property and franchises held under the national government and created by that government, for purposes connected with its own administration. The bank cannot exist, nor can any bank established by Congress exist, if this right to tax it exists in the state governments. If the law of Congress in establishing the bank is a constitutional act, it must be permitted to have its full and complete effects. Its operation cannot be either defeated or impeded by acts of state legislation. To hold otherwise, would be to declare, that Congress can only exercise its constitutional powers, subject to the controlling discretion, and under the sufferance, of the state governments.

C

See Rule above.

Gibbons v. Ogden
9 Wheat. (22 U.S.) 1 (1824)

FACTS

The Legislature of the State of New York granted to Robert R. Livingston and Robert Fulton the exclusive navigation rights along all the waters within the jurisdiction of New York State. Defendant-appellee Ogden was assigned this right from Livingston and Fulton, to operate a steamboat between New Jersey and New York. Livingston and Fulton had obtained exclusive rights to operate this maritime route for twenty years, as mandated by the New York Legislature. Plaintiff-appellant Gibbons was also running two boats between these same points, and he claimed they were properly licensed under the laws of the U.S. Article I, Sec. 8, cl. 3. Ogden brought an action to enjoin Gibbons from operating steamboats between the same two states (NY-NJ). Gibbons argued that he had a right to operate his steamship between on the contested waterways by virtue of a federal statute, irrespective of the stated rights bestowed upon Ogden. The New York courts held for Ogden and Gibbons appealed. Ogden urges that the federal government's power to regulate commerce coexists with that of the states' power. In support of this argument, Ogden advances the theory that state sovereignty existed prior to the formation of the constitution, and that the states still retain their power and sovereignty under the Tenth Amendment, unless it conflicts with Constitution. Moreover, Ogden argues that an affirmative grant of power by Congress is not exclusive, and that a state may also grant power in the same field occupied by the federal statute so long as the exercise of the states' power is not inconsistent with the grant, which New York's exercise is not. Gibbons disagrees and argues that full power to regulate a particular subject implies the whole power and leaves no residual power to the states; that a grant of the whole is incompatible with the existence of a right in another to any part of it.

I Is the New York statute regulating interstate commerce and granting exclusive use of the waterways to specific members of society, unconstitutional in that a state may not exercise power over the same subject matter as that proscribed by a Congressional statute even if those state powers (regulations) are not inconsistent and do not conflict with the federal law?

R Congress shall have power to regulate commerce with Foreign Nations, and among the Several States, and with the Indian Tribes such that federal commerce statutes invalidate any competing state statutes or licenses.

A The power to assess and collect taxes is, like the commerce power, made in general terms, and does not interfere with the states' right to do the same. But the two grants are not similar in nature. State governments form and remain an important part of our system of government and their power to tax is an indispensable part of their existence. When the federal government is exercising its powers of taxation, it is not exercising the States' power to tax. Conversely, when the state is exercising its power to tax, it doe not impede that of the federal government to do the same. But when a state exercises the commerce power, it is exercising the very power granted to the federal government. There is no analogy, then, between the tax and commerce powers. Gibbons argues that "to regulate" implies full power over the thing to be regulated, and excludes, necessarily, the actions of all others that would perform the same operation on the same thing. We think that there is great force in this argument, and we are not satisfied that Ogden has satisfactorily refuted it. When the states regulate their own purely internal affairs by way of their sovereign power to do so via the enactment of a state statute, and those laws interfere with an act of Congress pursuant to the Constitution, the Court will inquire whether the state law collides with a federal law thus depriving a citizen of a federal right. The laws of New York must yield to the federal law, and the privilege they confer upon Ogden is in error. The steamboat monopoly is in conflict with the federal statute, and the New York law is invalid under the Supremacy Clause. The injunction was dismissed.

C Reversed.

United States v. E.C. Knight Co.

156 U.S. 1 (1895)

FACTS

The material facts proved are that the American Sugar Refining Company, one of the defendants, is incorporated under the laws of New Jersey, and has authority to purchase, refine, and sell sugar; that the Franklin Sugar Refinery, the E. C. Knight Company, the Spreckels Sugar Refinery, and the Delaware Sugar House, were incorporated under the laws of Pennsylvania, and authorized to purchase, refine, and sell sugar; that the four latter Pennsylvania companies were located in Philadelphia, and, prior to March, 1892, produced about 33% of the total amount of sugar refined in the United States, and were in active competition with the American Sugar Refining Company, and with each other, selling their product wherever demand was found for it throughout the United States; that prior to March, 1892, the American Sugar Refining Company had obtained control of all refineries in the United States, excepting the four located in Philadelphia, and that of the Revere Company in Boston, the latter producing about two per cent. of the amount refined in this country; that in March, 1892, the American Sugar Refining Company entered into contracts (on different dates) with the stockholders of each of the Philadelphia corporations named, whereby it purchased their stock, paying therefor by transfers of stock in its company; that the American Sugar Refining Company thus obtained possession of the Philadelphia refineries and their business; that each of the purchases was made subject to the American Sugar Refining Company obtaining authority to increase its stock $25,000,000; that this assent was subsequently obtained, and the increase made; that there was no understanding or concert of action between the stockholders of the several Philadelphia companies respecting the sales, but that those of each company acted independently of those of the others, and in ignorance of what was being done by such others; that the stockholders of each company acted in concert with each other, understanding and intending that all the stock and property of the company should be sold; that the contract of sale in each instance left the sellers free to establish other refineries, [156 U.S. 1, 6] and continue the business if they should see fit to do so, and contained no provision respecting trade or commerce in sugar, and that no arrangement or provision on this subject has been made since; that since the purchase the Delaware Sugar House Refinery has been operated in conjunction with the Spreckels Refinery, and the E. C. Knight Refinery in connection with the Franklin, this combination being made apparently for reasons of economy in conducting the business; that the amount of sugar refined in Philadelphia has been increased since the purchases; that the price has been slightly advanced since that event, but is still lower than it had been for some years before, and up to within a few months of the sales; that about 10% of the sugar refined and sold in the United States is refined in other refineries than those controlled by the American Sugar Refining Company.

I

May Congress regulate the manufacture of goods before such goods enter the stream of commerce under it commerce powers?

R

Manufacturing is separate from "commerce" because it occurs before any goods are transported in interstate commerce - thus the federal government may not regulate manufacturing in and of itself.

United States v. E.C. Knight Co.

156 U.S. 1 (1895)

A Contracts, combinations, or conspiracies to control domestic enterprise in manufacture, agriculture, mining, production in all its forms, or to raise or lower prices or wages, might unquestionably tend to restrain external as well as domestic trade, but the restraint would be an indirect result, however inevitable, and whatever its extent, and such result would not necessarily determine the object of the contract, combination, or conspiracy. Again, all the authorities agree that, in order to vitiate a contract or combination, it is not essential that its result should be a complete monopoly - slight reflection will show that, if the national power extends to all contracts and combinations in manufacture, agriculture, mining, and other productive industries, whose ultimate result may affect external commerce, comparatively little of business operations and affairs would be left for state control. Here, Congress did not attempt thereby to assert the power to deal with monopoly directly as such; or to limit and restrict the rights of corporations created by the states or the citizens of the states in the acquisition, control, or disposition of property; or to regulate or prescribe the price or prices at which such property or the products thereof should be sold; or to make criminal the acts of persons in the acquisition and control of property which the states of their residence or creation sanctioned or permitted. The law struck at was combinations, contracts, and conspiracies to monopolize trade and commerce among the several states or with foreign nations; but the contracts and acts of the defendants related exclusively to the acquisition of the Philadelphia refineries and the business of sugar refining in Pennsylvania, and bore no direct relation to commerce between the states or with foreign nations. The object was manifestly private gain in the manufacture of the commodity, but not through the control of interstate or foreign commerce. It is true that the bill alleged that the products of these refineries were sold and distributed among the several states, and that all the companies were engaged in trade or commerce with the several states and with foreign nations; but this was no more than to say that trade and commerce served manufacture to fulfill its function. Nevertheless it does not follow that an attempt to monopolize, or the actual monopoly of, the manufacture was an attempt, whether executory or consummated, to monopolize commerce, even though, in order to dispose of the product, the instrumentality of commerce was necessarily invoked. There was nothing in the proofs to indicate any intention to put a restraint upon trade or commerce, and the fact, as we have seen, that trade or commerce might be indirectly affected, was not enough to entitle complainants to a decree. The subject-matter of the sale was shares of manufacturing stock, and the relief sought was the surrender of property which had already passed, and the suppression of the alleged monopoly in manufacture by the restoration of the status quo before the transfers; yet the act of congress only authorized the circuit courts to proceed by way of preventing and restraining violations of the act in respect of contracts, combinations, or conspiracies in restraint of interstate or international trade or commerce. The circuit court declined, upon the pleadings and proofs, to grant the relief prayed, and dismissed the bill, and we are of opinion that the circuit court of appears did not err in affirming that decree.

C Decree affirmed.

Carter v. Carter Coal Co.

298 U.S. 238 (1936)

FACTS

The purposes of the Bituminous Coal Conservation Act of 1935 involved in these suits, as declared by the title, are to stabilize the bituminous coal-mining industry and promote its interstate commerce; to provide for co-operative marketing of bituminous coal; to levy a tax on such coal and provide for a drawback under certain conditions; to declare the production, distribution, and use of such coal to be affected with a national public interest; to conserve the national resources of such coal; to provide for the general welfare, and for other purposes. The constitutional validity of the act is challenged in each of the suits. Nos. 636 and 651 are cross-writs of certiorari in a stockholder's suit, brought in the Supreme Court of the District of Columbia by Carter against the Carter Coal Company and some of its officers, Guy T. Helvering (Commissioner of Internal Revenue of the United States), and certain other officers of the United States, to enjoin the coal company and its officers named from filing an acceptance of the code provided for in said act, from paying any tax imposed upon the coal company under the authority of the act, and from complying with its provisions or the provisions f the code. The bill sought to enjoin the Commissioner of Internal Revenue and the other federal officials named from proceeding under the act in particulars specified, the details of which it is unnecessary to state. No. 649 is a suit brought in a federal District Court in Kentucky by petitioners against respondent collector of internal revenue for the district of Kentucky, to enjoin him from collecting or attempting to collect the taxes sought to be imposed upon them by the act, on the ground of its unconstitutionality. No. 650 is a stockholder's suit brought in the same court against the coal company and some of its officers, to secure a mandatory injunction against their refusal to accept and operate under the provisions of the Bituminous Coal Code prepared in pursuance of the act. By the terms of the act, every producer of bituminous coal within the United States is brought within its provisions.

I

Does Congress have the power under its Commerce powers to legislate in the area of labor-management relations, a purely local activity?

R

Congress may not legislate in areas which are purely local in nature, such as the negation of wages and working conditions, as they are outside of Congress' authority.

A

Certain recitals contained in the act plainly suggest that its makers were of opinion that its constitutionality could be sustained under some general federal power, thought to exist, apart from the specific grants of the Constitution. This view is a fallacy. Since the validity of the act depends upon whether it is a regulation of interstate commerce, the nature and extent of the power conferred upon Congress by the commerce clause becomes the determinative question in this branch of the case. The commerce clause vests in Congress the power 'To regulate Commerce with foreign Nations, and among the several States, and with the Indian Tribes.' The function to be exercised is that of regulation. The thing to be regulated is the commerce described. In exercising the authority conferred by this clause of the Constitution, Congress is powerless to regulate anything which is not commerce, as it is powerless to do anything about commerce which is not regulation. As used in the Constitution, the word 'commerce' is the equivalent of the phrase 'intercourse for the purposes of trade,' and includes transportation, purchase, sale, and exchange of commodities between the citizens of the different states. And the power to regulate commerce embraces the instruments by which commerce is carried on. That commodities produced or manufactured within a state are intended to be sold or transported outside the state does not render their production or manufacture subject to federal regulation under the commerce clause. The police power of a state is as broad and plenary as its taxing power, and property within the state is subject to the operations of the former so long as it is within the regulating restrictions of the latter. That the act, whatever it may be in form, in fact is compulsory clearly appears. We have already discussed section 3, which imposes the excise tax as a penalty to compel 'acceptance' of the code. Section 14 (15 U.S.C.A. 818) provides that the United States shall purchase no bituminous coal produced at any mine where the producer has not complied with the provisions of the code; and that each contract made by the United States shall contain a provision that the contractor will buy no bituminous coal to use on, or in the carrying out of, such contract unless the producer be a member of the code, as certified by the coal commission. In the light of these provisions we come to a consideration of subdivision (g) of part 3 of section 4, dealing with 'labor relations.' That subdivision delegates the power to fix maximum hours of labor to a part of the producers and the miners-namely, 'the producers of more than two-thirds the annual national tonnage production for the preceding calendar year' and 'more than one-half the mine workers employed'; and to producers of more than two-thirds of the district annual tonnage during the preceding calendar year and a majority of the miners, there is delegated the power to fix minimum wages for the district or group of districts. The effect, in respect of wages and hours, is to subject the dissentient minority, either of producers or miners or both, to the will of the stated majority, since, by refusing to submit, the minority at once incurs the hazard of enforcement of the drastic compulsory provisions of the act to which we have referred. To 'accept,' in these circumstances, is not to exercise a choice, but to surrender to force.

C

The decrees in Nos. 636, 649, and 650 must be reversed and the causes remanded for further consideration in conformity with this opinion. The decree in No. 651 will be affirmed.

Houston, East & West Texas Railway Co. v. United States

[the Shreveport Rate Cases] 234 U.S. 342 (1914)

FACTS

These suits were brought in the commerce court by the Houston, East & West Texas Railway Company and the Houston & Shreveport Railroad Company, and by the Texas & Pacific Railway Company, respectively, to set aside an order of the Interstate Commerce Commission, dated March 11, 1912, upon the ground that it exceeded the Commission's authority. Other railroad companies intervened in support of the petitions, and the Interstate Commerce Commission and the Railroad Commission of Louisiana intervened in opposition. The petitions were dismissed. The order of the Interstate Commerce Commission was made in a proceeding initiated in March, 1911, by the Railroad Commission of Louisiana. The complaint was that the appellants, and other interstate carriers, maintained unreasonable rates from Shreveport, Louisiana, to various points in Texas, and, further, that these carriers, in the adjustment of rates over their respective lines, unjustly discriminated in favor of traffic within the state of Texas, and against similar traffic between Louisiana and Texas. The carriers filed answers; numerous pleas of intervention by shippers and commercial bodies were allowed; testimony was taken and arguments were heard. The gravamen of the complaint, said the Interstate Commerce Commission, was that the carriers made rates out of Dallas and other Texas points into eastern Texas which were much lower than those which they extended into Texas from Shreveport.

I

May Congress regulate interstate commerce where it is found to affect interstate commerce?

R

Congress has the authority to regulate interstate commerce where it has the potential to affect interstate commerce where no federal regulation exists.

A

The point of the objection to the order is that, as the discrimination found by the Commission to be unjust arises out of the relation of intrastate rates, maintained under state authority, to interstate rates that have been upheld as reasonable, its correction was beyond the Commission's power. Manifestly the order might be complied with, and the discrimination avoided, either by reducing the interstate rates from Shreveport to the level of the competing intrastate rates, or by raising these intrastate rates to the level of the interstate rates, or by such reduction in the one case and increase in the other as would result in equality. But it is urged that, so far as the interstate rates were sustained by the Commission as reasonable, the Commission was without authority to compel their reduction in order to equalize them with the lower intrastate rates. The holding of the commerce court was that the order relieved the appellants from further obligation to observe the intrastate rates, and that they were at liberty to comply with the Commission's requirements by increasing these rates sufficiently to remove the forbidden discrimination. The invalidity of the order in this aspect is challenged upon two grounds: **(1)** That Congress is impotent to control the intrastate charges of an interstate carrier even to the extent necessary to prevent injurious discrimination against interstate traffic; and **(2)** That, if it be assumed that Congress has this power, still it has not been exercised, and hence the action of the Commission exceeded the limits of the authority which has been conferred upon it. It is unnecessary to repeat what has frequently been said by this court with respect to the complete and paramount character of the power confided to Congress to regulate commerce among the several states. It is of the essence of this power that, where it exists, it dominates. Interstate trade was not left to be destroyed or impeded by the rivalries of local government. The purpose was to make impossible the recurrence of the evils which had overwhelmed the Confederation, and to provide the necessary basis of national unity by insuring 'uniformity of regulation against conflicting and discriminating state legislation.' By virtue of the comprehensive terms of the grant, the authority of Congress is at all times adequate to meet the varying exigencies that arise, and to protect the national interest by securing the freedom of interstate commercial intercourse from local control. Congress is empowered to regulate - that is, to provide the law for the government of interstate commerce; to enact all appropriate legislation for its protection and advancement; to adopt measures to promote its growth and insure its safety; and to foster, protect, control, and restrain. Its authority, extending to these interstate carriers as instruments of interstate commerce, necessarily embraces the right to control their operations in all matters having such a close and substantial relation to interstate traffic that the control is essential or appropriate to the security of that traffic, to the efficiency of the interstate service, and to the maintenance of conditions under which interstate commerce may be conducted upon fair terms and without molestation or hindrance. As it is competent for Congress to legislate to these ends, unquestionably it may seek their attainment by requiring that the agencies of interstate commerce shall not be used in such manner as to cripple, retard, or destroy it. The fact that carriers are instruments of intrastate commerce, as well as of interstate commerce, does not derogate from the complete and paramount authority of Congress over the latter, or preclude the Federal power from being exerted to prevent the intrastate operations of such carriers from being made a means of injury to that which has been confided to Federal care. Wherever the interstate and intrastate transactions of carriers are so related that the government of the one involves the control of the other, it is Congress, and not the state, that is entitled to prescribe the final and dominant rule, for otherwise Congress would be denied the exercise of its constitutional authority, and the state, and not the nation, would be supreme within the national field.

C The decree of the Commerce Court is affirmed in each case.

A.L.A. Schechter Poultry Corp. v. United States

295 U.S. 495 (1935)

FACTS

Petitioners in No. 854 were convicted in the District Court of the United States for the Eastern District of New York on eighteen counts of an indictment charging violations of what is known as the "Live Poultry Code" and on an additional count for conspiracy to commit such violations. By demurrer to the indictment and appropriate motions on the trial, the defendants contended (1) that the code had been adopted pursuant to an unconstitutional delegation by Congress of legislative power; (2) that it attempted to regulate intrastate transactions which lay outside the authority of Congress; and (3) that in certain provisions it was repugnant to the due process clause of the Fifth Amendment. The Circuit Court of Appeals sustained the conviction on the conspiracy count and on sixteen counts for violation of the code, but reversed the conviction on two counts which charged violation of requirements as to minimum wages and maximum hours of labor, as these were not deemed to be within the congressional power of regulation. On the respective applications of the defendants (No. 854) and of the government (No. 864), the U.S. Supreme Court granted writs of certiorari.

I

Did the defendants' transactions directly 'affect' interstate commerce so as to be subject to federal regulation?

R

Once goods traveled in interstate commerce and have been bought and sold in the state of their final destination, they are no longer subject to federal law because they are no longer in interstate commerce.

A

The power of Congress extends, not only to the regulation of transactions which are part of interstate commerce, but to the protection of that commerce from injury. It matters not that the injury may be due to the conduct of those engaged in intrastate operations. Thus, Congress may protect the safety of those employed in interstate transportation, 'no matter what may be the source of the dangers which threaten it.' We said in *Mondou v. New York* that it is the 'effect upon interstate commerce,' not 'the source of the injury,' which is 'the criterion of congressional power.' We have held that, in dealing with common carriers engaged in both interstate and intrastate commerce, the dominant authority of Congress necessarily embraces the right to control their intrastate operations in all matters having such a close and substantial relation to interstate traffic that the control is essential or appropriate to secure the freedom of that traffic from interference or unjust discrimination and to promote the efficiency of the interstate service. Thus, combinations and conspiracies to restrain interstate commerce, or to monopolize any part of it, are nonetheless within the reach of the Anti-Trust Act because the conspirators seek to attain their end by means of intrastate activities. We recently had occasion, in *Local 167 v. United States*, to apply this principle in connection with the live poultry industry. That was a suit to enjoin a conspiracy to restrain and monopolize interstate commerce in violation of the Anti-Trust Act. It was shown that marketmen, teamsters, and slaughterers (shochtim) had conspired to burden the free movement of live poultry into the metropolitan area in and about New York City. In view of the proof of that conspiracy, we said that it was unnecessary to decide when interstate commerce ended and when intrastate commerce began. We found that the proved interference by the conspirators 'with the unloading, the transportation, the sales by marketmen to retailers, the prices charged, and the amount of profits exacted' operated 'substantially and directly to restrain and burden the untrammelled shipment and movement of the poultry,' while unquestionably it was in interstate commerce. The intrastate acts of the conspirators were included in the injunction because that was found to be necessary for the protection of interstate commerce against the attempted and illegal restraint. The instant case is not of that sort. This is not a prosecution for a conspiracy to restrain or monopolize interstate commerce in violation of the Anti-Trust Act. Defendants have been convicted, not upon direct charges of injury to interstate commerce or of interference with persons engaged in that commerce, but of violations of certain provisions of the Live Poultry Code and of conspiracy to commit these violations. Interstate commerce is brought in only upon the charge that violations of these provisions-as to hours and wages of employees and local sales-'affected' interstate commerce.

Thus, we are of the opinion that the attempt through the provisions of the code to fix the hours and wages of employees of defendants in their intrastate business was not a valid exercise of federal power. On both the grounds we have discussed, the attempted delegation of legislative power and the attempted regulation of intrastate transactions which affect interstate commerce only indirectly, we hold the code provisions here in question to be invalid and that the judgment of conviction must be reversed.

C No. 854 –reversed; No. 864-affirmed.

Hammer v. Dagenhart [The Child Labor Case]

247 U.S. 251 (1918)

FACTS

A bill was filed in the United States District Court for the Western District of North Carolina by a father in his own behalf and on behalf of his two minor sons, one under the age of fourteen years and the other between the ages of fourteen and sixteen years, employees in a cotton mill at Charlotte, North Carolina, to enjoin the enforcement of the act of Congress intended to prevent interstate commerce in the products of child labor. The District Court held the act unconstitutional and entered a decree enjoining its enforcement. An appeal was thereafter filed.

I

Is it within the authority of Congress in regulating commerce among the states to prohibit the transportation in interstate commerce of manufactured goods, the product of a factory in which, within thirty days prior to their removal therefrom, children under the age of fourteen have been employed or permitted to work, or children between the ages of 14 to 16 have been employed or permitted to work more than 8 hours in any day, or more than six days in any week?

R

Congress does not have the authority to regulate child labor, a purely state function, by way of preventing the interstate commerce of the products of child labor.

A

In interpreting the Constitution, it must never be forgotten that the nation is made up of states to which are entrusted the powers of local government. And to them and to the people the powers not expressly delegated to the national government are reserved. The power of the states to regulate their purely internal affairs by such laws as seem wise to the local authority is inherent and has never been surrendered to the general government. To sustain this statute would not be in our judgment a recognition of the lawful exertion of congressional authority over interstate commerce, but would sanction an invasion by the federal power of the control of a matter purely local in its character, and over which no authority has been delegated to Congress in conferring the power to regulate commerce among the states. We have neither authority nor disposition to question the motives of Congress in enacting this legislation. The purposes intended must be attained consistently with constitutional limitations and not by an invasion of the powers of the states. This court has no more important function than that which devolves upon it the obligation to preserve inviolate the constitutional limitations upon the exercise of authority federal and state to the end that each may continue to discharge, harmoniously with the other, the duties entrusted to it by the Constitution. In our view the necessary effect of this act is, by means of a prohibition against the movement in interstate commerce of ordinary commercial commodities to regulate the hours of labor of children in factories and mines within the states, a purely state authority. Thus the act in a two-fold sense is repugnant to the Constitution. It not only transcends the authority delegated to Congress over commerce but also exerts a power as to a purely local matter to which the federal authority does not extend. The far reaching result of upholding the act cannot be more plainly indicated than by pointing out that if Congress can thus regulate matters entrusted to local authority by prohibition of the movement of commodities in interstate commerce, all freedom of commerce will be at an end, and the power of the states over local matters may be eliminated, and thus our system of government be practically destroyed. For these reasons we hold that this law exceeds the constitutional authority of Congress. It follows that the decree of the District Court must be affirmed.

C

Affirmed.

Champion v. Ames [The Lottery Case]

188 U.S. 321 (1903)

FACTS

The general question arising upon this appeal involves the constitutionality of the 1st section of the act of Congress of March 2d, 1895, chap. 191, entitled 'An Act for the Suppression of Lottery Traffic through National and Interstate Commerce and the Postal Service, Subject to the Jurisdiction and Laws of the United States.' 28 Stat. at L. 963, U. S. Comp. Stat. 1901, p. 3178, which barred the interstate shipment of lottery tickets. The appeal was from an order of the circuit court of the United States for the northern district of Illinois dismissing a writ of habeas corpus brought by the appellant Champion, who complained that he was restrained of his liberty by the Marshal of the United States in violation of the Constitution and laws of the United States. It appears that the accused was under indictment in the district court of the United States for the northern district of Texas for conspiracy under 5440 of the Revised Statues. He was arrested at Chicago under a warrant based upon a complaint in writing, under oath, charging him with conspiring with others, at Dallas, in the northern district of Texas, to commit the offense denounced in the Lottery Act; and the object of the arrest was to compel his appearance in the Federal court in Texas to answer the indictment against him. Specifically, the indictment further charged that 'in pursuance to said conspiracy, and to effect the object thereof, W. F. Champion and Charles B. Park did unlawfully, knowingly, and feloniously, for the purpose of being carried from one state to another in the United States, from Dallas to Fresno, deposited, shipped and carried one certain box or package containing lottery tickets. It thus appears that the "carrying" in this case was by an incorporated express company, engaged in transporting freight and packages from one state to another. The commissioner who issued the warrant of arrest, having found that there was probable cause to believe that Champion was guilty of the offense charged, ordered that he give bond for his appearance for trial in the district court of the United States for the northern district of Texas, or in default thereof to be committed to jail.

I May Congress, pursuant to the Commerce Clause, prohibit the interstate shipment of things adjudged to evil or fatal in order to protect the commerce concerning all states?

R Congress may, pursuant to the Commerce Clause, prohibit the interstate shipment of things adjudged to evil or fatal in order to protect the commerce concerning all states.

A The appellant insists that the carrying of lottery tickets from one state to another state by an express company engaged in carrying freight and packages from state to state, although such tickets may be contained in a box or package, does not constitute, and cannot by any act of Congress be legally made to constitute, commerce among the states within the meaning of the clause of the Constitution of the United States providing that Congress shall have power 'to regulate commerce with foreign nations, and among the several states, and with the Indian tribes;' consequently, that Congress cannot make it an offense to cause such tickets to be carried from one state to another. The government insists that express companies, when engaged, for hire, in the business of transportation from one state to another, are instrumentalities of commerce among the states; that the carrying of lottery tickets from one state to another is commerce which Congress may regulate; and that as a means of executing the power to regulate interstate commerce Congress may make it an offense against the United States to cause lottery tickets to be carried from one state to another. We are of opinion that lottery tickets are subjects of traffic, and therefore are subjects of commerce, and the regulation of the carriage of such tickets from state to state, at least by independent carriers, is a regulation of commerce among the several states. But it is said that the statute in question does not regulate the carrying of lottery tickets from state to state, but by punishing those who cause them to be so carried Congress in effect prohibits such carrying; that in respect of the carrying from one state to another of articles or things that are, in fact, or according to usage in business, the subjects of commerce, the authority given Congress was not to prohibit, but only to regulate. It is said, however, that if, in order to suppress lotteries carried on through interstate commerce, Congress may exclude lottery tickets from such commerce, that principle leads necessarily to the conclusion that Congress may arbitrarily exclude from commerce among the states any article, commodity, or thing, of whatever kind or nature, or however useful or valuable, which it may choose, no matter with what motive, to declare shall not be carried from one state to another. The present case does not require the court to declare the full extent of the power that Congress may exercise in the regulation of commerce among the states. We may, however, repeat, in this connection, what the court has heretofore said, that the power of Congress to regulate commerce among the states, although plenary, cannot be deemed arbitrary, since it is subject to such limitations or restrictions as are prescribed by the Constitution. The whole subject is too important, and the questions suggested by its consideration are too difficult of solution, to justify any attempt to lay down a rule for determining in advance the validity of every statute that may be enacted under the commerce clause. We decide nothing more in the present case than that lottery tickets are subjects of traffic among those who choose to sell or buy them; that the carriage of such tickets by independent carriers from one state to another is therefore interstate commerce; that under its power to regulate commerce among the several states Congress-subject to the limitations imposed by the Constitution upon the exercise of the powers granted-has plenary authority over such commerce, and may prohibit the carriage of such tickets from state to state; and that legislation to that end, and of that character, is not inconsistent with any limitation or restriction imposed upon the exercise of the powers granted to Congress.

C The judgment is affirmed.

NLRB v. Jones & Laughlin Steel Corp.

301 U.S. 1 (1937)

FACTS

In a proceeding under the National Labor Relations Act, Plaintiff-petitioner National Labor Relations Board (NLRB) found that the Defendant-respondent Jones & Laughlin Steel Corporation, a large diversified steel producer and distributor, had violated the act by engaging in unfair labor practices affecting commerce. The proceeding was instituted by the Beaver Valley Lodge No. 200, a labor organization. The unfair labor practices charged that the corporation was discriminating against members of the union with regard to hire and tenure of employment and was coercing and intimidating its employees in order to interfere with their self-organization and involved the discharge of certain employees. The NLRB, sustained the charge and ordered the corporation to cease and desist from such discrimination and coercion, to offer reinstatement to ten of the employees, to make good their losses in pay, and to post notices for 30 days that the corporation would not discharge or discriminate against present/future labor union members. The corporation failed to comply, and the Board petitioned the Court of Appeals to enforce the order. The court denied the petition holding that the order lay beyond the range of federal power. The U.S. Supreme Court granted certiorari.

I

Is the National Labor Relations Act, which allows for the federal supervision of labor relations, an impermissible invasion of the States' powers as an attempt to regulate all industry?

R

Congressional power to protect interstate commerce is not limited to transactions which are an essential part of the "flow" of interstate or foreign commerce but may be additionally used to regulate those activities which have a substantial relation to interstate commerce; the control of which is essential or appropriate to protect commerce from burdens and obstructions.

A

Defendant-respondent Jones & Laughlin Steel challenges the Act as an attempt to regulate all industry, thus invading the reserved powers of the States. Congressional power to protect interstate commerce is not limited to transactions that are an essential part of the "flow" of interstate commerce but may be additionally used to regulate those activities which have a substantial relation to interstate commerce; the control of which is essential or appropriate to protect commerce from burdens and obstructions. In fact, Congressional power is plenary with regard to interstate commerce such that may be exerted to protect even <u>intra</u>state activity that bears substantial relation to interstate commerce. Here, the discriminatory activity against the employees for labor union activity would have an indirect but severe interstate effect on interstate commerce. When industries organize themselves nationally, making their relation to interstate commerce the dominant factor in their activities, the presence of potential industrial strife becomes an important national concern and the recognition of a right self-unionize is often an essential condition industrial peace.

C

Reversed.

United States v. Darby

312 U.S. 100 (1941)

FACTS

Plaintiff Darby, a Georgia lumber producer, challenged an indictment charging him with violating the Fair Labor Standards Act. Appellee demurred to an indictment found in the district court for southern Georgia charging him with violation of the Fair Labor Standards Act of 1938. The district court sustained the demurrer and quashed the indictment holding that the Act unconstitutionally regulated hours and wages of employees in local manufacturing activities. The case now comes before the U.S. Supreme Court on direct appeal under 238 of the Judicial Code as amended, which authorizes an appeal to the U.S. Supreme Court when the judgment sustaining the demurrer "is based upon the invalidity, or construction of the statute upon which the indictment is founded."

I

1) Does Congress have the power to prohibit the shipment in interstate commerce of lumber manufactured by employees whose wages do not meet a prescribed minimum, and 2) does it have the power to prohibit the employment of workmen engaged in the production of interstate commercial goods at other than prescribed wages and hours?

R

The power of congress over interstate commerce can neither be enlarge nor diminished by the exercise or non-exercise of state power, nor within the control of the Courts.

A

Congress' power to regulate commerce extends not only to regulations that aid and protect commerce, but also covers regulations which prohibit or inhibit commerce. Congress may prohibit or restrict articles from interstate commerce that are injurious to public health, safety or welfare. The Fair Labor Standards Act set up a comprehensive legislative scheme for preventing the shipment in interstate commerce of certain products and commodities produced in the United States under labor conditions as respects wages and hours which fail to conform to standards set up by the Act. Its purpose, as we judicially know from the declaration of policy and the reports of Congressional committees proposing the legislation is to exclude from interstate commerce goods produced for the commerce and to prevent their production for interstate commerce, under conditions detrimental to the maintenance of the minimum standards of living necessary for health and general well-being; and to prevent the use of interstate commerce as the means of competition in the distribution of goods so produced, and as the means of spreading and perpetuating such substandard labor conditions among the workers of the several states. The Act also sets up an administrative procedure whereby those standards may from time to time be modified generally as to industries subject to the Act or within an industry in accordance with specified standards, by an administrator acting in collaboration with 'Industry Committees' appointed by him. The demurrer, so far as now relevant to the appeal, challenged the validity of the Fair Labor Standards Act under the Commerce Clause, Art. 1, 8, cl. 3, and the Fifth and Tenth Amendments. The district court quashed the indictment in its entirety upon the broad grounds that the Act, which it interpreted as a regulation of manufacture within the states, is unconstitutional. It declared that manufacture is not interstate commerce and that the regulation by the Fair Labor

Standards Act of wages and hours of employment of those engaged in the manufacture of goods which it is intended at the time of production 'may or will be' after production 'sold in interstate commerce in part or in whole' is not within the Congressional power to regulate interstate commerce. The effect of the court's decision and judgment are thus to deny the power of Congress to prohibit shipment in interstate commerce of lumber produced for interstate commerce under the proscribed substandard labor conditions of wages and hours, its power to penalize the employer for his failure to conform to the wage and hour provisions in the case of employees engaged in the production of lumber which he intends thereafter to ship in interstate commerce in part or in whole according to the normal course of his business and its power to compel him to keep records of hours of employment as required by the statute and the regulations of the administrator. The case comes here on assignments by the Government that the district court erred insofar as it held that Congress was without constitutional power to penalize the acts set forth in the indictment, and appellees seek to sustain the decision below on the grounds that the prohibition by Congress of those Acts is unauthorized by the commerce clause and is prohibited by the Fifth Amendment. The appeals statute limits our jurisdiction on this appeal to a review of the determination of the district court so far only as it is based on the validity or construction of the statute. Hence we accept the district court's interpretation of the indictment and confine our decision to the validity and construction of the statute.

C

Reversed.

Wickard v. Filburn

317 U.S. 111 (1942)

FACTS

The appellee filed his complaint against the Secretary of Agriculture of the United States, three members of the County Agricultural Conservation Committee for Montgomery County, Ohio, and a member of the State Agricultural Conservation Committee for Ohio. He sought to enjoin enforcement against himself of the marketing penalty imposed by the amendment of May 26, 1941, to the Agricultural Adjustment Act of 1938, upon that part of his 1941 wheat crop which was available for marketing in excess of the marketing quota established for his farm. He also sought a declaratory judgment that the wheat marketing quota provisions of the Act as amended and applicable to him were unconstitutional because not sustainable under the Commerce Clause or consistent with the Due Process Clause of the Fifth Amendment. The Secretary moved to dismiss the action against him for improper venue but later waived his objection and filed an answer. The other appellants moved to dismiss on the ground that they had no power or authority to enforce the wheat marketing quota provisions of the Act, and after their motion was denied they answered, reserving exceptions to the ruling on their motion to dismiss. The case was submitted to the U.S. Supreme Court for decision on the pleadings and upon a stipulation of facts.

I

Does the Commerce Clause include the regulation of those items not intended for distribution nationally?

R

Congress may regulate to all activities having a substantial effect on interstate commerce; even those that do not have a substantial effect individually but do when viewed in the aggregate.

A

The general scheme of the Agricultural Adjustment Act of 1938 as related to wheat is to control the volume moving in interstate and foreign commerce in order to avoid surpluses and shortages and the consequent abnormally low or high wheat prices and obstructions to commerce. Within prescribed limits and by prescribed standards the Secretary of Agriculture is directed to ascertain and proclaim each year a national acreage allotment for the next crop of wheat, which is then apportioned to the states and their counties, and is eventually broken up into allotments for individual farms. Loans and payments to wheat farmers are authorized in stated circumstances. The Act provides further that whenever it appears that the total supply of wheat as of the beginning of any marketing year, beginning July 1, will exceed a normal year's domestic consumption and export by more than 35%, the Secretary shall so proclaim not later than May 15 prior to the beginning of such marketing year; and that during the marketing year a compulsory national marketing quota shall be in effect with respect to the marketing of wheat. Between the issuance of the proclamation and June 10, the Secretary must, however, conduct a referendum of farmers who will be subject to the quota to determine whether they favor or oppose it; and if more than one-third of the farmers voting in the referendum do oppose, the Secretary must prior to the effective date of the quota by proclamation suspend its operation. On May 19, 1941 the Secretary of Agriculture made a radio address to the wheat farmers of the United States in which he advocated approval of the quotas and called attention to the pendency of the amendment of May 26, 1941, which had at the time been sent by Congress to the White House, and pointed out its provision for an increase in the loans on wheat to 85 per cent of parity. He made no mention of the fact that it also increased the penalty from 15 cents a bushel to one-half of the parity loan rate of about 98 cents, but stated that 'Because of the uncertain world situation, we deliberately planted several million extra acres of wheat. ... Farmers should not be penalized because they have provided insurance against shortages of food.' Pursuant to the Act, the referendum of wheat growers was held on May 31, 1941. According to the required published statement of the Secretary of Agriculture, 81 per cent of those voting favored the marketing quota, with 19 per cent opposed. The court below held, with one judge dissenting, that the speech of the Secretary invalidated the referendum; and that the amendment of May 26, 1941, 'in so far as it increased the penalty for the farm marketing excess over the fifteen cents per bushel prevailing at the time of planting and subjected the entire crop to a lien for the payment thereof,' should not be applied to the appellee because as so applied it was retroactive and in violation of the Fifth Amendment; and, alternatively, because the equities of the case so required. Its judgment permanently enjoined appellants from collecting a marketing penalty of more than 15 cents a bushel on the farm marketing excess of appellee's 1941 wheat crop, from subjecting appellee's entire 1941 crop to a lien for the payment of the penalty, and from collecting a 15-cent penalty except in accordance with the provisions of 339 of the Act as that section stood prior to the amendment of May 26, 1941.10 The Secretary and his co-defendants have appealed.

The holding of the court below that the Secretary's speech invalidated the referendum is manifest error. Read as a whole and in the context of world events that constituted his principal theme, the penalties of which he spoke were more likely those in the form of ruinously low prices resulting from the excess supply rather than the penalties prescribed in the Act. But under any interpretation the speech cannot be given the effect of invalidating the referendum. There is no evidence that any voter put upon the Secretary's words the interpretation that impressed the court below or was in any way misled. There is no showing that the speech influenced the outcome of the referendum. The record in fact does not show that any, and does not suggest a basis for even a guess as to how many, of the voting farmers dropped work to listen to 'Wheat Farmers and the Battle for Democracy' at 11:30 in the morning of May 19th, which was a busy hour in one of the busiest of seasons. If this discourse intended reference to this legislation at all, it was of course a public Act, whose terms were readily available, and the speech did not purport to be an exposition of its provisions. To hold that a speech by a Cabinet officer, which failed to meet judicial ideals of clarity, precision, and exhaustiveness, may defeat a policy embodied in an Act of Congress, would invest communication between administrators and the people with perils heretofore unsuspected. Moreover, we should have to conclude that such an officer is able to do by accident what he has no power to do by design. Appellee's complaint, in so far as it is based on this speech, is frivolous, and the injunction, in so far as it rests on this ground, is unwarranted.

Dismissed.

Heart of Atlanta Motel Inc. v. United States

379 U.S. 241 (1964)

FACTS

Appellant, the owner of a large motel in Atlanta, Georgia, which restricts its clientele to white persons, three-fourths of whom are transient interstate travelers, sued for declaratory relief and to enjoin enforcement of the Civil Rights Act of 1964, contending that the prohibition of racial discrimination in places of public accommodation affecting commerce exceeded Congress' powers under the Commerce Clause and violated other parts of the Constitution. A three-judge District Court upheld the constitutionality of Title II, 201 (a), (b) (1) and (c) (1), the provisions attacked, and on appellees' counterclaim permanently enjoined appellant from refusing to accommodate Negro guests for racial reasons.

I

May Congress regulate local activities that can exert a substantial and harmful effect on interstate travel?

R

Under the Commerce Clause, Congress can regulate local activities that can exert a substantial and harmful effect on interstate travel.

A

Title II of the Civil Rights Act of 1964 is a valid exercise of Congress' power under the Commerce Clause as applied to a place of public accommodation serving interstate travelers. The interstate movement of persons is "commerce" which concerns more than one State. The protection of interstate commerce is within the regulatory power of Congress under the Commerce Clause whether or not the transportation of persons between States is "commercial." Congress' action in removing the disruptive effect which it found racial discrimination has on interstate travel is not invalidated because Congress was also legislating against what it considered to be moral wrongs. Congress had power to enact appropriate legislation with regard to a place of public accommodation such as appellant's motel even if it is assumed to be of a purely "local" character, as Congress' power over interstate commerce extends to the regulation of local incidents thereof which might have a substantial and harmful effect upon that commerce. The prohibition in Title II of racial discrimination in public accommodations affecting commerce does not violate the Fifth Amendment as being a deprivation of property or liberty without due process of law. Such prohibition does not violate the Thirteenth Amendment as being "involuntary servitude."

C

Affirmed.

Katzenback v. McClung

379 U.S. 294 (1964)

FACTS

Appellees, whose restaurant in Birmingham, Alabama, caters to local white customers with take-out service for Negroes, serving food a substantial portion of which has moved in interstate commerce, sued to enjoin appellants from enforcing against their restaurant and others Title II of the Civil Rights Act of 1964 which they claimed was unconstitutional. A three-judge District Court granted an injunction, holding that there was no demonstrable connection between food purchased in interstate commerce and sold in a restaurant and Congress' conclusion that discrimination in the restaurant would affect commerce so as to warrant regulation of local activities to protect interstate commerce.

I Can Congress regulate a commercial enterprise serving the public if that enterprise sells goods, a substantial portion of which move in interstate commerce?

R Congress has the authority to regulate any public enterprise selling goods that have moved in interstate commerce and/or served interstate travelers.

A Since interference with governmental action has occurred and the constitutionality of Title II is before the Court in a companion case, the Court reaches the merits of this case by considering the complaint as an application for declaratory judgment, instead of denying relief for want of equity jurisdiction as it would ordinarily do on the ground that appellees should have waited to pursue the statutory procedures for adjudication of their rights. Congress acted within its power to protect and foster commerce in extending coverage of Title II to restaurants serving food a substantial portion of which has moved in interstate commerce, since it had ample basis to conclude that racial discrimination by such restaurants burdened interstate trade.

C Reversed.

National League of Cities v. Usery

426 U.S. 833 (1976)

FACTS

The Fair Labor Standards Act was amended in 1974 so as to extend the Act's minimum wage and maximum hour provisions to almost all employees of States and their political subdivisions. Appellants (including a number of cities and States) in these cases brought an action against appellee Secretary of Labor challenging the validity of these 1974 amendments and seeking declaratory and injunctive relief. A three-judge District Court dismissed the complaint for failure to state a claim upon which relief might be granted.

I Does Congress have the authority to regulate the conduct of cities under the Commerce Clause?

R The Commerce Clause does not allow Congress to regulate the states or local governments in their integral governmental functions.

A Insofar as the 1974 amendments operate directly to displace the States' abilities to structure employer-employee relationships in areas of traditional governmental functions, such as fire prevention, police protection, sanitation, public health, and parks and recreation, they are not within the authority granted Congress by the Commerce Clause. In attempting to exercise its Commerce Clause power to prescribe minimum wages and maximum hours to be paid by the States in their sovereign capacities, Congress has sought to wield its power in a fashion that would impair the States' "ability to function effectively in a federal system," *Fry v. United States*, and this exercise of congressional authority does not comport with the federal system of government embodied in the Constitution. Congress may not exercise its power to regulate commerce so as to force directly upon the States its choices as to how essential decisions regarding the conduct of integral governmental functions are to be made. *Maryland v. Wirtz*, overruled.

C Reversed and remanded.

Garcia v. San Antonio Metropolitan Transit Authority
469 U.S. 528 (1985)

FACTS

Appellee San Antonio Metropolitan Transit Authority (SAMTA) is a public mass-transit authority that is the major provider of transportation in the San Antonio, Tex., metropolitan area. It has received substantial federal financial assistance under the Urban Mass Transportation Act of 1964. In 1979, the Wage and Hour Administration of the Department of Labor issued an opinion that SAMTA's operations are not immune from the minimum-wage and overtime requirements of the Fair Labor Standards Act (FLSA) under *National League of Cities v. Usery*, in which it was held that the Commerce Clause does not empower Congress to enforce such requirements against the States "in areas of traditional governmental functions." SAMTA then filed an action in Federal District Court, seeking declaratory relief. Entering judgment for SAMTA, the District Court held that municipal ownership and operation of a mass-transit system is a traditional governmental function and thus, under National League of Cities, is exempt from the obligations imposed by the FLSA.

I Under the Commerce Clause, can Congress regulate a city's mass transit employer-employee relations?

R Congress has been granted full authority under the Commerce Clause to regulate a state or city's traditional functions despite the 10th Amendment.

A In affording SAMTA employees the protection of the wage and hour provisions of the FLSA, Congress contravened no affirmative limit on its power under the Commerce Clause. The attempt to draw the boundaries of state regulatory immunity in terms of "traditional governmental functions" is not only unworkable but is also inconsistent with established principles of federalism and, indeed, with those very federalism principles on which National League of Cities purported to rest. That case, accordingly, is overruled. There is nothing in the overtime and minimum-wage requirements of the FLSA, as applied to SAMTA, that is destructive of state sovereignty or violative of any constitutional provision. The States' continued role in the federal system is primarily guaranteed not by any externally imposed limits on the commerce power, but by the structure of the Federal Government itself. In these cases, the political process effectively protected that role.

C Reversed and remanded.

United States v. Lopez

514 U.S. 549 (1995)

FACTS

After Defendant-respondent Lopez, then a 12th-grade student, carried a concealed handgun into his high school, he was charged with violating the Gun-Free School Zones Act of 1990, which forbids "any individual knowingly to possess a firearm at a place that [he] knows . . . is a school zone," 18 U.S.C. 922(q)(1)(A). The District Court denied his motion to dismiss the indictment, concluding that 922(q) is a constitutional exercise of Congress' power to regulate activities in and affecting commerce. In reversing, the Court of Appeals held that, in light of what it characterized as insufficient Congressional findings and legislative history, 922(q) is invalid as beyond Congress' power under the Commerce Clause.

I

Does a federal statute which regulates firearm possession on school grounds exceed Congress' power to regulate commerce based on the Commerce Clause?

R

Congressional authority based on the Commerce Clause extends to activities that implicate 1) the channels of interstate commerce; or 2) the instrumentalities of interstate commerce; or 3) activities having a substantial relationship to interstate commerce.

A

The Act exceeds Congress' Commerce Clause authority. First, although this Court has upheld a wide variety of Congressional Acts regulating intrastate economic activity that substantially affected interstate commerce, the possession of a gun in a local school zone is in no sense an economic activity that might, through repetition elsewhere, have such a substantial effect on interstate commerce. Section 922(q) is a criminal statute that by its terms has nothing to do with "commerce" or any sort of economic enterprise, however broadly those terms are defined. Nor is it an essential part of a larger regulation of economic activity, in which the regulatory scheme could be undercut unless the intrastate activity were regulated. It cannot, therefore, be sustained under the Court's cases upholding regulations of activities that arise out of or are connected with a commercial transaction, which viewed in the aggregate, substantially affects interstate commerce. Second, 922(q) contains no jurisdictional element which would ensure, through case-by-case inquiry, that the firearms possession in question has the requisite Page II nexus with interstate commerce. Defendant-respondent Lopez was a local student at a local school; there is no indication that he had recently moved in interstate commerce, and there is no requirement that his possession of the firearm have any concrete tie to interstate commerce. To uphold the Government's contention that 922(q) is justified because firearms possession in a local school zone does indeed substantially affect interstate commerce would require this Court to pile inference upon inference in a manner that would bid fair to convert Congressional Commerce Clause authority to a general police power of the sort held only by the States.

C

Affirmed.

United States v. Morrison

529 U.S. 598 (2000)

FACTS

Plaintiff-petitioner Brzonkala filed suit alleging, *inter alia,* that she was raped by Defendant-respondents while the three were students at the Virginia Polytechnic Institute (co-defendant-respondent), and that this attack violated 42 U. S. C. §13981, which provides a federal civil remedy for the victims of gender-motivated violence. Respondents moved to dismiss on the grounds that the complaint failed to state a claim and that §13981's civil remedy is unconstitutional. Petitioner United States intervened to defend the section's constitutionality. In dismissing the complaint, the District Court held that it stated a claim against respondents, but that Congress lacked authority to enact §13981 under either §8 of the Commerce Clause or §5 of the Fourteenth Amendment, which Congress had explicitly identified as the sources of federal authority for §13981. The en banc Fourth Circuit affirmed.

I

Can gender-motivated violence be regulated by Congress via the Commerce Clause?

R

No Congressional authority exists to regulate gender–motivated violence under the Commerce Clause.

A

Section 13981 cannot be sustained under the Commerce Clause or §5 of the Fourteenth Amendment. The Commerce Clause does not provide Congress with authority to enact §13981's federal civil remedy. A Congressional enactment will be invalidated only upon a plain showing that Congress has exceeded its constitutional bounds. Petitioners assert that §13981 can be sustained under Congress' commerce power as a regulation of activity that substantially affects interstate commerce. The proper framework for analyzing such a claim is provided by the principles the Court set out in *Lopez*. First, in *Lopez,* the non-economic, criminal nature of possessing a firearm in a school zone was central to the Court's conclusion that Congress lacks authority to regulate such possession. Similarly, gender-motivated crimes of violence are not, in any sense, economic activity. Second, like the statute at issue in *Lopez*, §13981 contains no jurisdictional element establishing that the federal cause of action is in pursuance of Congress' regulation of interstate commerce. Although *Lopez* makes clear that such a jurisdictional element would lend support to the argument that §13981 is sufficiently tied to interstate commerce to come within Congress' authority, Congress elected to cast §13981's remedy over a wider, and more purely intrastate, body of violent crime. Third, although §13981, unlike the *Lopez* statute, *is* supported by numerous findings regarding the serious impact of gender-motivated violence on victims and their families, these findings are substantially weakened by the fact that they rely on reasoning that this Court has rejected, namely a but-for causal chain from the initial occurrence of violent crime to every attenuated effect upon interstate commerce. If accepted, this reasoning would allow Congress to regulate any crime whose nationwide, aggregated impact has substantial effects on employment, production, transit, or consumption. Moreover, such reasoning will not limit Congress to regulating violence, but may be applied equally as well to family law and other areas of state regulation since the aggregate effect of marriage, divorce, and childrearing on the national economy is undoubtedly significant. The Constitution requires a distinction between what is truly national and what is truly local, and there is no better example of the police power, which the Founders undeniably left reposed in the States and denied the central government, than the suppression of violent crime and vindication of its victims. Congress therefore may not regulate non-economic, violent criminal conduct based solely on the conduct's aggregate effect on interstate commerce. Section 5 of the Fourteenth Amendment, which permits Congress to enforce by appropriate legislation the constitutional guarantee that no State shall deprive any person of life, liberty, or property, without due process or deny any person equal protection of the laws also does not give Congress the authority to enact §13981. Petitioners' assertion that there is pervasive bias in various state justice systems against victims of gender-motivated violence is supported by a voluminous Congressional record. However, the Fourteenth Amendment places limitations on the manner in which Congress may attack discriminatory conduct. Foremost among them is the principle that the Amendment prohibits only state action, not private conduct. This was the conclusion reached in *United States v. Harris* and the *Civil Rights Cases,* which were both decided shortly after the Amendment's adoption. The force of the doctrine of *stare decisis* behind these decisions stems not only from the length of time they have been on the books, but also from the insight attributable to the Members of the Court at that time, who all had intimate knowledge and familiarity with the events surrounding the Amendment's adoption. Neither *United States v. Guest* nor *District of Columbia v. Carter* casts any doubt on the enduring vitality of the *Civil Rights Cases* and *Harris.* Assuming that there has been gender-based disparate treatment by state authorities in this case, it would not be enough to save §13981's civil remedy, which is directed not at a State or state actor but at individuals who have committed criminal acts motivated by gender bias. Section 13981 visits no consequence on any Virginia public official involved in investigating or prosecuting Brzonkala's assault, and it is thus unlike any of the §5 remedies this Court has previously upheld. Section 13981 is also different from previously upheld remedies in that it applies uniformly throughout the Nation, even though Congress' findings indicate that the problem addressed does not exist in all, or even most, States. In contrast, the §5 remedy in *Katzenbach* was directed only to those States in which Congress found that there had been discrimination.

C

Affirmed.

Solid Waste Agency of Northern Cook County v. U.S. Army Corps of Engineers

531 U.S. 159 (2001)

FACTS

Petitioner, a consortium of suburban Chicago municipalities, selected as a solid waste disposal site an abandoned sand and gravel pit with excavation trenches that had evolved into permanent and seasonal ponds. Because the operation called for filling in some of the ponds, petitioner contacted federal respondents, including the Army Corps of Engineers (Corps), to determine if a landfill permit was required under §404(a) of the Clean Water Act (CWA), which authorizes the Corps to issue permits allowing the discharge of dredged or fill material into "navigable waters." The CWA defines "navigable waters" as "the waters of the United States," 33 U. S. C. §1362(7), and the Corps' regulations define such waters to include intrastate waters, "the use, degradation or destruction of which could affect interstate or foreign commerce," 33 CFR §328.3(a)(3). In 1986, the Corps attempted to clarify its jurisdiction, stating, in what has been dubbed the "Migratory Bird Rule," that §404(a) extends to intrastate waters that, *inter alia,* provide habitat for migratory birds. Asserting jurisdiction over the instant site pursuant to that Rule, the Corps refused to issue a §404(a) permit. When petitioner challenged the Corps' jurisdiction and the merits of the permit denial, the District Court granted respondents summary judgment on the jurisdictional issue. The Seventh Circuit held that Congress has authority under the Commerce Clause to regulate intrastate waters and that the Migratory Bird Rule is a reasonable interpretation of the CWA.

I

Does Congress have authority under the Commerce Clause to regulate intrastate waters?

R

Congress has authority under the Commerce Clause to regulate intrastate waters and that the Migratory Bird Rule is a reasonable interpretation of the CWA.

A

Title 33 CFR §328.3(a)(3), as clarified and applied to petitioner's site pursuant to the Migratory Bird Rule, exceeds the authority granted to respondents under §404(a) of the CWA. In *United States* v. *Riverside Bayview Homes, Inc.,* this Court held that the Corps had §404(a) jurisdiction over wetlands adjacent to a navigable waterway, noting that the term "navigable" is of "limited import" and that Congress evidenced its intent to "regulate at least some waters that would not be deemed `navigable' under [that term's] classical understanding," *id.,* at 133. But that holding was based in large measure upon Congress' unequivocal acquiescence to, and approval of, the Corps' regulations interpreting the CWA to cover wetlands adjacent to navigable waters. The Court expressed no opinion on the question of the Corps' authority to regulate wetlands not adjacent to open water, and the statute's text will not allow extension of the Corps' jurisdiction to such wetlands here. The Corps' *original* interpretation of the CWA in its 1974 regulations - which emphasized that a water body's capability of use by the public for transportation or commerce determines whether it is navigable - is inconsistent with that which it espouses here, yet respondents present no persuasive evidence that the Corps mistook Congress' intent in 1974.

Solid Waste Agency of Northern Cook County v. U.S. Army Corps of Engineers

531 U.S. 159 (2001)

Respondents contend that whatever its original aim, when Congress amended the CWA in 1977, it approved the more expansive definition of "navigable waters" found in the Corps' 1977 regulations. Specifically, respondents submit that Congress' failure to pass legislation that would have overturned the 1977 regulations and the extension of the Environmental Protection Agency's jurisdiction in §404(g) to include waters "other than" traditional "navigable waters" indicates that Congress recognized and accepted a broad definition of "navigable waters" that includes non-navigable, isolated, intrastate waters. This Court recognizes congressional acquiescence to administrative interpretations of a statute with extreme care. Failed legislative proposals are a particularly dangerous ground on which to rest an interpretation of a prior statute, *Central Bank of Denver, N. A.* v. *First Interstate Bank of Denver, N. A.*, because a bill can be proposed or rejected for any number of reasons. Here, respondents have failed to make the necessary showing that Congress' failure to pass legislation demonstrates acquiescence to the 1977 regulations or the 1986 Migratory Bird Rule. Section 404(g) is equally unenlightening, for it does not conclusively determine the construction to be placed on the use of the term "waters" elsewhere in the CWA. Even if §404(a) were not clear, this Court would not extend deference to the Migratory Bird Rule under *Chevron U. S. A. Inc.* v. *Natural Resources Defense Council, Inc.* Where an administrative interpretation of a statute would raise serious constitutional problems, the Court will construe the statute to avoid such problems unless the construction is plainly contrary to Congress' intent. The grant of authority to Congress under the Commerce Clause, though broad, is not unlimited. Respondents' arguments, *e.g.*, that the Migratory Bird Rule falls within Congress' power to regulate intrastate activities that substantially affect interstate commerce, raise significant constitutional questions, yet there is nothing approaching a clear statement from Congress that it intended §404(a) to reach an abandoned sand and gravel pit such as the one at issue. Permitting respondents to claim federal jurisdiction over ponds and mudflats falling within the Migratory Bird Rule would also result in a significant impingement of the States' traditional and primary power over land and water use. The Court thus reads the statute as written to avoid such significant constitutional and federalism questions and rejects the request for administrative deference.

C Reversed.

Pierce County, Washington v. Guillen

123 S. Ct. 720 (2003)

FACTS

As part of its effort to improve the safety of the Nation's highways, Congress adopted the Hazard Elimination Program (Program), 23 U. S. C. §152, which provides state and local governments with funding to improve the most dangerous sections of their roads. To be eligible for such funding, a government must undertake a thorough evaluation of its public roads. Because of States' concerns that the absence of confidentiality with respect to §152's compliance measures would increase the liability risk for accidents that took place at hazardous locations before improvements could be made and Department of Transportation's concerns that the States' reluctance to be forthcoming in their data collection efforts undermined the Program's effectiveness, Congress, in 1987, adopted §409, which provided that materials "compiled" for §152 purposes "shall not be admitted into evidence in Federal or State court." Responding to subsequent court decisions holding that §409 did not apply to pretrial discovery and protected only materials that an agency actually generated for §152 purposes, not documents that the agency collected to prepare its §152 application, Congress expressly made the statute applicable to pretrial discovery in 1991 and added the phrase "or collected" after the word "compiled" in 1995. Several months before respondent Ignacio Gullien's wife died in an automobile accident at an intersection in petitioner county, petitioner's §152 funding request for the intersection was denied. Its second request was approved three weeks after the accident. Petitioner declined to provide respondents' counsel with information about accidents at the intersection, asserting that any relevant information was protected by §409. Respondents then filed an action in Washington state court, alleging that petitioner's refusal to disclose violated the State's Public Disclosure Act (PDA). The trial court granted respondents summary judgment, ordering petitioner to disclose five documents and pay respondents' attorney's fees. While petitioner's appeal was pending, respondents filed another state-court action, alleging that petitioner had been negligent in failing to install proper traffic controls at the intersection. Petitioner refused to comply with their discovery request for information regarding accidents at the intersection, and respondents successfully sought an order to compel. The State Court of Appeals granted petitioner's motion for discretionary appellate review of the interlocutory order, consolidated this and the PDA appeals, and in large part affirmed, concluding that four of the documents requested in the PDA action were not protected. On further appeal, the Washington Supreme Court determined that disclosure under the relevant state laws would be appropriate only if the requested materials were not protected by §409; that protection under §409, as amended in 1995, turned on whether the documents were collected for §152 purposes, without regard to the identity of the documents' custodian; and that the 1995 amendment's adoption exceeded Congress' powers under the Spending, Commerce, and Necessary and Proper Clauses. It therefore vacated the lower court's judgment and remanded the case.

I Is §409, which protects information "compiled or collected" in connection with certain federal highway safety programs from being discovered or admitted in certain federal or state trials, a valid exercise of Congress's authority under the Constitution?

Pierce County, Washington v. Guillen

123 S. Ct. 720 (2003)

R §409, which protects information "compiled or collected" in connection with certain federal highway safety programs from being discovered or admitted in certain federal or state trials, is a valid exercise of Congress's authority under the Constitution.

A This Court lacks jurisdiction to hear the tort portion of the case but has jurisdiction to hear the PDA portion. Certain state-court judgments can be treated as final for jurisdictional purposes even though further proceedings are to take place in the state courts. *Cox Broadcasting Corp.* v. *Cohn,* (outlining four exceptions to the finality rule). In the tort action, the Washington Supreme Court resolved only a discovery dispute; it did not determine the litigation's final outcome. And the *Cox* exceptions do not apply to that action. Accordingly, this Court dismisses the writ of certiorari with respect to that action for want of jurisdiction. However, the PDA action falls squarely under the first *Cox* exception. The State Supreme Court's ruling that the 1995 amendment to §409 was invalid, which left four documents subject to disclosure under the PDA and only the amount of attorney's fees remaining to be decided on remand, is "conclusive" as to the federal issue and "the outcome of further proceedings preordained." Both the original §409 and the 1995 amendment fall within Congress' Commerce Clause power. Before addressing the constitutional question, this Court must determine §409's scope. Evidentiary privileges, such as §409, must be construed narrowly because they impede the search for the truth. This Court agrees with the United States that §409 protects only information compiled or collected for §152 purposes, but does not protect information that was compiled or collected for purposes unrelated to §152, as held by agencies that complied or collected that information, even if the information was at some point "collected" by another agency for §152 purposes. Although respondents offer the narrowest interpretation of §409 - that §409 protects only materials actually created by the agency responsible for seeking §152 funding - their reading leaves the 1995 amendment (changing "compiled" to "compiled or collected") with no real and substantial effect. By contrast, petitioner's reading--that a document initially prepared by an agency for purposes unrelated to §152, and held by that agency, becomes protected under §409 when a copy of that document is collected by another agency for §152 purposes--gives the statute too broad of a reach, thus conflicting with the rule that privileges should be construed narrowly. The Government's interpretation suffers from neither of these faults. It gives effect to the 1995 amendment by making clear that §409 protects not just the information an agency compiles for §152 purposes but also any information that an agency collects from other sources for those purposes. It also takes a narrower view of the privilege by making it inapplicable to information compiled or collected for purposes unrelated to §152 and held by agencies that are not pursuing §152 objectives. The Court's view of §409 is reinforced by the 1995 amendment's history. "[A]s collected" was added to address confusion about §409's proper scope and to overcome judicial reluctance to protect raw data collected for §152 purposes. Congress wished to make clear that §152 was not intended to be an effort-free tool in litigation against state and local governments, but §409's text evinces no intent to make plaintiffs worse off than they would have been had §152 funding never existed. Section 409 is a proper exercise of Congress' Commerce Clause authority to "regulate the use of the channels of interstate commerce" and "to regulate and protect the instrumentalities of interstate commerce," *United States* v. *Lopez*. Congress adopted §152 to assist state and local governments in reducing hazardous conditions in the Nations' channels of commerce, but that effort was impeded by the States' reluctance to comply fully with §152's requirements lest those governments become easier targets for negligence actions by providing a centralized location from which would-be plaintiffs could obtain much of the evidence necessary to sue. Because Congress could reasonably believe that adopting a measure eliminating an unforeseen side effect of §152's information-gathering requirement would result in more diligent collection efforts, more candid discussions of hazardous locations, better informed decisionmaking, and greater safety on the Nation's roads, both the original §409 and the 1995 amendment can be viewed as legislation aimed at improving safety in the channels of commerce and increasing protections for the instrumentalities of interstate commerce.

C

Certiorari dismissed in part; reversed and remanded.

New York v. United States

505 U.S. 144 (1992)

FACTS

Together with No. 91-558, *County of Allegany, New York v. United States et al.*, and No. 91-563, *County of Cortland, New York v. United States et al.*, also on certiorari to the same court. Faced with a looming shortage of disposal sites for low level radioactive waste in 31 States, Congress enacted the Low-Level Radioactive Waste Policy Amendments Act of 1985 (the "Act"), which, among other things, imposes upon States, either alone or in "regional compacts" with other States, the obligation to provide for the disposal of waste generated within their borders, and contains three provisions setting forth "incentives" to States to comply with that obligation. The first set of incentives - the monetary incentives - works in three steps: (1) States with disposal sites are authorized to impose a surcharge on radioactive waste received from other States; (2) the Secretary of Energy collects a portion of this surcharge and places it in an escrow account; and (3) States achieving a series of milestones in developing sites receive portions of this fund. The second set of incentives - the access incentives - authorizes sited States and regional compacts gradually to increase the cost of access to their sites, and then to deny access altogether, to waste generated in States that do not meet federal deadlines. The so-called third "incentive" - the "take-title" provision - specifies that a State or regional compact that fails to provide for the disposal of all internally generated waste by a particular date must, upon the request of the waste's generator or owner, take title to and possession of the waste and become liable for all damages suffered by the generator or owner as a result of the State's failure to promptly take possession. Plaintiff-petitioners, the State of New York and two of its Counties, filed this suit against the United States (Defendant-respondent), seeking a declaratory judgment that, *inter alia*, the three incentives provisions are inconsistent with the Tenth Amendment - which declares that "powers not delegated to the United States by the Constitution, nor prohibited by it to the States, are reserved to the States" - and with the Guarantee Clause of Article IV, 4 - which directs the United States to "guarantee to every State . . . a Republican Form of Government." The District Court dismissed the complaint, and the Court of Appeals affirmed.

I Does the use of a "take-title" provision which compels the states to follow federal guidelines amount to an unconstitutional exercise of federal authority?

R The "take-title" provision is unconstitutional as Congress may not "commandeer [the state] legislative processes by directly compelling them to enact and enforce a federal regulatory program."

A The Act's monetary incentives and access incentives provisions are consistent with the Constitution's allocation of power between the Federal and State Governments, but the "take-title" provision is not. In ascertaining whether any of the challenged provisions oversteps the boundary between federal and state power, the Court must determine whether it is authorized by the affirmative grants to Congress contained in Article I's Commerce and Spending Clauses or whether it invades the province of state sovereignty reserved by the Tenth Amendment. Although regulation of the interstate market in the disposal of low level radioactive waste is well within Congress' Commerce Clause authority and Congress could, if it wished, pre-empt entirely state regulation in this area, a review of this Court's decisions and the history of the Constitutional Convention, demonstrates that Congress may not commandeer the States' legislative processes by directly compelling them to enact and enforce a federal regulatory program, but must exercise legislative authority directly upon individuals. The United States' alternative arguments purporting to find limited circumstances in which Congressional compulsion of state regulation is constitutionally permissible - that such compulsion is justified where the federal interest is sufficiently important; that the Constitution does, in some circumstances, permit federal directives to state governments; and that the Constitution endows Congress with the power to arbitrate disputes between States in interstate commerce - are rejected. Also rejected is the sited state respondents' argument that the Act cannot be ruled an unconstitutional infringement of New York sovereignty because officials of that State lent their support, and consented, to the Act's passage. A departure from the Constitution's plan for the intergovernmental allocation of authority cannot be ratified by the "consent" of state officials, since the Constitution protects state sovereignty for the benefit of individuals, not States or their governments, and since the officials' interests may not coincide with the Constitution's allocation. Nor does New York's prior support estop it from asserting the Act's unconstitutionality. Even assuming that the Guarantee Clause provides a basis upon which a State or its subdivisions may sue to enjoin the enforcement of a federal statute, petitioners have not made out a claim that the Act's money incentives and access incentives provisions are inconsistent with that Clause. Neither the threat of loss of federal funds nor the possibility that the State's waste producers may find themselves excluded from other States' disposal sites can reasonably be said to deny New York a republican form of government. The take-title provision is severable from the rest of the Act, since severance will not prevent the operation of the rest of the Act or defeat its purpose of encouraging the States to attain local or regional self-sufficiency in low level radioactive waste disposal; since the Act still includes two incentives to encourage States along this road; since a State whose waste generators are unable to gain access to out-of-state disposal sites may encounter considerable internal pressure to provide for disposal, even without the prospect of taking title; and since any burden caused by New York's failure to secure a site will not be borne by other States' residents because the sited regional compacts need not accept New York's waste after the final transition period.

C

Affirmed in part and reversed in part.

Printz v. United States

521 U.S. 898 (1997)

FACTS

The Brady Handgun Violence Prevention Act ("The Brady Act") provisions require the Attorney General to establish a national system for instantly checking prospective handgun purchasers' backgrounds. While the system was being put in place, interim provisions required that a firearms dealer seek identifying information from the transferee and provide that information to the "chief law enforcement officer" (CLEO) of each local jurisdiction to conduct such checks and perform related tasks on an interim basis until the national system becomes operative. Plaintiff-petitioners Jay Printz and Richard Mack, the CLEOs for counties in Montana and Arizona, filed separate actions challenging the interim provisions' constitutionality. In each case, the District Court held that the background check provision was unconstitutional, but concluded that it was severable from the remainder of the Act, effectively leaving a voluntary background check system in place. The Ninth Circuit reversed, finding none of the interim provisions unconstitutional.

I

May an Act of Congress compel a state actor to implement federal statutes and/or guidelines?

R

Congress cannot force the states to enact or enforce a federal regulatory program and may not evade such a prohibition by tasking the State's actors directly.

A

The Brady Act's interim provision commanding CLEOs to conduct background checks, §922(s)(2), is unconstitutional. Extinguished with it is the duty implicit in the background check requirement that the CLEO accept completed handgun applicant statements (Brady Forms) from firearms dealers, §§922(s)(1)(A)(i)(III) and (IV). Because there is no constitutional text speaking to the precise question whether Congressional action compelling state officers to execute federal laws is unconstitutional, the answer to the CLEOs' challenge must be sought in historical understanding and practice, in the Constitution's structure, and in this Court's jurisprudence. Relevant constitutional practice tends to negate the existence of the Congressional power asserted here, but is not conclusive. Enactments of the early Congresses seem to contain no evidence of an assumption that the Federal Government may command the States' executive power in the absence of a particularized constitutional authorization. The early enactments establish, at most, that the Constitution was originally understood to permit imposition of an obligation on state judges to enforce federal prescriptions related to matters appropriate for the judicial power. The Government misplaces its reliance on portions of The Federalist suggesting that federal responsibilities could be imposed on state officers. None of these statements necessarily implies--what is the critical point here--that Congress could impose these responsibilities without the States' consent. They appear to rest on the natural assumption that the States would consent. Finally, there is an absence of executive commandeering federal statutes in the country's later history, at least until very recent years. Even assuming that newer laws represent an assertion of the Congressional power challenged here, they are of such recent vintage that they are not probative of a constitutional tradition. The Constitution's structure reveals a principle that controls these cases: the system of "dual sovereignty." Although the States surrendered many of their powers to the new Federal Government, they retained a residuary and inviolable sovereignty that is reflected throughout the Constitution's text. The Framers rejected the concept of a central government that would act upon and through the States, and instead designed a system in which the State and Federal Governments would exercise concurrent authority over the people. The Federal Government's power would be augmented immeasurably and impermissibly if it were able to impress into its service the police officers of the 50 States. Federal control of state officers would also have an effect upon the separation and equilibration of powers between the three branches of the Federal Government itself. The Brady Act effectively transfers the President's responsibility to administer the laws enacted by Congress, Art. II, §§2 and 3, to thousands of CLEOs in the 50 States, who are left to implement the program without meaningful Presidential control. The Federal Executive's unity would be shattered, and the power of the President would be subject to reduction, if Congress could simply require state officers to execute its laws. Contrary to the dissent's contention, the Brady Act's direction of the actions of state executive officials is not constitutionally valid under Art. I, §8, as a law "necessary and proper" to the execution of Congress's Commerce Clause power to regulate handgun sales. Where, as here, a law violates the state sovereignty principle, it is not a law "proper for carrying into Execution" delegated powers within the Necessary and Proper Clause's meaning. Finally, and most conclusively in these cases, the Court's jurisprudence makes clear that the Federal Government may not compel the States to enact or administer a federal regulatory program. The attempts of the Government and the dissent to distinguish *New York* - on grounds that the Brady Act's background check provision does not require state legislative or executive officials to make policy; that requiring state officers to perform discrete, ministerial federal tasks does not diminish the state or federal officials' accountability; and that the Brady Act is addressed to individual CLEOs while the provisions invalidated in New York were directed to the State itself - are not persuasive. A "balancing" analysis is inappropriate here, since the whole object of the law is to direct the functioning of the state executive, and hence to compromise the structural framework of dual sovereignty; it is the very principle of separate state sovereignty that such a law offends. With the Act's background check and implicit receipt of forms requirements invalidated, the Brady Act requirements that CLEOs destroy all Brady Forms and related records, §922(s)(6)(B)(i), and give would be purchasers written statements of the reasons for determining their ineligibility to receive handguns, §922(s)(6)(C), require no action whatsoever on the part of CLEOs such as petitioners, who are not voluntary participants in administration of the federal scheme. As to them, these provisions are not unconstitutional, but simply inoperative.

C

Reversed.

Reno v. Condon

528 U.S. 141 (2000)

FACTS

State departments of motor vehicles (DMVs) require drivers and automobile owners to provide personal information, which may include a person's name, address, telephone number, vehicle description, Social Security number, medical information, and photograph, as a condition of obtaining a driver's license or registering an automobile. Finding that many States sell this information to individuals and businesses for significant revenues, Congress enacted the Driver's Privacy Protection Act of 1994 (DPPA), which establishes a regulatory scheme that restricts the States' ability to disclose a driver's personal information without the driver's consent. South Carolina law conflicts with the DPPA's provisions. Following the DPPA's enactment, South Carolina and its Attorney General filed this suit, alleging that the DPPA violates the Tenth and Eleventh Amendments to the United States Constitution. Concluding that the DPPA is incompatible with the principles of federalism inherent in the Constitution's division of power between the States and the Federal Government, the District Court granted summary judgment for the State and permanently enjoined the DPPA's enforcement against the State and its officers. The Fourth Circuit affirmed, concluding that the Act violates constitutional principles of federalism.

I May Congress validly regulate state activities that impose costs that may be borne by the states?

R Congress may validly regulate state activities even when such regulations impose costs that may be borne by the states.

A In enacting the DPPA, Congress did not run afoul of the federalism principles enunciated in *New York v. United States* and *Printz v. United States.* The Federal Government correctly asserts that the DPPA is a proper exercise of Congress' authority to regulate interstate commerce under the Commerce Clause, U. S. Const., Art. I, §8, cl. 3. The motor vehicle information which the States have historically sold is used by insurers, manufacturers, direct marketers, and others engaged in interstate commerce to contact drivers with customized solicitations. The information is also used in the stream of interstate commerce by various public and private entities for matters related to interstate motoring. Because drivers' personal, identifying information is, in this context, an article of commerce, its sale or release into the interstate stream of business is sufficient to support congressional regulation. This does not conclusively resolve the DPPA's constitutionality because in *New York* and *Printz* the Court held that federal statutes were invalid, not because Congress lacked legislative authority over the subject matter, but because those statutes violated Tenth Amendment federalism principles. However, the DPPA does not violate those principles. This case is instead governed by *South Carolina* v. *Baker*, in which a statute prohibiting States from issuing unregistered bonds was upheld because it regulated state activities, rather than seeking to control or influence the manner in which States regulated private parties. Like that statute, the DPPA does not require the States in their sovereign capacity to regulate their own citizens; rather, it regulates the States as the owners of databases. It does not require the South Carolina Legislature to enact any laws or regulations, as did the statute at issue in *New York* , and it does not require state officials to assist in the enforcement of federal statutes regulating private individuals, as did the law considered in *Printz* . Thus, the DPPA is consistent with the principles set forth in those cases. The Court need not address South Carolina's argument that the DPPA unconstitutionally regulates the States exclusively rather than by means of a generally applicable law. The DPPA is generally applicable because it regulates the universe of entities that participate as suppliers to the market for motor vehicle information--the States as initial suppliers of the information in interstate commerce and private resellers or re-disclosers of that information in commerce.

C Reversed.

United States v. Butler

297 U.S. 1 (1936)

FACTS

The Agricultural Adjustment Act of 1933 was part of the New Deal measures which sought "to establish and maintain such balance between the production and consumption of agricultural commodities, and such marketing conditions therefore, as will reestablish prices to farmers at a level that will give agricultural commodities a purchasing power with respect to articles that farmers buy, equivalent to the purchasing power of agricultural commodities in the base period." The core intent of the Act was to stabilize farm prices by limiting agricultural production. The Secretary of Agriculture Secretary is not required, but is permitted, if, in his sole judgment, the policy of the Act will so be promoted, to make agreements with individual farmers for a reduction of acreage or production upon such terms as he may think fair and reasonable in exchange for benefit payments. The benefit payments were drawn out of funds obtained from a processing tax "levied, assessed, and collected upon the first domestic processing of the commodity, whether of domestic production or imported, and shall be paid by the processor." A processing tax on cotton was imposed upon the Hoosac Mills Corporation. Thereafter, Plaintiff-respondents Butler and other co-receivers for the company attacked the tax, claiming that it was an unconstitutional attempt to regulate agricultural production. The District Court found the taxes valid and ordered them paid. Upon appeal the Circuit Court of Appeals reversed the order. The judgment under review was entered prior to the adoption of the amending act of August 24, 1935, Title 5, so the U.S. Supreme Court was therefore concerned only with the original act.

I

May Congress' taxing power be used to raise funds to purchase a compliance in an area where Congress is powerless to command; that is, an area of concern reserved to the States?

R

Congress' taxing power may not be used to raise funds to purchase compliance in an area that Congress is powerless to command.

A

When an act of Congress is challenged in the courts as potentially unconstitutional, the function of the judiciary is lay the statute at issue next to the Constitution and decide whether the former squares with the latter. This Court neither condemns nor approves any legislative policy. Our function is to ascertain and declare whether the legislation is in accordance with, or in contravention of, the provisions of the Constitution. Having done that, our task is finished. The Government asserts that even if the respondents question the propriety of the appropriation embodied in the statute, their attack must fail because Article I, §8 of the Constitution authorizes the completed expenditure of the funds raised by the tax. The clause thought to authorize this act gives Congress the power to "lay and collect Taxes, Duties, Imposts and Excises, to pay the Debts and provide for the common Defense and general Welfare of the United States." The Government advances the argument that the clause grants power to provide for the general welfare independently of the taxing power. However, as Mr. Justice Story has pointed out, such a view has never been authoritatively accepted. We thus conclude, that the reading advocated by Hamilton and Justice Story is in fact the correct one: that while the power to tax is not unlimited, its confines are set in the clause that confers the power, rather than in §8 which bestows and defines the legislative powers of Congress. Thus, the power of Congress to authorize expenditure of public moneys for public purposes is not limited by the direct grants of legislative power found in the Constitution. We find further support for the unconstitutionality of the enforcement of the tax in another principle embedded in the Constitution: The Act invades that power reserved to the States. The statutory plan to regulate agricultural production is a matter beyond the reach of Congress. Consequently, the tax, the appropriation of funds raised and the directions for disbursement of the funds are but part of that unconstitutional plan and are themselves unconstitutional. If the taxing power may not be used to enforce regulation over matters of state concern [e.g., Child Labor Tax Case], it may not be used to raise funds to purchase compliance in an area that Congress is powerless to command. The Government asserts that the plan is constitutional because the end is accomplished by voluntary cooperation. We disagree on two fronts. First, the regulation is not voluntary because if farmers do not comply they will lose their benefits. The monetary amount of the benefits offered is intended to exert coercion by economic pressure. Second, even if the plan were voluntary, the contract for the reduction of acreage and the control of production are not with the sphere of power conferred to Congress by the Constitution. An appropriation to be expended by the United States under contracts calling for a violation of state law clearly offends the Constitution. At best, this is a scheme for purchasing with federal funds submission to federal regulation of a subject reserved to the states.

C Affirmed.

Sabri v. United States

541 U.S. 600 (2004)

FACTS

After petitioner Sabri offered three separate bribes to a Minneapolis councilman to facilitate construction in the city, Sabri was charged with violating 18 U. S. C. §666(a)(2), which proscribes bribery of state and local officials of entities, such as Minneapolis, that receive at least $10,000 in federal funds. Before trial, Sabri moved to dismiss the indictment on the ground that §666(a)(2) is unconstitutional on its face for failure to require proof of a connection between the federal funds and the alleged bribe, as an element of liability. The District Court agreed, but the Eighth Circuit reversed, holding that the absence of such an express requirement was not fatal, and that the statute was constitutional under the Constitution's Necessary and Proper Clause in serving the objects of the congressional spending power.

I

Is Section 666(a)(2) a valid exercise of Congress's Article I authority?

R

18 U.S.C. §666(a)(2), probscribing bribery of a state, local and tribal officials of entities that receive at least $10,000 in federal funds, is a valid exercise of Congress's Article I authority.

A

Section 666(a)(2) is a valid exercise of Congress's Article I authority. Sabri's "facial" challenge that §666(a)(2) must, as an element of the offense, require proof of connection with federal money is readily rejected. This Court does not presume the unconstitutionality of all federal criminal statutes from the absence of an explicit jurisdictional hook, and there is no occasion even to consider the need for such a requirement where there is no reason to suspect that enforcing a criminal statute would extend beyond a legitimate interest cognizable under Article I, §8. Congress has Spending Clause authority to appropriate federal moneys to promote the general welfare, Art. I, §8, cl. 1, and corresponding Necessary and Proper Clause authority, Art. I, §8, cl. 18, to assure that taxpayer dollars appropriated under that power are in fact spent for the general welfare, rather than frittered away in graft or upon projects undermined by graft. Congress does not have to accept the risk of getting poor performance for its money, owing to local and state administrators' improbity. Section 666(a)(2) addresses the problem at the sources of bribes, by rational means, to safeguard the integrity of federal dollar recipients. Although not every bribe offered or paid to covered government agents will be traceably skimmed from specific federal payments, or be found in the guise of a *quid pro quo* for some dereliction in spending a federal grant, these facts do not portend enforcement beyond the scope of federal interest, for the simple reason that corruption need not be so limited in order to affect that interest. Money is fungible, bribed officials are untrustworthy stewards of federal funds, and corrupt contractors do not deliver dollar-for-dollar value. It is enough that the statute condition the offense on a threshold amount of federal dollars to the government such as that provided here and a bribe that goes well beyond liquor and cigars. The legislative history confirms that §666(a)(2) is an instance of necessary and proper legislation. Neither of Sabri's arguments against §666(a)(2)'s constitutionality helps him. First, his claim that

§666 is of a piece with the legislation ruled unconstitutional in *United States* v. *Lopez* and *United States* v. *Morrison,* is unavailing because these precedents do not control here. In them, the Court struck down federal statutes regulating gun possession near schools and gender-motivated violence, respectively, because it found the effects of those activities on interstate commerce insufficiently robust. Here, in contrast, Congress was within its prerogative to ensure that the objects of spending are not menaced by local administrators on the take. Second, contrary to Sabri's argument, §666(a)(2) is not an unduly coercive, and impermissibly sweeping, condition on the grant of federal funds, but is authority to bring federal power to bear directly on individuals who convert public spending into unearned private gain. The Court disapproves Sabri's technique for challenging his indictment by facial attack on the underlying statute. If Sabri was making any substantive constitutional claim, it had to be seen as an overbreadth challenge; the most he could seriously say was that the statute could not be enforced against him, because it could not be enforced against someone else whose behavior would be outside the scope of Congress's Article I authority to legislate. Facial challenges of this sort are to be discouraged because they invite judgments on fact-poor records and entail a departure from the norms of federal-court adjudication by calling for relaxation of familiar standing requirements to allow a determination that the law would be unconstitutionally applied to different parties and different circumstances from those at hand. Thus, the Court has recognized the validity of facial attacks alleging overbreadth (though not necessarily using that term) in relatively few settings, and, generally, only on the strength of a specific reason, such as free speech, that is weighty enough to overcome the Court's well-founded reticence.

C

Affirmed and remanded.

South Dakota v. Dole

483 U.S. 203 (1987)

FACTS

20 U.S.C. §158 directs the Secretary of Transportation to withhold 5% of otherwise allocable federal highway funds from States "in which the purchase or public possession . . . of any alcoholic beverage by a person who is less than twenty-one years of age is lawful." South Dakota, which permits persons 19 years old or older to purchase beer containing up to 3.2% alcohol, sued in Federal District Court for a declaratory judgment that §158 violates the constitutional limitations on congressional exercise of the spending power under Art. I, 8, cl. 1, of the Constitution and violates the Twenty-first Amendment. The District Court rejected the State's claims and the Court of Appeals affirmed.

I May Congress constitutionally, but indirectly, achieve those regulatory goals (a conditional grant of federal highway funds) that it could not achieve directly through the use of its spending power?

R Congress may indirectly encourage a state via a "financial inducement" (the loss of 5% of funds otherwise obtainable under specific highway grant programs) to comply with those regulatory objectives through the use of its spending power that it could not achieve directly.

A Even if Congress, in view of the Twenty-first Amendment, might lack the power to impose directly a national minimum drinking age (a question not decided here), §158's indirect encouragement of state action to obtain uniformity in the States' drinking ages is a valid use of the spending power. Incident to the spending power, Congress may attach conditions on the receipt of federal funds. However, exercise of the power is subject to certain restrictions, including that it must be in pursuit of "the general welfare." Section 158 is consistent with such restriction, since the means chosen by Congress to address a dangerous situation - the interstate problem resulting from the incentive, created by differing state drinking ages, for young persons to combine drinking and driving - were reasonably calculated to advance the general welfare. Section 158 also is consistent with the spending power restrictions that, if Congress desires to condition the States' receipt of federal funds, it must do so unambiguously, enabling the States to exercise their choice knowingly, cognizant of the consequences of their participation; and that conditions on federal grants must be related to a national concern (safe interstate travel here). Nor is 158 invalidated by the spending power limitation that the conditional grant of federal funds must not be independently barred by other constitutional provisions (the Twenty-first Amendment here). Such limitation is not a prohibition on the indirect achievement of objectives which Congress is not empowered to achieve directly, but, instead, means that the power may not be used to induce the States to engage in activities that would themselves be unconstitutional. The relatively small financial inducement offered by Congress here - resulting from the State's loss of only 5% of federal funds otherwise obtainable under certain highway grant programs - is not so coercive as to be compulsive.

C Affirmed.

United States v. Morrison

529 U.S. 598 (2000)

FACTS

Plaintiff-petitioner Brzonkala filed suit alleging, *inter alia,* that she was raped by Defendant-respondents while the three were students at the Virginia Polytechnic Institute (co-defendant-respondent), and that this attack violated 42 U. S. C. §13981, which provides a federal civil remedy for the victims of gender-motivated violence. Respondents moved to dismiss on the grounds that the complaint failed to state a claim and that §13981's civil remedy is unconstitutional. Petitioner United States intervened to defend the section's constitutionality. In dismissing the complaint, the District Court held that it stated a claim against respondents, but that Congress lacked authority to enact §13981 under either §8 of the Commerce Clause or §5 of the Fourteenth Amendment, which Congress had explicitly identified as the sources of federal authority for §13981. The en banc Fourth Circuit affirmed.

I Can gender-motivated violence be regulated by Congress via the Commerce Clause?

R No Congressional authority exists to regulate gender–motivated violence under the Commerce Clause.

A Section 13981 cannot be sustained under the Commerce Clause or §5 of the Fourteenth Amendment. The Commerce Clause does not provide Congress with authority to enact §13981's federal civil remedy. A Congressional enactment will be invalidated only upon a plain showing that Congress has exceeded its constitutional bounds. Petitioners assert that §13981 can be sustained under Congress' commerce power as a regulation of activity that substantially affects interstate commerce. The proper framework for analyzing such a claim is provided by the principles the Court set out in *Lopez*. First, in *Lopez,* the non-economic, criminal nature of possessing a firearm in a school zone was central to the Court's conclusion that Congress lacks authority to regulate such possession. Similarly, gender-motivated crimes of violence are not, in any sense, economic activity. Second, like the statute at issue in *Lopez*, §13981 contains no jurisdictional element establishing that the federal cause of action is in pursuance of Congress' regulation of interstate commerce. Although *Lopez* makes clear that such a jurisdictional element would lend support to the argument that §13981 is sufficiently tied to interstate commerce to come within Congress' authority, Congress elected to cast §13981's remedy over a wider, and more purely intrastate, body of violent crime. Third, although §13981, unlike the *Lopez* statute, *is* supported by numerous findings regarding the serious impact of gender-motivated violence on victims and their families, these findings are substantially weakened by the fact that they rely on reasoning that this Court has rejected, namely a but-for causal chain from the initial occurrence of violent crime to every attenuated effect upon interstate commerce. If accepted, this reasoning would allow Congress to regulate any crime whose nationwide, aggregated impact has substantial effects on employment, production, transit, or consumption. Moreover, such reasoning will not limit Congress to regulating violence, but may be applied equally as well to family law and other areas of state regulation since the aggregate effect of marriage, divorce, and childrearing on the national economy is undoubtedly significant. The Constitution requires a distinction between what is truly national and what is truly local, and there is no better example of the police power, which the Founders undeniably left reposed in the States and denied the central government, than the suppression of violent crime and vindication of its victims. Congress therefore may not regulate non-economic, violent criminal conduct based solely on the conduct's aggregate effect on interstate commerce. Section 5 of the Fourteenth Amendment, which permits Congress to enforce by appropriate legislation the constitutional guarantee that no State shall deprive any person of life, liberty, or property, without due process or deny any person equal protection of the laws also does not give Congress the authority to enact §13981. Petitioners' assertion that there is pervasive bias in various state justice systems against victims of gender-motivated violence is supported by a voluminous Congressional record. However, the Fourteenth Amendment places limitations on the manner in which Congress may attack discriminatory conduct. Foremost among them is the principle that the Amendment prohibits only state action, not private conduct. This was the conclusion reached in *United States v. Harris* and the *Civil Rights Cases,* which were both decided shortly after the Amendment's adoption. The force of the doctrine of *stare decisis* behind these decisions stems not only from the length of time they have been on the books, but also from the insight attributable to the Members of the Court at that time, who all had intimate knowledge and familiarity with the events surrounding the Amendment's adoption. Neither *United States v. Guest* nor *District of Columbia v. Carter* casts any doubt on the enduring vitality of the *Civil Rights Cases* and *Harris.* Assuming that there has been gender-based disparate treatment by state authorities in this case, it would not be enough to save §13981's civil remedy, which is directed not at a State or state actor but at individuals who have committed criminal acts motivated by gender bias. Section 13981 visits no consequence on any Virginia public official involved in investigating or prosecuting Brzonkala's assault, and it is thus unlike any of the §5 remedies this Court has previously upheld. Section 13981 is also different from previously upheld remedies in that it applies uniformly throughout the Nation, even though Congress' findings indicate that the problem addressed does not exist in all, or even most, States. In contrast, the §5 remedy in *Katzenbach* was directed only to those States in which Congress found that there had been discrimination.

C Affirmed.

Katzenback v. Morgan and Morgan

384 U.S. 641 (1966)

FACTS

Appellees, registered voters in New York City, brought this suit to challenge the constitutionality of §4(e) of the Voting Rights Act of 1965 to the extent that the provision prohibits enforcement of the statutory requirement for literacy in English as applied to numerous New York City residents from Puerto Rico who, because of that requirement, had previously been denied the right to vote. Section 4(e) provides that no person who has completed the sixth grade in a public school, or an accredited private school, in Puerto Rico in which the language of instruction was other than English shall be disfranchised for inability to read or write English. A three-judge District Court granted appellees declaratory and injunctive relief, holding that in enacting §4(e) Congress had exceeded its powers.

I

When a state enacts its own voting regulations, may Congress enact legislation which encroaches upon the states' promulgation of those laws by authority granted to the latter by the Fourteenth Amendment?

R

Congress has the power and authority to supersede a state law if there exists a reasonable basis for it to believe that the state law violates equal protection.

A

Section 4(e) is a proper exercise of the powers under §5 of the 14th Amendment. And by virtue of the Supremacy Clause, New York's English literacy requirement cannot be enforced to the extent it conflicts with §4(e). Though the States have power to fix voting qualifications, they cannot do so contrary to the 14th Amendment or any other constitutional provision. Congress' power under §5 of the 14th Amendment to enact legislation prohibiting enforcement of a state law is not limited to situations where the state law has been adjudged to violate the provisions of the Amendment which Congress sought to enforce. It is therefore the Court's task here to determine, not whether New York's English literacy requirement as applied violates the Equal Protection Clause, but whether §4(e)'s prohibition against that requirement is "appropriate legislation" to enforce the Clause. Section 5 of the 14th Amendment is a positive grant of legislative power authorizing Congress to exercise its discretion in determining the need for and nature of legislation to secure 14th Amendment guarantees. Section 4(e) was enacted to enforce the Equal Protection Clause as a measure to secure nondiscriminatory treatment by government for numerous Puerto Ricans residing in New York. Congress had an adequate basis for deciding that §4(e) was plainly adapted to that end. Section 4(e) does not itself invidiously discriminate in violation of the Fifth Amendment for failure to extend relief to those educated in non-American flag schools. A reform measure such as §4(e) is not invalid because Congress might have gone further than it did and did not eliminate all the evils at the same time.

C

Reversed.

City of Boerne v. Flores

521 U.S. 507 (1997)

FACTS

Respondent, the Catholic Archbishop of San Antonio, applied for a building permit to enlarge a church in Boerne, Texas. When local zoning authorities denied the permit, relying on an ordinance governing historic preservation in a district which, they argued, included the church, the Archbishop brought this suit challenging, amongst other things, the permit denial under, the Religious Freedom Restoration Act of 1993 (RFRA). The District Court concluded that by enacting RFRA Congress exceeded the scope of its enforcement power under §5 of the Fourteenth Amendment. The court certified its order for interlocutory appeal, and the Fifth Circuit reversed, finding RFRA to be constitutional.

I Does Congress have the power to enact RFRA, which would call for Congress to interpret the meaning of certain constitutional provisions within the Act?

R The power to interpret the meaning of constitutional provision is beyond the reach of Congress' power; however, it may take strong remedial measures to prohibit violations of the Constitution.

A RFRA exceeds Congress' power. Congress enacted RFRA in direct response to *Employment Div., Dept. of Human Resources of Ore. v. Smith*, in which the Court upheld against a free exercise challenge a state law of general applicability criminalizing peyote use, as applied to deny unemployment benefits to Native American Church members who lost their jobs because of such use. In so ruling, the Court declined to apply the balancing test of *Sherbert v. Verner*, which asks whether the law at issue substantially burdens a religious practice and, if so, whether the burden is justified by a compelling government interest. RFRA prohibits "government" from "substantially burdening" a person's exercise of religion even if the burden results from a rule of general applicability unless the government can demonstrate the burden "1) is in furtherance of a compelling governmental interest; and 2) is the least restrictive means of furthering that . . . interest." RFRA's mandate applies to any branch of Federal or State Government, to all officials, and to other persons acting under color of law. Its universal coverage includes "all Federal and State law and the implementation of that law, whether statutory or otherwise and whether adopted before or after [RFRA's enactment]." In imposing RFRA's requirements on the States, Congress relied on the Fourteenth Amendment, which guarantees that no State shall make or enforce any law depriving any person of "life, liberty, or property, without due process of law." Respondent and the United States as *amicus* contend that RFRA is permissible enforcement legislation under §5. Although Congress certainly can enact legislation enforcing the constitutional right to the free exercise of religion, its §5 power "to enforce" is only preventive or "remedial." The Amendment's design and §5's text are inconsistent with any suggestion that Congress has the power to decree the substance of the Amendment's restrictions on the States. Legislation which alters the Free Exercise Clause's meaning cannot be said to be enforcing the Clause. Congress does not enforce a constitutional right by changing what the right is. While the line between measures that remedy or prevent unconstitutional actions and measures that make a substantive change in the governing law is not easy to discern, and Congress must have wide latitude in determining where it lies, the distinction exists and must be observed. There must be a congruence and proportionality between the injury to be prevented or remedied and the means adopted to that end. Lacking such a connection, legislation may become substantive in operation and effect. The need to distinguish between remedy and substance is supported by the Fourteenth Amendment's history and this Court's case law. The Amendment's design has proved significant also in maintaining the traditional separation of powers between Congress and the Judiciary, depriving Congress of any power to interpret and elaborate on its meaning by conferring self executing substantive rights against the States and thereby leaving the interpretive power with the Judiciary. RFRA is not a proper exercise of Congress' §5 enforcement power because it contradicts vital principles necessary to maintain separation of powers and the federal state balance. An instructive comparison may be drawn between RFRA and the Voting Rights Act of 1965. In contrast to the record of widespread and persisting racial discrimination which confronted Congress and the Judiciary in those cases, RFRA's legislative record lacks examples of any instances of generally applicable laws passed because of religious bigotry in the past 40 years. Rather, the emphasis of the RFRA hearings was on laws like the one at issue that place incidental burdens on religion. It is difficult to maintain that such laws are based on animus or hostility to the burdened religious practices or that they indicate some widespread pattern of religious discrimination in this country. RFRA's most serious shortcoming, however, lies in the fact that it is so out of proportion to a supposed remedial or preventive object that it cannot be understood as responsive to, or designed to prevent, unconstitutional behavior. It appears, instead, to attempt a substantive change in constitutional protections, proscribing state conduct that the Fourteenth Amendment itself does not prohibit. Its sweeping coverage ensures its intrusion at every level of government, displacing laws and prohibiting official actions of almost every description and regardless of subject matter. Its restrictions apply to every government agency and official and to all statutory or other law, whether adopted before or after its enactment. It has no termination date or termination mechanism. Any law is subject to challenge at any time by any individual who claims a substantial burden on his or her free exercise of religion. Such a claim will often be difficult to contest. Requiring a State to demonstrate a compelling interest and show that it has adopted the least restrictive means of achieving that interest is the most demanding test known to constitutional law. Furthermore, the least restrictive means requirement was not used in the pre-Smith jurisprudence RFRA purported to codify. All told, RFRA is a considerable congressional intrusion into the States' traditional prerogatives and general authority to regulate for the health and welfare of their citizens, and is not designed to identify and counteract state laws likely to be unconstitutional because of their treatment of religion.

C

Reversed.

Fitzpatrick v. Bitzer

427 U.S. 445 (1976)

FACTS

Present and retired male employees of the State of Connecticut (petitioners in No. 75-251) brought this class action alleging, inter alia, that certain provisions of the State's statutory retirement benefit plan discriminated against them because of their sex, in violation of Title VII of the Civil Rights Act of 1964, which, as amended, extends coverage to the States as employers. The District Court ruled in their favor and entered prospective injunctive relief against respondent state officials. But the court denied petitioners' request for an award of retroactive retirement benefits as compensation for losses caused by the State's discrimination, as well as "a reasonable attorney's fee as part of the costs," as provided in Title VII, holding that both would constitute recovery of money damages from the State's treasury and were thus precluded by the Eleventh Amendment and by this Court's decision in *Edelman v. Jordan*, where the District Court's award for welfare benefits wrongfully withheld was held to violate that Amendment, there being no authorization in the Social Security Act for a citizen to sue a State. The Court of Appeals reversed in the matter of attorneys' fees, the award of which was deemed to have only an "ancillary effect" on the state treasury of the sort permitted by Edelman, but otherwise affirmed.

I

May Congress use its power under §5 to create a federal cause of action against a state or government?

R

Congress may provide for a private cause of action in the federal courts against a state government as a means of enforcing the rights found in the 14th Amendment.

A

The Eleventh Amendment does not bar a backpay award to petitioners in No. 75-251, since that Amendment and the principle of state sovereignty that it embodies are limited by the enforcement provisions of 5 of the Fourteenth Amendment, which grants Congress authority to enforce "by appropriate legislation" the substantive provisions of the Fourteenth Amendment, which themselves embody significant limitations on state authority. Congress in determining what legislation is appropriate for enforcing the Fourteenth Amendment may, as it has done in Title VII, provide for suits against States that are constitutionally impermissible in other contexts. The "threshold fact of congressional authorization" for a citizen to sue his state employer, which was absent in Edelman, supra, is thus present here. Congress's exercise of power in allowing reasonable attorneys' fees is similarly not barred by the Eleventh Amendment.

C

Affirmed in part, reversed in part.

Seminole Tribe of Florida v. Florida

517 U.S. 44 (1996)

FACTS

The Indian Gaming Regulatory Act, passed by Congress pursuant to the Indian Commerce Clause, allows an Indian tribe to conduct certain gaming activities only in conformance with a valid compact between the tribe and the State in which the gaming activities are located. 25 U.S.C. 2710(d)(1)(C). Under the Act, States have a duty to negotiate in good faith with a tribe toward the formation of a compact, 2710(d)(3)(A), and a tribe may sue a State in federal court in order to compel performance of that duty, 2710(d)(7). In this 2710(d)(7) suit, respondents, Florida and its Governor, moved to dismiss petitioner Seminole Tribe's complaint on the ground that the suit violated Florida's sovereign immunity from suit in federal court. The District Court denied the motion, but the Court of Appeals reversed, finding that the Indian Commerce Clause did not grant Congress the power to abrogate the States' Eleventh Amendment immunity and that *Ex parte Young*, does not permit an Indian tribe to force good faith negotiations by suing a State's Governor.

I Can Congress annul the States' sovereign immunity under the 11th Amendment in an effort to enforce constitutional provisions falling outside the scope of the 14th Amendment?

R Congress may not authorize federal lawsuits against the states in abrogation of the 11th Amendment's guarantee of state sovereign immunity.

A The Eleventh Amendment prevents Congress from authorizing suits by Indian tribes against States to enforce legislation enacted pursuant to the Indian Commerce Clause. The Eleventh Amendment presupposes that each State is a sovereign entity in our federal system and that "`[i]t is inherent in the nature of sovereignty not to be amenable to the suit of an individual without [a State's] consent.'" However, Congress may abrogate the States' sovereign immunity if it has "unequivocally expresse[d] its intent to abrogate the immunity" and has acted "pursuant to a valid exercise of power." Here, through the numerous references to the "State" in 2710(d)(7)(B)'s text, Congress provided an "unmistakably clear" statement of its intent to abrogate. The inquiry into whether Congress has the power to abrogate unilaterally the States' immunity from suit is narrowly focused on a single question: Was the Act in question passed pursuant to a constitutional provision granting Congress such power? This Court has found authority to abrogate under only two constitutional provisions: the Fourteenth Amendment, see, e.g., *Fitzpatrick v. Bitzer*, and, in a plurality opinion, the Interstate Commerce Clause, *Pennsylvania v. Union Gas Co*. The Union Gas plurality found that Congress' power to abrogate came from the States' session of their sovereignty when they gave Congress plenary power to regulate commerce. Under the rationale of Union Gas, the Indian Commerce Clause is indistinguishable from the Interstate Commerce Clause. However, in the five years since it was decided, Union Gas has proven to be a solitary departure from established law. Reconsidering that decision, none of the policies underlying stare decisis require this Court's continuing adherence to its holding. The decision has been of questionable precedential value, largely because a majority of the Court expressly disagreed with the plurality's rationale. Moreover, the deeply fractured decision has created confusion among the lower courts that have sought to understand and apply it. The plurality's rationale also deviated sharply from this Court's established federalism jurisprudence and essentially eviscerated the Court's decision in Hans, since the plurality's conclusion - that Congress could under Article I expand the scope of the federal courts' Article III jurisdiction - contradicted the fundamental notion that Article III sets forth the exclusive catalog of permissible federal-court jurisdiction. Thus, Union Gas was wrongly decided and is overruled. The Eleventh Amendment restricts the judicial power under Article III, and Article I cannot be used to circumvent the constitutional limitations placed upon federal jurisdiction. The doctrine of *Ex parte Young* may not be used to enforce 2710(d)(3) against a state official. That doctrine allows a suit against a state official to go forward, notwithstanding the Eleventh Amendment's jurisdictional bar, where the suit seeks prospective injunctive relief in order to end a continuing federal-law violation. However, where, as here, Congress has prescribed a detailed remedial scheme for the enforcement against a State of a statutorily created right, a court should hesitate before casting aside those Page III limitations and permitting an *Ex parte Young* action. The intricate procedures set forth in 2710(d)(7) show that Congress intended not only to define, but also significantly to limit, the duty imposed by 2710(d)(3). The Act mandates only a modest set of sanctions against a State, culminating in the Secretary of the Interior prescribing gaming regulations where an agreement is not reached through negotiation or mediation. In contrast, an *Ex parte Young* action would expose a state official to a federal court's full remedial powers, including, presumably, contempt sanctions. Enforcement through an *Ex parte Young* suit would also make 2710(d)(7) superfluous, for it is difficult to see why a tribe would suffer through 2710(d)(7)'s intricate enforcement scheme if Ex parte Young's more complete and more immediate relief were available. The Court is not free to rewrite the statutory scheme in order to approximate what it thinks Congress might have wanted had it known that 2710(d)(7) was beyond its authority. Pp. 27-30.

C

Affirmed.

Alden v. Maine

527 U.S. 706 (1999)

FACTS

After this Court decided, in *Seminole Tribe of Fla.* v. *Florida,* that Congress lacks power under Article I to abrogate the States' sovereign immunity in federal court, the Federal District Court dismissed a Fair Labor Standards Act of 1938 suit filed by petitioners against their employer, respondent Maine. Subsequently, petitioners filed the same action in state court. Although the FLSA purports to authorize private actions against States in their own courts, the trial court dismissed the suit on the ground of sovereign immunity. The Maine Supreme Judicial Court affirmed.

I Does the Constitution, by delegating to Congress the power to establish the supreme law of the land when acting within its enumerated powers, foreclose a State from asserting immunity to claims arising under federal law merely because that law derives not from the State itself but from the national power?

R The Constitution, by delegating to Congress the power to establish the supreme law of the land when acting within its enumerated powers, does not foreclose a State from asserting immunity to claims arising under federal law merely because that law derives not from the State itself but from the national power.

A The Constitution, by delegating to Congress the power to establish the supreme law of the land when acting within its enumerated powers, does not foreclose a State from asserting immunity to claims arising under federal law merely because that law derives not from the State itself but from the national power. Moreover, the specific Article I powers delegated to Congress do not necessarily include the incidental authority to subject States to private suits as a means of achieving objectives otherwise within the enumerated powers' scope. Isolated statements in some of this Court's cases suggest that the Eleventh Amendment is inapplicable in state courts. This is a truism as to the Amendment's literal terms. However, the Amendment's bare text is not an exhaustive description of States' constitutional immunity, and the cases do not decide the question whether States retain immunity in their own courts notwithstanding an attempted abrogation by Congress. A review of the essential principles of federalism and the state courts' special role in the constitutional design leads to the conclusion that a congressional power to subject nonconsenting States to private suits in their own courts is inconsistent with the Constitution's structure. Federalism requires that Congress accord States the respect and dignity due them as residuary sovereigns and joint participants in the Nation's governance. Immunity from suit in federal courts is not enough to preserve that dignity, for the indignity of subjecting a nonconsenting State to the coercive process of judicial tribunals at the instance of private parties exists regardless of the forum. In some ways, a congressional power to authorize suits against States in their own courts would be even more offensive to state sovereignty than a power to authorize suits in a federal forum, since a sovereign's immunity in its own courts has always been understood to be within the sole control of the sovereign itself. Further, because the Federal Government retains its own immunity from suit in state and federal court, this Court is reluctant to conclude that States are not entitled to a reciprocal privilege. Underlying constitutional form are considerations of great substance. Private suits against nonconsenting States may threaten their financial integrity, and the surrender of immunity carries with it substantial costs to the autonomy, decisionmaking ability, and sovereign capacity of the States. A general federal power to authorize private suits for money damages would also strain States' ability to govern in accordance with their citizens' will, for judgment creditors compete with other important needs and worthwhile ends, necessitating difficult decisions involving the most sensitive and political of judgments. A national power to remove these decisions regarding the allocation of scarce resources from the political processes established by the citizens of the States and commit their resolution to judicial decrees mandated by the Federal Government and invoked by the private citizen would blur not only the State and National Governments' distinct responsibilities but also the separate duties of the state government's judicial and political branches. Congress cannot abrogate States' sovereign immunity in federal court; were the rule different here, the National Government would wield greater power in state courts than in federal courts. This anomaly cannot be explained by reference to the state courts' special role in the constitutional design. It would be unprecedented to infer from the fact that Congress may declare federal law binding and enforceable in state courts the further principle that Congress' authority to pursue federal objectives through state courts exceeds not only its power to press other branches of the State into its service but also its control over federal courts. The constitutional provisions upon which this Court has relied in finding state courts peculiarly amendable to federal command, moreover, do not distinguish those courts from the Federal Judiciary. No constitutional precept would admit of a congressional power to require state courts to entertain federal suits which are not within the United States' judicial power and could not be heard in federal courts. Maine has not waived its immunity. It adheres to the general rule that a specific legislative enactment is required to waive sovereign immunity. Although petitioners contend that Maine discriminated against federal rights by claiming immunity from this suit, there is no evidence that it has manipulated its immunity in a systematic fashion to discriminate against federal causes of action. To the extent Maine has chosen to consent to certain classes of suits while maintaining its immunity from others, it has done no more than exercise a privilege of sovereignty. The States' immunity from private suit in their own courts is beyond congressional power to abrogate by Article I legislation. Congress may exercise its Article I powers to subject States to private suits in their own courts only if there is compelling evidence that States were required to surrender this power to Congress pursuant to the constitutional design. Neither the Constitution's text nor the Court's recent sovereign immunity decisions establish that States were required to relinquish this portion of their sovereignty.

C

Affirmed.

Youngstown Sheet & Tube Co. v. Sawyer

343 U.S. 579 (1952)

FACTS

During the Korean War and to avert a nation-wide strike of steel workers in April 1952, which he believed would jeopardize national defense, the President Harry Truman issued Executive Order 10340, directing the Secretary of Commerce to seize and operate most of the steel mills. The Order was not based upon any specific statutory authority but was based generally upon all powers vested in the President by the Constitution and as Commander in Chief of the Armed Forces. The Secretary issued an order seizing the steel mills and directing their presidents to operate them as operating managers for the United States in accordance with his regulations and directions. The President promptly reported these events to Congress; but Congress took no action. It had provided other methods of dealing with such situations and had refused to authorize governmental seizures of property to settle labor disputes. The steel companies sued the Secretary in Federal District Court, praying for a declaratory judgment and injunctive relief. The District Court issued a preliminary injunction, which the Court of Appeals stayed.

I

May the President of the United States constitutionally order the seizure of the nation's steel mills?

R

The seizure of private property to prevent the consequences of labor dispute by the President of the United States is an unconstitutional act.

A

Although this case has proceeded no further than the preliminary injunction stage, it is ripe for determination of the constitutional validity of the Executive Order on the record presented. Under prior decisions of this Court, there is doubt as to the right to recover in the Court of Claims on account of properties unlawfully taken by government officials for public use. Seizure and governmental operation of these going businesses were bound to result in many present and future damages that are difficult, if not incapable, of measurement. The Executive Order was not authorized by the Constitution or laws of the United States; and it cannot stand. There is no statute which expressly or impliedly authorizes the President to take possession of this property as he did here. Authority of the President to issue such an order in the circumstances of this case cannot be implied from the aggregate of his powers under Article II of the Constitution. The Order cannot properly be sustained as an exercise of the President's military power as Commander in Chief. The power here sought to be exercised is the lawmaking power, which the Constitution vests in the Congress alone.

C

Affirmed.

U.S. v. Nixon

418 U.S. 683 (1974)

FACTS

During the 1972 presidential campaign, the Democratic National Headquarters in the Watergate Hotel was burglarized. Investigation of the burglary revealed White House involvement, and several Nixon associates were indicted on charges of conspiracy to obstruct justice and other offenses. Following indictment, the Special Prosecutor filed a motion under Fed. Rule Crim. Proc. 17(c) for a subpoena duces tecum (a command to a witness to produce documents) for the production before trial of certain tapes and documents relating to precisely identified conversations and meetings between the President and others. The President, claiming executive privilege, filed a motion to quash the subpoena. The District Court, after treating the subpoenaed material as presumptively privileged, concluded that the Special Prosecutor had made a sufficient showing to rebut the presumption and that the requirements of Rule 17 (c) had been satisfied. The court thereafter issued an order for an in camera examination of the subpoenaed material, having rejected the President's contentions (a) that the dispute between him and the Special Prosecutor was nonjusticiable as an "intra-executive" conflict and (b) that the judiciary lacked authority to review the President's assertion of executive privilege. The court stayed its order pending appellate review, which the President then sought in the Court of Appeals. The Special Prosecutor then filed in this Court a petition for a writ of certiorari before judgment (No. 73-1766) and the President filed a cross-petition for such a writ challenging the grand-jury action (No. 73-1834). The U.S. Supreme Court granted both petitions.

I

Can the President of the U.S. be compelled to produce certain tape recordings and documents relating to his conversations with his aids or does he enjoy an absolute privilege of confidentiality for all presidential communications?

R

The president does not enjoy an absolute, global and indiscriminate privilege of confidentiality allowing him to withhold any and all documents and recordings from a subpoena in a criminal proceeding.

A

We reject the President's claims of absolute privilege, lack of jurisdiction and failure to satisfy the requirements of Rule 17(c). Jurisdiction was proper. The District Court's order was appealable as a "final" order under 28 U.S.C. 1291, was therefore properly "in" the Court of Appeals, 28 U.S.C. 1254, when the petition for certiorari before judgment was filed in this Court, and is now properly before this Court for review. The dispute between the Special Prosecutor and the President presents a justiciable controversy. The mere assertion of an "intra-branch dispute," without more, does not defeat federal jurisdiction. The Attorney General by regulation has conferred upon the Special Prosecutor unique authority to represent the United States and has given the Special Prosecutor explicit power to contest the invocation of executive privilege in seeking evidence deemed relevant to the performance of his specially delegated duties. While the regulation remains in effect, the Executive Branch is bound by it. The action of the Special Prosecutor within the scope of his express authority seeking specified evidence preliminarily determined to be relevant and admissible in the pending criminal case, and the President's assertion of privilege in opposition thereto, present issues "of a type which are traditionally justiciable," and the fact that both litigants are officers of the Executive Branch is not a bar to justiciability. From this Court's examination of the material submitted by the Special Prosecutor in support of his motion for the subpoena, much of which is under seal, it is clear that the District Court's denial of the motion to quash comported with Rule 17(c) and that the Special Prosecutor has made a sufficient showing to justify a subpoena for production before trial. Neither the doctrine of separation of powers nor the generalized need for confidentiality of high-level communications, without more, can sustain an absolute, unqualified Presidential privilege of immunity from judicial process under all circumstances. Absent a claim of need to protect military, diplomatic, or sensitive national security secrets, the confidentiality of Presidential communications is not significantly diminished by producing material for a criminal trial under the protected conditions of in camera inspection, and any absolute executive privilege under Art. II of the Constitution would plainly conflict with the function of the courts under the Constitution. Although the courts will afford the utmost deference to Presidential acts in the performance of an Art. II function, when a claim of Presidential privilege as to materials subpoenaed for use in a criminal trial is based, as it is here, not on the ground that military or diplomatic secrets are implicated, but merely on the ground of a generalized interest in confidentiality, the President's generalized assertion of privilege must yield to the specific need for evidence in a pending criminal trial. On the basis of this Court's examination of the record, it cannot be concluded that the District Court erred in ordering in camera examination of the subpoenaed material, which shall now forthwith be transmitted to the District Court. Since a President's communications encompass a vastly wider range of sensitive material than would be true of an ordinary individual, the public interest requires that Presidential confidentiality be afforded the greatest protection. Presidential conversations irrelevant to or inadmissible in the criminal prosecution be accorded the high degree of respect due a President and that such material be returned under seal to its lawful custodian. Until released to the Special Prosecutor no *in camera* material is to be released to anyone.

C

No. 73-1766 affirmed; No. 73-1834, certiorari dismissed as improvidently granted.

Clinton v. New York

524 U.S. 417 (1998)

FACTS

[This case represents the consolidation of two cases] In 1997, then President Clinton exercised his authority under the Line Item Veto Act of 1996 by canceling §4722(c) of the Balanced Budget Act of 1997, which waived the Federal Government's statutory right to recoup as much as $2.6 billion in taxes that the State of New York had levied against Medicaid providers, and §968 of the Taxpayer Relief Act of 1997, which permitted the owners of certain food refiners and processors to defer recognition of capital gains if they sold their stock to eligible farmers' cooperatives. The Line Item Veto Act (the Act) gave the president the power to cancel in whole three types of provisions that had been signed into law: "(1) any dollar amount of discretionary budget authority; (2) any item of new direct spending; or (3) any limited tax benefit." The Act required the President to carefully consider any cancellations, making sure that each would reduce the deficit, not impair essential government functions, and not harm the national interest. The President was to notify Congress of any use of his line item veto within five days of a particular bill's enactment. Congress could then override the cancellations by passing a disapproval bill with a majority vote in each house. The President, under the Act, retained his constitutional power to veto the entire bill but could not cancel a disapproval bill. Several parties who claimed that they would be harmed by the cancellations, including New York City and a farmers' cooperative, filed separate actions against the President and other officials challenging the cancellations. The plaintiffs in the first case are the City of New York, two hospital associations, one hospital, and two unions representing health care employees. The plaintiffs in the second are the Snake River farmers' cooperative and one of its individual members. The District Court consolidated the cases, determined that at least one of the plaintiffs in each had standing under Article III, and ruled, *inter alia*, that the Act's cancellation procedures violate the Presentment Clause, Art. I, §7, cl. 2. The U.S. Supreme Court expedited its review.

I

May the President use a line item veto to selectively strike provisions of bills that have already been signed into law?

R

The Line Item Veto Act of 1996's cancellation provisions (the line item veto) violate Article I, §7 of the Constitutional and is thus unconstitutional.

A

The appellees have standing to challenge the Act's constitutionality. They invoked the District Court's jurisdiction under a section entitled "Expedited Review," which, among other things, expressly authorizes "any individual adversely affected" to bring a constitutional challenge. The Government's argument that none of them except the individual Snake River member is an "individual" within §692(a)(1)'s meaning is rejected because, in the context of the entire section, it is clear that Congress meant that word to be construed broadly to include corporations and other entities. The Court is also unpersuaded by the Government's argument that appellees' challenge is nonjusticiable. Here, the President's exercise of his cancellation authority has removed any concern about the dispute's ripeness and because the parties have alleged a "personal stake" in having an actual injury redressed, rather than an "institutional injury" that is "abstract and widely dispersed." There is no merit to the Government's contention that the appellees have not suffered actual injury because their claims are too speculative and, in any event, are advanced by the wrong parties. Because New York State now has a multibillion dollar contingent liability that had been eliminated by §4722(c), the State, and the appellees, suffered an immediate, concrete injury the moment the President canceled the section and deprived them of its benefits. The argument that New York's claim belongs to the State, not appellees, fails in light of New York statutes demonstrating that both New York City and the appellee providers will be assessed for substantial portions of any recoupment payments the State has to make. The Act's cancellation procedures violate the Presentment Clause. The Act empowers the President to cancel an "item of new direct spending" such as §4722(c) of the Balanced Budget Act and a "limited tax benefit" such as §968 of the Taxpayer Relief Act, §691(a), specifying that such cancellation prevents a provision "from having legal force or effect." Thus, in both legal and practical effect, the presidential actions at issue have amended two Acts of Congress by repealing a portion of each. Statutory repeals must conform with Art. I, but there is no constitutional authorization for the President to amend or repeal. Under the Presentment Clause, after a bill has passed both Houses, but "before it become[s] a Law," it must be presented to the President, who "shall sign it" if he approves it, but "return it [a/k/a veto it]" if he does not. There are important differences between such a "return [a/k/a veto]" and cancellation under the Act: The constitutional return is of the entire bill and takes place before it becomes law, whereas the statutory cancellation occurs after the bill becomes law and affects it only in part. The Court rejects two related Government arguments. First, the contention that the cancellations were merely exercises of the President's discretionary authority under the Balanced Budget Act and the Taxpayer Relief Act, read in light of the previously enacted Line Item Veto Act, is unpersuasive. *Field v. Clark*, on which the Government relies, suggests critical differences between this cancellation power and the President's statutory power to suspend import duty exemptions that was there upheld: such suspension was contingent on a condition that did not predate its statute, the duty to suspend was absolute once the President determined the contingency had arisen. In contrast, the Act at issue authorizes the President himself to effect the repeal of laws, for his own policy reasons, without observing Article I, §7, procedures. Second, the contention that the cancellation authority is no greater than the President's traditional statutory authority to decline to spend appropriated funds or to implement specified tax measures fails because this Act, unlike the earlier laws, gives the President the unilateral power to change the text of duly enacted statutes.

Affirmed.

A.L.A. Schechter Poultry Corp. v. United States

295 U.S. 495 (1935)

FACTS

Petitioners in No. 854 were convicted in the District Court of the United States for the Eastern District of New York on eighteen counts of an indictment charging violations of what is known as the "Live Poultry Code" and on an additional count for conspiracy to commit such violations. By demurrer to the indictment and appropriate motions on the trial, the defendants contended (1) that the code had been adopted pursuant to an unconstitutional delegation by Congress of legislative power; (2) that it attempted to regulate intrastate transactions which lay outside the authority of Congress; and (3) that in certain provisions it was repugnant to the due process clause of the Fifth Amendment. The Circuit Court of Appeals sustained the conviction on the conspiracy count and on sixteen counts for violation of the code, but reversed the conviction on two counts which charged violation of requirements as to minimum wages and maximum hours of labor, as these were not deemed to be within the congressional power of regulation. On the respective applications of the defendants (No. 854) and of the government (No. 864), the U.S. Supreme Court granted writs of certiorari.

I Can Congress delegate unrestrained lawmaking authority onto the Executive branch?

R Congress may not delegate unrestrained lawmaking authority onto the Executive branch.

A The power of Congress extends, not only to the regulation of transactions which are part of interstate commerce, but to the protection of that commerce from injury. It matters not that the injury may be due to the conduct of those engaged in intrastate operations. Thus, Congress may protect the safety of those employed in interstate transportation, 'no matter what may be the source of the dangers which threaten it.' We said in *Mondou v. New York* that it is the 'effect upon interstate commerce,' not 'the source of the injury,' which is 'the criterion of congressional power.' We have held that, in dealing with common carriers engaged in both interstate and intrastate commerce, the dominant authority of Congress necessarily embraces the right to control their intrastate operations in all matters having such a close and substantial relation to interstate traffic that the control is essential or appropriate to secure the freedom of that traffic from interference or unjust discrimination and to promote the efficiency of the interstate service. Thus, combinations and conspiracies to restrain interstate commerce, or to monopolize any part of it, are nonetheless within the reach of the Anti-Trust Act because the conspirators seek to attain their end by means of intrastate activities. We recently had occasion, in *Local 167 v. United States*, to apply this principle in connection with the live poultry industry. That was a suit to enjoin a conspiracy to restrain and monopolize interstate commerce in violation of the Anti-Trust Act. It was shown that marketmen, teamsters, and slaughterers (shochtim) had conspired to burden the free movement of live poultry into the metropolitan area in and about New York City. In view of the proof of that conspiracy, we said that it was unnecessary to decide when interstate commerce ended and when intrastate commerce began. We found that the proved interference by the conspirators 'with the unloading, the transportation, the sales by marketmen to retailers, the prices charged, and the amount of profits exacted' operated 'substantially and directly to restrain and burden the untrammelled shipment and movement of the poultry,' while unquestionably it was in interstate commerce. The intrastate acts of the conspirators were included in the injunction because that was found to be necessary for the protection of interstate commerce against the attempted and illegal restraint. The instant case is not of that sort. This is not a prosecution for a conspiracy to restrain or monopolize interstate commerce in violation of the Anti-Trust Act. Defendants have been convicted, not upon direct charges of injury to interstate commerce or of interference with persons engaged in that commerce, but of violations of certain provisions of the Live Poultry Code and of conspiracy to commit these violations. Interstate commerce is brought in only upon the charge that violations of these provisions-as to hours and wages of employees and local sales-'affected' interstate commerce. Thus, we are of the opinion that the attempt through the provisions of the code to fix the hours and wages of employees of defendants in their intrastate business was not a valid exercise of federal power. On both the grounds we have discussed, the attempted delegation of legislative power and the attempted regulation of intrastate transactions which affect interstate commerce only indirectly, we hold the code provisions here in question to be invalid and that the judgment of conviction must be reversed.

C No. 854 –reversed; No. 864-affirmed.

Panama Refining Co. v. Ryan

293 U.S. 388 (1935)

FACTS

On July 11, 1933, the President, by Executive Order No. 6199 (15 USCA 709 note), prohibited 'the transportation in interstate and foreign commerce of petroleum and the products thereof produced or withdrawn from storage in excess of the amount permitted to be produced or withdrawn from storage by any State law or valid regulation or order prescribed thereunder, by any board, commission, officer, or other duly authorized agency of a State.' This action was based on section 9(c) of title 1 of the National Industrial Recovery Act of June 16, 1933. On July 14, 1933, the President, by Executive Order No. 6204 authorized the Secretary of the Interior to exercise all the powers vested in the President 'for the purpose of enforcing Section 9(c) of said act. On July 15, 1933, the Secretary of the Interior issued regulations to carry out the President's orders of July 11 and 14, 1933. These regulations were amended by orders of July 25, 1933, and August 21, 1933, prior to the commencement of these suits. Regulation IV provided, in substance, that every producer of petroleum should file a monthly statement under oath, beginning August 15, 1933, with the Division of Investigations of the Department of the Interior giving information with respect to the residence and post office address of the producer, the location of his producing properties and wells, the allowable production as prescribed by state authority, the amount of daily production, all deliveries of petroleum, and declaring that no part of the petroleum or products produced and shipped had been produced or withdrawn from storage in excess of the amount permitted by state authority. Oil refiners brought suit to enjoin government officials from enforcing the Executive Order and implementing the regulations. The District Court granted the injunction; the Court of Appeals reversed.

I

May Congress delegate unrestrained lawmaking authority to the President?

R

Congress may not delegate unrestrained lawmaking authority to the President as it is a violation of the separation of powers if not standards are imposed limiting such a grant of authority.

A

Section 9(c) is brief and unambiguous. It does not attempt to control the production of petroleum and petroleum products within a state. It does not seek to lay down rules for the guidance of state Legislatures or state officers. It leaves to the states and to their constituted authorities the determination of what production shall be permitted. It does not qualify the President's authority by reference to the basis or extent of the state's limitation of production. Section 9(c) does not state whether or in what circumstances or under what conditions the President is to prohibit the transportation of the amount of petroleum or petroleum products produced in excess of the state's permission. It establishes no criterion to govern the President's course. It does not require any finding by the President as a condition of his action. The Congress in section 9(c) thus declares no policy as to the transportation of the excess production. So far as this section is concerned, it gives to the President an unlimited authority to determine the policy and to lay down the prohibition, or not to lay it down, as he may see fit. And disobedience to his order is made a crime punishable by fine and imprisonment. Thus, in every case in which the question has been raised, the Court has recognized that there are limits of delegation which there is no constitutional authority to transcend. We think that section 9(c) goes beyond those limits. As to the transportation of oil production in excess of state permission, the Congress has declared no policy, has established no standard, has laid down no rule. There is no requirement, no definition of circumstances and conditions in which the transportation is to be allowed or prohibited. We see no escape from the conclusion that the Executive Orders of July 11, 1933, and July 14, 1933, and the regulations issued by the Secretary of the Interior thereunder, are without constitutional authority. The decrees of the Circuit Court of Appeals are reversed, and the causes are remanded to the District Court, with direction to modify its decrees in conformity with this opinion so as to grant permanent injunctions, restraining the defendants from enforcing those orders and regulations.

Reversed and remanded.

Whitman v. American Trucking Assn. Inc.

531 U.S. 457 (2001)

FACTS

Section 109(a) of the Clean Air Act (CAA) requires the Environmental Protection Agency (EPA) Administrator to promulgate national ambient air quality standards (NAAQS) for each air pollutant for which "air quality criteria" have been issued under §108. Pursuant to §109(d)(1), the Administrator in 1997 revised the ozone and particulate matter NAAQS. Respondents in No. 99-1257, private parties and several States (hereinafter respondents), challenged the revised NAAQS on several grounds. The District of Columbia Circuit found that, under the Administrator's interpretation, §109(b)(1) - which instructs the EPA to set standards "the attainment and maintenance of which ... are requisite to protect the public health" with "an adequate margin of safety" - delegated legislative power to the Administrator in contravention of the Federal Constitution, and it remanded the NAAQS to the EPA. The Court of Appeals also declined to depart from its rule that the EPA may not consider implementation costs in setting the NAAQS. And it held that, although certain implementation provisions for the ozone NAAQS contained in Part D, Subpart 2, of Title I of the CAA did not prevent the EPA from revising the ozone standard and designating certain areas as "non-attainment areas," those provisions, rather than more general provisions contained in Subpart 1, constrained the implementation of the new ozone NAAQS. The court rejected the EPA's argument that it lacked jurisdiction to reach the implementation question because there had been no "final" implementation action.

I

Does §109(a) of the Clean Air Act delegate legislative power to the Administrator of the EPA?

R

Section 109(a) of the Clean Air Act does not delegate legislative power to the Administrator of the EPA in contravention of the Constitution; however, the Administrator has discretion to "determine criterion" for saying how much of the regulated harm is too much - that is, make judgments of degree [in the context of determining air quality].

A

Section 109(b) does not permit the Administrator to consider implementation costs in setting NAAQS. Because the CAA often expressly grants the EPA the authority to consider implementation costs, a provision for costs will not be inferred from its ambiguous provisions. And since §109(b)(1) is the engine that drives nearly all of Title I of the CAA, the textual commitment of costs must be clear; Congress does not alter a regulatory scheme's fundamental details in vague terms or ancillary provisions. Respondents' arguments founder upon this principle. It is implausible that §109(b)(1)'s modest words "adequate margin" and "requisite" give the EPA the power to determine whether implementation costs should moderate national air quality standards. And the cost factor is *both* so indirectly related to public health *and* so full of potential for canceling the conclusions drawn from direct health effects that it would have been expressly mentioned in §§108 and 109 had Congress meant it to be considered. Other CAA provisions, which do require cost data, have no bearing upon whether costs are to be taken into account in setting the NAAQS. Because the text of §109(b)(1) in its context is clear, the canon of construing texts to avoid serious constitutional problems is not applicable. Section 109(b)(1) does not delegate legislative power to the EPA. When conferring decisionmaking authority upon agencies, Congress must lay down an intelligible principle to which the person or body authorized to act is directed to conform. An agency cannot cure an unlawful delegation of legislative power by adopting in its discretion a limiting construction of the statute. The limits that §109(b)(1) imposes on the EPA's discretion are strikingly similar to the ones approved in, *e.g., Touby* v. *United States,* and the scope of discretion that §109(b)(1) allows is well within the outer limits of the Court's non-delegation precedents, see, *e.g., Panama Refining Co.* v. *Ryan.* Statutes need not provide a determinate criterion for saying how much of a regulated harm is too much to avoid delegating legislative power. The Court of Appeals had jurisdiction to consider the implementation issue under §307 of the CAA. The implementation policy constitutes final agency action under §307 of the CAA because it marked the consummation of the EPA's decisionmaking process. The decision is also ripe for review. The question is purely one of statutory interpretation that would not benefit from further factual development; review will not interfere with further administrative development; and the hardship on respondent States in developing state implementation plans satisfies the CAA's special judicial-review provision permitting pre-enforcement review. The implementation issue was also fairly included within the challenges to the final ozone rule that were before the Court of Appeals, which all parties agree is final agency action ripe for review. The implementation policy is unlawful. Under *Chevron U. S. A. Inc.* v. *Natural Resources Defense Council, Inc.,* if the statute resolves the question whether Subpart 1 or Subpart 2 applies to revised ozone NAAQS, that ends the matter; but if the statute is ambiguous, the Court must defer to a reasonable agency interpretation. Here, the statute is ambiguous concerning the interaction between Subpart 1 and Subpart 2, but the Court cannot defer to the EPA's interpretation, which would render Subpart 2's carefully designed restrictions on EPA discretion nugatory once a new ozone NAAQS has been promulgated. The principal distinction between the subparts is that Subpart 2 eliminates regulatory discretion allowed by Subpart 1. The EPA may not construe the statute in a way that completely nullifies textually applicable provisions meant to limit its discretion. In addition, although Subpart 2 was obviously written to govern implementation for some time into the future, nothing in the EPA's interpretation would have prevented the agency from aborting the subpart the day after it was enacted. It is left to the EPA to develop a reasonable interpretation of the non-attainment implementation provisions insofar as they apply to revised ozone NAAQS.

C Affirmed in part, reversed in part, and remanded.

INS v. Chadha

462 U.S. 919 (1983)

FACTS

Section 244(c)(2) of the Immigration and Nationality Act (Act) authorizes either House of Congress, by resolution, to invalidate the decision of the Executive Branch, pursuant to authority delegated by Congress to the Attorney General, to allow a particular deportable alien to remain in the United States. Plaintiff-appellant Chadha, an East Indian alien who had been lawfully admitted to the United States on a nonimmigrant student visa, remained in the United States after his visa had expired and was ordered by the Immigration and Naturalization Service (INS) to show cause why he should not be deported. He then applied for suspension of the deportation, and, after a hearing, an Immigration Judge, acting pursuant to 244(a)(1) of the Act, which authorizes the Attorney General, in his discretion, to suspend deportation, ordered the suspension, and reported the suspension to Congress as required by 244(c)(1). Thereafter, the House of Representatives passed a resolution pursuant to 244(c)(2) vetoing the suspension, and the Immigration Judge reopened the deportation proceedings. Chadha moved to terminate the proceedings on the ground that 244(c)(2) is unconstitutional, but the judge held that he had no authority to rule on its constitutionality and ordered Chadha deported pursuant to the House Resolution. Chadha's appeal to the Board of Immigration Appeals was dismissed, the Board also holding that it had no power to declare 244(c)(2) unconstitutional. Chadha then filed a petition for review of the deportation order in the Court of Appeals, and the INS joined him in arguing that 244(c)(2) is unconstitutional. The Court of Appeals held that 244(c)(2) violates the constitutional doctrine of separation of powers, and accordingly directed the Attorney General to cease taking any steps to deport Chadha based upon the House Resolution.

I

May one house of Congress unilaterally invalidate a decision by the executive branch?

R

One House of Congress may unilaterally act if the act is not a use of legislative power and falls within one of four provisions of the Constitution explicit and unambiguous on the subject or where Congress has narrowly and precisely defined the procedure for such an action.

A

We first address the jurisdiction issue. This Court has jurisdiction to entertain the INS's appeal under 28 U.S.C. §1252, which provides that "[a]ny party" may appeal to the Supreme Court from a judgment of "any court of the United States" holding an Act of Congress unconstitutional in "any civil action, suit, or proceeding" to which the United States or any of its agencies is a party. A court of appeals is "a court of the United States" for purposes of 1252, the proceeding below was a "civil action, suit, or proceeding," the INS is an agency of the United States and was a party to the proceeding below, and the judgment below held an Act of Congress unconstitutional. We next turn to the issue of petitioner's standing, or lack thereof. Chadha has standing to challenge the constitutionality of 244(c)(2) since he has demonstrated "injury in fact and a substantial likelihood that the judicial relief requested will prevent or redress the claimed injury." The fact that Chadha may have other statutory relief available to him does not preclude him from challenging the constitutionality of 244(c)(2). Here, Chadha's deportation stands or falls on the validity of the challenged veto, the final deportation order having been entered only to implement that veto. A case or controversy is presented by these cases. From the time of the House's formal intervention, there was concrete adverseness, and prior to such intervention, there was adequate Art. III adverseness even though the only parties were the INS and Chadha. The INS's agreement with Chadha's position does not alter the fact that the INS would have deported him absent the Court of Appeals' judgment. Moreover, Congress is the proper party to defend the validity of a statute when a Government agency, as a defendant charged with enforcing the statute, agrees with plaintiffs that the statute is unconstitutional. These cases do not present a nonjusticiable political question on the asserted ground that Chadha is merely challenging Congress' authority under the Naturalization and Necessary and Proper Clauses of the Constitution. The presence of constitutional issues with significant political overtones does not automatically invoke the political question doctrine. Resolution of litigation challenging the constitutional authority of one of the three branches cannot be evaded by the courts simply because the issues have political implications. The congressional veto provision in 244(c)(2) is unconstitutional. The prescription for legislative action in Art. I requiring all legislative powers to be vested in a Congress consisting of a Senate and a House of Representatives, and 7, requiring every bill passed by the House and Senate, before becoming law, to be presented to the President, and, if he disapproves, to be repassed by two-thirds of the Senate and House, represents the Framers' decision that the legislative power of the Federal Government be exercised in accord with a single, finely wrought and exhaustively considered procedure. This procedure is an integral part of the constitutional design for the separation of powers. Here, the action taken by the House pursuant to 244(c)(2) was essentially legislative in purpose and effect and thus was subject to the procedural requirements of Art. I, 7, for legislative action: passage by a majority of both Houses and presentation to the President. The one-House veto operated to overrule the Attorney General and mandate Chadha's deportation. The veto's legislative character is confirmed by the character of the congressional action it supplants; i. e., absent the veto provision of 244(c)(2), neither the House nor the Senate, or both acting together, could effectively require the Attorney General to deport an alien once the Attorney General, in the exercise of legislatively delegated authority, had determined that the alien should remain in the United States. Without the veto provision, this could have been achieved only by legislation requiring deportation. A veto by one House under 244(c)(2) cannot be justified as an attempt at amending the standards set out in 244(a)(1), or as a repeal of 244 as applied to Chadha. The nature of the decision implemented by the one-House veto further manifests its legislative character. Congress must abide by its delegation of authority to the Attorney General until that delegation is legislatively altered or revoked. Finally, the veto's legislative character is confirmed by the fact that when the Framers intended to authorize either House of Congress to act alone and outside of its prescribed bicameral legislative role, they narrowly and precisely defined the procedure for such action in the Constitution.

C

Affirmed.

Morrison v. Olsen

487 U.S. 654 (1988)

FACTS

This case presents the question of the constitutionality of the independent counsel provisions of the Ethics in Government Act of 1978 (Act). It arose when the House Judiciary Committee began an investigation into the Justice Department's role in a controversy between the House and the Environmental Protection Agency (EPA) with regard to the Agency's limited production of certain documents that had been subpoenaed during an earlier House investigation. The Judiciary Committee's Report suggested that an official of the Attorney General's Office (appellee Olson) had given false testimony during the earlier EPA investigation, and that two other officials of that Office (appellees Schmults and Dinkins) had obstructed the EPA investigation by wrongfully withholding certain documents. A copy of the Report was forwarded to the Attorney General with a request, pursuant to the Act, that he seek appointment of an independent counsel to investigate the allegations against appellees. Ultimately, pursuant to the Act's provisions, the Special Division (a special court created by the Act) appointed Appellant Morrison as independent counsel with respect to Olson only, and gave her jurisdiction to investigate whether Olson's testimony, or any other matter related thereto, violated federal law, and to prosecute any violations. When a dispute arose between independent counsel and the Attorney General, who refused to furnish as "related matters" the Judiciary Committee's allegations against Schmults and Dinkins, the Special Division ruled that its grant of jurisdiction to counsel was broad enough to permit inquiry into whether Olson had conspired with others, including Schmults and Dinkins, to obstruct the EPA investigation. Appellant then caused a grand jury to issue subpoenas on appellees who moved in Federal District Court to quash the subpoenas, claiming that the Act's independent counsel provisions were unconstitutional and that appellant accordingly had no authority to proceed. The court upheld the Act's constitutionality, denied the motions, and later ordered that appellees be held in contempt for continuing to refuse to comply with the subpoenas. The Court of Appeals reversed, holding that the Act violated the Appointments Clause of the Constitution, Art. II, 2, cl. 2; the limitations of Article III; and the principle of separation of powers by interfering with the President's authority under Article II.

I

Does an act which provides for the appointment of an independent counsel violate separation of powers?

R

The Ethics in Government Act of 1978 does not violate separation of powers because it gives the executive branch adequate control over the independent counsel to enable the Executive to faithfully execute the laws of the United States.

A

There is no merit to Appellant Morrison's contention, based on *Blair v. United States,* which limited the issues that may be raised by a person who has been held in contempt for failure to comply with a grand jury subpoena, that the constitutional issues addressed by the Court of Appeals cannot be raised on this appeal from the District Court's contempt judgment. The Court of Appeals ruled that, because appellant had failed to object to the District Court's consideration of the merits of appellees' constitutional claims, she had waived her opportunity to contend on appeal that Blair barred review of those claims. Appellant's contention is not "jurisdictional" in the sense that it cannot be waived by failure to raise it at the proper time and place. Nor is it the sort of claim which would defeat jurisdiction in the District Court by showing that an Article III "Case or Controversy" is lacking. It does not violate the Appointments Clause for Congress to vest the appointment of independent counsel in the Special Division. Appellant is an "inferior" officer for purposes of the Clause, which, after providing for the appointment of certain federal officials ("principal" officers) by the President with the Senate's advice and consent, states that "the Congress may by Law vest the Appointment of such inferior Officers, as they think proper, in the President alone, in the Courts of Law, or in the Heads of Departments." Moreover, appellant is empowered by the Act to perform only certain, limited duties, restricted primarily to investigation and, if appropriate, prosecution for certain federal crimes. There is no merit to appellees' argument that, even if appellant is an "inferior" officer, the Clause does not empower Congress to place the power to appoint such an officer outside the Executive Branch (to make "interbranch appointments"). The Clause's language as to "inferior" officers admits of no limitation on interbranch appointments, but instead seems clearly to give Congress significant discretion to determine whether it is "proper" to vest the appointment of, for example, executive officials in the "courts of Law." The powers vested in the Special Division do not violate Article III, under which executive or administrative duties of a nonjudicial nature may not be imposed on judges holding office under Article III. There can be no Article III objection to the Special Division's exercise of the power, under the Act, to appoint independent counsel, since the power itself derives from the Appointments Clause, a source of authority for judicial action that is independent of Article III. The Act simply does not give the Division power to "supervise" the independent counsel in the exercise of counsel's investigative or prosecutorial authority. And, the functions that the Division is empowered to perform are not inherently "Executive," but are directly analogous to functions that federal judges perform in other contexts. The Special Division's power to terminate an independent counsel's office when counsel's task is completed - although "administrative" to the extent that it requires the Division to monitor the progress of counsel's proceedings and to decide whether counsel's job is "completed" - is not such a significant judicial encroachment upon executive power or upon independent counsel's prosecutorial discretion as to require that the Act be invalidated as inconsistent with Article III. The Act's termination provisions do not give the Division anything approaching the power to remove the counsel while an investigation or court proceeding is still underway - this power is vested solely in the Attorney General. The Act's provision restricting the Attorney General's power to remove the independent counsel to only those instances in which he can show "good cause," taken by itself, does not impermissibly interfere with the President's exercise of his constitutionally appointed functions. Even though counsel is to some degree "independent" and free from Executive Branch supervision, the Act gives the Executive Branch sufficient control over the independent counsel to ensure that the President is able to perform his constitutionally assigned duties.

C

Reversed.

United States v. Curtiss-Wright Export Corp.

299 U.S. 304 (1936)

FACTS

On January 27, 1936, an indictment was returned in the court below, the first count of which charges that appellees, beginning with the 29th day of May, 1934, conspired to sell in the United States certain arms of war, namely, fifteen machine guns, to Bolivia, a country then engaged in armed conflict in the Chaco, in violation of the Joint Resolution of Congress approved May 28, 1934, and the provisions of a proclamation issued on the same day by the President of the United States pursuant to authority conferred by section 1 of the resolution. In pursuance of the conspiracy, the commission of certain overt acts was alleged, details of which need not be stated.

I

May Congress delegate lawmaking authority to the Executive with respect to foreign affairs?

R

Congress may validly delegate lawmaking authority to the Executive with respect to foreign affairs.

A

Whether, if the Joint Resolution had related solely to internal affairs, it would be open to the challenge that it constituted an unlawful delegation of legislative power to the Executive, we find it unnecessary to determine. The whole aim of the resolution is to affect a situation entirely external to the United States, and falling within the category of foreign affairs. The determination which we are called to make, therefore, is whether the Joint Resolution, as applied to that situation, is vulnerable to attack under the rule that forbids a delegation of the lawmaking power. Not only is the federal power over external affairs in origin and essential character different from that over internal affairs, but participation in the exercise of the power is significantly limited. In this vast external realm, with its important, complicated, delicate and manifold problems, the President alone has the power to speak or listen as a representative of the nation. He makes treaties with the advice and consent of the Senate; but he alone negotiates. Into the field of negotiation the Senate cannot intrude; and Congress itself is powerless to invade it. The result of holding that the joint resolution here under attack is void and unenforceable as constituting an unlawful delegation of legislative power would be to stamp this multitude of comparable acts and resolutions as likewise invalid. And while this court may not, and should not, hesitate to declare acts of Congress, however many times repeated, to be unconstitutional if beyond all rational doubt it finds them to be so, an impressive array of legislation such as we have just set forth, enacted by nearly every Congress from the beginning of our national existence to the present day, must be given unusual weight in the process of reaching a correct determination of the problem. A legislative practice such as we have here, evidenced not by only occasional instances, but marked by the movement of a steady stream for a century and a half of time, goes a long way in the direction of proving the presence of unassailable ground for the constitutionality of the practice, to be found in the origin and history of the power involved, or in its nature, or in both combined. We deem it unnecessary to consider, seriatim, the several clauses which are said to evidence the unconstitutionality of the Joint Resolution as involving an unlawful delegation of legislative power. It is enough to summarize by saying that, both upon principle and in accordance with precedent, we conclude there is sufficient warrant for the broad discretion vested in the President to determine whether the enforcement of the statute will have a beneficial effect upon the re-establishment of peace in the affected countries; whether he shall make proclamation to bring the resolution into operation; whether and when the resolution shall cease to operate and to make proclamation accordingly; and to prescribe limitations and exceptions to which the enforcement of the resolution shall be subject. The judgment of the court below must be reversed and the cause remanded for further proceedings in accordance with the foregoing opinion.

C

Reversed and remanded.

Dames & Moore v. Regan

453 U.S. 654 (1981)

FACTS

In response to the seizure of American personnel as hostages at the American Embassy in Tehran, Iran, on November 4, 1979, then President Jimmy Carter, pursuant to the International Emergency Economic Powers Act (IEEPA), declared a national emergency on November 14, 1979, and blocked the removal or transfer of all property and interests in property of the Government of Iran which were subject to the jurisdiction of the United States. The Treasury Department then issued implementing regulations providing that "[u]nless licensed or authorized . . . any attachment, judgment, decree, lien, execution, garnishment, or other judicial process is null and void with respect to any property in which on or since [November 14, 1979,] there existed an interest of Iran," and that any licenses or authorizations granted could be "amended, modified, or revoked at any time." The President then granted a general license that authorized certain judicial proceedings, including prejudgment attachments, against Iran but did not allow the entry of any judgment or decree. On December 19, 1979, Plaintiff-petitioner Dames & Moore filed suit in Federal District Court against a number of defendants including the Government of Iran, the Atomic Energy Organization of Iran and a number of Iranian banks, alleging that it was owed a certain amount of money for services performed under a contract with the Atomic Energy Organization. The District Court issued orders of attachment against the defendants' property, and property of certain Iranian banks was then attached to secure any judgment that might be entered against them. Subsequently, on January 19, 1981, the Americans held hostage were released by Iran pursuant to an agreement with the United States. Under this agreement the United States was obligated to terminate all legal proceedings in United States courts involving claims of United States nationals against Iran, to nullify all attachments and judgments obtained therein, and to bring about the termination of such claims through binding arbitration in an Iran-United States Claims Tribunal. The President at the same time issued implementing Executive Orders revoking all licenses that permitted the exercise of "any right, power, or privilege" with regard to Iranian funds, nullifying all non-Iranian interests in such assets acquired after the blocking order of November 14, 1979, and requiring banks holding Iranian assets to transfer them to the Federal Reserve Bank of New York to be held or transferred as directed by the Secretary of the Treasury. On February 24, 1981, President Reagan issued an Executive Order which ratified President Carter's Executive Orders and "suspended" all claims that may be presented to the Claims Tribunal. Meanwhile, the District Court granted summary judgment for petitioner and awarded it the amount claimed under the contract plus interest, but stayed execution of the judgment pending appeal by the defendants, and ordered that all prejudgment attachments against the defendants be vacated and that further proceedings against the bank defendants be stayed. Petitioner then filed an action in Federal District Court against the United States and the Secretary of the Treasury, seeking to prevent enforcement of the various Executive Orders and regulations implementing the agreement with Iran. The District Court dismissed the complaint for failure to state a claim upon, but entered an injunction pending appeal prohibiting the United States from requiring the transfer of Iranian property.

I

Does a President constitutionally permitted to suspend claims pending in U.S. Courts against foreign governments by U.S. citizens?

Dames & Moore v. Regan

453 U.S. 654 (1981)

R The President has the power and authority to constitutionally suspend pending claims against foreign governments where such action is necessary to resolve a major foreign policy dispute between the U.S. and another sovereign, where there is no contrary indication of legislative intent and where there is a history of Congressional acquiescence.

A The President was authorized to nullify the attachments and order the transfer of Iranian assets by the provision of the IEEPA, 50 U.S.C. 1702 (a) (1) (B), which empowers the President to "compel," "nullify," or "prohibit" any "transfer" with respect to, or transactions involving, any property subject to the jurisdiction of the United States, in which any foreign country has any interest. Nothing in the legislative history of either 1702 or 5(b) of the Trading With the Enemy Act (TWEA), from which 1702 was directly drawn, requires reading out of 1702 all meaning to the words "transfer," "compel," or "nullify," and limiting the President's authority in this case only to continuing the freeze, as petitioner claims. To the contrary, both the legislative history and cases interpreting the TWEA fully sustain the President's broad authority when acting under such congressional grant of power. And the changes brought about by the enactment of the IEEPA did not in any way affect the President's authority to take the specific action taken here. By the time petitioner brought the instant action, the President had already entered the freeze order, and petitioner proceeded against the blocked assets only after the Treasury Department had issued revocable licenses authorizing such proceedings and attachments. The attachments obtained by petitioner, being subject to revocation, were specifically made subordinate to further actions which the President might take under the IEEPA. Blocking orders, such as the one here, permit the President to maintain foreign assets at his disposal for use in negotiating the resolution of a declared national emergency, and the frozen assets serve as a "bargaining chip" to be used by the President when dealing with a hostile country. To limit the President's authority, as petitioner urges, would mean that claimants could minimize or eliminate this "bargaining chip" through attachments or similar encumbrances. Petitioner's interest in its attachments was conditional and revocable and as such the President's action nullifying the attachments and ordering the transfer of the assets did not effect a taking of property in violation of the Fifth Amendment absent just compensation.

C Affirmed.

Hamdi v. Rumsfeld

124 S.Ct. 2633 (2004)

FACTS

After Congress passed a resolution, the Authorization for Use of Military Force (AUMF), empowering the President to "use all necessary and appropriate force" against "nations, organizations, or persons" that he determines "planned, authorized, committed, or aided" in the September 11, 2001, al Qaeda terrorist attacks, the President ordered the Armed Forces to Afghanistan to subdue al Qaeda and quell the supporting Taliban regime. Plaintiff-petitioner Yasir Esam Hamdi, an American citizen born in Louisiana and raised in Saudi Arabia, whom the Government has classified as an "enemy combatant" for allegedly taking up arms with the Taliban during the conflict, was captured in Afghanistan and presently is detained at a naval brig in Charleston, S.C. Hamdi's father filed this habeas petition on his behalf under 28 U. S. C. §2241, alleging, among other things, that the Government holds his son in violation of the Fifth and Fourteenth Amendments. Although the petition did not elaborate on the factual circumstances of Hamdi's capture and detention, his father has asserted in other documents in the record that Hamdi went to Afghanistan to do "relief work" less than two months before September 11 and could not have received military training. The Government attached to its response to the petition a declaration from Michael Mobbs (the "Mobbs Declaration"), a Defense Department official. The Mobbs Declaration alleges various details regarding Hamdi's trip to Afghanistan, his affiliation there with a Taliban unit during a time when the Taliban was battling U. S allies, and his subsequent surrender of an assault rifle. The District Court found that the Mobbs Declaration, standing alone, did not support Hamdi's detention and ordered the Government to turn over numerous materials for *in camera* review. The Court of Appeals for the Fourth Circuit reversed, stressing that, because it was undisputed that Hamdi was captured in an active combat zone, no factual inquiry or evidentiary hearing allowing Hamdi to be heard or to rebut the Government's assertions was necessary or proper. Concluding that the factual averments in the Mobbs Declaration, if accurate, provided a sufficient basis upon which to conclude that the President had constitutionally detained Hamdi, the court ordered the habeas petition dismissed. The Appeals Court held that, assuming that express congressional authorization of the detention was required by 18 U. S. C. §4001(a) which provides that "[n]o citizen shall be imprisoned or otherwise detained by the United States except pursuant to an Act of Congress." It also concluded that Hamdi is entitled only to a limited judicial inquiry into his detention's legality under the war powers of the political branches, and not to a searching review of the factual determinations underlying his seizure.

I

1) Does the President have authority to detain U.S. citizens as enemy combatants? 2) Does a U.S. citizen have a due process right to challenge his classification and detention as an enemy combatant?

R

The government may detain U.S. citizens as "enemy combatants," but due process mandates that they receive notice of the factual basis for their classification and a fair opportunity to rebut the government's factual decisions before a neutral decisionmaker.

Hamdi v. Rumsfeld

124 S. Ct. 2633 (2004)

A The question for us to determine is how much process should a U.S. citizen be afforded, if any, when he/she disputes his/her status as an enemy combatant. To answer this threshold question, we must weigh the individual's personal interest affected by the official action against the government's claimed countervailing interest. In this case, both the government and petitioner have substantial interests at stake. Hamdi's private interest is the most fundamental of all liberty interests – to be free from physical detention by one's own government. On the other side, is the governmental interest in preventing captured individuals from returning to the field and taking up arms against the U.S. once again. In order to strike the proper balance, we hold that citizen-detainees seeking to challenge their classifications as enemy combatants must receive 1) notice of the factual basis for their classification and 2) a fair opportunity to rebut the government's factual decisions before a neutral decisionmaker. At the same time, emergency circumstances may demand that enemy combatant proceedings be tailored to alleviate their potential burdens on the government. Hearsay, for example, may need to be accepted as the most reliable evidence. We note the parties captured on the field need not receive the process we have discussed here; that process is due only when the determination is made to hold those that have been seized. All in all, there remains the possibility that a military tribunal could meet the due process standards we set forth. However, if they can not, a court receiving a habeas petition from an enemy combatant must see to it that due process is realized.

C Vacated and remanded.

Nixon v. Fitzgerald

457 U.S. 731 (1982)

FACTS

During the waning months of the Presidency of Lyndon B. Johnson in 1968, respondent, a management analyst with the Department of the Air Force, testified before a congressional Subcommittee about cost-overruns and unexpected technical difficulties concerning the development of a particular airplane. In January 1970, during the Presidency of petitioner Richard M. Nixon, respondent was dismissed from his job during a departmental reorganization and reduction in force, in which his job was eliminated. Respondent complained to the Civil Service Commission, alleging that his separation represented unlawful retaliation for his congressional testimony. The Commission rejected this claim, but concluded that respondent's dismissal offended applicable regulations because it was motivated by "reasons purely personal to" respondent. Respondent thereafter filed suit for damages in Federal District Court against various Defense Department officials and White House aides allegedly responsible for his dismissal. An amended complaint later named petitioner as a defendant. After earlier judicial rulings and extensive pretrial discovery, only three defendants were involved: petitioner and two White House aides. Denying the defendants' motion for summary judgment, the court held that respondent had stated triable causes of action under two federal statutes and the First Amendment, and that petitioner was not entitled to claim absolute Presidential immunity. Petitioner took a collateral appeal of the immunity decision to the Court of Appeals, which dismissed summarily.

I Does the President enjoy absolute immunity from law suits for actions taken in his official capacity?

R The President enjoys absolute immunity from civil liability for acts committed in his official capacity.

A This Court has jurisdiction to determine the immunity question. The case was "in" the Court of Appeals for purposes of 28 U.S.C. 1254, which authorizes this Court's review of "[c]ases in" the courts of appeals. The Court of Appeals here dismissed the appeal for lack of jurisdiction. However, petitioner's appeal to the Court of Appeals falls within the "collateral order" doctrine of *Cohen v. Beneficial Industrial Loan Corp.*, as raising a "serious and unsettled question" of law. Although the Court of Appeals had previously ruled in another case that the President was not entitled to absolute immunity, this Court had never so held. Nor was the controversy mooted by an agreement to liquidate damages entered into between the parties after the petition for certiorari was filed and respondent had entered his opposition. Under the terms of the agreement, petitioner paid respondent $142,000; respondent agreed to accept liquidated damages of $28,000 if this Court ruled that petitioner was not entitled to absolute immunity; and no further payments would be made if the decision upheld petitioner's immunity claim. The limited agreement left both parties with a considerable financial stake in the resolution of the question presented in this Court. Petitioner, as a former President of the United States, is entitled to absolute immunity from damages liability predicated on his official acts. Although there is no blanket recognition of absolute immunity for all federal executive officials from liability for civil damages resulting from constitutional violations, certain officials - such as judges and prosecutors - because of the special nature of their responsibilities require absolute exemption from liability. Determination of the immunity of particular officials is guided by the Constitution, federal statutes, history, and public policy. The President's absolute immunity is a functionally mandated incident of his unique office, rooted in the constitutional tradition of the separation of powers and supported by the Nation's history. Because of the singular importance of the President's duties, diversion of his energies by concern with private lawsuits would raise unique risks to the effective functioning of government. While the separation-of-powers doctrine does not bar every exercise of jurisdiction over the President, a court, before exercising jurisdiction, must balance the constitutional weight of the interest to be served against the dangers of intrusion on the authority and functions of the Executive Branch. The exercise of jurisdiction is not warranted in the case of merely private suits for damages based on a President's official acts. The President's absolute immunity extends to all acts within the "outer perimeter" of his duties of office. A rule of absolute immunity for the President does not leave the Nation without sufficient protection against his misconduct. There remains the constitutional remedy of impeachment, as well as the deterrent effects of constant scrutiny by the press and vigilant oversight by Congress. Other incentives to avoid misconduct may include a desire to earn reelection, the need to maintain prestige as an element of Presidential influence, and a President's traditional concern for his historical stature.

C

Reversed and remanded.

Clinton v. Jones

520 U.S. 681 (1997)

FACTS

Plaintiff-respondent Paula Jones sued under 42 U.S.C. §§1983 and 1985 and Arkansas law to recover damages from petitioner, former President of the United States Bill Clinton, alleging, *inter alia*, that while he was Governor of Arkansas, petitioner made "abhorrent" sexual advances to her, and that her rejection of those advances led to punishment by her supervisors in the state job she held at the time. Petitioner promptly advised the Federal District Court that he would file a motion to dismiss on Presidential immunity grounds, and requested that all other pleadings and motions be deferred until the immunity issue was resolved. After the court granted that request, petitioner filed a motion to dismiss without prejudice and to toll any applicable statutes of limitation during his Presidency. The District Judge denied dismissal on immunity grounds and ruled that discovery could go forward, but ordered any trial stayed until petitioner's Presidency ended. The Eighth Circuit affirmed the dismissal denial, but reversed the trial postponement as the "functional equivalent" of a grant of temporary immunity to which petitioner was not constitutionally entitled. The court explained that the President, like other officials, is subject to the same laws that apply to all citizens, that no case had been found in which an official was granted immunity from suit for his unofficial acts, and that the rationale for official immunity is inapposite where only personal, private conduct by a President is at issue. The court also rejected the argument that, unless immunity is available, the threat of judicial interference with the Executive Branch would violate separation of powers.

I May a sitting President defer civil litigation brought against him and based on unofficial acts, until after he leaves office?

R The Constitution does not automatically grant the President of the United States immunity from civil lawsuits based on his private conduct nor will he be afforded temporary immunity from those lawsuits until after he has left office.

A This Court need not address two important constitutional issues not encompassed within the questions presented by the certiorari petition: 1) whether a claim comparable to petitioner's assertion of immunity might succeed in a state tribunal, and 2) whether a court may compel the President's attendance at any specific time or place. Deferral of this litigation until petitioner's Presidency ends is not constitutionally required. Petitioner's principal submission, that in all but the most exceptional cases the Constitution affords the President temporary immunity from civil damages litigation arising out of events that occurred before he took office, cannot be sustained on the basis of precedent. The principal rationale for affording Presidents immunity from damages actions based on their official acts provides no support for immunity for *unofficial* conduct. Moreover, immunities for acts clearly within official capacity are grounded in the nature of the function performed, not the identity of the actor who performed it. We are also not persuaded by petitioner's historical evidence, which sheds little light on the question at issue, and is largely canceled by conflicting evidence that is itself consistent with both the doctrine of presidential immunity and rejection of the immunity claim in this case. The separation of powers doctrine does not require federal courts to stay all private actions against the President until he leaves office. Even accepting the unique importance of the Presidency in the constitutional scheme, it does not follow that that doctrine would be violated by allowing this action to proceed. The doctrine provides a self executing safeguard against the encroachment or aggrandizement of one of the three co equal branches of Government at the expense of another. But in this case there is no suggestion that the Federal Judiciary is being asked to perform any function that might in some way be described as "executive." Respondent is merely asking the courts to exercise their core Article III jurisdiction to decide cases and controversies, and, whatever the outcome, there is no possibility that the decision here will curtail the scope of the Executive Branch's official powers. The Court rejects petitioner's contention that this case may place unacceptable burdens on the President that will hamper the performance of his official duties. That assertion finds little support either in history, as evidenced by the paucity of suits against sitting Presidents for their private actions, or in the relatively narrow compass of the issues raised in this particular case. Of greater significance, it is settled that the Judiciary may severely burden the Executive Branch by reviewing the legality of the President's official conduct, and may direct appropriate process to the President himself. It must follow that the federal courts have power to determine the legality of the President's unofficial conduct. The reasons for rejecting a categorical rule requiring federal courts to stay private actions during the President's term apply as well to a rule that would, in petitioner's words, require a stay "in all but the most exceptional cases." Contrary to the Eighth Circuit's ruling, the District Court's stay order was not the "functional equivalent" of an unconstitutional grant of temporary immunity. Rather, the District Court has broad discretion to stay proceedings as an incident to its power to control its own docket. Moreover, the potential burdens on the President posed by this litigation are appropriate matters for that court to evaluate in its management of the case, and the high respect owed the Presidency is a matter that should inform the conduct of the entire proceeding. Nevertheless, the District Court's stay decision was an abuse of discretion because it took no account of the importance of respondent's interest in bringing the case to trial, and because it was premature in that there was nothing in the record to enable a judge to assess whether postponement of trial after the completion of discovery would be warranted. The Court is not persuaded of the seriousness of the alleged risks that this decision will generate a large volume of politically motivated harassing and frivolous litigation and that national security concerns might prevent the President from explaining a legitimate need for a continuance, and has confidence in the ability of federal judges to deal with both concerns. If Congress deems it appropriate to afford the President stronger protection, it may respond with legislation.

C

Affirmed.

Lorillard Tobacco Co. v. Reilly

533 U.S. 525 (2001)

FACTS

After the Attorney General of Massachusetts (Attorney General) promulgated comprehensive regulations governing the advertising and sale of cigarettes, smokeless tobacco, and cigars, petitioners, a group of tobacco manufacturers and retailers, filed this suit asserting, among other things, the Supremacy Clause claim that the cigarette advertising regulations are pre-empted by the Federal Cigarette Labeling and Advertising Act (FCLAA), which prescribes mandatory health warnings for cigarette packaging and advertising, 15 U. S. C. §1333, and pre-empts similar state regulations, §1334(b); and a claim that the regulations violate the First and Fourteenth Amendments to the Federal Constitution. In large measure, the District Court upheld the regulations. Among its rulings, the court held that restrictions on the location of advertising were not pre-empted by the FCLAA, and that neither the regulations prohibiting outdoor advertising within 1,000 feet of a school or playground nor the sales practices regulations restricting the location and distribution of tobacco products violated the First Amendment. The court ruled, however, that the point-of-sale advertising regulations requiring that indoor advertising be placed no lower than five feet from the floor were invalid because the Attorney General had not provided sufficient justification for that restriction. The First Circuit affirmed the District Court's rulings that the cigarette advertising regulations are not pre-empted by the FCLAA and that the outdoor advertising regulations and the sales practices regulations do not violate the First Amendment under *Central Hudson Gas & Elec. Corp.* v. *Public Serv. Comm'n of N. Y.*, but reversed the lower court's invalidation of the point-of-sale advertising regulations, concluding that the Attorney General is better suited than courts to determine what restrictions are necessary.

I

Are certain state cigarette advertising regulations pre-empted by the Federal Cigarette Labeling and Advertising Act (FCLAA)?

R

Certain state cigarette advertising regulations are pre-empted by the Federal Cigarette Labeling and Advertising Act (FCLAA).

A

The FCLAA pre-empts Massachusetts' regulations governing outdoor and point-of-sale cigarette advertising. Congress pre-empted state cigarette advertising regulations like the Attorney General's because they would upset federal legislative choices to require specific warnings and to impose the ban on cigarette advertising in electronic media in order to address concerns about smoking and health. In holding that the FCLAA does not nullify the Massachusetts regulations, the First Circuit concentrated on whether they are "with respect to" advertising and promotion, concluding that the FCLAA only pre-empts regulations of the content of cigarette advertising. The court also reasoned that the regulations are a form of zoning, a traditional area of state power, and, therefore, a presumption against pre-emption applied. We reject the notion that the regulations are not "with respect to" cigarette advertising and promotion. There is no question about an indirect relationship between the Massachusetts regulations and cigarette advertising: The regulations expressly target such advertising. The Attorney General's argument that the regulations are not "based on smoking and health" since they do not involve health-related content, but instead target youth exposure to cigarette advertising, is unpersuasive because, at bottom, the youth exposure concern is intertwined with the smoking and health concern. Also unavailing is the Attorney General's claim that the regulations are not pre-empted because they govern the location, not the content, of cigarette advertising. The content/location distinction cannot be squared with the pre-emption provision's language, which reaches *all* "requirements" and "prohibitions" "imposed under State law." Although the First Circuit decided that the restriction's burden on speech is very limited, there is no *de minimis* exception for a speech restriction that lacks sufficient tailoring or justification. Assuming that petitioners have a cognizable speech interest in a particular means of displaying their products, the regulations requiring retailers to place tobacco products behind counters and requiring customers to have contact with a salesperson before they are able to handle such a product withstand First Amendment scrutiny. The State has demonstrated a substantial interest in preventing access to tobacco products by minors and has adopted an appropriately narrow means of advancing that interest. Because unattended displays of such products present an opportunity for access without the proper age verification required by law, the State prohibits self-service and other displays that would allow an individual to obtain tobacco without direct contact with a salesperson. It is clear that the regulations leave open ample communication channels. They do not significantly impede adult access to tobacco products, and retailers have other means of exercising any cognizable speech interest in the presentation of their products. The Court presumes that vendors may place empty tobacco packaging on open display, and display actual tobacco products so long as that display is only accessible to sales personnel. As for cigars, there is no indication that a customer is unable to examine a cigar prior to purchase, so long as that examination takes place through a salesperson. The Court declines to address the cigar petitioners' First Amendment challenge to a regulation prohibiting sampling or promotional giveaways of cigars and little cigars. That claim was not sufficiently briefed and argued before this Court.

C Affirmed in part, reversed in part, and remanded.

Florida Lime & Avocado Growers v. Paul

373 U.S. 132 (1963)

FACTS

Appellants, who are engaged in the business of growing packing and marketing Florida avocados in interstate commerce, sued in a Federal District Court to enjoin appellees, state officers of California, from enforcing 792 of the California Agricultural Code, which prohibits the transportation or sale in California of avocados containing less than 8% of oil by weight, against Florida avocados certified as mature under federal regulations issued under the Federal Agricultural Marketing Agreement Act of 1937. They contended that 792 of the California statute, as so applied, was unconstitutional, because (1) under the Supremacy Clause, it must be deemed displaced by the federal standard for determining the maturity of avocados grown in Florida; (2) its application to Florida avocados denied appellants the equal protection of the laws in violation of the Fourteenth Amendment; and (3) its application to them unreasonably burdened or discriminated against interstate marketing of Florida avocados in violation of the Commerce Clause. A three-judge District Court denied an injunction on the ground that the proofs did not establish that 792 violated any provision of the Federal Constitution.

I

When a federal law was just setting the minimum standard, the floor regulation, does is a stricter state law, not in conflict with the federal law, pre-empted?

R

When a federal law was just setting the minimum standard, the floor regulation, a stricter state law, not in conflict with the federal law, is not pre-empted.

A

Section 792 is not invalid under the Supremacy Clause, because there is no actual conflict between the two schemes of regulation that both cannot stand in the same area, nor is there evidence of a congressional design to preempt the field. The subject matter of the California regulation, while not concerned with health or safety, is one traditionally within the scope of the power of the States to prevent deception of consumers in the retail marketing of foodstuffs. Neither the terms nor the history of the Federal Agricultural Marketing Agreement Act of 1937 discloses a congressional intent to displace traditional state powers to regulate the retail distribution of agricultural commodities. Section 792 does not violate the Equal Protection Clause of the Fourteenth Amendment because it does not work an irrational discrimination between persons or groups of persons. Therefore, the judgment is reversed in this respect and the case is remanded to the District Court for a new trial of appellants' contentions that 792 unreasonably burdens or discriminates against interstate commerce in Florida avocados. Since the appellants showed sufficient injury to warrant at least a trial of their allegations, the District Court properly refused to dismiss the complaint for want of equity jurisdiction.

C

Affirmed in part, reversed in part, and remanded.

Pacific Gas & Electric Co. v. State Energy Resources Conservation & Development Commission

461 U.S. 190 (1983)

FACTS

Section 25524.1(b) of the California Public Resources Code provides that before a nuclear power plant may be built, the State Energy Resources Conservation and Development Commission must determine on a case-by-case basis that there will be "adequate capacity" for interim storage of the plant's spent fuel at the time the plant requires such storage. Section 25524.2 imposes a moratorium on the certification of new nuclear plants until the State Commission finds that there has been developed, and that the United States through its authorized agency has approved, a demonstrated technology or means for the permanent and terminal disposal of high-level nuclear wastes. Petitioner electric utilities filed an action in Federal District Court seeking a declaration that these provisions, *inter alia*, are invalid under the Supremacy Clause because they were pre-empted by the Atomic Energy Act of 1954. The District Court, after finding that the issues presented by the two provisions were ripe for adjudication, held that they were pre-empted by and in conflict with the Atomic Energy Act. The Court of Appeals agreed that the challenge to 25524.2 was ripe for review, but found that the challenge to 25524.1(b) was not because it could not be known whether the State Commission will ever find a nuclear plant's storage capacity to be inadequate. The court went on to hold that 25524.2 was not designed to provide protection against radiation hazards but was adopted because uncertainties in the nuclear fuel cycle make nuclear power an uneconomical and uncertain source of energy, and therefore that the section was not pre-empted because 271 and 274(k) of the Atomic Energy Act constituted authorization for States to regulate nuclear power plants for purposes other than protection against radiation hazards. The court further held that 25524.2 was not invalid as a barrier to fulfillment of the federal goal of encouraging the development of atomic energy.

I Is a state statute which imposes a moratorium on the certification of nuclear plants until a safe method of disposal is developed preempted by the Atomic Energy Act of 1954, whose purpose it is to promote the use of nuclear energy?

R How a state law is characterized by the courts will often decide whether a state law clashes with a federal law, necessitating preemption, when such a determination is not clear on its face.

A The challenge to 25524.2 is ripe for judicial review, but the questions concerning 25524.1(b) are not. The question of ripeness turns "on the fitness of the issues for judicial decision" and "the hardship to the parties of withholding court consideration." Both of these factors counsel in favor of finding the challenge to 25524.2 ripe for adjudication. The question of pre-emption is predominantly legal and to require the industry to proceed without knowing whether the moratorium imposed by 25524.2 is valid would impose a considerable hardship on the utilities, and may ultimately work harm on the citizens of California. Moreover, if 25524.2 is found void as hindering commercial development of atomic energy, delayed resolution would frustrate one of the key purposes of the Atomic Energy Act. Under circumstances where it is uncertain whether the State Commission will ever find a nuclear plant's interim storage capacity to be inadequate, and where, because of this Court's holding that 25524.2 is not pre-empted by federal law, it is unlikely that industry behavior would be uniquely affected by such uncertainty surrounding the interim storage provision, a court should not stretch to reach an early, and perhaps a premature, decision respecting 25524.1(b). Section 25524.2 is not pre-empted by the Atomic Energy Act. From the passage of the Atomic Energy Act in 1954, through several revisions, and to the present day, Congress has preserved the dual regulation of nuclear-powered electricity generation: the Federal Government maintains complete control of the safety and "nuclear" aspects of energy generation, whereas the States exercise their traditional authority over economic questions such as the need for additional generating capacity, the type of generating facilities to be licensed, land use, and ratemaking. This Court accepts California's avowed economic rather than safety purpose as the rationale for enacting 25524.2, and accordingly the statute lies outside the federally occupied field of nuclear safety regulation. Section 25524.2 does not conflict with federal regulation of nuclear waste disposal, with the decision of the Nuclear Regulatory Commission (NRC) that it is permissible to continue to license reactors, notwithstanding uncertainty surrounding the waste disposal problem, or with Congress' recent passage of the Nuclear Waste Policy Act of 1982 directed at that problem. Because the NRC's decision does not and could not compel a utility to develop a nuclear plant, compliance with both that decision and 25524.2 is possible. Moreover, because the NRC's regulations are aimed at insuring that plants are safe, not necessarily that they are economical, 25524.2 does not interfere with the objective of those regulations. And as there is no attempt on California's part to enter the field of developing and licensing nuclear waste disposal technology, a field occupied by the Federal Government, 25524.2 is not pre-empted any more by the NRC's obligations in the waste disposal field than by its licensing power over the plants themselves. Nor does it appear that Congress intended through the Nuclear Waste Policy Act of 1982 to make the decision for the States as to whether there is now sufficient federal commitment to fuel storage and waste disposal that licensing of nuclear reactors may resume. Moreover, that Act can be interpreted as being directed at solving the nuclear waste disposal problem for existing reactors without necessarily encouraging or requiring that future plant construction be undertaken. Section 25524.2 does not frustrate the Atomic Energy Act's purpose to develop the commercial use of nuclear power. Promotion of nuclear power is not to be accomplished "at all costs." Moreover, Congress has given the States authority to determine, as a matter of economics, whether a nuclear plant *vis-a-vis* a fossil fuel plant should be built. California's decision to exercise that authority does not, in itself, constitute a basis for pre-emption.

C Affirmed.

Himes v. Davidowitz

312 U.S. 52 (1941)

FACTS

This case involves the validity of an Alien Registration Act adopted by the Commonwealth of Pennsylvania. The Act, passed in 1939, requires every alien 18 years or over, with certain exceptions, to register once each year; provide such information as is required by the statute, plus any 'other information and details' that the Department of Labor and Industry may direct; pay $1 as an annual registration fee; receive an alien identification card and carry it at all times; show the card whenever it may be demanded by any police officer or any agent of the Department of Labor and Industry; and exhibit the card as a condition precedent to registering a motor vehicle in his name or obtaining a license to operate one. The Department of Labor and Industry is charged with the duties of classifying the registrations for 'the purpose of ready reference', and furnishing a copy of the classification to the Pennsylvania Motor Police. Nonexempt aliens who fail to register are subject to a fine of not more than $100 or imprisonment for not more than 60 days, or both. For failure to carry an identification card or for failure to show it upon proper demand, the punishment is a fine of not more than $10, or imprisonment for not more than 10 days, or both. A three-judge District Court enjoined enforcement of the Act, holding that it denied aliens equal protection of the laws, and that it encroached upon legislative powers constitutionally vested in the federal government. It is that judgment we are here called upon to review. But in 1940, after the court had held that Pennsylvania Act invalid, Congress enacted a federal Alien Registration Act.

I If the federal government exercises superior authority in a particular field, can states enact laws which interfere with, curtail or complement the federal law?

R If the federal government exercises superior authority in a particular field, the states cannot enact laws which interfere with, curtail or complement the federal law.

A The federal Act provides for a single registration of aliens 14 years of age and over; detailed information specified by the Act, plus 'such additional matters as may be prescribed by the Commissioner, with the approval of the Attorney General'; fingerprinting of all registrants; and secrecy of the federal files, which can be 'made available only to such persons or agencies as may be designated by the Commissioner, with the approval of the Attorney General.' No requirement that aliens carry a registration card to be exhibited to police or others is embodied in the law, and only the willful failure to register is made a criminal offense; punishment is fixed at a fine of not more than $ 1000, imprisonment for not more than 6 months, or both. The basic subject of the state and federal laws is identical- registration of aliens as a distinct group. Appellants urge that the Pennsylvania law "was constitutional when passed", and that "The only question is whether the state act is in abeyance or whether the state and Federal Government have concurrent jurisdiction to register aliens for the protection of inhabitants and property." The supremacy of the national power in the general field of foreign affairs, including power over immigration, naturalization and deportation, is made clear by the Constitution was pointed out by authors of The Federalist in 1787, and has since been given continuous recognition by this Court. When the national government by treaty or statute has established rules and regulations touching the rights, privileges, obligations or burdens of aliens as such, the treaty or statute is the supreme law of the land. No state can add to or take from the force and effect of such treaty or statute. The Federal Government, representing as it does the collective interests of the forty-eight states, is entrusted with full and exclusive responsibility for the conduct of affairs with foreign sovereignties. Our system of government is such that the interest of the cities, counties and states, no less than the interest of the people of the whole nation, imperatively requires that federal power in the field affecting foreign relations be left entirely free from local interference. We have already adverted to the conditions which make the treatment of aliens, in whatever state they may be located, a matter of national moment. And whether or not registration of aliens is of such a nature that the Constitution permits only of one uniform national system, it cannot be denied that the Congress might validly conclude that such uniformity is desirable. The legislative history of the Act indicates that Congress was trying to steer a middle path, realizing that any registration requirement was a departure from our traditional policy of not treating aliens as a thing apart, but also feeling that the Nation was in need of the type of information to be secured. Having the constitutional authority so to do, it has provided a standard for alien registration in a single integrated and all- embracing system in order to obtain the information deemed to be desirable in connection with aliens. When it made this addition to its uniform naturalization and immigration laws, it plainly manifested a purpose to do so in such a way as to protect the personal liberties of law-abiding aliens through one uniform national registration system, and to leave them free from the possibility of inquisitorial practices and police surveillance that might not only affect our international relations but might also generate the very disloyalty which the law has intended guarding against. Under these circumstances, the Pennsylvania Act cannot be enforced. Accordingly, the judgment below is affirmed.

C

Affirmed.

H.P. Hood & Sons v. Du Mond

336 U.S. 529 (1939)

FACTS

This case concerns the power of the State of New York to deny additional facilities to acquire and ship milk in interstate commerce where the grounds of denial are that such limitation upon interstate business will protect and advance local economic interests. H. P. Hood & Sons, Inc., a Massachusetts corporation, has long distributed milk and its products to inhabitants of Boston. That city obtains about 90% of its fluid milk from states other than Massachusetts. Dairies located in New York State since about 1900 have been among the sources of Boston's supply, their contribution having varied but during the last ten years approximately 8%. The area in which Hood has been denied an additional license to make interstate purchases has been developed as a part of the Boston milkshed from which both the Hood Company and a competitor have shipped to Boston. The state courts have held and it is conceded here that Hood's entire business in New York, present and proposed, is interstate commerce. This Hood has conducted for some time by means of three receiving depots, where it takes raw milk from farmers. The milk is not processed in New York but is weighed, tested and, if necessary, cooled and on the same day shipped as fluid milk to Boston. These existing plants have been operated under license from the State and are not in question here as the State has licensed Hood to continue them. The controversy concerns a proposed additional plant for the same kind of operation at Greenwich, New York. Article 21 of the Agriculture and Markets Law of New York, forbids a dealer to buy milk from producers unless licensed to do so by the Commissioner of Agriculture and Markets. For the license he must pay a substantial fee and furnish a bond to assure prompt payment to producers for milk. Under 258, the Commissioner may not grant a license unless satisfied 'that the applicant is qualified by character, experience, financial responsibility and equipment to properly conduct the proposed business.' The Hood Company concededly has met all the foregoing tests and license for an additional plant was not denied for any failure to comply with these requirements. Upon the hearing pursuant to the statute, milk dealers competing with Hood as buyers in the area opposed licensing the proposed Greenwich plant. They complained that Hood, by reason of conditions under which it sold in Boston, had competitive advantages under applicable federal milk orders, Boston health regulations, and OPA ceiling prices. There was also evidence of a temporary shortage of supply in the Troy, New York market during the fall and winter of 1945-46. The Commissioner was urged not to allow Hood to compete for additional supplies to milk or to take on producers then delivering to their dealers. The Commissioner found that Hood, if licensed at Greenwich, would permit its present suppliers, at their option, to deliver at the new plant rather than the old ones and for a substantial number this would mean shorter hauls and savings in delivery costs. The new plant also would attract twenty to thirty producers, some of whose milk Hood anticipates will or may be diverted from other buyers. Other large milk distributors have plants within the general area and dealers serving Troy obtain milk in the locality. He found that Troy was inadequately supplied during the preceding short season. Thus, the Commissioner denied the application for expanded facilities. Denial of the license was sustained by the Court of Appeals over constitutional objections duly urged under the Commerce Clause.

I May a state deny a license for a new plant to acquire and ship milk via interstate commerce on grounds that such a limitation will protect and advance local interests?

H.P. Hood & Sons v. Du Mond

336 U.S. 529 (1939)

R A state may not enact laws which will protect and advance local interests if such laws will also burden interstate commerce.

A Our review of the history, sections and reports of Congress indicate that it is the deliberate policy of the Congress to prevent federal officers from placing barriers in the way of the interstate flow of milk. While a statutory prohibition against federal interference with certain phases of it may not always imply that the state too is precluded, it is obvious that a state limitation on export for the benefit of its own consumers is not authorized by this Federal Act. The purpose as expressed in 1, 7 U.S.C. 601, 7 U.S.C.A. 601, is to avoid conditions which burden and obstruct the normal channels of interstate commerce. The object of the federal program to raise and stabilize the price of products was to stimulate interstate commerce. The order of the Commissioner avows itself to have the opposite effect. It can claim neither federal sponsorship nor congressional sanction. Since the statute as applied violates the Commerce Clause and is not authorized by federal legislation pursuant to that Clause, it cannot stand. The judgment is reversed and the cause remanded for proceedings not inconsistent with this opinion. It is so ordered.

C Reversed and remanded.

Aaron B. Cooley v. The Board of Wardens of the Port of Philadelphia

53 U.S. (*12 How.*) 299 (1851)

FACTS

A law in Pennsylvania required that all ships entering or leaving the port must be accompanied by a guide, to guide them through the harbor or pay a fine. The guides must be local pilots. Apparently, Plaintiff Cooley challenged the constitutionality of the law arguing that the Commerce Clause gave Congress gave Congress exclusive jurisdiction over commerce such that Congress could not re-grant that authority to the state. Thus, any state law regulating commerce is invalid.

I

Is the power to regulate commerce by Congress exclusive of all state powers to regulate it?

R

The power to regulate commerce by Congress is not exclusive of all state powers to regulate it.

A

If the grant of commercial power in the Constitution has deprived the states of all power to legislate for the regulation of pilots, if their laws on this subject are mere usurpations upon the exclusive power of the general government, and utterly void, it may be doubted whether Congress could, with propriety, recognize them as laws, and adopt them as its own acts; and how are the legislatures of the states to proceed in future, to watch over and amend these laws, as the progressive wants of a growing commerce will require, when the members of those legislatures are made aware that they cannot legislate on this subject without violating the oaths they have taken to support the Constitution of the United States? We are of opinion that this state law was enacted by virtue of a power, residing in the state to legislate; that it is not in conflict with any law of Congress; that it does not interfere with any system which Congress has established by making regulations, or by intentionally leaving individuals to their own unrestricted action; that this law is therefore valid, and the judgment of the Supreme Court of Pennsylvania in each case must be affirmed.

C

See Rule above.

South Carolina State Highway Dept. v. Barnwell Bros.

303 U.S. 177 (1938)

FACTS

Act No. 259 of the General Assembly of South Carolina, of April 28, 1933, prohibits use on the state highways of motor trucks and 'semi-trailer motor trucks' whose width exceeds 90 inches, and whose weight including load exceeds 20,000 pounds. For purposes of the weight limitation, section 2 of the statute provides that a semi-trailer motortruck, which is a motor propelled truck with a trailer whose front end is designed to be attached to and supported by the truck, shall be considered a single unit. The principal question for decision is whether these prohibitions impose an unconstitutional burden upon interstate commerce. Appellees include the original plaintiffs below, who are truckers and interstate shippers; the Interstate Commerce Commission; and certain others who were permitted to intervene as parties plaintiff. The suit was brought in the District Court for Eastern South Carolina against various state officials, to enjoin them from enforcing sections 4 and 6 of the act among others,1 on the ground that they have been superseded by the Federal Motor Carrier Act of 1935; that they infringe the due process clause of the Fourteenth Amendment; and that they impose an unconstitutional burden on interstate commerce. Certain railroads interested in restricting the competition of interstate motor carriers were permitted to intervene as parties defendant. The District Court of three judges, after hearing evidence, ruled that the challenged provisions of the statute have not been superseded by the Federal Motor Carrier Act, 49 U.S.C.A. 301-327, and adopted as its own the ruling of the state Supreme Court in *State ex rel. Daniel v. John P. Nutt Co.*, that the challenged provisions, being an exercise of the state's power to regulate the use of its highways so as to protect them from injury and to insure their safe and economical use, do not violate the Fourteenth Amendment. But it held that the weight and width prohibitions place an unlawful burden on interstate motor traffic passing over specified highways of the state, which for the most part are of concrete or a concrete base surfaced with asphalt. In accordingly enjoined the enforcement of the weight provision against interstate motor carriers on the specified highway, and also the width limitation of 90 inches, except in the case of vehicles exceeding 96 inches in width. It exempted from the operation of the decree, bridges on those highways 'not constructed with sufficient strength to support the heavy trucks of modern traffic or too narrow to accommodate such traffic safely,' provided the state highway department should place at each end of the bridge proper notices warning that the use of the bridge is forbidden by trucks exceeding the weight or width limits and provided the proper authorities take the necessary steps to enforce the law against such use of the bridges. The case comes before the U.S. Supreme Court on appeal under section 266 of the Judicial Code, as amended.

I Does a state law which places width and weight limitation on truck passing along its highways impose an unconstitutional burden on interstate commerce?

R There is no violation of the Commerce Clause when a state law places width and weight limitation on truck passing along its highways.

South Carolina State Highway Dept. v. Barnwell Bros.

303 U.S. 177 (1938)

A The trial court rested its decision that the statute unreasonably burdens interstate commerce. To reach this conclusion the court weighed conflicting evidence and made its own determinations as to the weight and width of motortrucks commonly used in interstate traffic and the capacity of the specified highways of the state to accommodate such traffic without injury to them or danger to their users. Congress, in the exercise of its plenary power to regulate interstate commerce, may determine whether the burdens imposed on it by state regulation are too great. In the absence of such legislation the judicial function, under the commerce clause, as well as the 14th Amendment, stops with the inquiry whether the state Legislature in adopting regulations such as the present has acted within its province. Here the first inquiry has already been resolved by our decisions that a state may impose nondiscriminatory restrictions with respect to the character of motor vehicles moving in interstate commerce as a safety measure and as a means of securing the economical use of its highways. In reviewing the present determination, we examine the record, not to see whether the findings of the court below are supported by evidence, but to ascertain upon the whole record whether it is possible to say that the legislative choice is without rational basis. Not only does the record fail to exclude that possibility but it shows affirmatively that there is adequate support for the legislative judgment. There is testimony to show that the axle or wheel weight limitation is the more easily enforced through resort to weighing devices adapted to ascertaining readily the axle or wheel weight. While the report of the National Conference on State and Highway Safety, on which the court below relied, suggested a wheel weight limitation of 8,000 or 9,000 pounds, it also suggested that a gross weight limitation might be adopted and should be subject to the recommended wheel limitation. Only a word need be said as to the width limitation. While a large part of the highways in question are from 18 to 20 feet in width, approximately 100 miles are only 16 feet wide. The use of a 96-inch truck leaves but a narrow margin for passing. On the road 16 feet wide it leaves none. The 90-inch limitation has been in force in South Carolina since 1920, and the concrete highways which it has built appear to be adapted to vehicles of that width. The record shows without contradiction that the use of heavy loaded trucks on the highways tends to force other traffic off the concrete surface onto the shoulders of the road adjoining its edges, and to increase repair costs materially. It appears also that as the width of trucks is increased it obstructs the view of the highway, causing much inconvenience and increased hazard in its use. It plainly cannot be said that the width of trucks used on the highways in South Carolina is unrelated to their safety and cost of maintenance, or that a 90-inch width limitation, adopted to safeguard the highways of the state, is not within the range of the permissible legislative choice. The regulatory measures taken by South Carolina are within its legislative power. They do not infringe the Fourteenth Amendment, and the resulting burden on interstate commerce is not forbidden.

C Judgment reversed.

Southern Pacific Co. v. Arizona

325 U.S. 761 (1945)

FACTS

The Arizona Train Limit Law of 1912 makes it unlawful for any person or corporation to operate within the state a railroad train of more than 14 passenger or 70 freight cars, and authorizes the state to recover a money penalty for each violation of the Act. In 1940 the State of Arizona (plaintiff-appellee) brought suit in the Arizona Superior Court against Defendant-appellant, the Southern Pacific Company, to recover the statutory penalties for operating within the state two interstate trains. Appellant answered, admitting the train operations, but defended on the ground that the statute offends against the commerce clause and the due process clause of the 14th Amendment and conflicts with federal legislation. After a trial without a jury, the court made findings of fact and gave judgment for the railroad company. The Supreme Court of Arizona reversed and directed judgment for the state. Southern Pacific appealed to the U.S. Supreme Court.

I

Has Congress, by legislative enactment, restricted the power of the states to regulate the length of interstate trains as a safety measure and, if not, does the statute contravenes the Commerce Clause of the federal Constitution?

R

The court will perform a cost-benefit analysis in deciding whether an alleged safety ordinance violates the Commerce Clause; weighing the benefits of the statute/ordinance against the burdens it imposes on commerce.

A

We leave undisturbed the findings of the trial court and made no new findings and hold that the power of the state to regulate the length of interstate trains had not been restricted by Congressional action. We uphold the Act as a safety measure to reduce the number of accidents attributed to the operation of trains of more than the statutory maximum length, enacted by the state legislature in the exercise of its "police power" in the interests of local health, safety and well-being of its citizens. The state statute, enacted in the exercise of the state's police power and bearing some reasonable relation to the health, safety and well-being of the people of the state, of which the state legislature is the judge, is not to be judicially overturned, notwithstanding its admittedly adverse effect on the operation of interstate trains. The trial court found that the Arizona law imposes a serious burden on interstate commerce, and inevitably results in an impairment of national uniformity in efficient railroad operation. It further found that the law has no reasonable relation to safety, as the safety benefit of reducing the train size is offset by the dangers from the increased number of trains required when train lengths are reduced. We agree. Here, Arizona's interest is outweighed by the national interest in efficient railway service. We arrive at this conclusion by considering the nature of the subject of the regulation and the states interest in it, and then balance those state interests against the countervailing national interests.

C

See above.

City of Philadelphia v. New Jersey

437 U.S. 617 (1978)

FACTS

In early 1974, a New Jersey statute (ch. 363) took effect which provided that "No person shall bring into this State any solid or liquid waste which originated or was collected outside the territorial limits of the State, except garbage to be fed to swine in the State of New Jersey, until the commissioner [of the State Department of Environmental Protection] shall determine that such action can be permitted without endangering the public health, safety and welfare and has promulgated regulations permitting and regulating the treatment and disposal of such waste in this State." As authorized, the Commissioner promulgated regulations permitting four categories of waste to enter the State. Apart from these narrow exceptions, however, New Jersey closed its borders to all waste from other States. Immediately affected by these developments were the operators of private landfills in New Jersey, and several cities in other States that had agreements with these operators for waste disposal. They brought suit against New Jersey and its Department of Environmental Protection in state court, attacking the statute and regulations on a number of state and federal grounds. In an oral opinion granting the plaintiffs' motion for summary judgment, the trial court declared the law unconstitutional because it discriminated against interstate commerce. The New Jersey Supreme Court consolidated this case with another reaching a different conclusion. It found that the statute advanced vital health and environmental objectives with no economic discrimination against, and with little burden upon, interstate commerce, and that the law was therefore permissible under the Commerce Clause of the Constitution. The court also found no congressional intent to pre-empt. The plaintiffs then appealed to the U.S. Supreme Court.

I

Does a state statute which prohibits the importation of most "solid or liquid waste which originated or was collected outside the territorial limits of the State" violative the Commerce Clause of the United States Constitution?

R

A state statute which prohibits the importation of most "solid or liquid waste which originated or was collected outside the territorial limits of the State" violates the Commerce Clause of the United States Constitution if it is basically an economic protectionist measure; however, if it directed at legitimate local concerns that have only incidental effects on interstate commerce, it ***may*** be valid and non-violative of the Commerce clause.

A

The New Jersey statute (ch. 363) at issue prohibits the importation of most "solid or liquid waste which originated or was collected outside the territorial limits of the State . . ." and is thus held to violate the Commerce Clause of the United States Constitution. All objects of interstate trade merit Commerce Clause protection and none is excluded from the definition of "commerce" at the outset; hence, contrary to the suggestion of the court below, there can be no doubt that the banning of "valueless" out-of-state wastes by ch. 363 implicates constitutional protection. The crucial inquiry here must be directed to determining whether ch. 363 is basically an economic protectionist measure, and thus virtually *per se* invalid, or a law directed at legitimate local concerns that has only incidental effects on interstate commerce. Since the evil of protectionism can reside in legislative means as well as legislative ends, it is immaterial whether the legislative purpose of ch. 363 is to protect New Jersey's environment or its economy, for whatever the purpose, it may not be accomplished by discriminating against articles of commerce coming from outside the State unless there is some reason, apart from their origin, to treat them differently. Both on its face and in its plain effect ch. 363 violates this principle of non-discrimination. A State may not attempt to isolate itself from a problem common to many by erecting a barrier against the movement of interstate trade, as ch. 363 seeks to do by imposing on out-of-state commercial interests the full burden of conserving New Jersey's remaining landfill space. The New Jersey statute cannot be likened to a quarantine law which bans importation of articles of commerce because of their innate harmfulness and not because of their origin. Though New Jersey concedes that out-of-state waste is no different from domestic waste, it has banned the former while leaving its landfill sites open to the latter, thus trying to saddle those outside the State with the entire burden of slowing the flow of wastes into New Jersey's remaining landfill sites.

C

Reversed.

C&A Carbone Inc. v. Clarkstown

511 U.S. 383 (1994)

FACTS

Respondent town, Clarkston, agreed to allow a private contractor to construct within town limits a solid waste transfer station to separate recyclable from non-recyclable items and to operate the facility for five years, at which time the town would buy it for one dollar. To finance the transfer station's cost, the town guaranteed a minimum waste flow to the facility, for which the contractor could charge the hauler a tipping fee which exceeded the disposal cost of unsorted solid waste on the private market. In order to meet the waste flow guarantee, the town adopted a flow control ordinance, requiring all non-hazardous solid waste within the town to be deposited at the transfer station. While recyclers like petitioners (collectively Carbone) may receive solid waste at their own sorting facilities, the ordinance requires them to bring non-recyclable residue to the transfer station, thus forbidding them to ship such waste themselves and requiring them to pay the tipping fee on trash that has already been sorted. After discovering that Carbone was shipping non-recyclable waste to out-of-state destinations, the town filed suit in state court, seeking an injunction requiring that this residue be shipped to the transfer station. The court granted summary judgment to the town, finding the ordinance constitutional, and the Appellate Division affirmed.

I

Is an ordinance requiring all non-hazardous solid waste within a town to be deposited at a central transfer station for a mandatory fee violative the commerce clause, when the ordinance also precludes a party from shipping the same waste by themselves either in-state or out-of state?

R

The flow control ordinance violates the Commerce Clause because it regulates interstate commerce.

A

The flow control ordinance violates the Commerce Clause. The ordinance regulates interstate commerce. While its immediate effect is to direct local transport of solid waste to a designated site within the local jurisdiction, its economic effects are interstate in reach. By requiring Carbone to send the Page II non-recyclable portion of waste it receives from out of State to the transfer station at an additional cost, the ordinance drives up the cost for out-of-state interests to dispose of their solid waste. It also deprives out-of-state businesses of access to the local market, by preventing everyone except the favored local operator from performing the initial processing step. The ordinance discriminates against interstate commerce, and thus is invalid. Although the ordinance erects no barrier to the import or export of any solid waste, the article of commerce here is not so much the waste itself, but rather the service of processing and disposing of it. With respect to this stream of commerce, the ordinance discriminates, for it allows only the favored operator to process waste that is within the town's limits. It is no less discriminatory because in-state or in-town processors are also covered by the prohibition. Favoring a single local proprietor makes the ordinance's protectionist effect even more acute, for it squelches competition in the waste-processing service altogether, leaving no room for outside investment. The town does not lack other means to advance a legitimate local interest. It could address alleged health and safety problems through nondiscriminatory alternatives, such as uniform safety regulations that would ensure that competitors do not underprice the market by cutting corners on environmental safety. Justifying the ordinance as a way to steer solid waste away from out-of-town disposal sites that the town might deem harmful to the environment would extend its police power beyond its jurisdictional boundaries. Moreover, the ordinance's revenue generating purpose by itself is not a local interest that can justify discrimination against interstate commerce. If special financing is needed to ensure the transfer station's long-term survival, the town may subsidize the facility through general taxes or municipal bonds, but it may not employ discriminatory regulation to give the project an advantage over rival out-of-state businesses.

C Reversed and remanded.

Hughes v. Oklahoma

441 U.S. 322 (1979)

FACTS

An Oklahoma statute prohibits transporting or shipping outside the State for sale natural minnows seined or procured from waters within the State. Appellant, who holds a Texas license to operate a commercial minnow business in Texas, was charged with violating the Oklahoma statute by transporting from Oklahoma to Texas a load of natural minnows purchased from a minnow dealer licensed to do business in Oklahoma. Appellant's defense that the Oklahoma statute was unconstitutional because it was repugnant to the Commerce Clause was rejected, and he was convicted and fined. The Oklahoma Court of Criminal Appeals affirmed, relying on *Geer v. Connecticut*, which had sustained against a Commerce Clause challenge a Connecticut statute forbidding the transportation beyond the State of game birds that had been lawfully killed within the State. The Geer decision rested on the holding that no interstate commerce was involved, because the State had the power, as representative for its citizens, who "owned" in common all wild animals within the State, to control the "ownership" of game that had been lawfully reduced to possession, and had exercised its power by prohibiting its removal from the State.

I

May a State enact laws to attempt to conserve natural resources for use by their own residents or is it a violation of the Commerce Clause?

R

A State may not enact laws to attempt to conserve natural resources for use by their own residents as such laws are a violation of the Commerce Clause.

A

The Oklahoma statute is repugnant to the Commerce Clause. *Geer v. Connecticut* is overruled. Challenges under the Commerce Clause to state regulations of wild animals should be considered according to the same general rule applied to state regulations of other natural resources. Under that general rule, this Court must inquire whether the challenged statute regulates evenhandedly with only "incidental" effects on interstate commerce, or discriminates against interstate commerce either on its face or in practical effect; whether the statute serves a legitimate local purpose; and, if so, whether alternative means could promote this local purpose as well without discriminating against interstate commerce. The Oklahoma statute on its face discriminates against interstate commerce by forbidding the transportation of natural minnows out of the State for purposes of sale and thus overtly blocking the flow of interstate commerce at the State's border. The statute is not a "last ditch" attempt at conservation after nondiscriminatory alternatives have proved unfeasible. It is rather a choice of the most discriminatory means even though nondiscriminatory alternatives are available. States may promote the legitimate purpose of protecting and conserving wild animal life within their borders only in ways consistent with the Constitution.

C

Reversed.

Hunt v. Washington State Apple Advertising Council

432 U.S. 333 (1977)

FACTS

Appellee Washington State Apple Advertising Council, a statutory agency for the promotion and protection of the Washington State apple industry and composed of 13 state growers and dealers chosen from electoral districts by their fellow growers and dealers, all of whom by mandatory assessments finance appellee's operations, brought this suit challenging the constitutionality of a North Carolina statute requiring that all apples sold or shipped into North Carolina in closed containers be identified by no grade on the containers other than the applicable federal grade or a designation that the apples are not graded. A three-judge District Court granted the requested injunctive and declaratory relief, holding that appellee had standing to challenge the statute, that the $10,000 jurisdictional amount of 28 U.S.C. 1331 was satisfied, and that the challenged statute unconstitutionally discriminated against commerce insofar as it affected the interstate shipment of Washington apples.

I

Does an association have standing to challenge a statute when it is not a grower, dealer or retailer but is part of the trade industry representing the aforementioned groups in some capacity?

R

An association has standing to bring suit on behalf of its members when 1) its members would otherwise have standing to sue in their own right; 2) the interests it seeks to protect are germane to the organization's purpose; and 3) neither the claim asserted nor the relief requested requires the participation in the lawsuit of each of the individual members.

A

Appellee has standing to bring this action in a representational capacity. An association has standing to bring suit on behalf of its members when 1) its members would otherwise have standing to sue in their own right; 2) the interests it seeks to protect are germane to the organization's purpose; and 3) neither the claim asserted nor the relief requested requires the participation in the lawsuit of each of the individual members, *Warth v. Seldin.* The prerequisites to associational standing described in *Warth* are clearly present here: (1) At the risk of otherwise losing North Carolina accounts, some Washington apple growers and dealers had obliterated Washington State grades from the large volume of North Carolina-bound containers; and they had stopped using preprinted containers, thus diminishing the efficiency of their marketing operations; (2) appellee's attempt to remedy these injuries is central to its purpose of protecting and enhancing the Washington apple market; and (3) neither appellee's constitutional claim nor the relief requested requires individualized proof. Though appellee is a state agency, it is not on that account precluded from asserting the claims of the State's apple growers and dealers since for all practical purposes appellee performs the functions of a traditional trade association. While the apple growers are not "members" of appellee in the traditional trade association sense, they possess all the indicia of organization membership (*viz.*, electing the members, being the only ones to serve on the Commission, and financing its activities), and it is of no consequence that membership assessments are mandatory. Appellee's own interests may be adversely affected by the outcome of this litigation, since the annual assessments that are used to support its activities and which are tied to the production of Washington apples could be reduced if the market for those apples declines as a result of the North Carolina statute. The requirements of 1331 are satisfied. Since appellee has standing to litigate its constituents' claims, it may rely on them to meet the requisite amount of $10,000 in controversy. And it does not appear "to a legal certainty" that the claims of at least some of the individual growers and dealers will not come to that amount in view of the substantial annual sales volume of Washington apples in North Carolina (over $2 million) and the continuing nature of the statute's interference with the Washington apple industry, coupled with the evidence in the record that growers and dealers have suffered and will continue to suffer losses of various types from the operation of the challenged statute. The North Carolina statute violates the Commerce Clause by burdening and discriminating against the interstate sale of Washington apples. The statute raises the costs of doing business in the North Carolina market for Washington growers and dealers while leaving unaffected their North Carolina counterparts, who were still free to market apples under the federal grade or none at all. The statute strips the Washington apple industry of the competitive and economic advantages it has earned for itself by an expensive, stringent mandatory state inspection and grading system that exceeds federal requirements. By requiring Washington apples to be sold under the inferior grades of their federal counterparts, the North Carolina statute offers the North Carolina apple industry the very sort of protection against out-of-state competition that the Commerce Clause was designed to prohibit. Even if the statute was not intended to be discriminatory and was enacted for the declared purpose of protecting consumers from deception and fraud because of the multiplicity of state grades, the statute does remarkably little to further that goal, at least with respect to Washington apples and grades, for it permits marketing of apples in closed containers under no grades at all and does nothing to purify the flow of information at the retail level. Moreover, Washington grades could not have led to the type of deception at which the statute was assertedly aimed, since those grades equal or surpass the comparable federal standards. Nondiscriminatory alternatives to the outright ban of Washington State grades are readily available.

C

Affirmed.

Exxon Corp. v. Governor of Maryland

437 U.S. 117 (1978)

FACTS

Responding to evidence that during the 1973 petroleum shortage oil producers or refiners were favoring company-operated gasoline stations, Maryland enacted a statute prohibiting producers or refiners from operating retail service stations within the State, and requiring them to extend all "voluntary allowances" (temporary price reductions granted to independent dealers injured by local competitive price reductions) uniformly to all stations they supply. In actions by several oil companies challenging the validity of the statute on various grounds, the Maryland trial court held the statute invalid primarily on substantive due process grounds, but the Maryland Court of Appeals reversed, upholding the validity of the statute against contentions, *inter alia*, that it violated the Commerce and Due Process Clauses and conflicted with 2(b) of the Clayton Act, as amended by the Robinson-Patman Act, which prohibits price discrimination, with the proviso that a seller can defend a price discrimination charge by showing that he charged a lower price in good faith to meet a competitor's equally low price.

I Does a State statue which prohibits producers or refiners from operating retail service stations within the State, and requiring them to extend all "voluntary allowances" (temporary price reductions granted to independent dealers injured by local competitive price reductions) uniformly to all stations they supply, violate the Due Process Clause?

R A State statue which prohibits producers or refiners from operating retail service stations within the State, and requiring them to extend all "voluntary allowances" uniformly to all stations they supply does not violate the Due Process Clause.

A The Maryland statute does not violate the Due Process Clause, since, regardless of the ultimate efficacy of the statute, it bears a reasonable relation to the State's legitimate purpose in controlling the gasoline retail market. The divestiture provisions of the statute do not violate the Commerce Clause. That the burden of such provisions falls solely on interstate companies does not, by itself, establish a claim of discrimination against interstate commerce. The statute creates no barrier against interstate independent dealers, nor does it prohibit the flow of interstate goods, place added costs upon them, or distinguish between in-state and out-of-state companies in the retail market. Nor does the fact that the burden of state regulation, which falls on interstate companies, show that the statute impermissibly burdens interstate commerce, even if some refiners were to stop selling in the State because of the divestiture requirement and even if the elimination of company-operated stations were to deprive consumers of certain special services. Interstate commerce is not subjected to an impermissible burden simply because an otherwise valid regulation causes some business to shift from one interstate supplier to another. The Commerce Clause protects the interstate market, not particular interstate firms, from prohibitive or burdensome regulations. The Commerce Clause does not, by its own force, pre-empt the field of retail gasoline marketing, but, absent a relevant congressional declaration of policy, or a showing of a specific discrimination against, or burdening of, interstate commerce, the States have the power to regulate in this area. The "voluntary allowances" requirement of the Maryland statute is not pre-empted by 2(b) the Clayton Act, as amended by the Robinson-Patman Act, or the Sherman Act. Any hypothetical "conflict" arising from the possibility that the Maryland statute may require uniformity in some situations in which the Robinson-Patman Act would permit localized price discrimination is not sufficient to warrant pre-emption. Neither 2(b) nor the federal policy favoring competition establishes a federal right to engage in discriminatory pricing in certain situations. Section 2(b)'s proviso is merely an exception to that statute's broad prohibition against discriminatory pricing and does not create any new federal right, but rather defines a specific, limited defense. While in the sense that the Maryland statute might have an anticompetitive effect there is a conflict between that statute and the Sherman Act's central policy of "economic liberty," nevertheless this sort of conflict cannot by itself constitute a sufficient reason for invalidating the Maryland statute, for if an adverse effect on competition were, in and of itself, enough to invalidate a state statute, the States' power to engage in economic regulation would be effectively destroyed.

C

Affirmed.

West Lynn Creamery Inc. v. Healy

512 U.S. 186 (1994)

FACTS

A Massachusetts pricing order subjects all fluid milk sold by dealers to Massachusetts retailers to an assessment. Although most of that milk is produced out of State, the entire assessment is distributed to Massachusetts dairy farmers. Petitioners - licensed dealers who purchase milk produced by out-of-state farmers and sell it within Massachusetts - sued to enjoin enforcement of the order on the ground that it violated the Federal Commerce Clause, but the state court denied relief. The Supreme Judicial Court of Massachusetts affirmed, concluding that the order was not facially discriminatory, applied evenhandedly, and only incidentally burdened interstate commerce, and that such burden was outweighed by the "local benefits" to the dairy industry.

I

Does a state's pricing order which subjects all fluid milk sold by dealers to Massachusetts retailers to an assessment violative of the commerce clause?

R

When a state order benefits local farmers at the expense of out-of state producers and is designed as a protectionist measure, it will be struck down as unconstitutionally discriminating against interstate commerce.

A

The pricing order unconstitutionally discriminates against interstate commerce. The order is clearly unconstitutional under this Court's decisions invalidating state laws designed to benefit local producers of goods by creating tariff-like barriers that neutralized the competitive and economic advantages possessed by lower cost out-of-state producers. The "premium payments" are effectively a tax making milk produced out of State more expensive. Although that tax also applies to milk produced in Massachusetts, its effect on Massachusetts producers is entirely (indeed more than) offset by the subsidy provided exclusively to Massachusetts dairy farmers, who are thereby empowered to sell at or below the price charged by lower cost out-of-state producers. Respondent's principal argument - that, because both the local subsidy and nondiscriminatory tax components of the order are valid, the combination of the two is equally valid - is rejected. Even granting respondent's assertion that both components of the pricing order would be constitutional standing alone, the order must still fall because it is funded principally from taxes on the sale of milk produced in other States, and therefore burdens interstate commerce. More fundamentally, the argument is logically flawed in its assumption that the lawfulness of each of two acts establishes the legality of their combination. Indeed, by conjoining a tax and a subsidy, Massachusetts has created a program more dangerous to interstate commerce than either part alone: The Commonwealth's political processes cannot be relied on to prevent legislative abuse where dairy farmers, one of the powerful in-state interests that would ordinarily be expected to lobby against the order premium as a tax raising milk prices, have been mollified by the subsidy. Respondent's second argument - that the order is not discriminatory because the dealers who pay premiums are not competitors of the farmers who receive disbursements - cannot withstand scrutiny. The imposition of a differential burden on any part of the stream of commerce - from wholesaler to retailer to consumer - is invalid because a burden placed at any point will result in a disadvantage to the out-of-state producer. If accepted, respondent's third argument - that the order is not protectionist because the program's costs are borne only by Massachusetts dealers and consumers and its benefits are distributed exclusively to Massachusetts farmers - would undermine almost every discriminatory tax case. State taxes are ordinarily paid by in-state businesses and consumers, yet, if they discriminate against out-of-state products, they are unconstitutional. More fundamentally, the argument ignores the fact that Massachusetts dairy farmers are part of an integrated interstate market. The obvious impact of the order on out-of-state production demonstrates that it is simply wrong to assume that it burdens only in-state consumers and dealers. Acceptance of respondent's final argument - that the order's incidental burden on commerce is justified by the local benefit of saving the financially distressed dairy industry - would make a virtue of the vice that the rule against discrimination condemns. Preservation of local industry by protecting it from the rigors of interstate competition is the hallmark of the economic protectionism that the Commerce Clause prohibits.

C

Reversed.

State of Minnesota v. Clover Leaf Creamery Co.

449 U.S. 456 (1981)

FACTS

For the stated purposes of promoting resource conservation, easing solid waste disposal problems, and conserving energy, the Minnesota Legislature enacted a statute banning the retail sale of milk in plastic nonreturnable, nonrefillable containers, but permitting such sale in other nonreturnable, nonrefillable containers, such as paperboard cartons. Respondents filed suit in Minnesota District Court, seeking to enjoin enforcement of the statute on constitutional grounds. The District Court held that the statute violated, inter alia, the Equal Protection Clause of the Fourteenth Amendment and the Commerce Clause. Finding that "the evidence conclusively demonstrate[d] that the discrimination against plastic nonrefillables [was] not rationally related to the Act's objectives," the Minnesota Supreme Court affirmed on the equal protection ground without reaching the Commerce Clause issue.

I

Can a state law, which is facially neutral, violate the Commerce Clause if it places an incidental burden on interstate commerce which is excessive in relation to its local benefits?

R

It is a violation of the Commerce Clause when a state law, which is facially neutral, places an incidental burden on interstate commerce which is excessive in relation to its local benefits.

A

The ban on plastic nonreturnable milk containers bears a rational relation to the State's objectives and must be sustained under the Equal Protection Clause. The Equal Protection Clause does not deny Minnesota the authority to ban one type of milk container conceded to cause environmental problems, merely because another already established type is permitted to continue in use. Whether in fact the statute will promote more environmentally desirable milk packaging is not the question. The Equal Protection Clause is satisfied if the Minnesota Legislature could rationally have decided that its ban on plastic milk jugs might foster greater use of environmentally desirable alternatives. The fact that the state legislature, having concluded that nonreturnable, nonrefillable milk containers pose environmental hazards, decided to ban the most recent entry in the field, and thus, in effect, "grandfathered" paperboard containers, at least temporarily, does not make the ban on plastic containers arbitrary or irrational. Where the evidence as to whether the statute would help to conserve energy was "at least debatable," the Minnesota Supreme Court erred in substituting its judgment for that of the legislature by finding, contrary to the legislature, that the production of plastic nonrefillable containers required less energy than production of paper containers. Similarly, the Minnesota Supreme Court erred in finding, contrary to the legislature's finding based on a reputable study, that plastic milk jugs take up less space in landfills and present fewer solid waste disposal problems than do paperboard containers. The statute does not violate the Commerce Clause as constituting an unreasonable burden on interstate commerce. The statute does not discriminate between interstate and intrastate commerce but regulates evenhandedly by prohibiting all milk retailers from selling their products in plastic containers, without regard to whether the milk, the containers, or the sellers are from outside the State. The incidental burden imposed on interstate commerce by the statute is not excessive in relation to the putative local benefits. Milk products may continue to move freely across the Minnesota border, and since most dairies package their products in more than one type of container, the inconvenience of having to conform to different packaging requirements in Minnesota and the surrounding States should be slight. Even granting that the out-of-state plastics industry is burdened relatively more heavily than the Minnesota pulpwood industry, this burden is not "clearly excessive" in light of the substantial state interest in promoting conservation of energy and other natural resources and easing solid waste disposal problems. These local benefits amply support Minnesota's decision under the Commerce Clause.

C

Reversed.

Dean Milk Co. v. Wisconsin

340 U.S. 349 (1951)

FACTS

An ordinance of a Wisconsin municipality forbids the sale of milk in the city as pasteurized unless it has been pasteurized and bottled at an approved pasteurization plant within five miles of the center of the city. Appellant, an Illinois corporation engaged in gathering and distributing milk from farms in Illinois and Wisconsin was denied a license to sell its products within the city solely because its pasteurization plants were more than five miles away.

I

Does a local health ordinance which places an incidental burden on interstate commerce violate the Commerce Clause when reasonable alternatives are available?

R

A local health ordinance which places an incidental burden on interstate commerce will violate the Commerce Clause when reasonable alternatives are available.

A

The ordinance unjustifiably discriminates against interstate commerce, in violation of the Commerce Clause of the Federal Constitution. Even in the exercise of its unquestioned power to protect the health and safety of its people, a municipality may not erect an economic barrier protecting a major local industry against competition from without the state, if reasonable nondiscriminatory alternatives, adequate to conserve legitimate local interests, are available. In view of the reasonable and adequate alternatives which are available for the protection of the health and safety of the people of the municipality, the discrimination against interstate commerce inherent in the ordinance violates the Commerce Clause. A second provision of the ordinance in question forbids the sale of milk, or the importation, receipt or storage of milk for sale, within the city except from a source of supply possessing a permit issued after inspection by city officials; and expressly relieves the city officials from any duty to inspect farms located beyond twenty-five miles from the city. Appellant's attack on the constitutional validity of this provision was dismissed by the state court for want of a justiciable controversy. As to the issue thus presented, the cause is remanded for further proceedings not inconsistent with the principles announced in the opinion of this Court.

C

Reversed.

Maine v. Taylor and United States

477 U.S. 131 (1986)

FACTS

Appellee, a bait dealer, arranged to have live baitfish imported into Maine, despite a Maine statute prohibiting such importation. He was indicted under a federal statute making it a federal crime to transport fish in interstate commerce in violation of state law. He moved to dismiss the indictment on the ground that the Maine statute unconstitutionally burdened interstate commerce, and Maine intervened to defend the validity of its statute. After an evidentiary hearing, the District Court denied the motion to dismiss and held the state statute constitutional. The court found that substantial uncertainties surrounded the effects that baitfish parasites and nonnative species would have on the State's wild fish population, and that less discriminatory means of protecting against those threats were currently unavailable. Appellee then entered a conditional guilty plea, reserving the right to appeal the District Court's constitutional ruling. The Court of Appeals reversed, concluding that the state statute was unconstitutional.

I

Does a state law that absolutely discriminates against interstate commerce in an attempt to prohibit significant damage to the state's environmental well-being violate the Commerce Clause?

R

A state law that absolutely discriminates against interstate commerce in an attempt to prohibit significant damage to the state's environmental well-being will not violate the Commerce Clause if it passes the strict scrutiny test.

A

Maine is entitled to invoke this Court's jurisdiction under 28 U.S.C. 1254(2). Nothing in the language or history of 1254(2) suggests that its scope is limited to civil litigation. The fact that Maine was only an intervenor in the District Court does not deprive it of standing to pursue this appeal, because its stake in the outcome is substantial and the controversy remains live, notwithstanding the Federal Government's decision to abandon its own appeal. The Maine statute is constitutional. The federal statute under which appellee was convicted did not waive the requirement of *Hughes v. Oklahoma*, that where a state statute, such a Maine's import ban, discriminates against interstate commerce either on its face or in practical effect, the State must show both that the statute serves a legitimate local purpose, and that this purpose cannot be served as well by available nondiscriminatory means. But the evidence amply supports the District Court's findings that Maine has made both showings. Under the "clearly erroneous" standard of review applicable to these findings, the Court of Appeals erred in setting them aside.

C

Reversed.

Loren J. Pike v. Bruce Church Inc.

397 U.S. 137 (1970)

FACTS

Appellee company grows cantaloupes of superior quality in Parker, Arizona. Since the company lacks packing sheds in Parker, it transports the cantaloupes to its nearby facilities in California, where they are sorted, inspected, packed, and shipped in containers that bear the name of the California packer. Appellant official, acting under the Arizona Fruit and Vegetable Standardization Act, which is designed to prevent deceptive packaging, entered an order prohibiting the company from shipping its cantaloupes outside the State unless they were packed in containers in a manner approved by appellant. Appellant contends that his order is necessary to ensure that the cantaloupes be identified as of Arizona origin. Appellee brought this suit for injunctive relief challenging the constitutionality of the order, which would have the effect of requiring appellee to build packing facilities in or near Parker at a cost of about $200,000. A three-judge District Court issued an injunction, holding that the order constituted an unlawful burden on interstate commerce.

I

Is the Dormant Commerce Clause violated by a nondiscriminatory state law?

R

Unless the burden imposed on commerce is clearly excessive in relation to the punitive local benefits, a state law which regulates even-handedly to effectuate local benefits to the public's health will be upheld.

A

Appellant's order burdens interstate commerce since the cantaloupes were destined to be shipped from Arizona to an ascertainable location in California immediately after harvest, and application of the challenged statute would require an operation now conducted outside the State to be performed within the State so it can be regulated there. The burden on interstate commerce imposed by appellant's order in unconstitutional since Arizona's minimal interest in identifying the origin of appellee's cantaloupes to enhance the reputation of Arizona producers cannot justify subjecting appellee to the substantial capital expenditure of building and operating in Arizona a packing plant that it does not need.

C

Affirmed.

BIBB, Dir., Dept. of Public Safety of Illinois v. Navajo Freight Lines Inc. 359 U.S. 520 (1959)

FACTS

As applied to interstate motor carriers operating under certificates of public convenience and necessity issued by the Interstate Commerce Commission, the Illinois statute here involved, which requires trucks and trailers operating on that State's highways to be equipped with a specified type of rear fender mudguard which would be illegal in Arkansas, which is different from those permitted in at least 45 other States, and which would seriously interfere with the "interline" operations of motor carriers, is invalid because it unduly and unreasonably burdens interstate commerce in violation of Art. I, sec. 8 of the U.S. Constitution.

I

Does a state's nondiscretionary highway safety law, which seriously interferes with interstate commerce and has a total marginal effect on safety, violate the dormant Commerce Clause?

R

A court will uphold a law unless the total effect of the law as a safety measure is so slight or problematic as not to outweigh the national interest in keeping interstate commerce free from interferences that impede it.

A

Even state safety regulations must yield when they run afoul of the policy of free trade reflected in the Commerce Clause. Interchanging mudguards on trucks and trailers at the border of Illinois is a time-consuming task; and the necessity to use welding might mean that some trucks or trailers would have to be unloaded and loaded again - all of which adds up to a serious burden on interstate commerce not justified by a compelling need for this new safety measure. The record in this case shows that this is one of those exceptional cases where a state safety regulation in the exercise of the police power places such a heavy burden on interstate commerce, uncompensated by compelling advantages of safety, that it violates the Commerce Clause.

C

Affirmed.

Raymond Kassel v. Con. Freight. Corp. of Delaware

455 U.S. 329 (1981)

FACTS

An Iowa statute restricts the length of trucks traveling on the highways to a maximum of 60 feet. Consolidated Freightways Corp of Delaware favors using 65-foot double or twin trucks, which have a larger capacity. Consolidated challenged the law on the ground that it violated the Commerce Clause because it burdened interstate commerce. Interstate 80 is a major East-West route linking New York, Chicago and the West coast, and Interstate 35 is a major North-South route. The state of Iowa defended arguing that the double trailers (65 feet and up) are more dangerous that the 55 foot ones. The court concluded that the doubles are as safe as the semi, and thus there was no valid safety reason for barring twin trailers from Iowa's highways.

I

May a state highway regulation offering only marginal safety benefits be held unconstitutional as a burden on interstate commerce?

R

State regulations concerning highway safety are strongly presumed to be valid, they may be held unconstitutional if they offer only marginal safety benefits or the burden on interstate commerce is substantial.

A

We conclude that the state law is an unconstitutional burden on interstate commerce. It substantially burdens the interstate flow of goods by truck. Where, as here, the state's safety interest has been found to be illusory, and is regulations significantly impair the federal government's interest in efficient and safe interstate transportation, the state law cannot be harmonized with the Commerce Clause and will be found unconstitutional.

C

See Rule above.

CTS Corp. v. Dynamics Corp. of America

481 U.S. 69 (1987)

FACTS

The federal Williams Act and implementing regulations govern hostile corporate stock tender offers by requiring, inter alia, that offers remain open for at least 20 business days. An Indiana Act applies to certain business corporations chartered in Indiana that have specified levels of shares or shareholders within the State and that opt into the Act's protection. The Indiana Act provides that the acquisition of "control shares" in such a corporation - shares that, but for the Act, would bring the acquiring entity's voting power to or above certain threshold levels - does not include voting rights unless a majority of all pre-existing disinterested shareholders so agree at their next regularly scheduled meeting. However, the stock acquiror can require a special meeting within 50 days by following specified procedures. Appellee Dynamics Corporation announced a tender offer that would have raised its ownership interest in CTS Corporation above the Indiana Act's threshold. Dynamics also filed suit in Federal District Court alleging federal securities violations by CTS. After CTS opted into the Indiana Act, Dynamics amended its complaint to challenge the Act's validity. The District Court granted Dynamics' motion for declaratory relief, ruling that the Act is pre-empted by the Williams Act and violates the Commerce Clause. The Court of Appeals affirmed, adopting the holding of the plurality opinion in *Edgar v. MITE Corp.*, that the Williams Act pre-empts state statutes that upset the balance between target company management and a tender offeror. The court based its pre-emption finding on the view that the Indiana Act, in effect, imposes at least a 50-day delay on the consummation of tender offers and that this conflicts with the minimum 20-day, hold-open period under the Williams Act. The court also held that the state Act violates the Commerce Clause since it deprives nonresidents of the valued opportunity to accept tender offers from nonresidents, and that it violates the conflict-of-laws "internal affairs" doctrine in that it has a direct, intended, and substantial effect on the interstate market in securities and corporate control.

I When a state law seeks to regulate he method of corporate takeovers, does the Commerce Clause invalidate it?

R A state law seeks to regulate the method of corporate takeovers does not violate the Commerce Clause if the law was equally applicable to in-state and out-of-state offerors; did not create inconsistent regulation by multiple states; and was applied domestically-incorporated corporations with substantial resident shareholders.

A The Indiana Act is consistent with the provisions and purposes of the Williams Act and is not pre-empted thereby. The Indiana Act protects independent shareholders from the coercive aspects of tender offers by allowing them to vote as a group, and thereby furthers the Williams Act's basic purpose of placing investors on an equal footing with takeover bidders. Moreover, the Indiana Act avoids the problems the plurality discussed in MITE, since it does not give either management or the offeror an advantage in communicating with shareholders, nor impose an indefinite delay on offers, nor allow the state government to interpose its views of fairness between willing buyers and sellers. Thus, the Act satisfies even the

MITE plurality's broad interpretation of the Williams Act. The possibility that the Indiana Act will delay some tender offers does not mandate pre-emption. The state Act neither imposes an absolute 50-day delay on the consummation of tender offers nor precludes offerors from purchasing shares as soon as federal law permits. If an adverse shareholder vote is feared, the tender offer can be conditioned on the shares' receiving voting rights within a specified period. Furthermore, even assuming that the Indiana Act does impose some additional delay, the MITE plurality found only that "unreasonable" delays conflict with the Williams Act. Here, it cannot be said that a 50-day delay is unreasonable since that period falls within a 60-day period Congress established for tendering shareholders to withdraw their unpurchased shares. If the Williams Act were construed to pre-empt any state statute that caused delays, it would pre-empt a variety of state corporate laws of hitherto unquestioned validity. The longstanding prevalence of state regulation in this area suggests that, if Congress had intended to pre-empt all such state laws, it would have said so. The Indiana Act does not violate the Commerce Clause. The Act's limited effect on interstate commerce is justified by the State's interests in defining attributes of its corporations' shares and in protecting shareholders. The Act does not discriminate against interstate commerce since it has the same effect on tender offers whether or not the offeror is an Indiana domiciliary or resident. That the Act might apply most often to out-of-state entities who launch most hostile tender offers is irrelevant, since a claim of discrimination is not established by the mere fact that the burden of a state regulation falls on some interstate companies. The Act does not create an impermissible risk of inconsistent regulation of tender offers by different States. It simply and evenhandedly exercises the State's firmly established authority to define the voting rights of shareholders in Indiana corporations, and thus subjects such corporations to the law of only one State. The Court of Appeals' holding that the Act unconstitutionally hinders tender offers ignores the fact that a State, in its role as overseer of corporate governance, enacts laws that necessarily affect certain aspects of interstate commerce, particularly with respect to corporations with shareholders in other States. A State has interests in promoting stable relationships among parties involved in its corporations and in ensuring that investors have an effective voice in corporate affairs. The Indiana Act validly furthers these interests by allowing shareholders collectively to determine whether the takeover is advantageous to them. The argument that Indiana has no legitimate interest in protecting nonresident shareholders is unavailing, since the Act applies only to corporations incorporated in Indiana that have a substantial number of shareholders in the State. Even if the Act should decrease the number of successful tender offers for Indiana corporations, this would not offend the Commerce Clause. The Act does not prohibit any resident or nonresident from offering to purchase, or from purchasing, shares in Indiana corporations, or from attempting thereby to gain control. It only provides regulatory procedures designed for the better protection of the corporations' shareholders. The Commerce Clause does not protect the particular structure or methods of operation in a market.

C

Reversed.

Western & Southern Life Insurance Co. v. State Board of Equalization of California 451 U.S. 648 (1981)

FACTS

California, in addition to imposing a premiums tax on both foreign and domestic insurance companies doing business in the State, imposes a "retaliatory" tax on such a foreign insurer when the insurer's State of incorporation imposes higher taxes on California insurers doing business in that State than California would otherwise impose on that State's insurers doing business in California. Appellant, an Ohio insurer doing business in California, after unsuccessfully filing administrative refund claims for California retaliatory taxes paid, brought a refund suit in California Superior Court, alleging that the retaliatory tax violates the Commerce Clause and the Equal Protection Clause of the Fourteenth Amendment. The Superior Court ruled the tax unconstitutional, but the California Court of Appeal reversed.

I

May Congress give States the power to enact laws that restrict the flow of interstate commerce?

R

Congress may give States the power to enact laws that restrict the flow of interstate commerce.

A

The retaliatory tax does not violate the Commerce Clause. The McCarran-Ferguson Act, which leaves the regulation and taxation of insurance companies to the States, removes entirely any Commerce Clause restriction upon California's power to tax the insurance business. Neither the language nor the history of that Act suggests that it does not permit, as appellant argues, "anti-competitive state taxation that discriminates against out-of-state insurers." Nor does the retaliatory tax violate the Equal Protection Clause. Whatever the extent of a State's authority to exclude foreign corporations from doing business within the State, that authority does not justify imposition of more onerous taxes or other burdens on foreign corporations than those imposed on domestic corporations, unless the discrimination between foreign and domestic corporations bears a rational relation to a legitimate state purpose. The purpose of the retaliatory tax to promote the interstate business of California insurers by deterring other States from imposing discriminatory or excessive taxes on California insurers is a legitimate state purpose. And the California Legislature rationally could have believed that the retaliatory tax would promote that purpose, it being immaterial whether in fact the tax will accomplish its objectives. Assuming that the lawmakers of each State are motivated in part by a desire to promote the interests of their domestic insurance industry, it is reasonable to suppose that California's retaliatory tax will induce other States to lower the burdens on California insurers in order to spare their domestic insurers the cost of the retaliatory tax in California.

C

Affirmed.

Reeves Inc. v. William Stake

447 U.S. 429 (1980)

FACTS

For more than 50 years, South Dakota has operated a cement plant that produced cement for both state residents and out-of-state buyers. In 1978, because of a cement shortage, the State Cement Commission announced a policy to confine the sale of cement by the state plant to residents of the State. This policy forced petitioner ready-mix concrete distributor, one of the out-of-state buyers, to cut its production severely. Petitioner then brought suit in Federal District Court, challenging the policy. The court granted injunctive relief on the ground that the policy violated the Commerce Clause. The Court of Appeals reversed on the ground that the State had simply acted in a proprietary capacity.

I

May a state give preference to in-state buyers when the state produces goods for sale to private buyers?

R

States may give preference to in-state buyers when the state produces goods for sale to private buyers (the state is acting as a "market participant").

A

South Dakota's resident-preference program for the sale of cement does not violate the Commerce Clause. The Commerce Clause responds principally to state taxes and regulatory measures impeding free private trade in the national market-place, and there is no indication of a constitutional plan to limit the ability of the States themselves to operate freely in the free market. State proprietary activities often are burdened with the same restrictions as private market participants. And, as this case illustrates, the competing considerations in cases involving state proprietary action often will be subtle, complex, politically charged, and difficult to assess under traditional Commerce Clause analysis. Given these factors, the adjustment of interests in this context is, as a rule, better suited for Congress than this Court. The arguments for invalidating South Dakota's resident-preference program - that the State, having long exploited the interstate market for cement, should not be permitted to withdraw from it when a shortage arises; that the program responds solely to the nongovernmental objective of protectionism; that hoarding may have undesirable consequences; that the program places South Dakota suppliers of ready-mix concrete at a competitive advantage in the out-of-state market; and that if South Dakota had not acted, free market forces would have generated an appropriate level of supply at free market prices for all buyers in the region - are weak at best. Whatever residual force inheres in them is more than offset by countervailing considerations of policy and fairness. To invalidate the program would discourage similar state projects and rob South Dakota of the intended benefit of its foresight, risk, and industry.

C

Affirmed.

South-Central Timber Dev. Inc. v. Wunnicke

467 U.S. 82 (1984)

FACTS

Pursuant to an Alaska statute, the Alaska Department of Natural Resources (defendant-appellee) published a notice that it would sell certain timber from state lands under a contract requiring "primary manufacture" (partial processing) of the timber within Alaska before the successful bidder could ship it outside of the State. Plaintiff-petitioner, South-Central Timber Development Inc., an Alaska corporation engaged in the business of purchasing timber and shipping the logs into foreign commerce, does not operate a mill in Alaska and customarily sells unprocessed logs. When it learned that the primary-manufacture requirement was to be imposed on the sale of state-owned timber involved here, petitioner filed an action in Federal District Court seeking an injunction on the ground that the requirement violated the negative implications of the Commerce Clause under which States may not enact laws imposing substantial burdens on interstate and foreign commerce unless authorized by Congress. The District Court agreed and issued an injunction, but the Court of Appeals reversed. That court found it unnecessary to reach the question whether, standing alone, the requirement would violate the Commerce Clause, because it found implicit congressional authorization in the federal policy of imposing a primary-manufacture requirement on timber taken from federal land in Alaska.

I May a state, acting as a market participant, impose "downstream" restrictions market participants, thus permissibly burdening interstate commerce?

R State-owned business may favor resident purchasers (market participant exception); however, they may not attach conditions to the sale of products that will burden interstate commerce.

A The Court of Appeals erred in holding that Congress has authorized Alaska's primary-manufacture requirement. Although there is a clearly delineated federal policy, endorsed by Congress, imposing primary-manufacture requirements as to timber taken from federal lands in Alaska for export from the United States or for shipment to other States, in order for a state regulation to be removed from the reach of the dormant Commerce Clause as being authorized by Congress, congressional intent must be *unmistakably clear.* The requirement that Congress affirmatively contemplate otherwise invalid state legislation is mandated by the policies underlying dormant Commerce Clause doctrine. The fact that Alaska's policy appears to be consistent with federal policy - or even that state policy furthers the goals that Congress had in mind - is an insufficient indicium of congressional intent. Congress acted only with respect to federal lands; it cannot be inferred from that fact that it intended to authorize a similar policy with respect to state lands. Although state-owned business may favor its own in-state, resident purchasers if the state is acting as a market participant rather than as a market regulator (the dormant Commerce Clause places no limitations on its activities), it still can not attach conditions to the sale of products that will burden interstate commerce. The doctrine, market participant doctrine, has only been applied in three cases of this Court to date; *Alexandria Scrap, Reeves,* and *White.*

South-Central Timber Dev. Inc. v. Wunnicke

467 U.S. 82 (1984)

Turning to the instant case, Defendant Alaska contends that its entry into the market is similar to the same type of subsidy approved in *Alexandria Scrap*. We disagree. In that case, when Maryland became involved in the scrap market, it was a *purchaser* of scrap. Here, when Alaska participates in the timber market, it is a *seller* and imposes conditions downstream in the timber-processing market. Alaska also contends that *Reeves* controls stating that "Reeves made it clear that the Commerce Clause imposes no limitation on Alaska's power to choose the terms on which it will sell its timber." In *Reeves*, we strongly endorsed the right of a state to deal with whomever it chooses when it participates in the market, however, we did not sanction the imposition of *any* terms the State might desire. Finally, Alaska contends that because the *White* ruling allowed a requirement to reach beyond the "boundary of formal privity of contract," then, for a stronger reason, the primary-manufacture requirement is permissible because the state is not regulating contracts for resale of timber or regulating the buying and selling of timber, but is instead "a seller of timber, pure and simple." However, Alaska is more than a pure seller of timber, since it attempts to impose further obligations on the buyer even after he has taken delivery of the product (post-sale). The market participant doctrine allows the State to impose burdens on commerce within the market in which it is a participant, and no further. A State may not impose conditions, whether by statute, regulation, or contract which have a substantial regulatory effect outside of that particular market.

C

The judgment is reversed, and the case is remanded.

Toomer v. Witsell

334 U.S. 385 (1948)

FACTS

This is a suit to enjoin as unconstitutional the enforcement of several South Carolina statutes governing commercial shrimp fishing in the three-mile maritime belt off the coast of that State. Appellants, who initiated the action, are five individual fishermen, all citizens and residents of Georgia, and a non-profit fish dealers' organization incorporated in Florida. Appellees are South Carolina officials charged with enforcement of the statutes. The three-judge Federal District Court which was convened to hear the case1 upheld the statutes, denied an injunction and dismissed the suit. On direct appeal from that judgment the U.S. Supreme Court noted probable jurisdiction.

I

Does a state law that discriminates against out-of-state residents violate the Privilege and Immunities Clause where its purpose is to conserve natural resources but creates a commercial monopoly instead?

R

In determining whether a state law violates the Privilege and Immunities Clause, the court must determine whether the law discriminates against out-of-state residents and, if so, whether there is a substantial reason for the discrimination beyond the plain fact that they are out-of-staters.

A

The fishery which South Carolina attempts to regulate by the statutes in question is part of a larger shrimp fishery extending from North Carolina to Florida. Most of the shrimp in this area are of a migratory type, swimming south in the late summer and fall and returning northward in the spring. Since there is no federal regulation of the fishery, the four States most intimately concerned have gone their separate ways in devising conservation and other regulatory measures. The statutes appellants challenge relate to shrimping during the open season in the three-mile belt: Section 3300 of the South Carolina Code provides that the waters in that area shall be 'a common for the people of the State for the taking of fish.' Section 3374 imposes a tax of 1/8 a pound on green, or raw, shrimp taken in those waters. Section 3379, as amended in 1947, requires payment of a license fee of $25 for each shrimp boat owned by a resident, and of $2,500 for each one owned by a non- resident. Another statute, not integrated in the Code, conditions the issuance of non-resident licenses for 1948 and the years thereafter on submission of proof that the applicants have paid South Carolina income taxes on all profits from operations in that State during the preceding year. And 3414 requires that all boats licensed to trawl for shrimp in the State's waters dock at a South Carolina port and unload, pack, and stamp their catch 'before shipping or transporting it to another State or the waters thereof.' Violation of the fishing laws involves suspension of the violator's license as well as a maximum of a $1,000 fine, imprisonment for a year, or a combination of a $ 500 fine and a year's imprisonment.

Appellants contend that 3374, which imposes a tax of 1/8 a pound on green shrimp taken in the maritime belt, taxes imports and unduly burdens interstate commerce in violation of 8 and 10 of Art. I. We agree with the court below that there is no merit in this position. Since South Carolina has power to regulate fishing in the three-mile belt, at least where the federal government has made no conflicting assertion of power, fish caught in that belt cannot be considered 'imports' in a realistic sense of the word.

Appellants' most vigorous attack is directed at 3379 which, as amended in 1947, requires non-residents of South Carolina to pay license fees one hundred times as great as those which residents must pay. The purpose and effect of this statute, they contend, is not to conserve shrimp, but to exclude non-residents and thereby create a commercial monopoly for South Carolina residents. As such, the statute is said to violate the privileges and immunities clause of Art. IV and the equal protection clause of the Fourteenth Amendment. By that statute South Carolina plainly and frankly discriminates against non-residents, and the record leaves little doubt but what the discrimination is so great that its practical effect is virtually exclusionary. As justification for the statute, appellees urge that the State's obvious purpose was to conserve its shrimp supply, and they suggest that it was designed to head off an impending threat of excessive trawling. The record casts some doubt on these statements. But in any event, appellees' argument assumes that any means adopted to attain valid objectives necessarily squares with the privileges and immunities clause. It overlooks the purpose of that clause, which, as indicated above, is to outlaw classifications based on the fact of non-citizenship unless there is something to indicate that non-citizens constitute a peculiar source of the evil at which the statute is aimed. Thus, 3379 must be held unconstitutional unless commercial shrimp fishing in the maritime belt falls within some unexpressed exception to the privileges and immunities clause. The record shows that a high proportion of the shrimp caught in the waters along the South Carolina coast, both by appellants and by others, is shipped in interstate commerce. In upholding this statute, the court below adduced a reason not advanced by appellees, that the requirements as to docking, unloading, packing, and affixing a tax stamp were a proper means of insuring collection of the 1/8 a pound tax. But the importance of having commerce between the forty-eight States flow unimpeded by local barriers persuades us that State restrictions inimical to the commerce clause should not be approved simply because they facilitate in some measure enforcement of a valid tax. Thus we hold that 3414 violates the commerce clause of the Constitution. To sum up, we hold that the District Court had jurisdiction to entertain the attacks pressed by the individual appellants, but not the corporate appellant, on all the statutes save the one relating to income taxes; that South Carolina has power, in the absence of a conflicting federal claim, to regulate fishing in the marginal sea; and that in 3374 of the South Carolina Code, though not in 3379 and 3414, the State has exercised that power in a manner consistent with restraints which the Constitution imposes upon the States. The District Court's judgment refusing equitable relief is affirmed with respect to 3374 and the income tax statute and reversed with respect to 3379 and 3414.

C

Affirmed in part and reversed in part.

United Building & Construction Trades Council v. Mayor and Council of Camden

465 U.S. 208 (1984)

FACTS

Acting pursuant to a statewide affirmative-action program, the city of Camden, N. J. (defendant-appellee) adopted an ordinance requiring that at least 40% of the employees of contractors and subcontractors working on city construction projects be Camden residents. After the ordinance was approved by the New Jersey Treasury Department, Plaintiff-appellant, United Building & Construction Trades Council, an association of labor organizations representing private employees in the building and construction trades, filed an appeal with the Appellate Division of the New Jersey Superior Court challenging the Treasury Department's approval of the ordinance. The New Jersey Supreme Court certified the appeal directly to that court and rejected appellant's challenges to the ordinance's validity, including the claim that the ordinance violated the Privileges and Immunities Clause of Art. IV of the Constitution. The court held that the Clause did not apply because the ordinance discriminated on the basis of municipal, not state, residency and had identical effects upon out-of-state citizens and New Jersey citizens not residing in Camden.

I

Does an ordinance requiring that at least 40% of the employees of contractors and subcontractors working on city construction projects be Camden residents violate the Privileges and Immunities clause of Article IV?

R

The Privileges and Immunities clause limits a State's discriminatory power against out-of-state residents with respect to their employment within the State.

A

The ordinance is properly subject to the strictures of the Privileges and Immunities Clause. That the ordinance is a municipal, rather than a state, law does not place it outside the Clause's scope. Here, municipal action cannot be distinguished easily from state action, since the ordinance would not have gone into effect without the Treasury Department's approval. Moreover, a municipality is merely a political subdivision of the State, and what would be unconstitutional if done directly by the State can no more readily be accomplished by a city deriving its authority from the State. The Clause applies not only to laws that discriminate on the basis of state citizenship, but also to laws that discriminate on the basis of municipal residency. For purposes of analysis of most cases under the Clause, the terms "citizen" and "resident" are essentially interchangeable. Camden's ordinance is not immune from constitutional review at the behest of out-of-state residents merely because in-state residents who do not live in Camden are similarly disadvantaged. While such in-state residents have no claim under the Clause, nevertheless they at least have a chance to remedy at the polls the discrimination against them. On remand, the determination of whether the Camden ordinance violates the Privileges and Immunities Clause should be made under the appropriate constitutional standard, which requires determination of whether the ordinance burdens one of those privileges and immunities protected by the Clause, and, if so, whether there is a "substantial reason" for the discrimination against citizens of other States. Although Camden may, without fear of violating the Commerce Clause, pressure private employers engaged in public works projects funded in whole or in part by the city to hire city residents, White v. Massachusetts Council of Construction Employers, Inc., an out-of-state resident's interest in employment by private employers on public works projects in another State is sufficiently fundamental to the promotion of interstate harmony and sufficiently basic to the livelihood of the Nation as to fall within the purview of the Privileges and Immunities Clause. However, it is impossible on the record as it now stands to evaluate Camden's contention that its ordinance is carefully tailored to counteract grave economic and social ills involving unemployment of city residents and a sharp decline in the city's population. On remand, the New Jersey Supreme Court may decide, consistent with state procedures, on the best method for making the necessary findings of fact.

C Reversed and remanded.

Lester Baldwin v. Fish & Game Comm. Of Montana
436 U.S. 371 (1978)

FACTS

Appellants brought this action for declaratory and other relief claiming that the Montana statutory elk-hunting license scheme, which imposes substantially higher (at least 7 1/2 times) license fees on nonresidents of the State than on residents, and which requires nonresidents (but not residents) to purchase a "combination" license in order to be able to obtain a single elk, denies nonresidents their constitutional rights guaranteed by the Privileges and Immunities Clause of Art. IV and by the Equal Protection Clause of the Fourteenth Amendment. A three-judge District Court denied all relief to appellants.

I

Does a state which makes a distinction between in-state residents and out-of-state residents with respect to recreational hunting violate or threaten a fundamental right under the Privileges and Immunities Clause.

R

A state which makes a distinction (imposes higher licensing fess for out-of – state persons than in-state persons) between in-state residents and out-of-state residents with respect to recreational hunting violates a fundamental right under the Privileges and Immunities Clause.

A

Access by nonresidents to recreational big-game hunting in Montana does not fall within the category of rights protected by the Privileges and Immunities Clause. Only with respect to those "privileges" and "immunities" bearing upon the vitality of the Nation as a single entity must a State treat all citizens, resident and nonresident, equally, and here equality in access to Montana elk is not basic to the maintenance or well-being of the Union. The statutory scheme is an economic means not unreasonably related to the preservation of a finite resource, elk, and a substantial regulatory interest of that State, and hence does not violate the Equal Protection Clause. In view of the fact that residents contribute to the costs of maintaining the elk-hunting program, the great increase in nonresident hunters in recent years, the limit in the elk supply, and the difficulties in supervising hunting practices, it cannot be said that either the license fee differentials or the required combination license for nonresidents is irrational.

C

Affirmed.

Supreme Court of New Hampshire v. Piper

470 U.S. 274 (1985)

FACTS

Appellee, a resident of Vermont, was allowed to take, and passed, the New Hampshire bar examination. But pursuant to Rule 42 of the New Hampshire Supreme Court, which limits bar admission to state residents, she was not permitted to be sworn in. After the New Hampshire Supreme Court denied appellee's request that an exception to the Rule be made in her case, she filed an action in Federal District Court, alleging that Rule 42 violates the Privileges and Immunities Clause of Art. IV of the U.S. Constitution. The District Court agreed and granted appellee's motion for a summary judgment. The Court of Appeals affirmed.

I

Does the practice of law constitute a fundamental right subject to protection under the Privileges and Immunities Clause?

R

The practice of law constitutes a fundamental right subject to protection under the Privileges and Immunities Clause because (1) there is no substantial reason for denying bar admission in the state to non-residents and (2) such discrimination does not bear a close relationship to the state's objectives.

A

Rule 42 violates the Privileges and Immunities Clause of Art. IV, 2. Derived, like the Commerce Clause, from the fourth of the Articles of Confederation, the Privileges and Immunities Clause was intended to create a national economic union. "[O]ne of the privileges which the Clause guarantees to citizens of State A is that of doing business in State B on terms of substantial equality with the citizens of that *State." Toomer v. Witsell.* Moreover, although a lawyer is "an officer of the court," he does not hold a position that can be entrusted only to a "full-fledged member of the political community" and thus is not an "officer" of the State in any political sense. *In re Griffiths*. Therefore, a nonresident's interest in practicing law is a "privilege" protected by the Clause. A State may discriminate against nonresidents only where its reasons are "substantial" and the difference in treatment bears a close or substantial relationship to those reasons. None of the reasons offered by appellant for its refusal to admit nonresidents to the bar - nonresidents would be less likely to keep abreast of local rules and procedures, to behave ethically, to be available for court proceedings, and to do pro bono and other volunteer work in the State - meets the test of "substantiality," and the means chosen do not bear the necessary relationship to the State's objectives.

C

Affirmed.

Barron v. Mayor & City Council of Baltimore

32 U.S. (*7 Pet.*) 243 (1833)

FACTS

Plaintiff Barron owned a wharf in Baltimore's harbor which was impaired when Defendant City of Baltimore diverted the flow of streams during street construction work causing a buildup of sand and earth under the wharf. Barron argued that this made the water too shallow for most vessels. Barron sued the City for ruining his wharf. The trial court awarded Barron $45,000, but the Baltimore Appellate Court reversed. Barron claimed that the state's action violated the Fifth Amendment's guarantee that private property shall not be taken for public use without just compensation and so sought review before the United States Supreme Court. The Supreme Court granted the review.

I Is the Fifth Amendment's prohibition against the seizure of private property by the federal government without just compensation applicable to the states?

R The Fifth Amendment's prohibition against the seizure of private property by the federal government without just compensation is not applicable to the states.

A The Fifth Amendment's prohibition against the seizure of private property by the Government without just compensation is not applicable to the states. The constitution was established by the people of the United States, for their own government, and not for the government of the individual states. In the 9th and 10th sections of Article I of the Bill of Rights, the Constitution draws a clear distinction between the limitations it imposes on the national and those imposed on state governments: The 9th section in the Bill of Rights imposes limitations on the powers of the federal government; the 10th section [of Article I] enumerates those which were to operate on the state legislatures. Had the framers of the Bill of Rights intended the Fifth Amendment to apply to the states, they would have they would have imitated the Framers of the original Constitution and clearly expressed that intention. Yet these amendments in the Bill of Rights contain no expression indicating an intention for the amendments to apply to state governments. Hence, we cannot so apply them. This court, therefore, has no jurisdiction of the cause, and it is dismissed.

C Case dismissed.

Slaughter-House Cases

16 Wall. (83 U.S.) 36 (1873)

FACTS

The legislature of Louisiana, on March 8, 1869, passed an act granting to a corporation the exclusive right, for twenty-five years, to have and maintain slaughterhouses, landings for cattle, and yards for inclosing cattle intended for sale or slaughter within the counties of Orleans, Jefferson, and St. Bernard, including the city of New Orleans, and prohibiting all other persons from building, keeping, or having slaughterhouses, landings for cattle, and yards for cattle intended for sale or slaughter, within those limits; requiring that all cattle and other animals intended for sale or slaughter in that district, should be brought to the yards and slaughterhouses of the corporation, and authorizing the corporation to exact certain prescribed fees for the use of its wharves and for each animal landed, and certain prescribed fees for each animal slaughtered. Some butchers brought suit arguing that the law deprived them of the right to freely exercise their trade in violation of the 13th Amendment because the act created an "involuntary servitude", and because it denied them equal protection, by depriving them of their property without due process in violation of the 14th Amendment in contravention of the privileges and immunities of citizens of the United States. The Louisiana Supreme Court sustained the law and the U.S. Supreme Court granted certiorari.

I

Do the 13th and 14th Amendments guarantee federal protection of individual rights against discrimination by their on state governments?

R

The 13th and 14th Amendments do not guarantee federal protection of individual rights against discrimination by their on state governments and are to be read narrowly to apply only to former slaves and African-Americans.

A

We hold that this grant of exclusive right or privilege, guarded by proper limitation of the prices to be charged, and imposing the duty of providing ample conveniences, with permission to all owners of stock to land, and of all butchers to slaughter at those places, was a police regulation for the health and comfort of the people within the power of the state legislatures, unaffected by the Constitution of the United States prior to the adoption of the thirteenth and fourteenth articles of amendment. The Parliament of Great Britain and the State legislatures of this country have always exercised the power of granting exclusive rights when they were necessary and proper to effectuate a purpose which had in view the public good, and the power here exercised is of that class, and has, until now, never been denied. Such power is not forbidden by the 13th Amendment or by the 14th Amendment. An examination of the history of the causes which led to the adoption of the amendments themselves demonstrates that the main purpose of all the three last amendments was the freedom of the African race, the security and perpetuation of that freedom, and their protection from the oppressions of the white men who had formerly held them in slavery. In giving construction to any of those articles, it is necessary to keep this main purpose squarely in mind, though the letter and spirit of those articles must apply to all cases coming within their purview, whether the party concerned be of African descent or not. While the 13th

Amendment was intended primarily to abolish African slavery, it equally forbids Mexican peonage or the Chinese coolie trade when they amount to slavery or involuntary servitude, and the use of the word "servitude" is intended to prohibit all forms of involuntary slavery of whatever class or name. The first clause of the 14th Amendment was primarily intended to confer citizenship on the negro race, and secondly to give definitions of citizenship of the United States and citizenship of the States, and it recognizes the distinction between citizenship of a State and citizenship of the United States by those definitions. The second clause protects from the hostile legislation of the States the privileges and immunities of citizens of the United States, as distinguished from the privileges and immunities of citizens of the States. The latter, as defined by Justice Washington in *Corfield v. Coryell*, and by this court in *Ward v. Maryland*, embrace generally those fundamental civil rights for the security and establishment of which organized society is instituted, and they remain, with certain exceptions mentioned in the Federal Constitution, under the care of the State governments, and of this class are those set up by plaintiffs. The privileges and immunities of citizens of the United States are those which arise out of the nature and essential character of the national government, the provisions of its Constitution, or its laws and treaties made in pursuance thereof, and it is these which are placed under the protection of Congress by this clause of the 13th Amendment. It is not necessary to inquire here into the full force of the clause forbidding a State to enforce any law which deprives a person of life, liberty, or property without due process of law, for that phrase has been often the subject of judicial construction, and is, under no admissible view of it, applicable to the present case. The clause which forbids a State to deny to any person the equal protection of the laws was clearly intended to prevent the hostile discrimination against the negro race so familiar in the States where he had been a slave, and, for this purpose, the clause confers ample power in Congress to secure his rights and his equality before the law.

C

Affirmed.

Saenz v. Roe

526 U.S. 489 (1999)

FACTS

California, which has the sixth highest welfare benefit levels in the country, sought to amend its Aid to Families with Dependent Children (AFDC) program in 1992 by limiting new residents, for the first year they live in the State, to the benefits they would have received in the State of their prior residence. Cal. Welf. & Inst. Code Ann. §11450.03. Although the Secretary of Health and Human Services approved the change--a requirement for it to go into effect--the Federal District Court enjoined its implementation, finding that, under *Shapiro* v. *Thompson* and *Zobel* v. *Williams,* it penalized "the decision of new residents to migrate to [California] and be treated [equally] with existing residents," *Green* v. *Anderson.* After the Ninth Circuit invalidated the Secretary's approval of §11450.03 in a separate proceeding, this Court ordered *Green* to be dismissed. The provision thus remained inoperative until after Congress enacted the Personal Responsibility and Work Opportunity Reconciliation Act of 1996 (PRWORA), which replaced AFDC with Temporary Assistance to Needy Families (TANF). PRWORA expressly authorizes any State receiving a TANF grant to pay the benefit amount of another State's TANF program to residents who have lived in the State for less than 12 months. Since the Secretary no longer needed to approve §11450.03, California announced that enforcement would begin on April 1, 1997. On that date, respondents filed this class action, challenging the constitutionality of §11450.03's durational residency requirement and PRWORA's approval of that requirement. In issuing a preliminary injunction, the District Court found that PRWORA's existence did not affect its analysis in *Green.* Without reaching the merits, the Ninth Circuit affirmed the injunction.

I

Does a statute providing lower benefits to families who have lived in a state for less than 12 months violate the Privileges and Immunities Clause?

R

A statute providing lower benefits to families who have lived in a state for less than 12 months does violate the Privileges and Immunities Clause; a state must provide the same benefits to new residents as it does to other residents.

A

Section 11450.03 violates Section 1 of the Fourteenth Amendment. In assessing laws denying welfare benefits to newly arrived residents, this Court held in *Shapiro* that a State cannot enact durational residency requirements in order to inhibit the migration of needy persons into the State, and that a classification that has the effect of imposing a penalty on the right to travel violates the Equal Protection Clause absent a compelling governmental interest. The right to travel embraces three different components: the right to enter and leave another State; the right to be treated as a welcome visitor while temporarily present in another State; and, for those travelers who elect to become permanent residents, the right to be treated like other citizens of that State. The right of newly arrived citizens to the same privileges and immunities enjoyed by other citizens of their new State--the third aspect of the right to travel--is at issue here. That right is protected by the new arrival's status as both a state citizen and a United States citizen, and it is plainly identified in the

Fourteenth Amendment's Privileges or Immunities Clause. That newly arrived citizens have both state and federal capacities adds special force to their claim that they have the same rights as others who share their citizenship. Since the right to travel embraces a citizen's right to be treated equally in her new State of residence, a discriminatory classification is itself a penalty. California's classifications are defined entirely by the period of residency and the location of the disfavored class members' prior residences. Within the category of new residents, those who lived in another country or in a State that had higher benefits than California are treated like lifetime residents; and within the broad subcategory of new arrivals who are treated less favorably, there are 45 smaller classes whose benefit levels are determined by the law of their former States. California's legitimate interest in saving money does not justify this discriminatory scheme. The Fourteenth Amendment's Citizenship Clause expressly equates citizenship with residence, and does not tolerate a hierarchy of subclasses of similarly situated citizens based on the location of their prior residences. PRWORA's approval of durational residency requirements does not resuscitate §11450.03. This Court has consistently held that Congress may not authorize the States to violate the Fourteenth Amendment. Moreover, the protection afforded to a citizen by that Amendment's Citizenship Clause limits the powers of the National Government as well as the States. Congress' Article I powers to legislate are limited not only by the scope of the Framers' affirmative delegation, but also by the principle that the powers may not be exercised in a way that violates other specific provisions of the Constitution.

C Affirmed.

Twining v. New Jersey

211 U.S. 78 (1908)

FACTS

Albert C. Twining and David C. Cornell, the plaintiffs in error, hereafter called the defendants, were indicted by the grand jury of Monmouth County, in the state of New Jersey. The indictment charged that the defendants, being directors of the Monmouth Trust & Safe Deposit Company, knowingly exhibited a false paper to Larue Vreedenberg, an examiner of the state banking department, with intent to deceive him as to the condition of the company. Such an act is made a misdemeanor by a statute of the state. The defendants were found guilty on March 1, 1904, by the verdict of a jury, and judgment upon the verdict, that the defendants be imprisoned for six and four years, respectively, was affirmed successively by the supreme court and the court of errors and appeals. There needs to be stated here only such part of what occurred at the trial as will describe the questions on which this court is authorized to pass. It appeared that in February, 1903, the company closed its doors. The bank examiner came at once to the place of business for the purpose of examining the affairs of the company, and found there Twining and Cornell, who were respectively president and treasurer as well as directors. Having soon discovered that, according to a book entry, there had been a recent payment of $44,875 for 381 shares of stock, the examiner inquired of the defendants by what authority this had been done, and was informed that it was done by authority of the board of directors, and the following paper was produced to him as a record of the transaction. On motion the meeting adjourned. This was the paper referred to in the indictment, and it was incumbent on the prosecution to prove that it was false and that it was 'knowingly' exhibited by the defendants to the examiner. There was evidence on the part of the prosecution tending to prove both these propositions. The defendants called no witnesses and did not testify themselves, although the law of New Jersey gave them the right to do so if they chose. In his charge to the jury the presiding judge charged the jury. The question duly brought here by writ of error is whether the parts of the charge are in violation of the 14th Amendment of the Constitution of the United States.

I

Does the 14th Amendment make the right against self-incrimination applicable to the states?

R

The provisions of the Bill of Rights may apply to the States under the Due Process Clause of the 14th Amendment if the provisions are necessary for due process of law.

A

In the view we take of the case we do not deem it necessary to consider whether, with respect to the Federal question, there is any difference in the situation of the two defendants. It is assumed, in respect of each, that the jury were instructed that they might draw an unfavorable inference against him from his failure to testify, where it was within his power, in denial of the evidence which tended to incriminate him. The law of the state, as declared in the case at bar, which accords with other decisions, permitted such an inference to be drawn. The general question, therefore, is, whether such a law violates the 14th Amendment, either by abridging the privileges or immunities of citizens of the United States, or by depriving persons of their life, liberty, or property without due process of law. In order to bring themselves within the protection of the Constitution it is incumbent on the defendants to prove two propositions: First, that the exemption from compulsory self- incrimination is guaranteed by the Federal Constitution against impairment by the states; and, second, if it be so guaranteed, that the exemption was in fact impaired in the case at bar. The first proposition naturally presents itself for earlier consideration. If the right here asserted is not a Federal right, that is the end of the case. We have no authority to go further and determine whether the state court has erred in the interpretation and enforcement of its own laws. The exemption from testimonial compulsion, that is, from disclosure as a witness of evidence against oneself, forced by any form of legal process, is universal in American law, though there may be differences as to its exact scope and limits. At the time of the formation of the Union the principle that no person could be compelled to be a witness against himself had become embodied in the common law and distinguished it from all other systems of jurisprudence. We have assumed only for the purpose of discussion that what was done in the case at bar was an infringement of the privilege against self- incrimination. We do not intend, however, to lend any countenance to the truth of that assumption. The courts of New Jersey, in adopting the rule of law which is complained of here, have deemed it consistent with the privilege itself, and not a denial of it. The reasoning by which this view is supported will be found in the cases cited from New Jersey and Maine,. The authorities upon the question are in conflict. We do not pass upon the conflict, because, for the reasons given, we think that the exemption from compulsory self-incrimination in the courts of the states is not secured by any part of the Federal Constitution.

C Judgment affirmed.

Duncan v. Louisiana

391 U.S. 145 (1968)

FACTS

Defendant-appellant Gary Duncan is a black man of 19 years at the time he was tried. While driving on Highway 23 in Plaquemines Parish on October 18, 1966, he saw two younger cousins engaged in a conversation by the side of the road with four white boys. Knowing his cousins, Negroes who had recently transferred to a formerly all-white high school, had reported the occurrence of racial incidents at the school, Duncan stopped the car, got out, and approached the six boys. At trial the white boys and a white onlooker testified, as did appellant and his cousins. The witnesses agreed that appellant and the white boys spoke to each other, that appellant encouraged his cousins to break off the encounter and enter his car. The whites testified that just before getting in the car appellant slapped Herman Landry, one of the white boys, on the elbow. The Negroes testified that appellant had not slapped Landry, but had merely touched him. The trial judge concluded that the State had proved beyond a reasonable doubt that Duncan had committed simple battery, and found him guilty. Duncan was convicted of simple battery in the Twenty-fifth Judicial District Court of Louisiana. Under Louisiana law simple battery is a misdemeanor, punishable by a maximum of two years' imprisonment and a $300 fine. Appellant sought trial by jury, but because the Louisiana Constitution grants jury trials only in cases in which capital punishment or imprisonment at hard labor may be imposed, the trial judge denied the request. Appellant was convicted and sentenced to serve 60 days in prison and pay a fine of $150. Appellant sought review in the Supreme Court of Louisiana, asserting that the denial of jury trial violated his constitutional rights. The Supreme Court denied appellant a writ of certiorari. Appellant then sought review in the U.S. Supreme Court, alleging that his Sixth and 14th Amendments were violated.

I

May a state deny a defendant the right to a trial by jury for a crime punishable by two years in prison?

R

The Sixth Amendment's right to jury trial is a fundamental right, which must be afforded recognition by the states, and which is applicable to crimes punishable by two or more years in prison.

A

Since trial by jury in criminal cases is fundamental to the American scheme of justice, the Fourteenth Amendment guarantees a right of jury trial in all criminal cases which, were they tried in a federal court, would come within the Sixth Amendment's guarantee of trial by jury. The penalty authorized for a particular crime is of major relevance in determining whether it is a serious one subject to the mandates of the Sixth Amendment, and it is sufficient here, without defining the boundary between petty offenses and serious crimes, to hold that a crime punishable by two years in prison is a serious crime and that appellant was entitled to a jury trial.

C

Reversed and remanded.

The Civil Rights Cases

109 U.S. 3 (1883)

FACTS

The Civil Rights Act of 1875 affirmed the equality of all persons in the enjoyment of transportation facilities, in hotels and inns, and in theaters and places of public amusement. Though privately owned, these businesses were like public utilities, exercising public functions for the benefit of the public and, thus, subject to public regulation. In five separate cases, a black person was denied the same accommodations as a white person in violation of the Act. These incidents were prosecuted and the result was four criminal indictments and one civil judgment.

I

Does the Civil Rights Act of 1875 violate the 10th Amendment of the Constitution which reserves all powers not granted to the national government to the states or to the people?

R

Congress may not prohibit private, individual acts of racial discrimination by private citizens.

A

The Fourteenth Amendment restrains only state action. And the fifth section of the Amendment empowers Congress only to enforce the prohibition on state action. The amendment did not authorize national legislation on subjects which are within the domain of the state. Private acts of racial discrimination were simply private wrongs that the national government was powerless to correct. The Fourteenth Amendment did not grant Congress the legislative power to enact the law in dispute here. The aggrieved parties also argue justification under the Thirteenth Amendment. That Amendment is not a mere prohibition of state action establishing and upholding slavery, rather it abolishes slavery or involuntary servitude throughout the United States. Congress does have the power to enact legislation to abolish all badges and incidents of slavery, and the aggrieved parties argue that this alone is sufficient justification. We disagree. An act of refusal has nothing to do with slavery or involuntary solitude. It would be running the slavery argument into the ground to make it apply to every act of private discrimination which a person sees fit to entertain. As far as we are aware, all states have laws prohibiting racial discrimination by innkeepers and public carriers. If these laws are discriminatory, Congress has the power, under the Fourteenth Amendment, to grant an aggrieved party a remedy under that amendment and under those conditions. When a man is free from the shackles of slavery and rises to the status of mere citizen, at some point he must cease to be a special favorite of the laws. The challenged law is unconstitutional.

C

Reversed.

Marsh v. Alabama

326 U.S. 501 (1946)

FACTS

The town, a suburb of Mobile, Alabama, known as Chickasaw, is owned by the Gulf Shipbuilding Corporation. Except for that it has all the characteristics of any other American town. The property consists of residential buildings, streets, a system of sewers, a sewage disposal plant and a 'business block' on which business places are situated. A deputy of the Mobile County Sheriff, paid by the company, serves as the town's policeman. Merchants and service establishments have rented the stores and business places on the business block and the United States uses one of the places as a post office from which six carriers deliver mail to the people of Chickasaw and the adjacent area. Appellant, a Jehovah's Witness, came onto the sidewalk we have just described, stood near the post-office and undertook to distribute religious literature. In the stores the corporation had posted a notice which read as follows: 'This Is Private Property, and Without Written Permission, No Street, or House Vendor, Agent or Solicitation of Any Kind Will Be Permitted.' Appellant was warned that she could not distribute the literature without a permit and told that no permit would be issued to her. She protested that the company rule could not be constitutionally applied so as to prohibit her from distributing religious writings. When she was asked to leave the sidewalk and Chickasaw she declined. The deputy sheriff arrested her and she was charged in the state court with violating Title 14, Section 426 of the 1940 Alabama Code which makes it a crime to enter or remain on the premises of another after having been warned not to do so. Appellant contended that to construe the state statute as applicable to her activities would abridge her right to freedom of press and religion contrary to the First and Fourteenth Amendments to the Constitution. This contention was rejected and she was convicted. The Alabama Court of Appeals affirmed the conviction, holding that the statute as applied was constitutional because the title to the sidewalk was in the corporation and because the public use of the sidewalk had not been such as to give rise to a presumption under Alabama law of its irrevocable dedication to the public. The State Supreme Court denied certiorari, and the case now comes before the U.S. Supreme Court on appeal.

I

Can a State, consistent with the First and Fourteenth Amendments, impose criminal punishment on a person who undertakes to distribute religious literature on the premises of a ***company-owned*** town contrary to the wishes of the town's management?

R

The actions of a private entity constitute state action subject to constitutional safegards when its primary function benefits the public.

A

Had the title to Chickasaw belonged not to a private but to a municipal corporation and had appellant been arrested for violating a municipal ordinance rather than a ruling by those appointed by the corporation to manage a company-town it would have been clear that appellant's conviction must be reversed. But this situation is slightly different. The town is a private not a municipal corporation. Our question thus narrows down to this: Can those people who live in or come to Chickasaw be denied freedom of press and religion simply because a single company has legal title to all the town? For it is the state's contention that the mere fact that all the property interests in the town are held by a single company is enough to give that company power, enforceable by a state statute, to abridge these freedoms. We do not agree that the corporation's property interests settle the question. The State urges in effect that the corporation's right to control the inhabitants of Chickasaw is coextensive with the right of a homeowner to regulate the conduct of his guests. We can not accept that contention. Ownership does not always mean absolute dominion. The more an owner, for his advantage, opens up his property for use by the public in general, the more do his rights become circumscribed by the statutory and constitutional rights of those who use it. Thus, the owners of privately held bridges, ferries, turnpikes and railroads may not operate them as freely as a farmer does his farm. Since these facilities are built and operated primarily to benefit the public and since their operation is essentially a public function, it is subject to state regulation. We do not think it makes any significant constitutional difference as to the relationship between the rights of the owner and those of the public that here the State, instead of permitting the corporation to operate a highway, permitted it to use its property as a town, operate a 'business block' in the town and a street and sidewalk on that business block. Whether a corporation or a municipality owns or possesses the town the public in either case has an identical interest in the functioning of the community in such manner that the channels of communication remain free. As we have already stated, the town of Chickasaw does not function differently from any other town; and the managers appointed by the corporation cannot curtail the liberty of press and religion of these people consistently with the purposes of the Constitutional guarantees, and a state statute, as the one here involved, which enforces such action by criminally punishing those who attempt to distribute religious literature clearly violates the First and Fourteenth Amendments to the Constitution. Many people in the United States live in company-owned towns. These people, just as residents of municipalities, are free citizens of their State and country. Just as all other citizens they must make decisions which affect the welfare of community and nation. To act as good citizens they must be informed. In order to enable them to be properly informed their information must be uncensored. There is no more reason for depriving these people of the liberties guaranteed by the First and Fourteenth Amendments than there is for curtailing these freedoms with respect to any other citizen. When we balance the Constitutional rights of owners of property against those of the people to enjoy freedom of press and religion, as we must here, we remain mindful of the fact that the latter occupy a preferred position. In our view the circumstance that the property rights to the premises where the deprivation of liberty, here involved, took place, were held by others than the public, is not sufficient to justify the State's permitting a corporation to govern a community of citizens so as to restrict their fundamental liberties and the enforcement of such restraint by the application of a State statute. Insofar as the State has attempted to impose criminal punishment on appellant for undertaking to distribute religious literature in a company town, its action cannot stand.

C

Reversed and remanded.

Jackson v. Metropolitan Edison Co.

419 U.S. 345 (1974)

FACTS

Plaintiff-Petitioner Catherine Jackson brought suit against Defendant-respondent Metropolitan Edison Co., a privately owned and operated utility corporation which holds a certificate of public convenience issued by the Pennsylvania Utility Commission (PUC), seeking damages and injunctive relief under 42 U.S.C. 1983 for termination of her electric service allegedly before she had been afforded notice, a hearing, and an opportunity to pay any amounts found due. Petitioner claimed that under state law she was entitled to reasonably continuous electric service and that respondent's termination for alleged nonpayment, permitted by a provision of its general tariff filed with the Commission, was state action depriving petitioner of her property without due process of law and giving rise to a cause of action under 1983. The Court of Appeals affirmed the District Court's dismissal of petitioner's complaint.

I

Does the heavy regulation of a public utility, which is privately owned, constitute state action?

R

A simple connection between the state and the private entity is not enough to implicate the state in the latter's discriminatory conduct, there must be something more, i.e., a sufficiently close nexus between the State and the challenged action.

A

Pennsylvania is not sufficiently connected with the challenged termination to make respondent's conduct attributable to the State for purposes of the Fourteenth Amendment, petitioner having shown no more than that respondent was a heavily regulated private utility with a partial monopoly and that it elected to terminate service in a manner that the Commission found permissible under state law. While the principle that private action is immune from the restrictions of the Fourteenth Amendment is well established and easily stated, the question whether particular conduct is "private," on the one hand, or "state action," on the other, frequently admits of no easy answer. Here the action complained of was taken by a utility company which is privately owned and operated, but which in many particulars of its business is subject to extensive state regulation. The mere fact that a business is subject to state regulation does not by itself convert its action into that of the State for purposes of the Fourteenth Amendment. Nor does the fact that the regulation is extensive and detailed, as in the case of most public utilities, do so. But the inquiry must be whether there is a sufficiently close nexus between the State and the challenged action of the regulated entity so that the action of the latter may be fairly treated as that of the State itself. The true nature of the State's involvement may not be immediately obvious, and detailed inquiry may be required in order to determine whether the test is met. Petitioner first argues that "state action" is present because of the monopoly status allegedly conferred upon Metropolitan by the State of Pennsylvania. As a factual matter, it may well be doubted that the State ever granted or guaranteed Metropolitan a monopoly. But assuming that it had, this fact is not determinative in considering whether Metropolitan's termination of service to petitioner was "state action" for purposes of the Fourteenth Amendment. Petitioner next urges that state action is present because respondent provides an essential public service required to be supplied on a reasonably continuous basis by Pennsylvania statute and hence performs a "public function." We have, of course, found state action present in the exercise by a private entity of powers traditionally exclusively reserved to the State. If we were dealing with the exercise by Metropolitan of some power delegated to it by the State which is traditionally associated with sovereignty, such as eminent domain, our case would be quite a different one. But while the Pennsylvania statute imposes an obligation to furnish service on regulated utilities, it imposes no such obligation on the State. Perhaps in recognition of the fact that the supplying of utility service is not traditionally the exclusive prerogative of the State, petitioner invites the expansion of the doctrine of this limited line of cases into a broad principle that all businesses "affected with the public interest" are state actors in all their actions. We decline the invitation for reasons stated long ago in *Nebbia v. New York,* in the course of rejecting a substantive due process attack on state legislation. Doctors, optometrists, lawyers, Metropolitan, and Nebbia's upstate New York grocery selling a quart of milk are all in regulated businesses, providing arguably essential goods and services, "affected with a public interest." We do not believe that such a status converts their every action, absent more, into that of the State. We also reject the notion that Metropolitan's termination is state action because the State "has specifically authorized and approved" the termination practice. We also find absent in the instant case the symbiotic relationship presented in *Burton v. Wilmington Parking Authority.* There where a private lessee, who practiced racial discrimination, leased space for a restaurant from a state parking authority in a publicly owned building, the Court held that the State had so far insinuated itself into a position of interdependence with the restaurant that it was a joint participant in the enterprise. We cautioned, however, that while "a multitude of relationships might appear to some to fall within the Amendment's embrace," differences in circumstances beget differences in law, limiting the actual holding to lessees of public property. Metropolitan is a privately owned corporation, and it does not lease its facilities from the State of Pennsylvania. It alone is responsible for the provision of power to its customers. In common with all corporations of the State it pays taxes to the State, and it is subject to a form of extensive regulation by the State in a way that most other business enterprises are not. All of petitioner's arguments, taken together, show no more than that Metropolitan was a heavily regulated, privately owned utility, enjoying at least a partial monopoly in the providing of electrical service within its territory, and that it elected to terminate service to petitioner in a manner which the Pennsylvania Public Utility Commission found permissible under state law. Under our decision this is not sufficient to connect the State of Pennsylvania with respondent's action so as to make the latter's conduct attributable to the State for purposes of the Fourteenth Amendment. We conclude that the State of Pennsylvania is not sufficiently connected with respondent's action in terminating petitioner's service so as to make respondent's conduct in so doing attributable to the State for purposes of the Fourteenth Amendment.

C

The judgment of the Court of Appeals for the Third Circuit is therefore affirmed.

Terry v. Adams

345 U.S. 461 (1953)

FACTS

Petitioners, qualified Negro voters of a Texas County, sued to determine the legality of their being excluded, solely because of their race and color, from voting in elections held by an Association consisting of all qualified white voters in the County. The Association held an election in each election year to select candidates for county offices to run for nomination in the official Democratic primary. The Association's elections were not governed by state laws and did not utilize state elective machinery or funds. Candidates elected by the Association were not certified by the Association as its candidates in the Democratic primary, but filed their own names as candidates. However, for more than 60 years, the Association's county-wide candidates had invariably been nominated in the Democratic primaries and elected to office. The District Court found that the Association was a political organization or party and that its chief object had always been to deny Negroes any voice or part in the election of county officials.

I Does a private political party that controls elections engage in state action, thereby making it subject to the 15th Amendment?

R A private political party that controls the outcome of elections engages in state action thereby making it subject to the 15th Amendment.

A The combined election machinery of the Association and the Democratic Party deprives petitioners of their right to vote on account of their race and color, contrary to the Fifteenth Amendment. The case is remanded to the District Court to enter such orders and decrees as are necessary and proper under the jurisdiction it has retained under 28 U.S.C. 2202. In exercising this jurisdiction, the District Court is left free to hold hearings to consider and determine what provisions are essential to afford Negro citizens of the County full protection from such future discriminatory election practices which deprive citizens of voting rights because of their color.

C Reversed.

Evans v. Newton

382 U.S. 296 (1966)

FACTS

A tract of land was willed in trust to the Mayor and City Council of Macon, Georgia, as a park for white people, to be controlled by a white Board of Managers. When the city ultimately desegregated the park, the individual Managers brought this suit in a state court against the city and the trustees of residuary beneficiaries and asked for the city's removal as trustee and the appointment of private trustees to enforce the racial limitations of the will. The city, which had alleged that it could not legally enforce segregation, asked to resign as trustee after intervention of Negro citizens who claimed that the racial limitations violated federal law. Other heirs of the testator who had also intervened asked along with the individual defendants for reversion of the property if the prayer of the petition was denied. The Georgia court, without passing on the heirs' other claims, accepted the city's resignation as trustee and appointed three new trustees. The Negro intervenors appealed. The Georgia Supreme Court affirmed, holding that the testator had a right to leave his property to a limited class and that charitable trusts are subject to the supervision of an equity court, which could appoint new trustees to avoid failure of the trust.

I

Does operating a park constitute a public function subjecting the owner to the 14th Amendment?

R

Operating a park is a public function subjecting the owner to the 14th Amendment.

A

Where private individuals or groups exercise powers or carry on functions governmental in nature, they become agencies or instrumentalities of the State and subject to the Fourteenth Amendment. Where the tradition of municipal control and maintenance had been perpetuated for many years, proof of the substitution of trustees is insufficient per se to divest the park of its public character. The services rendered by a park are municipal in nature and, under the circumstances of this case, the park is subject to the equal protection requirements of the Fourteenth Amendment.

C

The judgment is reversed.

Amalgamated Food Employees Union Local 590 v. Logan Valley Plaza Inc. 391 U.S. 308 (1968)

FACTS

Respondent Weis Markets owns and operates a supermarket in a large shopping center complex owned by respondent Logan Valley Plaza. In front of Weis' building is a covered porch and a parcel pickup zone. Members of petitioner union picketed Weis' store, confining the picketing almost entirely to the parcel pickup zone and the portion of the parking area adjacent thereto. The picketing was peaceful with some sporadic and infrequent congestion of the parcel pickup area. A Pennsylvania Court of Common Pleas enjoined "picketing and trespassing upon . . . the [Weis] storeroom, porch and parcel pick-up area . . . [and] the [Logan] parking area," thus preventing picketing inside the shopping center. That court held the injunction justified in order to protect respondents' property rights and because the picketing was unlawfully aimed at coercing Weis to compel its employees to join a union. The Pennsylvania Supreme Court affirmed the issuance of the injunction on the sole ground that petitioners' conduct constituted a trespass on respondents' property.

I

Does operating a shopping center constitute a public function subjecting the owner to the First Amendment?

R

Operating a shopping center constitutes a public function subjecting the owner to the First Amendment.

A

Peaceful picketing carried on in a location open generally to the public is, absent other factors involving the purpose or the manner of the picketing, protected by the First Amendment. Although there may be regulation of the manner in which handbilling, or picketing, is carried out, that does not mean that either can be barred under all circumstances on publicly owned property simply by recourse to traditional concepts of property law concerning the incidents of ownership of real property. Since the shopping center serves as the community business block "and is freely accessible and open to the people in the area and those passing through," *Marsh v. Alabama*, the State may not delegate the power, through the use of trespass laws, wholly to exclude those members of the public wishing to exercise their First Amendment rights on the premises in a manner and for a purpose generally consonant with the use to which the property is actually put.

C

Reversed and remanded.

Hudgens v. National Labor Relations Board

424 U.S. 507 (1976)

FACTS

When striking members of respondent union picketed in front of their employer's leased store located in petitioner's shopping center, the shopping center's general manager threatened them with arrest for criminal trespass if they did not depart, and they left. The union then filed unfair labor practice charges against petitioner, alleging that the threat constituted interference with rights protected by 7 of the National Labor Relations Act (NLRA). The National Labor Relations Board (NLRB), concluding that the NLRA had been violated, issued a cease-and-desist order against petitioner, and the Court of Appeals enforced the order. Petitioner and respondent union contend that the respective rights and liabilities of the parties are to be decided under the criteria of the NLRA alone, whereas the NLRB contends that such rights and liabilities must be measured under a First Amendment standard.

I

Does operating a shopping center constitute a public function subjecting the owner to the First Amendment?

R

Operating a privately-owned shopping center does not subject the owner to the First Amendment.

A

Under the present state of the law the constitutional guarantee of free expression has no part to play in a case such as this, and the pickets here did not have a First Amendment right to enter the shopping center for the purpose of advertising their strike against their employer. *Lloyd Corp. v. Tanner*. The rights and liabilities of the parties are dependent exclusively upon the NLRA, under which it is the NLRB's task, subject to judicial review, to resolve conflicts between 7 rights and private property rights and to seek accommodation of such rights "with as little destruction of one as is consistent with the maintenance of the other," *NLRB v. Babcock & Wilcox Co*. Hence, the case is remanded so that the NLRB may reconsider the case under the NLRA's statutory criteria alone.

C

Vacated and remanded.

Shelley v. Kraemer

334 U.S. 1 (1948)

FACTS

The first of these cases comes to this Court on certiorari to the Supreme Court of Missouri. On February 16, 1911, thirty out of a total of thirty-nine owners of property fronting both sides of Labadie Avenue between Taylor Avenue and Cora Avenue in the city of St. Louis, signed an agreement, which was subsequently recorded a racially restrictive covenant which provided that the houses could only be occupied by Caucasians. The entire district described in the agreement included fifty-seven parcels of land. The thirty owners who signed the agreement held title to forty-seven parcels, including the particular parcel involved in this case. At the time the agreement was signed, five of the parcels in the district were owned by Negroes. One of those had been occupied by Negro families since 1882, nearly thirty years before the restrictive agreement was executed. On August 11, 1945, pursuant to a contract of sale, petitioners Shelley, who are Negroes, for valuable consideration received from one Fitzgerald a warranty deed to the parcel in question. The trial court found that petitioners had no actual knowledge of the restrictive agreement at the time of the purchase. On October 9, 1945, respondents, as owners of other property subject to the terms of the restrictive covenant, brought suit in Circuit Court of the city of St. Louis praying that petitioners Shelley be restrained from taking possession of the property and that judgment be entered divesting title out of petitioners Shelley and revesting title in the immediate grantor or in such other person as the court should direct. The trial court denied the requested relief on the ground that the restrictive agreement, upon which respondents based their action, had never become final and complete because it was the intention of the parties to that agreement that it was not to become effective until signed by all property owners in the district, and signatures of all the owners had never been obtained. The Supreme Court of Missouri sitting en banc reversed and directed the trial court to grant the relief for which respondents had prayed. That court held the agreement effective and concluded that enforcement of its provisions violated no rights guaranteed to petitioners by the Federal Constitution. At the time the court rendered its decision, petitioners were occupying the property in question.

The second of the cases under consideration comes to this Court from the Supreme Court of Michigan. The circumstances presented do not differ materially from the Missouri case. In June, 1934, one Ferguson and his wife, who then owned the property located in the city of Detroit which is involved in this case, executed a contract providing in part that the property shall not be used or occupied by any person or persons except those of the Caucasian race and that the restriction shall not be effective unless at least eighty percent of the property fronting on both sides of the street in the block where our land is located is subjected to this or a similar restriction. The agreement provided that the restrictions were to remain in effect until January 1, 1960. The contract was subsequently recorded; and similar agreements were executed with respect to eighty percent of the lots in the block in which the property in question is situated. By deed dated November 30, 1944, petitioners, who were found by the trial court to be Negroes, acquired title to the property and thereupon entered into its occupancy. On January 30, 1945, respondents, as owners of property subject to the terms of the restrictive agreement, brought suit against petitioners in the Circuit Court of Wayne County. After a hearing, the court entered a decree directing petitioners to move from the property within ninety days. Petitioners were further enjoined and restrained from using or occupying the premises in the future.

Shelley v. Kraemer

334 U.S. 1 (1948)

On appeal, the Supreme Court of Michigan affirmed, deciding adversely to petitioners' contentions that they had been denied rights protected by the Fourteenth Amendment. Petitioners have placed primary reliance on their contentions, first raised in the state courts, that judicial enforcement of the restrictive agreements in these cases has violated rights guaranteed to petitioners by the Fourteenth Amendment of the Federal Constitution and Acts of Congress passed pursuant to that Amendment. Specifically, petitioners urge that they have been denied the equal protection of the laws, deprived of property without due process of law, and have been denied privileges and immunities of citizens of the United States.

I

Does a state court's action in enforcing private discrimination violate the Fourteenth Amendment?

R

When a court enforces a private discriminatory contractual agreement, that enforcement will be considered state action for Fourteenth Amendment purposes.

A

These cases present for our consideration questions relating to the validity of court enforcement of private agreements, generally described as restrictive covenants, which have as their purpose the exclusion of persons of designated race or color. Whether the equal protection clause of the 14th Amendment inhibits judicial enforcement by state courts of restrictive covenants based on race or color is a question which this Court has not heretofore been called upon to consider. Participation of the State consists in the enforcement of the restrictions so defined. The crucial issue with which we are here confronted is whether this distinction removes these cases from the operation of the prohibitory provisions of the 14th Amendment. Since the decision of this Court in the Civil Rights Cases of 1883, the principle has become firmly embedded in our constitutional law that the action inhibited by the first section of the Fourteenth Amendment is only such action as may fairly be said to be that of the States. That Amendment erects no shield against merely private conduct, however discriminatory or wrongful. We conclude, therefore, that the restrictive agreements standing alone cannot be regarded as a violation of any rights guaranteed to petitioners by the 14th Amendment. So long as the purposes of those agreements are effectuated by voluntary adherence to their terms, it would appear clear that there has been no action by the State and the provisions of the Amendment have not been violated. But here there was more. These are cases in which the purposes of the agreements were secured only by judicial enforcement by state courts of the restrictive terms of the agreements. The respondents urge that judicial enforcement of private agreements does not amount to state action; or, in any event, the participation of the State is so attenuated in character as not to amount to state action within the meaning of the Fourteenth Amendment. That the action of state courts and of judicial officers in their official capacities is to be regarded as action of the State within the meaning of the Fourteenth Amendment is a proposition which has long been established by decisions of this Court. Similar expressions, giving specific recognition to the fact that judicial action is to be regarded as action on the State for the purposes of the Fourteenth Amendment, are to be found in numerous cases which have been more recently decided. We have no doubt that there has been state action in these cases in the full and complete sense of the phrase. The undisputed facts disclose that petitioners were willing purchasers of properties; the owners of the properties were willing sellers; and contracts of sale were accordingly consummated. It is clear that but for the active intervention of the state courts, supported by state power, petitioners would have been free to occupy the properties in question without restraint. We hold that in granting judicial enforcement of the restrictive agreements in these cases, the States have denied petitioners the equal protection of the laws and that, therefore, the action of the state courts cannot stand. We have noted that freedom from discrimination by the States in the enjoyment of property rights was among the basic objectives sought to be effectuated by the framers of the Fourteenth Amendment. Because of the race or color of these petitioners they have been denied rights of ownership or occupancy enjoyed as a matter of course by other citizens of different race or color. It is, therefore, no answer to these petitioners to say that the courts may also be induced to deny white persons rights of ownership and occupancy on grounds of race or color. Equal protection of the laws is not achieved through indiscriminate imposition of inequalities. Nor do we find merit in the suggestion that property owners who are parties to these agreements are denied equal protection of the laws if denied access to the courts to enforce the terms of restrictive covenants and to assert property rights which the state courts have held to be created by such agreements. The Constitution confers upon no individual the right to demand action by the State which results in the denial of equal protection of the laws to other individuals. And it would appear beyond question that the power of the State to create and enforce property interests must be exercised within the boundaries defined by the Fourteenth Amendment. Upon full consideration, we have concluded that in these cases the States have acted to deny petitioners the equal protection of the laws guaranteed by the Fourteenth Amendment. Having so decided, we find it unnecessary to consider whether petitioners have also been deprived of property without due process of law or denied privileges and immunities of citizens of the United States. For the reasons stated, the judgment of the Supreme Court of Missouri and the judgment of the Supreme Court of Michigan must be reversed.

C Reversed – both judgments.

Lugar v. Edmondson Oil Co.

457 U.S. 922 (1982)

FACTS

This case consolidates two appeals. *Diedrich v. Commissioner of Internal Revenue.* In 1972 petitioners Victor and Frances Diedrich made gifts of approximately 85,000 shares of stock to their three children, using both a direct transfer and a trust arrangement. The gifts were subject to a condition that the donees pay the resulting federal and state gift taxes. There is no dispute concerning the amount of the gift tax paid by the donees. The donors' basis in the transferred stock was $51,073; the gift tax paid in 1972 by the donees was $62,992. Petitioners did not include as income on their 1972 federal income tax returns any portion of the gift tax paid by the donees. After an audit the Commissioner of Internal Revenue determined that petitioners had realized income to the extent that the gift tax owed by petitioners but paid by the donees exceeded the donors' basis in the property. Accordingly, petitioners' taxable income for 1972 was increased by $5,959. Petitioners filed a petition in the United States Tax Court for redetermination of the deficiencies. The Tax Court held for the taxpayers, concluding that no income had been realized.

United Missouri Bank of Kansas City v. Commissioner of Internal Revenue. In 1970 and 1971 Mrs. Frances Grant gave 90,000 voting trust certificates to her son on condition that he pay the resulting gift tax. Mrs. Grant's basis in the stock was $8,742.60; the gift tax paid by the donee was $232,620.09 As in Diedrich, there is no dispute concerning the amount of the gift tax or the fact of its payment by the donee pursuant to the condition. Like the Diedrichs, Mrs. Grant did not include as income on her 1970 or 1971 federal income tax returns any portion of the amount of the gift tax owed by her but paid by the donee. After auditing her returns, the Commissioner determined that the gift of stock to her son was part gift and part sale, with the result that Mrs. Grant realized income to the extent that the amount of the gift tax exceeded the adjusted basis in the property. Accordingly, Mrs. Grant's taxable income was increased by approximately $112,000. Mrs. Grant filed [457 U.S. 191, 194] a petition in the United States Tax Court for redetermination of the deficiencies. The Tax Court held for the taxpayer, concluding that no income had been realized.

The United States Court of Appeals for the Eighth Circuit consolidated the two appeals and reversed, concluding that "to the extent the gift taxes paid by donees" exceeded the donors' adjusted bases in the property transferred, "the donors realized taxable income." The Court of Appeals rejected the Tax Court's conclusion that the taxpayers merely had made a "net gift" of the difference between the fair market value of the transferred property and the gift taxes paid by the donees. The court reasoned that a donor receives a benefit when a donee discharges a donor's legal obligation to pay gift taxes. The Court of Appeals agreed with the Commissioner in rejecting the holding in *Turner v. Commissioner* and its progeny, and adopted the approach of *Johnson v. Commissioner* and *Estate of Levine v. Commissioner.* The U.S. Supreme Court granted certiorari to resolve this conflict.

I Under the 14th Amendment, does obtaining an ex parte writ of attachment constitute state action?

Lugar v. Edmondson Oil Co.

457 U.S. 922 (1982)

R

When the government and/or the court is used to seize property without due process of law, the 14th Amendment is implicated (state action is involved).

A

A donor (such as petitioner husband and wife and petitioner executor's decedent) who makes a gift of property on condition that the donee pay the resulting gift taxes realizes taxable income to the extent that the gift taxes paid by the donee exceed the donor's adjusted basis in the property. The substance, not the form, of the agreed transaction controls in determining whether taxable income was realized. When a donor makes a gift, he incurs a "debt" to the United States for the amount of whatever gift taxes are due, which are as much the donor's legal obligation as his income taxes. When conditional gifts, such as those in question here, are made, the donor realizes an immediate economic benefit by the donee's assumption of the donor's legal obligation to pay the gift taxes. Subjective intent, while relevant in determining whether a gift has been made, is not characteristically a factor in determining whether an individual has realized income. Even if intent were a factor, the donor's intent as to the condition shifting the gift tax obligation to the donee is plainly to relieve the donor of the debt owed to the United States. And the economic benefit realized by the donor is not diminished by the fact that the liability attaches during the course of the donative transfer, such benefit being indistinguishable from the benefit arising from discharge of a pre-existing obligation. Treating the amount by which the gift taxes exceed the donor's adjusted basis in the property as income is consistent with 1001 of the Internal Revenue Code, which provides that the gain from the disposition of property is the excess of the amount realized over the transferor's adjusted basis in the property.

C

Affirmed.

Edmonson v. Leesville Concrete Co.

500 U.S. 614 (1991)

FACTS

Petitioner Edmonson sued respondent Leesville Concrete Co. in the District Court, alleging that Leesville's negligence had caused him personal injury. During voir dire, Leesville used two of its three peremptory challenges authorized by statute to remove black persons from the prospective jury. Citing *Batson v. Kentucky*, Edmonson, who is black, requested that the court require Leesville to articulate a race-neutral explanation for the peremptory strikes. The court refused on the ground that Batson does not apply in civil proceedings, and the impaneled jury, which consisted of 11 white persons and 1 black, rendered a verdict unfavorable to Edmonson. The Court of Appeals affirmed, holding that a private litigant in a civil case can exercise peremptory challenges without accountability for alleged racial classifications.

I

Does the race-based exclusion of jurors in a civil action implicate the state (constitute state action)?

R

When a private citizen makes preemptory challenges based on race, he violates the Equal Protection Clause of the 14th Amendment.

A

A private litigant in a civil case may not use peremptory challenges to exclude jurors on account of race. Race-based exclusion of potential jurors in a civil case violates the excluded persons' equal protection rights. Although the conduct of private parties lies beyond the Constitution's scope in most instances, Leesville's exercise of peremptory challenges was pursuant to a course of state action, and is therefore subject to constitutional requirements under the analytical framework set forth in *Lugar v. Edmondson Oil Co.* First, the claimed constitutional deprivation results from the exercise of a right or privilege having its source in state authority, since Leesville would not have been able to engage in the alleged discriminatory acts without 28 U.S.C. 1870, which authorizes the use of peremptory challenges in civil cases. Second, Leesville must in all fairness be deemed a government actor in its use of peremptory challenges. Leesville has made extensive use of government procedures with the overt, significant assistance of the government, in that peremptory challenges have no utility outside the jury trial system, which is created and governed by an elaborate set of statutory provisions and administered solely by government officials, including the trial judge, himself a state actor, who exercises substantial control over *voir dire* and effects the final and practical denial of the excluded individual's opportunity to serve on the petit jury by discharging him or her. Moreover, the action in question involves the performance of a traditional governmental function, since the peremptory challenge is used in selecting the jury, an entity that is a quintessential governmental body having no attributes of a private actor. Furthermore, the injury allegedly caused by Leesville's use of peremptory challenges is aggravated in a unique way by the incidents of governmental authority, since the courtroom is a real expression of the government's constitutional authority, and racial exclusion within its confines compounds the racial insult inherent in judging a citizen by the color of his or her skin. A private civil litigant may raise the equal protection claim of a person whom the opposing party has excluded from jury service on account of race. Just as in the criminal context, see Powers, supra, all three of the requirements for third-party standing are satisfied in the civil context. First, there is no reason to believe that the daunting barriers to suit by an excluded criminal juror, would be any less imposing simply because the person was excluded from civil jury service. Second, the relation between the excluded venire person and the litigant challenging the exclusion is just as close in the civil as it is in the criminal context. Third, a civil litigant can demonstrate that he or she has suffered a concrete, redressable injury from the exclusion of jurors on account of race, in that racial discrimination in jury selection casts doubt on the integrity of the judicial process and places the fairness of the proceeding in doubt. The case is remanded for a determination whether Edmonson has established a prima facie case of racial discrimination under the approach set forth in *Batson*, such that Leesville would be required to offer race-neutral explanations for its peremptory challenges.

C

Reversed and remanded.

Burton v. Wilmington Parking Authority

365 U.S. 715 (1961)

FACTS

A restaurant, the Eagle Coffee Shoppe Inc. (Eagle), located in an automobile parking building refused to serve appellant food or drink solely because he was a Negro. The parking lot building was publicly owned and operated by Defendant Wilmington Parking Authority (the Authority). The building had been built with public funds for public purposes, and it was owned and operated by an agency of the State of Delaware, from which the private operator of the restaurant leased its premises. Claiming that refusal to serve him abridged his rights under the Equal Protection Clause of the 14th Amendment, Plaintiff-appellant Burton sued in a state court for declaratory and injunctive relief against the restaurant and the state agency. The Supreme Court of Delaware held that he was not entitled to relief, on the ground that the restaurant's action was not state action within the meaning of the Fourteenth Amendment and that the restaurant was not required by a Delaware statute to serve all persons entering its place of business. An appeal was taken to this Court on the ground that the state statute had been construed unconstitutionally.

I

When a lessee, who is a private party, acts discriminatorily against another, may the state, as the lessor of property, be implicated for a violation of the 14th Amendment?

R

A private party's racially discriminatory actions violate the Fourteenth Amendment when a state becomes so intertwined in a private party's dealings that the state may be considered a mutual partaker in the actions of the private party.

A

The appeal is dismissed, since the judgment did not depend for its ultimate support upon a determination of the constitutional validity of the state statute; but, treating the papers whereon the appeal was taken as a petition for writ of certiorari, certiorari is granted, since the case presents an important constitutional question under the Fourteenth Amendment. In view of all the circumstances of this case, including the facts that the restaurant was physically and financially an integral part of a public building, built and maintained with public funds, devoted to a public parking service, and owned and operated by an agency of the State for public purposes, the State was a joint participant in the operation of the restaurant, and its refusal to serve appellant violated the Equal Protection Clause of the Fourteenth Amendment. When a State leases public property in the manner and for the purpose shown to have been the case here, the proscriptions of the Fourteenth Amendment must be complied with by the lessee as certainly as though they were binding covenants written into the agreement itself.

C

Reversed.

Moose Lodge No. 107 v. Irvis

407 U.S. 163 (1972)

FACTS

Appellee Irvis, a Negro guest of a member of appellant, a private club, was refused service at the club's dining room and bar solely because of his race. In suing for injunctive relief, appellee contended that the discrimination was state action, and thus a violation of the Equal Protection Clause of the Fourteenth Amendment, because the Pennsylvania liquor board had issued appellant a private club liquor license. The District Court found appellant's membership and guest practices discriminatory, agreed with appellee's view that state action was present, and declared the liquor license invalid as long as appellant continued its discriminatory practices. Appellant's motion to have the final decree limited to its guest policy was opposed by appellee, and the court denied the motion. Following the District Court's decision, the applicable bylaws were amended to exclude as guests those who would be excluded as members.

I

Does a state's granting of a liquor license to a private entity which discriminates against others violate the equal protection clause?

R

The operation of a State's regulatory scheme enforced by the state liquor board does not sufficiently implicate the State in a private entity's discriminatory guest practices so as to make those practices "state action" within the purview of the Equal Protection Clause unless the regulation is intended overtly or covertly to encourage discrimination.

A

Appellee, who had not applied for or been denied membership in appellant private club, had no standing to contest appellant's membership practices. He did, however, have standing to litigate the constitutional validity of appellant's discriminatory policies toward members' guests, and his opposition to amendment of the judgment did not constitute a disclaimer of injunctive relief directed at appellant's guest policies. The operation of Pennsylvania's regulatory scheme enforced by the state liquor board, except as noted below, does not sufficiently implicate the State in appellant's discriminatory guest practices so as to make those practices "state action" within the purview of the Equal Protection Clause, and there is no suggestion in the record that the State's regulation of the sale of liquor is intended overtly or covertly to encourage discrimination. Pennsylvania liquor board's regulation requiring that "every club licensee shall adhere to all the provisions of its constitution and by-laws" in effect placed state sanctions behind the discriminatory guest practices that were enacted after the District Court's decision, and enforcement of that regulation should be enjoined to the extent that it requires appellant to adhere to those practices.

C

Reversed and remanded.

Norwood v. Harrison

413 U.S. 455 (1973)

FACTS

For more than three decades the state of Mississippi purchased textbooks and loaned them to both public and private schools. A class action was formed on behalf of all Mississippi students alleging that by supplying the books to students attending discriminatory private schools, the state provided aid to racially segregated schools. A three-judge District Court sustained the validity of a Mississippi statutory program, begun in 1940, under which textbooks are purchased by the State and lent to students in both public and private schools, without reference to whether any participating private school has racially discriminatory policies. The number of private secular schools in Mississippi, with a virtually all-white student population, has greatly increased in recent years.

I

Does providing governmental aid to a discriminatory private organization violate the 14th Amendment?

R

A state may not provide aid to private discriminatory institutions under the Equal Protections Clause of the 14th Amendment.

A

Private schools have the right to exist and to operate, but the State is not required by the Equal Protection Clause to provide assistance to private schools equivalent to that it provides to public schools without regard to whether the private schools discriminate on racial grounds. Free textbooks, like tuition grants directed to students in private schools, are a form of tangible financial assistance benefiting the schools themselves, and the State's constitutional obligation requires it to avoid not only operating the old dual system of racially segregated schools but also providing tangible aid to schools that practice racial or other invidious discrimination. Assistance carefully limited so as to avoid the prohibitions of the "effect" and "entanglement" tests may be confined to the secular functions of sectarian schools and does not substantially promote the religious mission of those schools in violation of the Establishment Clause. In this case, however, the legitimate educational function of private discriminatory schools cannot be isolated from their alleged discriminatory practices; discriminatory treatment exerts a pervasive influence on the entire educational process. The Establishment Clause permits a greater degree of state assistance to sectarian schools than may be given to private schools which engage in discriminatory practices. Proper injunctive relief can be granted without implying that all the private schools alleged to be receiving textbook aid have restrictive admission policies. The District Court can direct appellees to submit for approval a certification procedure whereby schools may apply for textbooks on behalf of pupils, affirmatively declaring admission policies and practices, and stating the number of their racially and religiously identifiable minority students, and other relevant data.

C

Vacated and remanded.

Rendell-Baker v. Kohn

457 U.S. 830 (1982)

FACTS

Respondent school is a privately operated school for maladjusted high school students. In recent years, nearly all of the students have been referred to the school by city school committees under a Massachusetts statute or by a state agency. When the students are referred to the school by the city committees, these cities pay for the students' education. The school also receives funds from a number of state and federal agencies. Public funds have recently accounted for at least 90% of the school's operating budget. To be eligible for tuition funding under the state statute, the school must comply with a variety of state regulations. Petitioners, a former vocational counselor and teachers at the school, brought separate actions in Federal District Court under 42 U.S.C. 1983, claiming that they had been discharged by the school in violation of their First, Fifth, and 14th Amendment rights. The court dismissed the counselor's action but denied a motion to dismiss the teachers' action, reaching conflicting conclusions as to whether the school had acted under color of state law so as to be subject to liability under 1983. On appeal the cases were consolidated, and the Court of Appeals held that it was error to conclude that the school acted under color of state law, since, although regulated by the State, it was not dominated by the State.

I

Is a private school considered a "state actor" for purposes of the 14th Amendment when it receives state financial aid?

R

Publicly-funded and regulated private organizations are not considered state actors under the 14th Amendment unless the state compels or exerts pressure on them.

A

Respondent school did not act under color of state law when it discharged petitioner employees, and hence petitioners have not stated a claim for relief under 1983. The ultimate issue in determining whether a person is subject to suit under 1983 is the same question posed in cases arising under the Fourteenth Amendment: Is the alleged infringement of federal rights fairly attributable to the State? The school's receipt of public funds does not make the discharge decisions acts of the State. The school is not fundamentally different from many private corporations whose business depends primarily on contracts with the government, and whose acts do not become acts of the government by reason of their significant or even total engagement in performing public contracts. The decision to discharge petitioners was not compelled or even influenced by any state regulation, and the fact that the school performs a public function in educating maladjusted high school students does not make its acts state action. Moreover, since the school's fiscal relationship with the State is not any different from that of many contractors performing services for the government, there is no "symbiotic relationship" between the school and the State.

C

Reversed.

Blum v. Yaretsky

457 U.S. 991 (1982)

FACTS

As a participating State in the Medicaid program established by the Social Security Act, New York provides Medicaid assistance to eligible persons who receive care in private nursing homes, which are designated as either "skilled nursing facilities" (SNF's) or "health related facilities" (HRF's), the latter providing less extensive, and generally less expensive, medical care than the former. The nursing homes are directly reimbursed by the State for the reasonable cost of health care services. To obtain Medicaid assistance, an individual must satisfy eligibility standards in terms of income or resources and must seek medically necessary services. As to the latter requirement, federal regulations require each nursing home to establish a utilization review committee (URC) of physicians whose functions include periodically assessing whether each patient is receiving the appropriate level of care, and thus whether the patient's continued stay in the facility is justified. Respondents, who were Medicaid patients in an SNF, instituted a class action in Federal District Court after the nursing home's URC decided that they should be transferred to a lower level of care in an HRF and so notified local officials, and after administrative hearings resulting in affirmance by state officials of the local officials' decision to discontinue benefits unless respondents accepted transfer to an HRF. Respondents alleged, inter alia, that they had not been afforded adequate notice either of the URC decisions and the reasons supporting them or of their right to an administrative hearing to challenge those decisions, as required by the Due Process Clause of the Fourteenth Amendment. Respondents later added claims as to procedural safeguards that should also apply to URC decisions transferring a patient to a higher level of care and to transfers of any kind initiated by the nursing homes themselves or by the patients' attending physicians. Ultimately the court approved a consent judgment establishing procedural rights applicable to URC-initiated transfers to lower levels of care, and ruled in respondents' favor as to transfers to higher levels of care and all transfers initiated by the facility or its agent. The court permanently enjoined petitioner state officials and all SNF's and HRF's in the State from permitting or ordering discharges of class members or their transfers to a different level of care, without prior written notice and an evidentiary hearing. The Court of Appeals affirmed, holding that URC-initiated transfers to a higher level of care and all discharges and transfers by nursing homes or attending physicians involved "state action" for purposes of the Fourteenth Amendment.

I Is the state responsible for the actions of private nursing homes that receive Medicaid funds?

R The state will not be held liable for decisions made by private parties when the state did not coerce or significantly encourage those decisions.

A Respondents have standing to challenge the procedural adequacy of facility-initiated discharges and transfers to lower levels of care. Although respondents were threatened only with URC-initiated transfers to lower levels of care, and although the consent judgment in the District Court halted implementation of such URC decisions, the threat that the nursing homes might determine, independently of the URC decisions, that respondents' continued stay at current levels of care was not medically necessary is not imaginary or speculative but is quite realistic. However, the threat of transfers to higher levels of care is not of sufficient immediacy and reality that respondents presently have standing to seek an adjudication of the procedures attending such transfers. Thus the District Court exceeded its authority under Art. III in adjudicating the procedures governing transfers to higher levels of care. Respondents failed to establish "state action" in the nursing homes' decisions to discharge or transfer Medicaid patients to lower levels of care and thus failed to prove that petitioners have violated rights secured by the Fourteenth Amendment. The mere fact that a private business is subject to state regulation does not by itself convert its action into that of the State for purposes of the Fourteenth Amendment. A State normally can be held responsible for a private decision only when it has exercised coercive power or has provided such significant encouragement that the choice must in law be deemed to be that of the State. The fact that the State responds to the nursing homes' discharge or transfer decisions by adjusting the patients' Medicaid benefits does not render it responsible for those decisions. Moreover, the pertinent statutes and regulations do not constitute affirmative commands by the State for summary discharge or transfer of Medicaid patients who are thought to be inappropriately placed in nursing facilities. The State, by requiring completion by physicians or nursing homes of forms relating to a patient's condition and discharge or transfer decisions, is not responsible for the decisions of the physicians or nursing homes. Those decisions ultimately turn on medical judgments made by private parties according to professional standards that are not established by the State. Similarly, regulations imposing penalties on nursing homes that fail to discharge or transfer patients whose continued stay is inappropriate do not themselves dictate the decision to discharge or transfer in a particular case. And even though the State subsidizes the cost of the facilities, pays the expenses of the patients, and licenses the facilities, the action of the nursing homes is not thereby converted into "state action." Nor do the nursing homes perform a function that has been "traditionally the exclusive prerogative of the State," *Jackson v. Metropolitan Edison Co.*, so as to establish the required nexus between the State and the challenged action.

C Reversed.

Reitman v. Mulkey

387 U.S. 369 (1967)

FACTS

The California Legislature, during the period 1959-1963, enacted several statutes regulating racial discrimination in housing. In 1964, pursuant to an initiative and referendum, Art. I, 26, was added to the state constitution. It provided in part that neither the State nor any agency thereof "shall deny, limit or abridge, directly or indirectly, the right of any person, who is willing or desires to sell, lease or rent any part or all of his real property, to decline to sell, lease or rent such property to such person or persons as he, in his absolute discretion, chooses." The California Supreme Court held that Art. I, 26, was designed to overturn state laws that bore on the right of private persons to discriminate, that it invalidly involved the State in racial discrimination in the housing market and that it changed the situation from one in which discriminatory practices were restricted to one where they are "encouraged," within the meaning of this Court's decisions. The court concluded that Art. I, 26, unconstitutionally involves the State in racial discrimination and is therefore invalid under the Equal Protection Clause of the Fourteenth Amendment.

I

Does a state constitutional law which prohibits private racial discrimination in housing unconstitutionally involve the state in the discrimination?

R

A state constitutional law which prohibits private racial discrimination in housing unconstitutionally involves the state in the discrimination and, as such, is a violation of the 14th Amendment.

A

The California Supreme Court believes that Art. I, 26, which does not merely repeal existing law forbidding private racial discrimination but authorizes racial discrimination in the housing market and establishes the right to discriminate as a basic state policy, will significantly encourage and involve the State in private discriminations. No persuasive considerations indicating that the judgments herein should be overturned have been presented, and they are affirmed. The question here is whether Art. I, 26, of the California Constitution denies "to any person . . . the equal protection of the laws" within the meaning of the Fourteenth Amendment of the Constitution of the United States. Section 26 of Art. I, an initiated measure submitted to the people as Proposition 14 in a statewide ballot in 1964, provides in part as follows: "Neither the State nor any subdivision or agency thereof shall deny, limit or abridge, directly or indirectly, the right of any person, who is willing or desires to sell, lease or rent any part or all of his real property, to decline to sell, lease or rent such property to such person or persons as he, in his absolute discretion, chooses." The real property covered by 26 is limited to residential property and contains an exception for state-owned real estate. The issue arose in two separate actions in the California courts, *Mulkey v. Reitman* and *Prendergast v. Snyder*. In *Reitman*, the Mulkeys, who are husband and wife and respondents here, sued under 51 and 52 of the California Civil Code alleging that petitioners had refused to rent them an apartment solely on account of their race. An injunction and damages were demanded. Petitioners moved for summary judgment on the ground that 51 and 52, insofar as they were the basis for the Mulkeys' action, had been rendered null and void by the adoption of Proposition 14 after the filing of the complaint. The trial court granted the motion and respondents took the case to the California Supreme Court. In the *Prendergast* case, respondents, husband and wife, filed suit in December 1964 seeking to enjoin eviction from their apartment; respondents alleged that the eviction was motivated by racial prejudice and therefore would violate 51 and 52 of the Civil Code. Petitioner Snyder cross-complained for a judicial declaration: that he was entitled to terminate the month-to-month tenancy even if his action was based on racial considerations. In denying petitioner's motion for summary [387 U.S. 369, 373] judgment the trial court found it unnecessary to consider the validity of Proposition 14 because it concluded that judicial enforcement of an eviction based on racial grounds would in any event violate the Equal Protection Clause of the United States Constitution. 4 The cross-complaint was dismissed with prejudice and petitioner Snyder appealed to the California Supreme Court which considered the case along with *Mulkey v. Reitman*. That court, in reversing the Reitman case, held that Art. I, 26, was invalid as denying the equal protection of the laws guaranteed by the Fourteenth Amendment. For similar reasons, the court affirmed the judgment in the Prendergast case. We granted certiorari because the cases involve an important issue arising under the Fourteenth Amendment. We affirm the judgments of the California Supreme Court. We first turn to the opinion of that court in *Reitman*, which quite properly undertook to examine the constitutionality of 26 in terms of its "immediate objective," its "ultimate effect" and its "historical context and the conditions existing prior to its enactment." Judgments such as these we have frequently undertaken ourselves. But here the California Supreme Court has addressed itself to these matters and we should give careful consideration to its views because they concern the purpose, scope, and operative effect of a provision of the California Constitution.

C Affirmed.

Brentwood Academy v. Tennessee Secondary School Athletic Assn. 531 U.S. 288 (2001)

FACTS

Respondent not-for-profit athletic association (Association) regulates interscholastic sport among Tennessee public and private high schools. Most of the State's public high schools are members, representing 84% of the Association's membership. School officials make up the voting membership of the Association's governing council and control board, which typically hold meetings during regular school hours. The Association is largely funded by gate receipts. Association staff, although not state employees, may join the state retirement system. The Association sets membership standards and student eligibility rules and has the power to penalize any member school that violates those rules. The State Board of Education (State Board) has long acknowledged the Association's role in regulating interscholastic competition in public schools, and its members sit as nonvoting members of the Association's governing bodies. When the Association penalized petitioner Brentwood Academy for violating a recruiting rule, Brentwood sued the Association and its executive director under 42 U. S. C. §1983, claiming that the rule's enforcement was state action that violated the First and Fourteenth Amendments. The District Court granted Brentwood summary judgment, enjoining the rule's enforcement, but the Sixth Circuit found no state action and reversed.

I

Can a private entity be considered a state actor under any circumstances?

R

A private entity will be considered a state actor when it is so "entwined" with the state as to be considered acting as the state itself (in terms of state actions).

A

The Association's regulatory activity is state action owing to the pervasive entwinement of state school officials in the Association's structure, there being no offsetting reason to see the Association's acts in any other way. State action may be found only if there is such a "close nexus between the State and the challenged action" that seemingly private behavior "may be fairly treated as that of the State itself." *Jackson* v. *Metropolitan Edison Co.* No one fact is a necessary condition for finding state action, nor is any set of circumstances sufficient, for there may be some countervailing reason against attributing activity to the government. The facts that can bear on an attribution's fairness - *e.g.,* a nominally private entity may be a state actor when it is entwined with governmental policies or when government is entwined in its management or control, *Evans* v. *Newton* - unequivocally show that a legal entity's character is determined neither by its expressly private characterization in statutory law, nor by the law's failure to acknowledge its inseparability from recognized government officials or agencies. In *National Collegiate Athletic Assn.* v. *Tarkanian,* this Court anticipated that state action could be found when there is public entwinement in the management or control of an organization whose member public schools are all within a single State. The necessarily fact-bound inquiry leads to the conclusion of state action here. The Association's nominally private character is overborne by the pervasive entwinement of public institutions and public officials in its composition and workings, and there is no substantial reason to claim unfairness in applying constitutional standards to it. To the extent of 84% of its membership, the Association is an organization of public schools represented by their officials acting in their official capacity to provide an integral element of secondary public schooling, interscholastic athletics. There would be no recognizable Association without the public school officials, who overwhelmingly determine and perform all but the Association's purely ministerial acts. Only the 16% minority of private school memberships keeps the entwinement of the Association and public schools from being total and their identities totally indistinguishable. To complement the entwinement from the bottom up, the State has provided entwinement from the top down: State Board members sit ex officio on the Association's governing bodies and Association employees participate in the state retirement system. Entwinement to the degree shown here requires that the Association be charged with a public character and judged by constitutional standards. Entwinement is also the answer to the Association's several arguments that the instant facts would not support a state action finding under various other criteria, *e.g.*, the public function test. Although facts showing public action may be outweighed in the name of a value at odds with finding public accountability in the circumstances, *e.g., Polk County* v. *Dodson*, no such countervailing value is present here. The Association's fear that reversing the judgment will trigger an epidemic of federal litigation is unfounded. Save for the Sixth Circuit, every Court of Appeals to consider a statewide athletic association like this one has found it to be a state actor, and there has been no litigation explosion in those jurisdictions; nor should the Association have dispensation merely because the public schools themselves are state actors subject to suit under §1983 and Title IX of the Education Amendments of 1972.

C

Reversed and remanded.

Allgeyer v. Louisiana

165 U.S. 578 (1897)

FACTS

Foreign corporations were conditionally banned from doing business with the state of Louisiana. Under that law, a foreign corporation can only conduct business within the state if (1) it has one or more known places of business and (2) has an authorized agent within the state. The rule was applied against Atlantic Mutual Insurance Company, whose business is confined with the state of New York. The suit is based upon a letter mailed from the New York Insurance Company to a Louisiana resident, one Allgeyer. The letter was a notice to the resident of property to be covered by an insurance contract entered into the state of New York and carried out within that state.

I

Can a state block a foreign corporation from conducting any and all business within it boards subject to its laws?

R

The 14th Amendment guarantees the right of "liberty" which includes the right of a citizen to be free from physical restraint and to enjoy all the facilities and to use them in lawful ways.

A

The 14th Amendment guarantees the right of "liberty" which includes the right of a citizen to be free from physical restraint and to enjoy all the facilities and to use them in lawful ways.

C

Reversed.

Lochner v. New York

198 U.S. 45 (1905)

FACTS

Defendant Lochner was convicted and fined for "wrongfully and unlawfully . . . [permit] an employee working for him in his biscuit, bread, and cake bakery and confectionery establishment, at the city of Utica, in this county, to work more than sixty hours in one week," pursuant to a law passed by the State of New York which prohibited such employees from working more than 10 hours a day (or 60 hours a week). The case eventually came before the U.S. Supreme Court for review.

I

Is a law that infringes on a person's freedom to contract unconstitutional when it lacks, for the most part, a reasonable relation to a legitimate legislative purpose?

R

The general right to make a contract in relation to his business is part of the liberty protected by the Fourteenth Amendment, and this includes the right to purchase and sell labor, except as controlled by the State in the legitimate exercise of its police power.

A

The indictment averred that the defendant 'wrongfully and unlawfully required and permitted an employee working for him in his biscuit, bread, and cake bakery and confectionery establishment, at the city of Utica, in this county, to work more than sixty hours in one week,' after having been theretofore convicted of a violation of the name act; and therefore, as averred, he committed the crime of misdemeanor, second offense. The plaintiff in error demurred to the indictment on several grounds, one of which was that the facts stated did not constitute a crime. The demurrer was overruled, and, the plaintiff in error having refused to plead further, a plea of not guilty was entered by order of the court and the trial commenced, and he was convicted of misdemeanor, second offense, as indicted, and sentenced to pay a fine of $ 50, and to stand committed until paid, not to exceed fifty days in the Oneida County jail. A certificate of reasonable doubt was granted by the county judge of Oneida County whereon an appeal was taken to the appellate division of the supreme court, fourth department, where the judgment of conviction was affirmed. A further appeal was then taken to the court of appeals, where the judgment of conviction was again affirmed. We now turn to the merits of the case. Liberty of contract relating to labor includes both parties to it; the one has as much right to purchase as the other to sell labor. There is no reasonable ground, on the score of health, for interfering with the liberty of the person or the right of free contract, by determining the hours of labor, in the occupation of a baker. Nor can a law limiting such hours be justified as a health law to safeguard the public health, or the health of the individuals following that occupation. Section 110 of the labor law of the State of New York, providing that no employees shall be required or permitted to work in bakeries more than sixty hours in a week, or ten hours a day, is not a legitimate exercise of the police power of the State, but an unreasonable, unnecessary and arbitrary interference with the right and liberty of the individual to contract in relation to labor, and, as such, it is in conflict with, and void under, the Federal Constitution. Yet the power of the state is not impotent in all instances. The state has power to prevent the individual from making certain kinds of contracts, and in regard to them the Federal Constitution offers no protection. If the contract be one which the state, in the legitimate exercise of its police power, has the right to prohibit, it is not prevented from prohibiting it by the 14th Amendment. Contracts in violation of a statute, either of the Federal or state government, or a contract to let one's property for immoral purposes, or to do any other unlawful act, could obtain no protection from the Federal Constitution, as coming under the liberty of person or of free contract. The judgment of the Court of Appeals of New York, as well as that of the Supreme Court and of the County Court of Oneida County, must be reversed and the case remanded to the County Court for further proceedings not inconsistent with this opinion.

C

Reversed.

Coppage v. Kansas

236 U.S. 1 (1915)

FACTS

The State of Kansas employed Plaintiff Coppage. Coppage was convicted upon an information charging him with violation of a state law which made it a crime for any employer offering employment to another on condition that that prospective employee not join a union.

I Is it a valid exercise of a state's police powers to made it a crime for any employer offering employment to another on condition that that prospective employee not join a union?

R The freedom to contract includes the right to make contracts affecting personal employment without arbitrary interference by the state.

A In *Adair v. United States*, this court had to deal with a question not distinguishable in principle from the one now presented. Congress had enacted 'that any employer subject to the provisions of this act, and any officer, agent, or receiver of such employer, who shall require any employee, or any person seeking employment, as a condition of such employment, to enter into an agreement, either written or verbal, not to become or remain a member of any labor corporation, association, or organization; or shall threaten any employee with loss of employment, or shall unjustly discriminate against any employee because of his membership in such a labor corporation, association, or organization . . . is hereby declared to be guilty of a misdemeanor, and, upon conviction thereof . . . shall be punished for each offense by a fine of not less than one hundred dollars and not more than one thousand dollars.' Adair was convicted upon an indictment charging that he, as agent of a common carrier subject to the provisions of the act, unjustly discriminated against a certain employee by discharging him from the employ of the carrier because of his membership in a labor organization. The court held that portion of the act upon which the conviction rested to be an invasion of the personal liberty as well as of the right of property guaranteed by the 5th Amendment, which declares that no person shall be deprived of liberty or property without due process of law. Speaking by Mr. Justice Harlan, the court said: 'While, as already suggested, the right of liberty and property guaranteed by the Constitution against deprivation without due process of law is subject to such reasonable restraints as the common good or the general welfare may require, it is not within the functions of government-at least, in the absence of contract between the parties-to compel any person in the course of his business and against his will to accept or retain the personal services of another, or to compel any person, against his will, to perform personal services for another. The right of a person to sell his labor upon such terms as he deems proper is, in its essence, the same as the right of the purchaser of labor to prescribe the conditions upon which he will accept such labor from the person offering to sell it. So the right of the employee to quit the service of the employer, for whatever reason, is the same as the right of the employer, for whatever reason, to dispense with the services of such employee. It was the legal right of the defendant Adair-however unwise such a course might have been-to discharge Coppage [the employee in that case] because of his being a member of a labor organization, as it was the legal right of Coppage, if he saw fit to do so,-however unwise such a course on his part might have been,-to quit the service in which he was engaged, because the defendant employed some persons who were not members of a labor organization. In all such particulars the employer and the employee have equality of right, and any legislation that disturbs that equality is an arbitrary interference with the liberty of contract, which no government can legally justify in a free land.' Unless it is to be overruled, this decision is controlling upon the present controversy; for if Congress is prevented from arbitrary interference with the liberty of contract because of the 'due process' provision of the 5th Amendment, it is too clear for argument that the states are prevented from the like interference by virtue of the corresponding clause of the 14th Amendment; and hence, if it be unconstitutional for Congress to deprive an employer of liberty or property for threatening an employee with loss of employment, or discriminating against him because of his membership in a labor organization, it is unconstitutional for a state to similarly punish an employer for requiring his employee, as a condition of securing or retaining employment, to agree not to become or remain a member of such an organization while so employed.

C

Reversed.

Muller v. Oregon

208 U.S. 412 (1908)

FACTS

On February 19, 1903, the legislature of the state of Oregon passed an act (Session Laws 1903, p. 148) the first section of which is in these words: 'Sec. 1. That no female (shall) be employed in any mechanical establishment, or factory, or laundry in this state more than ten hours during any one day. The hours of work may be so arranged as to permit the employment of females at any time so that they shall not work more than ten hours during the twenty-four hours of any one day.' Plaintiff Muller was convicted of violating the law.

I

Is a state law stetting the maximum allowable hours a woman could work in certain types of jobs a valid exercise of the state's police powers?

R

The right to contract is subject to reasonable restrictions placed upon it by the government; it is not absolute.

A

History discloses the fact that woman has always been dependent upon man. He established his control at the outset by superior physical strength, may, without conflicting with the provisions and this control in various forms, with diminishing intensity, has continued to the present. As minors, thought not to the same extent, she has been looked upon in the courts as needing especial care that her rights may be preserved. Education was long denied her, and while now the doors of the schoolroom are opened and her opportunities for acquiring knowledge are great, yet even with that and the consequent increase of capacity for business affairs it is still true that in the struggle for subsistence she is not an equal competitor with her brother. Though limitations upon personal and contractual rights may be removed by legislation, there is that in her disposition and habits of life which will operate against a full assertion of those rights. She will still be where some legislation to protect her seems necessary to secure a real equality of right. Doubtless there are individual exceptions, and there are many respects in which she has an advantage over him; but looking at it from the viewpoint of the effort to maintain an independent position in life, she is not upon an equality. Differentiated by these matters from the other sex, she is properly placed in a class by herself, and legislation designed for her protection may be sustained, even when like legislation is not necessary for men, and could not be sustained. It is impossible to close one's eyes to the fact that she still looks to her brother and depends upon him. Even though all restrictions on political, personal, and contractual rights were taken away, and she stood, so far as statutes are concerned, upon an absolutely equal plane with him, it would still be true that she is so constituted that she will rest upon and look to him for protection; that her physical structure and a proper discharge of her maternal functions-having in view not merely her own health, but the well-being of the race-justify legislation to protect her from the greed as well as the passion of man. The limitations which this statute places upon her contractual powers, upon her right to agree with her employer as to the time she shall labor, are not imposed solely for her benefit, but also largely for the benefit of all. Many words cannot make this plainer. The two sexes differ in structure of body, in the functions to be performed by each, in the amount of physical strength, in the capacity for long continued labor, particularly when done standing, the influence of vigorous health upon the future well-being of the race, the self-reliance which enables one to assert full rights, and in the capacity to maintain the struggle for subsistence. This difference [208 U.S. 412, 423] justifies a difference in legislation, and upholds that which is designed to compensate for some of the burdens which rest upon her. We have not referred in this discussion to the denial of the elective franchise in the state of Oregon, for while that may disclose a lack of political equality in all things with her brother, that is not of itself decisive. The reason runs deeper, and rests in the inherent difference between the two sexes, and in the different functions in life which they perform. For these reasons, and without questioning in any respect the decision in *Lochner v. New York*, we are of the opinion that it cannot be adjudged that the act in question is in conflict with the Federal Constitution, so far as it respects the work of a female in a laundry, and the judgment of the Supreme Court of Oregon is affirmed.

C

Affirmed.

Weaver v. Palmer Bros. Co.

270 U.S. 402 (1926)

FACTS

Appellee is a Connecticut corporation, and for more than 50 years it and its founders have manufactured comfortables in that state, and have sold them there and in other states. An act of the Legislature of Pennsylvania regulates the manufacture, sterilization, and sale of bedding and prohibits the selling of comfortables made with shoddy [woolen yarn made from scraps or used clothing, with some new wool added] materials. The act took effect January 1, 1924. Appellant is charged with its enforcement, and threatened to proceed against the appellee and its customers. January 29, 1924, appellee brought this suit to enjoin the enforcement of the act on the grounds, among others, that, as applied to the business of appellee, it is repugnant to the due process and equal protection clauses of the Fourteenth Amendment. An application under section 266 of the Judicial Code for a temporary injunction was denied. The decree was affirmed by this court. Later defendant answered, and there was a trial at which much evidence was introduced. The District Court found that the statute infringes appellee's constitutional rights in so far as it absolutely prohibits the use of shoddy in the manufacture of comfortables; and to that extent the decree restrains its enforcement. This appeal followed.

I

Is the provision purporting absolutely to forbid the use of shoddy in comfortables violative of the due process clause or the equal protection clause?

R

Laws protecting the public's health must be the only reasonable way of eliminating a known health threat.

A

The record shows that annually many million pounds of fabric, new and secondhand, are made into shoddy. The evidence is to the effect that practically all the woolen cloth woven in this country contains some shoddy. Comfortables made of secondhand shoddy sell at lower prices than those filled with other materials. Appellant claims that, in order properly to protect health, bedding material should be sterilized. The record shows that, for the sterilization of secondhand materials from which it makes shoddy, appellee uses effective steam sterilizers. There is no controversy between the parties as to whether shoddy may be rendered harmless by disinfection or sterilization. While it is sometimes made from filthy rags, and from other materials that have been exposed to infection, it stands undisputed that all dangers to health may be eliminated by appropriate treatment at low cost. There was no evidence that any sickness or disease was ever caused by the use of shoddy, and the record contains persuasive evidence, and by citation discloses the opinions of scientists eminent in fields related to public health that the transmission of disease-producing bacteria is almost entirely by immediate contact with, or close proximity to, infected persons; that such bacteria perish rapidly when separated from human or animal organisms; and that there is no probability that such bacteria or vermin likely to carry them survive after the period usually required for the gathering of the materials, the production of shoddy, and the manufacture and the shipping of comfortables. This evidence tends strongly to show that in the absence of sterilization or disinfection there would be little, if any, danger to the health of the users of comfortables filled with shoddy, new or secondhand; and confirms the conclusion that all danger from the use of shoddy may be eliminated by sterilization. The state has wide discretion in selecting things for regulation. We need not consider whether the mere failure to forbid the use of other filling materials that are mentioned in the act is sufficient in itself to invalidate the provision prohibiting the use of shoddy, as a violation of the equal protection clause. But the number and character of the things permitted to be used in such manufacture properly may be taken into account in deciding whether the prohibition of shoddy is a reasonable and valid regulation or is arbitrary and violative of the due process clause. Shoddy-filled comfortables made by appellee are useful articles for which there is much demand; and it is a matter of public concern that the production and sale of things necessary or convenient for use should not be forbidden. They are to be distinguished from things that the state is deemed to have power to suppress as inherently dangerous.

C

Decree affirmed.

Nebbia v. New York

291 U.S. 502 (1934)

FACTS

During 1932 the prices received by farmers for milk were much below the cost of production. The decline in prices during 1931 and 1932 was much greater than that of prices generally. The situation of the families of dairy producers had become desperate and called for state aid similar to that afforded the unemployed, if conditions should not improve. On March 10, 1932, the Legislature of New York established by chapter 158 of the Laws of 1933, a Milk Control Board with power, among other things to "fix minimum and maximum ... retail prices to be charged by ... stores to consumers for consumption off the premises where sold." The board fixed 9¢ as the price to be charged by a store for a quart of milk. Defendant-petitioner Nebbia, the proprietor of a grocery store in Rochester, New York, sold two quarts and a 5¢ loaf of bread for 18¢ and was convicted for violating the board's order. At his trial he asserted the statute and order contravene the equal protection clause and the due process clause of the Fourteenth Amendment, and renewed the contention in successive appeals to the county court and Court of Appeals. Both overruled his claim and affirmed the conviction. The U.S. Supreme Court granted review.

I

Does the Federal Constitution prohibit a state from so fixing the selling price of milk when its price control measures are nondiscriminatory and bear a reasonable relation to an important governmental purpose?

R

Price controls that are nondiscriminatory and bear a reasonable relation to a proper legislative purpose are constitutional.

A

The fluid milk industry is affected by factors of instability peculiar to itself which call for special methods of control. Under the best practicable adjustment of supply to demand the industry must carry a surplus of about 20%, because milk, an essential food, must be available as demanded by consumers every day in the year, and demand and supply vary from day to day and according to the reason; but milk is perishable and cannot be stored. Close adjustment of supply to demand is hindered by several factors difficult to control. Thus surplus milk presents a serious problem, as the prices which can be realized for it for other uses are much less than those obtainable for milk sold for consumption in fluid form or as cream. A satisfactory stabilization of prices for fluid milk requires that the burden of surplus milk be shared equally by all producers and all distributors in the milk shed. So long as the surplus burden is unequally distributed the pressure to market surplus milk in fluid form will be a serious disturbing factor. The fact that the larger distributors find it necessary to carry large quantities of surplus milk, while the smaller distributors do not, leads to price-cutting and other forms of destructive competition. Smaller distributors, who take no responsibility for the surplus, by purchasing their milk at the blended prices (i.e., an average between the price paid the producer for milk for sale as fluid milk, and the lower surplus milk price paid by the larger organizations) can undersell the larger distributors. Indulgence in this price-cutting often compels the larger dealer to cut the price to his own and the producer's detriment. Various remedies were suggested, and the

Legislature adopted chapter 158 as a method of correcting the evils. We turn now to the appellant's arguments. The appellant first urges that the order of the Milk Control Board denies him the equal protection of the laws. It is shown that the order requires him, if he purchases his supply from a dealer, to pay 8¢ per quart and 5¢ per pint, and to resell at not less than 9¢ and 6¢, whereas the same dealer may buy his supply from a farmer at lower prices and deliver milk to consumers at 10¢ the quart and 6¢ the pint. We disagree. Appellant purchased his supply of milk from a farmer as do distributors, or could have procured it from a dealer if he so desired. There is therefore no showing that the order placed him at a disadvantage, or in fact affected him adversely. This point alone is fatal to his claim of denial of equal protection. The appellant next argues that in the light of the conditions disclosed, the enforcement of section 312(e) denied the appellant the due process secured to him by the 14th Amendment. The Constitution does not guarantee the unrestricted privilege to engage in a business or to conduct it as one pleases. Certain kinds of business may be prohibited; and the right to conduct a business may be conditioned. Regulation of a business to prevent waste of the state's resources may be justified. And statutes prescribing the terms upon which those conducting certain businesses may contract are within the state's powers. So far as the requirement of due process is concerned, and in the absence of other constitutional restriction, a state is free to adopt whatever economic policy may reasonably be deemed to promote public welfare and to enforce that policy by legislation adapted to its purpose. The courts are without authority either to declare such policy, or, when it is declared by the legislature, to override it. If the laws passed are seen to have a reasonable relation to a proper legislative purpose, and are neither arbitrary nor discriminatory, the requirements of due process are satisfied, and judicial determination to that effect renders a court *functus officio* (something which once had life and power, but which now has no virtue whatsoever). And it is equally clear that if the legislative policy is to curb unrestrained and harmful competition by measures which are not arbitrary or discriminatory it does not lie with the courts to determine that the rule is unwise. If the lawmaking body, within its sphere of government, concludes that the conditions or practices in an industry make unrestricted competition an inadequate safeguard of the consumer's interests, produce waste harmful to the public, threaten ultimately to cut off the supply of a commodity needed by the public, appropriate statutes passed in an honest effort to correct the threatened consequences may not be set aside because the regulation adopted fixes prices reasonably deemed by the Legislature to be fair to those engaged in the industry and to the consuming public. And this is especially so where, as here, the economic maladjustment is one of price, which threatens harm to the producer at one end of the series and the consumer at the other. The Constitution does not secure to any one liberty to conduct his business in such fashion as to inflict injury upon the public at large, or upon any substantial group of the people. Price control, like any other form of regulation, is unconstitutional only if arbitrary, discriminatory, or demonstrably irrelevant to the policy the Legislature is free to adopt. Tested by these considerations we find no basis in the due process clause of the Fourteenth Amendment for condemning the provisions of the Agriculture and Markets Law here drawn into question.

C

The judgment is affirmed.

West Coast Hotel Co. v. Parrish

300 U.S. 379 (1937)

FACTS

This case presents the question of the constitutional validity of the minimum wage law of the state of Washington. The act, entitled 'Minimum Wages for Women,' authorizes the fixing of minimum wages for women and minors. The appellant conducts a hotel. The appellee Elsie Parrish was employed as a chambermaid and (with her husband) brought this suit to recover the difference between the wages paid her and the minimum wage fixed pursuant to the state law. The minimum wage was $14.50 per week of 48 hours. The appellant challenged the act as repugnant to the due process clause of the Fourteenth Amendment of the Constitution of the United States. The Supreme Court of the state, reversing the trial court, sustained the statute and directed judgment for the plaintiffs. The case now comes before the U.S. Supreme Court on appeal.

I

Is a state law setting the minimum wage a woman can earn a valid exercise of the state's police power?

R

Regulation that is reasonable in its relation to its subject and is adopted in the interests of the public comports with the Due Process Clause of the 14th Amendment.

A

The principle which must control our decision is not in doubt. The constitutional provision invoked is the due process clause of the Fourteenth Amendment governing the states, as the due process clause invoked in the *Adkins* Case governed Congress. In each case the violation alleged by those attacking minimum wage regulations for women is deprivation of freedom of contract. What is this freedom? The Constitution does not speak of freedom of contract. It speaks of liberty and prohibits the deprivation of liberty without due process of law. In prohibiting that deprivation, the Constitution does not recognize an absolute and uncontrollable liberty. Liberty in each of its phases has its history and connotation. But the liberty safeguarded is liberty in a social organization which requires the protection of law against the evils which menace the health, safety, morals, and welfare of the people. Liberty under the Constitution is thus necessarily subject to the restraints of due process, and regulation which is reasonable in relation to its subject and is adopted in the interests of the community is due process. This essential limitation of liberty in general governs freedom of contract in particular. More than twenty-five years ago we set forth the applicable principle in these words, after referring to the cases where the liberty guaranteed by the Fourteenth Amendment had been broadly described. We think that the views thus expressed are sound and that the decision in the Adkins Case was a departure from the true application of the principles governing the regulation by the state of the relation of employer and employed. Those principles have been reinforced by our subsequent decisions. Thus in *Radice v. New York,* we sustained the New York statute which restricted the employment of women in restaurants at night. In *O'Gorman & Young v. Hartford Fire Insurance Company*, which upheld an act regulating the commissions of insurance agents, we pointed to the presumption of the constitutionality of a statute dealing with a subject within the scope of the police power and to the absence of any factual foundation of record for deciding that the limits of power had been transcended.

West Coast Hotel Co. v. Parrish

300 U.S. 379 (1937)

In *Nebbia v. New York*, dealing with the New York statute providing for minimum prices for milk, the general subject of the regulation of the use of private property and of the making of private contracts received an exhaustive examination, and we again declared that if such laws 'have a reasonable relation to a proper legislative purpose, and are neither arbitrary nor discriminatory, the requirements of due process are satisfied'; that 'with the wisdom of the policy adopted, with the adequacy or practicability of the law enacted to forward it, the courts are both incompetent and unauthorized to deal'; that 'times without number we have said that the Legislature is primarily the judge of the necessity of such an enactment, that every possible presumption is in favor of its validity, and that though the court may hold views inconsistent with the wisdom of the law, it may not be annulled unless palpably in excess of legislative power.' With full recognition of the earnestness and vigor which characterize the prevailing opinion in the *Adkins* Case, we find it impossible to reconcile that ruling with these well-considered declarations. Our conclusion, therefore, is that the case of *Adkins v. Children's Hospital*, supra, should be, and it is, overruled. The judgment of the Supreme Court of the state of Washington is affirmed.

C

Affirmed.

United States v. Carolene Products Co.

304 U.S. 144 (1938)

FACTS

Appellee was indicted in the District Court for Southern Illinois for violation of the act by the shipment in interstate commerce of certain packages of 'Milnut,' a compound of condensed skimmed milk and coconut oil made in imitation or semblance of condensed milk or cream. The indictment states, in the words of the statute, section 2, 21 U.S.C.A. 62, that Milnut 'is an adulterated article of food, injurious to the public health,' and that it is not a prepared food product of the type excepted from the prohibition of the act. The trial court sustained a demurrer to the indictment on the authority of an earlier case in the same court. The case was brought here on appeal under the Criminal Appeals Act of March 2, 1907. The Court of Appeals for the Seventh Circuit has meanwhile, in another case, upheld the Filled Milk Act as an appropriate exercise of the commerce power in *Carolene Products Co. v. Evaporated Milk Association.*

I

Does the 'Filled Milk Act' of Congress, which prohibits the shipment in interstate commerce of skimmed milk compounded with any fat or oil other than milk fat, so as to resemble milk or cream, transcend the power of Congress to regulate interstate commerce or infringes the Fifth Amendment?

R

When reviewing legislation, the existence of facts supporting legislations must be presumed and not be pronounced unconstitutional unless the assumption to presume otherwise is supported by some rational basis.

A

Appellee assails the statute as beyond the power of Congress over interstate commerce, and hence an invasion of a field of action said to be reserved to the states by the Tenth Amendment. Appellee also complains that the statute denies to it equal protection of the laws, and in violation of the Fifth Amendment, deprives it of its property without due process of law, particularly in that the statute purports to make binding and conclusive upon appellee the legislative declaration that appellee's product 'is an adulterated article of food, injurious to the public health, and its sale constitutes a fraud on the public.' We disagree. The prohibition of shipment of appellee's product in interstate commerce does not infringe the Fifth Amendment. Twenty years ago this Court, in *Hebe Co. v. Shaw*, held that a state law which forbids the manufacture and sale of a product assumed to be wholesome and nutritive, made of condensed skimmed milk, compounded with coconut oil, is not forbidden by the Fourteenth Amendment. The power of the Legislature to secure a minimum of particular nutritive elements in a widely used article of food and to protect the public from fraudulent substitutions was not doubted; and the Court thought that there was ample scope for the legislative judgment that prohibition of the offending article was an appropriate means of preventing injury to the public. We see no persuasive reason for departing from that ruling here, where the Fifth Amendment is concerned; and since none is suggested, we might rest decision wholly on the presumption of constitutionality. But affirmative evidence also sustains the statute. In twenty years evidence has steadily accumulated of the danger to the public health from the general consumption of foods which have been stripped of elements essential to the maintenance of health. The Filled Milk Act was adopted by Congress after committee hearings, in the course of which eminent scientists and health experts testified. An extensive investigation was made of the commerce in milk compounds in which vegetable oils have been substituted for natural milk fat, and of the effect upon the public health of the use of such compounds as a food substitute for milk. The conclusions drawn from evidence presented at the hearings were embodied in reports of the House Committees on Agriculture. Both committees concluded, as the statute itself declares, that the use of filled milk as a substitute for pure milk is generally injurious to health and facilitates fraud on the public. The prohibition of shipment in interstate commerce of appellee's product, as described in the indictment, is a constitutional exercise of the power to regulate interstate commerce. As the statute is not unconstitutional on its face, the demurrer should have been overruled and the judgment will be reversed.

C

Affirmed.

Williamson v. Lee Optical

348 U.S. 483 (1955)

FACTS

An Oklahoma law (59 Okla. Stat. Ann. 941-947, Okla. Laws 1953, c. 13, 2-8) prohibits opticians and other persons who are not licensed optometrists or ophthalmologists from dispensing lenses or fitting lenses into frames, except upon a written prescription from an optometrist or ophthalmologist. The law also prohibits the solicitation for sale of eyeglass frames. A suit was instituted in the District Court to have the Oklahoma law declared unconstitutional and to enjoin state officials from enforcing it for the reason that it allegedly violated various provisions of the Federal Constitution. The matter was heard by a District Court of three judges, as required by 28 U.S.C. 2281. The District Court held unconstitutional portions of three sections of the Act. First, it held invalid under the Due Process Clause of the Fourteenth Amendment the portions of 2 which make it unlawful for any person not a licensed optometrist or ophthalmologist to fit lenses to a face or to duplicate or replace into frames lenses or other optical appliances, except upon written prescriptive authority of an Oklahoma licensed ophthalmologist or optometrist. The case comes before the U.S Supreme Court on Appeal pursuant to 28 U.S.C. 1253.

I

May an act of economic regulation be upheld if there is exists a minimal rational basis for the legislation?

R

As long as there is at least some conceivable justification for the legislation, states are free to regulate economic interests and the court will not overturn them.

A

An ophthalmologist is a duly licensed physician who specializes in the care of the eyes. An optometrist examines eyes for refractive error, recognizes (but does not treat) diseases of the eye, and fills prescriptions for eyeglasses. The optician is an artisan qualified to grind lenses, fill prescriptions, and fit frames. The effect of the statute is to forbid the optician from fitting or duplicating lenses without a prescription from an ophthalmologist or optometrist. In practical effect, it means that no optician can fit old glasses into new frames or supply a lens, whether it be a new lens or one to duplicate a lost or broken lens, without a prescription. The District Court conceded that it was in the competence of the police power of a State to regulate the examination of the eyes. But it resisted the notion that a State could require a prescription from an optometrist or ophthalmologist "to take old lenses and place them in new frames and then fit the completed spectacles to the face of the eyeglass wearer." It held that such a requirement was not "reasonably and rationally related to the health and welfare of the people." It was, accordingly, the opinion of that court that this provision of the law violated the Due Process Clause by arbitrarily interfering with the optician's right to do business. The Oklahoma law may exact a needless, wasteful requirement in many cases. But it is for the legislature, not the courts, to balance the advantages and disadvantages of the new requirement. It appears that in many cases the optician can easily supply the new frames or new lenses without reference to the old written prescription. It also appears that many written prescriptions contain no directive data in regard to fitting spectacles to the face. But in some cases the directions contained in the prescription are essential, if the glasses are to be fitted so as to correct the particular defects of vision or alleviate the eye condition. The legislature might have concluded that the frequency of occasions when a prescription is necessary was sufficient to justify this regulation of the fitting of eyeglasses. The law need not be in every respect logically consistent with its aims to be constitutional. It is enough that there is an evil at hand for correction, and that it might be thought that the particular legislative measure was a rational way to correct it. We reject also the District Court's view that the law violated the Equal Protection Clause of the 14th Amendment by subjecting opticians to this regulatory system and to exempt all sellers of ready-to-wear glasses. The prohibition of the Equal Protection Clause goes no further than the invidious discrimination. We cannot say that that point has been reached here. For all this record shows, the ready-to-wear branch of this business may not loom large in Oklahoma or may present problems of regulation distinct from the other branch. We similarly do not agree with the District Court's finding that that part of the law which makes it unlawful "to solicit the sale of . . . frames, mountings . . . or any other optical appliances" was unconstitutional as violative of the Due Process Clause. An eyeglass frame, considered in isolation, is only a piece of merchandise. But an eyeglass frame is not used in isolation; it is used with lenses; and lenses, pertaining as they do to the human eye, enter the field of health. Therefore, the legislature might conclude that to regulate one effectively it would have to regulate the other. Or it might conclude that both the sellers of frames and the sellers of lenses were in a business where advertising should be limited or even abolished in the public interest. We see no constitutional reason why a State may not treat all who deal with the human eye as members of a profession who should use no merchandising methods for obtaining customers. Last, we reject the District Court holding as unconstitutional and as violative of the Due Process Clause of the Fourteenth Amendment, the provision of the Act which provides that, "No person, firm, or corporation engaged in the business of retailing merchandise to the general public shall rent space, sublease departments, or otherwise permit any person purporting to do eye examination or visual care to occupy space in such retail store." It seems to us that this regulation is on the same constitutional footing as the denial to corporations of the right to practice dentistry. It is an attempt to free the profession, to as great an extent as possible, from all taints of commercialism. It certainly might be easy for an optometrist with space in a retail store to be merely a front for the retail establishment. In any case, the opportunity for that nexus may be too great for safety, if the eye doctor is allowed inside the retail store. Moreover, it may be deemed important to effective regulation that the eye doctor be restricted to geographical locations that reduce the temptations of commercialism. Geographical location may be an important consideration in a legislative program which aims to raise the treatment of the human eye to a strictly professional level. We cannot say that the regulation has no rational relation to that objective and therefore is beyond constitutional bounds.

C Affirmed in part and reversed in part.

BMW of North America v. Gore

517 U.S. 559 (1996)

FACTS

After respondent Gore purchased a new BMW automobile from an authorized Alabama dealer, he discovered that the car had been repainted. He brought this suit for compensatory and punitive damages against petitioner, the American distributor of BMW's, alleging, *inter alia*, that the failure to disclose the repainting constituted fraud under Alabama law. At trial, BMW acknowledged that it followed a nationwide policy of not advising its dealers, and hence their customers, of pre-delivery damage to new cars when the cost of repair did not exceed 3 percent of the car's suggested retail price. Gore's vehicle fell into that category. The jury returned a verdict finding BMW liable for compensatory damages of $4,000, and assessing $4 million in punitive damages. The trial judge denied BMW's post-trial motion to set aside the punitive damages award, holding, among other things, that the award was not "grossly excessive" and thus did not violate the Due Process Clause of the Fourteenth Amendment. The Alabama Supreme Court agreed, but reduced the award to $2 million on the ground that, in computing the amount, the jury had improperly multiplied Gore's compensatory damages by the number of similar sales in all States, not just those in Alabama.

I May a state constitutionally impose any amount of economic sanctions in the form of punitive damages?

R A state may not constitutionally impose any amount of economic sanctions in the form of punitive damages; where a punitive damage award is characterized as excessive (where the legitimate interests in deterring the conduct to be barred is arbitrary and excessive in relation to the conduct at issue) a violation of the due process clause of the 14th Amendment will be found.

A The $2 million punitive damages award is grossly excessive and therefore exceeds the constitutional limit. Because such an award violates due process only when it can fairly be categorized as "grossly excessive" in relation to the State's legitimate interests in punishing unlawful conduct and deterring its repetition, the federal excessiveness inquiry appropriately begins with an identification of the state interests that such an award is designed to serve. Principles of state sovereignty and comity forbid a State to enact policies for the entire Nation, or to impose its own policy choice on neighboring States. Accordingly, the economic penalties that a State inflicts on those who transgress its laws, whether the penalties are legislatively authorized fines or judicially imposed punitive damages, must be supported by the State's interest in protecting its own consumers and economy, rather than those of other States or the entire Nation. Gore's award must therefore be analyzed in the light of conduct that occurred solely within Alabama, with consideration being given only to the interests of Alabama consumers. Elementary notions of fairness enshrined in this Court's constitutional jurisprudence dictate that a person receive fair notice not only of the conduct that will subject him to punishment but also of the severity of the penalty that a State may impose. Three guideposts, each of which indicates that BMW did not receive adequate notice of the magnitude of the sanction that Alabama might impose, lead to the conclusion that the $2 million award is grossly excessive. None of the aggravating factors associated with the first (and perhaps most important) indicium of a punitive damages award's excessiveness - the degree of reprehensibility of the defendant's conduct - is present here. The harm BMW inflicted on Gore was purely economic; the presale repainting had no effect on the car's performance, safety features, or appearance; and BMW's conduct evinced no indifference to or reckless disregard for the health and safety of others. Gore's contention that BMW's nondisclosure was particularly reprehensible because it formed part of a nationwide pattern of tortious conduct is rejected, because a corporate executive could reasonably have interpreted the relevant state statutes as establishing safe harbors for nondisclosure of presumptively minor repairs, and because there is no evidence either that BMW acted in bad faith when it sought to establish the appropriate line between minor damage and damage requiring disclosure to purchasers, or that it persisted in its course of conduct after it had been adjudged unlawful. Finally, there is no evidence that BMW engaged in deliberate false statements, acts of affirmative misconduct, or concealment of evidence of improper motive. The second (and perhaps most commonly cited) indicium of excessiveness the ratio between the plaintiff's compensatory damages and the amount of the punitive damages also weighs against Gore because his $2 million award is 500 times the amount of his actual harm as determined by the jury, and there is no suggestion that he or any other BMW purchaser was threatened with any additional potential harm by BMW's nondisclosure policy. Although it is not possible to draw a mathematical bright line between the constitutionally acceptable and the constitutionally unacceptable that would fit every case, the ratio here is clearly outside the acceptable range. Gore's punitive damages award is not saved by the third relevant indicium of excessiveness - the difference between it and the civil or criminal Page III sanctions that could be imposed for comparable misconduct - because $2 million is substantially greater than Alabama's applicable $2,000 fine and the penalties imposed in other States for similar malfeasance, and because none of the pertinent statutes or interpretive decisions would have put an out-of-state distributor on notice that it might be subject to a multimillion dollar sanction. Moreover, in the absence of a BMW history of noncompliance with known statutory requirements, there is no basis for assuming that a more modest sanction would not have been sufficient. Thus, BMW's conduct was not sufficiently egregious to justify the severe punitive sanction imposed against it. Whether the appropriate remedy requires a new trial or merely an independent determination by the Alabama Supreme Court of the award necessary to vindicate Alabama consumers' economic interests is a matter for that court to address in the first instance.

C

Reversed and remanded.

State Farm Mutual Automobile Insurance v. Campbell

123 S.Ct. 1513 (2003)

FACTS

Although investigators and witnesses concluded that Curtis Campbell caused an accident in which one person was killed and another permanently disabled, his insurer, petitioner State Farm Mutual Automobile Insurance Company (State Farm), contested liability, declined to settle the ensuing claims for the $50,000 policy limit, ignored its own investigators' advice, and took the case to trial, assuring Campbell and his wife that they had no liability for the accident, that State Farm would represent their interests, and that they did not need separate counsel. In fact, a Utah jury returned a judgment for over three times the policy limit, and State Farm refused to appeal. The Utah Supreme Court denied Campbell's own appeal, and State Farm paid the entire judgment. The Campbells then sued State Farm for bad faith, fraud, and intentional infliction of emotional distress. The trial court's initial ruling granting State Farm summary judgment was reversed on appeal. On remand, the court denied State Farm's motion to exclude evidence of dissimilar out-of-state conduct. In the first phase of a bifurcated trial, the jury found unreasonable State Farm's decision not to settle. Before the second phase, this Court refused, in *BMW of North America, Inc.* v. *Gore,* to sustain a $2 million punitive damages award which accompanied a $4,000 compensatory damages award. The trial court denied State Farm's renewed motion to exclude dissimilar out-of-state conduct evidence. In the second phase, which addressed, *inter alia,* compensatory and punitive damages, evidence was introduced that pertained to State Farm's business practices in numerous States but bore no relation to the type of claims underlying the Campbells' complaint. The jury awarded the Campbells $2.6 million in compensatory damages and $145 million in punitive damages, which the trial court reduced to $1 million and $25 million respectively. Applying *Gore,* the Utah Supreme Court reinstated the $145 million punitive damages award.

I Are punitive damages awarded considered excessive and in violation of the Due Process Clause of the 14th Amendment when they are fixed at 145 times the amount of full compensatory damages?

R Punitive damages that are fixed at 145 times the amount of full compensatory damages (i.e. grossly excessive) violate the Due Process Clause - the Due Process Clause prohibits the imposition of grossly excessive or arbitrary punishments on a tortfeaser.

A A punitive damages award of $145 million, where full compensatory damages are $1 million, is excessive and violates the Due Process Clause of the Fourteenth Amendment. Compensatory damages are intended to redress a plaintiff's concrete loss, while punitive damages are aimed at the different purposes of deterrence and retribution. The Due Process Clause prohibits the imposition of grossly excessive or arbitrary punishments on a tortfeaser. Punitive damages awards serve the same purpose as criminal penalties. However, because civil defendants are not accorded the protections afforded criminal defendants, punitive damages pose an acute danger of arbitrary deprivation of property, which is heightened when the decisionmaker is presented with evidence having little bearing on the amount that should be awarded. Thus, this Court has instructed courts reviewing punitive damages to consider (1) the degree of reprehensibility of the defendant's misconduct, (2) the disparity between the actual or potential harm suffered by the plaintiff and the punitive damages award, and (3) the difference between the punitive damages awarded by the jury and the civil penalties authorized or imposed in comparable cases. A trial court's application of these guideposts is subject to *de novo* review. Under *Gore's* guideposts, this case is neither close nor difficult. In this case, State Farm's handling of the claims against the Campbells merits no praise, but a more modest punishment could have satisfied the State's legitimate objectives. Instead, this case was used as a platform to expose, and punish, the perceived deficiencies of State Farm's operations throughout the country. However, a State cannot punish a defendant for conduct that may have been lawful where it occurred. Nor does the State have a legitimate concern in imposing punitive damages to punish a defendant for unlawful acts committed outside of its jurisdiction. Due process does not permit courts to adjudicate the merits of other parties' hypothetical claims under the guise of the reprehensibility analysis. Punishment on these bases creates the possibility of multiple punitive damages awards for the same conduct, for nonparties are not normally bound by another plaintiff's judgment. For the same reasons, the Utah Supreme Court's decision cannot be justified on the grounds that State Farm was a recidivist. To justify punishment based upon recidivism, courts must ensure the conduct in question replicates the prior transgressions. There is scant evidence of repeated misconduct of the sort that injured the Campbells, and a review of the decisions below does not convince this Court that State Farm was only punished for its actions toward the Campbells. Because the Campbells have shown no conduct similar to that which harmed them, the only relevant conduct to the reprehensibility analysis is that which harmed them. With regard to the second *Gore* guidepost, the Court has been reluctant to identify concrete constitutional limits on the ratio between harm, or potential harm, to the plaintiff and the punitive damages award; but, in practice, few awards exceeding a single-digit ratio between punitive and compensatory damages will satisfy due process. Single-digit multipliers are more likely to comport with due process, while still achieving the State's deterrence and retribution goals, than are awards with 145-to-1 ratios, as in this case. Because there are no rigid benchmarks, ratios greater than those that this Court has previously upheld may comport with due process where a particularly egregious act has resulted in only a small amount of economic damages, but when compensatory damages are substantial, then an even lesser ratio can reach the outermost limit of the due process guarantee. Here, there is a presumption against an award with a 145-to-1 ratio; the $1 million compensatory award for a year and a half of emotional distress was substantial; and the distress caused by outrage and humiliation the Campbells suffered is likely a component of both the compensatory and punitive damages awards. The Utah Supreme Court sought to justify the massive award based on premises bearing no relation to the award's reasonableness or proportionality to the harm. The Court need not dwell on the third guidepost.

C

Reversed and remanded.

Home Building & Loan Ass'n v. Blasidell

290 U.S. 398 (1934)

FACTS

The Minnesota Mortgage Moratorium Law (the "Act") provides that during the emergency declared to exist (The Great Depression), local courts may grant relief from mortgage foreclosures and execution sales by extending the period of redemption from foreclosure sales. Relief may be had through authorized judicial proceedings with respect to foreclosures of mortgages, and execution sales, of real estate; that sales may be postponed and periods of redemption may be extended. The act does not apply to mortgages subsequently made or to those made previously which shall be extended for a period ending more than a year after the passage of the Act. There are separate provisions relating to homesteads, but these are to apply "only to cases not entitled to relief under some valid provision of Part One." The act is to remain in effect "only during the continuance of the emergency and in no event beyond May 1, 1935." No extension of the period for redemption and no postponement of sale is allowed which would have the effect of extending the period of redemption beyond that date. Invoking the relevant provision of the statute, Defendant-appellees (the "Blaisdells") applied to the district court for an order extending the period of redemption from a foreclosure sale. The court entered its judgment extending the period of redemption of May 1, 1935, subject to the condition that the appellees should pay to the appellant $40 a month through the extended period from May 2, 1933; that is, that in each of the months of August, September, and October, 1933, the payments should be $80, in two installments, and thereafter $40 a month, all these amounts to go to the payment of taxes, insurance, interest, and mortgage indebtedness. It is this judgment, sustained by the Supreme Court of the state, which Plainitff-appellant contests as offending both the contract clause and the due process and equal protection clauses of the Fourteenth Amendment of the Constitution and which is now under review before the U.S. Supreme Court.

I

Can a state impose restraints on the enforcement of private contracts while at the same time avoiding a violation of the Contracts Clause?

R

As long as a state's legislation reasonably relates to an important public interest and does not impair the fundamental value of the creditor's claim, a state may amend existing remedies for the collection of debts.

A

The state court upheld the statute as an emergency measure. Although conceding that the obligations of the mortgage contract were impaired, the court decided, notwithstanding the contract cause of the Constitution, that such a measure was within the police power of the state. The court said that in addition to the weight to be given to the Legislature determination that an economic emergency exists which demands relief, the court must take notice of other considerations. The members of the Legislature come from every community of the state and from all the walks of life. They are familiar with conditions generally in every calling, occupation, profession, and business in the state. Not only they, but the courts must be guided by what is common knowledge. It is common knowledge that in the last few years [during the Depression] land values have shrunk enormously. Loans made a few years ago upon the basis of the then going values cannot possibly be replaced on the basis of present values. It is common knowledge that when this law was enacted, the large financial companies, which had made it their business to invest in mortgages, had ceased to do so. No bank would directly or indirectly loan on real estate mortgages. Life insurance companies and large investors in such mortgages had even declared a moratorium as to the loan provisions of their policy contracts. The President had closed banks temporarily. The Congress, in addition to many extraordinary measures looking to the relief of the economic emergency, had passed an act to supply funds whereby mortgagors may be able within a reasonable time to refinance their mortgages or redeem from sales where the redemption has not expired. With this knowledge, the court could not hold that the Legislature had no basis in fact for the conclusion that an economic emergency existed which called for the exercise of the police power to grant relief. We agree, judgment affirmed.

C The judgment is affirmed.

Energy Reserves Group v. Kansas Power & Light Co.

459 U.S. 400 (1983)

FACTS

In 1975, appellee public utility entered into two intrastate contracts with appellant's predecessor-in-interest to purchase wellhead and residue gas from a certain gas field. Each contract contains a "governmental price escalator clause," which provides that if any governmental authority fixes a price for any natural gas that is higher than the contract price, the contract price shall be increased to that level, and a "price redetermination clause," which gives appellant the option to have the contract price redetermined no more than once every two years by averaging the prices being paid under three other gas contracts chosen by the parties. If the price is increased pursuant to either clause, each contract requires appellee, within specified time periods, to seek from the Kansas Corporation Commission (Commission) approval to pass the increase through to consumers. If pass-through approval is refused and appellee elects not to pay the increase, appellant has the option to terminate the agreement. Pursuant to the price redetermination clauses, the parties agreed on a higher price to be effective November 27, 1977, the Commission approved the pass-through of the increase to consumers, and appellee paid the new price through 1978. Effective December 1, 1978, the Natural Gas Policy Act of 1978 replaced earlier federal price controls for interstate natural gas with gradually increasing price ceilings, including a ceiling for newly discovered or newly produced gas (102) and a lower ceiling for categories of gas not otherwise covered by the Act (109). The Act also extended federal price regulation to the intrastate gas market, providing in 105(b)(1) that the ceiling price for intrastate gas shall be the lower of the 102 price and "the price under the terms of the existing contract, to which such natural gas was subject on [November 9, 1978]." As authorized by the federal Act, the Kansas Natural Gas Price Protection Act was enacted in May 1979, imposing price controls on the intrastate gas market with regard to contracts executed before April 20, 1977, and prohibiting consideration either of ceiling prices set by federal authorities or of prices paid in Kansas under other contracts in the application of governmental price escalator and price redetermination clauses. However, the Kansas Act permits indefinite price escalator clauses to operate after March 1, 1979, to raise the price of "old" intrastate gas up to the federal Act's 109 ceiling price. In November 1978 appellant notified appellee that gas prices would be escalated to the 102 price pursuant to the governmental price escalator clauses, but appellee, after failing to obtain pass-through approval because of its failure to file a timely application with the Commission, elected not to pay the higher price and appellant then sought to terminate the contracts. When appellee contended that the governmental price escalator clauses were not triggered by the federal Act and that the Kansas Act prohibited their activation, appellant filed suit in a Kansas state court, seeking a declaratory judgment that it had the contractual right to terminate the contracts. Appellee later rejected appellant's request under the price redetermination clauses for a price increase, to be effective in November 1979, contending that the Kansas Act had extinguished appellee's obligation to comply with those clauses. Appellant then filed an amended complaint, alleging that it was entitled to terminate the contracts because of appellee's refusal to redetermine the price. Appellee counter-claimed for a declaratory judgment that the contracts were still in effect. The trial court entered summary judgment for appellee, holding that the federal Act's imposition of price ceilings on intrastate gas did not trigger the governmental price escalator clauses, and that the Kansas Act did not violate the Contract Clause. The Kansas Supreme Court affirmed.

Energy Reserves Group v. Kansas Power & Light Co.

459 U.S. 400 (1983)

I

Does the Kansas Act impair appellant's contracts with appellee in violation of the Contract Clause?

R

The Kansas Act does not impair appellant's contracts with appellee in violation of the Contract Clause, and thus the contract price may be escalated.

A

The Kansas Act does not impair appellant's contracts with appellee in violation of the Contract Clause, and thus the contract price may be escalated under either escalator clause only to the ceiling under 109 of the federal Act, not to the 102 ceiling. The Contract Clause's prohibition of any state law impairing the obligation of contracts must be accommodated to the State's inherent police power to safeguard the vital interests of its people. The threshold inquiry is "whether the state law has, in fact, operated as a substantial impairment of a contractual relationship." *Allied Structural Steel Co. v. Spannaus*. If a substantial impairment is found, the State, in justification, must have a significant and legitimate public purpose behind the regulation. Once such a purpose has been identified, the adjustment of the contracting parties' rights and responsibilities must be based upon reasonable conditions and must be of a character appropriate to the public purpose justifying the legislation's adoption. Here, the Kansas Act has not impaired substantially appellant's contractual rights. The parties are operating in a heavily regulated industry, and the statement of intent in their contracts made clear that the escalator clauses were designed to guarantee price increases consistent with anticipated regulated increases in the value of appellant's gas, not that appellant expected to receive deregulated prices. Moreover, the contract provision making any contractual term subject to relevant present and future state and federal law suggests that appellant knew its contractual rights were subject to alteration by state price regulation. To the extent, if any, the Kansas Act impairs appellant's contractual interests, it rests on significant state interests in protecting consumers from the escalation of natural gas prices caused by deregulation and in correcting the imbalance between the interstate and intrastate markets by permitting the intrastate prices to rise only to the 109 level. Nor are the means chosen to implement these purposes deficient, particularly in light of the deference to which the Kansas Legislature's judgment is entitled. The Kansas Supreme Court did not err in holding that the enactment of 105 of the federal Act did not trigger the governmental price escalator clauses in these contracts so as to entitle appellant to a price increase on December 1, 1978. As a matter of federal statutory interpretation, the federal Act does not trigger such clauses automatically. By the language of 105(b)(1), Congress set a ceiling for the operation of contractual provisions; it did not prescribe a price. And the Kansas Supreme Court's holding that the particular governmental price escalator clauses involved here were insufficient to escalate the gas price is an interpretation of state law to which we defer.

C

Affirmed.

Allied Structural Steel Co. v. Spannaus

438 U.S. 234 (1978)

FACTS

Appellant, an Illinois corporation, maintained an office in Minnesota with 30 employees. Under appellant's pension plan, adopted in 1963 and qualified under 401 of the Internal Revenue Code, employees were entitled to retire and receive a pension at age 65 regardless of length of service, and an employee's pension right became vested if he satisfied certain conditions as to length of service and age. Appellant was the sole contributor to the pension trust fund, and each year made contributions to the fund based on actuarial predictions of eventual payout needs. But the plan neither required appellant to make specific contributions nor imposed any sanction on it for failing to make adequate contributions, and appellant retained a right not only to amend the plan but also to terminate it at any time and for any reason. In 1974, Minnesota enacted the Private Pension Benefits Protection Act (Act), under which a private employer of 100 employees or more (at least one of whom was a Minnesota resident) who provided pension benefits under a plan meeting the qualifications of 401 of the Internal Revenue Code, was subject to a "pension funding charge" if he terminated the plan or closed a Minnesota office. The charge was assessed if the pension funds were insufficient to cover full pensions for all employees who had worked at least 10 years, and periods of employment prior to the effective date of the Act were to be included in the 10-year employment criterion. Shortly thereafter, in a move planned before passage of the Act, appellant closed its Minnesota office, and several of its employees, who were then discharged, had no vested pension rights under appellant's plan but had worked for appellant for 10 years or more, thus qualifying as pension obligees under the Act. Subsequently, the State notified appellant that it owed a pension funding charge of $185,000 under the Act. Appellant then brought suit in Federal District Court for injunctive and declaratory relief, claiming that the Act unconstitutionally impaired its contractual obligations to its employees under its pension plan, but the court upheld the Act as applied to appellant.

I

May a state enact legislation that alters an employer's obligations with respect to its pension plan?

R

A state may not <u>unilaterally</u> enact legislation that alters an employer's obligations with respect to its pension plan without <u>reasonable justification</u> for doing so.

A

The application of the Act to appellant violates the Contract Clause of the Constitution, which provides that "[n]o State shall . . . pass any . . . law impairing the Obligation of Contracts." While the Contract Clause does not operate to obliterate the police power of the States, it does impose some limits upon the power of a State to abridge existing contractual relationships, even in the exercise of its otherwise legitimate police power. "Legislation adjusting the rights and responsibilities of contracting parties must be upon reasonable conditions and of a character appropriate to the public purpose justifying its adoption." *United States Trust Co. v. New Jersey*. The impact of the Act upon appellant's contractual obligations was both substantial and severe. Not only did the Act retroactively modify the compensation that appellant had agreed to pay its employees from 1963 to 1974, but it did so by changing appellant's obligations in an area where the element of reliance was vital - the funding of a pension plan. Moreover, the retroactive state-imposed vesting requirement was applied only to those employers who terminated their pension plans or who, like appellant, closed their Minnesota offices, thus forcing the employer to make all the retroactive changes in its contractual obligations at one time. The Act does not possess the attributes of those state laws that have survived challenge under the Contract Clause. It was not even purportedly enacted to deal with a broad, generalized economic or social problem, but has an extremely narrow focus and enters an area never before subject to regulation by the State.

C

Reversed.

United States Trust Co. v. New Jersey

431 U.S. 1 (1977)

FACTS

A 1962 statutory covenant between New Jersey and New York limited the ability of the Port Authority of New York and New Jersey to subsidize rail passenger transportation from revenues and reserves pledged as security for consolidated bonds issued by the Port Authority. A 1974 New Jersey statute, together with a concurrent and parallel New York statute, retroactively repealed the 1962 covenant. Appellant, both as a trustee for, and as a holder of, Port Authority bonds, brought suit in the New Jersey Superior Court for declaratory relief, claiming that the 1974 New Jersey statute impaired the obligation of the States' contract with the bondholders in violation of the Contract Clause of the United States Constitution. The Superior Court dismissed the complaint after trial, holding that the statutory repeal was a reasonable exercise of New Jersey's police power and was not prohibited by the Contract Clause. The New Jersey Supreme Court affirmed.

I

May a state enact legislation that abandons its own obligations?

R

A state may enact legislation that abandons its own obligations and such laws will be upheld as valid if it is both reasonable and necessary to serve the purposes claimed by the state.

A

The Contract Clause prohibits the retroactive repeal of the 1962 covenant. The outright repeal of the 1962 covenant totally eliminated an important security provision for the bondholders and thus impaired the obligation of the States' contract. The security provision of the 1962 covenant was purely a financial obligation and thus not necessarily a compromise of the States' reserved powers that cannot be contracted away. The repeal of the 1962 covenant cannot be sustained on the basis of *Faitoute Iron & Steel Co. v. City of Asbury Park*, and *W. B. Worthen Co. v. Kavanaugh*, simply because the bondholders' rights were not totally destroyed. An impairment of contract such as is involved in this case can only be upheld if it is both reasonable and necessary to serve an important public purpose, but here the impairment was neither necessary to achieve the States' plan to encourage private automobile users to shift to public transportation nor reasonable in light of changed circumstances. Total repeal of the 1962 covenant was not essential, since the States' plan could have been implemented with a less drastic modification of the covenant, and since, without modifying the covenant at all, the States could have adopted alternative means of achieving their twin goals of discouraging automobile use and improving mass transit. Nor can the repeal be claimed to be reasonable on the basis of the need for mass transportation, energy conservation, and environmental protection, since the 1962 covenant was adopted with knowledge of such concerns.

C

Reversed.

Loretto v. Teleprompter Manhattan CATV Corp.

458 U.S. 419 (1982)

FACTS

A New York statute provides that a landlord must permit a cable television (CATV) company to install its CATV facilities upon his property and may not demand payment from the company in excess of the amount determined by a State Commission to be reasonable. Pursuant to the statute, the Commission ruled that a one-time $1 payment was a reasonable fee. After purchasing a five-story apartment building in New York City, appellant landlord discovered that appellee CATV companies had installed cables on the building, both "crossovers" for serving other buildings and "noncrossovers" for serving appellant's tenants. Appellant then brought a class action for damages and injunctive relief in a New York state court, alleging, inter alia, that installation of the cables insofar as appellee companies relied on the New York statute constituted a taking without just compensation. Appellee New York City, which had granted the companies an exclusive franchise to provide CATV within certain areas of the city, intervened. Upholding the New York statute, the trial court granted summary judgment to appellees. The Appellate Division of the New York Court of Appeals also upheld the statute, holding that it serves the legitimate police power purpose of eliminating landlord fees and conditions that inhibit the development of CATV, which has important educational and community benefits. Rejecting appellant's argument that a physical occupation authorized by government is necessarily a taking, the court further held that the statute did not have an excessive economic impact upon appellant when measured against her aggregate property rights, did not interfere with any reasonable investment-backed expectations, and accordingly did not work a taking of appellant's property.

I

May a state validly authorize an intrusion onto the private property of a private landowner with paying just compensation?

R

Any permanent intrusion by the state (i.e. government) or intrusion authorized by it constitutes a taking for which just compensation must be paid.

A

The New York statute works a taking of a portion of appellant's property for which she is entitled to just compensation under the Fifth Amendment, as made applicable to the States by the Fourteenth Amendment. When the "character of the governmental action," *Penn Central Transportation Co. v. New York City*, is a permanent physical occupation of real property, there is a taking to the extent of the occupation without regard to whether the action achieves an important public benefit or has only minimal economic impact on the owner. To the extent that the government permanently occupies physical property, it effectively destroys the owner's rights to possess, use, and dispose of the property. Moreover, the owner suffers a special kind of injury when a stranger invades and occupies the owner's property. Such an invasion is qualitatively more severe than a regulation of the use of property, since the owner may have no control over the timing, extent, or nature of the invasion. And constitutional protection for the rights of private property cannot be made to depend on the size of the area permanently occupied. Here, the cable installation on appellant's building constituted a taking under the traditional physical occupation test, since it involved a direct physical attachment of plates, boxes, wires, bolts, and screws to the building, completely occupying space immediately above and upon the roof and along the building's exterior wall. There is no constitutional difference between a crossover and noncrossover installation, since portions of the installation necessary for both types of installation permanently appropriated appellant's property. The fact that the New York statute applies only to buildings used as rental property does not make it simply a regulation of the use of real property. Physical occupation of one type of property but not another is no less a physical occupation. The New York statute does not purport to give the tenant any enforceable property rights with respect to CATV installation, and thus cannot be construed as merely granting a tenant a property right as an appurtenance to his leasehold. Application of the physical occupation rule in this case will not have dire consequences for the government's power to adjust landlord-tenant relationships, since it in no way alters the usual analysis governing a State's power to require landlords to comply with building codes.

C

Reversed and remanded.

Pennsylvania Coal Co. v. Mahon

260 U.S. 393 (1922)

FACTS

This is a bill in equity brought by the defendants in error (Plaintiff Mahon) to prevent the Pennsylvania Coal Company (defendant) from mining under their property in such way as to remove the supports and cause a subsidence of the surface and of their house. The bill sets out a deed executed by the Coal Company in 1878, under which the plaintiffs claim. The deed conveys the surface but in express terms reserves the right to remove all the coal under the same and the grantee takes the premises with the risk and waives all claim for damages that may arise from mining out the coal. But the plaintiffs say that whatever may have been the Coal Company's rights, they were taken away by an Act of Pennsylvania, approved May 27, 1921, commonly known there as the Kohler Act. The statute forbids the mining of anthracite coal in such way as to cause the subsidence of, among other things, any structure used as a human habitation, with certain exceptions, including among them land where the surface is owned by the owner of the underlying coal and is distant more than one hundred and fifty feet from any improved property belonging to any other person. As applied to this case the statute is admitted to destroy previously existing rights of property and contract. The Court of Common Pleas found that if not restrained the defendant would cause the damage to prevent which the bill was brought but denied an injunction, holding that the statute if applied to this case would be unconstitutional. On appeal the Supreme Court of the State agreed that the defendant had contract and property rights protected by the Constitution of the United States, but held that the statute was a legitimate exercise of the police power and directed a decree for the plaintiffs. A writ of error was granted bringing the case to the U.S. Supreme Court.

I Does a statute which admittedly destroys previously existing rights of property and contract and severely restricts existing land use rights constitute an unconstitutional taking unless just compensation is paid?

R A regulation that severely restricts land use rights amounts to an unconstitutional taking unless just compensation is paid.

A This is the case of a single private house. Usually in ordinary private affairs, the public interest does not warrant this kind of interference. A source of damage to such a house is not a public nuisance even if similar damage is inflicted on others in different places. The damage is not common or public. The extent of the public interest is shown by the statute to be limited, since the statute ordinarily does not apply to land when the surface is owned by the owner of the coal. Furthermore, it is not justified as a protection of personal safety that could be provided for by notice. Indeed the very foundation of this bill is that the defendant gave timely notice of its intent to mine under the house. On the other hand the extent of the taking is great. It purports to abolish what is recognized in Pennsylvania as an estate in land, a very valuable estate, and what is declared by the Court below to be a contract hitherto binding the plaintiffs. It is our opinion that the act cannot be sustained as an exercise of the police power, so far as it affects the mining of coal under streets or cities in places where the right to mine such coal has been reserved. To make it commercially impracticable to mine certain coal has very nearly the same effect for constitutional purposes as appropriating or destroying it. The rights of the public in a street purchased or laid out by eminent domain are those that it has paid for. The protection of private property in the Fifth Amendment presupposes that it is wanted for public use, but provides that it shall not be taken for such use without compensation. A similar assumption is made in the decisions upon the Fourteenth Amendment. When this seemingly absolute protection is found to be qualified by the police power, the natural tendency of human nature is to extend the qualification more and more until at last private property disappears. But that cannot be accomplished in this way under the Constitution of the United States. The general rule at least is that while property may be regulated to a certain extent, if regulation goes too far it will be recognized as a taking. A strong public desire to improve the public condition is not enough to warrant achieving the desire by short cut than the constitutional way of paying for the change. As we already have said, this is a question of degree and therefore cannot be disposed of by general propositions. We assume of course that the statute was passed upon the conviction that an exigency existed that would warrant it, and we assume that an exigency exists that would warrant the exercise of eminent domain. But the question ultimately to be answered is upon whom the loss of the changes desired should fall. So far as private persons or communities have seen fit to take the risk of acquiring only surface rights, we cannot see that the fact that their risk has become a danger warrants the giving to them greater rights than they originally purchased.

C

Decree reversed.

Miller v. Schoene

276 U.S. 272 (1928)

FACTS

Acting under the Cedar Rust Act of Virginia, defendant in error, the state entomologist, ordered the plaintiffs in error to cut down a large number of ornamental red cedar trees growing on their property, as a means of preventing the communication of a rust or plant disease with which they were infected to the apple orchards in the vicinity. The plaintiffs in error appealed from the order to the circuit court of Shenandoah county which, after a hearing and a consideration of evidence, affirmed the order and allowed to plaintiffs in error $100 to cover the expense of removal of the cedars. Neither the judgment of the court nor the statute as interpreted allows compensation for the value of the standing cedars or the decrease in the market value of the realty caused by their destruction whether considered as ornamental trees or otherwise. But they allow the plaintiffs in error the privilege of using the trees when felled. On appeal the Supreme Court of Appeals of Virginia affirmed the judgment. Both in the circuit court and the Supreme Court of Appeals plaintiffs in error challenged the constitutionality of the statute under the due process clause of the Fourteenth Amendment and the case is properly here on writ of error.

I Can the state's police power be used to eliminate one form of property to prevent the destruction of other property and, if so, must the state compensate the owners of the destroyed property?

R When the destruction of one form of property threatens other property which is in the public's interest and of greater public value, the state may destroy that class of property and need not compensate the owners of the destroyed property.

A The Virginia statute presents a comprehensive scheme for the condemnation and destruction of red cedar trees infected by cedar rust. Cedar rust is an infectious plant disease in the form of a fungoid organism which is destructive of the fruit and foliage of the apple, but without effect on the value of the cedar. The only practicable method of controlling the disease and protecting apple trees from its ravages is the destruction of all red cedar trees, subject to the infection, located within two miles of apple orchards. The red cedar, aside from its ornamental use, has occasional use and value as lumber. It is indigenous to Virginia, is not cultivated or dealt in commercially on any substantial scale, and its value throughout the state is shown to be small as compared with that of the apple orchards of the state. Apple growing is one of the principal agricultural pursuits in Virginia. The apple is used there and exported in large quantities. Many millions of dollars are invested in the orchards, which furnish employment for a large portion of the population, and have induced the development of attendant railroad and cold storage facilities. On the evidence we may accept the conclusion of the Supreme Court of Appeals that the state was under the necessity of making a choice between the preservation of one class of property and that of the other wherever both existed in dangerous proximity. It would have been none the less a choice if, instead of enacting the present statute, the state, by doing nothing, had permitted serious injury to the apple orchards within its borders to go on unchecked.

When forced to such a choice the state does not exceed its constitutional powers by deciding upon the destruction of one class of property in order to save another which, in the judgment of the legislature, is of greater value to the public. It will not do to say that the case is merely one of a conflict of two private interests and that the misfortune of apple growers may not be shifted to cedar owners by ordering the destruction of their property; for it is obvious that there may be, and that here there is, a preponderant public concern in the preservation of the one interest over the other. And where the public interest is involved preferment of that interest over the property interest of the individual, to the extent even of its destruction, is one of the distinguishing characteristics of every exercise of the police power which affects property. We need not weigh with nicety the question whether the infected cedars constitute a nuisance according to the common law; or whether they may be so declared by statute. For where, as here, the choice is unavoidable, we cannot say that its exercise, controlled by considerations of social policy which are not unreasonable, involves any denial of due process. The objection of plaintiffs in error to the vagueness of the statute is without weight. The state court has held it to be applicable and that is enough when, by the statute, no penalty can be incurred or disadvantage suffered in advance of the judicial ascertainment of its applicability.

C

Affirmed.

Lucas v. South Carolina Coastal Council

505 U.S. 1003 (1992)

FACTS

In 1986, petitioner Lucas bought two residential lots on a South Carolina barrier island, intending to build single-family homes such as those on the immediately adjacent parcels. At that time, Lucas' lots were not subject to the State's coastal zone building permit requirements. In 1988, however, the state legislature enacted the Beachfront Management Act, which barred Lucas from erecting any permanent habitable structures on his parcels. He filed suit against respondent state agency, contending that, even though the Act may have been a lawful exercise of the State's police power, the ban on construction deprived him of all "economically viable use" of his property, and therefore effected a "taking" under the Fifth and Fourteenth Amendments that required the payment of just compensation. The state trial court agreed, finding that the ban rendered Lucas' parcels "valueless," and entered an award exceeding $1.2 million. In reversing, the State Supreme Court held itself bound, in light of Lucas' failure to attack the Act's validity, to accept the legislature's "uncontested . . . findings" that new construction in the coastal zone threatened a valuable public resource. The court ruled that, under the *Mugler v. Kansas* line of cases, when a regulation is designed to prevent "harmful or noxious uses" of property akin to public nuisances, no compensation is owed under the Takings Clause regardless of the regulation's effect on the property's value.

I Has the state effected a "taking" under the Fifth Amendment when it regulates land use to a degree which deprives the owner of all economically beneficial and productive use of it?

R A state has effected a "taking" under the Fifth Amendment when it regulates land use to an degree which deprives the owner of all economically beneficial and productive use of it.

A Lucas' takings claim is not rendered unripe by the fact that he may yet be able to secure a special permit to build on his property under an amendment to the Act passed after briefing and argument before the State Supreme Court, but prior to issuance of that court's opinion. Because it declined to rest its judgment on ripeness grounds, preferring to dispose of the case on the merits, the latter court's decision precludes, both practically and legally, any takings claim with respect to Lucas' pre-amendment deprivation. Lucas has properly alleged injury in fact with respect to this pre-amendment deprivation, and it would not accord with sound process in these circumstances to insist that he pursue the late-created procedure before that component of his takings claim can be considered ripe. The State Supreme Court erred in applying the "harmful or noxious uses" principle to decide this case. Regulations that deny the property owner all "economically viable use of his land" constitute one of the discrete categories of regulatory deprivations that require compensation without the usual case-specific inquiry into the public interest advanced in support of the restraint. Although the Court has never set forth the justification for this categorical rule, the practical - and economic - equivalence of physically appropriating and eliminating all beneficial use of land counsels its preservation. A review of the relevant decisions demonstrates that the "harmful or noxious use" principle was merely this Court's early formulation of the police power justification necessary to sustain (without compensation) any regulatory diminution in value; that the distinction between regulation that "prevents harmful use" and that which "confers benefits" is difficult, if not impossible, to discern on an objective, value-free basis; and that, therefore, noxious-use logic cannot be the basis for departing from this Court's categorical rule that total regulatory takings must be compensated. Rather, the question must turn, in accord with this Court's "takings" jurisprudence, on citizens' historic understandings regarding the content of, and the State's power over, the "bundle of rights" that they acquire when they take title to property. Because it is not consistent with the historical compact embodied in the Takings Clause that title to real estate is held subject to the State's subsequent decision to eliminate all economically beneficial use, a regulation having that effect cannot be newly decreed, and sustained, without compensation's being paid the owner. However, no compensation is owed - in this setting as with all takings claims - if the State's affirmative decree simply makes explicit what already inheres in the title itself, in the restrictions that background principles of the State's law of property and nuisance already place upon land ownership. Although it seems unlikely that common law principles would have prevented the erection of any habitable or productive improvements on Lucas' land, this state law question must be dealt with on remand. To win its case, respondent cannot simply proffer the legislature's declaration that the uses Lucas desires are inconsistent with the public interest, or the conclusory assertion that they violate a common law maxim such as *sic utere tuo ut alienum non laedas* ["use what is yours so as not to harm what is others"], but must identify background principles of nuisance and property law that prohibit the uses Lucas now intends in the property's present circumstances.

C

Reversed and remanded.

Dolan v. City of Tigard

512 U.S. 374 (1994)

FACTS

The City Planning Commission conditioned approval of petitioner Dolan's application to expand her store and pave her parking lot upon her compliance with dedication of land (1) for a public greenway along Fanno Creek to minimize flooding that would be exacerbated by the increases in impervious surfaces associated with her development and (2) for a pedestrian/bicycle pathway intended to relieve traffic congestion in the City's Central Business District. She appealed the Commission's denial of her request for variances from these standards to the Land Use Board of Appeals (LUBA), alleging that the land dedication requirements were not related to the proposed development, and therefore constituted an uncompensated taking of her property under the Fifth Amendment. LUBA found a reasonable relationship between (1) the development and the requirement to dedicate land for a greenway, since the larger building and paved lot would increase the impervious surfaces, and thus the runoff into the creek, and (2) alleviating the impact of increased traffic from the development and facilitating the provision of a pathway as an alternative means of transportation. Both the State Court of Appeals and the State Supreme Court affirmed.

I

May a municipality impose conditions on a building permit which result in a taking of private property use without paying the owner just compensation?

R

Permit conditions will only be upheld where there is an essential nexus between the legitimate state interest and the imposed permit conditions and where the government shows an individualized determination (not generalized) has been made that the required dedication is related both in nature and extent to the impact of the proposed development.

A

The city's dedication requirements constitute an uncompensated taking of property. Under the well settled doctrine of "unconstitutional conditions," the government may not require a person to give up a constitutional right in exchange for a discretionary benefit conferred by the government where the property sought has little or no relationship to the benefit. In evaluating Dolan's claim, it must be determined whether an "essential nexus" exists between a legitimate state interest and the permit condition. If one does, then it must be decided whether the degree of the exactions demanded by the permit conditions bears the required relationship to the projected impact of the proposed development. Preventing flooding along Fanno Creek and reducing traffic congestion in the District are legitimate public purposes; and a nexus exists between the first purpose and limiting development within the creek's floodplain and between the second purpose and providing for alternative means of transportation. In deciding the second question - whether the city's findings are constitutionally sufficient to justify the conditions imposed on Dolan's permit - the necessary connection required by the Fifth Amendment is "rough proportionality." No precise mathematical calculation is required, but the city must make some sort of individualized determination that the required dedication is related both in nature and extent to the proposed development's impact. This is essentially the "reasonable relationship" test adopted by the majority of the state courts. The findings upon which the city relies do not show the required reasonable relationship between the floodplain easement and Dolan's proposed building. The Community Development Code already required that Dolan leave 15% of her property as open space, and the undeveloped floodplain would have nearly satisfied that requirement. However, the city has never said why a public, as opposed to a private, greenway is required in the interest of flood control. The difference to Dolan is the loss of her ability to exclude others from her property, yet the city has not attempted to make any individualized determination to support this part of its request. The city has also not met its burden of demonstrating that the additional number of vehicle and bicycle trips generated by Dolan's development reasonably relates to the city's requirement for a dedication of the pathway easement. The city must quantify its finding beyond a conclusory statement that the dedication could offset some of the traffic demand generated by the development.

C

Reversed and remanded.

Palazzo v. Rhode Island

533 U.S. 606 (2001)

FACTS

In order to acquire the waterfront parcel of Rhode Island land that is here at issue, petitioner and associates formed Shore Gardens, Inc. (SGI), in 1959. After SGI purchased the property petitioner bought out his associates and became the sole shareholder. Most of the property was then, and is now, salt marsh subject to tidal flooding. The wet ground and permeable soil would require considerable fill before significant structures could be built. Over the years, SGI's intermittent applications to develop the property were rejected by various government agencies. After 1966, no further applications were made for over a decade. Two intervening events, however, become important to the issues presented. First, in 1971, the State created respondent Rhode Island Coastal Resources Management Council (Council) and charged it with protecting the State's coastal properties. The Council's regulations, known as the Rhode Island Coastal Resources Management Program (CRMP), designated salt marshes like those on SGI's property as protected "coastal wetlands" on which development is greatly limited. Second, in 1978 SGI's corporate charter was revoked, and title to the property passed to petitioner as the corporation's sole shareholder. In 1983, petitioner applied to the Council for permission to fill his entire marsh land area. The Council rejected the application, concluding, among other things, that it would conflict with the CRMP. In 1985 petitioner filed a new application with the Council, seeking permission to fill 11 of the property's 18 wetland acres in order to build a private beach club. The Council rejected this application as well, ruling that the proposal did not satisfy the standards for obtaining a "special exception" to fill salt marsh, whereby the proposed activity must serve a compelling public purpose. Subsequently, petitioner filed an inverse condemnation action in Rhode Island Superior Court, asserting that the State's wetlands regulations, as applied by the Council to his parcel, had taken the property without compensation in violation of the Fifth and Fourteenth Amendments. The suit alleged the Council's action deprived him of "all economically beneficial use" of his property, resulting in a total taking requiring compensation under *Lucas* v. *South Carolina Coastal Council* and sought $3,150,000 in damages. The court ruled against petitioner, and the State Supreme Court affirmed, holding that (1) petitioner's takings claim was not ripe; (2) he had no right to challenge regulations predating 1978, when he succeeded to legal ownership of the property; (3) he could not assert a takings claim based on the denial of all economic use of his property in light of undisputed evidence that he had $200,000 in development value remaining on an upland parcel of the property; and (4) because the regulation at issue predated his acquisition of title, he could have had no reasonable investment-backed expectation that he could develop his property, and, therefore, he could not recover under *Penn Central.*

I May a property owner who acquired title to the property after it was subject to wetlands regulations still bring a takings claim under the Fifth Amendment?

R A state may not regulate property into uselessness without paying compensation, simply because the owner acquired the property after the regulation became effective.

Palazzolo v. Rhode Island

533 U.S. 606 (2001)

A This case is ripe for review. A takings claim challenging application of land-use regulations is not ripe unless the agency charged with implementing the regulations has reached a final decision regarding their application to the property at issue. A final decision does not occur until the responsible agency determines the extent of permitted development on the land. Petitioner obtained such a final decision when the Council denied his 1983 and 1985 applications. The State Supreme Court erred in ruling that, notwithstanding those denials, doubt remained as to the extent of development the Council would allow on petitioner's parcel due to his failure to explore other uses for the property that would involve filling substantially less wetlands. Moreover, petitioner's acquisition of title after the regulations' effective date did not bar his takings claims. This Court rejects the State Supreme Court's sweeping rule that a purchaser or a successive title holder like petitioner is deemed to have notice of an earlier-enacted restriction and is barred from claiming that it effects a taking. Were the Court to accept that rule, the post-enactment transfer of title would absolve the State of its obligation to defend any action restricting land use, no matter how extreme or unreasonable. A State would be allowed, in effect, to put an expiration date on the Takings Clause. This ought not to be the rule. Future generations, too, have a right to challenge unreasonable limitations on the use and value of land. The State's notice justification does not take into account the effect on owners at the time of enactment, who are prejudiced as well. Should an owner attempt to challenge a new regulation, but not survive the process of ripening his or her claim (which, as this case demonstrates, will often take years), under the State's rule the right to compensation may not by asserted by an heir or successor, and so may not be asserted at all. The State's rule also would work a critical alteration to the nature of property, as the newly regulated landowner is stripped of the ability to transfer the interest which was possessed prior to the regulation. Further, the State Supreme Court did not err in finding that petitioner failed to establish a deprivation of all economic use, for it is undisputed that his parcel retains significant development value. Petitioner is correct that, assuming a taking is otherwise established, a State may not evade the duty to compensate on the premise that the landowner is left with a token interest. This is not the situation in this case, however. A regulation permitting a landowner to build a substantial residence on an 18-acre parcel does not leave the property "economically idle." Petitioner attempts to revive this part of his claim by arguing, for the first time, that the upland parcel is distinct from the wetlands portions, so he should be permitted to assert a deprivation limited to the latter. The Court will not explore the point here. Petitioner did not press the argument in the state courts, and the issue was not presented in his certiorari petition. The case comes to the Court on the premise that petitioner's entire parcel serves as the basis for his takings claim, and, so framed, the total deprivation argument fails. Because petitioner's claims under the *Penn Central* analysis were not examined below, the case is remanded.

C Affirmed in part, reversed in part, and remanded.

Tahoe-Sierra Preservation Council v. Tahoe Regional Planning Agency 535 U.S. 301 (2002)

FACTS

Respondent Tahoe Regional Planning Agency (TRPA) imposed two moratoria, totaling 32 months, on development in the Lake Tahoe Basin while formulating a comprehensive land-use plan for the area. Petitioners, real estate owners affected by the moratoria and an association representing such owners, filed parallel suits, later consolidated, claiming that TRPA's actions constituted a taking of their property without just compensation. The District Court found that TRPA had not effected a "partial taking" under the analysis set out in *Penn Central Transp. Co.* v. *New York City*; however, it concluded that the moratoria did constitute a taking under the categorical rule announced in *Lucas* v. *South Carolina Coastal Council,* because TRPA temporarily deprived petitioners of all economically viable use of their land. On appeal, TRPA successfully challenged the District Court's takings determination. Finding that the only question in this facial challenge was whether *Lucas*' rule applied, the Ninth Circuit held that because the regulations had only a temporary impact on petitioners' fee interest, no categorical taking had occurred; that *Lucas* applied to the relatively rare case in which a regulation permanently denies all productive use of an entire parcel, whereas the moratoria involved only a temporal slice of the fee interest; and that *First English Evangelical Lutheran Church of Glendale* v. *County of Los Angeles,* concerned the question whether compensation is an appropriate remedy for a temporary taking, not whether or when such a taking has occurred. The court also concluded that *Penn Central*'s ad hoc balancing approach was the proper framework for analyzing whether a taking had occurred, but that petitioners had not challenged the District Court's conclusion that they could not make out a claim under *Penn Central*'s factors.

I

Is an imposed moratoria of specific lengths of time considered a taking requiring payment of just compensation?

R

The moratoria ordered by TRPA are not *per se* takings of property requiring compensation under the Takings Clause; however, the restriction's duration is one factor for a court to consider in appraising regulatory takings claims, but with respect to that factor, the temptation to adopt *per se* rules in either direction must be resisted.

A

The longstanding distinction between physical and regulatory takings makes it inappropriate to treat precedent from one as controlling on the other. Petitioners rely on *First English* and *Lucas* - both regulatory takings cases - to argue for a categorical rule that whenever the government imposes a deprivation of all economically viable use of property, no matter how brief, it effects a taking. In *First English,* the Court addressed the separate remedial question of how compensation is measured once a regulatory taking is established, but not the different and prior question whether the temporary regulation was in fact a taking. To the extent that the Court referenced that antecedent question, it recognized that a regulation temporarily denying an owner all use of her property might not constitute a taking if the denial was part of the State's authority to enact safety regulations, or if it were one of the normal delays in obtaining building permits, changes in zoning ordinances, variances, and the like. Thus, *First English* did not approve, and implicitly rejected, petitioners' categorical approach. Nor is *Lucas* dispositive of the question presented. Its categorical rule--requiring compensation when a regulation permanently deprives an owner of "*all* economically beneficial uses" of his land does not answer the question whether a regulation prohibiting any economic use of land for 32 months must be compensated. Petitioners attempt to bring this case under the rule in *Lucas* by focusing exclusively on the property during the moratoria is unavailing. A permanent deprivation of all use is a taking of the parcel as a whole, but a temporary restriction causing a diminution in value is not, for the property will recover value when the prohibition is lifted. *Lucas* was carved out for the "extraordinary case" in which a regulation permanently deprives property of all use; the default rule remains that a fact specific inquiry is required in the regulatory taking context. For the reasons set out in *Justice O'Connor's* concurring opinion in *Palazzolo,* the better approach to a temporary regulatory taking claim requires careful examination and weighing of all the relevant circumstances - only one of which is the length of the delay. A narrower rule excluding normal delays in processing permits, or covering only delays of more than a year, would have a less severe impact on prevailing practices, but would still impose serious constraints on the planning process. Moratoria are an essential tool of successful development. The interest in informed decisionmaking counsels against adopting a *per se* rule that would treat such interim measures as takings regardless of the planners' good faith, the landowners' reasonable expectations, or the moratorium's actual impact on property values. The financial constraints of compensating property owners during a moratorium may force officials to rush through the planning process or abandon the practice altogether. And the interest in protecting the decisional process is even stronger when an agency is developing a regional plan than when it is considering a permit for a single parcel. Here, TRPA obtained the benefit of comments and criticisms from interested parties during its deliberations, but a categorical rule tied to the deliberations' length would likely create added pressure on decisionmakers to quickly resolve land-use questions, disadvantaging landowners and interest groups less organized or familiar with the planning process. Moreover, with a temporary development ban, there is less risk that individual landowners will be singled out to bear a special burden that should be shared by the public as a whole. It may be true that a moratorium lasting more than one year should be viewed with special skepticism, but the District Court found that the instant delay was not unreasonable. The restriction's duration is one factor for a court to consider in appraising regulatory takings claims, but with respect to that factor, the temptation to adopt *per se* rules in either direction must be resisted.

C

Affirmed.

Hawaii Housing Authority v. Midkiff

467 U.S. 229 (1984)

FACTS

To reduce the perceived social and economic evils of a land oligopoly traceable to the early high chiefs of the Hawaiian Islands, the Hawaii Legislature enacted the Land Reform Act of 1967 (Act), which created a land condemnation scheme whereby title in real property is taken from lessors and transferred to lessees in order to reduce the concentration of land ownership. Under the Act, lessees living on single-family residential lots within tracts at least five acres in size are entitled to ask appellant Hawaii Housing Authority (HHA) to condemn the property on which they live. When appropriate applications by lessees are filed, the Act authorizes HHA to hold a public hearing to determine whether the State's acquisition of the tract will "effectuate the public purposes" of the Act. If HHA determines that these public purposes will be served, it is authorized to designate some or all of the lots in the tract for acquisition. It then acquires, at prices set by a condemnation trial or by negotiation between lessors and lessees, the former fee owners'"right, title, and interest" in the land, and may then sell the land titles to the applicant lessees. After HHA had held a public hearing on the proposed acquisition of appellees' lands and had found that such acquisition would effectuate the Act's public purposes, it directed appellees to negotiate with certain lessees concerning the sale of the designated properties. When these negotiations failed, HHA ordered appellees to submit to compulsory arbitration as provided by the Act. Rather than comply with this order, appellees filed suit in Federal District Court, asking that the Act be declared unconstitutional and that its enforcement be enjoined. The court temporarily restrained the State from proceeding against appellees' estates, but subsequently, while holding the compulsory arbitration and compensation formulae provisions of the Act unconstitutional, refused to issue a preliminary injunction and ultimately granted partial summary judgment to HHA and private appellants who had intervened, holding the remainder of the Act constitutional under the Public Use Clause of the Fifth Amendment, made applicable to the States under the Fourteenth Amendment. After deciding that the District Court had properly not abstained from exercising its jurisdiction, the Court of Appeals reversed, holding that the Act violates the "public use" requirement of the Fifth Amendment.

I Can a state take land, with just compensation, for resale to private lessees without violating the Fifth Amendment?

R The legislature determines what constitutes public use – its determination will generally be upheld except in the narrowest of cases.

A The District Court was not required to abstain from exercising its jurisdiction. Abstention under *Railroad Comm'n v. Pullman Co.*, is unnecessary. Pullman's abstention is limited to uncertain questions of state law, and here there is no uncertain question of state law, since the Act unambiguously provides that the power to condemn is "for a public use and purpose." Thus, the question, uncomplicated by ambiguous language, is whether the Act on its face is unconstitutional. Nor is abstention required under *Younger v. Harris*. Younger abstention is required only when state-court proceedings are initiated before any proceedings of substance on the merits have occurred in federal court. Here, state judicial proceedings had not been initiated at the time proceedings of substance took place in the District Court, the District Court having issued a preliminary injunction before HHA filed its first state eminent domain suit in state court. And the fact that HHA's administrative proceedings occurred before the federal suit was filed did not require abstention, since the Act clearly states that those proceedings are not part of, or are not themselves, a judicial proceeding. The Act does not violate the "public use" requirement of the Fifth Amendment. That requirement is coterminous with the scope of a sovereign's police powers. This Court will not substitute its judgment for a legislature's judgment as to what constitutes "public use" unless the use is palpably without reasonable foundation. Where the exercise of the eminent domain power is rationally related to a conceivable public purpose, a compensated taking is not prohibited by the Public Use Clause. Here, regulating oligopoly and the evils associated with it is a classic exercise of a State's police powers, and redistribution of fees simple to reduce such evils is a rational exercise of the eminent domain power. The mere fact that property taken outright by eminent domain is transferred in the first instance to private beneficiaries does not condemn that taking as having only a private purpose. Government does not itself have to use property to legitimate the taking; it is only the taking's purpose, and not its mechanics, that must pass scrutiny under the Public Use Clause. And the fact that a state legislature, and not Congress, made the public use determination does not mean that judicial deference is less appropriate.

C

Reversed and remanded.

Brown v. Legal Foundation of Washington

538 U.S. 216 (2003)

FACTS

Every State uses interest on lawyers' trust accounts (IOLTA) to pay for legal services for the needy. In promulgating Rules establishing Washington's program, the State Supreme Court required that: (a) *all* client funds be deposited in interest-bearing trust accounts, (b) funds that cannot earn net interest for the client be deposited in an IOLTA account, (c) lawyers direct banks to pay the net interest on the IOLTA accounts to the Legal Foundation of Washington (Foundation), and (d) the Foundation use all such funds for tax-exempt law-related charitable and educational purposes. It seems apparent from the court's explanation of its IOLTA Rules that a lawyer who mistakenly uses an IOLTA account for money that could earn interest for the client would violate the Rule. That court subsequently made its IOLTA Rules applicable to Limited Practice Officers (LPOs), non-lawyers who are licensed to act as escrowees in real estate closings. Petitioners, who have funds that are deposited by LPOs in IOLTA accounts, and others sought to enjoin respondent state official from continuing this requirement, alleging, among other things, that the taking of the interest earned on their funds in IOLTA accounts violates the Just Compensation Clause of the Fifth Amendment, and that the requirement that client funds be placed in such accounts is an illegal taking of the beneficial use of those funds. The record suggests that petitioners' funds generated some interest that was paid to the Foundation, but that without IOLTA they would have produced no net interest for either petitioner. The District Court granted respondents summary judgment, concluding, as a factual matter, that petitioners could not make any net returns on the interest accrued in the accounts and, if they could, the funds would not be subject to the IOLTA program; and that, as a legal matter, the constitutional issue focused on what an owner has lost, not what the taker has gained, and that petitioners had lost nothing. While the case was on appeal, this Court decided in *Phillips* v. *Washington Legal Foundation,* that interest generated by funds held in IOLTA accounts is the private property of the owner of the principal. Relying on that case, a Ninth Circuit panel held that Washington's program caused an unconstitutional taking of petitioners' property and remanded the case for a determination whether they are entitled to just compensation. On reconsideration, the en banc Ninth Circuit affirmed the District Court's judgment, reasoning that, under the ad hoc approach applied in *Penn Central Transp. Co.* v. *New York City,* there was no taking because petitioners had suffered neither an actual loss nor an interference with any investment-backed expectations, and that if there were such a taking, the just compensation due was zero.

I

Is a state law requiring that client funds that could not otherwise generate net earnings for the client be deposited in an IOLTA account considered a regulatory taking?

R

A state law requiring that client funds that could not otherwise generate net earnings for the client be deposited in an IOLTA account is not a "regulatory taking," but a law requiring that the interest on those funds be transferred to a different owner for a legitimate public use could be a *per se* taking requiring the payment of "just compensation" to the client..

Brown v. Legal Foundation of Washington

538 U.S. 216 (2003)

A The Fifth Amendment imposes two conditions on the state's authority to confiscate private property: the taking must be for a "public use" and "just compensation" must be paid to the owner. In this case, the overall, dramatic success of IOLTA programs in serving the compelling interest in providing legal services to literally millions of needy Americans qualifies the Foundation's distribution of the funds as a "public use." The Court first addresses the type of taking that this case involves. The Court's jurisprudence concerning condemnations and physical takings involves the straightforward application of *per se* rules, while its regulatory takings jurisprudence is characterized by essentially ad hoc, factual inquiries designed to allow careful examination and weighing of all relevant circumstances. Even if viewed as the first step in a regulatory taking which should be analyzed under the *Penn Central* factors, it is clear that there would be no taking because the transaction had no adverse economic impact on petitioners and did not interfere with any investment-backed expectation. A *per se* approach is more consistent with the Court's reasoning in *Phillips* than *Penn Central*'s ad hoc analysis. Because interest earned in IOLTA accounts "is the 'private property' of the owner of the principal," the transfer of the interest to the Foundation here seems more akin to the occupation of a small amount of rooftop space in *Loretto* v. *Teleprompter Manhattan CATV Corp.,* which was a physical taking subject to *per se* rules. The Court therefore assumes that petitioners retained the beneficial ownership of at least a portion of their escrow deposits until the funds were disbursed at closings, that those funds generated interest in the IOLTA accounts, and that their interest was taken for a public use when it was turned over to the Foundation. This does not end the inquiry, however, for the Court must now determine whether any "just compensation" is due. Because "just compensation" is measured by the owner's pecuniary loss--which is zero whenever the Washington law is obeyed--there has been no violation of the Just Compensation Clause. This Court's consistent and unambiguous holdings support the conclusion that the "just compensation" required by the Fifth Amendment is measured by the property owner's loss rather than the government's gain. Applying the teachings of such cases to the question here, it is clear that neither petitioner is entitled to any compensation for the non-pecuniary consequences of the taking of the interest on his deposited funds and that any pecuniary compensation must be measured by his net losses rather than the value of the public's gain. Thus, if petitioners' net loss was zero, the compensation that is due is also zero. Because Washington's IOLTA program mandates a non-IOLTA account when net interest can be generated for the client, the compensation due petitioners for any taking of their property would be nil, and there was therefore no constitutional violation when they were not compensated.

C Affirmed.

Romer v. Evans

517 U.S. 620 (1996)

FACTS

After various Colorado municipalities passed ordinances banning discrimination based on sexual orientation in housing, employment, education, public accommodations, health and welfare services, and other transactions and activities, Colorado voters adopted by statewide referendum "Amendment 2" to the State Constitution, which precludes all legislative, executive, or judicial action at any level of state or local government designed to protect the status of persons based on their "homosexual, lesbian or bisexual orientation, conduct, practices or relationships." Respondents, who include aggrieved homosexuals and municipalities, commenced this litigation in state court against petitioner state parties to declare Amendment 2 invalid and enjoin its enforcement. The trial court's grant of a preliminary injunction was sustained by the Colorado Supreme Court, which held that Amendment 2 was subject to strict scrutiny under the Equal Protection Clause of the Fourteenth Amendment because it infringed the fundamental right of gays and lesbians to participate in the political process. On remand, the trial court found that the Amendment failed to satisfy strict scrutiny. It enjoined Amendment 2's enforcement, and the State Supreme Court affirmed.

I

Do laws enacted to strike down related laws that protect homosexuals from discrimination violate Equal Protection?

R

A law which strikes down all other laws which protect homosexuals broadly and invidiously seeks discriminate against homosexuals such that it will not pass a rational-basis review with respect to equal protection.

A

Amendment 2 violates the Equal Protection Clause. The State's principal argument that Amendment 2 puts gays and lesbians in the same position as all other persons by denying them special rights is rejected as implausible. The extent of the change in legal status effected by this law is evident from the authoritative construction of Colorado's Supreme Court - which establishes that the amendment's immediate effect is to repeal all existing statutes, regulations, ordinances, and policies of state and local entities barring discrimination based on sexual orientation, and that its ultimate effect is to prohibit any governmental entity from adopting similar, or more protective, measures in the future absent state constitutional amendment. Even if, as the State contends, homosexuals can find protection in laws and policies of general application, Amendment 2 goes well beyond merely depriving them of special rights. It imposes a broad disability upon those persons alone, forbidding them, but no others, to seek specific legal protection from injuries caused by discrimination in a wide range of public and private transactions. In order to reconcile the Fourteenth Amendment's promise that no person shall be denied equal protection with the practical reality that most legislation classifies for one purpose or another, the Court has stated that it will uphold a law that neither burdens a fundamental right nor targets a suspect class so long as the legislative classification bears a rational relation to some independent and legitimate legislative end. Amendment 2 fails, indeed defies, even this conventional inquiry. First, the amendment is at once too narrow and too broad, identifying persons by a single trait and then denying them the possibility of protection across the board. This disqualification of a class of persons from the right to obtain specific protection from the law is unprecedented and is itself a denial of equal protection in the most literal sense. Second, the sheer breadth of Amendment 2, which makes a general announcement that gays and lesbians shall not have any particular protections from the law, is so far removed from the reasons offered for it, i.e., respect for other citizens' freedom of association, particularly landlords or employers who have personal or religious objections to homosexuality, and the State's interest in conserving resources to fight discrimination against other groups, that the amendment cannot be explained by reference to those reasons; the Amendment raises the inevitable inference that it is born of animosity toward the class that it affects. Amendment 2 cannot be said to be directed to an identifiable legitimate purpose or discrete objective. It is a status-based classification of persons undertaken for its own sake, something the Equal Protection Clause does not permit.

C

Affirmed.

United States Railroad Retirement Board v. Fritz

449 U.S. 166 (1980)

FACTS

The Railroad Retirement Act of 1974 (1974 Act) fundamentally restructured the railroad retirement system under the predecessor 1937 Act, which had included provisions whereby a person who worked for both railroad and non-railroad employers and who qualified for both railroad retirement and social security benefits received benefits under both systems and an accompanying "windfall" benefit. Although providing that employees who lacked the requisite 10 years of railroad employment to qualify for railroad retirement benefits as of the January 1, 1975, changeover date would not receive any windfall benefits, the 1974 Act preserved windfall benefits for individuals who had retired and were receiving dual benefits as of the changeover date. A provision of the 1974 Act, 45 U.S.C. 231b (h) (1), also preserved windfall benefits for employees who had qualified for dual benefits as of the changeover date, but who had not yet retired, if they had (1) performed some railroad service in 1974 or (2) had a "current connection" with the railroad industry as of December 31, 1974, or their later retirement date, or (3) completed 25 years of railroad service as of December 31, 1974. The 1974 Act further provided, 45 U.S.C. 231b (h) (2), that employees who had qualified for railroad benefits as of the changeover date, but lacked a current connection with the railroad industry in 1974 and 25 years of railroad employment, could obtain a lesser amount of windfall benefits if they had qualified for social security benefits as of the year (prior to 1975) they left railroad employment. Appellee and others filed a class action in Federal District Court for a declaratory judgment that 231b (h) is unconstitutional under the Due Process Clause of the Fifth Amendment, contending that it was irrational for Congress to distinguish between employees who had more than 10 years but less than 25 years of railroad employment simply on the basis of whether they had a "current connection" with the railroad industry as of the changeover date or as of the date of retirement. The District Court certified a plaintiff class of all persons eligible to retire between January 1, 1975, and January 31, 1977, who were permanently insured under the Social Security Act as of December 31, 1974, but who were not eligible to receive any windfall benefits because they had left the railroad industry before 1974, had no "current connection" with it at the end of 1974, and had less than 25 years of railroad service. The court held that the differentiation based solely on whether an employee was "active" in the railroad business as of 1974 was not "rationally related" to the congressional purposes of insuring the solvency of the railroad retirement system and protecting vested benefits.

I When social and economic legislation enacted by Congress is challenged on equal protection grounds as being violative of the Fifth Amendment, is the rational-basis standard the appropriate standard of judicial review?

R When social and economic legislation enacted by Congress is challenged on equal protection grounds as being violative of the Fifth Amendment, the rational-basis standard is the appropriate standard of judicial review.

A The challenged provisions of the 1974 Act do not deny the plaintiff class equal protection of the laws guaranteed by the Fifth Amendment. When social and economic legislation enacted by Congress is challenged on equal protection grounds as being violative of the Fifth Amendment, the rational-basis standard is the appropriate standard of judicial review. If the classification has some "reasonable basis," it does not offend the Constitution simply because the classification is not made with mathematical nicety or because in practice it results in some inequality. This Court will not invalidate on equal protection grounds legislation that it simply deems unwise or unartfully drawn. Under such principles, 231b (h) does not violate the Fifth Amendment. Because Congress could have eliminated windfall benefits for all classes of employees, it is not constitutionally impermissible for Congress to have drawn lines between groups of employees for the purpose of phasing out those benefits. Congress did not achieve its purpose in a patently arbitrary or irrational way, since it could properly conclude that persons who had actually acquired statutory entitlement to windfall benefits while still employed in the railroad industry had a greater equitable claim to those benefits than the members of the plaintiff class who were no longer in railroad employment when they became eligible for dual benefits. Furthermore, the "current connection" test is not a patently arbitrary means for determining which employees are "career railroaders," the class for whom the 1974 Act was designed. Nor is there merit to the District Court's conclusion that Congress was unaware of what it accomplished or that it was misled by the groups that appeared before it. The language of the statute is clear, and it has been historically assumed that Congress intended what it enacted.

C

Reversed.

Railway Express Agency v. New York

336 U.S. 106 (1949)

FACTS

Section 124 of the Traffic Regulations of the City of New York promulgated by the Police Commissioner provides that No person shall operate upon any street an advertising vehicle, except that businesses may advertise their own products or services on their own vehicles. Appellant, Railway Express Agency ("Railway") is a company engaged in a nationwide express business. It operates about 1,900 trucks in New York City and sells the space on the exterior sides of these trucks for advertising. That advertising is for the most part unconnected with its own business. It was convicted in the Magistrate Court and fined for violating the statute. The judgment of conviction was sustained in the Court of Special Sessions. The Court of Appeals affirmed without opinion by a divided vote. The case is here on appeal.

I Can a state statute punishes one group for selling advertising space on the side of their trucks while leaving untouched another group who do the same of their own trucks, do so without violating the Equal Protection rights of the former group?

R If a statute that regulates economic activity bears a rational relationship to the purpose for which it was made, the statute will survive an equal protection challenge.

A We do not sit to weigh evidence on the due process issue in order to determine whether the regulation is sound or appropriate; nor is it our function to pass judgment on its wisdom. It is the judgment of the local authorities that it does have such a relation. And nothing has been advanced which shows that to be palpably false. The question of equal protection is our concern. It is pointed out that the regulation draws the line between advertisements of products sold by the owner of the truck and general advertisements. It is argued that unequal treatment on the basis of such a distinction is not justified by the aim and purpose of the regulation. It is said, for example, that one of appellant's trucks carrying the advertisement of a commercial house would not cause any greater distraction of pedestrians and vehicle drivers than if the commercial house carried the same advertisement on its own truck. Yet the regulation allows the latter to do what the former is forbidden from doing. It is therefore contended that the classification which the regulation makes has no relation to the traffic problem since a violation turns not on what kind of advertisements are carried on trucks but on whose trucks they are carried. The local authorities may well have concluded that those who advertised their own wares on their trucks do not present the same traffic problem in view of the nature or extent of the advertising which they use. If that judgment is correct, the advertising displays that are exempt impede traffic less than those of appellants. We cannot say that this is not the case. But if it is, the classification has relation to the purpose for which it is made and does not contain the kind of discrimination against which the Equal Protection Clause affords protection. It is by such practical considerations based on experience rather than by theoretical inconsistencies that the question of equal protection is to be answered. And the fact that New York City sees fit to eliminate from traffic this kind of distraction but leaves untouched s the vivid displays on Times Square, is immaterial. Equal protection does not mandate that all evils of the same kind be eradicated or not at all. The classification is related to the purpose for which the statute was made. Where traffic control and the use of highways are involved and where there is no conflicting federal regulation, great leeway is allowed local authorities, even though the local regulation materially interferes with interstate commerce.

C

Affirmed.

New York City Transit Authority v. Beazer

440 U.S. 568 (1979)

FACTS

Petitioner, New York City Transit Authority (TA), which, in operating the subway system and certain bus lines in New York City, employs about 47,000 persons, of whom many are employed in positions that involve danger to themselves or to the public, enforces a general policy against employing persons who use narcotic drugs. TA interprets its drug regulation to encompass current users of methadone, including those receiving methadone maintenance treatments for curing heroin addiction. Respondents, two former employees of TA who were dismissed while they were receiving methadone treatment, and two persons who were refused employment because they were receiving methadone treatment, brought a class action, alleging, *inter alia*, that TA's blanket exclusion of all former heroin addicts receiving methadone treatments was illegal under Title VII of the Civil Rights Act of 1964 and the Equal Protection Clause of the Fourteenth Amendment. The District Court found that TA's blanket methadone policy violates the Equal Protection Clause, and granted injunctive relief which, however, authorized TA to exclude methadone users from specific categories of safety-sensitive positions and also to condition eligibility on satisfactory performance in a methadone program for at least a year. Subsequently, the District Court also held that TA's drug policy violates Title VII because even though the policy was not adopted with a discriminatory purpose, it nevertheless was not related to any of TA's business needs. The Court of Appeals affirmed the District Court's constitutional holding without reaching the statutory question.

I

Can the government constitutionally exclude from employment an entire class of people based on their use of methadone, a narcotic drug?

R

The blanket exclusion of persons from governmental employment who regularly use narcotic drugs is constitutional when it is not directed against any specific individual or category of persons and does not define a class of persons characterized by some unpopular trait or association.

A

An amendment to the Rehabilitation Act of 1973 after certiorari was granted, even if construed to proscribe TA's enforcement of a general rule denying employment to methadone users, does not render the case moot, since respondents' claims arose even before that Act itself was passed, and they have been awarded monetary relief. More importantly, however this Court might construe that Act, the concerns that prompted the grant of certiorari - the lower courts' departure from the procedure normally followed in addressing statutory and constitutional questions in the same case, and the concern that those courts erroneously decided the merits of such questions - would still merit this Court's attention. The statistical evidence on which respondents and the District Court relied does not support the conclusion that TA's regulation prohibiting the use of narcotics, or its interpretation of that regulation to encompass users of methadone, violated Title VII. The statistic that 81% of the employees referred to TA's medical director for suspected violations of its narcotics rule were either black or Hispanic indicates nothing about the racial composition of the employees suspected of using methadone, and respondents have only challenged the rule to the extent that it is construed to apply to methadone users. Nor does the record provide any information about the number of black, Hispanic, or white persons who were dismissed for using methadone. The statistic that about 63% of the persons in New York City receiving methadone maintenance in public programs are black or Hispanic does not indicate how many of these persons ever worked or sought to work for TA; tells nothing about the class of otherwise-qualified applicants and employees who have participated in methadone maintenance programs for over a year, the only class improperly excluded by TA's policy under the District Court's analysis; and affords no data on the 14,000 methadone users in private programs, leaving open the possibility that the percentage of blacks and Hispanics in the class of methadone users is not significantly greater than the percentage of those minorities in the general population of New York City. Even if respondents' statistical showing is considered to be sufficient to establish a prima facie case of discrimination, it is rebutted by TA's demonstration that its narcotics rule (and the rule's application to methadone users) is "job related." The District Court's finding that the rule was not motivated by racial animus forecloses any claim that it was merely a pretext for intentional discrimination. TA's blanket exclusion of persons who regularly use narcotic drugs, including methadone, does not violate the Equal Protection Clause for failing to include more precise special rules for methadone users who have progressed satisfactorily with their treatment for one year and who, when examined individually, satisfy TA's employment criteria for non-sensitive jobs. An employment policy such as TA's that postpones eligibility for employment until the methadone treatment has been completed, rather than accepting an intermediate point on an uncertain line - such as one year of treatment - is rational and is neither unprincipled nor invidious in the sense that it implies disrespect for the excluded subclass. Even assuming that TA's rule is broader than necessary to exclude those methadone users who are not actually qualified to work for TA, and that it is probably unwise for a large employer like TA to rely on a general rule instead of individualized considerations of every job applicant, nevertheless under the circumstances of this case such assumptions concern matters of personnel policy that do not implicate the principle safeguarded by the Equal Protection Clause.

C

Reversed.

U.S. Department of Agriculture v. Moreno

413 U.S. 528 (1973)

FACTS

Section 3(e) of the Food Stamp Act of 1964, as amended in 1971, generally excludes from participation in the food stamp program any household containing an individual who is unrelated to any other household member. The Secretary of Agriculture issued regulations thereunder rendering ineligible for participation in the program any "household" whose members are not "all related to each other." Congress stated that the purposes of the Act were "to safeguard the health and well-being of the Nation's population and raise levels of nutrition among low-income households . . . [and] that increased utilization of food in establishing and maintaining adequate national levels of nutrition will promote the distribution . . . of our agricultural abundance and will strengthen our agricultural economy . . . ." The District Court held that the "unrelated person" provision of 3 (e) creates an irrational classification in violation of the equal protection component of the Due Process Clause of the Fifth Amendment. Held: The legislative classification here involved cannot be sustained, the classification being clearly irrelevant to the stated purposes of the Act and not rationally furthering any other legitimate governmental interest. In practical operation, the Act excludes, not those who are "likely to abuse the program." but, rather, only those who so desperately need aid that they cannot even afford to alter their living arrangements so as to retain their eligibility. This case requires us to consider the constitutionality of 3 (e) of the Food Stamp Act of 1964, 7 U.S.C. 2012 (e), as amended in 1971, 84 Stat. 2048, which, with certain exceptions, excludes from participation in the food stamp program any household containing an individual who is unrelated to any other member of the household. In practical effect, 3 (e) creates two classes of persons for food stamp purposes: one class is composed of those individuals who live in households all of whose members are related to one another, and the other class consists of those individuals who live in households containing one or more members who are unrelated to the rest. The latter class of persons is denied federal food assistance. A three-judge District Court for the District of Columbia held this classification invalid as violative of the Due Process Clause of the Fifth Amendment.

I

If a statute classifies persons in a manner which is irrelevant to the stated purpose of the law, can the statute be invalidated on the ground of rational basis review?

R

A challenged classification must rationally further some legitimate governmental interest.

A

The federal food stamp program was established in 1964 in an effort to alleviate hunger and malnutrition among the more needy segments of our society. Eligibility for participation in the program is determined on a household rather than an individual basis. As initially enacted, 3 (e) defined a "household" as "a group of related or non-related individuals, who are not residents of an institution or boarding house, but are living as one economic unit sharing common cooking facilities and for whom food is customarily purchased in common." In January

1971, however, Congress redefined the term "household" so as to include only groups of related individuals. Pursuant to this amendment, the Secretary of Agriculture promulgated regulations rendering ineligible for participation in the program any "household" whose members are not "all related to each other." Appellees in this case consist of several groups of individuals who allege that, although they satisfy the income eligibility requirements for federal food assistance, they have nevertheless been excluded from the program solely because the persons in each group are not "all related to each other." Appellees instituted a class action against the Department of Agriculture, its Secretary, and two other departmental officials, seeking declaratory and injunctive relief against the enforcement of the 1971 amendment of 3 (e) and its implementing regulations. In essence, appellees contend, and the District Court held, that the "unrelated person" provision of 3(e) creates an irrational classification in violation of the equal protection component of the Due Process Clause of the Fifth Amendment. We agree. Under traditional equal protection analysis, a legislative classification must be sustained if the classification itself is rationally related to a legitimate governmental interest. The challenged statutory classification (households of related persons versus households containing one or more unrelated persons) is clearly irrelevant to the stated purposes of the Act. As the District Court recognized, "[t]he relationships among persons constituting one economic unit and sharing cooking facilities have nothing to do with their abilities to stimulate the agricultural economy by purchasing farm surpluses, or with their personal nutritional requirements." Thus, if it is to be sustained, the challenged classification must rationally further some legitimate governmental interest other than those specifically stated in the congressional "declaration of policy." In practical operation, the 1971 amendment excludes from participation in the food stamp program, not those persons who are "likely to abuse the program" but, rather, only those persons who are so desperately in need of aid that they cannot even afford to alter their living arrangements so as to retain their eligibility. Traditional equal protection analysis does not require that every classification be drawn with precise "`mathematical nicety.'" *Dandridge v. Williams*. But the classification here in issue is not only "imprecise," it is wholly without any rational basis. The judgment of the District Court holding the "unrelated person" provision invalid under the Due Process Clause of the Fifth Amendment is therefore Affirmed.

C

Affirmed.

City of Cleburne v. Cleburne Living Center Inc.

473 U.S. 432 (1985)

FACTS

Respondent Cleburne Living Center, Inc. (CLC), which anticipated leasing a certain building for the operation of a group home for the mentally retarded, was informed by petitioner city that a special use permit would be required, the city having concluded that the proposed group home should be classified as a "hospital for the feebleminded" under the zoning ordinance covering the area in which the proposed home would be located. Accordingly, CLC applied for a special use permit, but the City Council, after a public hearing, denied the permit. CLC and others (also respondents here) then filed suit against the city and a number of its officials, alleging that the zoning ordinance, on its face and as applied, violated the equal protection rights of CLC and its potential residents. The District Court held the ordinance and its application constitutional. The Court of Appeals reversed, holding that mental retardation is a "quasi-suspect" classification; that, under the applicable "heightened-scrutiny" equal protection test, the ordinance was facially invalid because it did not substantially further an important governmental purpose; and that the ordinance was also invalid as applied.

I Is a local government ordinance requiring a group home for the mentally retarded to apply for and secure a special-use permit violate equal protection, when other groups are not required to do so?

R The class consisting of the mentally retarded is *not* a quasi-suspect class such that a regulation relating to them will be reviewed under a rational basis standard of review.

A The Court of Appeals erred in holding mental retardation a quasi-suspect classification calling for a more exacting standard of judicial review than is normally accorded economic and social legislation. Where individuals in a group affected by a statute have distinguishing characteristics relevant to interests a State has the authority to implement, the Equal Protection Clause requires only that the classification drawn by the statute be rationally related to a legitimate state interest. When social or economic legislation is at issue, the Equal Protection Clause allows the States wide latitude. Mentally retarded persons, who have a reduced ability to cope with and function in the everyday world, are thus different from other persons, and the States' interest in dealing with and providing for them is plainly a legitimate one. The distinctive legislative response, both national and state, to the plight of those who are mentally retarded demonstrates not only that they have unique problems, but also that the lawmakers have been addressing their difficulties in a manner that belies a continuing antipathy or prejudice and a corresponding need for more intrusive oversight by the judiciary than is afforded under the normal equal protection standard. Moreover, the legislative response, which could hardly have occurred and survived without public support, negates any claim that the mentally retarded are politically powerless in the sense that they have no ability to attract the attention of the lawmakers. The equal protection standard requiring that legislation be rationally related to a legitimate governmental purpose affords government the latitude necessary both to pursue policies designed to assist the retarded in realizing their full potential, and to freely and efficiently engage in activities that burden the retarded in what is essentially an incidental manner. Requiring a special use permit for the proposed group home here deprives respondents of the equal protection of the laws, and thus it is unnecessary to decide whether the ordinance's permit requirement is facially invalid where the mentally retarded are involved. Although the mentally retarded, as a group, are different from those who occupy other facilities - such as boarding houses and hospitals - that are permitted in the zoning area in question without a special permit, such difference is irrelevant unless the proposed group home would threaten the city's legitimate interests in a way that the permitted uses would not. The record does not reveal any rational basis for believing that the proposed group home would pose any special threat to the city's legitimate interests. Requiring the permit in this case appears to rest on an irrational prejudice against the mentally retarded, including those who would occupy the proposed group home and who would live under the closely supervised and highly regulated conditions expressly provided for by state and federal law.

C

Affirmed in part, vacated in part, and remanded.

Dred Scott v. Sandford

60 U.S. (*19 How.*) 393 (1856)

FACTS

Plaintiff Dred Scott, admittedly once a slave but now claiming to be a citizen of Missouri, brought an action in trespass in the Circuit Court of the United States for the District of Missouri against Defendant John F. A. Sanford [name misspelled in the official case], his owner and a citizen of New York. In 1834, Scott was taken by a former owner to Illinois, a free state, where he lived for two years. Two years later Scott and his owner moved to Minnesota, then part of the Louisiana Territory. In 1838, they returned to Missouri, where Scott was sold to Sanford. Scott brought suit seeking his freedom on the ground that he became free when he and his master lived in a free state and a free territory. Sanford argued that Scott was not free, and if he was, that he was not a citizen of Missouri and the court therefore lacked diversity of citizenship. The circuit court ruled for Scott and Sanford appealed.

I

Are slaves "citizens" within the meaning of the Constitution?

R

Slaves are not "citizens" within the meaning of the Constitution and a State cannot grant a slave such a right; nor can Congress cannot prohibit a citizen from owning slaves in a territory in which it is prohibited.

A

The Constitution never intended slaves to be included in the body of its citizens. Accordingly, slaves cannot claim any of the rights and privileges which the Constitution affords. It is not for us to decide whether issues of policy or injustice mandate a change - that is the province of the legislature. We are merely charged with interpreting the Constitution according to its true intent and meaning at the time it was adopted, which is what we have done here. Under the Constitution, Congress, and not the states, have the right to determine who can become a citizen of the United States. Consequently, no State can grant Scott the rights and privileges secured by citizens under the federal government. Therefore, he is not a citizen of the U.S. or of the State of Missouri, and as such cannot sue in the federal courts. Scott also seeks his freedom on the ground that he, for a period of four years, lived in a territory in which slavery is prohibited. Yet the act of Congress prohibiting the owning of slaves in the Louisiana Territory would deprive slave owners of the right to own their property. Congress cannot take away the right to own slaves and Scott's living in a free territory did not give him his freedom.

C

Reversed.

Korematsu v. United States

323 U.S. 214 (1944)

FACTS

Petitioner Korematsu, an American citizen of Japanese descent, was convicted in a federal district court for remaining in San Leandro, California, a 'Military Area', contrary to Civilian Exclusion Order No. 34 of the Commanding General of the Western Command, U.S. Army, which directed that after May 9, 1942, all persons of Japanese ancestry should be excluded from that area. No question was raised as to petitioner's loyalty to the United States. The Circuit Court of Appeals affirmed, and the importance of the constitutional question involved caused the U.S Supreme Court to grant certiorari.

I

Can race-based exclusions be constitutionally justified on account of military necessity?

R

Race-based exclusions can be constitutionally justified on account of military necessity but will be subjected to high level of scrutiny.

A

It should be noted, to begin with, that all legal restrictions which curtail the civil rights of a single racial group are immediately suspect. That is not to say that all such restrictions are unconstitutional. It is to say that courts must subject them to the most rigid scrutiny. Pressing public necessity may sometimes justify the existence of such restrictions; racial antagonism never can. In the instant case prosecution of the petitioner was begun by information charging violation of an Act of Congress which provides, in part, that ' . . . whoever shall enter, remain in, leave, or commit any act in any military area or military zone prescribed, under the authority of an Executive order of the President, by the Secretary of War, or by any military commander . . . knowingly . . . shall . . . be guilty of a misdemeanor and upon conviction shall be liable to a fine of not to exceed $5,000 or to imprisonment for not more than one year, or both, for each offense.' Like curfew, exclusion of those of Japanese origin was deemed necessary because of the presence of an unascertained number of disloyal members of the group, most of whom we have no doubt were loyal to this country. It was because we could not reject the finding of the military authorities that it was impossible to bring about an immediate segregation of the disloyal from the loyal that we sustained the validity of the curfew order as applying to the whole group. In the instant case, temporary exclusion of the entire group was rested by the military on the same ground. The judgment that exclusion of the whole group was for the same reason a military imperative answers the contention that the exclusion was in the nature of group punishment based on antagonism to those of Japanese origin. That there were members of the group who retained loyalties to Japan has been confirmed by investigations made subsequent to the exclusion. Approximately five thousand American citizens of Japanese ancestry refused to swear unqualified allegiance to the United States and to renounce allegiance to the Japanese Emperor, and several thousand evacuees requested repatriation to Japan. We uphold the exclusion order as of the time it was made and when the petitioner violated it. In doing so, we are not unmindful of the hardships imposed by it upon a large group of American citizens. But hardships are part of war, and war is an aggregation of hardships. All citizens alike, both in and out of uniform, feel the impact of war in greater or lesser measure. Citizenship has its responsibilities as well as its privileges, and in time of war the burden is always heavier. Compulsory exclusion of large groups of citizens from their homes, except under circumstances of direst emergency and peril, is inconsistent with our basic governmental institutions. But when under conditions of modern warfare our shores are threatened by hostile forces, the power to protect must be commensurate with the threatened danger.

C Affirmed.

Loving v. Virginia

388 U.S. 1 (1967)

FACTS

In June 1958, two residents of Virginia, Mildred Jeter, a Negro woman, and Richard Loving, a white man, were married in the District of Columbia pursuant to its laws. Shortly after their marriage, the Lovings returned to Virginia and established their marital abode in Caroline County. At the October Term, 1958, of the Circuit Court of Caroline County, a grand jury issued an indictment charging the Lovings with violating Virginia's ban on interracial marriages. On January 6, 1959, the Lovings pleaded guilty to the charge and were sentenced to one year in jail; however, the trial judge suspended the sentence for a period of 25 years on the condition that the Lovings leave the State and not return to Virginia together for 25 years. After their convictions, the Lovings took up residence in the District of Columbia. On November 6, 1963, they filed a motion in the state trial court to vacate the judgment and set aside the sentence on the ground that the statutes which they had violated were repugnant to the Fourteenth Amendment. The motion not having been decided by October 28, 1964, the Lovings instituted a class action in the United States District Court for the Eastern District of Virginia requesting that a three-judge court be convened to declare the Virginia statutes unconstitutional and to enjoin state officials from enforcing their convictions. On January 22, 1965, the state trial judge denied the motion to vacate the sentences, and the Lovings perfected an appeal to the Supreme Court of Appeals of Virginia. On February 11, 1965, the three-judge District Court continued the case to allow the Lovings to present their constitutional claims to the highest state court. The Supreme Court of Appeals upheld the constitutionality of the statutes and, after modifying the sentence, affirmed the convictions. The Lovings appealed this decision and the U.S. Supreme Court noted probable jurisdiction on December 12, 1966.

I

Does a statutory scheme adopted by the State of Virginia to prevent marriages between persons solely on the basis of racial classifications violate the Equal Protection and Due Process Clauses of the Fourteenth Amendment?

R

Laws that classify on the basis of race are reviewed under a strict scrutiny standard / equal protection analysis and will be stricken unless they are necessary to achieve a compelling state interest.

A

The two statutes under which appellants were convicted and sentenced are part of a comprehensive statutory scheme aimed at prohibiting and punishing interracial marriages. The Lovings were convicted of violating 20-58 of the Virginia Code. Virginia is now one of 16 States which prohibit and punish marriages on the basis of racial classifications. Penalties for miscegenation arose as an incident to slavery and have been common in Virginia since the colonial period. In upholding the constitutionality of these provisions in the decision below, the Supreme Court of Appeals of Virginia referred to its 1955 decision in *Naim v. Naim*, as stating the reasons supporting the validity of these laws. In *Naim*, the state court concluded that the State's legitimate purposes were "to preserve the racial integrity of its citizens," and to prevent "the corruption of blood," "a mongrel breed of citizens," and "the obliteration of racial pride," obviously an endorsement of the doctrine of White Supremacy. The State argues that the meaning of the Equal Protection Clause, as illuminated by the statements of the Framers, is only that state penal laws containing an interracial element as part of the definition of the offense must apply equally to whites and Negroes in the sense that members of each race are punished to the same degree. Thus, the State contends that, because its miscegenation statutes punish equally both the white and the Negro participants in an interracial marriage, these statutes, despite their reliance on racial classifications, do not constitute an invidious discrimination based upon race. The second argument advanced by the State assumes the validity of its equal application theory. The argument is that, if the Equal Protection Clause does not outlaw miscegenation statutes because of their reliance on racial classifications, the question of constitutionality would thus become whether there was any rational basis for a State to treat interracial marriages differently from other marriages. On this question, the State argues, the scientific evidence is substantially in doubt and, consequently, this Court should defer to the wisdom of the state legislature in adopting its policy of discouraging interracial marriages. Because we reject the notion that the mere "equal application" of a statute containing racial classifications is enough to remove the classifications from the Fourteenth Amendment's proscription of all invidious racial discriminations, we do not accept the State's contention that these statutes should be upheld if there is any possible basis for concluding that they serve a rational purpose. In the case at bar we deal with statutes containing racial classifications, and the fact of equal application does not immunize the statute from the very heavy burden of justification which the Fourteenth Amendment has traditionally required of state statutes drawn according to race. There is patently no legitimate overriding purpose independent of invidious racial discrimination which justifies this classification. The fact that Virginia prohibits only interracial marriages involving white persons demonstrates that the racial classifications must stand on their own justification, as measures designed to maintain White Supremacy. We have consistently denied the constitutionality of measures which restrict the rights of citizens on account of race. There can be no doubt that restricting the freedom to marry solely because of racial classifications violates the central meaning of the Equal Protection Clause. These statutes also deprive the Lovings of liberty without due process of law in violation of the Due Process Clause of the Fourteenth Amendment. The freedom to marry has long been recognized as one of the vital personal rights essential to the orderly pursuit of happiness by free men. Marriage is one of the "basic civil rights of man," fundamental to our very existence and survival. To deny this fundamental freedom on so unsupportable a basis as the racial classifications embodied in these statutes, classifications so directly subversive of the principle of equality at the heart of the Fourteenth Amendment, is surely to deprive all the State's citizens of liberty without due process of law. The Fourteenth Amendment requires that the freedom of choice to marry not be restricted by invidious racial discriminations. Under our Constitution, the freedom to marry, or not marry, a person of another race resides with the individual and cannot be infringed by the State. These convictions must be reversed. It is so ordered.

C

Reversed.

Palmore v. Sidoti

466 U.S. 429 (1984)

FACTS

When petitioner and respondent, both Caucasians, were divorced in Florida, petitioner, the mother, was awarded custody of their 3-year-old daughter. The following year respondent sought custody of the child by filing a petition to modify the prior judgment because of changed conditions, namely, that petitioner was then cohabiting with a Negro, whom she later married. The Florida trial court awarded custody to respondent, concluding that the child's best interests would be served thereby. Without focusing directly on the parental qualifications of petitioner, her present husband, or respondent, the court reasoned that although respondent's resentment at petitioner's choice of a black partner was insufficient to deprive petitioner of custody, there would be a damaging impact on the child if she remained in a racially mixed household. The Florida District Court of Appeal affirmed.

I

Can the effects of racial prejudice justify a racial classification removing an infant child from the custody of its natural mother?

R

The effects of racial prejudice, however real, cannot justify a racial classification removing an infant child from the custody of its natural mother.

A

The effects of racial prejudice, however real, cannot justify a racial classification removing an infant child from the custody of its natural mother. The Constitution cannot control such prejudice, but neither can it tolerate it. Private biases may be outside the reach of the law, but the law cannot, directly or indirectly, give them effect.

C

Reversed.

Plessy v. Ferguson

163 U.S. 537 (1896)

FACTS

An 1890 a Louisiana statute required railroad companies to provide white and non-white passengers with "equal but separate accommodations for the white and colored races." Under the statute, passengers using facilities for a different race were held criminally liable. Defendant Plessy, a professed octoroon [a person whose ancestry is one-eighth Black] was prosecuted under the statute after refusing to leave a portion of the train reserved for white persons. The Louisiana Supreme Court upheld the constitutionality of the statute.

I

Does a statute mandating the separation of whites and non-whites in public accommodations violate the 14th Amendment?

R

Even though the 14th Amendment was enacted to enforce the absolute equality of the races, it was not intended to abolish distinctions based on color, enforce social equality or force a commingling of the races.

R

Even though the 14th Amendment was enacted to enforce the absolute equality of the races, it was not intended to abolish distinctions based on color, enforce social equality or force a commingling of the races. Indeed, laws permitting and requiring separation of the races in places in which blacks and whites are likely to come into contact do not imply the inferiority of either race and do not result in a violation of the 14th Amendment. The most common instance of this rule is the segregation of schools, which is generally recognized by courts as a proper exercise of state legislative and police powers. Plessy suggests that this same argument will be used to justify all sorts of rules to keep blacks and whites separate, such as requiring them to walk on different sides of the street or to paint their houses different colors. The reply to this is that every exercise of the police power must be reasonable, and extend only to such laws as are enacted in good faith for the promotion of the public good, and not for the annoyance or oppression of a particular class. Plessy's argument is based on an assumption that the enforced separation of the two races places a badge of inferiority on colored people. We disagree. The argument assumes that social prejudices may be overcome only through the legislative process and that equal rights can only be secured by blacks through the forced commingling of the races. If one race be inferior to the other socially, the Constitution cannot put them on the same plane.

C

Affirmed.

Brown v. Board of Education [Brown I]

347 U.S. 483 (1954)

FACTS

These cases come to us from the States of Kansas, South Carolina, Virginia, and Delaware. They are premised on different facts and different local conditions, but a common legal question justifies their consideration together in this consolidated opinion. In each of the cases, minors of the Negro race, through their legal representatives, seek the aid of the courts in obtaining admission to the public schools of their community on a non-segregated basis. In each instance, they had been denied admission to schools attended by white children under laws requiring or permitting segregation according to race. This segregation was alleged to deprive the plaintiffs of the equal protection of the laws under the Fourteenth Amendment. In each of the cases other than the Delaware case, a three-judge federal district court denied relief to the plaintiffs on the so-called "separate but equal" doctrine announced by this Court in *Plessy v. Ferguson*. Under that doctrine, equality of treatment is accorded when the races are provided substantially equal facilities, even though these facilities be separate. In the Delaware case, the Supreme Court of Delaware adhered to that doctrine, but ordered that the plaintiffs be admitted to the white schools because of their superiority to the Negro schools. The plaintiffs contend that segregated public schools are not "equal" and cannot be made "equal," and that hence they are deprived of the equal protection of the laws. Because of the obvious importance of the question presented, the Court took jurisdiction. Argument was heard in the 1952 Term, and reargument was heard this Term on certain questions propounded by the Court.

I

Does segregation of children in public schools solely on the basis of race, even though the physical facilities and other "tangible" factors may be equal, deprive the children of the minority group of equal educational opportunities?

R

Segregation of white and Negro children in the public schools of a State solely on the basis of race, pursuant to state laws permitting or requiring such segregation, denies to Negro children the equal protection of the laws guaranteed by the Fourteenth Amendment.

A

Today, education is perhaps the most important function of state and local governments. Compulsory school attendance laws and the great expenditures for education both demonstrate our recognition of the importance of education to our democratic society. It is required in the performance of our most basic public responsibilities, even service in the armed forces. It is the very foundation of good citizenship. Such an opportunity, where the state has undertaken to provide it, is a right which must be made available to all on equal terms. We come then to the question presented: Does segregation of children in public schools solely on the basis of race, even though the physical facilities and other "tangible" factors may be equal, deprive the children of the minority group of equal educational opportunities? We believe that it does. In *Sweatt v. Painter*, in finding that a segregated law school for Negroes could not provide them equal educational opportunities, this Court relied in large part on "those qualities which are incapable of objective measurement but which make for greatness in a law school." In *McLaurin v. Oklahoma State Regents*, the Court, in requiring that a African American admitted to a white graduate school be treated like all other students, again resorted to intangible considerations: ". . . his ability to study, to engage in discussions and exchange views with other students, and, in general, to learn his profession." Such considerations apply with added force to children in grade and high schools. To separate them from others of similar age and qualifications solely because of their race generates a feeling of inferiority as to their status in the community that may affect their hearts and minds in a way unlikely ever to be undone. We conclude that in the field of public education the doctrine of "separate but equal" has no place. Separate educational facilities are inherently unequal. Therefore, we hold that the plaintiffs and others similarly situated for whom the actions have been brought are, by reason of the segregation complained of, deprived of the equal protection of the laws guaranteed by the Fourteenth Amendment. This disposition makes unnecessary any discussion whether such segregation also violates the Due Process Clause of the Fourteenth Amendment. Because these are class actions, because of the wide applicability of this decision, and because of the great variety of local conditions, the formulation of decrees in these cases presents problems of considerable complexity. On reargument, the consideration of appropriate relief was necessarily subordinated to the primary question - the constitutionality of segregation in public education. We have now announced that such segregation is a denial of the equal protection of the laws.

C

Reversed.

Washington v. Davis

426 U.S. 229 (1976)

FACTS

Plaintiff-respondents Harley and Sellers, both Negroes whose applications to become police officers in the District of Columbia had been rejected, in an action against District of Columbia officials (Defendant-petitioners) and others, claimed that the Police Department's recruiting procedures, including a written personnel test (Test 21), were racially discriminatory and violated the Due Process Clause of the Fifth Amendment. Test 21 is administered generally to prospective Government employees to determine whether applicants have acquired a particular level of verbal skill. Respondents contended that the test bore no relationship to job performance and excluded a disproportionately high number of Negro applicants. Focusing solely on Test 21, the parties filed cross-motions for summary judgment. The District Court, noting the absence of any claim of intentional discrimination, found that respondents' evidence supporting their motion warranted the conclusions that (a) the number of black police officers, while substantial, is not proportionate to the city's population mix; (b) a higher percentage of blacks fail the test than whites; and (c) the test has not been validated to establish its reliability for measuring subsequent job performance. While that showing sufficed to shift the burden of proof to the defendants in the action, the court concluded that respondents were not entitled to relief, and granted petitioners' motion for summary judgment, in view of the facts that 44% of new police recruits were black, a figure proportionate to the blacks on the total force and equal to the number of 20 to 29-year-old blacks in the recruiting area; that the Police Department had affirmatively sought to recruit blacks, many of whom passed the test but failed to report for duty; and that the test was a useful indicator of training school performance (precluding the need to show validation in terms of job performance) and was not designed to, and did not, discriminate against otherwise qualified blacks. Respondents, on appeal, contended that their summary judgment motion (which was based solely on the contention that Test 21 invidiously discriminated against Negroes in violation of the Fifth Amendment) should have been granted. The Court of Appeals reversed, and directed summary judgment in favor of respondents, having applied to the constitutional issue the statutory standards enunciated in *Griggs v. Duke Power Co.* which held that Title VII of the Civil Rights Act of 1964, as amended, prohibits the use of tests that operate to exclude members of minority groups, unless the employer demonstrates that the procedures are substantially related to job performance. The court held that the lack of discriminatory intent in the enactment and administration of Test 21 was irrelevant; that the critical fact was that four times as many blacks as whites failed the test; and that such disproportionate impact sufficed to establish a constitutional violation, absent any proof by petitioners that the test adequately measured job performance.

I

Can a violation of Equal Protection be evidenced by showing a disparate racial impact only?

R

The disproportionate impact of an otherwise official action, standing alone and without regard to whether it indicated a discriminatory purpose, is not sufficient to establish a constitutional violation.

Washington v. Davis

426 U.S. 229 (1976)

A The Court of Appeals erred in resolving the Fifth Amendment issue by applying standards applicable to Title VII cases. Though the Due Process Clause of the Fifth Amendment contains an equal protection component prohibiting the Government from invidious discrimination, it does not follow that a law or other official act is unconstitutional solely because it has a racially disproportionate impact regardless of whether it reflects a racially discriminatory purpose. The Constitution does not prevent the Government from seeking through Test 21 modestly to upgrade the communicative abilities of its employees rather than to be satisfied with some lower level of competence, particularly where the job requires special abilities to communicate orally and in writing; and respondents, as Negroes, could no more ascribe their failure to pass the test to denial of equal protection than could whites who also failed. The disproportionate impact of Test 21, which is neutral on its face, does not warrant the conclusion that the test was a purposely discriminatory device, and on the facts before it the District Court properly held that any inference of discrimination was unwarranted. The rigorous statutory standard of Title VII involves a more probing judicial review of, and less deference to, the seemingly reasonable acts of administrators and executives than is appropriate under the Constitution where, as in this case, special racial impact but no discriminatory purpose is claimed. Any extension of that statutory standard should await legislative prescription. Statutory standards similar to those obtaining under Title VII were also satisfied here. The District Court's conclusion that Test 21 was directly related to the requirements of the police training program and that a positive relationship between the test and that program was sufficient to validate the test (wholly aside from its possible relationship to actual performance as a police officer) is fully supported on the record in this case, and no remand to establish further validation is appropriate.

C Reversed.

McCleskey v. Kemp

481 U.S. 279 (1987)

FACTS

In 1978, petitioner, a black man, was convicted in a Georgia trial court of armed robbery and murder, arising from the killing of a white police officer during the robbery of a store. Pursuant to Georgia statutes, the jury at the penalty hearing considered the mitigating and aggravating circumstances of petitioner's conduct and recommended the death penalty on the murder charge. The trial court followed the recommendation, and the Georgia Supreme Court affirmed. After unsuccessfully seeking post-conviction relief in state courts, petitioner sought habeas corpus relief in Federal District Court. His petition included a claim that the Georgia capital sentencing process was administered in a racially discriminatory manner in violation of the Eighth and Fourteenth Amendments. In support of the claim, petitioner proffered a statistical study (the Baldus study) that purports to show a disparity in the imposition of the death sentence in Georgia based on the murder victim's race and, to a lesser extent, the defendant's race. The study is based on over 2,000 murder cases that occurred in Georgia during the 1970's, and involves data relating to the victim's race, the defendant's race, and the various combinations of such persons' races. The study indicates that black defendants who killed white victims have the greatest likelihood of receiving the death penalty. Rejecting petitioner's constitutional claims, the court denied his petition insofar as it was based on the Baldus study, and the Court of Appeals affirmed the District Court's decision on this issue. It assumed the validity of the Baldus study but found the statistics insufficient to demonstrate unconstitutional discrimination in the Fourteenth Amendment context or to show irrationality, arbitrariness, and capriciousness under Eighth Amendment analysis.

I Can statistical proof support the inference that Georgia's capital sentencing process is administered in a racially discriminatory manner in violation of the Eighth and Fourteenth Amendments?

R In order to show a violation of the 8th and 14th Amerndments, petitioner must prove that the Georgia Legislature enacted or maintained the death penalty statute to further a racially discriminatory purpose, or maintained the statute because of the racially disproportionate impact suggested by the Baldus study.

A The Baldus study does not establish that the administration of the Georgia capital punishment system violates the Equal Protection Clause. To prevail under that Clause, petitioner must prove that the decisionmakers in his case acted with discriminatory purpose. Petitioner offered no evidence specific to his own case that would support an inference that racial considerations played a part in his sentence, and the Baldus study is insufficient to support an inference that any of the decisionmakers in his case acted with discriminatory purpose. Because discretion is essential to the criminal justice process, exceptionally clear proof is required before this Court will infer that the discretion has been abused. There is no merit to petitioner's argument that the Baldus study proves that the State has violated the Equal Protection Clause by adopting the capital punishment statute and allowing it to remain in force despite its allegedly discriminatory application. For this claim to prevail, petitioner would have to prove that the Georgia Legislature enacted or maintained the death penalty statute because of an anticipated racially discriminatory effect. There is no evidence that the legislature either enacted the statute to further a racially discriminatory purpose, or maintained the statute because of the racially disproportionate impact suggested by the Baldus study. Petitioner's argument that the Baldus study demonstrates that the Georgia capital sentencing system violates the Eighth Amendment's prohibition of cruel and unusual punishment must be analyzed in the light of this Court's prior decisions under that Amendment. Decisions since *Furman v. Georgia*, have identified a constitutionally permissible range of discretion in imposing the death penalty. First, there is a required threshold below which the death penalty cannot be imposed, and the State must establish rational criteria that narrow the decisionmaker's judgment as to whether the circumstances of a particular defendant's case meet the threshold. Second, States cannot limit the sentencer's consideration of any relevant circumstance that could cause it to decline to impose the death penalty. In this respect, the State cannot channel the sentencer's discretion, but must allow it to consider any relevant information offered by the defendant. The Baldus study does not demonstrate that the Georgia capital sentencing system violates the Eighth Amendment. Because petitioner's sentence was imposed under Georgia sentencing procedures that focus discretion "on the particularized nature of the crime and the particularized characteristics of the individual defendant," it may be presumed that his death sentence was not "wantonly and freakishly" imposed, and thus that the sentence is not disproportionate within any recognized meaning under the Eighth Amendment. There is no merit to the contention that the Baldus study shows that Georgia's capital punishment system is arbitrary and capricious in application. The statistics do not prove that race enters into any capital sentencing decisions or that race was a factor in petitioner's case. The likelihood of racial prejudice allegedly shown by the study does not constitute the constitutional measure of an unacceptable risk of racial prejudice. The inherent lack of predictability of jury decisions does not justify their condemnation. On the contrary, it is the jury's function to make the difficult and uniquely human judgments that defy codification and that build discretion, equity, and flexibility into the legal system. At most, the Baldus study indicates a discrepancy that appears to correlate with race, but this discrepancy does not constitute a major systemic defect. Any mode for determining guilt or punishment has its weaknesses and the potential for misuse. Despite such imperfections, constitutional guarantees are met when the mode for determining guilt or punishment has been surrounded with safeguards to make it as fair as possible. Petitioner's claim, taken to its logical conclusion, throws into serious question the principles that underlie the entire criminal justice system. His claim easily could be extended to apply to other types of penalties and to claims based on unexplained discrepancies correlating to membership in other minority groups and even to gender. The Constitution does not require that a State eliminate any demonstrable disparity that correlates with a potentially irrelevant factor in order to operate a criminal justice system that includes capital punishment. Petitioner's arguments are best presented to the legislative bodies, not the courts.

C Affirmed.

City of Mobile v. Bolden

446 U.S. 55 (1980)

FACTS

Mobile, Alabama, is governed by a Commission consisting of three members elected at large who jointly exercise all legislative, executive, and administrative power in the city. Appellees brought a class action in Federal District Court against the city and the incumbent Commissioners on behalf of all Negro citizens of the city, alleging, *inter alia,* that the practice of electing the City Commissioners at large unfairly diluted the voting strength of Negroes in violation of the Fourteenth and Fifteenth Amendments. Although finding that Negroes in Mobile "register and vote without hindrance," the District Court nevertheless held that the at-large electoral system violated the Fifteenth Amendment and invidiously discriminated against Negroes in violation of the Equal Protection Clause of the Fourteenth Amendment, and ordered that the Commission be disestablished and replaced by a Mayor and a Council elected from single-member districts. The Court of Appeals affirmed.

I

Does Mobile's at-large electoral system violate the rights of the city's Negro voters in contravention of the Equal Protection Clause of the Fifteenth Amendment?

R

The Equal Protection Clause of the 14th Amendment does not require proportionate representation of Negro candidates elected but prohibits only purposefully discriminatory denial or abridgment by government of the freedom to vote "on account of race, color, or previous condition of servitude."

A

Mobile's at-large electoral system does not violate the rights of the city's Negro voters in contravention of the Fifteenth Amendment. Racially discriminatory motivation is a necessary ingredient of a Fifteenth Amendment violation. The Amendment does not entail the right to have Negro candidates elected but prohibits only purposefully discriminatory denial or abridgment by government of the freedom to vote "on account of race, color, or previous condition of servitude." Here, having found that Negroes in Mobile register and vote without hindrance, the courts below erred in believing that appellants invaded the protection of the Fifteenth Amendment. Nor does Mobile's at-large electoral system violate the Equal Protection Clause of the Fourteenth Amendment. Only if there is purposeful discrimination can there be a violation of the Equal Protection Clause. And this principle applies to claims of racial discrimination affecting voting just as it does to other claims of racial discrimination. Disproportionate effects alone are insufficient to establish a claim of unconstitutional racial vote dilution. Where the character of a law is readily explainable on grounds apart from race, as would nearly always be true where, as here, an entire system of local governance is brought into question, disproportionate impact alone cannot be decisive, and courts must look to other evidence to support a finding of discriminatory purpose. Even assuming that an at-large municipal electoral system such as Mobile's is constitutionally indistinguishable from the election of a few members of a state legislature in multimember districts, it is clear that the evidence in this case fell far short of showing that appellants "conceived or operated [a] purposeful devic[e] to further racial . . . discrimination," *Whitcomb v. Chavis.* The Equal Protection

Clause does not require proportional representation as an imperative of political organization. While the Clause confers a substantive right to participate in elections on an equal basis with other qualified voters, this right does not protect any "political group," however defined, from electoral defeat. Since Mobile is a unitary electoral district and the Commission elections are conducted at large, there can be no claim that the "one person, one vote" principle has been violated, and therefore nobody's vote has been "diluted" in the sense in which that word was used in *Reynolds v. Sims*.

C

The judgment is reversed, and the case is remanded.

Palmer v. Thompson

403 U.S. 217 (1971)

FACTS

Following the Court of Appeals' affirmance of a District Court judgment invalidating enforced segregation on equal protection grounds, the city council of Jackson, Mississippi, desegregated its public recreational facilities, including its five public parks, except for their swimming pools. Stating that the pools could not be operated safely and economically on an integrated basis, the council closed four city-owned pools and surrendered its lease on a fifth, which the lessor, the YMCA, continued to operate for whites only. Petitioners, Negro citizens of Jackson, then brought this action, mainly on equal protection grounds, to force the city to reopen and operate the pools on a desegregated basis. The District Court held that there was no denial of equal protection. The Court of Appeals affirmed, rejecting the contention that since the pools had been closed to avoid desegregation there was a denial of equal protection.

I

Can a legislative act which is racially motivated but facially race-neutral be invalidated under the 14th Amendment?

R

A governmental act can not be invalidated simply because it was motivated by a discriminatory intention.

A

The closing of the pools to all persons did not constitute a denial of equal protection of the laws under the Fourteenth Amendment to the Negroes. This case is distinguishable from *Griffin v. County School Board of Prince Edward County* and *Reitman v. Mulkey*, on both of which petitioners rely. In Griffin there were many facets of state involvement in the segregated operation of "private" schools; here there is no city involvement in the operation or funding of any pool. In *Reitman* the evidence was deemed sufficient to show that the State, by enacting a constitutional amendment establishing the right of private persons to discriminate in realty transactions, thereby repealing two housing anti-discrimination laws, was abetting refusal to rent apartments on racial grounds; here there was no evidence that the city conspired with the YMCA that its pool be segregated. In this case, where there was substantial evidence to support the council's stated reason for closing the pools and there was no evidence of state action affecting Negroes differently from whites, petitioners' contention that equal protection requirements were violated because the pool-closing decision was motivated by anti-integration considerations, must also fail since courts will not invalidate legislation based solely on asserted illicit motivation by the enacting legislative body. The city council's action in closing the pools instead of keeping them open on an integrated basis did not create a "badge or incident" of slavery in violation of the Thirteenth Amendment.

C

Affirmed.

Personnel Administrator of Massachusetts v. Feeney

442 U.S. 256 (1979)

FACTS

During her 12-year tenure as a state employee, appellee, who is not a veteran, had passed a number of open competitive civil service examinations for better jobs, but because of Massachusetts' veterans' preference statute, she was ranked in each instance below male veterans who had achieved lower test scores than appellee. Under the statute, all veterans who qualify for state civil service positions must be considered for appointment ahead of any qualifying non-veterans. The statutory preference, which is available to "any person, male or female, including a nurse," who was honorably discharged from the United States Armed Forces after at least 90 days of active service, at least one day of which was during "wartime," operates overwhelmingly to the advantage of males. Appellee brought an action in Federal District Court, alleging that the absolute-preference formula established in the Massachusetts statute inevitably operates to exclude women from consideration for the best state civil service jobs and thus discriminates against women in violation of the Equal Protection Clause of the Fourteenth Amendment. A three-judge court declared the statute unconstitutional and enjoined its operation, finding that while the goals of the preference were legitimate and the statute had not been enacted for the purpose of discriminating against women, the exclusionary impact upon women was so severe as to require the State to further its goals through a more limited form of preference. On an earlier appeal, this Court vacated the judgment and remanded the case for further consideration in light of the intervening decision in *Washington v. Davis*, which held that a neutral law does not violate the Equal Protection Clause solely because it results in a racially disproportionate impact and that, instead, the disproportionate impact must be traced to a purpose to discriminate on the basis of race. Upon remand, the District Court reaffirmed its original judgment, concluding that a veterans' hiring preference is inherently non-neutral because it favors a class from which women have traditionally been excluded, and that the consequences of the Massachusetts absolute-preference formula for the employment opportunities of women were too inevitable to have been "unintended."

I Is there a presumption that certain legislation was enacted for a discriminatory purpose if the government was aware of its discriminatory impact?

R A governmental act must have been mandated because of, not in spite of, it adverse discriminatory effects upon a particular group in order to be held purposefully discriminatory.

A Massachusetts, in granting an absolute lifetime preference to veterans, has not discriminated against women in violation of the Equal Protection Clause of the Fourteenth Amendment. Classifications based upon gender must bear a close and substantial relationship to important governmental objectives. Although public employment is not a constitutional right and the States have wide discretion in framing employee qualifications, any state law overtly or covertly designed to prefer males over females in public employment would require an exceedingly persuasive justification to withstand a constitutional challenge under the Equal Protection

Clause. When a statute gender-neutral on its face is challenged on the ground that its effects upon women are disproportionably adverse, a twofold inquiry is appropriate. The first question is whether the statutory classification is indeed neutral in the sense that it is not gender-based. If the classification itself, covert or overt, is not based upon gender, the second question is whether the adverse effect reflects invidious gender-based discrimination. Here, the appellee's concession and the District Court's finding that the Massachusetts statute is not a pretext for gender discrimination are clearly correct. Apart from the facts that the definition of "veterans" in the statute has always been neutral as to gender and that Massachusetts has consistently defined veteran status in a way that has been inclusive of women who have served in the military, this is not a law that can plausibly, or even rationally, be explained only as a gender-based classification. Significant numbers of non-veterans are men, and all non-veterans - male as well as female - are placed at a disadvantage. The distinction made by the Massachusetts statute is, as it seems to be, quite simply between veterans and non-veterans, not between men and women. Appellee's contention that this veterans' preference is "inherently non-neutral" or "gender-biased" in the sense that it favors a status reserved under federal military policy primarily to men is wholly at odds with the District Court's central finding that Massachusetts has not offered a preference to veterans for the purpose of discriminating against women; nor can it be reconciled with the assumption made by both the appellee and the District Court that a more limited hiring preference for veterans could be sustained, since the degree of the preference makes no constitutional difference. While it would be disingenuous to say that the adverse consequences of this legislation for women were unintended, in the sense that they were not volitional or in the sense that they were not foreseeable, nevertheless "discriminatory purpose" implies more than intent as volition or intent as awareness of consequences; it implies that the decisionmaker selected or reaffirmed a particular course of action at least in part "because of," not merely "in spite of," its adverse effects upon an identifiable group. When the totality of legislative actions establishing and extending the Massachusetts veterans' preference are considered, the law remains what it purports to be: a preference for veterans of either sex over non-veterans of either sex, not for men over women. Although absolute and permanent preferences have always been subject to the objection that they give the veteran more than a square deal, the Fourteenth Amendment "cannot be made a refuge from ill-advised . . . laws." *District of Columbia v. Brooke.* The substantial edge granted to veterans by the Massachusetts statute may reflect unwise policy, but appellee has simply failed to demonstrate that the law in any way reflects a purpose to discriminate on the basis of sex.

C

Reversed and remanded.

Village of Arlington Heights v. Metropolitan Housing Development Corp.

429 U.S. 252 (1977)

FACTS

Respondent Metropolitan Housing Development Corp. (MHDC), a nonprofit developer, contracted to purchase a tract within the boundaries of petitioner Village in order to build racially integrated low- and moderate-income housing. The contract was contingent upon securing rezoning as well as federal housing assistance. MHDC applied to the Village for the necessary rezoning from a single-family to a multiple-family (R-5) classification. At a series of Village Plan Commission public meetings, both supporters and opponents touched upon the fact that the project would probably be racially integrated. Opponents also stressed zoning factors that pointed toward denial of MHDC's application: The location had always been zoned single-family, and the Village's apartment policy called for limited use of R-5 zoning, primarily as a buffer between single-family development and commercial or manufacturing districts, none of which adjoined the project's proposed location. After the Village denied rezoning, MHDC and individual minority respondents filed this suit for injunctive and declaratory relief, alleging that the denial was racially discriminatory and violated, *inter alia*, the Equal Protection Clause of the Fourteenth Amendment and the Fair Housing Act. The District Court held that the Village's rezoning denial was motivated not by racial discrimination but by a desire to protect property values and maintain the Village's zoning plan. Though approving those conclusions, the Court of Appeals reversed, finding that the "ultimate effect" of the rezoning denial was racially discriminatory and observing that the denial would disproportionately affect blacks, particularly in view of the fact that the general suburban area, though economically expanding, continued to be marked by residential segregation.

I

Can an official action be held unconstitutional ***solely*** because it results in a racially disproportionate impact?

R

An official action will not be held unconstitutional solely because it results in a racially disproportionate impact – a racially discriminatory intent, as evidenced by such factors as disproportionate impact, the historical background of the challenged decision, the specific antecedent events, departures from normal procedures, and contemporary statements of the decisionmakers, must be shown.

A

MHDC and at least one individual respondent have standing to bring this action. MHDC has met the constitutional standing requirements by showing injury fairly traceable to petitioners' acts. The challenged action of the Village stands as an absolute barrier to constructing the housing for which MHDC had contracted, a barrier which could be removed if injunctive relief were granted. MHDC, despite the contingency provisions in its contract, has suffered economic injury based upon the expenditures it made in support of its rezoning petition, as well as non-economic injury from the defeat of its objective, embodied in its specific project, of making suitable low-cost housing available where such housing is scarce. Whether MHDC has standing to assert the constitutional rights of its prospective minority tenants need not be decided, for at least one of the individual respondents, a Negro working in the Village and desirous of securing low-cost housing there but who now lives 20 miles away, has standing. Focusing on the specific MHDC project, he has adequately alleged an "actionable causal relationship" between the Village's zoning practices and his asserted injury. Proof of a racially discriminatory intent or purpose is required to show a violation of the Equal Protection Clause of the Fourteenth Amendment, and respondents failed to carry their burden of proving that such an intent or purpose was a motivating factor in the Village's rezoning decision. Official action will not be held unconstitutional solely because it results in a racially disproportionate impact. "[Such] impact is not irrelevant, but it is not the sole touchstone of an invidious racial discrimination." *Washington v. Davis*. A racially discriminatory intent, as evidenced by such factors as disproportionate impact, the historical background of the challenged decision, the specific antecedent events, departures from normal procedures, and contemporary statements of the decisionmakers, must be shown. The evidence does not warrant overturning the concurrent findings of both courts below that there was no proof warranting the conclusion that the Village's rezoning decision was racially motivated. The statutory question whether the rezoning decision violated the Fair Housing Act of 1968 was not decided by the Court of Appeals and should be considered on remand.

C Reversed and remanded.

Brown v. Board of Education [Brown II]

349 U.S. 294 (1955)

FACTS

The U.S. Supreme Court, in appreciation of the national implication and importance of the *Brown I* decision as well as acknowledging the wide disparities in local conditions, placed the case back on the docket to address the question of appropriate relief afforded to the affected.

I

What is the appropriate relief to be given the Negro students for a violation of their equal protection rights?

R

The lower courts shall be charged with the responsibility for overseeing the implementation of *Brown;* however, because local conditions vary from place to place, it may not be practical to implement immediately, but nonetheless shall take place with deliberate speed.

A

These cases were decided on May 17, 1954. The opinions of that date, declaring the fundamental principle that racial discrimination in public education is unconstitutional, are incorporated herein by reference. All provisions of federal, state, or local law requiring or permitting such discrimination must yield to this principle. There remains for consideration the manner in which relief is to be accorded. Because these cases arose under different local conditions and their disposition will involve a variety of local problems, we requested further argument on the question of relief. In view of the nationwide importance of the decision, we invited the Attorney General of the United States and the Attorneys General of all states requiring or permitting racial discrimination in public education to present their views on that question. The parties, the United States, and the States of Florida, North Carolina, Arkansas, Oklahoma, Maryland, and Texas filed briefs and participated in the oral argument. These presentations were informative and helpful to the Court in its consideration of the complexities arising from the transition to a system of public education freed of racial discrimination. The presentations also demonstrated that substantial steps to eliminate racial discrimination in public schools have already been taken, not only in some of the communities in which these cases arose, but in some of the states appearing as *amici curiae*, and in other states as well. Substantial progress has been made in the District of Columbia and in the communities in Kansas and Delaware involved in this litigation. The defendants in the cases coming to us from South Carolina and Virginia are awaiting the decision of this Court concerning relief. Full implementation of these constitutional principles may require solution of varied local school problems. School authorities have the primary responsibility for elucidating, assessing, and solving these problems; courts will have to consider whether the action of school authorities constitutes good faith implementation of the governing constitutional principles. Because of their proximity to local conditions and the possible need for further hearings, the courts which originally heard these cases can best perform this judicial appraisal. Accordingly, we believe it appropriate to remand the cases to those courts. In fashioning and effectuating the decrees, the courts will be guided by equitable principles. Traditionally, equity has been characterized by a practical flexibility in shaping its remedies and by a facility for adjusting and reconciling public and private needs. These

---

cases call for the exercise of these traditional attributes of equity power. At stake is the personal interest of the plaintiffs in admission to public schools as soon as practicable on a nondiscriminatory basis. To effectuate this interest may call for elimination of a variety of obstacles in making the transition to school systems operated in accordance with the constitutional principles set forth in our May 17, 1954, decision. Courts of equity may properly take into account the public interest in the elimination of such obstacles in a systematic and effective manner. But it should go without saying that the vitality of these constitutional principles cannot be allowed to yield simply because of disagreement with them. While giving weight to these public and private considerations, the courts will require that the defendants make a prompt and reasonable start toward full compliance with our May 17, 1954, ruling. Once such a start has been made, the courts may find that additional time is necessary to carry out the ruling in an effective manner. The burden rests upon the defendants to establish that such time is necessary in the public interest and is consistent with good faith compliance at the earliest practicable date. To that end, the courts may consider problems related to administration, arising from the physical condition of the school plant, the school transportation system, personnel, revision of school districts and attendance areas into compact units to achieve a system of determining admission to the public schools on a nonracial basis, and revision of local laws and regulations which may be necessary in solving the foregoing problems. They will also consider the adequacy of any plans the defendants may propose to meet these problems and to effectuate a transition to a racially nondiscriminatory school system. During this period of transition, the courts will retain jurisdiction of these cases. The judgments below, except that in the Delaware case, are accordingly reversed and the cases are remanded to the District Courts to take such proceedings and enter such orders and decrees consistent with this opinion as are necessary and proper to admit to public schools on a racially nondiscriminatory basis with all deliberate speed the parties to these cases. The judgment in the Delaware case - ordering the immediate admission of the plaintiffs to schools previously attended only by white children - is affirmed on the basis of the principles stated in our May 17, 1954, opinion, but the case is remanded to the Supreme Court of Delaware for such further proceedings as that Court may deem necessary in light of this opinion. It is so ordered.

C

See Rule above.

Swann v. Charlotte-Mecklenburg Board of Education

402 U.S. 1 (1971)

FACTS

Together with No. 349, *Charlotte-Mecklenburg Board of Education et al. v. Swann et al.*, also on certiorari to the same court. The Charlotte-Mecklenburg school system, which includes the city of Charlotte, North Carolina, had more than 84,000 students in 107 schools in the 1968-1969 school year. Approximately 29% (24,000) of the pupils were Negro, about 14,000 of whom attended 21 schools that were at least 99% Negro. This resulted from a desegregation plan approved by the District Court in 1965, at the commencement of this litigation. In 1968 petitioner Swann moved for further relief based on *Green v. County School Board*, which required school boards to "come forward with a plan that promises realistically to work . . . now . . . until it is clear that state-imposed segregation has been completely removed." The District Court ordered the school board in April 1969 to provide a plan for faculty and student desegregation. Finding the board's submission unsatisfactory, the District Court appointed an expert to submit a desegregation plan. In February 1970, the expert and the board presented plans, and the court adopted the board's plan, as modified, for the junior and senior high schools, and the expert's proposed plan for the elementary schools. The Court of Appeals affirmed the District Court's order as to faculty desegregation and the secondary school plans, but vacated the order respecting elementary schools, fearing that the provisions for pairing and grouping of elementary schools would unreasonably burden the pupils and the board. The case was remanded to the District Court for reconsideration and submission of further plans. This Court granted certiorari and directed reinstatement of the District Court's order pending further proceedings in that court. On remand the District Court received two new plans, and ordered the board to adopt a plan, or the expert's plan would remain in effect. After the board "acquiesced" in the expert's plan, the District Court directed that it remain in effect.

I

Can federal district courts use their discretion to employ broad equitable powers to fashion a plan for desegregation once it has been shown that school officials have failed to do so?

R

Once it is shown that school officials have failed to do so, under *Brown v. Board of Education*, federal district courts use their discretion to employ broad equitable powers to fashion a plan for desegregation.

A

Today's objective is to eliminate from the public schools all vestiges of state-imposed segregation that was held violative of equal protection guarantees by *Brown v. Board of Education*. In default by the school authorities of their affirmative obligation to proffer acceptable remedies, the district courts have broad power to fashion remedies that will assure unitary school systems. Title IV of the Civil Rights Act of 1964 does not restrict or withdraw from the federal courts their historic equitable remedial powers. The proviso in 42 U.S.C. 2000c-6 was designed simply to foreclose any interpretation of the Act as expanding the existing powers of the federal courts to enforce the Equal Protection Clause. Policy and practice with regard to faculty, staff, transportation, extracurricular activities, and facilities are among the most important indicia of a segregated system, and the first remedial responsibility of school authorities is to eliminate invidious racial distinctions in those respects. Normal administrative practice should then produce schools of like quality, facilities, and staffs. The Constitution does not prohibit district courts from using their equity power to order assignment of teachers to achieve a particular degree of faculty desegregation. *United States v. Montgomery County Board of Education* was properly followed by the lower courts in this case. In devising remedies to eliminate legally imposed segregation, local authorities and district courts must see to it that future school construction and abandonment are not used and do not serve to perpetuate or re-establish a dual system. Four problem areas exist on the issue of student assignment: (1) Racial quotas. The constitutional command to desegregate schools does not mean that every school in the community must always reflect the racial composition of the system as a whole; here the District Court's very limited use of the racial ratio - not as an inflexible requirement, but as a starting point in shaping a remedy - was within its equitable discretion. (2) One-race schools. While the existence of a small number of one-race, or virtually one-race, schools does not in itself denote a system that still practices segregation by law, the court should scrutinize such schools and require the school authorities to satisfy the court that the racial composition does not result from present or past discriminatory action on their part. An optional majority-to-minority transfer provision has long been recognized as a useful part of a desegregation plan, and to be effective such arrangement must provide the transferring student free transportation and available space in the school to which he desires to move. (3) Attendance zones. The remedial altering of attendance zones is not, as an interim corrective measure, beyond the remedial powers of a district court. A student assignment plan is not acceptable merely because it appears to be neutral, for such a plan may fail to counteract the continuing effects of past school segregation. The pairing and grouping of noncontiguous zones is a permissible tool; judicial steps going beyond contiguous zones should be examined in light of the objectives to be sought. No rigid rules can be laid down to govern conditions in different localities. (4) Transportation. The District Court's conclusion that assignment of children to the school nearest their home serving their grade would not effectively dismantle the dual school system is supported by the record, and the remedial technique of requiring bus transportation as a tool of school desegregation was within that court's power to provide equitable relief. An objection to transportation of students may have validity when the time or distance of travel is so great as to risk either the health of the children or significantly impinge on the educational process; limits on travel time will vary with many factors, but probably with none more than the age of the students. Neither school authorities nor district courts are constitutionally required to make year-by-year adjustments of the racial composition of student bodies once a unitary system has been achieved.

C

431 F.2d 138, affirmed as to those parts in which it affirmed the District Court's judgment. The District Court's order of August 7, 1970, is also affirmed.

Milliken v. Bradley

418 U.S. 717 (1974)

FACTS

Together with No. 73-435, *Allen Park Public Schools et al. v. Bradley et al.*, and No. 73-436, *Grosse Pointe Public School System v. Bradley et al.*, also on certiorari to the same court. Respondents brought this class action, alleging that the Detroit public school system is racially segregated as a result of the official policies and actions of petitioner state and city officials, and seeking implementation of a plan to eliminate the segregation and establish a unitary nonracial school system. The District Court, after concluding that various acts by the petitioner Detroit Board of Education had created and perpetuated school segregation in Detroit, and that the acts of the Board, as a subordinate entity of the State, were attributable to the State, ordered the Board to submit Detroit-only desegregation plans. The court also ordered the state officials to submit desegregation plans encompassing the three-county metropolitan area, despite the fact that the 85 outlying school districts in these three counties were not parties to the action and there was no claim that they had committed constitutional violations. Subsequently, outlying school districts were allowed to intervene, but were not permitted to assert any claim or defense on issues previously adjudicated or to reopen any issue previously decided, but were allowed merely to advise the court as to the propriety of a metropolitan plan and to submit any objections, modifications, or alternatives to any such plan. Thereafter, the District Court ruled that it was proper to consider metropolitan plans, that Detroit-only plans submitted by the Board and respondents were inadequate to accomplish desegregation, and that therefore it would seek a solution beyond the limits of the Detroit School District, and concluded that "[s]chool district lines are simply matters of political convenience and may not be used to deny constitutional rights." Without having evidence that the suburban school districts had committed acts of de jure segregation, the court appointed a panel to submit a plan for the Detroit schools that would encompass an entire designated desegregation area consisting of 53 of the 85 suburban school districts plus Detroit, and ordered the Detroit Board to acquire at least 295 school buses to provide transportation under an interim plan to be developed for the 1972-1973 school year. The Court of Appeals, affirming in part, held that the record supported the District Court's finding as to the constitutional violations committed by the Detroit Board and the state officials; that therefore the District Court was authorized and required to take effective measures to desegregate the Detroit school system; and that a metropolitan area plan embracing the 53 outlying districts was the only feasible solution and was within the District Court's equity powers. The court remanded so that all suburban school districts that might be affected by a metropolitan remedy could be made parties and have an opportunity to be heard.

I May a federal court impose a multidistrict, area-wide remedy for single-district de jure school segregation violations where there is no finding that the other included school districts have failed to operate unitary school systems or have committed acts that effected segregation within the other districts?

R A federal court may not impose a multidistrict, area-wide remedy for single-district de jure school segregation violations where there is no finding that the other included school districts have failed to operate unitary school systems or have committed acts that effected segregation within the other districts, there is no claim or finding that the school district boundary lines were established with the purpose of fostering racial segregation, and there is no meaningful opportunity for the included neighboring school districts to present evidence or be heard on the propriety of a multidistrict remedy or on the question of constitutional violations by those districts.

A The relief ordered by the District Court and affirmed by the Court of Appeals was based upon erroneous standards and was unsupported by record evidence that acts of the outlying districts had any impact on the discrimination found to exist in the Detroit schools. A federal court may not impose a multidistrict, area-wide remedy for single-district de jure school segregation violations where there is no finding that the other included school districts have failed to operate unitary school systems or have committed acts that effected segregation within the other districts, there is no claim or finding that the school district boundary lines were established with the purpose of fostering racial segregation, and there is no meaningful opportunity for the included neighboring school districts to present evidence or be heard on the propriety of a multidistrict remedy or on the question of constitutional violations by those districts. The District Court erred in using as a standard the declared objective of development of a metropolitan area plan which, upon implementation, would leave "no school, grade or classroom . . . substantially disproportionate to the overall pupil racial composition" of the metropolitan area as a whole. Before the boundaries of separate and autonomous school districts may be set aside by consolidating the separate units for remedial purposes or by imposing a cross-district remedy, it must be first shown that there has been a constitutional violation within one district that produces a significant segregative effect in another district; i. e., specifically, it must be shown that racially discriminatory acts of the state or local school districts, or of a single school district have been a substantial cause of interdistrict segregation. With no showing of significant violation by the 53 outlying school districts and no evidence of any interdistrict violation or effect, the District Court transcended the original theory of the case as framed by the pleadings, and mandated a metropolitan area remedy, the approval of which would impose on the outlying districts, not shown to have committed any constitutional violation, a standard not previously hinted at in any holding of this Court. Assuming, arguendo, that the State was derivatively responsible for Detroit's segregated school conditions, it does not follow that an interdistrict remedy is constitutionally justified or required, since there has been virtually no showing that either the State or any of the 85 outlying districts engaged in any activity that had a cross-district effect. An isolated instance of a possible segregative effect as between two of the school districts involved would not justify the broad metropolitan-wide remedy contemplated, particularly since that remedy embraced 52 districts having no responsibility for the arrangement and potentially involved 503,000 pupils in addition to Detroit's 276,000 pupils.

C Reversed and remanded.

Board of Education of Oklahoma City Public Schools v. Dowell 498 U.S. 237 (1991)

FACTS

In 1972, finding that previous efforts had not been successful at eliminating de jure segregation, the District Court entered a decree imposing a school desegregation plan on petitioner Oklahoma City Board of Education (Board). In 1977, finding that the school district had achieved "unitary" status, the court issued an order terminating the case which respondents, black students and their parents, did not appeal. In 1984, the Board adopted its Student Reassignment Plan (SRP), under which a number of previously desegregated schools would return to primarily one-race status for the asserted purpose of alleviating greater busing burdens on young black children caused by demographic changes. The District Court thereafter denied respondents' motion to reopen the terminated case, holding, inter alia, that its 1977 unitariness finding was res judicata. The Court of Appeals reversed, holding that respondents could challenge the SRP because the school district was still subject to the desegregation decree, nothing in the 1977 order having indicated that the 1972 injunction itself was terminated. On remand, the District Court dissolved the injunction, finding, among other things, that the original plan was no longer workable, that the Board had complied in good faith for more than a decade with the court's orders, and that the SRP was not designed with discriminatory intent. The Court of Appeals again reversed, holding that a desegregation decree remains in effect until a school district can show "`grievous wrong evoked by new and unforeseen conditions,'" *United States v. Swift & Co.*, and that circumstances had not changed enough to justify modification of the 1972 decree.

I Can a court reinstate a desegregation decree even after it has been shown that local authorities have been in full compliance with the order?

R A desegregation decree should be dissolved after it has been shown that local authorities have been in full compliance with the court order.

A Respondents may contest the District Court's order dissolving the 1972 injunction. Although respondents did not appeal from the court's 1977 order, that order did not dissolve the desegregation decree, and, since the order is unclear with respect to what it meant by "unitary" and the necessary result of that finding, it is too ambiguous to bar respondents from challenging later action by the Board. If a desegregation decree is to be terminated or dissolved, the parties are entitled to a rather precise statement to that effect from the court. The Court of Appeals' test for dissolving a desegregation decree is more stringent than is required either by this Court's decisions dealing with injunctions or by the Equal Protection Clause of the Fourteenth Amendment. Considerations based on the allocation of powers within the federal system demonstrate that the Swift test does not provide the proper standard to apply to injunctions entered in school desegregation cases. Such decrees, unlike the one in Swift, are not intended to operate in perpetuity, federal supervision of local school systems always having been intended as a temporary measure to remedy past discrimination. The legal justification for displacement of local authority in such cases is a violation of the

Constitution and dissolution of a desegregation decree after local authorities have operated in compliance with it for a reasonable period is proper. Thus, in this case, a finding by the District Court that the school system was being operated in compliance with the Equal Protection Clause, and that it was unlikely that the Board would return to its former ways, would be a finding that the purposes of the desegregation litigation had been fully achieved, and no additional showing of "grievous wrong evoked by new and unforeseen conditions" would be required of the Board. The Court of Appeals also erred in relying on *United States v. W.T. Grant Co.* for the proposition that "compliance alone cannot become the basis for modifying or dissolving an injunction." That case did not involve the dissolution of an injunction, but the question whether an injunction should be issued in the first place in light of the wrongdoer's promise to comply with the law. Although a district court need not accept at face value a school board's profession that it will cease to intentionally discriminate in the future, the board's compliance with previous court orders is obviously relevant in deciding whether to modify or dissolve a desegregation decree, since the passage of time results in changes in board personnel and enables the court to observe the board's good faith in complying with the decree. The Court of Appeals' test would improperly condemn a school district to judicial tutelage for the indefinite future. In deciding whether the Board made a sufficient showing of constitutional compliance as of 1985, when the SRP was adopted, to allow the injunction to be dissolved, the District Court, on remand, should address itself to whether the Board had complied in good faith with the desegregation decree since it was entered, and whether, in light of every facet of school operations, the vestiges of past de jure segregation had been eliminated to the extent practicable. If it decides that the Board was entitled to have the decree terminated, the court should proceed to decide whether the Board's decision to implement the SRP complies with appropriate equal protection principles.

C

Reversed and remanded.

Richmond v. J.A. Croson Co.

488 U.S. 469 (1989)

FACTS

Appellant city adopted a Minority Business Utilization Plan (Plan) requiring prime contractors awarded city construction contracts to subcontract at least 30% of the dollar amount of each contract to one or more "Minority Business Enterprises" (MBE's), which the Plan defined to include a business from anywhere in the country at least 51% of which is owned and controlled by black, Spanish-speaking, Oriental, Indian, Eskimo, or Aleut citizens. Pursuant to the Plan, the city adopted rules requiring individualized consideration of each bid or request for a waiver of the 30% set-aside, and providing that a waiver could be granted only upon proof that sufficient qualified MBE's were unavailable or unwilling to participate. After Appellee J.A. Croson Co., a construction company and the sole bidder on a city contract was denied a waiver and lost its contract, it brought suit under 42 U.S.C. 1983, alleging that the Plan was unconstitutional under the Fourteenth Amendment's Equal Protection Clause. The Federal District Court upheld the Plan in all respects, and the Court of Appeals affirmed, applying a test derived from the principal opinion in *Fullilove*, which accorded great deference to Congress' findings of past societal discrimination in holding that a 10% minority set-aside for certain federal construction grants did not violate the equal protection component of the Fifth Amendment. However, on appellee's petition for certiorari in this case, this Court vacated and remanded for further consideration in light of its intervening decision in *Wygant v. Jackson Board of Education*, which the plurality applied a strict scrutiny standard in holding that a race-based layoff program agreed to by a school board and the local teachers' union violated the Fourteenth Amendment's Equal Protection Clause. On remand, the Court of Appeals held that the city's Plan violated both prongs of strict scrutiny, in that (1) the Plan was not justified by a compelling governmental interest, since the record revealed no prior discrimination by the city itself in awarding contracts, and (2) the 30% set-aside was not narrowly tailored to accomplish a remedial purpose.

I When a city guarantees minority owned businesses 30% of certain city contracts on account of race, does it also violate the Equal Protection clause?

R Only when a race-based classification are narrowly tailored to achieve a compelling governmental interest may state and local governments favor one group over another on the basis of race classifications.

A The city has failed to demonstrate a compelling governmental interest justifying the Plan, since the factual predicate supporting the Plan does not establish the type of identified past discrimination in the city's construction industry that would authorize race-based relief under the 14th Amendment's Equal Protection Clause. A generalized assertion that there has been past discrimination in the entire construction industry cannot justify the use of an unyielding racial quota, since it provides no guidance for the city's legislative body to determine the precise scope of the injury it seeks to remedy and would allow race-based decisionmaking essentially limitless in scope and duration. The city's argument that it is attempting to remedy various forms of past societal discrimination that are alleged to be responsible for the small number of minority entrepreneurs in the local contracting industry fails, since the city also lists a host of nonracial factors which would seem to face a member of any racial group seeking to establish a new business enterprise. None of the "facts" cited by the city or relied on by the District Court, singly or together, provide a basis for a *prima facie* case of a constitutional or statutory violation by anyone in the city's construction industry. The fact that the Plan declares itself to be "remedial" is insufficient, since the mere recitation of a "benign" or legitimate purpose for a racial classification is entitled to little or no weight. Similarly, the views of Plan proponents as to past and present discrimination in the industry are highly conclusory and of little probative value. Reliance on the disparity between the number of prime contracts awarded to minority businesses and the city's minority population is also misplaced, since the proper statistical evaluation would compare the percentage of MBE's in the relevant market that are qualified to undertake city subcontracting work with the percentage of total city construction dollars that are presently awarded to minority subcontractors, neither of which is known to the city. The Plan is not narrowly tailored to remedy the effects of prior discrimination, since it entitles a black, Hispanic, or Oriental entrepreneur from anywhere in the country to an absolute preference over other citizens based solely on their race. There is no evidence that the city considered using alternative, race-neutral means to increase minority participation in city contracting. Moreover, the Plan's rigid 30% quota rests upon the completely unrealistic assumption that minorities will choose to enter construction in lockstep proportion to their representation in the local population. Given the fact that the city must already consider bids and waivers on a case-by-case basis, the city's only interest in maintaining a quota system rather than investigating the need for remedial action in particular cases would seem to be simply administrative convenience, which, standing alone, cannot justify the use of a suspect classification under equal protection strict scrutiny. If the city could identify past discrimination in the local construction industry with the particularity required by the Equal Protection Clause, it would have the power to adopt race-based legislation designed to eradicate the effects of that discrimination. The principal opinion in *Fullilove* cannot be read to relieve the city of the necessity of making the specific findings of discrimination required by the Clause. Since the Plan denies certain citizens the opportunity to compete for a fixed percentage of public contracts based solely on their race, *Wygant's* strict scrutiny standard of review must be applied. Even if the level of equal protection scrutiny could be said to vary according to the ability of different groups to defend their interests in the representative process, heightened scrutiny would still be appropriate in the circumstances of this case, since blacks constitute approximately 50% of the city's population and hold five of nine seats on the City Council, thereby raising the concern that the political majority may have acted to disadvantage a minority. Even in the absence of evidence of discrimination in the local construction industry, the city has at its disposal an array of race-neutral devices to increase the accessibility of city contracting opportunities to small entrepreneurs of all races who have suffered the effects of past societal discrimination.

C

Affirmed.

Adarand Constructors Inc. v. Pena

515 U.S. 200 (1995)

FACTS

Most federal agency contracts must contain a subcontractor compensation clause, which gives a prime contractor a financial incentive to hire subcontractors certified as small businesses controlled by socially and economically disadvantaged individuals, and requires the contractor to presume that such individuals include minorities or any other individuals found to be disadvantaged by the Small Business Administration (SBA). The prime contractor under a federal highway construction contract containing such a clause awarded a subcontract to a company that was certified as a small disadvantaged business. The record does not reveal how the company obtained its certification, but it could have been by any one of three routes: under one of two SBA programs - known as the 8(a) and 8(d) programs - or by a state agency under relevant Department of Transportation regulations. Petitioner Adarand Constructors Inc., which submitted the low bid on the subcontract but was not a certified business, filed suit against respondent federal officials claiming that the race-based presumptions used in subcontractor compensation clauses violate the equal protection component of the Fifth Amendment's Due Process Clause. The District Court granted respondents summary judgment. In affirming, the Court of Appeals assessed the constitutionality of the federal race-based action under a lenient standard, resembling intermediate scrutiny, which it determined was required by *Fullilove* and *Metro Broadcasting, Inc.*

I

Are federal racial classifications subject to strict scrutiny review?

R

All racial classifications must be narrowly tailored to further a compelling governmental interest.

A

Adarand has standing to seek forward-looking relief. It has met the requirements necessary to maintain its claim by alleging an invasion of a legally protected interest in a particularized manner, and by showing that it is very likely to bid, in the relatively near future, on another Government contract offering financial incentives to a prime contractor for hiring disadvantaged subcontractors. All racial classifications, imposed by whatever federal, state, or local governmental actor, must be analyzed by a reviewing court under strict scrutiny. In *Richmond v. J. A. Croson Co.*, a majority of the Court held that the Fourteenth Amendment requires strict scrutiny of all race-based action by state and local governments. While *Croson* did not consider what standard of review the Fifth Amendment requires for such action taken by the Federal Government, the Court's cases through *Croson* had established three general propositions with respect to governmental racial classifications. First, skepticism, consistency and congruence. Taken together, these propositions lead to the conclusion that any person, of whatever race, has the right to demand that any governmental actor subject to the Constitution justify any racial classification subjecting that person to unequal treatment under the strictest judicial scrutiny. However, a year after *Croson*, the Court in *Metro Broadcasting*, upheld two federal race-based policies against a Fifth Amendment challenge. The Court repudiated the long-held notion that "it would be unthinkable that the same Constitution would impose a lesser duty on the Federal Government" than it does on a State to afford equal protection of the laws by holding that congressionally mandated "benign" racial classifications need only satisfy intermediate scrutiny. By adopting that standard, *Metro Broadcasting* departed from prior cases in two significant respects. First, it turned its back on *Croson's* explanation that strict scrutiny of governmental racial classifications Page III is essential because it may not always be clear that a so-called preference is in fact benign. Second, it squarely rejected one of the three propositions established by this Court's earlier cases, namely, congruence between the standards applicable to federal and state race-based action, and in doing so also undermined the other two. The propositions undermined by *Metro Broadcasting* all derive from the basic principle that the Fifth and Fourteenth Amendments protect persons, not groups. It follows from that principle that all governmental action based on race - a group classification long recognized as in most circumstances irrelevant and therefore prohibited - should be subjected to detailed judicial inquiry to ensure that the personal right to equal protection has not been infringed. Thus, strict scrutiny is the proper standard for analysis of all racial classifications, whether imposed by a federal, state, or local actor. To the extent that *Metro Broadcasting* is inconsistent with that holding, it is overruled. The decision here makes explicit that federal racial classifications, like those of a State, must serve a compelling governmental interest, and must be narrowly tailored to further that interest. Thus, to the extent that *Fullilove* held federal racial classifications to be subject to a less rigorous standard, it is no longer controlling. Requiring strict scrutiny is the best way to ensure that courts will consistently give racial classifications a detailed examination, as to both ends and means. When race-based action is necessary to further a compelling interest, such action is within constitutional constraints if it satisfies the "narrow tailoring" test set out in this Court's previous cases. Because this decision alters the playing field in some important respects, the case is remanded to the lower courts for further consideration.

C

The judgment is vacated, and the case is remanded.

Grutter v. Bollinger

539 U.S. 306 (2003)

FACTS

The University of Michigan Law School (Law School), one of the Nation's top law schools, follows an official admissions policy that seeks to achieve student body diversity through compliance with *Regents of Univ. of Cal.* v. *Bakke*. Focusing on students' academic ability coupled with a flexible assessment of their talents, experiences, and potential, the policy requires admissions officials to evaluate each applicant based on all the information available in the file. The policy does not define diversity solely in terms of racial and ethnic status but it does reaffirm the Law School's commitment to diversity with special reference to the inclusion of African-American, Hispanic, and Native-American students, who otherwise might not be represented in the student body in meaningful numbers. By enrolling a "critical mass" of underrepresented minority students, the policy seeks to ensure their ability to contribute to the Law School's character and to the legal profession. When the Law School denied admission to petitioner Grutter, a white Michigan resident with a 3.8 GPA and 161 LSAT score, she filed this suit, alleging that respondents had discriminated against her on the basis of race in violation of the Fourteenth Amendment, Title VI of the Civil Rights Act of 1964, and 42 U. S. C. §1981; that she was rejected because the Law School uses race as a "predominant" factor, giving applicants belonging to certain minority groups a significantly greater chance of admission than students with similar credentials from disfavored racial groups; and that respondents had no compelling interest to justify that use of race. The District Court found the Law School's use of race as an admissions factor unlawful. The Sixth Circuit reversed, holding that Justice Powell's opinion in *Bakke* was binding precedent establishing diversity as a compelling state interest, and that the Law School's use of race was narrowly tailored because race was merely a "potential 'plus' factor" and because the Law School's program was virtually identical to the Harvard admissions program described approvingly by Justice Powell and appended to his *Bakke* opinion.

I

Did the Law School's admissions policy violate the Equal Protection Clause by using an enrollment plan based on a flexible "critical mass" of underrepresented minority students?

R

A law school's admission policy will not violate the Equal Protection Clause if it uses race or ethnicity as a "plus factor" in admissions but does not insulate each category of applicants with certain desired qualifications from competition with all other applicants.

A

The Law School's narrowly tailored use of race in admissions decisions to further a compelling interest in obtaining the educational benefits that flow from a diverse student body is not prohibited by the Equal Protection Clause, Title VI, or §1981. In the landmark *Bakke* case, this Court reviewed a medical school's racial set-aside program that reserved 16 out of 100 seats for members of certain minority groups. The decision produced six separate opinions, none of which commanded a majority. Justice Powell emphasized that "[t]he diversity that furthers a compelling state interest encompasses a far broader array of qualifications and characteristics of which racial or ethnic origin is but a single though important element." Since *Bakke*, Justice Powell's opinion has been the touchstone for constitutional analysis of race-conscious admissions policies. Public and private universities across the Nation have modeled their own admissions programs on Justice Powell's views. Courts, however, have struggled to discern whether Justice Powell's diversity rationale is binding precedent. The Court finds it unnecessary to decide this issue because the Court endorses Justice Powell's view that student body diversity is a compelling state interest in the context of university admissions. All government racial classifications must be analyzed by a reviewing court under strict scrutiny. But not all such uses are invalidated by strict scrutiny. Race-based action necessary to further a compelling governmental interest does not violate the Equal Protection Clause so long as it is narrowly tailored to further that interest. The Court endorses Justice Powell's view that student body diversity is a compelling state interest that can justify using race in university admissions. Attaining a diverse student body is at the heart of the Law School's proper institutional mission, and its "good faith" is "presumed" absent "a showing to the contrary." Enrolling a "critical mass" of minority students simply to assure some specified percentage of a particular group merely because of its race or ethnic origin would be patently unconstitutional. But the Law School defines its critical mass concept by reference to the substantial, important, and laudable educational benefits that diversity is designed to produce, including cross-racial understanding and the breaking down of racial stereotypes. The Law School's claim is further bolstered by numerous expert studies and reports showing that such diversity promotes learning outcomes and better prepares students for an increasingly diverse workforce, for society, and for the legal profession. The Law School's admissions program bears the hallmarks of a narrowly tailored plan. To be narrowly tailored, a race-conscious admissions program cannot "insulat[e] each category of applicants with certain desired qualifications from competition with all other applicants." Instead, it may consider race or ethnicity only as a " 'plus' in a particular applicant's file"; *i.e.,* it must be "flexible enough to consider all pertinent elements of diversity in light of the particular qualifications of each applicant, and to place them on the same footing for consideration, although not necessarily according them the same weight," The Law School's admissions program satisfies these requirements. Moreover, the program is flexible enough to ensure that each applicant is evaluated as an individual and not in a way that makes race or ethnicity the defining feature of the application. The Law School engages in a highly individualized, holistic review of each applicant's file, giving serious consideration to all the ways an applicant might contribute to a diverse educational environment. There is no policy, either *de jure* or *de facto*, of automatic acceptance or rejection based on any single "soft" variable. Because the Law School's use of race in admissions decisions is not prohibited by Equal Protection Clause, petitioner's statutory claims based on Title VI and §1981 also fail.

C

Affirmed.

Gratz v. Bollinger

539 U.S. 244 (2003)

FACTS

Petitioners Gratz and Hamacher, both of whom are white Michigan residents, applied for admission to the University of Michigan's (University) College of Literature, Science, and the Arts (LSA) in 1995 and 1997, respectively. Although the LSA considered Gratz to be well qualified and Hamacher to be within the qualified range, both were denied admission. In order to promote consistency in the review of the many applications received, the University's Office of Undergraduate Admissions (OUA) uses written guidelines for each academic year. The OUA considers a number of factors in making admissions decisions, including high school grades, standardized test scores, high school quality, curriculum strength, geography, alumni relationships, leadership, and race. During all relevant periods, the University has considered African-Americans, Hispanics, and Native Americans to be "underrepresented minorities," and it is undisputed that the University admits virtually every qualified applicant from these groups. The current guidelines use a selection method under which every applicant from an underrepresented racial or ethnic minority group is automatically awarded 20 points of the 100 needed to guarantee admission. Petitioners filed this class action alleging that the University's use of racial preferences in undergraduate admissions violated the Equal Protection Clause of the Fourteenth Amendment, Title VI of the Civil Rights Act of 1964, and 42 U. S. C. §1981. The District Court granted petitioners' motion to certify a class consisting of individuals who applied for and were denied admission to the LSA for academic year 1995 and forward and who are members of racial or ethnic groups that respondents treated less favorably on the basis of race. Hamacher was designated as the class representative. On cross-motions for summary judgment, respondents relied on Justice Powell's principal opinion in *Bakke*, which expressed the view that the consideration of race as a factor in admissions might in some cases serve a compelling government interest. Respondents contended that the LSA has just such an interest in the educational benefits that result from having a racially and ethnically diverse student body and that its program is narrowly tailored to serve that interest. The court agreed with respondents and granted them summary judgment in that respect. However, the court also found that the LSA's admissions guidelines for 1995 through 1998 operated as the functional equivalent of a quota and thus granted petitioners summary judgment with respect to respondents' admissions programs for those years. While interlocutory appeals were pending in the Sixth Circuit, that court issued an opinion in *Grutter* v. *Bollinger,* upholding the admissions program used by the University's Law School. The U.S. Supreme Court granted certiorari in both cases, even though the Sixth Circuit had not yet rendered judgment in this one.

I Is a university's point-based affirmative action program unconstitutional or is the program narrowly tailored to achieve educational diversity thus making it constitutional?

R The Equal Protection Clause will be violated by a university's affirmative action program which awards a set amount of points to racial minorities applying for admission because such a policy does not provide for "sufficiently individualized consideration."

Gratz v. Bollinger

539 U.S. 244 (2003)

A Petitioners have standing to seek declaratory and injunctive relief. In bringing his equal protection challenge against the University's use of race in undergraduate admissions, Hamacher alleged that the University had denied him the opportunity to compete for admission on an equal basis. The District Court's carefully considered decision to certify this class action is correct. Hamacher's personal stake, in view of both his past injury and the potential injury he faced at the time of certification, demonstrates that he may maintain the action. For the reasons set forth in *Grutter* v. *Bollinger*, the Court has today rejected petitioners' argument that diversity cannot constitute a compelling state interest. However, the Court finds that the University's current policy, which automatically distributes 20 points, or one-fifth of the points needed to guarantee admission, to every single "underrepresented minority" applicant solely because of race, is not narrowly tailored to achieve educational diversity and thus violates the Equal Protection Clause. In *Bakke*, Justice Powell explained his view that it would be permissible for a university to employ an admissions program in which "race or ethnic background may be deemed a 'plus' in a particular applicant's file." He emphasized, however, the importance of considering each particular applicant as an individual, assessing all of the qualities that individual possesses, and in turn, evaluating that individual's ability to contribute to the unique setting of higher education. The admissions program Justice Powell described did not contemplate that any single characteristic automatically ensured a specific and identifiable contribution to a university's diversity. The current LSA policy does not provide the individualized consideration Justice Powell contemplated. Moreover, unlike Justice Powell's example, where the race of a "particular black applicant" could be considered without being decisive, the LSA's 20-point distribution has the effect of making "the factor of race ... decisive" for virtually every minimally qualified underrepresented minority applicant. The fact that the LSA has created the possibility of an applicant's file being flagged for individualized consideration only emphasizes the flaws of the University's system as a whole. Also, this individualized review is only provided *after* admissions counselors automatically distribute the University's version of a "plus" that makes race a decisive factor for virtually every minimally qualified underrepresented minority applicant. The Court rejects respondents' contention that the volume of applications and the presentation of applicant information make it impractical for the LSA to use the admissions system upheld today in *Grutter*. The fact that the implementation of a program capable of providing individualized consideration might present administrative challenges does not render constitutional an otherwise problematic system. Nothing in Justice Powell's *Bakke* opinion signaled that a university may employ whatever means it desires to achieve diversity without regard to the limits imposed by strict scrutiny. Because the University's use of race in its current freshman admissions policy violates the Equal Protection Clause, it also violates Title VI and §1981. Accordingly, the Court reverses that portion of the District Court's decision granting respondents summary judgment with respect to liability.

C Reversed in part and remanded.

Easley v. Cromartie

532 U.S. 234 (2001)

FACTS

After this Court found that North Carolina's legislature violated the Constitution by using race as the predominant factor in drawing its Twelfth Congressional District's 1992 boundaries, *Shaw* v. *Hunt,* the State redrew those boundaries. A three-judge District Court subsequently granted appellees summary judgment, finding that the new 1997 boundaries had also been created with racial considerations dominating all others. This Court reversed, finding that there was a genuine issue of material fact as to whether the evidence was consistent with a race-based objective or the constitutional political objective of creating a safe Democratic seat. Among other things, this Court relied on evidence proposed to be submitted by appellants to conclude that, because the State's African-American voters overwhelmingly voted Democratic, one could not easily distinguish a legislative effort to create a majority-minority district from a legislative effort to create a safely Democratic one; that data showing voter registration did not indicate how voters would actually vote; and that data about actual behavior could affect the litigation's outcome. On remand, the District Court again held, after a 3-day trial, that the legislature had used race driven criteria in drawing the 1997 boundaries. It based that conclusion on three findings--the district's shape, its splitting of towns and counties, and its heavily African-American voting population - that this Court had considered when it found summary judgment inappropriate, and on the new finding that the legislature had drawn the boundaries to collect precincts with a high racial, rather than political, identification.

I Is there adequate support for the District Court's finding that race, rather than politics, drove the legislature's districting decision?

R Where majority-minority districts are at issue and racial identification correlates highly with political affiliation, the party attacking the boundaries must show at the least that the legislature could have achieved its legitimate political objectives in alternative ways that are comparably consistent with traditional districting principles and that those alternatives would have brought about significantly greater racial balance.

A The District Court's conclusion that the State violated the Equal Protection Clause in drawing the 1997 boundaries is based on clearly erroneous findings. The issue here is evidentiary: whether there is adequate support for the District Court's finding that race, rather than politics, drove the legislature's districting decision. Those attacking the district have the demanding burden of proof to show that a facially neutral law is unexplainable on grounds other than race. Because the underlying districting decision falls within a legislature's sphere of competence, courts must exercise extraordinary caution in adjudicating claims such as this one, especially where, as here, the State has articulated a legitimate political explanation for its districting decision and the voting population is one in which race and political affiliation are highly coordinated. This Court will review the District Court's findings only for "clear error," asking whether "on the entire evidence" the Court is "left with the definite and firm conviction that a mistake has been committed." *United States*

v. *United States Gypsum Co.* An extensive review of the District Court's findings is warranted here because there was no intermediate court review, the trial was not lengthy, the key evidence consisted primarily of documents and expert testimony, and credibility evaluations played a minor role. The critical District Court determination that "race, not politics," predominantly explains the 1997 boundaries rests upon the three findings that this Court found insufficient to support summary judgment, and which cannot in and of themselves, as a matter of law, support the District Court's judgment here. Its determination also rests upon five new subsidiary findings, which this Court also cannot accept as adequate. First, the District Court primarily relied on evidence of voting registration, not voting behavior, which is precisely the kind of evidence that this Court found inadequate the last time the case was here. White registered Democrats "cross-over" to vote Republican more often than do African-Americans, who register and vote Democratic between 95% and 97% of the time. Thus, a legislature trying to secure a safe Democratic seat by placing reliable Democratic precincts within a district may end up with a district containing more heavily African-American precincts for political, not racial, reasons. Second, the evidence to which appellees' expert, Dr. Weber, pointed that a reliably Democratic voting population of 60% is necessary to create a safe Democratic seat, but this district was 63% reliable; that certain white-Democratic precincts were excluded while African-American-Democratic precincts were included; that one precinct was split between Districts 9 and 12; and that other plans would have created a safely Democratic district with fewer African-American precincts simply does not provide significant additional support for the District Court's conclusion. Also, portions of Dr. Weber's testimony not cited by the District Court undercut his conclusions. Third, the District Court, while not accepting the contrary conclusion of appellants' expert, Dr. Peterson, did not (and as far as the record reveals, could not) reject much of the significant supporting factual information he provided, which showed that African-American Democratic voters were more reliably Democratic and that District 12's boundaries were drawn to include reliable Democrats. Fourth, a statement about racial balance made by Senator Cooper, the legislative redistricting leader, shows that the legislature considered race along with other partisan and geographic considerations, but says little about whether race played a predominant role. And an e-mail sent by Gerry Cohen, a legislative staff member responsible for drafting districting plans, offers some support for the District Court's conclusion, but is less persuasive than the kinds of direct evidence that this Court has found significant in other redistricting cases. Fifth, appellees' maps summarizing voting behavior evidence tend to refute the District Court's "race, not politics," conclusion. The modicum of evidence supporting the District Court's conclusion, taken together, does not show that racial considerations predominated in the boundaries' drawing, because race in this case correlates closely with political behavior. Because appellees failed to make any such showing here, the District Court's contrary findings are clearly erroneous.

C Reversed.

Frontiero v. Richardson

411 U.S. 677 (1973)

FACTS

A married woman Air Force officer (hereafter appellant) sought increased benefits for her husband as a "dependent" under 37 U.S.C. 401, 403, and 10 U.S.C. 1072, 1076. Those statutes provide, solely for administrative convenience, that spouses of male members of the uniformed services are dependents for purposes of obtaining increased quarters allowances and medical and dental benefits, but that spouses of female members are not dependents unless they are in fact dependent for over one-half of their support. When her application was denied for failure to satisfy the statutory dependency standard, appellant and her husband brought this suit in District Court, contending that the statutes deprived servicewomen of due process. From that Court's adverse ruling, they took a direct appeal.

I

Does the difference in treatment with respect to benefits constitute an unconstitutional discrimination against servicewomen in violation of the Due Process Clause of the Fifth Amendment?

R

The difference in treatment with respect to benefits does constitute an unconstitutional discrimination against servicewomen in violation of the Due Process Clause of the Fifth Amendment.

A

The question before us concerns the right of a female member of the uniformed services to claim her spouse as a "dependent" for the purposes of obtaining increased quarters allowances and medical and dental benefits under 37 U.S.C. 401, 403, and 10 U.S.C. 1072, 1076, on an equal footing with male members. Under these statutes, a serviceman may claim his wife as a "dependent" without regard to whether she is in fact dependent upon him for any part of her support. A servicewoman, on the other hand, may not claim her husband as a "dependent" under these programs unless he is in fact dependent upon her for over one-half of his support. Thus, the question for decision is whether this difference in treatment constitutes an unconstitutional discrimination against servicewomen in violation of the Due Process Clause of the Fifth Amendment. A three-judge District Court for the Middle District of Alabama, one judge dissenting, rejected this contention and sustained the constitutionality of the provisions of the statutes making this distinction. At the outset, appellants contend that classifications based upon sex, like classifications based upon race, alienage, and national origin, are inherently suspect and must therefore be subjected to close judicial scrutiny. Since sex, like race and national origin, is an immutable characteristic determined solely by the accident of birth, the imposition of special disabilities upon the members of a particular sex because of their sex would seem to violate "the basic concept of our system that legal burdens should bear some relationship to individual responsibility . . . ." And what differentiates sex from such non-suspect statuses as intelligence or physical disability, and aligns it with the recognized suspect criteria, is that the sex characteristic frequently bears no relation to ability to perform or contribute to society. As a result, statutory distinctions between the sexes often have the effect of invidiously relegating the entire class of females to inferior legal status without regard to the actual capabilities of its individual members. We might also note that, over the past decade, Congress has itself manifested an increasing sensitivity to sex-based classifications. In Tit. VII of the Civil Rights Act of 1964, for example, Congress expressly declared that no employer, labor union, or other organization subject to the provisions of the Act shall discriminate against any individual on the basis of "race, color, religion, sex, or national origin." Similarly, the Equal Pay Act of 1963 provides that no employer covered by the Act "shall discriminate . . . between employees on the basis of sex." And 1 of the Equal Rights Amendment, passed by Congress on March 22, 1972, and submitted to the legislatures of the States for ratification, declares that "[e]quality of rights under the law shall not be denied or abridged by the United States or by any State on account of sex." Thus, Congress itself has concluded that classifications based upon sex are inherently invidious, and this conclusion of a coequal branch of Government is not without significance to the question presently under consideration. With these considerations in mind, we can only conclude that classifications based upon sex, like classifications based upon race, alienage, or national origin, are inherently suspect, and must therefore be subjected to strict judicial scrutiny. Applying the analysis mandated by that stricter standard of review, it is clear that the statutory scheme now before us is constitutionally invalid. The sole basis of the classification established in the challenged statutes is the sex of the individuals involved. Thus, under 37 U.S.C. 401, 403, and 10 U.S.C. 1072, 1076, a female member of the uniformed services seeking to obtain housing and medical benefits for her spouse must prove his dependency in fact, whereas no such burden is imposed upon male members. We therefore conclude that, by according differential treatment to male and female members of the uniformed services for the sole purpose of achieving administrative convenience, the challenged statutes violate the Due Process Clause of the Fifth Amendment insofar as they require a female member to prove the dependency of her husband.

C Reversed.

Craig v. Boren

429 U.S. 190 (1976)

FACTS

Appellant Craig, a male then between 18 and 21 years old, and appellant Whitener, a licensed vendor of 3.2% beer, brought this action for declaratory and injunctive relief, claiming that an Oklahoma statutory scheme prohibiting the sale of "non-intoxicating" 3.2% beer to males under the age of 21 and to females under the age of 18 constituted a gender-based discrimination that denied to males 18-20 years of age the equal protection of the laws. Recognizing that later cases establish that classification by gender must substantially further important governmental objectives, a three-judge District Court held that appellees' statistical evidence regarding young males' drunk-driving arrests and traffic injuries demonstrated that the gender-based discrimination was substantially related to the achievement of traffic safety on Oklahoma roads.

I

Is a statute violative of equal protection if it treats males and females within the same age group differently based solely on their gender?

R

Gender-based classifications which discriminate based solely on sex and are not substantially related to an important governmental objective (intermediate scrutiny standard) violate equal protection.

A

Since only declaratory and injunctive relief against enforcement of the gender-based differential was sought, the controversy has been mooted as to Craig, who became 21 after this Court had noted probable jurisdiction. Whitener has standing to make the equal protection challenge. Whitener in any event independently has established third-party standing. She suffers "injury in fact" since the challenged statutory provisions are addressed to vendors like her, who either must obey the statutory provisions and incur economic injury or disobey the statute and suffer sanctions. In such circumstances, vendors may resist efforts to restrict their operations by advocating the rights of third parties seeking access to their market. Oklahoma's gender-based differential constitutes an invidious discrimination against males 18-20 years of age in violation of the Equal Protection Clause. Appellees' statistics (the most relevant of which show only that .18% of females and 2% of males in the 18-20-year-old age group were arrested for driving while under the influence of liquor) do not warrant the conclusion that sex represents an accurate proxy for the regulation of drinking and driving. The operation of the Twenty-first Amendment does not alter the application of equal protection standards that otherwise govern this case. The Court has never recognized that application of that Amendment can defeat an otherwise established claim under the Equal Protection Clause, the principles of which cannot be rendered inapplicable here by reliance upon statistically measured but loose-fitting generalities concerning the drinking tendencies of aggregate groups.

C

Reversed.

United States v. Virginia

518 U.S. 515 (1996)

FACTS

Virginia Military Institute (VMI) is the sole single-sex school among Virginia's public institutions of higher learning. VMI's distinctive mission is to produce "citizen-soldiers," men prepared for leadership in civilian life and in military service. Using an "adversative method" of training not available elsewhere in Virginia, VMI endeavors to instill physical and mental discipline in its cadets and impart to them a strong moral code. Reflecting the high value alumni place on their VMI training, VMI has the largest per-student endowment of all undergraduate institutions in the Nation. The United States sued Virginia and VMI, alleging that VMI's exclusively male admission policy violated the Fourteenth Amendment's Equal Protection Clause. The District Court ruled in VMI's favor. The Fourth Circuit reversed and ordered Virginia to remedy the constitutional violation. In response, Virginia proposed a parallel program for women: Virginia Women's Institute for Leadership (VWIL), located at Mary Baldwin College, a private liberal arts school for women. The District Court found that Virginia's proposal satisfied the Constitution's equal protection requirement, and the Fourth Circuit affirmed. The appeals court deferentially reviewed Virginia's plan and determined that provision of single-gender educational options was a legitimate objective. Maintenance of single-sex programs, the court concluded, was essential to that objective. The court recognized, however, that its analysis risked bypassing equal protection scrutiny, so it fashioned an additional test, asking whether VMI and VWIL students would receive "substantively comparable" benefits. Although the Court of Appeals acknowledged that the VWIL degree lacked the historical benefit and prestige of a VMI degree, the court nevertheless found the educational opportunities at the two schools sufficiently comparable.

I

Is an equal protection right(s) violated when women are denied admission to a state school based solely on their gender?

R

Unless there is an "exceedingly persuasive justification" for doing so, a state may not discriminate based on gender.

A

Parties who seek to defend gender-based government action must demonstrate an "exceedingly persuasive justification" for that action. To meet the burden of justification, a State must show at least that the [challenged] classification serves "important governmental objectives and that the discriminatory means employed are substantially related to the achievement of those objectives." The justification must be genuine, not hypothesized or invented post hoc in response to litigation. And it must not rely on overbroad generalizations about the different talents, capacities, or preferences of males and females. The heightened review standard applicable to sex-based classifications does not make sex a proscribed classification, but it does mean that categorization by sex may not be used to create or perpetuate the legal, social, and economic inferiority of women. Virginia's categorical exclusion of women from the educational opportunities VMI provides denies equal protection to women. Virginia contends that single-sex education yields important educational benefits and that provision of an option for such education fosters diversity in educational approaches. Benign justifications proffered in defense of categorical exclusions, however, must describe actual state purposes, not rationalizations for actions in fact differently grounded. Virginia has not shown that VMI was established, or has been maintained, with a view to diversifying, by its categorical exclusion of women, educational opportunities within the State. The constitutional violation in this case is the categorical exclusion of women, in disregard of their individual merit, from an extraordinary educational opportunity afforded men. Virginia chose to leave untouched VMI's exclusionary policy, and proposed for women only a separate program, different in kind from VMI and unequal in tangible and intangible facilities. VWIL affords women no opportunity to experience the rigorous military training for which VMI is famed. Kept away from the pressures, hazards, and psychological bonding characteristic of VMI's adversative training, VWIL students will not know the feeling of tremendous accomplishment commonly experienced by VMI's successful cadets. Virginia maintains that methodological differences are justified by the important differences between men and women in learning and developmental needs, but generalizations about "the way women are," estimates of what is appropriate for most women, no longer justify denying opportunity to women whose talent and capacity place them outside the average description. In myriad respects other than military training, VWIL does not qualify as VMI's equal. The VWIL program is a pale shadow of VMI in terms of the range of curricular choices and faculty stature, funding, prestige, alumni support and influence. Virginia has not shown substantial equality in the separate educational opportunities the State supports at VWIL and VMI. The Fourth Circuit failed to inquire whether the proposed remedy placed women denied the VMI advantage in the position they would have occupied in the absence of discrimination and considered instead whether the State could provide, with fidelity to equal protection, separate and unequal educational programs for men and women. In declaring the substantially different and significantly unequal VWIL program satisfactory, the appeals court displaced the exacting standard developed by this Court with a deferential standard, and added an inquiry of its own invention, the "substantive comparability" test. The Fourth Circuit plainly erred in exposing Virginia's VWIL plan to such a deferential analysis, for "all gender based classifications today" warrant "heightened scrutiny." Women seeking and fit for a VMI-quality education cannot be offered anything less, under the State's obligation to afford them genuinely equal protection.

C

Reversed and remanded.

Geduldig v. Aiello

417 U.S. 484 (1974)

FACTS

California has a disability insurance system for private employees temporarily disabled from working by an injury or illness not covered by workmen's compensation, under which an employee contributes to an Unemployment Compensation Disability Fund one percent of his salary up to an annual maximum of $85. A disability lasting less than eight days is not compensable, except when the employee is hospitalized. Benefits are not payable for a single disability exceeding 26 weeks. A disability resulting from an individual's court commitment as a dipsomaniac, drug addict, or sexual psychopath is not compensable, nor are certain disabilities attributable to pregnancy. Appellees, four women otherwise qualified under the program who have suffered employment disability because of pregnancies, only one of which was normal, challenged the pregnancy exclusion. A three-judge District Court upheld their contention that the exclusion violated the Equal Protection Clause. The court denied a motion to reconsider based on a state appellate court ruling, in which appellant who administers the program has acquiesced, confining the exclusion to only normal pregnancies. The California program, in terms of the level of benefits and risks insured, is structured to maintain the solvency of the Disability Fund at a one-percent annual level of contribution. The District Court acknowledged that coverage of disabilities resulting from normal pregnancies would entail substantial additional expense. But it concluded that this increased cost could be accommodated through adjustments in the rate of employee contribution, the maximum benefits payable, "and the other variables affecting the solvency of the program."

I Does discrimination on the basis of pregnancy amount to an invidious discrimination under the Equal Protection Clause?

R Discrimination on the basis of pregnancy is not in itself considered invidious discrimination under the Equal Protection Clause.

A The appellate ruling and administrative guidelines excluding only normal pregnancies have mooted the case as to the three appellees who had abnormal pregnancies and whose claims have now been paid. California's decision not to insure under its program the risk of disability resulting from normal pregnancy does not constitute an invidious discrimination violative of the Equal Protection Clause. The program does not discriminate with respect to the persons or groups eligible for its protection, and there is no evidence that it discriminates against any definable group or class in terms of the aggregate risk protection derived from the program. The sole contention is the asserted underinclusiveness of the program's coverage as a result of the exclusion of disabilities resulting from normal pregnancy. The State is not required by the Equal Protection Clause to sacrifice the self-supporting nature of the program, reduce the benefits payable for covered disabilities, or increase the maximum employee contribution rate just to provide protection against another risk of disability, such as normal pregnancy. "[T]he Equal Protection Clause does not require that a State must choose between attacking every aspect of a problem or not attacking the problem at all." *Dandridge v. Williams.*

C

Reversed.

Orr v. Orr

440 U.S. 268 (1979)

FACTS

Following a stipulation between appellant husband and appellee wife, in which appellant agreed to pay appellee alimony, an Alabama court, acting pursuant to state alimony statutes under which husbands but not wives may be required to pay alimony upon divorce, ordered appellant to make monthly alimony payments. Some two years thereafter appellee filed a petition seeking to have appellant adjudged in contempt for failing to maintain the alimony payments. At the hearing on the petition appellant, though not claiming that he was entitled to an alimony award from appellee, made the contention (advanced for the first time in that proceeding) that the Alabama statutes, by virtue of their reliance on a gender-based classification, violated the Equal Protection Clause of the Fourteenth Amendment. The trial court, ruling adversely to appellant on that issue, entered judgment against him, which was affirmed on appeal.

I

Can a state provide that only men are required to pay alimony to their ex-spouses?

R

A state may not enact a law which provides that only men are required to pay alimony to their ex-spouses.

A

This Court has jurisdiction over appellant's appeal. Appellant's failure to ask for alimony for himself does not deprive him of standing to attack the constitutionality of the Alabama statutes for underinclusiveness. That attack holds the only promise of relief from the burden deriving from the challenged statutes, and appellant has therefore "alleged such a personal stake in the outcome of the controversy as to assure that concrete adverseness which sharpens the presentation of issues upon which th[is] court so largely depends for illumination of difficult constitutional questions." *Baker v. Carr.* Had the courts below refused to entertain appellant's constitutional contention on the ground that it was not timely made under applicable state procedures this Court might have lacked jurisdiction to consider the contention; but no timeliness point was raised or considered below and the constitutional issue was decided on the merits. Under these circumstances it is irrelevant whether the decision below could have been based upon an adequate and independent state ground. No point was raised or considered below that appellant by virtue of the stipulation was obliged to make the alimony payments under state contract law. "Where the state court does not decide against [an] appellant upon an independent state ground, but deeming the federal question to be before it, actually . . . decides that question adversely to the federal right asserted, this Court has jurisdiction to review the judgment if, as here, it is . . . final . . ." The Alabama statutory scheme of imposing alimony obligations on husbands but not wives violates the Equal Protection Clause of the Fourteenth Amendment. "To withstand scrutiny" under the Equal Protection Clause, "'classifications by gender must serve important governmental objectives and must be substantially related to achievement of those objectives.'" *Califano v. Webster.* The statutes cannot be validated on the basis of the State's preference for an allocation of family responsibilities under which the wife plays a dependent role. "No longer is the female destined solely for the home and the rearing of the family, and only the male for the marketplace and the world of ideas." *Stanton v. Stanton.* Though it could be argued that the Alabama statutory scheme is designed to provide help for needy spouses, using sex as a proxy for need, and to compensate women for past discrimination during marriage, which assertedly has left them unprepared to fend for themselves in the working world following divorce, these considerations would not justify that scheme because under the Alabama statutes individualized hearings at which the parties' relative financial circumstances are considered already occur. Since such hearings can determine which spouses are needy as well as which wives were in fact discriminated against, there is no reason to operate by generalization. "Thus, the gender-based distinction is gratuitous . . . ." *Weinberger v. Wiesenfeld.* Use of a gender classification, moreover, actually produces perverse results in this case because only a financially secure wife whose husband is in need derives an advantage from the Alabama scheme as compared to a gender-neutral one. The question remains open on remand whether appellant's stipulated agreement to pay alimony, or other grounds of gender-neutral state law, bind him to continue his alimony payments.

C

Reversed and remanded.

Mississippi University for Women v. Hogan

458 U.S. 718 (1982)

FACTS

In 1884, the Mississippi Legislature created the Mississippi Industrial Institute and College for the Education of White Girls of the State of Mississippi, known today as Mississippi University for Women (MUW). It has, from its inception, limited its enrollment to women. In 1971, MUW established a School of Nursing, initially offering a 2-year associate degree. Three years later, the school instituted a 4-year baccalaureate program in nursing and today also offers a graduate program. The School of Nursing has its own faculty and administrative officers and establishes its own criteria for admission. Respondent, Joe Hogan, is a registered nurse but does not hold a baccalaureate degree in nursing. Since 1974, he has worked as a nursing supervisor in a medical center in Columbus, the city in which MUW is located. In 1979, Hogan applied for admission to the MUW School of Nursing's baccalaureate program. Although he was otherwise qualified, he was denied admission to the School of Nursing solely because of his sex. School officials informed him that he could audit the courses in which he was interested, but could not enroll for credit. Hogan filed an action in the United States District Court for the Northern District of Mississippi, claiming the single-sex admissions policy of MUW's School of Nursing violated the Equal Protection Clause of the Fourteenth Amendment. Hogan sought injunctive and declaratory relief, as well as compensatory damages. Following a hearing, the District Court denied preliminary injunctive relief. The Court of Appeals for the Fifth Circuit reversed, holding that, because the admissions policy discriminates on the basis of gender, the District Court improperly used a "rational relationship" test to judge the constitutionality of the policy. Instead, the Court of Appeals stated, the proper test is whether the State has carried the heavier burden of showing that the gender-based classification is substantially related to an important governmental objective. The U.S. Supreme Court granted certiorari and affirmed the judgment of the Court of Appeals.

I May a state-sponsored nursing school deny admission to males?

R A state-sponsored nursing school may not deny admission to males; it may, however, designate educational opportunities to members of only one sex to remedy past discrimination against that sex.

A The policy of petitioner Mississippi University for Women (MUW), a state-supported university which has from its inception limited its enrollment to women, of denying otherwise qualified males (such as respondent) the right to enroll for credit in its School of Nursing violates the Equal Protection Clause of the Fourteenth Amendment. The party seeking to uphold a statute that classifies individuals on the basis of their gender must carry the burden of showing an "exceedingly persuasive justification" for the classification. The burden is met only by showing at least that the classification serves "important governmental objectives and that the discriminatory means employed" are "substantially related to the achievement of those objectives." The test must be applied free of fixed notions concerning the roles and abilities of males and females. The single-sex admissions policy of MUW's School of Nursing cannot be justified on the asserted ground that it compensates for discrimination against women and, therefore, constitutes educational affirmative action. A State can evoke a compensatory purpose to justify an otherwise discriminatory classification only if members of the gender benefited by the classification actually suffer a disadvantage related to the classification. Rather than compensating for discriminatory barriers faced by women, MUW's policy tends to perpetuate the stereotyped view of nursing as an exclusively woman's job. Moreover, the State has not shown that the gender-based classification is substantially and directly related to its proposed compensatory objective. To the contrary, MUW's policy of permitting men to attend classes as auditors fatally undermines its claim that women, at least those in the School of Nursing, are adversely affected by the presence of men. Thus, the State has fallen far short of establishing the "exceedingly persuasive justification" needed to sustain the gender-based classification. Nor can the exclusion of men from MUW's School of Nursing be justified on the basis of the language of 901(a)(5) of Title IX of the Education Amendments of 1972, which exempts from 901(a)'s general prohibition of gender discrimination in federally funded education programs the admissions policies of public institutions of undergraduate higher education "that traditionally and continually from [their] establishment [have] had a policy of admitting only students of one sex." It is not clear that, as argued by the State, Congress enacted the statute pursuant to its power granted by 5 of the Fourteenth Amendment to enforce that Amendment, and thus placed a limitation upon the broad prohibitions of the Equal Protection Clause. Rather, Congress apparently intended, at most, to create an exemption from Title IX's requirements. In any event, Congress' power under 5 "is limited to adopting measures to enforce the guarantees of the Amendment; 5 grants Congress no power to restrict, abrogate, or dilute these guarantees." *Katzenbach v. Morgan.*

C

Affirmed.

Michael M. v. Superior Court of Sonoma County

450 U.S. 464 (1981)

FACTS

Petitioner, then a 17 ½ year-old male, was charged with violating California's "statutory rape" law, which defines unlawful sexual intercourse as "an act of sexual intercourse accomplished with a female not the wife of the perpetrator, where the female is under the age of 18 years." Prior to trial, petitioner sought to set aside the information on both state and federal constitutional grounds, asserting that the statute unlawfully discriminated on the basis of gender since men alone were criminally liable thereunder. The trial court and the California Court of Appeal denied relief, and on review the California Supreme Court upheld the statute.

I Does a statutory rape law violate Equal Protection if it is applicable to men only who have sex with under-aged women?

R A statutory rape law does not violate Equal Protection even if it is applicable to men only who have sex with under-aged women because the purpose of such laws, among other things, is to address teen pregnancy and teen sex.

A The statute does not violate the Equal Protection Clause of the Fourteenth Amendment. Gender-based classifications are not "inherently suspect" so as to be subject to so-called "strict scrutiny," but will be upheld if they bear a "fair and substantial relationship" to legitimate state ends. Because the Equal Protection Clause does not "demand that a statute necessarily apply equally to all persons" or require "things which are different in fact . . . to be treated in law as though they were the same," a statute will be upheld where the gender classification is not invidious, but rather realistically reflects the fact that the sexes are not similarly situated in certain circumstances. One of the purposes of the California statute in which the State has a strong interest is the prevention of illegitimate teenage pregnancies. The statute protects women from sexual intercourse and pregnancy at an age when the physical, emotional, and psychological consequences are particularly severe. Because virtually all of the significant harmful and identifiable consequences of teenage pregnancy fall on the female, a legislature acts well within its authority when it elects to punish only the participant who, by nature, suffers few of the consequences of his conduct. There is no merit in petitioner's contention that the statute is impermissibly underinclusive and must, in order to pass judicial scrutiny, be broadened so as to hold the female as criminally liable as the male. The relevant inquiry is not whether the statute is drawn as precisely as it might have been, but whether the line chosen by the California Legislature is within constitutional limitations. In any event, a gender-neutral statute would frustrate the State's interest in effective enforcement since a female would be less likely to report violations of the statute if she herself would be subject to prosecution. The Equal Protection Clause does not require a legislature to enact a statute so broad that it may well be incapable of enforcement. Nor is the statute impermissibly overbroad because it makes unlawful sexual intercourse with prepubescent females, incapable of becoming pregnant. Aside from the fact that the statute could be justified on the grounds that very young females are particularly susceptible to physical injury from sexual intercourse, the Constitution does not require the California Legislature to limit the scope of the statute to older teenagers and exclude young girls. And the statute is not unconstitutional as applied to petitioner who, like the girl involved, was under 18 at the time of sexual intercourse, on the asserted ground that the statute presumes in such circumstances that the male is the culpable aggressor. The statute does not rest on such an assumption, but instead is an attempt to prevent illegitimate teenage pregnancy by providing an additional deterrent for men. The age of the man is irrelevant since young men are as capable as older men of inflicting the harm sought to be prevented.

C

Affirmed.

Rostker v. Goldberg

453 U.S. 57 (1981)

FACTS

The Military Selective Service Act (Act) authorizes the President to require the registration for possible military service of males but not females, the purpose of registration being to facilitate any eventual conscription under the Act. Registration for the draft was discontinued by Presidential Proclamation in 1975 (the Act was amended in 1973 to preclude conscription), but as the result of a crisis in Southwestern Asia, President Carter decided in 1980 that it was necessary to reactivate the registration process, and sought Congress' allocation of funds for that purpose. He also recommended that Congress amend the Act to permit the registration and conscription of women as well as men. Although agreeing that it was necessary to reactivate the registration process, Congress allocated only those funds necessary to register males and declined to amend the Act to permit the registration of women. Thereafter, the President ordered the registration of specified groups of young men. In a lawsuit brought by several men challenging the Act's constitutionality, a three-judge District Court ultimately held that the Act's gender-based discrimination violated the Due Process Clause of the Fifth Amendment and enjoined registration under the Act.

I Is it a violation of the Equal Protection Clause to authorize the president to require registration of men, but not women, for selective service?

R Congress does not violate Equal Protection by authorizing the president to require registration of men, but not women, for selective service.

A The Act's registration provisions do not violate the Fifth Amendment. Congress acted well within its constitutional authority to raise and regulate armies and navies when it authorized the registration of men and not women. The customary deference accorded Congress' judgments is particularly appropriate when, as here, Congress specifically considered the question of the Act's constitutionality, and perhaps in no area has the Court accorded Congress greater deference than in the area of national defense and military affairs. While Congress is not free to disregard the Constitution when it acts in the area of military affairs, this Court must be particularly careful not to substitute its judgment of what is desirable for that of Congress, or its own evaluation of evidence for a reasonable evaluation by the Legislative Branch. Congress carefully considered whether to register only males for potential conscription or whether to register both sexes, and its broad constitutional authority [453 U.S. 57, 58] cannot be ignored in considering the constitutionality of its studied choice of one alternative in preference to the other. The question of registering women was extensively considered by Congress in hearings held in response to the President's request for authorization to register women, and its decision to exempt women was not the accidental byproduct of a traditional way of thinking about women. Since Congress thoroughly reconsidered the question of exempting women from the Act in 1980, the Act's constitutionality need not be considered solely on the basis of the views expressed by Congress in 1948, when the Act was first enacted in its modern form. Congress' determination that any future draft would be characterized by a need for combat troops was sufficiently supported by testimony adduced at the hearings so that the courts are not free to make their own judgment on the question. And since women are excluded from combat service by statute or military policy, men and women are simply not similarly situated for purposes of a draft or registration for a draft, and Congress' decision to authorize the registration of only men, therefore, does not violate the Due Process Clause. The testimony of executive and military officials before Congress showed that the argument for registering women was based on considerations of equity, but Congress was entitled, in the exercise of its constitutional powers, to focus on the question of military need rather than "equity." The District Court, undertaking an independent evaluation of the evidence, exceeded its authority in ignoring Congress' conclusions that whatever the need for women for noncombat roles during mobilization, it could be met by volunteers, and that staffing noncombat positions with women during a mobilization would be positively detrimental to the important goal of military flexibility.

C

Reversed.

Califao v. Webster

430 U.S. 313 (1977)

FACTS

Under 215 of the Social Security Act, old-age benefits are computed on the basis of a wage earner's "average monthly wage" earned during his "benefit computation years" which are the "elapsed years" (reduced by five) during which his covered wages were highest. Until 1972, when the statute was amended to eliminate the distinction, "elapsed years" depended upon the wage earner's sex. Section 215(b)(3) prescribed that the number of "elapsed years" for a male wage earner would be three higher than for an otherwise similarly situated female wage earner; for a male, the number of "elapsed years" equaled the number of years that elapsed after 1950 and before the year in which he became 65, whereas for a female the number of "elapsed years" equaled the number of years that elapsed after 1950 and before the year in which she became 62. Accordingly, a female could exclude from the computation of her "average monthly wage" three more lower earning years than a similarly situated male could exclude, and this would result in a slightly higher "average monthly wage" and correspondingly higher monthly old-age benefits for the retired female wage earner. On review of a denial of the request of appellee male wage earner, the District Court held that the statutory scheme violated the equal protection component of the Due Process Clause of the Fifth Amendment.

I

May the government enact a gender-based classification in an effort to remedy past economic disparity between men and women arising from prior discrimination against women?

R

The government may enact a gender-based classification in an effort to remedy past economic disparity between men and women arising from prior discrimination against women because such an interest is sufficiently important to justify such a classification.

A

"[C]lassifications by gender must serve important governmental objectives and must be substantially related to the achievement of those objectives," *Craig v. Boren*. The statutory scheme itself, and the legislative history of former 215 (b) (3), demonstrate that the statute was deliberately enacted to "redres[s] our society's longstanding disparate treatment of women," *Califano v. Goldfarb*, and was not "the accidental byproduct of a traditional way of thinking about females." The statute operated directly to compensate women for past economic discrimination by allowing them to eliminate additional low-earning years from the calculation of their retirement benefits, and in no way penalized women wage earners. The failure to make the 1972 amendment retroactive does not constitute discrimination on the basis of date of birth. Old-age benefits are not constitutionally immunized against alterations of this kind, but Congress may replace one constitutional computation formula with another and make the new formula prospective only.

C

Reversed.

Nguyen v. Immigration & Naturalization Service
533 U.S. 53 (2001)

FACTS

Petitioner Tuan Anh Nguyen was born out of wedlock in Vietnam to a Vietnamese citizen and copetitioner Joseph Boulais, a United States citizen. Nguyen became a lawful permanent United States resident at age six and was raised by Boulais. At age 22, Nguyen pleaded guilty in a Texas state court to two counts of sexual assault on a child. Subsequently, respondent Immigration and Naturalization Service initiated deportation proceedings against him based on his serious criminal offenses. The Immigration Judge ordered him deportable. Boulais obtained an order of parentage from a state court while Nguyen's appeal was pending before the Board of Immigration Appeals, but the Board dismissed the appeal, rejecting Nguyen's citizenship claim because he had not complied with 8 U. S. C. §1409(a)'s requirements for one born out of wedlock and abroad to a citizen father and a noncitizen mother. On appeal, the Fifth Circuit rejected petitioners' claim that §1409 violates equal protection by providing different citizenship rules for children born abroad and out of wedlock depending on whether the citizen parent is the mother or the father.

I Can a gender-based classification withstand equal protection scrutiny if it serves important governmental objectives and the discriminatory means employed are substantially related to the achievement of those objectives?

R A gender-based classification withstands equal protection scrutiny if it serves important governmental objectives and the discriminatory means employed are substantially related to the achievement of those objectives.

A Section 1409 is consistent with the equal protection guarantee embedded in the Fifth Amendment's Due Process Clause. A child born abroad and out of wedlock acquires at birth the nationality status of a citizen mother who meets a specified residency requirement. §1409(c). However, when the father is the citizen parent, *inter alia,* one of three affirmative steps must be taken before the child turns 18: legitimization, a declaration of paternity under oath by the father, or a court order of paternity. §1409(a)(4). The failure to satisfy this section renders Nguyen ineligible for citizenship. A gender-based classification withstands equal protection scrutiny if it serves important governmental objectives and the discriminatory means employed are substantially related to the achievement of those objectives. Congress' decision to impose different requirements on unmarried fathers and unmarried mothers is based on the significant difference between their respective relationships to the potential citizen at the time of birth and is justified by two important governmental interests. The first such interest is the importance of assuring that a biological parent-child relationship exists. The mother's relation is verifiable from the birth itself and is documented by the birth certificate or hospital records and the witnesses to the birth. However, a father need not be present at the birth, and his presence is not incontrovertible proof of fatherhood. Because fathers and mothers are not similarly situated with regard to proof of biological parenthood, the imposition of different rules for each is neither surprising nor troublesome from a constitutional perspective. Congress is well within its authority in refusing, absent proof of an opportunity for a relationship to develop, to commit this country to embracing a child as a citizen. Contrary to petitioners' argument, §1409 does not embody a gender-based stereotype. There is nothing irrational or improper in recognizing that at the moment of birth, a critical event in the statutory scheme and tradition of citizenship law, the mother's knowledge of the child and the fact of parenthood have been established in a way not guaranteed to the unwed father. The means Congress chose substantially relate to its interest in facilitating a parent-child relationship. First, various statutory provisions, in addition to §1409(a), require that some act linking a child to the United States occur before the child turns 18. Second, petitioners' argument that §1409(a)(4) reflects a stereotype that women are more likely than men to actually establish the required relationship misconceives both the governmental interest's nature and the equal protection inquiry. As to the former, Congress could have chosen to advance the interest of ensuring a meaningful relationship in every case, but it enacted instead an easily administered scheme to promote the different but still substantial interest of ensuring an opportunity for that relationship to develop. Petitioners' argument confuses the equal protection inquiry's means and ends; §1409(a)(4) should not be invalidated because Congress elected to advance an interest that is less demanding to satisfy than some alternative. Even if one conceives of Congress' real interest as the establishment of a meaningful relationship, it is almost axiomatic that a policy seeking to foster the opportunity for meaningful parent-child bonds to develop has a close and substantial bearing on the governmental interest in that bond's formation. Here, Congress' means are in substantial furtherance of an important governmental objective, and the fit between the means and that end is exceedingly persuasive. Section 1409(a)(4) imposes a minimal obligation. Only the least onerous of its three options must be satisfied; and it can be satisfied on the day of birth, or the next day, or for the next 18 years. Section 1409(a), moreover, is not the sole means of attaining citizenship for the child, who can seek citizenship in his or her own right, rather than via reliance on parental ties. Because the statute satisfies the equal protection scrutiny applied to gender-based qualifications, this Court need not consider whether it can confer citizenship on terms other than those specified by Congress or assess the implications of statements in earlier cases regarding the wide deference afforded to Congress in exercising its immigration and naturalization power.

C Affirmed.

Graham v. Richardson

403 U.S. 365 (1971)

FACTS

Appellee Carmen Richardson, at the institution of this suit in July 1969, was 64 years of age. She is a lawfully admitted resident alien. She emigrated from Mexico in 1956 and since then has resided continuously in Arizona. She became permanently and totally disabled. She also met all other requirements for eligibility for APTD benefits except the 15-year residency specified for aliens by 46-233 (A) (1). She applied for benefits but was denied relief solely because of the residency provision. Mrs. Richardson instituted her class action in the District of Arizona against the Commissioner of the State's Department of Public Welfare seeking declaratory relief, an injunction against the enforcement of 46-233 (A) (1), 46-252 (2), and 46-272 (4), and the award of amounts allegedly due. She claimed that Arizona's alien residency requirements violate the Equal Protection Clause and the constitutional right to travel; that they conflict with the Social Security Act and are thus overborne by the Supremacy Clause; and that the regulation of aliens has been pre-empted by Congress. The three-judge court upheld Mrs. Richardson's motion for summary judgment on equal protection grounds. It did so in reliance on this Court's opinions in *Takahashi v. Fish & Game Comm'n*, and *Shapiro v. Thompson*. The Commissioner appealed. The judgment was stayed as to all parties plaintiff other than Mrs. Richardson.

I Does the Equal Protection Clause of the Fourteenth Amendment prevent a State from conditioning welfare benefits either (a) upon the beneficiary's possession of United States citizenship, or (b) if the beneficiary is an alien, upon his having resided in this country for a specified number of years?

R A state statute that denies welfare benefits to resident aliens and one that denies them to aliens who have not resided in the United States for a specified number of years violate the Equal Protection Clause.

A State statutes, like the Arizona and Pennsylvania statutes here involved, that deny welfare benefits to resident aliens or to aliens who have not resided in the United States for a specified number of years are violative of the Equal Protection Clause and encroach upon the exclusive federal power over the entrance and residence of aliens; and there is no authorization for Arizona's 15-year durational residency requirement in 1402 (b) of the Social Security Act. Under traditional equal protection principles, a State retains broad discretion to classify as long as its classification has a reasonable basis. But the Court's decisions have established that classifications based on alienage, like those based on nationality or race, are inherently suspect and subject to close judicial scrutiny. Aliens as a class are a prime example of a "discrete and insular" minority (see *United States v. Carolene Products Co.*) for whom such heightened judicial solicitude is appropriate. Accordingly, it was said in *Takahashi* that "the power of a state to apply its laws exclusively to its alien inhabitants as a class is confined within narrow limits." Arizona and Pennsylvania seek to justify their restrictions on the eligibility of aliens for public assistance solely on the basis of a State's "special public interest" in favoring its own citizens over aliens in the distribution of limited resources such as welfare benefits. It is true that this Court on occasion has upheld state statutes that treat citizens and noncitizens differently, the ground for distinction having been that such laws were necessary to protect special interests of the State or its citizens. *Takahashi v. Fish & Game Comm'n*, however, cast doubt on the continuing validity of the special public-interest doctrine in all contexts. Whatever may be the contemporary vitality of the special public-interest doctrine in other contexts after Takahashi, we conclude that a State's desire to preserve limited welfare benefits for its own citizens is inadequate to justify Pennsylvania's making noncitizens ineligible for public assistance, and Arizona's restricting benefits to citizens and longtime resident aliens. Since an alien as well as a citizen is a "person" for equal protection purposes, a concern for fiscal integrity is no more compelling a justification for the questioned classification in these cases than it was in *Shapiro*. Accordingly, we hold that a state statute that denies welfare benefits to resident aliens and one that denies them to aliens who have not resided in the United States for a specified number of years violate the Equal Protection Clause.

C

Affirmed.

Foley v. Connelie

435 U.S. 291 (1978)

FACTS

The appellant, Edmund Foley, is an alien eligible in due course to become a naturalized citizen, who is lawfully in this country as a permanent resident. He applied for appointment as a New York State trooper, a position which is filled on the basis of competitive examinations. Pursuant to a New York statute, state authorities refused to allow Foley to take the examination. The statute provides: "No person shall be appointed to the New York state police force unless he shall be a citizen of the United States." Appellant then brought this action in the United States District Court for the Southern District of New York, seeking a declaratory judgment that the State's exclusion of aliens from its police force violates the Equal Protection Clause of the Fourteenth Amendment. After Foley was certified as representative of a class of those similarly situated, a three-judge District Court was convened to consider the merits of the claim. The District Court held the statute to be constitutional.

I Does a New York statute limiting appointment of members of state police force to citizens of the United States violate the Equal Protection Clause of the Fourteenth Amendment?

R A New York statute limiting appointment of members of state police force to citizens of the United States does not violate the Equal Protection Clause of the Fourteenth Amendment?

A A New York statute limiting appointment of members of state police force to citizens of the United States held not to violate the Equal Protection Clause of the Fourteenth Amendment. Citizenship may be a relevant qualification for fulfilling those "important nonelective . . . positions" held by "officers who participate directly in the formulation, execution, or review of broad public policy," *Sugarman v. Dougall*. Strict equal protection scrutiny is not required to justify classifications applicable to such positions; a State need only show some rational relationship between the interest sought to be protected and the limiting classification. In deciding what level of scrutiny is to be applied, each position in question must be examined to determine whether it involves discretionary decisionmaking, or execution of policy, which substantially affects members of the political community. Police officials are clothed with authority to exercise an almost infinite variety of discretionary powers, calling for a very high degree of judgment and discretion, the exercise of which can seriously affect individuals. Police officers fall within the category of "important nonelective . . . officers who participate directly in the . . . execution . . . of broad public policy." *Dougall* (emphasis added). In the enforcement and execution of the laws the police function is one where citizenship bears a rational relationship to the special demands of the particular position, and a State may therefore confine the performance of this important public responsibility to those who are citizens.

C Affirmed.

Ambach v. Norwick

441 U.S. 68 (1979)

FACTS

New York Education Law 3001 forbids certification as a public school teacher of any person who is not a citizen of the United States, unless that person has manifested an intention to apply for citizenship. The Commissioner of Education is authorized to create exemptions from this prohibition, and has done so with respect to aliens who are not yet eligible for citizenship. Unless a teacher obtains certification, he may not work in a public elementary or secondary school in New York. Appellee Norwick was born in Scotland and is a subject of Great Britain. She has resided in this country since 1965 and is married to a United States citizen. Appellee Dachinger is a Finnish subject who came to this country in 1966 and also is married to a United States citizen. Both Norwick and Dachinger currently meet all of the educational requirements New York has set for certification as a public school teacher, but they consistently have refused to seek citizenship in spite of their eligibility to do so. Norwick applied in 1973 for a teaching certificate covering nursery school through sixth grade, and Dachinger sought a certificate covering the same grades in 1975. Both applications were denied because of appellees' failure to meet the requirements of 3001 (3). Norwick then filed this suit seeking to enjoin the enforcement of 3001 (3), and Dachinger obtained leave to intervene as a plaintiff. A three-judge District Court was convened pursuant to 28 U.S.C. 2281 (1970 ed.). Applying the "close judicial scrutiny" standard, the court held that 3001 (3) discriminated against aliens in violation of the Equal Protection Clause. The court believed that the statute was overbroad, because it excluded all resident aliens from all teaching jobs regardless of the subject sought to be taught, the alien's nationality, the nature of the alien's relationship to this country, and the alien's willingness to substitute some other sign of loyalty to this Nation's political values, such as an oath of allegiance.

I Can a State, consistent with the Equal Protection Clause of the Fourteenth Amendment, refuse to employ as elementary and secondary school teachers aliens who are eligible for United States citizenship but who refuse to seek naturalization?

R A New York statute forbidding permanent certification as a public school teacher of any person who is not a United States citizen unless that person has manifested an intention to apply for citizenship, does not violate the Equal Protection Clause of the Fourteenth Amendment.

A As a general principle some state functions are so bound up with the operation of the State as a governmental entity as to permit exclusion from those functions of all persons who have not become part of the process of self-government. Accordingly, a State is required to justify its exclusion of aliens from such governmental positions only "by a showing of some rational relationship between the interest sought to be protected and the limiting classification," *Foley v. Connelie*. This rule for governmental functions, which is an exception to the stricter general standard applicable to classifications based on alienage, rests on important principles inherent in the Constitution. The distinction between citizens and aliens, though ordinarily irrelevant to private activity, is fundamental to the definition and government of a State, and the references to such distinction in the Constitution itself indicate that the status of citizenship was meant to have significance in the structure of our government. It is because of this special significance of citizenship that governmental entities, when exercising the functions of government, have wider latitude in limiting the participation of noncitizens. Taking into consideration the role of public education and the degree of responsibility and discretion teachers possess in fulfilling that role, it is clear that public school teachers come well within the "governmental function" principle recognized in *Sugarman v. Dougall*, and *Foley v. Connelie*, and, accordingly, the Constitution requires only that a citizenship requirement applicable to teaching in the public school bear a rational relationship to a legitimate state interest. Here, the statute in question does bear a rational relationship to the State's interest in furthering its educational goals, especially with respect to regarding all teachers as having an obligation to promote civic virtues and understanding in their classes, regardless of the subject taught.

C Reversed.

Plyler v. Doe
457 U.S. 202 (1982)

FACTS

This is a class action, filed in the United States District Court for the Eastern District of Texas in September 1977, on behalf of certain school-age children of Mexican origin residing in Smith County, Tex., who could not establish that they had been legally admitted into the United States. The action complained of the exclusion of plaintiff children from the public schools of the Tyler Independent School District. The Superintendent and members of the Board of Trustees of the School District were named as defendants; the State of Texas intervened as a party-defendant. After certifying a class consisting of all undocumented school-age children of Mexican origin residing within the School District, the District Court preliminarily enjoined defendants from denying a free education to members of the plaintiff class. In December 1977, the court conducted an extensive hearing on plaintiffs' motion for permanent injunctive relief.

I Can Texas constitutionally deny to undocumented school-age children the free public education that it provides to children who are citizens of the United States or legally admitted aliens?

R A Texas statute which withholds from local school districts any state funds for the education of children who were not "legally admitted" into the United States, and which authorizes local school districts to deny enrollment to such children, violates the Equal Protection Clause of the Fourteenth Amendment.

A A Texas statute which withholds from local school districts any state funds for the education of children who were not "legally admitted" into the United States, and which authorizes local school districts to deny enrollment to such children, violates the Equal Protection Clause of the Fourteenth Amendment. The illegal aliens who are plaintiffs in these cases challenging the statute may claim the benefit of the Equal Protection Clause, which provides that no State shall "deny to any person within its jurisdiction the equal protection of the laws." Whatever his status under the immigration laws, an alien is a "person" in any ordinary sense of that term. This Court's prior cases recognizing that illegal aliens are "persons" protected by the Due Process Clauses of the Fifth and Fourteenth Amendments, which Clauses do not include the phrase "within its jurisdiction," cannot be distinguished on the asserted ground that persons who have entered the country illegally are not "within the jurisdiction" of a State even if they are present within its boundaries and subject to its laws. Nor do the logic and history of the Fourteenth Amendment support such a construction. Instead, use of the phrase "within its jurisdiction" confirms the understanding that the Fourteenth Amendment's protection extends to anyone, citizen or stranger, who is subject to the laws of a State, and reaches into every corner of a State's territory. The discrimination contained in the Texas statute cannot be considered rational unless it furthers some substantial goal of the State. Although undocumented resident aliens cannot be treated as a "suspect class," and although education is not a "fundamental right," so as to require the State to justify the statutory classification by showing that it serves a compelling governmental interest, nevertheless the Texas statute imposes a lifetime hardship on a discrete class of children not accountable for their disabling status. These children can neither affect their parents' conduct nor their own undocumented status. The deprivation of public education is not like the deprivation of some other governmental benefit. Public education has a pivotal role in maintaining the fabric of our society and in sustaining our political and cultural heritage; the deprivation of education takes an inestimable toll on the social, economic, intellectual, and psychological well-being of the individual, and poses an obstacle to individual achievement. In determining the rationality of the Texas statute, its costs to the Nation and to the innocent children may properly be considered. The undocumented status of these children does not establish a sufficient rational basis for denying them benefits that the State affords other residents. It is true that when faced with an equal protection challenge respecting a State's differential treatment of aliens, the courts must be attentive to congressional policy concerning aliens. But in the area of special constitutional sensitivity presented by these cases, and in the absence of any contrary indication fairly discernible in the legislative record, no national policy is perceived that might justify the State in denying these children an elementary education. Texas' statutory classification cannot be sustained as furthering its interest in the "preservation of the state's limited resources for the education of its lawful residents." While the State might have an interest in mitigating potentially harsh economic effects from an influx of illegal immigrants, the Texas statute does not offer an effective method of dealing with the problem. Even assuming that the net impact of illegal aliens on the economy is negative, charging tuition to undocumented children constitutes an ineffectual attempt to stem the tide of illegal immigration, at least when compared with the alternative of prohibiting employment of illegal aliens. Nor is there any merit to the suggestion that undocumented children are appropriately singled out for exclusion because of the special burdens they impose on the State's ability to provide high-quality public education. The record does not show that exclusion of undocumented children is likely to improve the overall quality of education in the State. Neither is there any merit to the claim that undocumented children are appropriately singled out because their unlawful presence within the United States renders them less likely than other children to remain within the State's boundaries and to put their education to productive social or political use within the State.

C

Affirmed.

Massachusetts Board of Retirement v. Murgia

427 U.S. 307 (1976)

FACTS

Appellee Robert Murgia was a Massachusetts State Police officer. The Massachusetts Board of Retirement retired him upon his 50th birthday. Appellee brought this civil action in the U.S. District Court, alleging that the operation of 26(3)(a) denied him equal protection of the laws and requesting the convening of a three-judge court under 28 U.S.C. 2281, 2284. The District Judge dismissed appellee's complaint on the ground that the complaint did not allege a substantial constitutional question. On appeal, the U.S. First Circuit Court of Appeals, in an unreported memorandum, set aside the District Court judgment and remanded the case with direction to convene a three-judge court. Upon a record consisting of depositions, affidavits, and other evidence submitted by the parties, the three-judge court filed an opinion that declared 26 (3) (a) unconstitutional on the ground that "a classification based on age 50 alone lacks a rational basis in furthering any substantial state interest," and enjoined enforcement of the statute.

I

Can a state force its police officers to retire at a certain age?

R

Classifications based on age need only be rationally related to a legitimate governmental purpose.

A

A Massachusetts statute making it mandatory for a uniformed state police officer to retire at age 50 does not deny equal protection in violation of the Fourteenth Amendment. Rationality, rather than strict scrutiny, is the proper standard for determining whether the statute violates equal protection. Equal protection analysis requires strict scrutiny of a legislative classification only when it impermissibly interferes with the exercise of a fundamental right or operates to the peculiar disadvantage of a suspect class. Here mandatory retirement at 50 does not implicate any fundamental right of a uniformed state police officer over that age, since a right of governmental employment per se is not fundamental, and the class of such officers over 50 does not constitute a suspect class, since classifications based on age are not considered suspect. Since physical ability generally declines with age, mandatory retirement at 50 serves to remove from police service those whose fitness for uniformed police work has presumptively diminished with age and is, therefore, rationally related to the State's announced legitimate objective of protecting the public by assuring the physical preparedness of its uniformed police. While the State perhaps has not chosen the best means to accomplish its purpose, where rationality is the test, a statute "does not violate the Equal Protection Clause merely because the classifications made by [it] are imperfect," *Dandridge v. Williams*.

C

Reversed.

Zablocki v. Redhail

434 U.S. 378 (1978)

FACTS

Wisconsin statute providing that any resident of that State "having minor issue not in his custody and which he is under obligation to support by any court order or judgment" may not marry without a court approval order, which cannot be granted absent a showing that the support obligation has been met and that children covered by the support order "are not then and are not likely thereafter to become public charges," held to violate the Equal Protection Clause of the Fourteenth Amendment.

I

Can a state place restrictions on marriage such that a person owing child support and whose payments are not current cannot obtain a marriage certificate (i.e. cannot marry)?

R

Marriage is a fundamental right such that the interference of it cannot be upheld unless the reason for denying the right is narrowly tailored to serve a compelling state objective.

A

Since the right to marry is of fundamental importance, and the statutory classification involved here significantly interferes with the exercise of that right, "critical examination" of the state interests advanced in support of the classification is required. The state interests assertedly served by the challenged statute unnecessarily impinge on the right to marry. If the statute is designed to furnish an opportunity to counsel persons with prior child-support obligations before further such obligations are incurred, it neither expressly requires counseling nor provides for automatic approval after counseling is completed. The statute cannot be justified as encouraging an applicant to support his children. By the proceeding the State, which already possesses numerous other means for exacting compliance with support obligations, merely prevents the applicant from getting married, without ensuring support of the applicant's prior children. Though it is suggested that the statute protects the ability of marriage applicants to meet prior support obligations before new ones are incurred, the statute is both under-inclusive (as it does not limit new financial commitments other than those arising out of the contemplated marriage) and over-inclusive (since the new spouse may better the applicant's financial situation).

C

Affirmed.

Michael H. v. Gerald D.

491 U.S. 110 (1989)

FACTS

In May 1981, appellant Victoria D. was born to Carole D., who was married to, and resided with, appellee Gerald D. in California. Although Gerald was listed as father on the birth certificate and has always claimed Victoria as his daughter, blood tests showed a 98.07% probability that appellant Michael H., with whom Carole had had an adulterous affair, was Victoria's father. During Victoria's first three years, she and her mother resided at times with Michael, who held her out as his own, at times with another man, and at times with Gerald, with whom they have lived since June 1984. In November 1982, Michael filed a filiation action in California Superior Court to establish his paternity and right to visitation. Victoria, through her court-appointed guardian ad litem, filed a cross-complaint asserting that she was entitled to maintain filial relationships with both Michael and Gerald. The court ultimately granted Gerald summary judgment on the ground that there were no triable issues of fact as to paternity under Cal. Evid. Code 621, which provides that a child born to a married woman living with her husband, who is neither impotent nor sterile, is presumed to be a child of the marriage, and that this presumption may be rebutted only by the husband or wife, and then only in limited circumstances. Moreover, the court denied Michael's and Victoria's motions for visitation pending appeal under Cal. Civ. Code 4601, which provides that a court may, in its discretion, grant "reasonable visitation rights . . . to any . . . person having an interest in the [child's] welfare." The California Court of Appeal affirmed, rejecting Michael's procedural and substantive due process challenges to 621 as well as Victoria's due process and equal protection claims. The court also rejected Victoria's assertion of a right to continued visitation with Michael under 4601, on the ground that California law denies visitation against the wishes of the mother to a putative father who has been prevented by 621 from establishing his paternity.

I Are there any restrictions on what type of interests can receive constitutional protection under the Due Process Clause of the 14th Amendment?

R The asserted liberty interest must be both a fundamental interest and one that has traditionally been protected by society in order to receive the protections afforded by due process under the 14th Amendment.

A The 621 presumption does not infringe upon the due process rights of a man wishing to establish his paternity of a child born to the wife of another man. Michael's contention that procedural due process requires that he be afforded an opportunity to demonstrate his paternity in an evidentiary hearing fundamentally misconceives the nature of 621. Although phrased in terms of a presumption, 621 expresses and implements a substantive rule of law declaring it to be generally irrelevant for paternity purposes whether a child conceived during, and born into, an existing marriage was begotten by someone other than the husband and had a prior relationship with him, based on the state legislature's determination as a matter of overriding social policy that the husband should be held responsible for the child and that the integrity and privacy of the family unit should not be impugned. Because Michael's complaint is that the statute categorically denies all men in his circumstances an opportunity to establish their paternity, his challenge is not accurately viewed as procedural. There is no merit to Michael's substantive due process claim that he has a constitutionally protected "liberty" interest in the parental relationship he has established with Victoria, and that protection of Gerald's and Carole's marital union is an insufficient state interest to support termination of that relationship. Michael has failed to meet his burden of proving that his claimed "liberty" interest is one so deeply imbedded within society's traditions as to be a fundamental right. Not only has he failed to demonstrate that the interest he seeks to vindicate has traditionally been accorded protection by society, but the common-law presumption of legitimacy, and even modern statutory and decisional law, demonstrate that society has historically protected, and continues to protect, the marital family against the sort of claim Michael asserts. The 621 presumption does not infringe upon any constitutional right of a child to maintain a relationship with her natural father. Victoria's assertion that she has a due process right to maintain filial relationships with both Michael and Gerald is, at best, the obverse of Michael's claim and fails for the same reasons. Nor is there any merit to her claim that her equal protection rights have been violated because, unlike her mother and presumed father, she had no opportunity to rebut the presumption of her legitimacy, since the State's decision to treat her differently from her parents pursues the legitimate end of preventing the disruption of an otherwise peaceful union by the rational means of not allowing anyone but the husband or wife to contest legitimacy.

C

Affirmed.

Moore v. City of East Cleveland, Ohio

431 U.S. 494 (1977)

FACTS

Appellant lives in her East Cleveland, Ohio, home with her son and two grandsons (who are first cousins). An East Cleveland housing ordinance limits occupancy of a dwelling unit to members of a single family, but defines "family" in such a way that appellant's household does not qualify. Appellant was convicted of a criminal violation of the ordinance. Her conviction was upheld on appeal over her claim that the ordinance is unconstitutional. Appellee city contends that the ordinance should be sustained under *Village of Belle Terre v. Boraas*, which upheld an ordinance imposing limits on the types of groups that could occupy a single dwelling unit.

I

Is an ordinance imposing limits on the types of groups that could occupy a single dwelling unit constitutional?

R

An ordinance imposing limits on the types of groups that could occupy a single dwelling unit constitutional.

A

The ordinance deprived appellant of her liberty in violation of the Due Process Clause of the Fourteenth Amendment. This case is distinguishable from *Belle Terre*, where the ordinance affected only unrelated individuals. The ordinance here expressly selects certain categories of relatives who may live together and declares that others may not, in this instance making it a crime for a grandmother to live with her grandson. When the government intrudes on choices concerning family living arrangements, the usual deference to the legislature is inappropriate; and the Court must examine carefully the importance of the governmental interests advanced and the extent to which they are served by the challenged regulation. The ordinance at best has but a tenuous relationship to the objectives cited by the city: avoiding overcrowding, traffic congestion, and an undue financial burden on the school system. The strong constitutional protection of the sanctity of the family established in numerous decisions of this Court extends to the family choice involved in this case and is not confined within an arbitrary boundary drawn at the limits of the nuclear family (essentially a couple and their dependent children). Appropriate limits on substantive due process come not from drawing arbitrary lines but from careful "respect for the teachings of history [and] solid recognition of the basic values that underlie our society," *Griswold v. Connecticut*. The history and tradition of this Nation compel a larger conception of the family.

C

Judgment is reversed.

Meyer v. Nebraska

262 U.S. 390 (1923)

FACTS

Plaintiff in error was tried and convicted in the district court for Hamilton county, Nebraska, under an information which charged that on May 25, 1920, while an instructor in Zion Parochial School he unlawfully taught the subject of reading in the German language to Raymond Parpart, a child of 10 years, who had not attained and successfully passed the eighth grade. The information is based upon 'An act relating to the teaching of foreign languages in the state of Nebraska,' approved April 9, 1919. The Supreme Court of the state affirmed the judgment of conviction. It declared the offense charged and established was 'the direct and intentional teaching of the German language as a distinct subject to a child who had not passed the eighth grade,' in the parochial school maintained by Zion Evangelical Lutheran Congregation, a collection of Biblical stories being used therefore. And it held that the statute forbidding this did not conflict with the Fourteenth Amendment, but was a valid exercise of the police power.

I

Does the Constitution prohibit the teaching of children in languages other than English?

R

The Constitution provides that the government may not interfere with a person liberty by legislative action that is arbitrary or devoid of a reasonable relation to some legitimate governmental interest.

A

The challenged statute forbids the teaching in school of any subject except in English; also the teaching of any other language until the pupil has attained and successfully passed the eighth grade, which is not usually accomplished before the age of twelve. The Supreme Court of the state has held that 'the so-called ancient or dead languages' are not 'within the spirit or the purpose of the act.' Latin, Greek, Hebrew are not proscribed; but German, French, Spanish, Italian, and every other alien speech are within the ban. Evidently the Legislature has attempted materially to interfere with the calling of modern language teachers, with the opportunities of pupils to acquire knowledge, and with the power of parents to control the education of their own. It is said the purpose of the legislation was to promote civic development by inhibiting training and education of the immature in foreign tongues and ideals before they could learn English and acquire American ideals, and 'that the English language should be and become the mother tongue of all children reared in this state.' It is also affirmed that the foreign born population is very large, that certain communities commonly use foreign words, follow foreign leaders, move in a foreign atmosphere, and that the children are thereby hindered from becoming citizens of the most useful type and the public safety is imperiled. The desire of the Legislature to foster a homogeneous people with American ideals prepared readily to understand current discussions of civic matters is easy to appreciate. Unfortunate experiences during the late war and aversion toward every character of truculent adversaries were certainly enough to quicken that aspiration. But the means adopted, we think, exceed the limitations upon the power of the state and conflict with rights assured to plaintiff in error. The interference is plain enough and no adequate reason therefore in time of peace and domestic tranquility has been shown. The power of the state to compel attendance at some school and to make reasonable regulations for all schools, including a requirement that they shall give instructions in English, is not questioned. Nor has challenge been made of the state's power to prescribe a curriculum for institutions which it supports. Those matters are not within the present controversy. Our concern is with the prohibition approved by the Supreme Court. *Adams v. Tanner*, pointed out that mere abuse incident to an occupation ordinarily useful is not enough to justify its abolition, although regulation may be entirely proper. No emergency has arisen which renders knowledge by a child of some language other than English so clearly harmful as to justify its inhibition with the consequent infringement of rights long freely enjoyed. We are constrained to conclude that the statute as applied is arbitrary and without reasonable relation to any end within the competency of the state. As the statute undertakes to interfere only with teaching which involves a modern language, leaving complete freedom as to other matters, there seems no adequate foundation for the suggestion that the purpose was to protect the child's health by limiting his mental activities. It is well known that proficiency in a foreign language seldom comes to one not instructed at an early age, and experience shows that this is not injurious to the health, morals or understanding of the ordinary child. The judgment of the court below must be reversed and the cause remanded for further proceedings not inconsistent with this opinion.

Reversed.

Troxel v. Granville

530 U.S. 57 (2000)

FACTS

Washington Rev. Code §26.10.160(3) permits "[a]ny person" to petition for visitation rights "at any time" and authorizes state superior courts to grant such rights whenever visitation may serve a child's best interest. Petitioners Troxel petitioned for the right to visit their deceased son's daughters. Respondent Granville, the girls' mother, did not oppose all visitation, but objected to the amount sought by the Troxels. The Superior Court ordered more visitation than Granville desired, and she appealed. The State Court of Appeals reversed and dismissed the Troxels' petition. In affirming, the State Supreme Court held, *inter alia,* that §26.10.160(3) unconstitutionally infringes on parents' fundamental right to rear their children. Reasoning that the Federal Constitution permits a State to interfere with this right only to prevent harm or potential harm to the child, it found that §26.10.160(3) does not require a threshold showing of harm and sweeps too broadly by permitting any person to petition at any time with the only requirement being that the visitation serve the best interest of the child.

I

Does a statute which allows any person to petition a court for visitation rights with a child and then gives the petitioned court indiscriminate authority to decide the issue without giving any weight to the position of the child's parents, constitutional?

R

Parents have a fundamental right to make decisions concerning the welfare of their children; any state interference with that right must pass close scrutiny by the courts.

A

§26.10.160(3), as applied to Granville and her family, violates her due process right to make decisions concerning the care, custody, and control of her daughters. The Fourteenth Amendment's Due Process Clause has a substantive component that "provides heightened protection against government interference with certain fundamental rights and liberty interests," *Washington* v. *Glucksberg,* including parents' fundamental right to make decisions concerning the care, custody, and control of their children. Washington's breathtakingly broad statute effectively permits a court to disregard and overturn *any* decision by a fit custodial parent concerning visitation whenever a third party affected by the decision files a visitation petition, based solely on the judge's determination of the child's best interest. A parent's estimation of the child's best interest is accorded no deference. The State Supreme Court had the opportunity, but declined, to give §26.10.160(3) a narrower reading. A combination of several factors compels the conclusion that §26.10.160(3), as applied here, exceeded the bounds of the Due Process Clause. First, the Troxels did not allege, and no court has found, that Granville was an unfit parent. There is a presumption that fit parents act in their children's best interests, there is normally no reason for the State to inject itself into the private realm of the family to further question fit parents' ability to make the best decisions regarding their children. The problem here is not that the Superior Court intervened, but that when it did so, it gave no special weight to Granville's determination of her daughters' best interests. More importantly, that court appears to have applied the opposite presumption, favoring grandparent visitation. In effect, it placed on Granville the burden of *disproving* that visitation would be in her daughters' best interest and thus failed to provide any protection for her fundamental right. The court also gave no weight to Granville's having assented to visitation even before the filing of the petition or subsequent court intervention. These factors, when considered with the Superior Court's slender findings, show that this case involves nothing more than a simple disagreement between the court and Granville concerning her children's best interests, and that the visitation order was an unconstitutional infringement on Granville's right to make decisions regarding the rearing of her children. Because the instant decision rests on §26.10.160(3)'s sweeping breadth and its application here, there is no need to consider the question whether the Due Process Clause requires all non-parental visitation statutes to include a showing of harm or potential harm to the child as a condition precedent to granting visitation or to decide the precise scope of the parental due process right in the visitation context. There is also no reason to remand this case for further proceedings. The visitation order clearly violated the Constitution, and the parties should not be forced into additional litigation that would further burden Granville's parental right.

C Affirmed.

Skinner v. Oklahoma

316 U.S. 535 (1942)

FACTS

The statute involved is Oklahoma's Habitual Criminal Sterilization Act. The Act defines an 'habitual criminal' as a person who, having been convicted two or more times for crimes 'amounting to felonies involving moral turpitude' either in an Oklahoma court or in a court of any other State, is thereafter convicted of such a felony in Oklahoma and is sentenced to a term of imprisonment in an Oklahoma penal institution. Machinery is provided for the institution by the Attorney General of a proceeding against such a person in the Oklahoma courts for a judgment that such person shall be rendered sexually sterile. Notice, an opportunity to be heard, and the right to a jury trial are provided. The issues triable in such a proceeding are narrow and confined. If the court or jury finds that the defendant is an 'habitual criminal' and that he 'may be rendered sexually sterile without detriment to his or her general health', then the court 'shall render judgment to the effect that said defendant be rendered sexually sterile' by the operation of vasectomy in case of a male and of salpingectomy in case of a female. Only one other provision of the Act is material here provides that 'offenses arising out of the violation of the prohibitory laws, revenue acts, embezzlement, or political offenses, shall not come or be considered within the terms of this Act.' Petitioner was convicted in 1926 of the crime of stealing chickens and was sentenced to the Oklahoma State Reformatory. In 1929 he was convicted of the crime of robbery with fire arms and was sentenced to the reformatory. In 1934 he was convicted again of robbery with firearms and was sentenced to the penitentiary. He was confined there in 1935 when the Act was passed. In 1936 the Attorney General instituted proceedings against him. Petitioner in his answer challenged the Act as unconstitutional by reason of the Fourteenth Amendment. A jury trial was had. The court instructed the jury that the crimes of which petitioner had been convicted were felonies involving moral turpitude and that the only question for the jury was whether the operation of vasectomy could be performed on petitioner without detriment to his general health. The jury found that it could be. A judgment directing that the operation of vasectomy be performed on petitioner was affirmed by the Supreme Court of Oklahoma. Several objections to the constitutionality of the Act have been pressed upon us. It is urged that the Act cannot be sustained as an exercise of the police power in view of the state of scientific authorities respecting inheritability of criminal traits. It is argued that due process is lacking because the defendant is given no opportunity to be heard on the issue as to whether he is the probable potential parent of socially undesirable offspring. It is also suggested that the Act is penal in character and that the sterilization provided for is cruel and unusual punishment. We pass those points without intimating an opinion on them; we deal only whether, constitutionally speaking, a law may lawfully provide different punishments for criminal offenders who have committed essentially the same crime.

I Is a law which provides different punishments for criminal offenders who have committed essentially the same crime Constitutional?

R A law which provides different punishments for criminal offenders who have committed essentially the same crime is invidiously discriminatory.

Skinner v. Oklahoma

316 U.S. 535 (1942)

A The instant legislation runs afoul of the equal protection clause, though we give Oklahoma that large deference which the rule of the foregoing cases requires. We are dealing here with legislation which involves one of the basic civil rights of man. Marriage and procreation are fundamental to the very existence and survival of the race. The power to sterilize, if exercised, may have subtle, far reaching and devastating effects. In evil or reckless hands it can cause races or types which are inimical to the dominant group to wither and disappear. There is no redemption for the individual whom the law touches. Any experiment which the State conducts is to his irreparable injury. He is forever deprived of a basic liberty. We mention these matters not to reexamine the scope of the police power of the States. We advert to them merely in emphasis of our view that strict scrutiny of the classification which a State makes in a sterilization law is essential, lest unwittingly or otherwise invidious discriminations are made against groups or types of individuals in violation of the constitutional guaranty of just and equal laws. The guaranty of 'equal protection of the laws is a pledge of the protection of equal laws.' Thus, when the law lays an unequal hand on those who have committed intrinsically the same quality of offense and sterilizes one and not the other, it has made as an invidious discrimination as if it had selected a particular race or nationality for oppressive treatment. Sterilization of those who have thrice committed grand larceny with immunity for those who are embezzlers is a clear, pointed, unmistakable discrimination. Oklahoma makes no attempt to say that he who commits larceny by trespass or trick or fraud has biologically inheritable traits which he who commits embezzlement lacks. Oklahoma's line between larceny by fraud and embezzlement is determined, as we have noted, 'with reference to the time when the fraudulent intent to convert the property to the taker's own use' arises. In terms of fines and imprisonment the crimes of larceny and embezzlement rate the same under the Oklahoma code. Only when it comes to sterilization are the pains and penalties of the law different. The equal protection clause would indeed be a formula of empty words if such conspicuously artificial lines could be drawn. It is true that the Act has a broad severability clause. But we will not endeavor to determine whether its application would solve the equal protection difficulty. The Supreme Court of Oklahoma sustained the Act without reference to the severability clause. We have therefore a situation where the Act as construed and applied to petitioner is allowed to perpetuate the discrimination which we have found to be fatal. Whether the severability clause would be so applied as to remove this particular constitutional objection is a question which may be more appropriately left for adjudication by the Oklahoma court. That is reemphasized here by our uncertainty as to what excision, if any, would be made as a matter of Oklahoma law. It is by no means clear whether if an excision were made, this particular constitutional difficulty might be solved by enlarging on the one hand or contracting on the other the class of criminals who might be sterilized.

C Reversed.

Griswold v. Connecticut

381 U.S. 479 (1965)

FACTS

Defendant-appellants, the Executive Director of the Planned Parenthood League of Connecticut, one Griswold, and its medical director, a licensed physician, were convicted as accessories for giving married couples information and medical advice on how to prevent conception and, following examination, prescribing a contraceptive device or material for the wife's use. One Connecticut statute (53-32) makes it a crime for any person to use any drug or article to prevent conception. Another statute (54-196) makes it illegal to abet or counsel another person to commit any offense. Appellants were found guilty and fined $100 each (Griswold was convicted under this accessory statute for counseling individuals to violate the contraception law). Appellants claimed that the accessory statute as applied violated the Fourteenth Amendment. An intermediate appellate court and the State's highest court affirmed the judgment.

I Does the Constitution protect the right of marital privacy against state restrictions on a couple's ability to be counseled in the use of contraceptives?

R While the Constitution does not explicitly protect a general right to privacy, the range of guarantees within the Bill of Rights create penumbras, or zones, that establish a right to privacy which cannot be invaded unless the state can show that the legislation is necessary to vindicate a compelling governmental interest.

A We think that appellants have standing to raise the constitutional rights of the married people with whom they had a professional relationship. This case is more akin to *Truax v. Raich*, where an employee was permitted to assert the rights of his employer; to *Pierce v. Society of Sisters*, where the owners of private schools were entitled to assert the rights of potential pupils and their parents; and to *Barrows v. Jackson*, where a white defendant, party to a racially restrictive covenant, who was being sued for damages by the covenantors because she had conveyed her property to Negroes, was allowed to raise the issue that enforcement of the covenant violated the rights of prospective Negro purchasers to equal protection, although no Negro was a party to the suit. Coming to the merits, we are met with a wide range of questions that implicate the Due Process Clause of the Fourteenth Amendment. We do not sit as a super-legislature to determine the wisdom, need, and propriety of laws that touch economic problems, business affairs, or social conditions. This law, however, operates directly on an intimate relation of husband and wife and their physician's role in one aspect of that relation. The association of people is not mentioned in the Constitution nor in the Bill of Rights. The right to educate a child in a school of the parents' choice, whether public or private or parochial, is also not mentioned. Nor is the right to study any particular subject or any foreign language. Yet the First Amendment has been construed to include certain of those rights. The present case concerns a relationship lying within the zone of privacy created by several fundamental constitutional guarantees. And it concerns a law which, in forbidding the use of contraceptives rather than regulating their manufacture or sale, seeks to achieve its goals by means having a maximum destructive impact upon that relationship. Such a law cannot stand in light of the familiar principle, so often applied by this Court, that a "governmental purpose to control or prevent activities constitutionally subject to state regulation may not be achieved by means which sweep unnecessarily broadly and thereby invade the area of protected freedoms." Would we allow the police to search the sacred precincts of marital bedrooms for telltale signs of the use of contraceptives? The very idea is repulsive to the notions of privacy surrounding the marriage relationship. We deal with a right of privacy older than the Bill of Rights, older than our political parties, older than our school system. Marriage is a coming together for better or for worse, hopefully enduring, and intimate to the degree of being sacred. It is an association that promotes a way of life, not causes; a harmony in living, not political faiths; a bilateral loyalty, not commercial or social projects. Yet it is an association for as noble a purpose as any involved in our prior decisions.

C Reversed.

Eisenstadt v. Baird

405 U.S. 438 (1972)

FACTS

Appellee attacks his conviction of violating Massachusetts law for giving a woman a contraceptive foam at the close of his lecture to students on contraception. That law makes it a felony for anyone to give away a drug, medicine, instrument, or article for the prevention of conception except in the case of (1) a registered physician administering or prescribing it for a married person or (2) an active registered pharmacist furnishing it to a married person presenting a registered physician's prescription. The District Court dismissed appellee's petition for a writ of habeas corpus. The Court of Appeals vacated the dismissal, holding that the statute is a prohibition on contraception *per se* and conflicts "with fundamental human rights" under *Griswold v. Connecticut.* Appellant, *inter alia,* argues that appellee lacks standing to assert the rights of unmarried persons denied access to contraceptives because he was neither an authorized distributor under the statute nor a single person unable to obtain contraceptives.

I

Can a state constitutionally distribute contraceptives to married person but make their distribution illegal to unmarried persons?

R

The right of privacy is a right to be free from governmental intrusion into matters fundamentally affecting a person which include whether to carry or conceive a child, married or not.

A

If, as the Court of Appeals held, the statute under which appellee was convicted is not a health measure, appellee may not be prevented, because he was not an authorized distributor, from attacking the statute in its alleged discriminatory application to potential distributees. Appellee, furthermore, has standing to assert the rights of unmarried persons denied access to contraceptives because their ability to obtain them will be materially impaired by enforcement of the statute. By providing dissimilar treatment for married and unmarried persons who are similarly situated, the statute violates the Equal Protection Clause of the Fourteenth Amendment. The deterrence of fornication, a 90-day misdemeanor under Massachusetts law, cannot reasonably be regarded as the purpose of the statute, since the statute is riddled with exceptions making contraceptives freely available for use in premarital sexual relations and its scope and penalty structure are inconsistent with that purpose. Similarly, the protection of public health through the regulation of the distribution of potentially harmful articles cannot reasonably be regarded as the purpose of the law, since, if health were the rationale, the statute would be both discriminatory and overbroad, and federal and state laws already regulate the distribution of drugs unsafe for use except under the supervision of a licensed physician. Nor can the statute be sustained simply as a prohibition on contraception per se, for whatever the rights of the individual to access to contraceptives may be, the rights must be the same for the unmarried and the married alike. If under Griswold, supra, the distribution of contraceptives to married persons cannot be prohibited, a ban on distribution to unmarried persons would be equally impermissible, since the constitutionally protected right of privacy inheres in the individual, not the marital couple. If, on the other hand, Griswold is no bar to a prohibition on the distribution of contraceptives, a prohibition limited to unmarried persons would be underinclusive and invidiously discriminatory.

C Affirmed.

Roe v. Wade

410 U.S. 113 (1991)

FACTS

A pregnant single woman (Jane Roe) brought a class action challenging the constitutionality of the Texas criminal abortion laws, which proscribe procuring or attempting an abortion except on medical advice for the purpose of saving the mother's life. A licensed physician, one Hallford, who had two state abortion prosecutions pending against him, was permitted to intervene. A childless married couple (John and Mary Doe), the wife not being pregnant, separately attacked the laws, basing alleged injury on the future possibilities of contraceptive failure, pregnancy, unpreparedness for parenthood, and impairment of the wife's health. A three-judge District Court, which consolidated the actions, held that Roe and Hallford, and members of their classes, had standing to sue and presented justiciable controversies. Ruling that declaratory, though not injunctive, relief was warranted, the court declared the abortion statutes void as vague and overbroadly infringing those plaintiffs' Ninth and Fourteenth Amendment rights. The court ruled the Does' complaint not justiciable. Appellants (Jane Roe, the Does and Hallford) directly appealed to this Court on the injunctive rulings, and appellee (the State of Texas) cross-appealed from the District Court's grant of declaratory relief to Roe and Hallford. The Supreme Court granted certiorari.

I

Does a pregnant woman have a constitutional right to terminate her pregnancy as she chooses?

R

The 14th Amendment entitles a pregnant woman to terminate her pregnancy; however, regulate the abortion procedure in ways that are reasonably related to maternal health.

A

While 28 U.S.C. 1253 authorizes no direct appeal to this Court from the grant or denial of declaratory relief alone, review is not foreclosed when the case is properly before the Court on appeal from specific denial of injunctive relief and the arguments as to both injunctive and declaratory relief are necessarily identical. Roe has standing to sue; the Does and Hallford do not. Contrary to appellee's (Texas') contention, the natural termination of Roe's pregnancy did not moot her suit. Litigation involving pregnancy, which is "capable of repetition, yet evading review," is an exception to the usual federal rule that an actual controversy must exist at review stages and not simply when the action is initiated. The District Court correctly refused injunctive, but erred in granting declaratory relief to Hallford. The Does' complaint, based as it is on contingencies, any one or more of which may not occur, is too speculative to present an actual case or controversy. State criminal abortion laws, like those involved here, that except from criminality only a life-saving procedure on the mother's behalf without regard to the stage of her pregnancy and other interests involved violate the Due Process Clause of the Fourteenth Amendment, which protects against state action the right to privacy, including a woman's qualified right to terminate her pregnancy. Though the State cannot override that right, it has legitimate interests in protecting both the pregnant woman's health and the potentiality of human life, each of which interests grows and reaches a "compelling" point at various stages of the woman's approach to term. For the stage prior to approximately the end of the first trimester, the abortion decision and its effectuation must be left to the medical judgment of the pregnant woman's attending physician. For the stage subsequent to approximately the end of the first trimester, the State, in promoting its interest in the health of the mother, may, if it chooses, regulate the abortion procedure in ways that are reasonably related to maternal health. For the stage subsequent to viability the State, in promoting its interest in the potentiality of human life may, if it chooses, regulate, and even proscribe, abortion except where necessary, in appropriate medical judgment, for the preservation of the life or health of the mother. The State may define the term "physician" to mean only a physician currently licensed by the State, and may proscribe any abortion by a person who is not a physician as so defined. It is unnecessary to decide the injunctive relief issue since the Texas authorities will doubtless fully recognize the Court's ruling that the Texas criminal abortion statutes are unconstitutional.

C

Affirmed in part and reversed in part.

Planned Parenthood of Southern Pa. v. Casey

505 U.S. 833 (1992)

FACTS

At issue are five provisions of the Pennsylvania Abortion Control Act of 1982 which imposed several restrictions on abortions: 3205, which requires that a woman seeking an abortion give her informed consent prior to the procedure, and specifies that she be provided with certain information at least 24 hours before the abortion is performed; 3206, which mandates the informed consent of one parent for a minor to obtain an abortion, but provides a judicial bypass procedure; 3209, which commands that, unless certain exceptions apply, a married woman seeking an abortion must sign a statement indicating that she has notified her husband; 3203, which defines a "medical emergency" that will excuse compliance with the foregoing requirements; and 3207(b), 3214(a), and 3214(f), which impose certain reporting requirements on facilities providing abortion services. Before any of the provisions took effect, the petitioners, five abortion clinics and a physician representing himself and a class of doctors who provide abortion services, brought this suit seeking a declaratory judgment that each of the provisions was unconstitutional on its face, as well as injunctive relief. The District Court held all the provisions unconstitutional, and permanently enjoined their enforcement. The Court of Appeals affirmed in part and reversed in part, striking down the husband notification provision but upholding the others. The case was brought before the U.S. Supreme Court.

I

1) Should the essential holding of *Roe v. Wade* be reaffirmed? 2) Should *Roe's* rigid trimester framework be upheld?

R

The essential holding of *Roe v. Wade* remains untouched; however, the rigid trimester frame work and strict scrutiny standard are replaced by the undue burden test.

A

We conclude that consideration of the fundamental constitutional question resolved by *Roe v. Wade*, principles of institutional integrity, and the rule of stare decisis require that *Roe's* essential holding be retained and reaffirmed as to each of its three parts: 1) a recognition of a woman's right to choose to have an abortion before fetal viability and to obtain it without undue interference from the State, whose pre-viability interests are not strong enough to support an abortion prohibition or the imposition of substantial obstacles to the woman's effective right to elect the procedure; 2) a confirmation of the State's power to restrict abortions after viability, if the law contains exceptions for pregnancies endangering a woman's life or health; and 3) the principle that the State has legitimate interests from the outset of the pregnancy in protecting the health of the woman and the life of the fetus that may become a child. *Roe* determined that a woman's decision to terminate her pregnancy is a "liberty" protected against state interference by the substantive component of the Due Process Clause. The adjudication of substantive due process claims may require this Court to exercise its reasoned judgment in determining the boundaries between the individual's liberty and the demands of organized society. The Court's decisions have afforded constitutional protection to personal decisions relating to marriage, child rearing and education, and contraception, and have recognized the right of the individual to be free from unwarranted governmental intrusion into matters so fundamentally affecting a person as the decision whether to bear a child. *Roe's* central holding properly invoked the reasoning and tradition of these precedents. Application of the doctrine of *stare decisis* confirms that *Roe's* essential holding should be reaffirmed. Although *Roe* has engendered opposition, it has in no sense proven unworkable. The *Roe* rule's limitation on state power could not be repudiated without serious inequity to people who have made choices that define their views of themselves in reliance on the availability of abortion in the event that contraception should fail. The ability of women to participate equally in the economic and social life of the Nation has been facilitated by their ability to control their reproductive lives. The Constitution serves human values, and while the effect of reliance on *Roe* cannot be exactly measured, neither can the certain costs of overruling *Roe* for people who have ordered their thinking and living around that case be dismissed. No change in Roe's factual underpinning has left its central holding obsolete, and none supports an argument for its overruling. Although subsequent maternal health care advances allow for later abortions safe to the pregnant woman, and post-*Roe* neonatal care developments have advanced viability to a point somewhat earlier, these facts go only to the scheme of time limits on the realization of competing interests and have no bearing on the validity of its central holding. The soundness or unsoundness of that constitutional judgment in no sense turns on when viability occurs. Overruling Roe's central holding would not only reach an unjustifiable result under *stare decisis* principles, but would seriously weaken the Court's capacity to exercise the judicial power and to function as the Supreme Court of the Nation. To protect the central right recognized by *Roe* while at the same time accommodating the State's profound interest in potential life, the undue burden standard should be employed. An undue burden exists, and therefore a provision of law is invalid, if its purpose or effect is to place substantial obstacles in the path of a woman seeking an abortion before the fetus attains viability. *Roe's* rigid trimester framework is rejected. To promote the State's interest in potential life throughout pregnancy, the State may take measures to ensure that the woman's choice is informed. Measures designed to advance this interest should not be invalidated if their purpose is to persuade the woman to choose childbirth over abortion. These measures must not be an undue burden on the right. As with any medical procedure, the State may enact regulations to further the health or safety of a woman seeking an abortion, but may not impose unnecessary health regulations that present a substantial obstacle to a woman seeking an abortion. Adoption of the undue burden standard does not disturb *Roe's* holding that, regardless of whether exceptions are made for particular circumstances, a State may not prohibit any woman from making the ultimate decision to terminate her pregnancy before viability. Roe's holding that "subsequent to viability, the State, in promoting its interest in the potentiality of human life, may, if it chooses, regulate, and even proscribe, abortion except where it is necessary, in appropriate medical judgment, for the preservation of the life or health of the mother" is also reaffirmed.

C Affirmed.

Stenberg v. Carhart

530 U.S. 914 (2000)

FACTS

The Constitution offers basic protection to a woman's right to choose whether to have an abortion. Before fetal viability, a woman has a right to terminate her pregnancy, and a state law is unconstitutional if it imposes on the woman's decision an "undue burden," *i.e.*, if it has the purpose or effect of placing a substantial obstacle in the woman's path. Post-viability, the State, in promoting its interest in the potentiality of human life, may regulate, and even proscribe, abortion except where "necessary, in appropriate medical judgment, for the preservation of the [mother's] life or health." The Nebraska law at issue prohibits any "partial birth abortion" unless that procedure is necessary to save the mother's life. It defines "partial birth abortion" as a procedure in which the doctor "partially delivers vaginally a living unborn child before killing the . . . child," and defines the latter phrase to mean "intentionally delivering into the vagina a living unborn child, or a substantial portion thereof, for the purpose of performing a procedure that the [abortionist] knows will kill the ... child and does kill the ... child." Violation of the law is a felony, and it provides for the automatic revocation of a convicted doctor's state license to practice medicine. Respondent Carhart, a Nebraska physician who performs abortions in a clinical setting, brought this suit seeking a declaration that the statute violates the Federal Constitution. The District Court held the statute unconstitutional. The Eighth Circuit affirmed.

I

Does a state law which bans partial birth abortions place an undue burden on a woman's light to obtain an abortion?

R

A law banning partial birth abortion creates an undue burden on a woman's right to obtain an abortion and is thus unconstitutional.

A

Nebraska's statute criminalizing the performance of "partial birth abortion[s]" violates the Federal Constitution, as interpreted in *Casey* and *Roe.* Because the statute seeks to ban one abortion method, the Court discusses several different abortion procedures, as described in the evidence below and the medical literature. During a pregnancy's second trimester (12 to 24 weeks), the most common abortion procedure is "dilation and evacuation" (D&E), which involves dilation of the cervix, removal of at least some fetal tissue using non-vacuum surgical instruments, and (after the 15th week) the potential need for instrumental dismemberment of the fetus or the collapse of fetal parts to facilitate evacuation from the uterus. When such dismemberment is necessary, it typically occurs as the doctor pulls a portion of the fetus through the cervix into the birth canal. The risks of mortality and complication that accompany D&E are significantly lower than those accompanying induced labor procedures (the next safest mid-second-trimester procedures). A variation of D&E, known as "intact D&E," is used after 16 weeks. It involves removing the fetus from the uterus through the cervix "intact," *i.e.*, in one pass rather than several passes. The intact D&E proceeds in one of two ways, depending on whether the fetus presents head first or feet first. The feet-first method is known as "dilation and extraction" (D&X). D&X is ordinarily associated with the term "partial birth abortion." The District Court concluded that clear and convincing evidence established that Carhart's D&X procedure is superior to, and safer than, the D&E and other abortion procedures used during the relevant gestational period in the 10 to 20 cases a year that present to Carhart. Moreover, materials presented at trial emphasize the potential benefits of the D&X procedure in certain cases. Proponents of the statute argue that it lacks the requisite exception "for the preservation of the ... health of the mother." The State may promote but not endanger a woman's health when it regulates the methods of abortion. We disagree. The Court rejects Nebraska's contention that there is no need for a health exception here because safe alternatives remain available and a ban on partial-birth abortion/D&X would create no risk to women's health. The parties strongly contested this factual question in the District Court; and the findings and evidence support Dr. Carhart. Proponents next argue that the Nebraska statute imposes an "undue burden" on a woman's ability to choose an abortion. Nebraska does not deny that the statute imposes an "undue burden" *if* it applies to the more commonly used D&E procedure as well as to D&E This Court agrees with the Eighth Circuit that the D&E procedure falls within the statutory prohibition of intentionally delivering into the vagina a living fetus, or "a substantial portion thereof," for the purpose of performing a procedure that the perpetrator knows will kill the fetus. Because the evidence makes clear that D&E will often involve a physician pulling an arm, leg, or other "substantial portion" of a still living fetus into the vagina prior to the fetus' death, the statutory terms do not to distinguish between D&E and D&X. The statute's language does not track the medical differences between D&E and D&X, but covers both. Using the law's statutory terms, it is impossible to distinguish between D&E (where a foot or arm is drawn through the cervix) and D&X (where the body up to the head is drawn through the cervix). Both procedures can involve the introduction of a "substantial portion" of a still living fetus, through the cervix, into the vagina--the very feature of an abortion that leads to characterizing such a procedure as involving "partial birth." Moreover, the Court rejects the Nebraska Attorney General's arguments that the state law does differentiate between the two procedures - *i.e.,* that the words "substantial portion" mean "the child up to the head," such that the law is inapplicable where the physician introduces into the birth canal anything less than the entire fetal body - and that the Court must defer to his views. The Court's case law makes clear that the Attorney General's narrowing interpretation cannot be given controlling weight. For one thing, this Court normally follows lower federal-court interpretations of state law. Also, the statutory words, "substantial portion," indicate that the statute does not include the Attorney General's restriction - "the child up to the head." The Nebraska Legislature's debates hurt the Attorney General's argument more than they help it, indicating that as small a portion of the fetus as a foot would constitute a "substantial portion." Even assuming that the distinction the Attorney General seeks to draw between the overall abortion procedure itself and the separate procedure used to kill an unborn child would help him make the D&E/D&X distinction he seeks, there is no language in the statute that supports it.

C

Affirmed.

Maher v. Roe

432 U.S. 464 (1977)

FACTS

Appellees, two indigent women who were unable to obtain a physician's certificate of medical necessity, brought this action attacking the validity of a Connecticut Welfare Department regulation that limits state Medicaid benefits for first trimester abortions to those that are "medically necessary." A three-judge District Court held that the Equal Protection Clause of the Fourteenth Amendment forbids the exclusion of non-therapeutic abortions from a state welfare program that generally subsidizes the medical expenses incident to pregnancy and childbirth. The court found implicit in *Roe v. Wade* and *Doe v. Bolton*, the view that "abortion and childbirth . . . are simply two alternative medical methods of dealing with pregnancy. . ."

I

Can the constitution require states to pay for non-therapeutic abortions when they make a decision to pay for children?

R

The Constitution does not require the government to subsidize abortions, even when it chooses to subsidize childbirth.

A

The Equal Protection Clause does not require a State participating in the Medicaid program to pay the expenses incident to non-therapeutic abortions for indigent women simply because it has made a policy choice to pay expenses incident to childbirth. Financial need alone does not identify a suspect class for purposes of equal protection analysis. The Connecticut regulation does not impinge upon the fundamental right of privacy recognized in *Roe* that protects a woman from unduly burdensome interference with her freedom to decide whether or not to terminate her pregnancy. That right implies no limitation on State's authority to make a value judgment favoring childbirth over abortion and to implement that judgment by the allocation of public funds. An indigent woman desiring an abortion is not disadvantaged by Connecticut's decision to fund childbirth; she continues as before to be dependent on private abortion services. A State is not required to show a compelling interest for its policy choice to favor normal childbirth. Connecticut's regulation is rationally related to and furthers its "strong and legitimate interest in encouraging normal childbirth," *Beal v. Doe*. The subsidizing of costs incident to childbirth is a rational means of encouraging childbirth. Since it is not unreasonable for a State to insist upon a prior showing of medical necessity to insure that its money is being spent only for authorized purposes, the District Court erred in invalidating the requirements of prior written request by the pregnant woman and prior authorization by the Department of Social Services for abortions. Although similar requirements are not imposed for other medical procedures, such procedures do not involve the termination of a potential human life.

C

Reversed and remanded.

Planned Parenthood v. Casey

505 U.S. 833 (1992)

FACTS

At issue are five provisions of the Pennsylvania Abortion Control Act of 1982 which imposed several restrictions on abortions: 3205, which requires that a woman seeking an abortion give her informed consent prior to the procedure, and specifies that she be provided with certain information at least 24 hours before the abortion is performed; 3206, which mandates the informed consent of one parent for a minor to obtain an abortion, but provides a judicial bypass procedure; 3209, which commands that, unless certain exceptions apply, a married woman seeking an abortion must sign a statement indicating that she has notified her husband; 3203, which defines a "medical emergency" that will excuse compliance with the foregoing requirements; and 3207(b), 3214(a), and 3214(f), which impose certain reporting requirements on facilities providing abortion services. Before any of the provisions took effect, the petitioners, five abortion clinics and a physician representing himself and a class of doctors who provide abortion services, brought this suit seeking a declaratory judgment that each of the provisions was unconstitutional on its face, as well as injunctive relief. The District Court held all the provisions unconstitutional, and permanently enjoined their enforcement. The Court of Appeals affirmed in part and reversed in part, striking down the husband notification provision but upholding the others. The case was brought before the U.S. Supreme Court.

I

1) Should the essential holding of *Roe v. Wade* be reaffirmed? 2) Should *Roe's* rigid trimester framework be upheld?

R

The essential holding of *Roe v. Wade* remains untouched; however, the rigid trimester frame work and strict scrutiny standard are replaced by the undue burden test.

A

We conclude that consideration of the fundamental constitutional question resolved by *Roe v. Wade*, principles of institutional integrity, and the rule of stare decisis require that *Roe's* essential holding be retained and reaffirmed as to each of its three parts: 1) a recognition of a woman's right to choose to have an abortion before fetal viability and to obtain it without undue interference from the State, whose pre-viability interests are not strong enough to support an abortion prohibition or the imposition of substantial obstacles to the woman's effective right to elect the procedure; 2) a confirmation of the State's power to restrict abortions after viability, if the law contains exceptions for pregnancies endangering a woman's life or health; and 3) the principle that the State has legitimate interests from the outset of the pregnancy in protecting the health of the woman and the life of the fetus that may become a child. *Roe* determined that a woman's decision to terminate her pregnancy is a "liberty" protected against state interference by the substantive component of the Due Process Clause. The adjudication of substantive due process claims may require this Court to exercise its reasoned judgment in determining the boundaries between the individual's liberty and the demands of organized society. The Court's decisions have afforded constitutional protection to personal decisions relating to marriage, child rearing and education, and contraception, and have recognized the right of the individual to be free from unwarranted governmental intrusion into matters so fundamentally affecting a person as the decision whether to bear a child. *Roe's* central holding properly invoked the reasoning and tradition of these precedents. Application of the doctrine of *stare decisis* confirms that *Roe's* essential holding should be reaffirmed. Although *Roe* has engendered opposition, it has in no sense proven unworkable. The *Roe* rule's limitation on state power could not be repudiated without serious inequity to people who have made choices that define their views of themselves in reliance on the availability of abortion in the event that contraception should fail. The ability of women to participate equally in the economic and social life of the Nation has been facilitated by their ability to control their reproductive lives. The Constitution serves human values, and while the effect of reliance on *Roe* cannot be exactly measured, neither can the certain costs of overruling *Roe* for people who have ordered their thinking and living around that case be dismissed. No change in Roe's factual underpinning has left its central holding obsolete, and none supports an argument for its overruling. Although subsequent maternal health care advances allow for later abortions safe to the pregnant woman, and post-*Roe* neonatal care developments have advanced viability to a point somewhat earlier, these facts go only to the scheme of time limits on the realization of competing interests and have no bearing on the validity of its central holding. The soundness or unsoundness of that constitutional judgment in no sense turns on when viability occurs. Overruling Roe's central holding would not only reach an unjustifiable result under *stare decisis* principles, but would seriously weaken the Court's capacity to exercise the judicial power and to function as the Supreme Court of the Nation. To protect the central right recognized by *Roe* while at the same time accommodating the State's profound interest in potential life, the undue burden standard should be employed. An undue burden exists, and therefore a provision of law is invalid, if its purpose or effect is to place substantial obstacles in the path of a woman seeking an abortion before the fetus attains viability. *Roe's* rigid trimester framework is rejected. To promote the State's interest in potential life throughout pregnancy, the State may take measures to ensure that the woman's choice is informed. Measures designed to advance this interest should not be invalidated if their purpose is to persuade the woman to choose childbirth over abortion. These measures must not be an undue burden on the right. As with any medical procedure, the State may enact regulations to further the health or safety of a woman seeking an abortion, but may not impose unnecessary health regulations that present a substantial obstacle to a woman seeking an abortion. Adoption of the undue burden standard does not disturb *Roe's* holding that, regardless of whether exceptions are made for particular circumstances, a State may not prohibit any woman from making the ultimate decision to terminate her pregnancy before viability. Roe's holding that "subsequent to viability, the State, in promoting its interest in the potentiality of human life, may, if it chooses, regulate, and even proscribe, abortion except where it is necessary, in appropriate medical judgment, for the preservation of the life or health of the mother" is also reaffirmed.

C

Affirmed.

Bellotti v. Baird

443 U.S. 622 (1979)

FACTS

A Massachusetts statute requires parental consent before an abortion can be performed on an unmarried woman under the age of 18. If one or both parents refuse such consent, however, the abortion may be obtained by order of a judge of the superior court "for good cause shown." In appellees' class action challenging the constitutionality of the statute, a three-judge District Court held it unconstitutional. Subsequently, this Court vacated the District Court's judgment holding that the District Court should have abstained and certified to the Massachusetts Supreme Judicial Court appropriate questions concerning the meaning of the statute. On remand, the District Court certified several questions to the Supreme Judicial Court. Among the questions certified was whether the statute permits any minors - mature or immature - to obtain judicial consent to an abortion without any parental consultation whatsoever. The Supreme Judicial Court answered that, in general, it does not; that consent must be obtained for every non-emergency abortion unless no parent is available; and that an available parent must be given notice of any judicial proceedings brought by a minor to obtain consent for an abortion. Another question certified was whether, if the superior court finds that the minor is capable of making, and has, in fact, made and adhered to, an informed and reasonable decision to have an abortion, the court may refuse its consent on a finding that a parent's, or its own, contrary decision is a better one. The Supreme Judicial Court answered in the affirmative. Following the Supreme Judicial Court's judgment, the District Court again declared the statute unconstitutional and enjoined its enforcement.

I

Can a state give parents an absolute right over a minor child's decision to obtain an abortion?

R

If a state chooses to require a minor who is pregnant to obtain an abortion only with one or both of her parents consent, that state must also offer alternate procedure(s) whereby parental consent is not required.

A

There are three reasons justifying the conclusion that the constitutional rights of children cannot be equated with those of adults: the peculiar vulnerability of children; their inability to make critical decisions in an informed, mature manner; and the importance of the guiding role of parents in the upbringing of their children. The abortion decision differs in important ways from other decisions facing minors, and the State is required to act with particular sensitivity when it legislates to foster parental involvement in this matter. If a State decides to require a pregnant minor to obtain one or both parents' consent to an abortion, it also must provide an alternative procedure whereby authorization for the abortion can be obtained. A pregnant minor is entitled in such a proceeding to show either that she is mature enough and well enough informed to make her abortion decision, in consultation with her physician, independently of her parents' wishes, or that even if she is not able to make this decision independently, the desired abortion would be in her best interests. Such a procedure must ensure that the provision requiring parental consent does not in fact amount to an impermissible "absolute, and possibly arbitrary, veto," *Planned Parenthood of Central*

Bellotti v. Baird

443 U.S. 622 (1979)

Missouri v. Danforth. The Massachusetts statute, as authoritatively interpreted by the Supreme Judicial Court, unduly burdens the right to seek an abortion. The statute falls short of constitutional standards in two respects. First, it permits judicial authorization for an abortion to be withheld from a minor who is found by the superior court to be mature and fully competent to make this decision independently. Second, it requires parental consultation or notification in every instance, whether or not in the pregnant minor's best interests, without affording her an opportunity to receive an independent judicial determination that she is mature enough to consent or that an abortion would be in her best interests.

Affirmed.

Cruzan v. Director, Missouri Dept. of Health

497 U.S. 261 (1990)

FACTS

Petitioner Nancy Cruzan is incompetent, having sustained severe injuries in an automobile accident, and now lies in a Missouri state hospital in what is referred to as a persistent vegetative state: generally, a condition in which a person exhibits motor reflexes but evinces no indications of significant cognitive function. The State is bearing the cost of her care. Hospital employees refused, without court approval, to honor the request of Cruzan's parents, co-petitioners here, to terminate her artificial nutrition and hydration, since that would result in death. A state trial court authorized the termination, finding that a person in Cruzan's condition has a fundamental right under the State and Federal Constitutions to direct or refuse the withdrawal of death-prolonging procedures, and that Cruzan's expression to a former housemate that she would not wish to continue her life if sick or injured unless she could live at least halfway normally suggested that she would not wish to continue on with her nutrition and hydration. The State Supreme Court reversed. While recognizing a right to refuse treatment embodied in the common-law doctrine of informed consent, the court questioned its applicability in this case. It also declined to read into the State Constitution a broad right to privacy that would support an unrestricted right to refuse treatment and expressed doubt that the Federal Constitution embodied such a right. The court then decided that the State Living Will statute embodied a state policy strongly favoring the preservation of life, and that Cruzan's statements to her housemate were unreliable for the purpose of determining her intent. It rejected the argument that her parents were entitled to order the termination of her medical treatment, concluding that no person can assume that choice for an incompetent in the absence of the formalities required by the Living Will statute or clear and convincing evidence of the patient's wishes.

I Does the U.S. Constitution forbid Missouri to require that evidence of an incompetent's wishes as to the withdrawal of life-sustaining treatment be proved by clear and convincing evidence?

R The United States Constitution does not forbid Missouri to require that evidence of an incompetent's wishes as to the withdrawal of life-sustaining treatment be proved by clear and convincing evidence.

A The United States Constitution does not forbid Missouri to require that evidence of an incompetent's wishes as to the withdrawal of life-sustaining treatment be proved by clear and convincing evidence. Most state courts have based a right to refuse treatment on the common law right to informed consent or on both that right and a constitutional privacy right. In addition to relying on state constitutions and the common law, state courts have also turned to state statutes for guidance. However, these sources are not available to this Court, where the question is simply whether the Federal Constitution prohibits Missouri from choosing the rule of law which it did. A competent person has a liberty interest under the Due Process Clause in refusing unwanted medical treatment. However, the question whether that constitutional right has been violated must be determined by balancing the liberty interest against relevant state interests. For purposes of this case, it is assumed that a competent person would have a constitutionally protected right to refuse lifesaving hydration and nutrition. This does not mean that an incompetent person should possess the same right, since such a person is unable to make an informed and voluntary choice to exercise that hypothetical right or any other right. While Missouri has in effect recognized that, under certain circumstances, a surrogate may act for the patient in electing to withdraw hydration and nutrition and thus cause death, it has established a procedural safeguard to assure that the surrogate's action conforms as best it may to the wishes expressed by the patient while competent. It is permissible for Missouri, in its proceedings, to apply a clear and convincing evidence standard, which is an appropriate standard when the individual interests at stake are both particularly important and more substantial than mere loss of money. Here, Missouri has a general interest in the protection and preservation of human life, as well as other, more particular interests, at stake. It may legitimately seek to safeguard the personal element of an individual's choice between life and death. The State is also entitled to guard against potential abuses by surrogates who may not act to protect the patient. Similarly, it is entitled to consider that a judicial proceeding regarding an incompetent's wishes may not be adversarial, with the added guarantee of accurate factfinding that the adversary process brings with it. The State may also properly decline to make judgments about the "quality" of a particular individual's life, and simply assert an unqualified interest in the preservation of human life to be weighed against the constitutionally protected interests of the individual. It is self-evident that these interests are more substantial, both on an individual and societal level, than those involved in a common civil dispute. The clear and convincing evidence standard also serves as a societal judgment about how the risk of error should be distributed between the litigants. Missouri may permissibly place the increased risk of an erroneous decision on those seeking to terminate life-sustaining treatment. An erroneous decision not to terminate results in a maintenance of the status quo, with at least the potential that a wrong decision will eventually be corrected or its impact mitigated by an event such as an advancement in medical science or the patient's unexpected death. However, an erroneous decision to withdraw such treatment is not susceptible of correction. Although Missouri's proof requirement may have frustrated the effectuation of Cruzan's not-fully-expressed desires, the Constitution does not require general rules to work flawlessly. The State Supreme Court did not commit constitutional error in concluding that the evidence adduced at trial did not amount to clear and convincing proof of Cruzan's desire to have hydration and nutrition withdrawn. The trial court had not adopted a clear and convincing evidence standard, and Cruzan's observations that she did not want to live life as a "vegetable" did not deal in terms with withdrawal of medical treatment or of hydration and nutrition. The Due Process Clause does not require a State to accept the "substituted judgment" of close family members in the absence of substantial proof that their views reflect the patient's. Nancy Cruzan's parents would surely be qualified to exercise such a right of "substituted judgment" were it required by the Constitution. However, for the same reasons that Missouri may require clear and convincing evidence of a patient's wishes, it may also choose to defer only to those wishes.

C

Affirmed.

Washington v. Glucksberg

521 U.S. 702 (1997)

FACTS

It has always been a crime to assist a suicide in the State of Washington. The State's present law makes "[p]romoting a suicide attempt" a felony and provides that "a person is guilty of [that crime] when he knowingly causes or aids another person to attempt suicide." Washington's Natural Death Act stated that the withholding or withdrawal of life-sustaining treatment at a patient's discretion shall not constitute a suicide. Respondents, four Washington physicians who occasionally treat terminally ill, suffering patients, declare that they would assist these patients in ending their lives if not for the State's assisted suicide ban. These respondents, along with three gravely ill plaintiffs who have since died and a nonprofit organization that counsels people considering physician assisted suicide, filed this suit against petitioners, the State and its Attorney General, seeking a declaration that the ban is, on its face, unconstitutional. They assert a liberty interest protected by the Fourteenth Amendment's Due Process Clause which extends to a personal choice by a mentally competent, terminally ill adult to commit physician assisted suicide. Relying primarily on *Planned Parenthood* and *Cruzan v. Director*, the Federal District Court agreed, concluding that Washington's assisted suicide ban is unconstitutional because it places an undue burden on the exercise of that constitutionally protected liberty interest. The en banc Ninth Circuit affirmed. The Supreme Court of the U.S. granted certiorari.

I

Is a statute that bans assisted suicide unconstitutional?

R

A ban on assisted suicide is not unconstitutional, either on its face or as applied to the terminally who wish for it.

A

Washington's prohibition against "caus[ing]" or "aid[ing]" a suicide does not violate the Due Process Clause. An examination of our Nation's history, legal traditions, and practices demonstrates that Anglo-American common law has punished or otherwise disapproved of assisting suicide for over 700 years; that rendering such assistance is still a crime in almost every State; that such prohibitions have never contained exceptions for those who were near death. In light of that history, this Court's decisions lead to the conclusion that respondents' asserted "right" to assistance in committing suicide is not a fundamental liberty interest protected by the Due Process Clause. The Court's established method of substantive due process analysis has two primary features: First, the Court has regularly observed that the Clause specially protects those fundamental rights and liberties which are, objectively, deeply rooted in this Nation's history and tradition. Second, the Court has required a "careful description" of the asserted fundamental liberty interest. The Ninth Circuit's and respondents' various descriptions of the interest here at stake - a right to "determin[e] the time and manner of one's death," the "right to die," a "liberty to choose how to die," a right to "control of one's final days," "the right to choose a humane, dignified death," and "the liberty to shape death" - run counter to that second requirement. Since the Washington statute prohibits "aid[ing] another person to attempt suicide," the question before the Court is more properly characterized as whether the "liberty" specially protected by the Clause includes a right to commit suicide which itself includes a right to assistance in doing so. This asserted right has no place in our Nation's traditions, given the country's consistent, almost universal, and continuing rejection of the right, even for terminally ill, mentally competent adults. To hold for respondents, the Court would have to reverse centuries of legal doctrine and practice, and strike down the considered policy choice of almost every State. Respondents' contention that the asserted interest is consistent with this Court's substantive due process cases, if not with this Nation's history and practice, is unpersuasive. The constitutionally protected right to refuse lifesaving hydration and nutrition that was discussed in Cruzan, supra, at 279, was not simply deduced from abstract concepts of personal autonomy, but was instead grounded in the Nation's history and traditions, given the common law rule that forced medication was a battery, and the long legal tradition protecting the decision to refuse unwanted medical treatment. And although Casey recognized that many of the rights and liberties protected by the Due Process Clause sound in personal autonomy, it does not follow that any and all important, intimate, and personal decisions are so protected. The constitutional requirement that Washington's assisted suicide ban be rationally related to legitimate government interests is unquestionably met here. These interests include prohibiting intentional killing and preserving human life; preventing the serious public health problem of suicide, especially among the young, the elderly, and those suffering from untreated pain or from depression or other mental disorders; protecting the medical profession's integrity and ethics and maintaining physicians' role as their patients' healers; protecting the poor, the elderly, disabled persons, the terminally ill, and persons in other vulnerable groups from indifference, prejudice, and psychological and financial pressure to end their lives; and avoiding a possible slide towards voluntary and perhaps even involuntary euthanasia. The relative strengths of these various interests need not be weighed exactingly, since they are unquestionably important and legitimate, and the law at issue is at least reasonably related to their promotion and protection.

C

Reversed and remanded.

Laurence v. Texas

539 U.S. 558 (2003)

FACTS

Responding to a reported weapons disturbance in a private residence, Houston police entered petitioner Lawrence's apartment and saw him and another adult man, petitioner Garner, engaging in a private, consensual sexual act of sodomy. Petitioners were arrested and convicted of deviate sexual intercourse in violation of a Texas statute forbidding two persons of the same sex to engage in certain intimate sexual conduct. In affirming, the State Court of Appeals held, *inter alia*, that the statute was not unconstitutional under the Due Process Clause of the Fourteenth Amendment. The court considered *Bowers* v. *Hardwick* controlling on that point. The U.S. Supreme Court granted review.

I

Does the Texas sodomy statute violate the right to liberty under the Due Process Clause?

R

When two consenting adults engage in private, sexual conduct, their liberty rights under the Due Process Clause will be violated by an act, like Texas's sodomy statute, which seeks to criminalize their behavior.

A

The Texas statute making it a crime for two persons of the same sex to engage in certain intimate sexual conduct violates the Due Process Clause. Resolution of this case depends on whether petitioners were free as adults to engage in private conduct in the exercise of their liberty under the Due Process Clause. For this inquiry the Court deems it necessary to reconsider its *Bowers* holding. The *Bowers* Court failed to appreciate the extent of the liberty at stake. To say that the issue in *Bowers* was simply the right to engage in certain sexual conduct demeans the claim the individual put forward, just as it would demean a married couple were it said that marriage is just about the right to have sexual intercourse. Although the laws involved in *Bowers* and here purport to do not more than prohibit a particular sexual act, their penalties and purposes have more far-reaching consequences, touching upon the most private human conduct, sexual behavior, and in the most private of places, the home. They seek to control a personal relationship that, whether or not entitled to formal recognition in the law, is within the liberty of persons to choose without being punished as criminals. The liberty protected by the Constitution allows homosexual persons the right to choose to enter upon relationships in the confines of their homes and their own private lives and still retain their dignity as free persons. Having misapprehended the liberty claim presented to it, the *Bowers* Court stated that proscriptions against sodomy have ancient roots. But the Nation's laws and traditions in the past half century are most relevant here. They show an emerging awareness that liberty gives substantial protection to adult persons in deciding how to conduct their private lives in matters pertaining to sex. *Bowers'* deficiencies became even more apparent in the years following its announcement. The 25 States with laws prohibiting the conduct referenced in *Bowers* are reduced now to 13, of which 4 enforce their laws only against homosexual conduct. In those States, including Texas, that still proscribe sodomy there is a pattern of non-enforcement with respect to consenting adults acting in private. The stigma the Texas criminal statute imposes is not trivial. Although the offense is but a minor misdemeanor, it remains a criminal offense with all that imports for the dignity of the persons charged, including notation of convictions on their records and on job application forms, and registration as sex offenders under state law. This case does not involve minors, persons who might be injured or coerced, those who might not easily refuse consent, or public conduct or prostitution. It does involve two adults who, with full and mutual consent, engaged in sexual practices common to a homosexual lifestyle. Petitioners' right to liberty under the Due Process Clause gives them the full right to engage in private conduct without government intervention. The Texas statute furthers no legitimate state interest which can justify its intrusion into the individual's personal and private life.

C

Reversed and remanded.

Whalen v. Roe

429 U.S. 589 (1977)

FACTS

Responding to a concern that drugs were being diverted into unlawful channels, the New York Legislature in 1972 enacted a statutory scheme to correct defects in the previous law. The 1972 statute classifies potentially harmful drugs and provides that prescriptions for the category embracing the most dangerous legitimate drugs (Schedule II) be prepared on an official form. One copy of the form, which requires identification of the prescribing physician, dispensing pharmacy, drug and dosage, and the patient's name, address, and age, must be filed with the State Health Department, where pertinent data are recorded on tapes for computer processing. All forms are retained for a five-year period under a system to safeguard their security, and are thereafter destroyed. Public disclosure of the patient's identity is prohibited, and access to the files is confined to a limited number of health department and investigatory personnel. Appellees, including a group of patients regularly receiving Schedule II drugs and prescribing doctors, brought this action challenging the constitutionality of the Schedule II patient-identification requirements. Holding that "the doctor-patient relationship is one of the zones of privacy accorded constitutional protection" and that the Act's patient-identification provisions invaded that zone with "a needlessly broad sweep," since appellant had been unable to demonstrate the need for those requirements a three-judge District Court enjoined the enforcement of the challenged provisions.

I

Can a state record the names and addresses of all persons who have obtained certain prescription drugs without violating the Constitution?

R

The disclosure of private medical information to insurance companies, public health agencies and medical personnel does not amount to a *per se* violation of the Constitution on invasion of privacy grounds.

A

The patient-identification requirement is a reasonable exercise of the State's broad police powers, and the District Court's finding that the necessity for the requirement had not been proved is not a sufficient reason for holding the statute unconstitutional. Neither the immediate nor the threatened impact of the patient-identification requirement on either the reputation or the independence of patients for whom Schedule II drugs are medically indicated suffices to constitute an invasion of any right or liberty protected by the Fourteenth Amendment. The possibility that a doctor or pharmacist may voluntarily reveal information on a prescription form, which existed under prior law, is unrelated to the computerized data bank. There is no support in the record or in the experience of the two States that the New York program emulates for assuming that the statute's security provisions will be improperly administered. The remote possibility that judicial supervision of the evidentiary use of particular items of stored information will not provide adequate protection against unwarranted disclosure is not a sufficient reason for invalidating the entire patient-identification program. Though it is argued that concern about disclosure may induce patients to refuse needed medication, the 1972 statute does not deprive the public of access to Schedule II drugs, as is clear from the fact that about 100,000 prescriptions for such drugs were filed each month before the District Court's injunction was entered. Appellee doctors' contention that the 1972 statute impairs their right to practice medicine free from unwarranted state interference is without merit, whether it refers to the statute's impact on their own procedures, which is no different from the impact of the prior statute, or refers to the patients' concern about disclosure that the Court has rejected.

C

Reversed.

Saenz v. Roe

526 U.S. 489 (1999)

FACTS

California sought to amend its Aid to Families with Dependent Children (AFDC) program in 1992 by limiting new residents, for the first year they live in the State, to the benefits they would have received in the State of their prior residence (Cal. Code §11450.03). Although the Secretary of Health and Human Services approved the change, a requirement for it to go into effect, the Federal District Court enjoined its implementation, finding that, under *Shapiro v. Thompson,* and *Zobel v. Williams,* it penalized "the decision of new residents to migrate to [California] and be treated [equally] with existing residents," *Green* v. *Anderson*. After the Ninth Circuit invalidated the Secretary's approval of §11450.03 in a separate proceeding, this Court ordered *Green* to be dismissed. The provision thus remained inoperative until after Congress enacted the Personal Responsibility and Work Opportunity Reconciliation Act of 1996 (PRWORA), which replaced AFDC with Temporary Assistance to Needy Families (TANF). PRWORA expressly authorizes any State receiving a TANF grant to pay the benefit amount of another State's TANF program to residents who have lived in the State for less than 12 months. Since the Secretary no longer needed to approve §11450.03, California announced that enforcement would begin on April 1, 1997. On that date, respondents filed this class action, challenging the constitutionality of §11450.03's durational residency requirement and PRWORA's approval of that requirement. In issuing a preliminary injunction, the District Court found that PRWORA's existence did not affect its analysis in *Green.* Without reaching the merits, the Ninth Circuit affirmed the injunction. The Court of Appeals affirmed the District Court's issuance of a preliminary injunction and the case went before the U.S. Supreme Court.

I Does a state statute, authorizing states receiving Temporary Assistance to Needy Families to pay the benefit amount of another State's TANF to its first year residents, violate the Fourteenth Amendment's right-to-travel protections?

R A State must treat new residents the same as those who live within their boarders for less than a year and must provide them the same rights under the 14th Amendments as it would its own citizens.

A By paying first-year residents the same TNF benefits they received in their state of origin, states treated new residents differently than others who have lived in their borders for over one year. As such, enforcement of the PRWORA power unconstitutionally discriminated among residents. Section 11450.03 violates §1 of the 14th Amendment. In assessing laws denying welfare benefits to newly arrived residents, this Court held in *Shapiro* that a State cannot enact durational residency requirements in order to inhibit the migration of needy persons into the State, and that a classification that has the effect of imposing a penalty on the right to travel violates the Equal Protection Clause absent a compelling governmental interest. The right to travel embraces three different components: the right to enter and leave another State; the right to be treated as a welcome visitor while temporarily present in another State; and, for those travelers who elect to become permanent residents, the right to be treated like other citizens of that State. The right of newly arrived citizens to the same privileges and immunities enjoyed by other citizens of their new State, the third aspect of the right to travel, is at issue here. That right is protected by the new arrival's status as both a state citizen and a United States citizen, and it is plainly identified in the Fourteenth Amendment's Privileges or Immunities Clause, see *Slaughter-House Cases*. That newly arrived citizens have both state and federal capacities adds special force to their claim that they have the same rights as others who share their citizenship. Since the right to travel embraces a citizen's right to be treated equally in her new State of residence, a discriminatory classification is itself a penalty. California's classifications are defined entirely by the period of residency and the location of the disfavored class members' prior residences. Within the category of new residents, those who lived in another country or in a State that had higher benefits than California are treated like lifetime residents; and within the broad subcategory of new arrivals who are treated less favorably, there are 45 smaller classes whose benefit levels are determined by the law of their former States. California's legitimate interest in saving money does not justify this discriminatory scheme. The Fourteenth Amendment's Citizenship Clause expressly equates citizenship with residence and does not tolerate a hierarchy of subclasses of similarly situated citizens based on the location of their prior residences. PRWORA's approval of durational residency requirements does not resuscitate §11450.03. This Court has consistently held that Congress may not authorize the States to violate the Fourteenth Amendment. Moreover, the protection afforded to a citizen by that Amendment's Citizenship Clause limits the powers of the National Government as well as the States. Congress' Article I powers to legislate are limited not only by the scope of the Framers' affirmative delegation, but also by the principle that the powers may not be exercised in a way that violates other specific provisions of the Constitution.

C

Affirmed.

Harper v. Virginia State Board of Elections

383 U.S 663 (1966)

FACTS

Appellants, Virginia residents, brought this action to have Virginia's poll tax declared unconstitutional. The three-judge District Court dismissed the complaint on the basis of *Breedlove v. Suttles*, which upheld a Georgia poll tax.

I

May a state impose a poll tax as a condition of voting?

R

A State's conditioning of the right to vote on the payment of a fee or tax violates the Equal Protection Clause of the Fourteenth Amendment.

A

A State's conditioning of the right to vote on the payment of a fee or tax violates the Equal Protection Clause of the Fourteenth Amendment. Once the franchise is granted to the electorate, lines which determine who may vote may not be drawn so as to cause invidious discrimination. Fee payments or wealth, like race, creed, or color, are unrelated to the citizen's ability to participate intelligently in the electoral process. The interest of the State, when it comes to voting registration, is limited to the fixing of standards related to the applicant's qualifications as a voter. Lines drawn on the basis of wealth or property, like those of race, are traditionally disfavored. Classifications which might impinge on fundamental rights and liberties - such as the franchise - must be closely scrutinized. To the extent that *Breedlove* sanctioned the use of poll taxes as a prerequisite for voting, it is overruled.

C

Judgment affirmed.

Kramer v. Union Free School District

395 U.S. 621 (1969)

FACTS

Section 2012 of the New York Education Law provides that in certain school districts residents who are otherwise eligible to vote in state and federal elections may vote in the school district elections only if they own or lease taxable realty in the district or are parents or custodians of children enrolled in the local public schools. Plaintiff-appellant Kramer, a 21 year old bachelor who lived with his parents and who neither owns nor leases taxable real property, challenged the constitutionality of the section on equal protection grounds. New York (defendant-appellee) argued that it had a legitimate interest in limiting school district elections to those primarily interested in those elections, and that, at any rate, the offices being voted on could have been filled through appointment if the legislature had wished. A three-judge district court ruled §2012 constitutional.

I

May a state law restrict the voting in its school districts to owners or lessees of taxable property or those parents who have children enrolled in the local school district?

R

It is a violation of equal protection to restrict the voting in school district elections to owners or lessees of taxable property or those parents who have children enrolled in the local school district.

A

Section 2012 violates the Equal Protection Clause of the Fourteenth Amendment. Where a state statute grants the right to vote to some bona fide residents of requisite age and citizenship and denies the franchise to others, it must be determined whether the exclusions are necessary to promote a compelling state interest. Assuming, arguendo ("for the sake of argument"), that New York legitimately might limit the franchise in these school district elections to those "primarily interested in school affairs," the §2012 classifications do not accomplish this purpose with sufficient precision to justify denying the franchise to appellant and members of his class, since the classifications include many persons at best only remotely interested in school affairs and exclude others directly interested.

C

Reversed and remanded.

Ball v. James

451 U.S. 355 (1981)

FACTS

The Salt River Project Agricultural Improvement and Power District (District), a governmental entity, stores and delivers untreated water to the owners of 236,000 acres of land in central Arizona, and, to subsidize its water operations, sells electricity to hundreds of thousands of people in an area including a large part of metropolitan Phoenix. Under state law, the system for electing the District's directors limits voting eligibility to landowners and apportions voting power according to the number of acres owned. A class of registered voters living within the District but owning either no land or less than an acre of land there, filed suit, claiming that the election scheme violated the Equal Protection Clause of the Fourteenth Amendment. They alleged that because the District has such governmental powers as the authority to condemn land and sell tax-exempt bonds, and because it sells electricity to virtually half the State's population and exercises significant influence on flood control and environmental management, its policies and actions substantially affect all District residents, regardless of property ownership. The District Court upheld the constitutionality of the voting scheme, but the Court of Appeals reversed. It held that the case was governed by the one-person, one-vote principle established in *Reynolds v. Sims*, rather than by the exception to that principle established in *Salyer Land Co. v. Tulare Lake Basin Water Storage Dist.*, which upheld a state law permitting only landowners to vote for directors of a water district because of its special limited purpose and the disproportionate effect of its activities on landowners as a group.

I Can a local government be released from the strict one-person, one-vote principles of the Equal Protection Clause because of that local government's special relationship to one class of citizens?

R States may, under special conditions, limit the right to vote in a particular election to only those voters who are primarily affected by or have a special interest in the outcome of the election.

A The District's purpose is sufficiently specialized and narrow and its activities bear on landowners so disproportionately as to release it from the strict demands of the Reynolds principle. As in *Salyer*, the voting scheme for the District is constitutional because it bears a reasonable relationship to its statutory objectives. The distinctions between the more diverse and extensive services furnished by the District here and those furnished by the water district involved in *Salyer* do not amount to a constitutional difference. The District does not exercise the sort of governmental powers that invoke the strict demands of Reynolds. It cannot impose ad valorem property taxes or sales taxes or enact laws governing citizens' conduct. Nor does it administer normal government functions such as the maintenance of streets, the operation of schools, or sanitation, health, or welfare services. The District's water functions, which constitute its primary and originating purpose, are relatively narrow. Although unlike in *Salyer*, as much as 40% of the water delivered by the District goes for nonagricultural, urban purposes, the constitutionally relevant fact is that all water is distributed according to land ownership and the District cannot control the use to which the water is put by the landowners. Nor is the legality of the District's property-based voting scheme affected by the fact that as one of the largest suppliers of electric power in the State it meets most of its capital and operating costs by the selling of such power. The provision of electricity is not in itself the sort of general or important governmental function that would make the government provider subject to the Reynolds doctrine. And, in any event, the District's electric power functions are only incidental to, and thus cannot change the character of, its water functions. And the District's functions bear a disproportionate relationship to the specific class of people whom the system makes eligible to vote. Voting landowners are the only residents of the District whose lands are subject to liens to secure District bonds, who are subject to the District's acreage-based taxing power, and who committed capital to the District.

C

Reversed and remanded.

Reynolds v. Sims

379 U.S. 870 (1964)

FACTS

Charging that mal-apportionment of the Alabama Legislature deprived them and others similarly situated of rights under the Equal Protection Clause of the Fourteenth Amendment and the Alabama Constitution, voters in several Alabama counties brought suit against various officials having state election duties. Complaints sought a declaration that the existing state legislative apportionment provisions were unconstitutional; an injunction against future elections pending reapportionment in accordance with the State Constitution; or, absent such reapportionment, a mandatory injunction requiring holding the 1962 election for legislators at large over the entire State. The complaint alleged serious discrimination against voters in counties whose populations had grown proportionately far more than others since the 1900 census. A three-judge Federal District Court declined ordering the May 1962 primary election to be held at large, stating that it should not act before the legislature had further opportunity to take corrective measures before the general election. Finding after a hearing that neither of two apportionment plans which the legislature thereafter adopted would cure the gross inequality and invidious discrimination of the existing representation, the District Court ordered temporary reapportionment for the 1962 general election by combining features of the two plans adopted by the legislature, and enjoined officials from holding future elections under any of the invalid plans. The officials appealed, claiming that the District Court erred in holding unconstitutional the existing and proposed reapportionment plans and that a federal court lacks power affirmatively to reapportion a legislature.

I

With respect to its own legislature, must a State elect and allocate its legislature according to population or may it weigh votes differently according to where citizens happen to reside?

R

The seats in both houses of a bicameral legislature must, under the Equal Protection Clause, be apportioned substantially on a population basis.

A

The right of suffrage is denied by debasement or dilution of a citizen's vote in a state or federal election. Under the Equal Protection Clause a claim of debasement of the right to vote through mal-apportionment presents a justiciable controversy; and the Equal Protection Clause provides manageable standards for lower courts to determine the constitutionality of a state legislative apportionment scheme. The Equal Protection Clause requires substantially equal legislative representation for all citizens in a State regardless of where they reside. Legislators represent people, not areas. Weighting votes differently according to where citizens happen to reside is discriminatory. The seats in both houses of a bicameral legislature must under the Equal Protection Clause be apportioned substantially on a population basis. The District Court correctly held that the existing Alabama apportionment scheme and both of the proposed plans are constitutionally invalid since neither legislative house is or would thereunder be apportioned on a population basis. The superficial resemblance between one of the Alabama apportionment plans and the legislative representation scheme of the Federal Congress affords no proper basis for sustaining that plan since the historical circumstances which gave rise to the congressional system of representation, arising out of compromise among sovereign States, are unique and without relevance to the allocation of seats in state legislatures. The federal constitutional requirement that both houses of a state legislature must be apportioned on a population basis means that, as nearly as practicable, districts be of equal population, though mechanical exactness is not required. Somewhat more flexibility may be constitutionally permissible for state legislative apportionment than for congressional districting. A state legislative apportionment scheme may properly give representation to various political subdivisions and provide for compact districts of contiguous territory if substantial equality among districts is maintained. Some deviations from a strict equal-population principle are constitutionally permissible in the two houses of a bicameral state legislature, where incident to the effectuation of a rational state policy, so long as the basic standard of equality of population among districts is not significantly departed from. Considerations of history, economic or other group interests, or area alone do not justify deviations from the equal-population principle. Insuring some voice to political subdivisions in at least one legislative body may, within reason, warrant some deviations from population-based representation in state legislatures. In admitting States into the Union, Congress does not purport to pass on all constitutional questions concerning the character of state governmental organization, such as whether a state legislature's apportionment departs from the equal-population principle; in any case, congressional approval could not validate an unconstitutional state legislative apportionment. States consistently with the Equal Protection Clause can properly provide for periodic revision of reapportionment schemes, though revision less frequent than decennial would be constitutionally suspect. Courts should attempt to accommodate the relief ordered to the apportionment provisions of state constitutions as far as possible, provided that such provisions harmonize with the Equal Protection Clause. A court in awarding or withholding immediate relief should consider the proximity of a forthcoming election and the mechanics and complexities of election laws, and should rely on general equitable principles. The District Court properly exercised its judicial power in this case by ordering reapportionment of both houses of the Alabama Legislature for purposes of 1962 elections as a temporary measure by using the best parts of the two proposed plans, each of which it had found, as a whole, invalid, and in retaining jurisdiction while deferring a hearing on the issuance of a final injunction to give the reapportioned legislature an opportunity to act effectively.

C

Affirmed and remanded for further proceedings.

Bush v. Gore

531 U.S. 98 (2000)

FACTS

On November 8, 2000, the day following the Presidential election, the Florida Division of Elections reported that petitioner, Governor Bush, had received 2,909,135 votes, and respondent, Vice President Gore, had received 2,907,351 votes, a margin of 1,784 for Governor Bush. Because Governor Bush's margin of victory was less than "one-half of a percent . . . of the votes cast," an automatic machine recount was conducted under §102.141(4) of the election code, the results of which showed Governor Bush still winning the race but by a diminished margin. Vice President Gore then sought manual recounts in Volusia, Palm Beach, Broward, and Miami-Dade Counties, pursuant to Florida's election protest provisions. A dispute arose concerning the deadline for local county canvassing boards to submit their returns to the Secretary of State (Secretary). The Secretary declined to waive the November 14 deadline imposed by statute. The Florida Supreme Court, however, set the deadline at November 26. On December 8, 2000, the Supreme Court of Florida ordered that the Circuit Court of Leon County tabulate by hand 9,000 ballots in Miami-Dade County. It also ordered the inclusion in the certified vote totals of 215 votes identified in Palm Beach County and 168 votes identified in Miami-Dade County for Vice President Albert Gore, Jr., and Senator Joseph Lieberman, Democratic Candidates for President and Vice President. The Supreme Court noted that petitioner, Governor George W. Bush asserted that the net gain for Vice President Gore in Palm Beach County was 176 votes, and directed the Circuit Court to resolve that dispute on remand. The court further held that relief would require manual recounts in all Florida counties where so-called "undervotes" had not been subject to manual tabulation. The court ordered all manual recounts to begin at once. Governor Bush and Richard Cheney, Republican Candidates for the Presidency and Vice Presidency, filed an emergency application for a stay of this mandate. On December 9, the U.S. Supreme Court granted the application, treated the application as a petition for a writ of certiorari, and granted certiorari.

I

1) Did the Florida Supreme Court establish new standards for resolving Presidential election contests, thereby violating Art. II, §1, cl. 2, of the United States Constitution and failing to comply with 3 U.S.C. §5; and 2) whether the use of standardless manual recounts violates the Equal Protection and Due Process Clauses?

R

When a court establishes arbitrary, new standards for resolving elections, Art. II is violated and the use of standardless manual recounts violates the Equal Protection and Due Process Clauses.

A

With respect to the equal protection question, we find a violation of the Equal Protection Clause. The right to vote is protected in more than the initial allocation of the franchise. Equal protection applies as well to the manner of its exercise. Having once granted the right to vote on equal terms, the State may not, by later arbitrary and disparate treatment, value one person's vote over that of another. There is no difference between the two sides of the present controversy: Respondents say that the very purpose of vindicating the right to vote justifies the recount procedures now at issue. The question before us, however, is whether the recount procedures the Florida Supreme Court has adopted are consistent with its obligation to avoid arbitrary and disparate treatment of the members of its electorate. Much of the controversy seems to revolve around ballot cards designed to be perforated by a stylus but which, either through error or deliberate omission, have not been perforated with sufficient precision for a machine to count them. The Florida Supreme Court has ordered that the intent of the voter be discerned from such ballots. For purposes of resolving the equal protection challenge, it is not necessary to decide whether the Florida Supreme Court had the authority under the legislative scheme for resolving election disputes to define what a legal vote is and to mandate a manual recount implementing that definition. The recount mechanisms implemented in response to the decisions of the Florida Supreme Court do not satisfy the minimum requirement for non-arbitrary treatment of voters necessary to secure the fundamental right. Florida's basic command for the count of legally cast votes is to consider the "intent of the voter." This is unobjectionable as an abstract proposition. The problem inheres in the absence of specific standards to ensure its equal application. The formulation of uniform rules to determine intent based on these recurring circumstances is practicable and, we conclude, necessary. The want of those rules here has led to unequal evaluation of ballots in various respects. As seems to have been acknowledged at oral argument, the standards for accepting or rejecting contested ballots might vary not only from county to county but indeed within a single county from one recount team to another. The State Supreme Court ratified this uneven treatment. It mandated that the recount totals from two counties, Miami-Dade and Palm Beach, be included in the certified total. The State has not shown that its procedures include the necessary safeguards. The problem, for instance, of the estimated 110,000 overvotes has not been addressed. Upon due consideration of the difficulties identified to this point, it is obvious that the recount cannot be conducted in compliance with the requirements of equal protection and due process without substantial additional work. It would require not only the adoption (after opportunity for argument) of adequate statewide standards for determining what is a legal vote, and practicable procedures to implement them, but also orderly judicial review of any disputed matters that might arise. In addition, the Secretary of State has advised that the recount of only a portion of the ballots requires that the vote tabulation equipment be used to screen out undervotes, a function for which the machines were not designed. The Supreme Court of Florida has said that the legislature intended the State's electors to "participate fully in the federal electoral process." That statute, in turn, requires that any controversy or contest that is designed to lead to a conclusive selection of electors be completed by December 12. That date is upon us, and there is no recount procedure in place under the State Supreme Court's order that comports with minimal constitutional standards. Because it is evident that any recount seeking to meet the December 12 date will be unconstitutional for the reasons we have discussed, we reverse the judgment of the Supreme Court of Florida ordering a recount to proceed. It is so ordered.

C

The judgment of the Supreme Court of Florida is reversed, and the case is remanded for further proceedings not inconsistent with this opinion.

Boddie v. Connecticut

401 U.S. 371 (1971)

FACTS

Appellants, welfare recipients residing in the State of Connecticut, brought this action in the Federal District Court for the District of Connecticut on behalf of themselves and others similarly situated, challenging, as applied to them, certain state procedures for the commencement of litigation, including requirements for payment of court fees and costs for service of process, that restrict their access to the courts in their effort to bring an action for divorce. It appears from the briefs and oral argument that the average cost to a litigant for bringing an action for divorce is $60. Section 52-259 of the Connecticut General Statutes provides: "There shall be paid to the clerks of the supreme court or the superior court, for entering each civil cause, forty-five dollars . . . ." An additional $15 is usually required for the service of process by the sheriff, although as much as $40 or $50 may be necessary where notice must be accomplished by publication. Appellants thereafter commenced this action in the Federal District Court seeking a judgment declaring that Connecticut's statute and service of process provisions unconstitutional. A three-judge court was convened pursuant to 28 U.S.C. 2281 concluded that "a state [may] limit access to its civil courts and particularly in this instance, to its divorce courts, by the requirement of a filing fee or other fees which effectively bar persons on relief from commencing actions therein."

I Does due process prohibit a State from denying, solely because of inability to pay, access to its courts to individuals who seek judicial dissolution of their marriages?

R A State may not, consistent with the obligations imposed on it by the Due Process Clause of the Fourteenth Amendment, pre-empt the right to dissolve this legal relationship without affording all citizens access to the means it has prescribed for doing so.

A Our conclusion is that, given the basic position of the marriage relationship in this society's hierarchy of values and the concomitant state monopolization of the means for legally dissolving this relationship, due process does prohibit a State from denying, solely because of inability to pay, access to its courts to individuals who seek judicial dissolution of their marriages. Thus, although they assert here due process rights as would-be plaintiffs, we think appellants' plight, because resort to the state courts is the only avenue to dissolution of their marriages, is akin to that of defendants faced with exclusion from the only forum effectively empowered to settle their disputes. Resort to the judicial process by these plaintiffs is no more voluntary in a realistic sense than that of the defendant called upon to defend his interests in court. For both groups this process is not only the paramount dispute-settlement technique, but, in fact, the only available one. In concluding that the Due Process Clause of the Fourteenth Amendment requires that these appellants be afforded an opportunity to go into court to obtain a divorce, we wish to re-emphasize that we go no further than necessary to dispose of the case before us, a case where the bona fides of both appellants' indigency and desire for divorce are here beyond dispute. We do not decide that access for all individuals to the courts is a right that is, in all circumstances, guaranteed by the Due Process Clause of the Fourteenth Amendment so that its exercise may not be placed beyond the reach of any individual, for, as we have already noted, in the case before us this right is the exclusive precondition to the adjustment of a fundamental human relationship. The requirement that these appellants resort to the judicial process is entirely a state-created matter. Thus we hold only that a State may not, consistent with the obligations imposed on it by the Due Process Clause of the Fourteenth Amendment, pre-empt the right to dissolve this legal relationship without affording all citizens access to the means it has prescribed for doing so.

C

Reversed.

United States v. Kras

409 U.S. 434 (1973)

FACTS

The Bankruptcy Act and one of this Court's complementary Orders in Bankruptcy impose fees and make the payment of those fees a condition to a discharge in voluntary bankruptcy. Appellee Kras, an indigent petitioner in bankruptcy, challenged the fees on Fifth Amendment grounds. Upon receiving notice of the constitutional issue in the District Court, the Government moved to intervene as of right under 28 U.S.C. 2403 and Rule 24 (a) of the Federal Rules of Civil Procedure. Leave to intervene was granted. The District Court held the fee provisions to be unconstitutional as applied to Kras. It reached this conclusion in the face of an earlier contrary holding by a unanimous First Circuit. Appellee, an indigent who filed a voluntary petition in bankruptcy, sought discharge without payment of the fees, aggregating no more than $50, that are a precondition to discharge in such a proceeding. The District Court, relying primarily on *Boddie v. Connecticut,* (where the Court held that a State could not consistently with due process and equal protection requirements, deny access to divorce courts to indigents unable to pay filing and other fees), held the bankruptcy fee provisions, as applied to appellee, an unconstitutional denial of Fifth Amendment rights of due process, including equal protection.

I

Can a state make payment of a court fee a requirement to obtaining a divorce with violating the Constitution?

R

The Due Process prohibits the states from denying individuals seeking dissolution of their mirages access to the courts based solely on that persons inability to pay.

A

This case is not controlled by *Boddie,* supra. For here access to courts is not the only conceivable relief available to bankrupts; the filing-fee requirement does not deny an indigent the equal protection of the laws, since there is no constitutional right to obtain a discharge of one's debts in bankruptcy; the right to a discharge in bankruptcy is not a "fundamental" right demanding a compelling governmental interest as a precondition to regulation; and there is a rational basis for the fee requirement.

C

Reversed.

M.L.B. v. S.J.L.

519 U.S. 102 (1996)

FACTS

In a decree forever terminating Plaintiff-petitioner M.L.B.'s parental rights to her two minor children, a Mississippi Chancery Court recited a segment of the governing Mississippi statute and stated, without elaboration, that respondents, the children's natural father and his second wife, had met their burden of proof by "clear and convincing evidence." The Chancery Court, however, neither described the evidence nor otherwise revealed precisely why M.L.B. was decreed a stranger to her children. M.L.B. filed a timely appeal from the termination decree, but Mississippi law conditioned her right to appeal on prepayment of record preparation fees estimated at $2,352.36. Lacking funds to pay the fees, M.L.B. sought leave to appeal in forma pauperis (Latin meaning "in the form of a pauper." The party who has their filing fees waived because they filed a declaration stating that they do not have the money to pay the fees). The Supreme Court of Mississippi denied her application on the ground that, under its precedent, there is no right to proceed in forma pauperis in civil appeals. Urging that the size of her pocketbook should not be dispositive when "an interest far more precious than any property right" is at stake, M.L.B. contends in this Court that a State may not, consistent with the Due Process and Equal Protection Clauses of the Fourteenth Amendment, condition appeals from trial court decrees terminating parental rights on the affected parent's ability to pay record preparation fees.

I

May a State deny an appeal to an indigent party because she cannot afford to pay the cost of the required trial transcript in an action adjudicating her parental rights with respect to a child or children?

R

A State deny an appeal to an indigent party because she cannot afford to pay the cost of the required trial transcript in an action adjudicating her parental rights as such a denial is a violation of Equal Protection prohibits.

A

Just as a State may not block an indigent petty offender's access to an appeal afforded others, so Mississippi may not deny M.L.B., because of her poverty, appellate review of the sufficiency of the evidence on which the trial court based its parental termination decree. The foundation case in the relevant line of decisions is *Griffin v. Illinois*, in which the Court struck down an Illinois rule that effectively conditioned thoroughgoing appeals from criminal convictions on the defendant's procurement of a transcript of trial proceedings. Of prime relevance to the question presented by M.L.B., is that *Griffin's* principle has not been confined only to cases in which imprisonment is at stake, but extends to appeals from convictions that are "quasi criminal" in nature. In contrast, an indigent defendant's right to counsel at state expense does not extend to non-felony trials if no term of imprisonment is actually imposed. We have also recognized a narrow category of civil cases in which the State must provide access to its judicial processes without regard to a party's ability to pay court fees. Making clear, however, that a constitutional requirement to waive court fees in civil cases is the exception, not the general rule, the Court has refused to extend *Griffin* to the broad array of civil cases. But the Court has consistently set apart from the plethora of civil cases those involving state controls or intrusions on family relationships. In that domain, to guard against undue official intrusion, the Court has examined closely and contextually the importance of the governmental interest advanced in defense of the intrusion. Permanently severing a parent-child bond demands the close consideration. Guided by *Lassiter*, *Santosky*, and other decisions acknowledging the primacy of the parent-child relationship, the Court agrees with M.L.B. that her parental termination appeal must be treated as the Court has treated petty offense appeals, and Mississippi may not withhold the transcript she needs to gain review of the order ending her parental status. The Court's decisions concerning access to judicial processes, commencing with *Griffin* and running through *Mayer*, reflect both equal protection and due process concerns. Placing this case within the framework established by the Court's past decisions in this area, the Court inspects the character and intensity of the individual interest at stake, on the one hand, and the State's justification for its exaction, on the other. The stakes for M.L.B. are high. Parental status termination is "irretrievably destructive" of the most fundamental family relationship. Mississippi has, consistent with *Santosky*, adopted a "clear and convincing proof" standard for parental status termination cases, but the Chancellor's order in this case simply recites statutory language; it describes no evidence, and otherwise details no reasons for finding M.L.B. "clearly and convincingly" unfit to be a parent. Only a transcript can reveal the sufficiency, or insufficiency, of the evidence to support that stern judgment. Mississippi's countervailing interest in offsetting the costs of its court system is unimpressive when measured against the stakes for M.L.B. While the Court does not question the general rule, stated in *Ortwein*, that fee requirements ordinarily are examined only for rationality, the Court's cases solidly establish two exceptions to that rule. The basic right to participate in political processes as voters and candidates cannot be limited to those who can pay for a license. Nor may access to judicial processes in cases criminal or "quasi criminal" in nature turn on ability to pay. Contrary to respondents' contention, cases in which the Court has held that government need not provide funds so that people can exercise even fundamental rights are inapposite here. Complainants in those cases sought state aid to subsidize their privately initiated action or to alleviate the consequences of differences in economic circumstances that existed apart from state action. M.L.B.'s complaint is of a different order. She is endeavoring to defend against the State's destruction of her family bonds, and to resist the brand associated with a parental unfitness adjudication. Like a defendant resisting criminal conviction, she seeks to be spared from the State's devastatingly adverse action. A failure rigidly to restrict *Griffin* to cases typed "criminal" will not result in the opening of judicial floodgates, as respondents urge. This Court has repeatedly distinguished parental status termination decrees from the plethora of civil actions on the basis of the unique deprivation termination decrees work: permanent destruction of all legal recognition of the parental relationship. Thus, Mississippi may not withhold from M.L.B. "a record of sufficient completeness to permit proper [appellate] consideration of [her] claims."

C

Reversed and remanded.

Lewis v. Casey
518 U.S. 343 (1996)

FACTS

Respondents, who are inmates of various prisons operated by the Arizona Department of Corrections (ADOC), brought a class action against petitioners, ADOC officials, alleging that petitioners were furnishing them with inadequate legal research facilities and thereby depriving them of their right of access to the courts, in violation of *Bounds v. Smith.* The District Court found petitioners to be in violation of Bounds and issued an injunction mandating detailed, system-wide changes in ADOC's prison law libraries and in its legal assistance programs. The Ninth Circuit affirmed both the finding of a Bounds violation and the injunction's major terms.

I

Does the existence of a sub-par law library per se limit the ability of prisoners to access the courts in violation of the Constitution?

R

A sub-par law library does not limit the ability of prisoners (constitutionally speaking) to access the courts in violation of the Constitution.

A

The success of respondents' systemic challenge was dependent on their ability to show widespread actual injury, and the District Court's failure to identify anything more than isolated instances of actual injury renders its finding of a systemic Bounds violation invalid. Bounds did not create an abstract, free-standing right to a law library or legal assistance; rather, the right that Bounds acknowledged was the right of access to the courts. Thus, to establish a Bounds violation, the ``actual injury" that an inmate must demonstrate is that the alleged shortcomings in the prison library or legal assistance program have hindered, or are presently hindering, his efforts to pursue a non-frivolous legal claim. This requirement derives ultimately from the doctrine of standing. Although Bounds made no mention of an actual injury requirement, it can hardly be thought to have eliminated that constitutional prerequisite. Statements in Bounds suggesting that prison authorities must also enable the prisoner to discover grievances, and to litigate effectively once in court have no antecedent in this Court's pre-Bounds cases, and are now disclaimed. Moreover, Bounds does not guarantee inmates the wherewithal to file any and every type of legal claim, but requires only that they be provided with the tools to attack their sentences, directly or collaterally, and to challenge the conditions of their confinement. It found that ADOC's failures with respect to illiterate prisoners had resulted in the dismissal with prejudice of inmate Bartholic's lawsuit and the inability of inmate Harris to file a legal action. These findings as to injury do not support the system-wide injunction ordered by the District Court. The remedy must be limited to the inadequacy that produced the injury-in-fact that the plaintiff has established; that this is a class action changes nothing, for even named plaintiffs in a class action must show that they personally have been injured. Only one named plaintiff, Bartholic, was found to have suffered actual injury-as a result of ADOC's failure to provide the special services he would have needed, in light of his particular disability (illiteracy), to avoid dismissal of his case. Eliminated from the proper scope of the injunction, therefore, are provisions directed at special services or facilities required by non-English-speakers, by prisoners in lockdown, and by the inmate population at large. Furthermore, the inadequacy that caused actual injury to illiterate inmates Bartholic and Harris was not sufficiently widespread to justify systemwide relief. There is no finding, and no evidence discernible from the record, that in ADOC prisons other than those occupied by Bartholic and Harris illiterate inmates cannot obtain the minimal help necessary to file legal claims. There are further reasons why the order here cannot stand. In concluding that ADOC's restrictions on lockdown inmates were unjustified, the District Court failed to accord the judgment of prison authorities the substantial deference required by cases such as *Turner v. Safley*. The court also failed to leave with prison officials the primary responsibility for devising a remedy. The result of this improper procedure was an inordinately intrusive order.

C Reversed and remanded.

San Antonio Indep. School District. v. Rodriguez

411 U.S. 1 (1973)

FACTS

The financing of public elementary and secondary schools in Texas is a product of state and local participation. Almost half of the revenues are derived from a largely state-funded program designed to provide a basic minimum educational offering in every school. Each district supplements state aid through an ad valorem tax (a tax which varies based on the value of the property on which it is levied) on property within its jurisdiction. Appellees brought this class action on behalf of schoolchildren said to be members of poor families who reside in school districts having a low property tax base, making the claim that the Texas system's reliance on local property taxation favors the more affluent and violates equal protection requirements because of substantial inter-district disparities in per-pupil expenditures resulting primarily from differences in the value of assessable property among the districts. The District Court, finding that wealth is a "suspect" classification and that education is a "fundamental" right, concluded that the system could be upheld only upon a showing, which appellants failed to make, that there was a compelling state interest for the system. The court also concluded that appellants failed even to demonstrate a reasonable or rational basis for the State's system.

I

Does a state's public education financing system violate equal protection because it spends more per pupil on students who live in affluent districts than those who live in poor districts?

R

The Texas system of financing public education does not operate to the disadvantage of some suspect class or impinge upon a fundamental right explicitly or implicitly protected by the Constitution, thereby requiring strict judicial scrutiny; even though the program leads to some disparity in spending per pupil across districts, it bears some rational relationship to a legitimate governmental purpose: funding education.

A

This is not a proper case in which to examine a State's laws under standards of strict judicial scrutiny, since that test is reserved for cases involving laws that operate to the disadvantage of suspect classes or interfere with the exercise of fundamental rights and liberties explicitly or implicitly protected by the Constitution. The Texas system does not disadvantage any suspect class. It has not been shown to discriminate against any definable class of "poor" people or to occasion discriminations depending on the relative wealth of the families in any district. And, insofar as the financing system disadvantages those who, disregarding their individual income characteristics, reside in comparatively poor school districts, the resulting class cannot be said to be suspect. Nor does the Texas school-financing system impermissibly interfere with the exercise of a "fundamental" right or liberty. Though education is one of the most important services performed by the State, it is not within the limited category of rights recognized by this Court as guaranteed by the Constitution. Even if some identifiable quantum of education is arguably entitled to constitutional protection to make meaningful the exercise of other constitutional rights, here there is no showing that the Texas system fails to provide the basic minimal skills necessary for that purpose. Moreover, this is an inappropriate case in which to invoke strict scrutiny since it involves the most delicate and difficult questions of local taxation, fiscal planning, educational policy, and federalism, considerations counseling a more restrained form of review. The Texas system does not violate the Equal Protection Clause of the Fourteenth Amendment. Though concededly imperfect, the system bears a rational relationship to a legitimate state purpose. While assuring a basic education for every child in the State, it permits and encourages participation in and significant control of each district's schools at the local level.

C

Reversed.

Daniels v. Williams

474 U.S. 327 (1986)

FACTS

Petitioner brought an action in Federal District Court under 42 U.S.C. 1983, seeking to recover damages for injuries allegedly sustained when, while an inmate in a Richmond, Virginia, jail, he slipped on a pillow negligently left on a stairway by respondent sheriff's deputy. Petitioner contends that such negligence deprived him of his "liberty" interest in freedom from bodily injury "without due process of law" within the meaning of the Due Process Clause of the Fourteenth Amendment. The District Court granted respondent's motion for summary judgment, and the Court of Appeals affirmed.

I Can a tort lawsuit based on a theory of negligence of a government employee be prosecuted by the Due Process Clause?

R A tort lawsuit based on a theory of negligence of a government employee does not generally implicate the Due Process Clause.

A The Due Process Clause is not implicated by a state official's negligent act causing unintended loss of or injury to life, liberty, or property. The Due Process Clause was intended to secure an individual from an abuse of power by government officials. Far from an abuse of power, lack of due care, such as respondent's alleged negligence here, suggests no more than a failure to measure up to the conduct of a reasonable person. To hold that injury caused by such conduct is a deprivation within the meaning of the Due Process Clause would trivialize the centuries-old principle of due process of law. *Parratt v. Taylor* is overruled to the extent that it states otherwise. The Constitution does not purport to supplant traditional tort law in laying down rules of conduct to regulate liability for injuries that attend living together in society. While the Due Process Clause speaks to some facets of the relationship between jailers and inmates, its protections are not triggered by lack of due care by the jailers. Jailers may owe a special duty of care under state tort law to those in their custody, but the Due Process Clause does not embrace such a tort law concept.

C Affirmed.

County of Sacramento v. Lewis

523 U.S. 833 (1998)

FACTS

After petitioner James Smith, a county sheriff's deputy, responded to a call along with another officer, Murray Stapp, the latter returned to his patrol car and saw a motorcycle approaching at high speed, driven by Brian Willard, and carrying Philip Lewis, respondents' decedent, as a passenger. Stapp turned on his rotating lights, yelled for the cycle to stop, and pulled his car closer to Smith's in an attempt to pen the cycle in, but Willard maneuvered between the two cars and sped off. Smith immediately switched on his own emergency lights and siren and began high-speed pursuit. The chase ended after the cycle tipped over. Smith slammed on his brakes, but his car skidded into Lewis, causing massive injuries and death. Respondents brought this action under 42 U.S.C. § 1983 alleging a deprivation of Lewis's Fourteenth Amendment substantive due process right to life. The District Court granted summary judgment for Smith, but the Ninth Circuit reversed, holding, inter alia, that the appropriate degree of fault for substantive due process liability for high-speed police pursuits is deliberate indifference to, or reckless disregard for, a person's right to life and personal security.

I

Does a police officer violate the 14th Amendment guarantee of due process when he causes a death through deliberate or reckless indifference to life in a high-speed automobile chase?

R

A police officer does not violate the 14th Amendment guarantee of due process when he causes a death through deliberate or reckless indifference to life in a high-speed automobile chase; to reach that level, there must be evidence of intent to harm.

A

A police officer does not violate substantive due process by causing death through deliberate or reckless indifference to life in a high speed automobile chase aimed at apprehending a suspected offender. The "more-specific-provision" rule of *Graham v. Connor*, does not bar respondents' suit. Graham simply requires that if a constitutional claim is covered by a specific constitutional provision, the claim must be analyzed under the standard appropriate to that specific provision, not under substantive due process. Substantive due process analysis is therefore inappropriate here only if, as *amici argue*, respondents' claim is "covered by" the Fourth Amendment. It is not. That Amendment covers only "searches and seizures," neither of which took place here. No one suggests that there was a search, and this Court's cases foreclose finding a seizure, since Smith did not terminate Lewis's freedom of movement through means intentionally applied. Respondents' allegations are insufficient to state a substantive due process violation. Protection against governmental arbitrariness is the core of due process, including substantive due process, but only the most egregious executive action can be said to be "arbitrary" in the constitutional sense; the cognizable level of executive abuse of power is that which shocks the conscience. The conscience-shocking concept points clearly away from liability, or clearly toward it, only at the ends of the tort law's culpability spectrum: Liability for negligently inflicted harm is categorically beneath the constitutional due process threshold, while conduct deliberately intended to injure in some way unjustifiable by any government interest is the sort of official action most likely to rise to the conscience-shocking level. Whether that level is reached when culpability falls between negligence and intentional conduct is a matter for closer calls. The Court has recognized that deliberate indifference is egregious enough to state a substantive due process claim in one context, that of deliberate indifference to the medical needs of pretrial detainees, but rules of due process are not subject to mechanical application in unfamiliar territory, and the need to preserve the constitutional proportions of substantive due process demands an exact analysis of context and circumstances before deliberate indifference is condemned as conscience-shocking. Attention to the markedly different circumstances of normal pretrial custody and high-speed law enforcement chases shows why the deliberate indifference that shocks in the one context is less egregious in the other. In the circumstances of a high-speed chase aimed at apprehending a suspected offender, where unforeseen circumstances demand an instant judgment on the part of an officer who feels the pulls of competing obligations, only a purpose to cause harm unrelated to the legitimate object of arrest will satisfy the shocks-the-conscience test. Such chases with no intent to harm suspects physically or to worsen their legal plight do not give rise to substantive due process liability. The fault claimed on Smith's part fails to meet this test. Smith was faced with a course of lawless behavior for which the police were not to blame. They had done nothing to cause Willard's high-speed driving in the first place, nothing to excuse his flouting of the commonly understood police authority to control traffic, and nothing (beyond a refusal to call off the chase) to encourage him to race through traffic at breakneck speed. Willard's outrageous behavior was practically instantaneous, and so was Smith's instinctive response. While prudence would have repressed the reaction, Smith's instinct was to do his job, not to induce Willard's lawlessness, or to terrorize, cause harm, or kill. Prudence, that is, was subject to countervailing enforcement considerations, and while Smith exaggerated their demands, there is no reason to believe that they were tainted by an improper or malicious motive.

C

Reversed.

DeShaney v. Winnebago County Dept. of School Serv.

489 U.S. 189 (1989)

FACTS

Petitioner is a child who was subjected to a series of beatings by his father, with whom he lived. Respondents, a county department of social services and several of its social workers, received complaints that petitioner was being abused by his father and took various steps to protect him; they did not, however, act to remove petitioner from his father's custody. Petitioner's father finally beat him so severely that he suffered permanent brain damage and was rendered profoundly retarded. Petitioner and his mother sued respondents under 42 U.S.C. 1983, alleging that respondents had deprived petitioner of his liberty interest in bodily integrity, in violation of his rights under the substantive component of the Fourteenth Amendment's Due Process Clause, by failing to intervene to protect him against his father's violence. The District Court granted summary judgment for respondents, and the Court of Appeals affirmed.

I

Does the Due Process Clause require the State to protect the life, liberty and property of its citizens against invasions by private actors?

R

The Due Process Clause does not require the State to protect the life, liberty and property of its citizens against invasions by private actors.

A

Respondents' failure to provide petitioner with adequate protection against his father's violence did not violate his rights under the substantive component of the Due Process Clause. A State's failure to protect an individual against private violence generally does not constitute a violation of the Due Process Clause, because the Clause imposes no duty on the State to provide members of the general public with adequate protective services. The Clause is phrased as a limitation on the State's power to act, not as a guarantee of certain minimal levels of safety and security; while it forbids the State itself to deprive individuals of life, liberty, and property without due process of law, its language cannot fairly be read to impose an affirmative obligation on the State to ensure that those interests do not come to harm through other means. There is no merit to petitioner's contention that the State's knowledge of his danger and expressions of willingness to protect him against that danger established a "special relationship" giving rise to an affirmative constitutional duty to protect. While certain "special relationships" created or assumed by the State with respect to particular individuals may give rise to an affirmative duty, enforceable through the Due Process Clause, to provide adequate protection the affirmative duty to protect arises not from the State's knowledge of the individual's predicament or from its expressions of intent to help him, but from the limitations which it has imposed on his freedom to act on his own behalf, through imprisonment, institutionalization, or other similar restraint of personal liberty. No such duty existed here, for the harms petitioner suffered occurred not while the State was holding him in its custody, but while he was in the custody of his natural father, who was in no sense a state actor. While the State may have been aware of the dangers that he faced, it played no part in their creation, nor did it do anything to render him more vulnerable to them. Under these circumstances, the Due

Process Clause did not impose upon the State an affirmative duty to provide petitioner with adequate protection. It may well be that by voluntarily undertaking to provide petitioner with protection against a danger it played no part in creating, the State acquired a duty under state tort law to provide him with adequate protection against that danger. But the Due Process Clause does not transform every tort committed by a state actor into a constitutional violation.

C

Affirmed.

Goldberg v. Kelly

397 U.S. 254 (1970)

FACTS

Appellees are New York City residents receiving financial aid under the federally assisted Aid to Families with Dependent Children program or under New York State's general Home Relief program who allege that officials administering these programs terminated, or were about to terminate, such aid without prior notice and hearing, thereby denying them due process of law. The District Court held that only a pre-termination evidentiary hearing would satisfy the constitutional command, and rejected the argument of the welfare officials that the combination of the existing post-termination "fair hearing" and informal pre-termination review was sufficient.

I

When a state terminates public assistance payments without giving the recipient the opportunity for an evidentiary hearing, is procedural due process denied?

R

The degree and extent of due process afforded to a person is commensurate with the extent of the loss suffered.

A

Welfare benefits are a matter of statutory entitlement for persons qualified to receive them and procedural due process is applicable to their termination. The interest of the eligible recipient in the uninterrupted receipt of public assistance, which provides him with essential food, clothing, housing, and medical care, coupled with the State's interest that his payments not be erroneously terminated, clearly outweighs the State's competing concern to prevent any increase in its fiscal and administrative burdens. A pre-termination evidentiary hearing is necessary to provide the welfare recipient with procedural due process. Such hearing need not take the form of a judicial or quasi-judicial trial, but the recipient must be provided with timely and adequate notice detailing the reasons for termination, and an effective opportunity to defend by confronting adverse witnesses and by presenting his own arguments and evidence orally before the decisionmaker. Counsel need not be furnished at the pre-termination hearing, but the recipient must be allowed to retain an attorney if he so desires. The decisionmaker need not file a full opinion or make formal findings of fact or conclusions of law but should state the reasons for his determination and indicate the evidence he relied on. The decisionmaker must be impartial, and although prior involvement in some aspects of a case will not necessarily bar a welfare official from acting as decision maker, he should not have participated in making the determination under review.

C

Affirmed.

Board of Regents v. Roth

408 U.S. 564 (1972)

FACTS

Respondent, hired for a fixed term of one academic year to teach at a state university, was informed without explanation that he would not be rehired for the ensuing year. A statute provided that all state university teachers would be employed initially on probation and that only after four years' continuous service would teachers achieve permanent employment "during efficiency and good behavior," with procedural protection against separation. University rules gave a non-tenured teacher "dismissed" before the end of the year some opportunity for review of the "dismissal," but provided that no reason need be given for non-retention of a non-tenured teacher, and no standards were specified for reemployment. Respondent brought this action claiming deprivation of his Fourteenth Amendment rights, alleging infringement of (1) his free speech right because the true reason for his non-retention was his criticism of the university administration, and (2) his procedural due process right because of the university's failure to advise him of the reason for its decision. The District Court granted summary judgment for the respondent on the procedural issue. The Court of Appeals affirmed.

I Does a governmental employee have a 14th Amendment liberty or property interest in continued employment?

R A governmental employee does not have a 14th Amendment liberty or property interest in continued employment when he is not hired or rehired for a government job but remains free to seek other employment.

A The Fourteenth Amendment does not require opportunity for a hearing prior to the non-renewal of a non-tenured state teacher's contract, unless he can show that the non-renewal deprived him of an interest in "liberty" or that he had a "property" interest in continued employment, despite the lack of tenure or a formal contract. Here the non-retention of respondent, absent any charges against him or stigma or disability foreclosing other employment, is not tantamount to a deprivation of "liberty," and the terms of respondent's employment accorded him no "property" interest protected by procedural due process. The courts below therefore erred in granting summary judgment for the respondent on the procedural due process issue.

C Reversed and remanded.

Goss v. Lopez

419 U.S. 565 (1975)

FACTS

Appellee Ohio public high school students, who had been suspended from school for misconduct for up to 10 days without a hearing, brought a class action against appellant school officials seeking a declaration that the Ohio statute permitting such suspensions was unconstitutional and an order enjoining the officials to remove the references to the suspensions from the students' records. A three-judge District Court declared that appellees were denied due process of law in violation of the Fourteenth Amendment because they were "suspended without hearing prior to suspension or within a reasonable time thereafter," and that the statute and implementing regulations were unconstitutional, and granted the requested injunction.

I

Do students facing temporary suspension from a public school have property and liberty interests that qualify for protection under the Due Process Clause of the Fourteenth Amendment?

R

Students facing temporary suspension from a public school have property and liberty interests that qualify for protection under the Due Process Clause of the Fourteenth Amendment.

A

Having chosen to extend the right to an education to people of appellees' class generally, Ohio may not withdraw that right on grounds of misconduct, absent fundamentally fair procedures to determine whether the misconduct has occurred, and must recognize a student's legitimate entitlement to a public education as a property interest that is protected by the Due Process Clause, and that may not be taken away for misconduct without observing minimum procedures required by that Clause. Since misconduct charges if sustained and recorded could seriously damage the students' reputation as well as interfere with later educational and employment opportunities, the State's claimed right to determine unilaterally and without process whether that misconduct has occurred immediately collides with the Due Process Clause's prohibition against arbitrary deprivation of liberty. A 10-day suspension from school is not *de minimis* and may not be imposed in complete disregard of the Due Process Clause. Neither the property interest in educational benefits temporarily denied nor the liberty interest in reputation is so insubstantial that suspensions may constitutionally be imposed by any procedure the school chooses, no matter how arbitrary. Due process requires, in connection with a suspension of 10 days or less, that the student be given oral or written notice of the charges against him and, if he denies them, an explanation of the evidence the authorities have and an opportunity to present his version. Generally, notice and hearing should precede the student's removal from school, but if prior notice and hearing are not feasible, as where the student's presence endangers persons or property or threatens disruption of the academic process, the necessary notice and hearing should follow.

C

Affirmed.

Paul v. Davis

424 U.S. 693 (1976)

FACTS

A photograph of respondent bearing his name was included in a "flyer" of "active shoplifters," after he had been arrested on a shoplifting charge in Louisville, Ky. After that charge had been dismissed respondent brought this action under 42 U.S.C. 1983 against petitioner police chiefs, who had distributed the flyer to area merchants, alleging that petitioners' action under color of law deprived him of his constitutional rights. The District Court granted petitioners' motion to dismiss. The Court of Appeals reversed, relying on *Wisconsin v. Constantineau.*

I Can the deformation of a person that stems directly from some governmental act serve as the basis for a civil rights suit against the government under 42 U.S.C. §1983?

R The 14th Amendment's guarantee against depravations of liberty or property without due process does not apply to the deformation of a person that stems directly from some governmental act and can not serve as the basis for a civil rights suit against the government under 42 U.S.C. §1983.

A Petitioners' action in distributing the flyer did not deprive respondent of any "liberty" or "property" rights secured against state deprivation by the Due Process Clause of the Fourteenth Amendment. The Due Process Clause does not *ex proprio vigore* extend to a person a right to be free of injury wherever the State may be characterized as the tortfeasor. Reputation alone, apart from some more tangible interests such as employment, does not implicate any "liberty" or "property" interests sufficient to invoke the procedural protection of the Due Process Clause; hence to establish a claim under 1983 and the Fourteenth Amendment more must be involved than simply defamation by a state official. Kentucky law does not extend to respondent any legal guarantee of present enjoyment of reputation that has been altered by petitioners' actions, and the interest in reputation alone is thus quite different from the "liberty" or "property" recognized in such decisions as *Bell v. Burson*, and *Morrissey v. Brewer*, where the guarantee of due process required certain procedural safeguards before the State could alter the status of the complainants. Respondent's contention that petitioners' defamatory flyer deprived him of his constitutional right to privacy is without merit, being based not upon any challenge to the State's ability to restrict his freedom of action in a sphere contended to be "private" but on a claim that the State may not publicize a record of an official act like an arrest.

C Reversed.

Mathews v. Eldridge

424 U.S. 319 (1976)

FACTS

In order to establish initial and continued entitlement to disability benefits under the Social Security Act (Act), a worker must demonstrate that, among other things, he is unable "to engage in any substantial gainful activity by reason of any medically determinable physical or mental impairment . . . ." The worker bears the continuing burden of showing, by means of "medically acceptable . . . techniques" that his impairment is of such severity that he cannot perform his previous work or any other kind of gainful work. A state agency makes the continuing assessment of the worker's eligibility for benefits, obtaining information from the worker and his sources of medical treatment. The agency may arrange for an independent medical examination to resolve conflicting information. If the agency's tentative assessment of the beneficiary's condition differs from his own, the beneficiary is informed that his benefits may be terminated, is provided a summary of the evidence, and afforded an opportunity to review the agency's evidence. The state agency then makes a final determination, which is reviewed by the Social Security Administration (SSA). If the SSA accepts the agency determination it gives written notification to the beneficiary of the reasons for the decision and of his right to de novo state agency reconsideration. Upon acceptance by the SSA, benefits are terminated effective two months after the month in which recovery is found to have occurred. If, after reconsideration by the state agency and SSA review, the decision remains adverse to the recipient, he is notified of his right to an evidentiary hearing before an SSA administrative law judge. If an adverse decision results, the recipient may request discretionary review by the SSA Appeals Council, and finally may obtain judicial review. If it is determined after benefits are terminated that the claimant's disability extended beyond the date of cessation initially established, he is entitled to retroactive payments. Retroactive adjustments are also made for overpayments. A few years after respondent was first awarded disability benefits he received and completed a questionnaire from the monitoring state agency. After considering the information contained therein and obtaining reports from his doctor and an independent medical consultant, the agency wrote respondent that it had tentatively determined that his disability had ceased in May 1972 and advised him that he might request a reasonable time to furnish additional information. In a reply letter respondent disputed one characterization of his medical condition and indicated that the agency had enough evidence to establish his disability. The agency then made its final determination reaffirming its tentative decision. This determination was accepted by the SSA, which notified respondent in July that his benefits would end after that month and that he had a right to state agency reconsideration within six months. Instead of requesting such reconsideration respondent brought this action challenging the constitutionality of the procedures for terminating disability benefits and seeking reinstatement of benefits pending a hearing. The District Court, relying in part on *Goldberg v. Kelly*, held that the termination procedures violated procedural due process and concluded that prior to termination of benefits respondent was entitled to an evidentiary hearing of the type provided welfare beneficiaries under Title IV of the Act. The Court of Appeals affirmed. Petitioner contends that the District Court is barred from considering respondent's action by *Weinberger v. Salfi*, which held that district courts are precluded from exercising jurisdiction over an action seeking a review of a decision of the Secretary of Health, Education, and Welfare regarding benefits under the Act except as provided in 42 U.S.C.

405 (g), which grants jurisdiction only to review a "final" decision of the Secretary made after a hearing to which he was a party.

I

Is an evidentiary hearing required prior to the termination of Social Security disability payments such that the denial of such administrative procedures prescribed under the Act do not comport with due process?

R

An evidentiary hearing is not required prior to the termination of Social Security disability payments and the administrative procedures prescribed under the Act fully comport with due process - the constitutional sufficiency of administrative procedures prior to the initial termination of benefits and pending review requires consideration of three factors: (1) the private interest that will be affected by the official action; (2) the risk of an erroneous deprivation of such interest through the procedures used, and probable value, if any, of additional procedural safeguards; and (3) the Government's interest, including the fiscal and administrative burdens that the additional or substitute procedures would entail.

A

The District Court had jurisdiction over respondent's constitutional claim, since the denial of his request for benefits was a final decision with respect to that claim for purposes of 405(g) jurisdiction. The 405(g) finality requirement consists of the waivable requirement that the administrative remedies prescribed by the Secretary be exhausted and the nonwaivable requirement that a claim for benefits shall have been presented to the Secretary. Respondent's answers to the questionnaire and his letter to the state agency specifically presented the claim that his benefits should not be terminated because he was still disabled, and thus satisfied the nonwaivable requirement. Although respondent concededly did not exhaust the Secretary's internal-review procedures and ordinarily only the Secretary has the power to waive exhaustion, this is a case where the claimant's interest in having a particular issue promptly resolved is so great that deference to the Secretary's judgment is inappropriate. The facts that respondent's constitutional challenge was collateral to his substantive claim of entitlement and that (contrary to the situation in *Salfi*) he colorably claimed that an erroneous termination would damage him in a way not compensable through retroactive payments warrant the conclusion that the denial of his claim to continued benefits was a sufficiently "final decision" with respect to his constitutional claim to satisfy the statutory exhaustion requirement. An evidentiary hearing is not required prior to the termination of Social Security disability payments and the administrative procedures prescribed under the Act fully comport with due process. "[D]ue process is flexible and calls for such procedural protections as the particular situation demands," *Morrissey v. Brewer*. Resolution of the issue here involving the constitutional sufficiency of administrative procedures prior to the initial termination of benefits and pending review, requires consideration of three factors: (1) the private interest that will be affected by the official action; (2) the risk of an erroneous deprivation of such interest through the procedures used, and probable value, if any, of additional procedural safeguards; and (3) the Government's interest, including the fiscal and administrative burdens that the additional or substitute procedures would entail. The private interest that will be adversely affected by an erroneous termination of benefits is likely to be less in the case of a disabled worker than in the case of a welfare recipient, like the claimants in Goldberg, supra. Eligibility for disability payments is not based on financial need, and although hardship may be imposed upon the erroneously terminated disability recipient, his need is likely less than the welfare recipient. In view of other forms of government assistance available to the terminated disability recipient, there is less reason than in Goldberg to depart from the ordinary principle that something less than an evidentiary hearing is sufficient prior to adverse administrative action. The medical assessment of the worker's condition implicates a more sharply focused and easily documented decision than the typical determination of welfare entitlement. The decision whether to discontinue disability benefits will normally turn upon "routine, standard, and unbiased medical reports by physician specialists." In a disability situation the potential value of an evidentiary hearing is thus substantially less than in the welfare context. Written submissions provide the disability recipient with an effective means of communicating his case to the decisionmaker. The detailed questionnaire identifies with particularity the information relevant to the entitlement decision. Information critical to the decision is derived directly from medical sources. Finally, prior to termination of benefits, the disability recipient or his representative is afforded full access to the information relied on by the state agency, is provided the reasons underlying its tentative assessment, and is given an opportunity to submit additional arguments and evidence. Requiring an evidentiary hearing upon demand in all cases prior to the termination of disability benefits would entail fiscal and administrative burdens out of proportion to any countervailing benefits. The judicial model of an evidentiary hearing is neither a required, nor even the most effective, method of decisionmaking in all circumstances, and here where the prescribed procedures not only provide the claimant with an effective process for asserting his claim prior to any administrative action but also assure a right to an evidentiary hearing as well as subsequent judicial review before the denial of his claim becomes final, there is no deprivation of procedural due process.

C

Reversed.

Turner Broadcasting System v. FCC

512 U.S. 622 (1994)

FACTS

Concerned that a competitive imbalance between cable television and over-the-air broadcasters was endangering the broadcasters' ability to compete for a viewing audience, and thus for necessary operating revenues, Congress passed the Cable Television Consumer Protection and Competition Act of 1992. Sections 4 and 5 of the Act require cable television systems to devote a specified portion of their channels to the transmission of local commercial and public broadcast stations. Soon after the Act became law, appellants, numerous cable programmers and operators, challenged the constitutionality of the must-carry provisions. The District Court granted the United States and intervenor defendants summary judgment, ruling that the provisions are consistent with the First Amendment. The court rejected appellants' argument that the provisions warrant strict scrutiny as a content-based regulation and sustained them under the intermediate standard of scrutiny set forth in *United States v. O'Brien* concluding that they are sufficiently tailored to serve the important governmental interest in the preservation of local broadcasting.

I Is a federal law requiring cable TV providers to devote some channels to local, educational broadcasters a content-based speech regulation subject to a strict scrutiny level of review?

R A federal law requiring cable TV providers to devote some channels to local, educational broadcasters a content-based speech regulation is not subject to a strict scrutiny level of review; rather it is subject to intermediate scrutiny.

A The appropriate standard by which to evaluate the constitutionality of the must-carry provisions is the intermediate level of scrutiny applicable to content-neutral restrictions that impose an incidental burden on speech. Because the must-carry provisions impose special obligations Page II upon cable operators and special burdens upon cable programmers, heightened First Amendment scrutiny is demanded. The less rigorous standard of scrutiny now reserved for broadcast regulation should not be extended to cable regulation, since the rationale for such review - the dual problems of spectrum scarcity and signal interference - does not apply in the context of cable. Nor is the mere assertion of dysfunction or failure in the cable market, without more, sufficient to shield a speech regulation from the First Amendment standards applicable to non-broadcast media. Moreover, while enforcement of a generally applicable law against members of the press may sometimes warrant only rational basis scrutiny, laws that single out the press for special treatment pose a particular danger of abuse by the State and are always subject to some degree of heightened scrutiny. The must-carry rules are content-neutral, and thus are not subject to strict scrutiny. They are neutral on their face, because they distinguish between speakers in the television programming market based only upon the manner in which programmers transmit their messages to viewers, not the messages they carry. The purposes underlying the must-carry rules are also unrelated to content. Congress' overriding objective was not to favor programming of a particular content, but rather to preserve access to free television programming for the 40 % of Americans without cable. The challenged provisions' design and operation confirm this purpose. Congress' acknowledgement that broadcast television stations make a valuable contribution to the Nation's communications structure does not indicate that Congress regarded broadcast programming to be more valuable than cable programming; rather, it reflects only the recognition that the services provided by broadcast television have some intrinsic value, and are worth preserving against the threats posed by cable. It is also incorrect to suggest that Congress enacted must-carry in an effort to exercise content control over what subscribers view on cable television, given the minimal extent to which the Federal Communications Commission and Congress influence the programming offered by broadcast stations. None of appellants' additional arguments suffices to require strict scrutiny in this case. The provisions do not intrude on the editorial control of cable operators. They are content-neutral in application, and they do not force cable operators to alter their own messages to respond to the broadcast programming they must carry. In addition, the physical connection between the television set and the cable network gives cable operators bottleneck, or Page III gatekeeper control over most programming delivered into subscribers' homes. Strict scrutiny is also not triggered by Congress' preference for broadcasters over cable operators, since it is based not on the content of the programming each group offers, but on the belief that broadcast television is in economic peril. Nor is such scrutiny warranted by the fact that the provisions single out certain members of the press - here, cable operators - for disfavored treatment. Such differential treatment is justified by the special characteristics of the cable medium - namely, the cable operators' bottleneck monopoly and the dangers this power poses to the viability of broadcast television - and because the must-carry provisions are not structured in a manner that carries the inherent risk of undermining First Amendment interests. Under *O'Brien*, a content-neutral regulation will be sustained if it furthers an important governmental interest that is unrelated to the suppression of free expression and the incidental restriction on alleged First Amendment freedoms is no greater than is essential to the furtherance of that interest. Viewed in the abstract, each of the governmental interests asserted-preserving the benefits of free, over-the-air local broadcast stations, promoting the widespread dissemination of information from a multiplicity of sources, and promoting fair competition in the market for television programming-is important.

C The judgment is vacated, and the case is remanded.

Boos v. Barry

485 U.S. 312 (1988)

FACTS

District of Columbia Code 22-1115 makes it unlawful, within 500 feet of a foreign embassy, either to display any sign that tends to bring the foreign government into "public odium" or "public disrepute" (display clause), or to congregate and refuse to obey a police dispersal order (congregation clause). Petitioners, who wish to engage in conduct that would violate both clauses, filed suit in Federal District Court against respondent city officials, asserting a facial First Amendment challenge to 22-1115. The court granted respondents' motion for summary judgment, and the Court of Appeals affirmed, concluding that both clauses were constitutional.

I

Is a federal law banning anti-governmental signs near foreign embassies a content-based regulation of speech violative of the Constitution?

R

A federal law banning anti-governmental signs near foreign embassies is a content-based regulation and thus subject to a strict scrutiny standard of review.

A

Section 22-1115's display clause is facially violative of the First Amendment, since it is a content-based restriction on political speech in a public forum, which is not narrowly tailored to serve a compelling state interest. Assuming, without deciding, that protecting the dignity of foreign diplomats by shielding them from criticism of their governments is a "compelling" interest for First Amendment purposes, the ready availability of a significantly less restrictive alternative - 18 U.S.C. 112, which prohibits intimidating, coercing, or harassing foreign officials or obstructing them in the performance of their duties - amply demonstrates that the display clause is not sufficiently narrowly tailored to withstand exacting scrutiny. Respondents' defense of the clause is further undercut by 1302 of the Omnibus Diplomatic Security and Anti-terrorism Act of 1986, in which Congress requested that the District of Columbia review and revise 22-1115 in the interest of protecting First Amendment rights, and the District responded by repealing the section, contingent on the prior extension of 112 to the District. This Court may rely on the judgment of Congress, the body primarily responsible for implementing international law obligations, that 112 adequately satisfies the Government's interest in protecting diplomatic personnel and that, accordingly, 22-1115's display clause is not narrowly tailored. Section 22-1115's congregation clause, as construed by the Court of Appeals, is not facially violative of the First Amendment. The clause is not overbroad, even though its actual language is problematic both because it applies to any congregation for any reason within 500 feet of an embassy and because it appears to place no limits on police dispersal authority. These difficulties are alleviated by the Court of Appeals' narrowing construction that the clause permits dispersal only of congregations that are directed at an embassy and only when the police reasonably believe that the embassy's "security or peace" is threatened. Thus, the clause does not reach a substantial amount of constitutionally protected conduct, since it merely regulates the place and manner of certain demonstrations, is site specific to areas within 500 feet of embassies, and does not prohibit peaceful congregations. Nor is the clause, as narrowed, impermissibly vague simply because the Court of Appeals has not defined or limited the word "peace." Given the particular context for which the clause is crafted, it is apparent that the prohibited quantum of disturbance is determined by whether normal embassy activities have been or are about to be disrupted. The contention that, since 22-1116 excludes labor picketing from 22-1115's general prohibitions, both of 22-1115's clauses require unequal treatment of non-labor and labor activities in violation of the Equal Protection Clause is without merit. Section 22-1116's primary function of ensuring that the display clause did not prohibit labor picketing is largely pre-empted by this Court's conclusion that that clause violates the First Amendment. Moreover, under the Court of Appeals' construction of the congregation clause as applying only to congregations that threaten an embassy's security or peace, any peaceful congregation, including a peaceful labor congregation, is permitted. This Court will not adopt the unreasonable interpretation that 22-1116's sole purpose is to protect violent labor congregations. Thus, 22-1116 does not violate equal protection.

C

The judgment is affirmed in part and reversed in part.

Republican Party of Minnesota v. White

536 U.S. 765 (2002)

FACTS

The Minnesota Supreme Court has adopted a canon of judicial conduct that prohibits a "candidate for a judicial office" from "announc[ing] his or her views on disputed legal or political issues" (hereinafter announce clause). While running for associate justice of that court, petitioner Gregory Wersal (and others) filed this suit seeking a declaration that the announce clause violates the First Amendment and an injunction against its enforcement. The District Court granted respondent officials summary judgment, and the Eighth Circuit affirmed.

I

Is a canon of judicial conduct that prohibits a "candidate for a judicial office" from "announc[ing] his or her views on disputed legal or political issues" violative of the First Amendment?

R

The announce clause both prohibits speech based on its content and burdens a category of speech that is at the core of First Amendment freedoms - speech about the qualifications of candidates for public office.

A

The announce clause violates the First Amendment. The record demonstrates that the announce clause prohibits a judicial candidate from stating his views on any specific non-fanciful legal question within the province of the court for which he is running, except in the context of discussing past decisions - and in the latter context as well, if he expresses the view that he is not bound by *stare decisis*. The announce clause both prohibits speech based on its content and burdens a category of speech that is at the core of First Amendment freedoms - speech about the qualifications of candidates for public office. The Eighth Circuit concluded, and the parties do not dispute, that the proper test to be applied to determine the constitutionality of such a restriction is strict scrutiny, under which respondents have the burden to prove that the clause is (1) narrowly tailored, to serve (2) a compelling state interest. That court found that respondents had established two interests as sufficiently compelling to justify the announce clause: preserving the state judiciary's impartiality and preserving the appearance of that impartiality. Under any definition of "impartiality," the announce clause fails strict scrutiny. First, it is plain that the clause is not narrowly tailored to serve impartiality (or its appearance) in the traditional sense of the word, *i.e.,* as a lack of bias for or against either party to the proceeding. Indeed, the clause is barely tailored to serve that interest at all, inasmuch as it does not restrict speech for or against particular parties, but rather speech for or against particular issues. Second, although "impartiality" in the sense of a lack of preconception in favor of or against a particular legal view may well be an interest served by the announce clause, pursuing this objective is not a compelling state interest, since it is virtually impossible, and hardly desirable, to find a judge who does not have preconceptions about the law. Third, the Court need not decide whether achieving "impartiality" (or its appearance) in the sense of open mindedness is a compelling state interest because, as a means of pursuing this interest, the announce clause is so woefully underinclusive that the Court does not believe it was adopted for that purpose. Respondents have not carried the burden imposed by strict scrutiny of establishing that statements made during an election campaign are uniquely destructive of open mindedness. A universal and long-established tradition of prohibiting certain conduct creates a strong presumption that the prohibition is constitutional. However, the practice of prohibiting speech by judicial candidates is neither ancient nor universal. The Court knows of no such prohibitions throughout the 19th and the first quarter of the 20th century, and they are still not universally adopted. This does not compare well with the traditions deemed worthy of attention in. There is an obvious tension between Minnesota's Constitution, which requires judicial elections, and the announce clause, which places most subjects of interest to the voters off limits. The First Amendment does not permit Minnesota to leave the principle of elections in place while preventing candidates from discussing what the elections are about.

C Reversed and remanded.

City of Renton v. Playtime Theatres Inc.

475 U.S. 41 (1986)

FACTS

Respondents purchased two theaters in Renton, Washington, with the intention of exhibiting adult films and, at about the same time, filed suit in Federal District Court, seeking injunctive relief and a declaratory judgment that the First and Fourteenth Amendments were violated by a city ordinance that prohibits adult motion picture theaters from locating within 1,000 feet of any residential zone, single- or multiple-family dwelling, church, park, or school. The District Court ultimately entered summary judgment in the city's favor, holding that the ordinance did not violate the First Amendment. The Court of Appeals reversed, holding that the ordinance constituted a substantial restriction on First Amendment interests, and remanded the case for reconsideration as to whether the city had substantial governmental interests to support the ordinance.

I

Is a zoning ordinance restricting pornographic theaters' placement a content-based restriction on speech violative of the First Amendment?

R

A zoning ordinance restricting pornographic theaters' placement must be analyzed as a content-neutral, "time, place and manner" regulation in order to find it content-based restriction violative of the First Amendment.

A

The ordinance is a valid governmental response to the serious problems created by adult theaters and satisfies the dictates of the First Amendment. Since the ordinance does not ban adult theaters altogether, it is properly analyzed as a form of time, place, and manner regulation. "Content-neutral" time, place, and manner regulations are acceptable so long as they are designed to serve a substantial governmental interest and do not unreasonably limit alternative avenues of communication. The District Court found that the Renton City Council's "predominate" concerns were with the secondary effects of adult theaters on the surrounding community, not with the content of adult films themselves. This finding is more than adequate to establish that the city's pursuit of its zoning interests was unrelated to the suppression of free expression, and thus the ordinance is a "content-neutral" speech regulation. The Renton ordinance is designed to serve a substantial governmental interest while allowing for reasonable alternative avenues of communication. A city's interest in attempting to preserve the quality of urban life, as here, must be accorded high respect. Although the ordinance was enacted without the benefit of studies specifically relating to Renton's particular problems, Renton was entitled to rely on the experiences of, and studies produced by, the nearby city of Seattle and other cities. Nor was there any constitutional defect in the method chosen by Renton to further its substantial interests. Cities may regulate adult theaters by dispersing them, or by effectively concentrating them, as in Renton. Moreover, the ordinance is not "underinclusive" for failing to regulate other kinds of adult businesses, since there was no evidence that, at the time the ordinance was enacted, any other adult business was located in, or was contemplating moving into, Renton. As required by the First Amendment, the ordinance allows for reasonable alternative avenues of communication. Although respondents argue that in general there are no "commercially viable" adult theater sites within the limited area of land left open for such theaters by the ordinance, the fact that respondents must fend for themselves in the real estate market, on an equal footing with other prospective purchasers and lessees, does not give rise to a violation of the First Amendment, which does not compel the Government to ensure that adult theaters, or any other kinds of speech-related businesses, will be able to obtain sites at bargain prices.

C

Reversed.

National Endowment For The Arts v. Finley

524 U.S. 569 (1988)

FACTS

The National Foundation on the Arts and Humanities Act vests the National Endowment for the Arts (NEA) with substantial discretion to award financial grants to support the arts; it identifies only the broadest funding priorities, including "artistic and cultural significance, giving emphasis to . . . creativity and cultural diversity," "professional excellence," and the encouragement of "public . . . education . . . and appreciation of the arts." See 20 U.S.C. § 954(c)(1)-(10). Applications for NEA funding are initially reviewed by advisory panels of experts in the relevant artistic field. The panels report to the National Council on the Arts (Council), which, in turn, advises the NEA Chairperson. In 1989, controversial photographs that appeared in two NEA-funded exhibits prompted public outcry over the agency's grant-making procedures. Congress reacted to the controversy by inserting an amendment into the NEA's 1990 reauthorization bill. The amendment became §954(d)(1), which directs the Chairperson to ensure that "artistic excellence and artistic merit are the criteria by which [grant] applications are judged, taking into consideration general standards of decency and respect for the diverse beliefs and values of the American public." The NEA has not promulgated an official interpretation of the provision, but the Council adopted a resolution to implement §954(d)(1) by ensuring that advisory panel members represent geographic, ethnic, and aesthetic diversity. The four individual respondents are performance artists who applied for NEA grants before §954(d)(1) was enacted. An advisory panel recommended approval of each of their projects, but the Council subsequently recommended disapproval, and funding was denied. They filed suit for restoration of the recommended grants or reconsideration of their applications, asserting First Amendment and statutory claims. When Congress enacted §954(d)(1), respondents, joined by the National Association of Artists' Organizations, amended their complaint to challenge the provision as void for vagueness and impermissibly viewpoint based. The District Court granted summary judgment in favor of respondents on their facial constitutional challenge to §954(d)(1). The Ninth Circuit affirmed, holding that §954(d)(1), on its face, impermissibly discriminates on the basis of viewpoint and is void for vagueness under the First and Fifth Amendments.

I

Does a statute which allows the government to fund the arts based on its [the government's] assessment of artistic content a violation of the First Amendment?

R

A statute which allows the government to fund the arts based on its [the government's] assessment of artistic content does not violate the First Amendment as long as it does not abuse its discretion by penalizing disfavored viewpoints.

A

Section 954(d)(1) is facially valid, as it neither inherently interferes with First Amendment rights nor violates constitutional vagueness principles. Respondents confront a heavy burden in advancing their facial constitutional challenge, and they have not demonstrated a substantial risk that application of §954(d)(1) will lead to the suppression of free expression. The premise of respondents' claim is that §954(d)(1) constrains the agency's ability to fund certain categories of artistic expression. The provision, however, simply adds "considerations" to the grant-making process; it does not preclude awards to projects that might be deemed "indecent" or "disrespectful," nor place conditions on grants, or even specify that those factors must be given any particular weight in reviewing an application. Regardless whether the NEA's view that the formulation of diverse advisory panels is sufficient to comply with Congress' command is in fact a reasonable reading, §954(d)(1)'s plain text clearly does not impose a categorical requirement. Given the varied interpretations of the "decency and respect" criteria urged by the parties, and the provision's vague exhortation to "take them into consideration," it seems unlikely that §954(d)(1) will significantly compromise First Amendment values. The NEA's enabling statute contemplates a number of indisputably constitutional applications for both the "decency" and the "respect" prong of §954(d)(1). It is well established that "decency" is a permissible factor where "educational suitability" motivates its consideration. And the statute already provides that the agency must take "cultural diversity" into account. References to permissible applications would not alone be sufficient to sustain the statute, but neither is the Court persuaded that, in other applications, the language of §954(d)(1) itself will give rise to the suppression of protected expression. Any content-based considerations that may be taken into account are a consequence of the nature of arts funding; the NEA has limited resources to allocate among many "artistically excellent" projects, and it does so on the basis of a wide variety of subjective criteria. Respondent's reliance on *Rosenberger v. Rector and Visitors of Univ. of Va.* in which the Court overturned a public university's objective decision denying funding to all student publications having religious editorial viewpoints-is therefore misplaced. The NEA's mandate is to make aesthetic judgments, and the inherently content-based "excellence" threshold for NEA support sets it apart from the subsidy at issue in Rosenberger. Moreover, although the First Amendment applies in the subsidy context, Congress has wide latitude to set spending priorities. Unless and until §954(d)(1) is applied in a manner that raises concern about the suppression of disfavored viewpoints, the Court will uphold it. The lower courts also erred in invalidating §954(d)(1) as unconstitutionally vague. The First and Fifth Amendments protect speakers from arbitrary and discriminatory enforcement of vague standards. Section 954(d)(1)'s terms are undeniably opaque, and if they appeared in a criminal statute or regulatory scheme, they could raise substantial vagueness concerns. It is unlikely, however, that speakers will be compelled to steer too far clear of any forbidden area in the context of NEA grants. As a practical matter, artists may conform their speech to what they believe to be the NEA decisionmaking criteria in order to acquire funding. But when the Government is acting as patron rather than sovereign, the consequences of imprecision are not constitutionally severe. In the context of selective subsidies, it is not always feasible for Congress to legislate with clarity. Indeed, to accept respondents' vagueness argument would be to call into question the constitutionality of the many valuable Government programs awarding scholarships and grants on the basis of subjective criteria such as "excellence."

C

Reversed and remanded.

United States v. American Library Assn. Inc.

539 U.S. 194 (2003)

FACTS

Two forms of federal assistance help public libraries provide patrons with Internet access: discounted rates under the E-rate program and grants under the Library Services and Technology Act (LSTA). Upon discovering that library patrons, including minors, regularly search the Internet for pornography and expose others to pornographic images by leaving them displayed on Internet terminals or printed at library printers, Congress enacted the Children's Internet Protection Act (CIPA), which forbids public libraries to receive federal assistance for Internet access unless they install software to block obscene or pornographic images and to prevent minors from accessing material harmful to them. Appellees, a group of libraries, patrons, Web site publishers, and related parties, sued the Government, challenging the constitutionality of CIPA's filtering provisions. Ruling that CIPA is facially unconstitutional and enjoining the Government from withholding federal assistance for failure to comply with CIPA, the District Court held, *inter alia*, that Congress had exceeded its authority under the Spending Clause because any public library that complies with CIPA's conditions will necessarily violate the First Amendment; that the CIPA filtering software constitutes a content-based restriction on access to a public forum that is subject to strict scrutiny; and that, although the Government has a compelling interest in preventing the dissemination of obscenity, child pornography, or material harmful to minors, the use of software filters is not narrowly tailored to further that interest.

I

Is Children's Internet Protection Act (CIPA), which forbids public libraries to receive federal assistance for Internet access unless they install software to block obscene or pornographic images and to prevent minors from accessing material harmful to them, constitutional?

R

The CIPA, which forbids public libraries to receive federal assistance for Internet access unless they install software to block obscene or pornographic images and to prevent minors from accessing material harmful to them, is constitutional and not subject to strict scrutiny.

A

Because public libraries' use of Internet filtering software does not violate their patrons' First Amendment rights, CIPA does not induce libraries to violate the Constitution, and is a valid exercise of Congress' spending power. Congress has wide latitude to attach conditions to the receipt of federal assistance to further its policy objectives, but may not "induce" the recipient "to engage in activities that would themselves be unconstitutional." To determine whether libraries would violate the First Amendment by employing the CIPA filtering software, the Court first examines their societal role. To fulfill their traditional missions of facilitating learning and cultural enrichment, public libraries must have broad discretion to decide what material to provide to their patrons. This Court has held in two analogous contexts that the Government has broad discretion to make content-based judgments in deciding what private speech to make available to the public. Just as forum analysis and heightened judicial scrutiny were incompatible with the role of public television stations in the former case and the role of the National Endowment for the Arts in the latter, so are they incompatible with the broad discretion that public libraries must have to consider content in making collection decisions. Thus, the public forum principles on which the

District Court relied are out of place in the context of this case. Internet access in public libraries is neither a "traditional" nor a "designated" public forum. Unlike the "Student Activity Fund" at issue in *Rosenberger* v. *Rector and Visitors of Univ. of Va.,* Internet terminals are not acquired by a library in order to create a public forum for Web publishers to express themselves. Rather, a library provides such access for the same reasons it offers other library resources: to facilitate research, learning, and recreational pursuits by furnishing materials of requisite and appropriate quality. The fact that a library reviews and affirmatively chooses to acquire every book in its collection, but does not review every Web site that it makes available, is not a constitutionally relevant distinction. The decisions by most libraries to exclude pornography from their print collections are not subjected to heightened scrutiny; it would make little sense to treat libraries' judgments to block online pornography any differently. Moreover, because of the vast quantity of material on the Internet and the rapid pace at which it changes, libraries cannot possibly segregate, item by item, all the Internet material that is appropriate for inclusion from all that is not. While a library could limit its Internet collection to just those sites it found worthwhile, it could do so only at the cost of excluding an enormous amount of valuable information that it lacks the capacity to review. Given that tradeoff, it is entirely reasonable for public libraries to reject that approach and instead exclude certain categories of content, without making individualized judgments that everything made available has requisite and appropriate quality. Assuming that appellees may assert an "unconstitutional conditions" claim, that claim would fail on the merits. When the Government appropriates public funds to establish a program, it is entitled to broadly define that program's limits. As in *Rust*, the Government here is not denying a benefit to anyone, but is instead simply insisting that public funds be spent for the purpose for which they are authorized: helping public libraries fulfill their traditional role of obtaining material of requisite and appropriate quality for educational and informational purposes. Especially because public libraries have traditionally excluded pornographic material from their other collections, Congress could reasonably impose a parallel limitation on its Internet assistance programs. As the use of filtering software helps to carry out these programs, it is a permissible condition under *Rust.* Appellees mistakenly contend, in reliance on *Legal Services Corporation* v. *Velazquez,* that CIPA's filtering conditions distort the usual functioning of public libraries. In contrast to the lawyers who furnished legal aid to the indigent under the program at issue in *Velazquez*, public libraries have no role that pits them against the Government, and there is no assumption, as there was in that case, that they must be free of any conditions that their benefactors might attach to the use of donated funds.

C

Reversed.

Near v. Minnesota

283 U.S. 697 (1931)

FACTS

Chapter 285 of the Session Laws of Minnesota for the year 19251 provides for the abatement, as a public nuisance, of a "malicious, scandalous and defamatory newspaper, magazine or other periodical." Under this statute, the county attorney of Hennepin County (plaintiff) brought this action to enjoin the publication of what was described as a "malicious, scandalous and defamatory newspaper, magazine or other periodical," known as The Saturday Press published by the defendants in the city of Minneapolis. The complaint alleged that the defendants, on September 24, 1927, and on eight subsequent dates in October and November, 1927, published and circulated editions of that periodical which stated that "a Jewish gangster was in control of gambling, bootlegging and racketeering in Minneapolis, and that law enforcing officers and agencies were not energetically performing their duties." Most of the charges were directed against the chief of police; he was charged with gross neglect of duty, illicit relations with gangsters, and with participation in graft. The county attorney was charged with knowing the existing conditions and with failure to take adequate measures to remedy them. The mayor was accused of inefficiency and dereliction. On member of the grand jury was stated to be in sympathy with the gangsters. The defendants demurred to the complaint upon the ground that it did not state facts sufficient to constitute a cause of action, and on this demurrer challenged the constitutionality of the statute. The district court overruled the demurrer and certified the question of constitutionality to the Supreme Court of the state. The plaintiff moved that the court direct the issue of a permanent injunction and the court permanently enjoined the newspaper from publishing "any publication whatsoever which is a malicious, scandalous or defamatory newspaper." The district court made findings of fact, which followed the allegations of the complaint and found in general terms that the editions in question were "chiefly devoted to malicious, scandalous and defamatory articles" concerning the individuals named. The court further found that the defendants through these publications "did engage in the business of regularly and customarily producing, publishing and circulating a malicious, scandalous and defamatory newspaper," and that 'the said publication" "under said name of The Saturday Press, or any other name, constitutes a public nuisance under the laws of the State." Defendant-appellant Near appealed from this judgment to the Supreme Court of the State, again asserting his right under the Federal Constitution, and the judgment was affirmed upon the authority of the former decision. From the judgment as thus affirmed, Defendant-appellant Near (owner of The Saturday Press) appealed to the U.S. Supreme Court.

I Can a state constitutionally restrict the publication of a newspaper which contains "malicious, scandalous and defamatory" material directed toward others without violating the First Amendment [freedom of the press]?

R The protection against prior restraints is at the very heart of the First Amendment guarantees of the freedom of the press such that, notwithstanding some narrow exceptions, the government can not censor or otherwise prohibit a publication in advance, even though the communication might be punishable after publication in a criminal or other proceeding.

Near v. State of Minnesota

283 U.S. 697 (1931)

A The fact that for approximately 150 years there has been almost an entire absence of attempts to impose previous restraints upon publications relating to the malfeasance of public officers is significant of the deep-seated conviction that such restraints would violate constitutional rights. Liberty of the press is within the liberty safeguarded by the due process clause of the Fourteenth Amendment from invasion by state action. Liberty of the press is not an absolute right, and the State may punish its abuse. In passing upon the constitutionality of the statute, the court has regard for substance, and not for form; the statute must be tested by its operation and effect. Cutting through mere details of procedure, the operation and effect of the statute is that public authorities may bring a publisher before a judge upon a charge of conducting a business of publishing scandalous and defamatory matter -- in particular, that the matter consists of charges against public officials of official dereliction -- and, unless the publisher is able and disposed to satisfy the judge that the charges are true and are published with good motives and for justifiable ends, his newspaper or periodical is suppressed and further publication is made punishable as a contempt. This is the essence of censorship. A statute authorizing such proceedings in restraint of publication is inconsistent with the conception of the liberty of the press as historically conceived and guaranteed. The chief purpose of the guaranty is to prevent previous restraints upon publication. The libeler, however, remains criminally and civilly responsible for his libels. There are undoubtedly limitations upon the immunity from previous restraint of the press, but they are not applicable in this case. The liberty of the press has been especially cherished in this country as respects publications censuring public officials and charging official misconduct. Public officers find their remedies for false accusations in actions for redress and punishment under the libel laws, and not in proceedings to restrain the publication of newspapers and periodicals. The fact that the liberty of the press may be abused by miscreant purveyors of scandal does not make any the less necessary the immunity from previous restraint in dealing with official misconduct. Characterizing the publication of charges of official misconduct as a "business," and the business as a nuisance, does not avoid the constitutional guaranty; nor does it matter that the periodical is largely or chiefly devoted to such charges. The guaranty against previous restraint extends to publications charging official derelictions that amount to crimes. Permitting the publisher to show in defense that the matter published is true and is published with good motives and for justifiable ends does not justify the statute, nor can it be sustained as a measure for preserving the public peace and preventing assaults and crime.

C Judgment reversed.

New York Times Co. v. United States

403 U.S. 713 (1971)

FACTS

This case was decided together with *United States v. Washington Post Co.* During the early 1970's, the New York Times (defendant) and the Washington Post (defendant) began publishing portions of a secret Department of Defense study entitled "History of U.S. Decision-Making Process on Viet Nam Policy;" commonly known as the "Pentagon Papers." This classified Defense Department study reviewed in great detail the history of United States' activities in Vietnam and detailed the formulation of American Policy toward Indochina, including military operations and diplomatic negotiations. The Nixon Administration (Plaintiff - United States) attempted to prevent both newspapers from publishing the material arguing that such publication would interfere with national security, undermine the diplomatic process and prolong the Vietnam War. The district courts in both cases held that the United States had not met its burden. On appeal to the courts of appeal, the court of appeals in the Washington Post case held that the United States had not met its burden, but court of appeals in the New York Times case held that the government had. A stay of publication was entered pending the outcome of both cases. The U.S. Supreme court granted certiorari in both cases.

I

Can the government impose prior restraints on expression to prevent the publication of what it termed "classified information" in the interests of national security, or does such a restrain on the press violate the First Amendment?

R

Prior restraints on expression will only be permitted when the government meets the heavy burden of showing that the restraint is justified since such prior restraints are viewed as presumptively unconstitutional.

A

The United States, which brought these actions to enjoin publication in the New York Times and in the Washington Post of certain classified material, has not met the heavy burden of showing justification for the enforcement of such a prior restraint. "Any system of prior restraints of expression comes to this Court bearing a heavy presumption against its constitutional validity." The Government "thus carries a heavy burden of showing justification for the imposition of such a restraint." The District Court for the Southern District of New York in the New York Times case and the District Court for the District of Columbia and the Court of Appeals for the District of Columbia Circuit in the Washington Post case held that the Government had not met that burden. We agree. The judgment of the Court of Appeals for the District of Columbia Circuit is therefore affirmed. The order of the Court of Appeals for the Second Circuit is reversed and the case is remanded with directions to enter a judgment affirming the judgment of the District Court for the Southern District of New York. The stays entered June 25, 1971, by the Court are vacated. The judgments shall issue forthwith. So ordered.

C

See above.

Nebraska Press Assn. v. Stuart

427 U.S. 539 (1976)

FACTS

Respondent Nebraska state trial judge, in anticipation of a trial for a multiple murder which had attracted widespread news coverage, entered an order which, as modified by the Nebraska Supreme Court, restrained petitioner newspaper, broadcasters, journalists, news media associations, and national newswire services from publishing or broadcasting accounts of confessions or admissions made by the accused to law enforcement officers or third parties, except members of the press, and other facts "strongly implicative" of the accused. The modification of the order had occurred in the course of an action by petitioners, which had sought a stay of the trial court's original order and in which the accused and the State of Nebraska intervened. This Court granted certiorari to determine whether the order violated the constitutional guarantee of freedom of the press. The order expired by its own terms when the jury was impaneled. Respondent was convicted; his appeal is pending in the Nebraska Supreme Court.

I

Is a court order limiting the media's pretrial publicity a violation of the First Amendment?

R

Court orders that bar publicity by the media must be analyzed by considering the extent and prejudicial nature of the publicity; whether other means would mitigate the publicity's effects; ho effective such an order would be; and the order's specific provisions.

A

The case is not moot simply because the order has expired, since the controversy between the parties is "capable of repetition, yet evading review." While the guarantees of freedom of expression are not an absolute prohibition under all circumstances, the barriers to prior restraint remain high and the presumption against its use continues intact. Although it is unnecessary to establish a priority between First Amendment rights and the Sixth Amendment right to a fair trial under all circumstances, as the authors of the Bill of Rights themselves declined to do, the protection against prior restraint should have particular force as applied to reporting of criminal proceedings. The heavy burden imposed as a condition to securing a prior restraint was not met in this case. On the pretrial record the trial judge was justified in concluding that there would be intense and pervasive pretrial publicity concerning the case, and he could also reasonably conclude, based on common human experience, that publicity might impair the accused's right to a fair trial. His conclusion as to the impact of such publicity on prospective jurors was of necessity speculative, however, dealing as he was with factors unknown and unknowable. There is no finding that measures short of prior restraint on the press and speech would not have protected the accused's rights; the Nebraska Supreme Court no more than implied that alternative measures might not suffice, and the record lacks evidence that would support such a finding. It is not clear that prior restraint on publication would have effectively protected the accused's rights, in view of such practical problems as the limited territorial jurisdiction of the trial court issuing the restraining order, the difficulties inherent in predicting what information will in fact undermine the jurors' impartiality, the problem of drafting an order that will effectively keep prejudicial information from prospective jurors, and the fact that in this case the events occurred in a small community where rumors would travel swiftly by word of mouth. To the extent that the order prohibited the reporting of evidence adduced at the open preliminary hearing held to determine whether the accused should be bound over for trial, it violated the settled principle that "there is nothing that proscribes the press from reporting events that transpire in the courtroom," *Sheppard v. Maxwell*, and the portion of the order restraining publication of other facts "strongly implicative" of the accused is too vague and too broad to survive the scrutiny given to restraints on First Amendment rights.

C Reversed.

Alexander v. United States

509 U.S. 544 (1993)

FACTS

After a full criminal trial, petitioner, the owner of numerous businesses dealing in sexually explicit materials, was convicted of, inter alia, violating federal obscenity laws and the Racketeer Influenced and Corrupt Organizations Act (RICO). The obscenity convictions, based on a finding that seven items sold at several stores were obscene, were the predicates for his RICO convictions. In addition to imposing a prison term and fine, the District Court ordered petitioner, as punishment for the RICO violations, to forfeit his businesses and almost $9 million acquired through racketeering activity. In affirming the forfeiture order, the Court of Appeals rejected petitioner's arguments that RICO's forfeiture provisions constitute a prior restraint on speech and are overbroad. The court also held that the forfeiture did not violate the Eighth Amendment, concluding that proportionality review is not required of any sentence less than life imprisonment without the possibility of parole. It did not consider whether the forfeiture was disproportionate or "excessive."

I Is a seizure of a business convicted of obscenity violations considered a prior restraint and, thus, unconstitutional?

R A seizure of a business convicted of obscenity violations is not considered a prior restraint and, thus, is not unconstitutional.

A RICO's forfeiture provisions, as applied here, did not violate the First Amendment. The forfeiture here is a permissible criminal punishment, not a prior restraint on speech. The distinction between prior restraints and subsequent punishments is solidly grounded in this Court's cases. The term "prior restraint" describes orders forbidding certain communications that are issued before the communications occur. However, the order here imposes no legal impediment to petitioner's ability to engage in any expressive activity; it just prevents him from financing those activities with assets derived from his prior racketeering offenses. RICO is oblivious to the expressive or non-expressive nature of the assets forfeited. Petitioner's assets were forfeited because they were directly related to past racketeering violations, and thus they differ from material seized or restrained on suspicion of being obscene without a prior judicial obscenity determination, as occurred in, e.g., *Marcus v. Search Warrant*. Nor were his assets ordered forfeited without the requisite procedural safeguards. His claim is also inconsistent with *Arcara v. Cloud Books, Inc.*, in which the Court rejected a claim that the closure of an adult bookstore under a general nuisance statute was an improper prior restraint. His definition of prior restraint also would undermine the time-honored distinction between barring future speech and penalizing past speech. Since the RICO statute does not criminalize constitutionally protected speech, it is materially different from the statutes at issue in this Court's overbreadth cases. In addition, the threat of forfeiture has no more of a "chilling" effect on free expression than threats of a prison term or large fine, which are constitutional under *Fort Wayne Books*. Nor can the forfeiture be said to offend the First Amendment based on

Alexander v. United States

509 U.S. 544 (1993)

Arcara's analysis that criminal sanctions with some incidental effect on First Amendment activities are subject to First Amendment scrutiny where it was the expressive conduct that drew the legal remedy. While the conduct drawing the legal remedy here may have been expressive, "obscenity" can be regulated or actually proscribed consistent with the Amendment. The case is remanded for the Court of Appeals to consider petitioner's claim that the forfeiture, considered atop his prison term and fine, is "excessive" within the meaning of the Excessive Fines Clause of the Eighth Amendment. The Court of Appeals rejected petitioner's Eighth Amendment challenge with a statement that applies only to the Amendment's prohibition against "cruel and unusual punishments." The Excessive Fines Clause limits the Government's power to extract payments as punishment for an offense, and the *in personam* criminal forfeiture at issue here is clearly a form of monetary punishment no different, for Eighth Amendment purposes, from a traditional "fine." The question whether or not the forfeiture was excessive must be considered in light of the extensive criminal activities that petitioner apparently conducted through his enormous racketeering enterprise over a substantial period of time, rather than the number of materials actually found to be obscene.

C

Vacated and remanded.

Watchtower v. Village of Stratton

536 U.S. 150 (2002)

FACTS

Respondent Village of Stratton (Village) promulgated an ordinance that, *inter alia,* prohibits "canvassers" from "going in and upon" private residential property to promote any "cause" without first obtaining a permit from the mayor's office by completing and signing a registration form. Petitioners, a society and a congregation of Jehovah's Witnesses that publish and distribute religious materials, brought this action for injunctive relief, alleging that the ordinance violates their First Amendment rights to the free exercise of religion, free speech, and freedom of the press. The District Court upheld most provisions of the ordinance as valid, content-neutral regulations, although it did require the Village to accept narrowing constructions of several provisions. The Sixth Circuit affirmed. Among its rulings, that court held that the ordinance was content neutral and of general applicability and therefore subject to intermediate scrutiny; rejected petitioners' argument that the ordinance is overbroad because it impairs the right to distribute pamphlets anonymously that was recognized in *McIntyre* v. *Ohio Elections Comm'n,* concluded that the Village's interests in protecting its residents from fraud and undue annoyance and its desire to prevent criminals from posing as canvassers in order to defraud its residents were sufficient bases on which to justify the regulation; and distinguished this Court's earlier cases protecting the Jehovah's Witnesses ministry.

I Does the ordinance's provisions making it a misdemeanor to engage in door-to-door advocacy without first registering with the mayor and receiving a permit violate the First Amendment as it applies to religious proselytizing, anonymous political speech, and the distribution of handbills?

R The ordinance's provisions making it a misdemeanor to engage in door-to-door advocacy without first registering with the mayor and receiving a permit violate the First Amendment as it applies to religious proselytizing, anonymous political speech, and the distribution of handbills.

A For over 50 years, this Court has invalidated on First Amendment grounds restrictions on door-to-door canvassing and pamphleteering by Jehovah's Witnesses. Although those cases do not directly control the question at issue, they yield several themes that guide the Court. Among other things, those cases emphasize that the hand distribution of religious tracts is ages old and has the same claim as more orthodox practices to the guarantees of freedom of religion, speech, and press, discuss extensively the historical importance of door-to-door canvassing and pamphleteering as vehicles for the dissemination of ideas, but recognize the legitimate interests a town may have in some form of regulation, particularly when the solicitation of money is involved, or the prevention of burglary is a legitimate concern, make clear that there must be a balance between such interests and the effect of the regulations on First Amendment rights; and demonstrate that the Jehovah's Witnesses have not struggled for their rights alone, but for those many who are poorly financed and rely extensively upon this method of communication, including nonreligious groups and individuals. The Court need not resolve the parties' dispute as to what standard of review to use here because the breadth of speech affected by the ordinance and the nature of the regulation make it clear that the Sixth Circuit erred in upholding it. There is no doubt that the interests the ordinance assertedly serves - the prevention of fraud and crime and the protection of residents' privacy - are important and that the Village may seek to safeguard them through some form of regulation of solicitation activity. However, the amount of speech covered by the ordinance raises serious concerns. Had its provisions been construed to apply only to commercial activities and the solicitation of funds, arguably the ordinance would have been tailored to the Village's interest in protecting its residents' privacy and preventing fraud. Yet, the Village's administration of its ordinance unquestionably demonstrates that it applies to a significant number of noncommercial "canvassers" promoting a wide variety of "causes." The pernicious effect of the permit requirement is illustrated by, *e.g.*, the requirement that a canvasser be identified in a permit application filed in the mayor's office and made available for public inspection, which necessarily results in a surrender of the anonymity this Court has protected. Also central to the Court's conclusion that the ordinance does not pass First Amendment scrutiny is that it is not tailored to the Village's stated interests. Even if the interest in preventing fraud could adequately support the ordinance insofar as it applies to commercial transactions and the solicitation of funds, that interest provides no support for its application to petitioners, to political campaigns, or to enlisting support for unpopular causes. The Village's argument that the ordinance is nonetheless valid because it serves the two additional interests of protecting residents' privacy and the prevention of crime is unpersuasive. As to the former, an unchallenged ordinance section authorizing residents to post "No Solicitation" signs, coupled with their unquestioned right to refuse to engage in conversation with unwelcome visitors, provides ample protection for unwilling listeners. As to the latter, it seems unlikely that the lack of a permit would preclude criminals from knocking on doors and engaging in conversations not covered by the ordinance, and, in any event, there is no evidence in the record of a special crime problem related to door-to-door solicitation.

C Reversed and remanded.

Thomas and Windy City Hemp Dev. Board v. Chicago Park District 534 U.S. 316 (2002)

FACTS

Respondent Chicago Park District adopted an ordinance requiring individuals to obtain a permit before conducting large-scale events in public parks. The ordinance provides that the Park District may deny a permit on any of 13 specified grounds, must process applications within 28 days, and must explain its reasons for a denial. An unsuccessful applicant may appeal, first, to the Park District's general superintendent and then to state court. Petitioners, dissatisfied that the Park District has denied some, though not all, of their applications for permits to hold rallies advocating the legalization of marijuana, filed a 42 U. S. C. §1983 suit, alleging, *inter alia,* that the ordinance is unconstitutional on its face. The District Court granted the Park District summary judgment, and the Seventh Circuit affirmed.

I

Is an ordinance requiring individuals to obtain a permit before conducting large-scale events in public parks violative of the First Amendment?

R

An ordinance requiring individuals to obtain a permit before conducting large-scale events in public parks is not violative of the First Amendment so long as it is based upon a content-neutral permit scheme regulating such uses.

A

A content-neutral permit scheme regulating uses (including speech uses) of a public forum need not contain the procedural safeguards described in *Freedman* v. *Maryland. Freedman* is inapposite because, unlike the motion picture censorship scheme in that case, the Park District's ordinance is not subject-matter censorship but content-neutral time, place, and manner regulation of the use of a public forum. None of the grounds for denying a permit has anything to do with the content of speech. Indeed, the ordinance is not directed at communicative activity as such, but to all activity in a public park. Its object is not to exclude particular communication, but to coordinate multiple uses of limited space; assure preservation of park facilities; prevent dangerous, unlawful, or impermissible uses; and assure financial accountability for damage caused by an event. A content-neutral time, place, and manner regulation can be applied in such a manner as to stifle free expression. It thus must contain adequate standards to guide an official's decision and render that decision subject to effective judicial review. The Park District's ordinance meets this test. That the ordinance describes grounds on which the Park District "may" deny a permit does not mean that it allows the Park District to waive requirements for some favored speakers. Such a waiver would be unconstitutional, but this abuse must be dealt with if and when a pattern of unlawful favoritism appears, rather than by insisting upon a rigid, no-waiver application of the permit requirements.

C

Affirmed.

City of Littleton v. Z.J. Gifts D-4 LLC

514 U.S. 774 (2004)

FACTS

Under petitioner city's "adult business license" ordinance, the city's decision to deny a license may be appealed to the state district court pursuant to Colorado Rules of Civil Procedure. Respondent Z. J. Gifts D-4, L. L. C. (hereinafter ZJ), opened an adult bookstore in a place not zoned for adult businesses. Instead of applying for a license, ZJ filed suit attacking the ordinance as facially unconstitutional. The Federal District Court rejected ZJ's claims, but the Tenth Circuit held, as relevant here, that state law does not assure the constitutionally required "prompt final judicial *decision*."

I

Does the ordinance meet the First Amendment's requirement that such a licensing scheme assure prompt judicial review of an administrative decision denying a license?

R

The ordinance meets the First Amendment's requirement that such a licensing scheme assure prompt judicial review of an administrative decision denying a license.

A

The Court rejects the city's claim that its licensing scheme need only provide prompt access to judicial review, but not a "prompt judicial determination," of an applicant's legal claim. The city concedes that *Freedman* v. *Maryland,* in listing constitutionally necessary "safeguards" applicable to a motion picture censorship statute, spoke of the need to assure a "prompt final judicial decision," but adds that *Justice* O'C*onnor*'s controlling plurality opinion in *FW/PBS, Inc.* v. *Dallas,* which addressed an adult business licensing scheme, did not use the word "decision," instead speaking only of the "*possibility of prompt judicial review.*" *Justice* O'C*onnor*'s *FW/PBS* opinion, however, points out that *Freedman*'s "judicial review" safeguard is meant to prevent "undue delay," which includes *judicial*, as well as *administrative,* delay. A delay in issuing a judicial decision, no less than a delay in obtaining access to a court, can prevent a license from being "issued within a reasonable period of time." However, the Court accepts the city's claim that Colorado law satisfies any "prompt judicial determination" requirement, agreeing that the Court should modify *FW/PBS,* withdrawing its implication that *Freedman*'s special judicial review rules - *e.g.*, strict time limits - apply in this case. Colorado's ordinary "judicial review" rules suffice to assure a prompt judicial *decision,* as long as the courts remain sensitive to the need to prevent First Amendment harms and administer those procedures accordingly. Whether the courts do so is a matter normally fit for case-by-case determination rather than a facial challenge. Four considerations support this conclusion. First, ordinary court procedural rules and practices give reviewing courts judicial tools sufficient to avoid delay-related First Amendment harm. Indeed, courts may arrange their schedules to "accelerate" proceedings, and higher courts may grant expedited review. Second, there is no reason to doubt state judges' willingness to exercise these powers wisely so as to avoid serious threats of delay-induced First Amendment harm. And federal remedies would provide an additional safety valve in the event of any such problem. Third, the typical First Amendment harm at issue here differs from that at issue in *Freedman*, diminishing the need in the typical case for procedural rules imposing special decisionmaking time limits.

Unlike in *Freedman*, this ordinance does not seek to *censor* material. And its licensing scheme applies reasonably objective, nondiscretionary criteria unrelated to the content of the expressive materials that an adult business may sell or display. These criteria are simple enough to apply and their application simple enough to review that their use is unlikely in practice to suppress totally any specific item of adult material in the community. And the criteria's simple objective nature means that in the ordinary case, judicial review, too, should prove simple, hence expeditious. Finally, nothing in *FW/PBS* or *Freedman* requires a city or State to place judicial review safeguards all in the city ordinance that sets forth a licensing scheme.

C Reversed.

United States v. National Treasury Employees Union

513 U.S. 454 (1995)

FACTS

The Government assessed a tax against Jerrold Rabin and placed a lien on all of his property, including his interest in the home he jointly owned with respondent Lori Williams, his then-wife. Before the Government recorded its lien, Rabin transferred his interest in the home to Williams, as part of a division of assets in contemplation of divorce. Although Williams was not personally liable for the tax, she paid it under protest to remove the lien and sued for a refund under 28 U.S.C. 1346(a)(1), which waives the Government's sovereign immunity from suit in "[a]ny civil action . . . for the recovery of any internal-revenue tax alleged to have been erroneously or illegally assessed or collected." The Government responded that it was irrelevant whether the Government had a right to Williams' money because she lacked standing to seek a refund under 1346(a)(1). According to the Government, that provision authorizes refund actions only by the assessed party, i.e., Rabin. The District Court accepted this jurisdictional argument, but the Court of Appeals reversed.

I

Does a law barring federal employees from being paid for speech violate the First Amendment?

R

Legislation which forbids payment for certain speech implicates the First Amendment.

A

Section 1346(a)(1) authorizes a refund suit by a party who, though not assessed a tax, paid the tax under protest to remove a federal tax lien from her property. Williams' plea falls squarely within 1346(a)(1)'s broad and unequivocal language authorizing suit for "any . . . tax .... erroneously . . . collected." The Government's strained reliance on the interaction of three other provisions to narrow 1346(a)(1)'s waiver of sovereign immunity is rejected. The Government argues: Under 26 U.S.C. 7422, a party may not bring a refund action without first exhausting administrative remedies; under 26 U.S.C. 6511, only a "taxpayer" may Page II exhaust; under 26 U.S.C. 7701(a)(14), Williams is not a taxpayer. The Government's argument fails at two statutory junctures. First, the word "taxpayer" in 6511(a) - the provision governing administrative claims cannot bear the weight the Government puts on it. This provision's plain terms provide only a deadline for filing for administrative relief, not a limit on who may file. Further, the Government's claim that Williams is not at this point a "taxpayer" is unpersuasive. In placing a lien on her home and then accepting the tax payment she made under protest, the Government surely subjected Williams to a tax, even though she was not the assessed party. The Government's strained reading of 1346(a)(1) would leave people in Williams' position without a remedy. This consequence reinforces the conclusion that Congress did not intend refund actions under 1346(a)(1) to be unavailable to persons situated as Lori Williams is. Though the Government points to the levy, quiet-title, and separate-fund remedies authorized by 26 U.S.C. 7426, 28 U.S.C. 2410(a) (12), and 26 U.S.C. 6325(b)(3), respectively, none of those realistically would be available to Williams or others in her situation. Moreover, because those remedies offer pre-deprivation relief, they do not become superfluous if some third party suits are authorized by 1346(a)(1), a post-deprivation remedy available only if the taxpayer has paid the Government in full. The principle, on which the Government relies, that parties generally may not challenge the tax liabilities of others, is not unyielding. The burden on that principle is mitigated here because Williams' main challenge is to the existence of a lien against her property, rather than to the underlying assessment on her husband. Moreover, the Government's forecast that allowing her to sue will lead to rampant abuse by parties volunteering to pay others' taxes seems implausible. In any event, the disposition herein does not address the circumstances, if any, under which a party who volunteers to pay a tax assessed against someone else may seek a refund under 1346(a).

C

Affirmed.

West Virginia State Board of Education v. Barnette

319 U.S. 624 (1943)

FACTS

Following the decision by this Court on June 3, 1940, in *Minersville School District v. Gobitis*, the West Virginia legislature amended its statutes to require all schools therein to conduct courses of instruction in history, civics, and in the Constitutions of the United States and of the State 'for the purpose of teaching, fostering and perpetuating the ideals, principles and spirit of Americanism, and increasing the knowledge of the organization and machinery of the government.' Appellant Board of Education was directed, with advice of the State Superintendent of Schools, to 'prescribe the courses of study covering these subjects' for public schools. The Act made it the duty of private, parochial and denominational schools to prescribe courses of study 'similar to those required for the public schools.' The Board of Education on January 9, 1942, adopted a resolution containing recitals taken largely from the Court's *Gobitis* opinion and ordering that the salute to the flag become 'a regular part of the program of activities in the public schools,' that all teachers and pupils 'shall be required to participate in the salute honoring the Nation represented by the Flag; provided, however, that refusal to salute the Flag be regarded as an Act of insubordination, and shall be dealt with accordingly.' The resolution originally required the 'commonly accepted salute to the Flag' which it defined. Objections to the salute as 'being too much like Hitler's' were raised by the Parent and Teachers Association, the Boy and Girl Scouts, the Red Cross, and the Federation of Women's Clubs. Some modification appears to have been made in deference to these objections, but no concession was made to Jehovah's Witnesses. What is now required is the 'stiff-arm' salute, the saluter to keep the right hand raised with palm turned up while the following is repeated: 'I pledge allegiance to the Flag of the United States of America and to the Republic for which it stands; one Nation, indivisible, with liberty and justice for all.' Failure to conform is 'insubordination' dealt with by expulsion. Readmission is denied by statute until compliance. Meanwhile the expelled child is 'unlawfully absent' and may be proceeded against as a delinquent. His parents or guardians are liable to prosecution, and if convicted are subject to fine not exceeding $50 and jail term not exceeding thirty days. Appellees, citizens of the United States and of West Virginia, brought suit in the United States District Court for themselves and others similarly situated asking its injunction to restrain enforcement of these laws and regulations against Jehovah's Witnesses. The Board of Education moved to dismiss the complaint alleging that the law and regulations are an unconstitutional denial of religious freedom and of freedom of speech, and are invalid under the 'due process' and 'equal protection' clauses of the 14th Amendment to the Federal Constitution. The cause was submitted on the pleadings to a District Court of three judges. It restrained enforcement as to the plaintiffs and those of that class. The case comes to the U.S. Supreme Court by direct appeal.

I May a state require school personnel to salute the American flag?

R The government cannot compel silence or speech, verbal or symbolic, expect to prevent a "clear and present danger."

West Virginia State Board of Education v. Barnette

319 U.S. 624 (1943)

A If there is any fixed star in our constitutional constellation, it is that no official, high or petty, can prescribe what shall be orthodox in politics, nationalism, religion, or other matters of opinion or force citizens to confess by word or act their faith therein. If there are any circumstances which permit an exception, they do not now occur to us. We think the action of the local authorities in compelling the flag salute and pledge transcends constitutional limitations on their power and invades the sphere of intellect and spirit which it is the purpose of the First Amendment to our Constitution to reserve from all official control. The decision of this Court in *Minersville School District v. Gobitis* and the holdings of those few *per curiam* decisions which preceded and foreshadowed it are overruled, and the judgment enjoining enforcement of the West Virginia Regulation is affirmed.

C Affirmed.

McIntyre v. Ohio Elections Comm.

514 U.S. 334 (1995)

FACTS

After petitioner's decedent distributed leaflets purporting to express the views of "CONCERNED PARENTS AND TAX PAYERS" opposing a proposed school tax levy, she was fined by respondent for violating 3599.09(A) of the Ohio Code, which prohibits the distribution of campaign literature that does not contain the name and address of the person or campaign official issuing the literature. The Court of Common Pleas reversed, but the Ohio Court of Appeals reinstated the fine. In affirming, the State Supreme Court held that the burdens 3599.09(A) imposed on voters' First Amendment rights were "reasonable and "nondiscriminatory" and therefore valid. Declaring that 3599.09(A) is intended to identify persons who distribute campaign materials containing fraud, libel, or false advertising and to provide voters with a mechanism for evaluating such materials, the court distinguished *Talley v. California*, in which this Court invalidated an ordinance prohibiting all anonymous leafleting.

I

Is a law banning anonymous communications in connection with elections consistent with, or violative of, the First Amendment?

R

The government cannot compel anonymous speakers to reveal their identities.

A

Section 3599.09(A)'s prohibition of the distribution of anonymous campaign literature abridges the freedom of speech in violation of the First Amendment. The freedom to publish anonymously is protected by the First Amendment, and, as Talley indicates, extends beyond the literary realm to the advocacy of political causes. This Court's precedents make abundantly clear that the Ohio Supreme Court's reasonableness standard is significantly more lenient than is appropriate in a case of this kind. Although Talley concerned a different limitation than 3599.09(A) and thus does not necessarily control here, the First Amendment's protection of anonymity nevertheless applies. Section 3599.09(A) is not simply an Page II election code provision subject to the "ordinary litigation" test set forth in *Anderson v. Celebrezze*, and similar cases. Rather, it is a regulation of core political speech. Moreover, the category of documents it covers is defined by their content - only those publications containing speech designed to influence the voters in an election need bear the required information. When a law burdens such speech, the Court applies "exacting scrutiny," upholding the restriction only if it is narrowly tailored to serve an overriding state interest. Section 3599.09(A)'s anonymous speech ban is not justified by Ohio's asserted interests in preventing fraudulent and libelous statements and in providing the electorate with relevant information. The claimed informational interest is plainly insufficient to support the statute's disclosure requirement, since the speaker's identity is no different from other components of a document's contents that the author is free to include or exclude, and the author's name and address add little to the reader's ability to evaluate the document in the case of a handbill written by a private citizen unknown to the reader. Moreover, the state interest in preventing fraud and libel (which Ohio vindicates by means of other, more direct prohibitions) does not justify 3599.09(A)'s extremely broad prohibition of anonymous leaflets. The statute encompasses all documents, regardless of whether they are arguably false or misleading. Although a State might somehow demonstrate that its enforcement interests justify a more limited identification requirement, Ohio has not met that burden here. This Court's opinions in *Bellotti*, which commented in dicta on the prophylactic effect of requiring identification of the source of corporate campaign advertising - and *Buckley v. Valeo*, which approved mandatory disclosure of campaign-related expenditures - do not establish the constitutionality of 3599.09(A), since neither case involved a prohibition of anonymous campaign literature.

C Reversed.

Buckley v. American Constitutional Law Foundation

525 U.S. 182 (1999)

FACTS

Colorado allows its citizens to make laws directly through initiatives placed on election ballots. The complaint in this federal action challenged six of the State's many controls on the initiative-petition process. Plaintiffs-respondents, the American Constitutional Law Foundation, Inc., and several individuals (collectively, ACLF), charged that the following prescriptions of Colorado's law governing initiative petitions violate the First Amendment's freedom of speech guarantee: (1) the requirement that petition circulators be at least 18 years old, Colo. Rev. Stat. §1-40-112(1); (2) the further requirement that they be registered voters; (3) the limitation of the petition circulation period to six months, §1-40-108; (4) the requirement that petition circulators wear identification badges stating their names, their status as "VOLUNTEER" or "PAID," and if the latter, the name and telephone number of their employer, §1-40-112(2); (5) the requirement that circulators attach to each petition section an affidavit containing, *inter alia* , the circulator's name and address, §1-40-111(2); and (6) the requirements that initiative proponents disclose (a) at the time they file their petition, the name, address, and county of voter registration of all paid circulators, the amount of money proponents paid per petition signature, and the total amount paid to each circulator, and (b) on a monthly basis, the names of the proponents, the name and address of each paid circulator, the name of the proposed ballot measure, and the amount of money paid and owed to each circulator during the month, §1-40-121. The District Court struck down the badge requirement and portions of the disclosure requirements, but upheld the age, affidavit, and registration requirements, and the six-month limit on petition circulation. The Tenth Circuit affirmed in part and reversed in part. That court properly sought guidance from this Court's recent decisions on ballot access and on hand-bill distribution. The Tenth Circuit upheld, as reasonable regulations of the ballot-initiative process, the age restriction, the six-month limit on petition circulation, and the affidavit requirement. The court struck down the requirement that petition circulators be registered voters, and also held portions of the badge and disclosure requirements invalid as trenching unnecessarily and improperly on political expression.

I

Can the government require electioneers to wear name badges and disclose their identities?

R

The government cannot compel electioneers to reveal their identities by requiring name badges or mandatory disclosure.

A

The Tenth Circuit correctly separated necessary or proper ballot access controls from restrictions that unjustifiably inhibit the circulation of ballot-initiative petitions. States have considerable leeway to protect the integrity and reliability of the ballot-initiative process, as they have with respect to election processes generally. The Court is satisfied that, as in *Meyer*, the restrictions in question significantly inhibit communication with voters about proposed political change, and are not warranted by the state interests (administrative efficiency, fraud detection, informing voters) alleged to justify those restrictions. This judgment is informed by other means Colorado employs to accomplish its regulatory purposes. Beyond question, Colorado's registration requirement drastically reduces the number of persons, both volunteer and paid, available to circulate petitions. That requirement produces a speech diminution of the very kind produced by the ban on paid circulators at issue in *Meyer.* The ease with which qualified voters may register to vote does not lift the burden on speech at petition circulation time. The Tenth Circuit held the badge requirement invalid insofar as it requires circulators to display their names. The District Court found from evidence ACLF presented that compelling circulators to wear identification badges inhibits participation in the petitioning process. Colorado's interest in enabling the public to identify, and the State to apprehend, petition circulators who engage in misconduct is addressed by the requirement that circulators disclose their names and addresses on affidavits submitted with each petition section. Unlike a name badge worn at the time a circulator is soliciting signatures, the affidavit is separated from the moment the circulator speaks, when reaction to the message is immediate and may be the most intense, emotional, and unreasoned. Because the badge requirement compels personal name identification at the precise moment when the circulator's interest in anonymity is greatest, it does not qualify for inclusion among "the more limited [election process] identification requirement[s]" to which this Court alluded in *McIntyre.* Like the Tenth Circuit, this Court expresses no opinion on the constitutionality of the additional requirements that the badge disclose whether the circulator is paid or volunteer, and if paid, by whom. The Tenth Circuit invalidated the requirement that ballot-initiative proponents file a final report when the initiative petition is submitted insofar as that requirement compels disclosure of each paid circulator by name and address, and the total amount paid to each circulator. In ruling on these disclosure requirements, the Court of Appeals looked primarily to this Court's decision in *Buckley v. Valeo.* In *Buckley*, the Court stated that "exacting scrutiny" is necessary when compelled disclosure of campaign-related payments is at issue, but nevertheless upheld, as substantially related to important governmental interests, the reporting and disclosure provisions of the Federal Election Campaign Act of 1971. Disclosure of the names of initiative sponsors, and the amounts they have spent to gather support for their initiatives, responds to Colorado's substantial interest in controlling domination of the initiative process by affluent special interest groups. This Court expresses no opinion whether other monthly report prescriptions regarding which the Tenth Circuit identified no infirmity would, standing alone, survive review. Through less problematic measures, Colorado can and does meet the State's substantial interest in regulating the ballot-initiative process. To deter fraud and diminish corruption, Colorado retains an arsenal of safeguards. To inform the public about the source of funding for ballot initiatives, the State legitimately requires sponsors of ballot initiatives to disclose who pays petition circulators, and how much..

C

Affirmed.

Rust v. Sullivan

500 U.S. 173 (1991)

FACTS

Section 1008 of the Public Health Service Act specifies that none of the federal funds appropriated under the Act's Title X for family-planning services "shall be used in programs where abortion is a method of family planning." In 1988, respondent Secretary of Health and Human Services issued new regulations that, inter alia, prohibit Title X projects from engaging in counseling concerning, referrals for, and activities advocating abortion as a method of family planning, and require such projects to maintain an objective integrity and independence from the prohibited abortion activities by the use of separate facilities, personnel, and accounting records. Before the regulations could be applied, petitioners - Title X grantees and doctors who supervise Title X funds - filed suits, which were consolidated, challenging the regulations' facial validity and seeking declaratory and injunctive relief to prevent their implementation. In affirming the District Court's grant of summary judgment to the Secretary, the Court of Appeals held that the regulations were a permissible construction of the statute and consistent with the First and Fifth Amendments.

I Can the government fund a program providing family planning services but disallow recipients from making abortion-related speeches?

R The government may selectively fund programs which support certain activities with funding alternative approaches.

A The regulations are a permissible construction of Title X. Because 1008 is ambiguous, in that it does not speak directly to the issues of abortion counseling, referral, and advocacy, or to "program integrity," the Secretary's construction must be accorded substantial deference as the interpretation of the agency charged with administering the statute, and may not be disturbed as an abuse of discretion if it reflects a plausible construction of the statute's plain language and does not otherwise conflict with Congress' expressed intent. Title X's broad language plainly allows the abortion counseling, referral, and advocacy regulations. Since the Title neither defines 1008's "method of family planning" phrase nor enumerates what types of medical and counseling services are entitled to funding, it cannot be said that the Secretary's construction of the 1008 prohibition to require a ban on such activities within Title X projects is impermissible. Moreover, since the legislative history is ambiguous as to Congress' intent on these issues, this Court will defer to the Secretary's expertise. The Secretary's view, that the requirements are necessary to ensure that Title X grantees apply federal funds only to authorized purposes and avoid creating the appearance of governmental support for abortion-related activities, is not unreasonable in light of 1008's express prohibitory language and is entitled to deference. Petitioners' contention is unpersuasive that the requirements frustrate Congress' intent, clearly expressed in the Act and the legislative history, that Title X programs be an integral part of a broader, comprehensive, health care system that envisions the efficient use of non-Title X funds. The statements relied on are highly generalized and do not directly address the scope of

1008 and, therefore, cannot form the basis for enjoining the regulations. The regulations do not violate the First Amendment free speech rights of private Title X fund recipients, their staffs, or their patients by impermissibly imposing viewpoint-discriminatory conditions on Government subsidies. There is no question but that 1008's prohibition is constitutional, since the Government may make a value judgment favoring childbirth over abortion, and implement that judgment by the allocation of public funds. In so doing, the Government has not discriminated on the basis of viewpoint; it has merely chosen to fund one activity to the exclusion of another. Similarly, in implementing the statutory prohibition by forbidding counseling, referral, and the provision of information regarding abortion as a method of family planning, the regulations simply ensure that appropriated funds are not used for activities, including speech, that are outside the federal program's scope. Although it could be argued that the traditional doctor-patient relationship should enjoy First Amendment protection from Government regulation, even when subsidized by the Government that question need not be resolved here, since the Title X program regulations do not significantly impinge on the doctor-patient relationship. The regulations do not violate a woman's Fifth Amendment right to choose whether to terminate her pregnancy. The Government has no constitutional duty to subsidize an activity merely because it is constitutionally protected, and may validly choose to allocate public funds for medical services relating to childbirth but not to abortion. That allocation places no governmental obstacle in the path of a woman wishing to terminate her pregnancy, and leaves her with the same choices as if the Government had chosen not to fund family planning services at all. Nor do the regulations place restrictions on the patient-doctor dialogue which violate a woman's right to make an informed and voluntary choice under *Akron v. Akron Center for Reproductive Health, Inc.* and *Thornburgh v. American College of Obstetricians and Gynecologists*. Unlike the laws invalidated in those cases, which required all doctors to provide all pregnant patients contemplating abortion with specific antiabortion information, here, a doctor's ability to provide, and a woman's right to receive, abortion-related information remains unfettered outside the context of the Title X project. The fact that most Title X clients may be effectively precluded by indigency from seeing a health care provider for abortion-related services does not affect the outcome here, since the financial constraints on such a woman's ability to enjoy the full range of constitutionally protected freedom of choice are the product not of governmental restrictions, but of her indigency.

C Affirmed.

Legal Services Corp. v. Velazquez

531 U.S. 533 (2001)

FACTS

The Legal Services Corporation Act authorizes petitioner Legal Services Corporation (LSC) to distribute funds appropriated by Congress to local grantee organizations providing free legal assistance to indigent clients in, *inter alia,* welfare benefits claims. In every annual appropriations Act since 1996, Congress has prohibited LSC funding of any organization that represented clients in an effort to amend or otherwise challenge existing welfare law. Grantees cannot continue representation in a welfare matter even where a constitutional or statutory validity challenge becomes apparent after representation is well under way. Respondents - lawyers employed by LSC grantees, together with others - filed suit to declare, *inter alia,* the restriction invalid. The District Court denied them a preliminary injunction, but the Second Circuit invalidated the restriction, finding it impermissible viewpoint discrimination that violated the First Amendment.

I

Does a funding restriction, which prohibits LSC funding of any organization that represented clients in an effort to amend or otherwise challenge existing welfare law, violate the First Amendment?

R

The funding restriction violates the First Amendment; the LSC Act funds constitutionally protected expression.

A

The funding restriction violates the First Amendment. LSC and the Government, also a petitioner, claim that *Rust* v. *Sullivan,* in which this Court upheld a restriction prohibiting doctors employed by federally funded family planning clinics from discussing abortion with their patients, supports the restriction here. However, the Court has since explained that the *Rust* counseling activities amounted to governmental speech, sustaining viewpoint-based funding decisions in instances in which the government is itself the speaker, or instances, like *Rust,* in which the government uses private speakers to transmit information pertaining to its own program, *Rosenberger* v. *Rector and Visitors of Univ. of Va.* Although the government has the latitude to ensure that its own message is being delivered, neither that latitude nor its rationale applies to subsidies for private speech in every instance. Like the *Rosenberger* program, the LSC program was designed to facilitate private speech, not to promote a governmental message. An LSC attorney speaks on behalf of a private, indigent client in a welfare benefits claim, while the Government's message is delivered by the attorney defending the benefits decision. The attorney's advice to the client and advocacy to the courts cannot be classified as governmental speech even under a generous understanding of that concept. In this vital respect this suit is distinguishable from *Rust.* The private nature of the instant speech and the extent of LSC's regulation of private expression are indicated further by the circumstance that the Government seeks to control an existing medium of expression in ways which distort its usual functioning. Cases involving a limited forum, though not controlling, provide instruction for evaluating restrictions in governmental subsidies. Here the program presumes that private, nongovernmental speech is necessary, and a substantial restriction is placed upon that speech. By providing subsidies to LSC, the Government seeks to facilitate suits for benefits by using the State and Federal Judiciaries and the independent bar on which they depend for the proper performance of their duties and responsibilities. Restricting LSC attorneys in advising their clients and in presenting arguments and analyses to the courts distorts the legal system by altering the attorneys' traditional role in much the same way broadcast systems or student publication networks were changed in the limited forum cases of *Arkansas Ed. Television Comm'n* v. *Forbes,* and *Rosenberger* v. *Rector and Visitors of Univ. of Va., supra.* The Government may not design a subsidy to effect such a serious and fundamental restriction on the advocacy of attorneys and the functioning of the judiciary. An informed, independent judiciary presumes an informed, independent bar. However, the instant restriction prevents LSC attorneys from advising the courts of serious statutory validity questions. It also threatens severe impairment of the judicial function by sifting out cases presenting constitutional challenges in order to insulate the Government's laws from judicial inquiry. The result of this restriction would be two tiers of cases. There would be lingering doubt whether an LSC attorney's truncated representation had resulted in complete analysis of the case, full advice to the client, and proper presentation to the court; and the courts and the public would come to question the adequacy and fairness of professional representations when the attorney avoided all reference to statutory validity and constitutional authority questions. A scheme so inconsistent with accepted separation-of-powers principles is an insufficient basis to sustain or uphold the restriction on speech. That LSC attorneys can withdraw does not make the restriction harmless, for the statute is an attempt to draw lines around the LSC program to exclude from litigation arguments and theories Congress finds unacceptable but which by their nature are within the courts' province to consider. The restriction is even more problematic because in cases where the attorney withdraws, the indigent client is unlikely to find other counsel. There may be no alternative source of vital information on the client's constitutional or statutory rights, in stark contrast to *Rust,* where a patient could receive both governmentally subsidized counseling and consultation with independent or affiliate organizations. Finally, notwithstanding Congress' purpose to confine and limit its program, the restriction insulates current welfare laws from constitutional scrutiny and certain other legal challenges, a condition implicating central First Amendment concerns. There can be little doubt that the LSC Act funds constitutionally protected expression; and there is no programmatic message of the kind recognized in *Rust* and which sufficed there to allow the Government to specify the advice deemed necessary for its legitimate objectives. The Court of Appeals concluded that the funding restriction could be severed from the statute, leaving the remaining portions operative. Because that determination was not contested here, the Court in the exercise of its discretion and prudential judgment declines to address it.

C Affirmed.

Schenck v. United States

249 U.S. 47 (1919)

FACTS

This is an indictment in three counts. The first two counts charged Defendant Schenck with conspiracy to cause insubordination by circulating anti-conscription leaflets and conspiracy to use the postal service in such a way to violate the 1917 Espionage Act. The third count charged an unlawful use of the mail systems in violation of the Act. It is argued that the evidence, if admissible, was not sufficient to prove that the defendant Schenck was involved with the sending of the documents. According to the testimony Schenck said he was general secretary of the Socialist party and had charge of the Socialist headquarters from which the documents were sent. The circular, which Schenck distributed, stated that the Conscription Act violated the principles of the 13th Amendment. It intimated that the draft was tyranny in its worse form, and compared draftees to convicts. Yet the flyer called only for peaceful measures. The backside of the circular was entitled "Assert Your Rights" and declared it to be a constitutional right and duty of citizens to assert their opposition to the draft. Despite raising the First Amendment as a defense, Schenck was convicted on all three counts. Schenck appealed to the United States Supreme Court.

I

Does the Constitution permit punishment of speech?

R

The Constitution allows for the punishment of speech when the words uttered are used to create a clear and present danger and will bring about the type of evil that Congress has a right to prevent.

A

The Constitution allows for the punishment of speech when the words uttered are used to create a clear and present danger and will bring about the type of evil that Congress has a right to prevent. Schenck sent the document intending it to have a specific effect. As such, the only reasonable substantive effect the flyer would have on persons subject to the draft is that of influencing them to obstruct the draft. Schenck argues protection by the First Amendment even if that that was the effect of the circular. While this may be true in some cases involving free speech, the character of every act depends is judged against the circumstances in which it is performed. The test in every case is whether the words, in the attendant circumstances, are of such a nature as to create a clear and present danger that they will bring about substantive evils. Here, such words during peacetime may be permissible but during wartime may hinder to our nation's efforts to recruit or keep those recruited in the fight during the war. Such words cannot be protected as a constitutional right.

C

Affirmed.

Frohwerk v. United States

249 U.S. 204 (1919)

FACTS

This is an indictment in thirteen counts. The first alleges a conspiracy between the plaintiff in error and one Carl Gleeser, they then being engaged in the preparation and publication of a newspaper, the Missouri Staats Zeitung, to violate the Espionage Act of June 15, 1917. It alleges as overt acts the preparation and circulation of twelve articles &c. in the said newspaper at different dates from July 6, 1917, to December 7 of the same year. The other counts allege attempts to cause disloyalty, mutiny and refusal of duty in the military and naval forces of the United States, by the same publications, each count being confined to the publication of a single date. Motion to dismiss and a demurrer on constitutional and other grounds especially that of the First Amendment as to free speech, were overruled, subject to exception, and the defendant refusing to plead the Court ordered a plea of not guilty to be filed. There was a trial and Frohwerk was found guilty on all the counts except the seventh, which needs no further mention. He was sentenced to a fine and to ten years imprisonment on each count, the imprisonment on the later counts to run concurrently with that on the first. Frohwerk applied to this Court for leave to file a petition for a writ of mandamus requiring the judge to sign a proper bill of exceptions, but a case was not stated that would warrant the issuing of the writ and leave was denied.

I Is an anti-draft speech, made during wartime, protected by the First Amendment?

R An anti-draft speech, made during wartime, is not protected by the First Amendment if it creates a "clear and present danger" of inciting illegal activity.

A The First Amendment does not protect such speech under the circumstances; where there is a "clear and present danger" of inciting illegal activity. It is said that the first count is bad because it does not allege the means by which the conspiracy was to be carried out. But a conspiracy to obstruct recruiting would be criminal even if no means were agreed upon specifically by which to accomplish the intent. It is enough if the parties agreed to set to work for that common purpose. That purpose could be accomplished or aided by persuasion as well as by false statements, and there was no need to allege that false reports were intended to be made or made. The conspiracy is the crime. Without pursuing the matter further we are of opinion that the indictment must stand. There is nothing before us that makes it possible to say that the judge's discretion was wrongly exercised. Upon the whole case we are driven to the conclusion that the record shows no ground upon which the judgment can be reversed.

C Judgment affirmed.

Debs v. United States

249 U.S. 211 (1919)

FACTS

This is an indictment under the Espionage Act of June 15, 1917, as amended. It has been cut down to two counts, originally the third and fourth. The former of these alleges that on or about June 16, 1918, at Canton, Ohio, the defendant caused and incited and attempted to cause and incite insubordination, disloyalty, mutiny and refusal of duty in the military and naval forces of the United States and with intent so to do delivered, to an assembly of people, a public speech, set forth. The fourth count alleges that he obstructed and attempted to obstruct the recruiting and enlistment service of the United States and to that end and with that intent delivered the same speech, again set forth. There was a demurrer to the indictment on the ground that the statute is unconstitutional as interfering with free speech, contrary to the First Amendment, and to the several counts as insufficiently stating the supposed offence. This was overruled, subject to exception. There were other exceptions to the admission of evidence with which we shall deal. The defendant was found guilty and was sentenced to ten years' imprisonment on each of the two counts, the punishment to run concurrently on both. The main theme of the speech was Socialism, its growth, and a prophecy of its ultimate success and later he expressed opposition to Prussian militarism in a way that naturally might have been thought to be intended to include the mode of proceeding in the United States.

I

Is an anti-draft speech punishable under the Espionage Act of 1917 if it was made to recently-drafted men?

R

The First Amendment does not protect speech which creates a "clear and present danger" of inciting illegal activity.

A

Without going into further particulars we are of opinion that the verdict on the fourth count, for obstructing and attempting to obstruct the recruiting service of the United States, must be sustained. Therefore it is less important to consider whether that upon the third count, for causing and attempting to cause insubordination, in the military and naval forces, is equally impregnable. The jury was instructed that for the purposes of the statute the persons designated by the Act of May 18, 1917 registered and enrolled under it, and thus subject to be called into the active service, were a part of the military forces of the United States. The Government presents a strong argument from the history of the statutes that the instruction was correct and in accordance with established legislative usage. We see no sufficient reason for differing from the conclusion but think it unnecessary to discuss the question in detail.

C

Judgment affirmed.

Abrams v. United States

250 U.S. 616 (1919)

FACTS

On a single indictment, containing four counts, the five plaintiffs in error, hereinafter designated the defendants, were convicted of conspiring to violate provisions of the Espionage Act of Congress, as amended by May 16, 1918 Act. Each of the first three counts charged the defendants with conspiring, when the United States was at war with Germany, to unlawfully utter, print, write and publish "disloyal, scurrilous and abusive language about the form of government of the United States" and "intended to bring the form of government of the United States into contempt, scorn, contumely, and disrepute" and "intended to incite, provoke and encourage resistance to the United States in said war." The charge in the fourth count was that the defendants conspired "when the United States was at war with the German Government, ... unlawfully and willfully, by utterance, writing, printing and publication to urge, incite and advocate curtailment of production of things and products, to wit, ordnance and ammunition, necessary and essential to the prosecution of the war.' The offenses were charged in the language of the act of Congress. It was charged in each count of the indictment that it was a part of the conspiracy that the defendants would attempt to accomplish their unlawful purpose by printing, writing and distributing in the city of New York many copies of a leaflet or circular, printed in English and Yiddish, copies of which, properly identified, were attached to the indictment. All of the five defendants were born in Russia. They were intelligent, had considerable schooling, and at the time they were arrested they had lived in the United States terms varying from five to ten years, but none of them had applied for naturalization. Four of them testified as witnesses in their own behalf and of these three frankly avowed that they were "rebels," "revolutionists," "anarchists," that they did not believe in government in any form, and they declared that they had no interest whatever in the government of the United States. The fourth defendant testified that he was a 'Socialist and believed in a proper kind of government, not capitalistic," but in his classification the government of the United States was "capitalistic." Under the new amendment to the Espionage Act, the Russian immigrants were convicted of intending to encourage resistance to the U.S., and conspiring to curtail the production of ammunition necessary for executing the war against Germany. The Abrams defendants appealed.

I When persons act with intent to cause an impediment in the government's prosecution of the war, will the First Amendment provide protection to them?

R The First Amendment provides no protection to those who intend to impede the government's prosecution of the war such that their punishment under the Espionage Act is constitutional under such circumstances.

A A distinction is made between disloyal and abusive language applied to the form of our government on the one hand, and language intended to bring our government into contempt and disrepute on the other. Here, it is unnecessary for us to do so for the language of these circulars was obviously intended to provoke and to encourage resistance to the United States in the war, as the defendants plainly urged and advocated a resort to a general strike of workers in ammunition factories for the purpose of curtailing the production of ordnance and munitions necessary and essential to the prosecution of the war as is charged in the fourth count. The Abrams defendants were self-described "revolutionists" and "anarchists," and must have intended the results which their acts were likely to produce, even if it was not their primary purpose. Their intent and goal was to assist the Russian revolution by distributing leaflets, the purpose of which was to excite sedition, riots and revolution in the U.S. at volatile time of war. Thus it is clear that there was a lot of persuasive evidence before the jury tending to prove that the defendants were guilty as charged with respect to all counts such that the judgment of the District Court must be affirmed.

C Affirmed.

Gitlow v. New York

268 U.S. 652 (1925)

FACTS

Benjamin Gitlow was indicted in the Supreme Court of New York, with three others, for the statutory crime of criminal anarchy under New York's Anarchy Law. He was separately tried, convicted, and sentenced to imprisonment. The judgment was affirmed by the Appellate Division and by the Court of Appeals. The case is here on writ of error to the Supreme Court, to which the record was remitted. The contention here is that the statute, by its terms and as applied in this case, violates the due process clause of the Fourteenth Amendment. The indictment was in two counts. The first charged that the defendant had advocated, advised and taught the duty, necessity and propriety of overthrowing and overturning organized government by force, violence and unlawful means, by certain writings therein set forth entitled "The Left Wing Manifesto." The second charged that he had printed, published and knowingly circulated and distributed a certain paper called "The Revolutionary Age," containing the writings set forth in the first count advocating, advising and teaching the doctrine that organized government should be overthrown by force, violence and unlawful means. At the outset of the trial the defendant's counsel objected to the introduction of any evidence under the indictment on the grounds that, as a matter of law, the Manifesto "is not in contravention of the statute," and that "the statute is in contravention of" the due process clause of the Fourteenth Amendment. This objection was denied. They also moved, at the close of the evidence, to dismiss the indictment and direct an acquittal on the grounds stated in the first objection to evidence, and again on the grounds that the indictment does not charge an offense and the evidence does not show an offense. These motions were also denied. The court, among other things, charged the jury, in substance, that they must determine what was the intent, purpose and fair meaning of the Manifesto; that its words must be taken in their ordinary meaning, as they would be understood by people whom it might reach; and that a mere statement or analysis of social and economic facts and historical incidents, but with no teaching, advice or advocacy of action, would not constitute the advocacy, advice or teaching of a doctrine for the overthrow of government within the meaning of the statute. Gitlow objected to the jury instructions, arguing the instructions lacked a requirement that the Manifesto called for *immediate* acts against the government and also argued that the New York law was inconsistent with Due Process under the 14th Amendment because the statute punishes the mere utterance of anarchy without any proof of incitement. His arguments were rejected and Gitlow was convicted. On appeal, the Court of Appeals held that the Manifesto "advocated the overthrow of this government by violence, or by unlawful means;" and both the Appellate Division and the Court of Appeals held the statute constitutional.

I Does the clear and present danger test [whether the words used are used in such circumstances and are of such a nature as to create a clear and present danger that they will bring about the substantive evils] of *Schenck v. United States* apply to state laws (New York's Anarchy Law) where the state legislature has made a determination that a certain kinds of expressions involve a punishable danger?

Gitlow v. New York

268 U.S. 652 (1925)

R The clear and present danger test does not apply to state laws.

A The statute does not penalize the utterance or publication of abstract "doctrine" or academic discussion having no quality of incitement to any concrete action. It is not aimed against mere historical or philosophical essays. It does not restrain the advocacy of changes in the form of government by constitutional and lawful means. What it prohibits is language advocating, advising or teaching the overthrow of organized government by unlawful means. These words imply urging to action. "A mere grouping of historical events and a prophetic deduction from them would neither constitute advocacy, advice or teaching of a doctrine for the overthrow of government by force, violence or unlawful means. [And] if it were a mere essay on the subject, as suggested by counsel, based upon deductions from alleged historical events, with no teaching, advice or advocacy of action, it would not constitute a violation of the statute. ..." The Manifesto, plainly, is neither the statement of abstract doctrine nor, as suggested by counsel, mere prediction that industrial disturbances and revolutionary mass strikes will result spontaneously in an inevitable process of evolution in the economic system. It advocates and urges in fervent language mass action which shall progressively foment industrial disturbances and through political mass strikes and revolutionary mass action overthrow and destroy organized parliamentary government. This is not the expression of philosophical abstraction, the mere prediction of future events; it is the language of direct incitement. The means advocated for bringing about the destruction of organized parliamentary government, namely, mass industrial revolts usurping the functions of municipal government, political mass strikes directed against the parliamentary state, and revolutionary mass action for its final destruction, necessarily imply the use of force and violence, and in their essential nature are inherently unlawful in a constitutional government of law and order. That the jury were warranted in finding that the Manifesto advocated not merely the abstract doctrine of overthrowing organized government by force, violence and unlawful means, but action to that end, is clear. For present purposes we may and do assume that freedom of speech and of the press-which are protected by the First Amendment from abridgment by Congress-are among the fundamental personal rights and 'liberties' protected by the due process clause of the Fourteenth Amendment from impairment by the States. The freedom of speech and of the press which is secured by the Constitution, does not confer an absolute right to speak or publish, without responsibility, whatever one may choose, or an unrestricted and unbridled license that gives immunity for every possible use of language and prevents the punishment of those who abuse this freedom. A State in the exercise of its police power may punish those who abuse this freedom by utterances inimical to the public welfare, tending to corrupt public morals, incite to crime, or disturb the public peace, is not open to question. By enacting the present statute, the State has determined, through its legislative body that utterances advocating the overthrow of organized government by force, violence and unlawful means, are so inimical to the general welfare and involve such danger of substantive evil that they may be penalized in the exercise of its police power. That determination must be given great weight. Every presumption is to be indulged in favor of the validity of the statute. That utterances inciting to the overthrow of organized government by unlawful means, present a sufficient danger of substantive evil to bring their punishment within the range of legislative discretion, is clear. Such utterances, by their very nature, involve danger to the public peace and to the security of the State. They threaten breaches of the peace and ultimate revolution. And the immediate danger is none the less real and substantial, because the effect of a given utterance cannot be accurately foreseen. The State cannot reasonably be required to measure the danger from every such utterance in the nice balance of a jeweler's scale. A single revolutionary spark may kindle a fire that, smoldering for a time, may burst into a sweeping and destructive conflagration. We cannot hold that the present statute is an arbitrary or unreasonable exercise of the police power of the State unwarrantably infringing the freedom of speech or press; and we must and do sustain its constitutionality. When the legislative body has determined generally, in the constitutional exercise of its discretion, that utterances of a certain kind involve such danger of substantive evil that they may be punished, the question whether any specific utterance coming within the prohibited class is likely, in and of itself, to bring about the substantive evil, is not open to consideration. It is sufficient that the statute itself be constitutional and that the use of the language comes within its prohibition. The defendant's brief does not separately discuss any of the rulings of the trial court. It is only necessary to say that, applying the general rules already stated, we find that none of them involved any invasion of the constitutional rights of the defendant. It was not necessary, within the meaning of the statute, that the defendant should have advocated 'some definite or immediate act or acts' of force, violence or unlawfulness. It was sufficient if such acts were advocated in general terms; and it was not essential that their immediate execution should have been advocated. Nor was it necessary that the language should have been 'reasonably and ordinarily calculated to incite certain persons' to acts of force, violence or unlawfulness. The advocacy need not be addressed to specific persons. Thus, the publication and circulation of a newspaper article may be an encouragement or endeavor to persuade to murder, although not addressed to any person in particular. We need not enter upon a consideration of the English common law rule of seditious libel or the Federal Sedition Act of 1798, to which reference is made in the defendant's brief. These are so unlike the present statute, that we think the decisions under them cast no helpful light upon the questions here. And finding, for the reasons stated, that the statute is not in itself unconstitutional, and that it has not been applied in the present case in derogation of any constitutional right, the judgment of the Court of Appeals is affirmed.

C

Affirmed.

Whitney v. California

274 U.S. 357 (1927)

FACTS

In 1919, Anita Whitney (defendant a/k/a plaintiff-in-error) attended a national convention of the Socialist Party as a delegate from the Oakland branch. The convention split between "radicals" and the old-line democratic socialists, the so-called "moderates." The radicals, including Whitney, formed the Communist Labor Party (CLP). Later in 1919, Whitney participated as a delegate at a convention called to organize a California unit of the CLP. As a member of the resolutions committee, she supported a moderate resolution proposing the achievement of the CLP's goals through traditional political processes. The proposal was defeated in favor of a more militant program. Nevertheless, Whitney remained a member though she later testified that she did not intend that the CLP of California be an instrument of terrorism or violence. By a criminal Information filed in the Superior Court of Alameda County, California, the plaintiff in error was charged, in five counts, with violations of the Criminal Syndicalism Act of that State, which punished those who helped organize and who knowingly became members of an association organized to advocate, teach and aid criminal syndicalism. She was tried, convicted on the first count, and sentenced to imprisonment. The judgment was affirmed by the District Court of Appeal. Her petition to have the case heard by the Supreme Court was denied. And the case was brought before the U.S. Supreme Court on a writ of error which was allowed by the Presiding Justice of the Court of Appeal, the highest court of the State in which a decision could be had. On the first hearing to the U.S. Supreme Court, the writ of error was dismissed for want of jurisdiction. Thereafter, a petition for rehearing was granted, and the case was again heard and reargued both as to the jurisdiction and the merits.

I May a state validly and constitutionally punish a person for knowingly joining, aiding and abetting an organization which advocates unlawful and violent means to advance its agenda?

R The freedom of speech which is secured by the Constitution does not confer an absolute right to speak such that a state may punish utterances hostile to the public welfare as inciting crime, disturbing the public peace, or threatening the unlawful overthrow of organized governments.

A It is clear that the Syndicalism Act does not violate the due process clause by reason of vagueness and uncertainty of definition. The language of §2 of the Act under which the plaintiff in error was convicted is clear; the definition of "criminal syndicalism" specific. The Act plainly meets the essential requirement of due process that a penal statute be "sufficiently explicit to inform those who subject to it what conduct on their part will render them liable to its penalties," and be couched in terms that are not "so vague that men of common intelligence must necessarily guess at its meaning and differ as to its application." Neither is the Syndicalism Act violative of the equal protection clause on the ground that as its penalties are confined to those who advocate a resort to violent and unlawful methods as a means of changing industrial and political conditions, it arbitrarily discriminates between such persons and those who may advocate a resort to these methods as a means of maintaining such conditions. It is settled by repeated decisions of this Court that the equal protection clause does not take from a State the power to classify in the adoption of police laws, but admits of the exercise of a wide scope of discretion, and avoids what is done only when it is without any reasonable basis and therefore is purely arbitrary; and that one who assails the classification must carry the burden of showing that it does not rest upon any reasonable basis, but is essentially arbitrary. A statute does not violate the equal protection clause merely because it is not all-embracing. A state may properly direct its legislation against what it deems an existing evil without covering the whole field of possible abuses. The statute must be presumed to be aimed at an evil where experience shows it to be most felt. And it is not open to objection unless the classification is so lacking in any adequate or reasonable basis as to preclude the assumption that it was made in the exercise of the legislative judgment and discretion. The Syndicalism Act is not class legislation; it affects all alike, no matter what their business associations or callings, who come within its terms and do the things prohibited. And there is no substantial basis for the contention that the Legislature has arbitrarily or unreasonably limited its application to those advocating the use of violent and unlawful methods to effect changes in industrial and political conditions; there being nothing indicating any ground to apprehend that those desiring to maintain existing industrial and political conditions did or would advocate such methods. That there is a wide-spread conviction of the necessity for legislation of this character is indicated by the adoption of similar statutes in several other States. Nor is the Syndicalism Act as applied in this case violative of the due process clause as a restraint of the rights of free speech, assembly, and association. That the freedom of speech which is secured by the Constitution does not confer an absolute right to speak, without responsibility, whatever one may choose, or an unrestricted and unbridled license giving immunity for every possible use of language and preventing the punishment of those who abuse this freedom; and that a State in the exercise of its police power may punish those who abuse this freedom by utterances inimical to the public welfare, tending to incite to crime, disturb the public peace, or endanger the foundations of organized government and threaten its overthrow by unlawful means, is not open to question. By enacting the provisions of the Syndicalism Act the State has declared, through its legislative body, that to knowingly be or become a member of or assist in organizing an association to advocate, teach or aid and abet the commission of crimes or unlawful acts of force, violence or terrorism as a means of accomplishing industrial or political changes, involves such danger to the public peace and the security of the State, that these acts should be penalized in the exercise of its police power. That determination must be given great weight. Every presumption is to be indulged in favor of the validity of the statute, and it may not be declared unconstitutional unless it is an arbitrary or unreasonable attempt to exercise the authority vested in the State in the public interest. We find no repugnancy in the Syndicalism Act as applied in this case to either the due process or equal protection clauses of the 14th Amendment on any of the grounds upon which its validity has been here challenged.

C The order dismissing the writ of error will be vacated and set aside, and the judgment of the Court of Appeal is affirmed.

Dennis v. United States

341 U.S. 494 (1951)

FACTS

In 1948, petitioners, leaders of the Communist Party in this country, including one Dennis, were indicted in a federal district court under 3 of the Smith Act for willfully and knowingly conspiring 1) to organize as the Communist Party a group of persons to teach and advocate the overthrow and destruction of the Government of the United States by force and violence, and 2) knowingly and willfully to advocate and teach the duty and necessity of overthrowing and destroying the Government of the United States by force and violence. As construed and applied in this case, 2 (a)(1), 2(a)(3) and 3 of the Smith Act, makes it a crime for any person knowingly or willfully to advocate the overthrow or destruction of the Government of the United States by force or violence, to organize or help to organize any group which does so, or to conspire to do so. The trial judge instructed the jury that they could not convict unless they found that petitioners intended to overthrow the Government "as speedily as circumstances would permit" but that, if they so found, then, as a matter of law, there was sufficient danger of a substantive evil that Congress has a right to prevent to justify application of the statute under the First Amendment. Petitioners were convicted and the convictions were sustained by the Court of Appeals. The U.S. Supreme Court granted certiorari.

I 1) Whether either 2 or 3 of the Smith Act, inherently or as construed and applied in the instant case, violates the First Amendment and other provisions of the Bill of Rights; and 2) whether either 2 or 3, inherently or as construed and applied in the instant case, violates the First and Fifth Amendments because of indefiniteness.

R When speech or publication creates a "clear and present danger" of attempting or accomplishing the overthrow of the Government or any unlawful activity, irrespective of its probability of success, the government may constitutionally restrict that speech and a conviction related thereto may be sustained.

A Congress may constitutionally prohibit acts intended to overthrow the Government by force or violence. Here, we are called upon to decide whether Dennis' conviction violated his First Amendment right to speak freely. We hold that it does not. To that end, we apply the clear and present danger test to determine whether speech or press present a "clear and present danger" of causing unlawful activity to occur. In applying the test, courts must weigh the gravity of the evil advocated in the speech against an invasion of free speech; and whether the latter is necessary to avoid the danger. Here, it is apparent that the government's attack on Dennis's freedom to speak was essential to avoid the danger of the overthrow of the government. The Communist Party in this country, which Dennis and others had formed, was part of a highly-organized conspiracy that had the capability and the resolve to act in the overthrow of the U.S. Government. A "'clear and present danger" was present; and we must therefore reject the argument that success or probability of success should be the decisive factor. We hold that 2 (a)(1), 2(a)(3) and 3 of the Smith Act do not inherently, or as construed or applied in the instant case, violate the First Amendment and other provisions of the Bill of Rights, or the First and Fifth Amendments because of indefiniteness. Petitioners intended to overthrow the Government of the United States as speedily as the circumstances would permit. Their conspiracy [341 U.S. 494, 517] to organize the Communist Party and to teach and advocate the overthrow of the Government of the United States by force and violence created a "clear and present danger" of an attempt to overthrow the Government by force and violence. They were properly and constitutionally convicted for violation of the Smith Act.

C

The judgments of conviction are affirmed.

Brandenburg v. Ohio

395 U.S. 444 (1969)

FACTS

The record shows that a man, identified at trial as the Defendant-appellant Brandenburg, a leader of a Ku Klux Klan group, telephoned an announcer-reporter on the staff of a Cincinnati television station and invited him to come to a Ku Klux Klan "rally" to be held at a farm in Hamilton County. With the cooperation of the organizers, the reporter and a cameraman attended the meeting and filmed the events. Portions of the films were later broadcast on the local station and on a national network. The prosecution's case consisted of films and testimony identifying the appellant as the person who communicated with the reporter and who spoke at the rally. The State also introduced into evidence several articles appearing in the film, including a pistol, a rifle, a shotgun, ammunition, a Bible, and a red hood worn by the speaker in the films. One film showed 12 hooded figures, some of whom carried firearms. They were gathered around a large wooden cross, which they burned. No one was present other than the participants and the newsmen who made the film. Most of the words uttered during the scene were incomprehensible when the film was projected, but scattered phrases could be understood that were derogatory of Negroes and, in one instance, of Jews. Another scene on the same film showed the appellant, in Klan regalia, making a speech. The appellant repeated a speech very similar to that recorded on the first of two films. At one point during the rally, Brandenburg (D) also stated, "Personally, I believe the nigger should be returned to Africa, the Jew returned to Israel." Though some of the figures in the films carried weapons, the speaker did not. The appellant was convicted under the Ohio Criminal Syndicalism statute for "advocating . . . the duty, necessity, or propriety of crime, sabotage, violence, or unlawful methods of terrorism as a means of accomplishing industrial or political reform" and for "voluntarily assembling with any society, group, or assemblage of persons formed to teach or advocate the doctrines of criminal syndicalism." Ohio Rev. Code Ann. 2923.13. He was fined $1,000 and sentenced to one to 10 years imprisonment. The appellant challenged the constitutionality of the criminal syndicalism statute under the First and Fourteenth Amendments to the United States Constitution, but the intermediate appellate court of Ohio affirmed his conviction without opinion. The Supreme Court of Ohio dismissed his appeal, "for the reason that no substantial constitutional question exists herein." It did not file an opinion or explain its conclusions. Appeal was taken to the U.S. Supreme Court which noted probable jurisdiction.

I

Can the states still constitutionally restrict speech that advocates violent overthrow of the government when that speech constitutes "teaching" but is not likely to incite immediate lawless action in the wake of the erosion of the *Whitney v. California* holding?

R

First Amendment free speech guarantees do not allow a state to forbid the encouragement of the use of force or to violate the law unless such sponsorship is directed to inciting or producing imminent lawless action and is likely to do so.

A

The Ohio Criminal Syndicalism Statute was enacted in 1919. From 1917 to 1920, identical or quite similar laws were adopted by 20 States and two territories. In 1927, this Court sustained the constitutionality of California's

Criminal Syndicalism Act, the text of which is quite similar to that of the laws of Ohio. The Court upheld the statute relying on *Whitney v. California* in that, without more, "advocating" violent means to effect political and economic change involves such danger to the security of the State that the State may outlaw it. But *Whitney* has been thoroughly discredited by later decisions. These later decisions have fashioned the principle that the constitutional guarantees of free speech and free press do not permit a State to forbid or proscribe advocacy of the use of force or of law violation except where such advocacy is directed to inciting or producing imminent lawless action and is likely to incite or produce such action. A statute which fails to draw this distinction impermissibly intrudes upon the freedoms guaranteed by the First and Fourteenth Amendments. It sweeps within its condemnation speech which our Constitution has immunized from governmental control. Measured by this test, Ohio's Criminal Syndicalism Act cannot be sustained. The Act punishes persons who "advocate or teach the duty, necessity, or propriety" of violence "as a means of accomplishing industrial or political reform"; or who publish or circulate or display any book or paper containing such advocacy; or who "justify" the commission of violent acts "with intent to exemplify, spread or advocate the propriety of the doctrines of criminal syndicalism"; or who "voluntarily assemble" with a group formed "to teach or advocate the doctrines of criminal syndicalism." Neither the indictment nor the trial judge's instructions to the jury in any way refined the statute's bald definition of the crime in terms of mere advocacy not distinguished from incitement to imminent lawless action. Accordingly, we are here confronted with a statute which, by its own words and as applied, purports to punish mere advocacy and to forbid, on pain of criminal punishment, assembly with others merely to advocate the described type of action. Such a statute falls within the condemnation of the First and Fourteenth Amendments. The contrary teaching of *Whitney v. California,* cannot be supported, and that decision is therefore overruled.

C

Reversed.

Chaplinsky v. New Hampshire

315 U.S. 568 (1942)

FACTS

Defendant-appellant Chaplinsky, a member of the sect known as Jehovah's Witnesses, was convicted in the municipal court of Rochester, New Hampshire, for violation of Chapter 378, Section 2, of the Public Laws of New Hampshire which provides: "No person shall address any offensive, derisive or annoying word to any other person who is lawfully in any street or other public place, nor call him by any offensive or derisive name, nor make any noise or exclamation in his presence and hearing with intent to deride, offend or annoy him, or to prevent him from pursuing his lawful business or occupation." The complaint charged that appellant unlawfully repeated the words, "You are a God damned racketeer" and "a damned Fascist and the whole government of Rochester are Fascists or agents of Fascists" with respect to the Marshal and with reference to the City of Rochester. Upon appeal there was a trial de novo of appellant before a jury in the Superior Court. He was found guilty and the judgment of conviction was affirmed by the Supreme Court of the state.

I

May the state constitutionally punish certain words likely to cause a breach of the peace?

R

Fighting words, which tend to incite an immediate breach of peace, are not constitutionally protected.

A

There is no substantial dispute over the facts. Chaplinsky was distributing the literature of his sect on the streets of Rochester on a busy Saturday afternoon. Members of the local citizenry complained to the City Marshal that Chaplinsky was denouncing all religion as a "racket." The Marshal told them that Chaplinsky was lawfully engaged, and then warned Chaplinsky that the crowd was getting restless. Some time later a disturbance occurred and the traffic officer on duty took Chaplinsky to the police station, but did not inform him that he was under arrest or that he was going to be arrested. On the way they encountered the Marshal who had been advised that a riot was under way and was therefore hurrying to the scene. The Marshal repeated his earlier warning to Chaplinsky who then cursed him. Appellant assails the statute as a violation of all three freedoms, speech, press and worship, but only an attack on the basis of free speech is warranted. We turn, therefore, to an examination of the statute itself. Allowing the broadest scope to the language and purpose of the Fourteenth Amendment, it is well understood that the right of free speech is not absolute at all times and under all circumstances. There are certain well-defined and narrowly limited classes of speech, the prevention and punishment of which has never been thought to raise any Constitutional problem. These include the lewd and obscene, the profane, the libelous, and the insulting or 'fighting' words-those which by their very utterance inflict injury or tend to incite an immediate breach of the peace. It has been well observed that such utterances are no essential part of any exposition of ideas, and are of such slight social value as a step to truth that any benefit that may be derived from them is clearly outweighed by the social interest in order and morality. We are unable to say that the limited scope of the statute as thus construed contravenes the constitutional right of free expression. It is a statute narrowly drawn and limited to define and punish specific conduct lying within the domain of state power, the use in a public place of words likely to cause a breach of the peace. This conclusion necessarily disposes of appellant's contention that the statute is so vague and indefinite as to render a conviction thereunder a violation of due process. A statute punishing verbal acts, carefully drawn so as not unduly to impair liberty of expression, is not too vague for a criminal law. Nor can we say that the application of the statute to the facts disclosed by the record substantially or unreasonably impinges upon the privilege of free speech. Argument is unnecessary to demonstrate that the appellations 'damn racketeer' and 'damn Fascist' are epithets likely to provoke the average person to retaliation, and thereby cause a breach of the peace. The refusal of the state court to admit evidence of provocation and evidence bearing on the truth or falsity of the utterances is open to no Constitutional objection. Whether the facts sought to be proved by such evidence constitute a defense to the charge or may be shown in mitigation are questions for the state court to determine. Our function is fulfilled by a determination that the challenged statute, on its face and as applied, does not contravene the Fourteenth Amendment.

C

Affirmed.

Gooding v. Wilson

405 U.S. 518 (1972)

FACTS

Appellee was convicted in Superior Court, Fulton County, Georgia, on two counts of using opprobrious words and abusive language in violation of a Georgia Code which provides: "Any person who shall, without provocation, use to or of another, and in his presence . . . opprobrious words or abusive language, tending to cause a breach of the peace . . . shall be guilty of a misdemeanor." Appellee appealed the conviction to the Supreme Court of Georgia on the ground, among others, that the statute violated the First and Fourteenth Amendments because vague and overbroad. The Georgia Supreme Court rejected that contention and sustained the conviction. Appellee then sought federal habeas corpus relief in the District Court for the Northern District of Georgia. The District Court found that, because appellee had failed to exhaust his available state remedies as to the other grounds he relied upon in attacking his conviction, only the contention that the statute was facially unconstitutional was ripe for decision. On the merits of that question, the District Court, in disagreement with the Georgia Supreme Court, held that 26-6303 [the applicable Georgia statute at issue] on its face was unconstitutionally vague and broad and set aside appellee's conviction. The Court of Appeals for the Fifth Circuit affirmed. The U.S. Supreme Court noted probable jurisdiction of the State's appeal.

I Can a statute which punishes speech which is offensive withstand a facial attack in a constitutional sense?

R A statute must be carefully drawn or be authoritatively construed to punish only unprotected speech and not be susceptible of application to protected expression.

A Section 26-6303 punishes only spoken words. It can therefore withstand appellee's attack upon its facial constitutionality only if, as authoritatively construed by the Georgia courts, it is not susceptible of application to speech, although vulgar or offensive, that is protected by the First and Fourteenth Amendments. "The line between speech unconditionally guaranteed and speech which may legitimately be regulated, suppressed, or punished is finely drawn" and "in every case the power to regulate must be so exercised as not, in attaining a permissible end, unduly to infringe the protected freedom." In other words, the statute must be carefully drawn or be authoritatively construed to punish only unprotected speech and not be susceptible of application to protected expression. "Because First Amendment freedoms need breathing space to survive, government may regulate in the area only with narrow specificity." Appellant does not challenge these principles but contends that the Georgia statute is narrowly drawn to apply only to a constitutionally unprotected class of words - "fighting" words - "those which by their very utterance inflict injury or tend to incite an immediate breach of the peace." We conclude that "[t]he separation of legitimate from illegitimate speech calls for more sensitive tools than [Georgia] has supplied." The most recent decision of the Georgia Supreme Court, *Wilson v. State*, in rejecting appellee's attack on the constitutionality of 26-6303, stated that the statute "conveys a definite meaning as to the conduct forbidden, measured by common understanding and practice." Because earlier appellate decisions applied 26-6303 to utterances where there was no likelihood that the person addressed would make an immediate violent response, it is clear that the standard allowing juries to determine guilt "measured by common understanding and practice" does not limit the application of 26-6303 to "fighting" words defined by Chaplinsky. Rather, that broad standard effectively "licenses the jury to create its own standard in each case." Accordingly, we agree with the conclusion of the District Court, "[t]he fault of the statute is that it leaves wide open the standard of responsibility, so that it is easily susceptible to improper application." Unlike the construction of the New Hampshire statute by the New Hampshire Supreme Court, the Georgia appellate courts have not construed 26-6303 "so as to avoid all constitutional difficulties."

C

Affirmed.

R.A.V. v. City of St. Paul

505 U.S. 377 (1992)

FACTS

On June 21, 1990, after allegedly burning a cross on a black family's lawn, Defendant-petitioner R.A.V., a teenager, was charged under the St. Paul, Minnesota, Bias-Motivated Crime Ordinance, which prohibits the display of a symbol which one knows or has reason to know "arouses anger, alarm or resentment in others on the basis of race, color, creed, religion or gender." The trial court dismissed this charge on the ground that the ordinance was substantially overbroad and impermissibly content based, but the State Supreme Court reversed. It rejected the overbreadth claim because the phrase "arouses anger, alarm or resentment in others" had been construed in earlier state cases to limit the ordinance's reach to "fighting words" within the meaning of the U.S. Supreme Court's decision in *Chaplinsky v. New Hampshire,* a category of expression not protected by the First Amendment. The State Supreme Court also concluded that the ordinance was not impermissibly content based, because it was narrowly tailored to serve a compelling governmental interest in protecting the community against bias-motivated threats to public safety and order. R.A.V. appealed.

I

Can the government constitutionally, under the First Amendment, regulate offensive speech, including fighting words, based on its content?

R

The Government may not regulate speech, including fighting words, based on opposition to or a preference towards the underlying message conveyed.

A

The ordinance is facially invalid under the First Amendment. This Court is bound by the state court's construction of the ordinance as reaching only expressions constituting "fighting words." However, R.A.V.'s request that the scope of the *Chaplinsky* formulation be modified, thereby invalidating the ordinance as substantially overbroad, need not be reached, since the ordinance unconstitutionally prohibits speech on the basis of the subjects the speech addresses. A few limited categories of speech, such as obscenity, defamation, and fighting words, may be regulated because of their constitutionally proscribable content. However, these categories are not entirely invisible to the Constitution, and government may not regulate them based on hostility, or favoritism, towards a nonproscribable message they contain. Thus, the regulation of "fighting words" may not be based on nonproscribable content. It may, however, be underinclusive, addressing some offensive instances and leaving other equally offensive ones alone, so long as the selective prescription is not based on content, or there is no realistic possibility that regulation of ideas is afoot. The ordinance, even as narrowly construed by the State Supreme Court, is facially unconstitutional, because it imposes special prohibitions on those speakers who express views on the disfavored subjects of "race, color, creed, religion or gender." At the same time, it permits displays containing abusive invective if they are not addressed to those topics. Moreover, in its practical operation, the ordinance goes beyond mere content, to actual viewpoint, discrimination. Displays containing "fighting words" that do not invoke the disfavored subjects would seemingly be useable *ad libitum* by those arguing in favor of racial, color, etc., tolerance and equality, but not by their opponents. St. Paul's desire to communicate to minority groups that it does not condone the "group hatred" of bias-motivated speech does not justify selectively silencing speech on the basis of its content. The content-based discrimination reflected in the ordinance does not rest upon the very reasons why the particular class of speech at issue is proscribable, it is not aimed only at the "secondary effects" of speech within the meaning of *Renton v. Playtime Theatres, Inc.*, and it is not for any other reason the sort that does not threaten censorship of ideas. In addition, the ordinance's content discrimination is not justified on the ground that the ordinance is narrowly tailored to serve a compelling state interest in ensuring the basic human rights of groups historically discriminated against, since an ordinance not limited to the favored topics would have precisely the same beneficial effect.

C

Reversed and remanded.

Feiner v. New York

340 U.S. 315 (1951)

FACTS

On the evening of March 8, 1949, Defendant-petitioner Irving Feiner was addressing an open-air meeting in the City of Syracuse. At approximately 6:30 p.m., the police received a telephone complaint concerning the meeting and two officers were sent to investigate. They found a crowd of about 75 people, both Negro and white, filling the sidewalk and spreading out into the street. Petitioner, standing on a large wooden box on the sidewalk, was addressing the crowd through a loud-speaker system attached to an automobile. Although the purpose of his speech was to urge his listeners to attend a meeting to be held that night in the Syracuse Hotel, in its course he was making derogatory remarks concerning President Truman, the Mayor of Syracuse, and other local political officials. The police officers made no effort to interfere with petitioner's speech, but were first concerned with the effect of the crowd on both pedestrian and vehicular traffic. At this time, petitioner was speaking in a "loud, high-pitched voice." He gave the impression that he was endeavoring to arouse the Negro people against the whites, urging that they rise up in arms and fight for equal rights. The statements "stirred up a little excitement." Some of the onlookers made remarks to the police about their inability to handle the crowd and at least one person threatened violence if the police did not act. There were others who appeared to be favoring petitioner's arguments. Because of the feeling that existed in the crowd both for and against the speaker, the officers finally "stepped in to prevent it from resulting in a fight." One of the officers approached the petitioner, not for the purpose of arresting him, but to get him to break up the crowd. He asked petitioner to get down off the box, but the latter refused to accede to his request and continued talking. The officer waited for a minute and then demanded that he cease talking. Although the officer had thus twice requested petitioner to stop over the course of several minutes, petitioner not only ignored him but continued talking. During all this time, the crowd was pressing closer around petitioner and the officer. Finally, the officer told petitioner he was under arrest and ordered him to get down from the box. Petitioner stepped down. In all, the officer had asked petitioner to get down off the box three times over a space of four or five minutes. Petitioner had been speaking for over a half hour. On these facts, petitioner was specifically charged with violation of 722 of the Penal Law of New York for ". . . ignoring and refusing to heed and obey reasonable police orders issued at the time and place mentioned in the Information to regulate and control said crowd and to prevent a breach or breaches of the peace and to prevent injury to pedestrians attempting to use said walk, and being forced into the highway adjacent to the place in question, and prevent injury to the public generally." The bill of particulars supported the charge of disorderly conduct. Petitioner was convicted of the offense of disorderly conduct, a misdemeanor under the New York penal laws, in the Court of Special Sessions of the City of Syracuse and was sentenced to thirty days in the county penitentiary. The conviction was affirmed by the Onondaga County Court and the New York Court of Appeals. The case comes before the U.S. Supreme Court on certiorari; petitioner having claimed that the conviction is in violation of his right of free speech rights under the Fourteenth Amendment.

I

May the police constitutionally suppress free speech when the tenor of a public speaker's verbal communication moves from protected speech to incitement to riot?

Feiner v. New York

340 U.S. 315 (1951)

R When a public speaker moves from protected speech, such as argument or persuasion, to incitement to riot, the police may step in and stop the speaker from communicating in the interest of the public's safety and welfare even if it means a suppression of the speaker's ideas.

A The conviction is sustained against a claim that it violated petitioner's right of free speech under the First and 14th Amendments. Petitioner was neither arrested nor convicted for the making or the content of his speech but for the reaction which it actually engendered. The police cannot be used as an instrument for the suppression of unpopular views; but, when a speaker passes the bounds of argument or persuasion and undertakes incitement to riot, the police may act to prevent a breach of the peace. We are not faced here with arbitrary police action. Petitioner was accorded a full, fair trial. The trial judge heard testimony and after weighing this contradictory evidence, the trial judge reached the conclusion that the police officers were justified in taking action to prevent a breach of the peace. The exercise of the police officers' proper discretionary power to prevent a breach of the peace was thus approved by the trial court and later by two courts on review. Petitioner was thus neither arrested nor convicted for the making or the content of his speech. Rather, it was the reaction which it actually engendered. When clear and present danger of riot, disorder, interference with traffic upon the public streets, or other immediate threat to public safety, peace, or order, appears, the power of the State to prevent or punish is obvious. The findings of the New York courts as to the condition of the crowd and the refusal of petitioner to obey the police requests, supported as they are by the record of this case, are persuasive that the conviction of petitioner for violation of public peace, order and authority does not exceed the bounds of proper state police action. This Court respects, as it must, the interest of the community in maintaining peace and order on its streets. We cannot say that the preservation of that interest here encroaches on the constitutional rights of this petitioner. We are well aware that the ordinary objections of a hostile audience cannot be allowed to silence a speaker, and are also mindful of the possible danger of giving overzealous police complete discretion to break up otherwise lawful public meetings. But we are not faced here with such a situation. It is one thing to say that the police cannot be used as an instrument for the suppression of unpopular views, and another to say that, when as here the speaker passes the bounds of argument or persuasion and undertakes incitement to riot, they are powerless to prevent a breach of the peace. Nor in this case can we condemn the considered judgment of three New York courts approving the means which the police, faced with a crisis, used in the exercise of their power and duty to preserve peace and order. The findings of the state courts as to the existing situation and the imminence of greater disorder coupled with petitioner's deliberate defiance of the police officers convince us that we should not reverse this conviction in the name of free speech.

C Affirmed.

Beauharnais v. Illinois

343 U.S. 250 (1952)

FACTS

Over his claim that the statute violated the liberty of speech and of the press guaranteed as against the States by the Due Process Clause of the Fourteenth Amendment and was void for vagueness, petitioner Beauharnais was convicted in a state court for distributing on the streets of Chicago anti-Negro leaflets in violation of Ill. Rev. Stat., 1949, c. 38, 471, which makes it a crime to exhibit in any public place any publication which "portrays depravity, criminality, unchastity, or lack of virtue of a class of citizens, of any race, color, creed or religion" which "exposes the citizens of any race, color, creed or religion to contempt, derision, or obloquy."

I

Is a state statute which prohibits and punishes those who engage in libel directed toward a specific racial group of people, constitutional?

R

A state statute which prohibits and punishes those who engage in libel directed toward a specific racial group of people is constitutional.

A

As construed and applied in this case, the statute does not violate the liberty of speech and of the press guaranteed as against the States by the Due Process Clause of the Fourteenth Amendment. As construed and applied in this case, the statute is not void for vagueness. Since petitioner did not, by appropriate steps in the trial court, seek to justify his utterance as "fair comment" or as privileged as a means for redressing grievances, those hypothetical defenses cannot be considered by this Court. Since the Illinois Supreme Court construed this statute as a form of criminal libel law, and truth of the utterance is not a defense to a charge of criminal libel under Illinois law unless the publication is also made "with good motives and for justifiable ends," petitioner was not denied due process by the trial court's rejection of a proffer of proof which did not satisfy this requirement. Since libelous utterances are not within the area of constitutionally protected speech, it is not necessary for this Court to consider the issues raised by the denial of petitioner's request that the jury be instructed that, in order to convict, they must find that the publication complained of was likely to produce a "clear and present danger" of a substantial evil.

C

Affirmed.

Virginia v. Black

538 U.S. 343 (2003)

FACTS

Defendant-Respondents, including one Black, were convicted separately of violating a Virginia statute that makes it a felony "for any person . . . with the intent of intimidating any person or group . . . to burn ... a cross on the property of another, a highway or other public place," and specifies that "any such burning . . . shall be prima facie evidence of an intent to intimidate a person or group." When respondent Black objected on First Amendment grounds to his trial court's jury instruction that cross burning by itself is sufficient evidence from which the required "intent to intimidate" could be inferred, the prosecutor responded that the instruction was taken straight out of the Virginia Model Instructions. Respondent O'Mara pleaded guilty to charges of violating the statute, but reserved the right to challenge its constitutionality. At respondent Elliott's trial, the judge instructed the jury as to what the Commonwealth had to prove, but did not give an instruction on the meaning of the word "intimidate" nor on the statute's prima facie evidence provision. Consolidating all three cases, the Virginia Supreme Court held that the cross-burning statute is unconstitutional on its face; that it is analytically indistinguishable from the ordinance found unconstitutional in *R.A.V. v. St. Paul;* that it discriminates on the basis of content and viewpoint since it selectively chooses only cross burning because of its distinctive message; and that the prima facie evidence provision renders the statute overbroad because the enhanced probability of prosecution under the statute chills the expression of protected speech.

I

Does a state's cross-burning statute, which targets cross burning with an intent to discriminate, violate the First Amendment when it treats cross burning as prima facie evidence of intent to intimidate?

R

A state may ban cross burning carried out with the intent to intimidate, but cross burning may not, by itself, be treated as prima facie evidence of intent to intimidate.

A

Burning a cross in the United States is inextricably intertwined with the history of the Ku Klux Klan, which, following its formation in 1866, imposed a reign of terror throughout the South, whipping, threatening, and murdering blacks, southern whites who disagreed with the Klan, and "carpetbagger" northern whites. The Klan has often used cross burnings as a tool of intimidation and a threat of impending violence, although such burnings have also remained potent symbols of shared group identity and ideology, serving as a central feature of Klan gatherings. To this day, however, regardless of whether the message is a political one or is also meant to intimidate, the burning of a cross is a "symbol of hate." While cross burning does not inevitably convey a message of intimidation, often the cross burner intends that the recipients of the message fear for their lives. And when a cross burning is used to intimidate, few if any messages are more powerful. The protections the First Amendment affords speech and expressive conduct are not absolute. This Court has long recognized that the government may regulate certain categories of expression consistent with the Constitution. For example, the First Amendment permits a State to ban "true threats" which encompass those statements where the speaker means to communicate a serious expression of an intent to commit an act of unlawful violence to a particular individual or group of individuals. The speaker need not actually intend to carry out the threat. Rather, a prohibition on true threats protects individuals from the fear of violence and the disruption that fear engenders, as well as from the possibility that the threatened violence will occur. *R. A. V., supra,* at 388. Intimidation in the constitutionally proscribable sense of the word is a type of true threat, where a speaker directs a threat to a person or group of persons with the intent of placing the victim in fear of bodily harm or death. Respondents do not contest that some cross burnings fit within this meaning of intimidating speech, and rightly so. As the history of cross burning in this country shows, that act is often intimidating, intended to create a pervasive fear in victims that they are a target of violence. The First Amendment permits Virginia to outlaw cross burnings done with the intent to intimidate because burning a cross is a particularly virulent form of intimidation. Instead of prohibiting all intimidating messages, Virginia may choose to regulate this subset of intimidating messages in light of cross burning's long and pernicious history as a signal of impending violence. A ban on cross burning carried out with the intent to intimidate is fully consistent with this Court's holding in *R.A.V.* Contrary to the Virginia Supreme Court's ruling, *R.A V.* did not hold that the First Amendment prohibits *all* forms of content-based discrimination within a proscribable area of speech. Rather, the Court specifically stated that a particular type of content discrimination does not violate the First Amendment when the basis for it consists entirely of the very reason its entire class of speech is proscribable. For example, it is permissible to prohibit only that obscenity that is most patently offensive in its prurience - *i.e.,* that which involves the most lascivious displays of sexual activity. Similarly, Virginia's statute does not run afoul of the First Amendment insofar as it bans cross burning with intent to intimidate. Unlike the statute at issue in *R.A.V.*, the Virginia statute does not single out for opprobrium only that speech directed toward "one of the specified disfavored topics." It does not matter whether an individual burns a cross with intent to intimidate because of the victim's race, gender, or religion, or because of the victim's "political affiliation, union membership, or homosexuality." Thus, just as a State may regulate only that obscenity which is the most obscene due to its prurient content, so too may a State choose to prohibit only those forms of intimidation that are most likely to inspire fear of bodily harm.

C

Affirmed in part, vacated in part, and remanded.

Roth v. United States

354 U.S. 476 (1957)

FACTS

Defendant Roth conducted a business in New York in the publication and sale of books, photographs and magazines. He used circulars and advertising matter to solicit sales. He was convicted by a jury in the District Court for the Southern District of New York upon 4 counts of a 26-count indictment charging him with mailing obscene circulars and advertising, and an obscene book, in violation of the federal obscenity statute. His conviction was affirmed by the Court of Appeals for the Second Circuit. The U.S. Supreme Court granted certiorari. Defendant Alberts conducted a mail-order business from Los Angeles. He was convicted by the Judge of the Municipal Court of the Beverly Hills Judicial District (having waived a jury trial) under a misdemeanor complaint which charged him with lewdly keeping for sale obscene and indecent books, and with writing, composing and publishing an obscene advertisement of them, in violation of the California Penal Code. The conviction was affirmed by the Appellate Department of the Superior Court of the State of California in and for the County of Los Angeles. The U.S. Supreme Court noted probable jurisdiction.

I

Is obscenity within the area of speech and press protected by the First Amendment?

R

The government is constitutionally permitted, without violating the protections afforded by the First Amendment's Free Speech Clause, to regulate material considered obscene when the average person applying contemporary community standards considers the dominant theme of the material, taken as a whole, appeals to prurient interests.

A

In the Roth case, the constitutionality of 18 U.S.C. 1461, which makes punishable the mailing of material that is "obscene, lewd, lascivious, or filthy . . . or other publication of an indecent character," and Roth's conviction thereunder for mailing an obscene book and obscene circulars and advertising, are sustained. In the *Alberts* case, the constitutionality of 311 of West's California Penal Code Ann., 1955, which makes it a misdemeanor to keep for sale, or to advertise, material that is "obscene or indecent," and Alberts' conviction thereunder for lewdly keeping for sale obscene and indecent books and for writing, composing, and publishing an obscene advertisement of them, are sustained. Obscenity is not within the area of constitutionally protected freedom of speech or press - either 1) under the First Amendment, as to the Federal Government, or 2) under the Due Process Clause of the Fourteenth Amendment, as to the States. In the light of history, it is apparent that the unconditional phrasing of the First Amendment was not intended to protect every utterance. The protection given speech and press was fashioned to assure unfettered interchange of ideas for the bringing about of political and social changes desired by the people. All ideas having even the slightest redeeming social importance - unorthodox ideas, controversial ideas, even ideas hateful to the prevailing climate of opinion - have the full protection of the guaranties, unless excludable because they encroach upon the limited area of more important interests; but implicit in the history of the First Amendment is the rejection of obscenity as utterly without redeeming social importance.

Roth v. United States

354 U.S. 476 (1957)

Since obscenity is not protected, constitutional guaranties were not violated in these cases merely because, under the trial judges' instructions to the juries, convictions could be had without proof either that the obscene material would perceptibly create a clear and present danger of antisocial conduct, or probably would induce its recipients to such conduct. Sex and obscenity are not synonymous. Obscene material is material which deals with sex in a manner appealing to prurient interest - i. e., material having a tendency to excite lustful thoughts. It is vital that the standards for judging obscenity safeguard the protection of freedom of speech and press for material which does not treat sex in a manner appealing to prurient interest. The standard for judging obscenity, adequate to withstand the charge of constitutional infirmity, is whether, to the average person, applying contemporary community standards, the dominant theme of the material, taken as a whole, appeals to prurient interest. In these cases, both trial courts sufficiently followed the proper standard and used the proper definition of obscenity. When applied according to the proper standard for judging obscenity, 18 U.S.C. 1461, which makes punishable the mailing of material that is "obscene, lewd, lascivious, or filthy . . . or other publication of an indecent character," does not 1) violate the freedom of speech or press guaranteed by the First Amendment, or 2) violate the constitutional requirements of due process by failing to provide reasonably ascertainable standards of guilt. When applied according to the proper standard for judging obscenity, 311 of West's California Penal Code Ann., 1955, which, *inter alia*, makes it a misdemeanor to keep for sale or to advertise material that is "obscene or indecent," does not 1) violate the freedom of speech or press guaranteed by the Fourteenth Amendment against encroachment by the States, or 2) violate the constitutional requirements of due process by failing to provide reasonably ascertainable standards of guilt. The federal obscenity statute, 18 U.S.C. 1461, punishing the use of the mails for obscene material, is a proper exercise of the postal power delegated to Congress by Art. I, 8, cl. 7; and it does not unconstitutionally encroach upon the powers reserved to the States by the Ninth and Tenth Amendments. The California obscenity statute here involved is not repugnant to Art. I, 8, cl. 7, since it does not impose a burden upon, or interfere with, the federal postal functions - even when applied to a mail-order business.

C

Affirmed..

Paris Adult Theatre I v. Slaton

413 U.S. 49 (1973)

FACTS

Plaintiff-respondents Slaton and others sued under Georgia civil law to enjoin the exhibiting by Defendant-petitioners Paris Adult Theatre I and one other adult cinema of two allegedly obscene films. In a jury-waived trial, the trial court (which did not require "expert" affirmative evidence of obscenity) viewed the films and thereafter dismissed the complaints on the ground that the display of the films in commercial theaters to consenting adult audiences (reasonable precautions having been taken to exclude minors) was "constitutionally permissible." The Georgia Supreme Court reversed, holding that the films constituted "hard core" pornography not within the protection of the First Amendment. Paris Adult Theatre I appealed to the United States Supreme Court.

I

Can the states constitutionally restrict theaters from exhibiting obscene or pornographic films to consenting adults?

R

When states have a legitimate interest in stemming the tide of commercialized obscenity in public places, they can do so even when the material is not available to minors but is available to consenting adults.

A

Obscene material is not speech entitled to First Amendment protection. States have a legitimate interest in regulating commerce in obscene material and its exhibition in places of public accommodation, including "adult" theaters. There is a proper state concern with safeguarding against crime and the other arguably ill effects of obscenity by prohibiting the public or commercial exhibition of obscene material. Though conclusive proof is lacking, the States may reasonably determine that a nexus does or might exist between antisocial behavior and obscene material, just as States have acted on unprovable assumptions in other areas of public control. Though States are free to adopt a laissez-faire policy toward commercialized obscenity, they are not constitutionally obliged to do so. Exhibition of obscene material in places of public accommodation is not protected by any constitutional doctrine of privacy. A commercial theater cannot be equated with a private home; nor is there here a privacy right arising from a special relationship, such as marriage. Nor can the privacy of the home be equated with a "zone" of "privacy" that follows a consumer of obscene materials wherever he goes. Preventing the unlimited display of obscene material is not thought control. Not all conduct directly involving "consenting adults" only has a claim to constitutional protection. The Georgia obscenity laws involved herein should now be re-evaluated in the light of the First Amendment standards newly enunciated by the Court in *Miller v. California*.

C

Vacated and remanded.

Miller v. California

413 U.S. 15 (1973)

FACTS

Defendant-appellant Miller was convicted of mailing unsolicited sexually explicit material in violation of a California statute §311.2(a) for knowingly distributing five unsolicited advertising brochures by mail. The brochures advertised the sale of illustrated adult books, and themselves contained descriptive printed material as well as drawings and pictures that explicitly depicted men and women in groups engaging in a variety of sexual activities with their genitals often prominently displayed. The trial court instructed the jury to evaluate the materials by the contemporary community standards of California. Appellant's conviction was affirmed on appeal.

I

May the states regulate the distribution of obscene material without violating the First Amendment?

R

Obscene material can be regulated by the States if the material is utterly without any redeeming social value, and if the laws restricting the dissemination of the material specifically define what is inappropriate, are narrowly drawn, and act in accordance with constitutional standards for defining obscenity.

A

Obscene material is not protected by the First Amendment. A work may be subject to state regulation where that work, taken as a whole, appeals to the prurient interest in sex; portrays, in a patently offensive way, sexual conduct specifically defined by the applicable state law; and, taken as a whole, does not have serious literary, artistic, political, or scientific value. The basic guidelines for the trier of fact must be: (a) whether "the average person, applying contemporary community standards" would find that the work, taken as a whole, appeals to the prurient interest, (b) whether the work depicts or describes, in a patently offensive way, sexual conduct specifically defined by the applicable state law, and (c) whether the work, taken as a whole, lacks serious literary, artistic, political, or scientific value. If a state obscenity law is thus limited, First Amendment values are adequately protected by ultimate independent appellate review of constitutional claims when necessary. The test of "utterly without redeeming social value" articulated in Memoirs, supra, is rejected as a constitutional standard. The jury may measure the essentially factual issues of prurient appeal and patent offensiveness by the standard that prevails in the forum community, and need not employ a "national standard." Vacated and remanded. In this case, the California statute at issue does not meet with these Constitutional requirements, and therefore the decision of the prior court is vacated and remanded.

C

Vacated and remanded.

New York v. Ferber

458 U.S. 747 (1982)

FACTS

A New York statute prohibits persons from knowingly promoting a sexual performance by a child under the age of 16 by distributing material which depicts such a performance. The statute defines "sexual performance" as any performance that includes sexual conduct by such a child, and "sexual conduct" is in turn defined as actual or simulated sexual intercourse, deviate sexual intercourse, sexual bestiality, masturbation, sado-masochistic abuse, or lewd exhibition of the genitals. Respondent bookstore proprietor was convicted under the statute for selling films depicting young boys masturbating, and the Appellate Division of the New York Supreme Court affirmed. The New York Court of Appeals reversed, holding that the statute violated the First Amendment as being the explicit inclusion of an obscenity standard in a companion statute banning the knowing dissemination of similarly defined material, the statute in question could not be construed to include an obscenity standard, and therefore would prohibit the promotion of materials traditionally entitled to protection under the First Amendment.

I

May the state regulate child pornography?

R

The state may regulate child pornography if it is a visual depiction of sexual conduct specifically described by the state by children below the specified age and made with some scienter.

A

As applied to respondent and others who distribute similar material, the statute in question does not violate the First Amendment as applied to the States through the Fourteenth Amendment. The States are entitled to greater leeway in the regulation of pornographic depictions of children for the following reasons: (1) the legislative judgment that the use of children as subjects of pornographic materials is harmful to the physiological, emotional, and mental health of the child, easily passes muster under the First Amendment; (2) the standard of *Miller v. California*, for determining what is legally obscene is not a satisfactory solution to the child pornography problem; (3) the advertising and selling of child pornography provide an economic motive for and are thus an integral part of the production of such materials, an activity illegal throughout the Nation; (4) the value of permitting live performances and photographic reproductions of children engaged in lewd exhibitions is exceedingly modest, if not *de minimis*; and (5) recognizing and classifying child pornography as a category of material outside the First Amendment's protection is not incompatible with this Court's decisions dealing with what speech is unprotected. When a definable class of material, such as that covered by the New York statute, bears so heavily and pervasively on the welfare of children engaged in its production, the balance of competing interests is clearly struck, and it is permissible to consider these materials as without the First Amendment's protection. The New York statute describes a category of material the production and distribution of which is not entitled to First Amendment protection. Accordingly, there is nothing unconstitutionally "under-inclusive" about the statute, and the State is not barred by the First Amendment from prohibiting the distribution of such unprotected materials produced outside the State. Nor is the New York statute unconstitutionally overbroad as forbidding the distribution of material with serious literary, scientific, or educational value. The substantial overbreath rule of *Broadrick v. Oklahoma,* applies. This is the paradigmatic case of a state statute whose legitimate reach dwarfs its arguably impermissible applications. "[W]hatever overbreadth may exist should be cured through case-by-case analysis of the fact situations to which [the statute's] sanctions, assertedly, may not be applied." *Broadrick v. Oklahoma.*

C

Reversed and remanded.

Ashcroft v. Free Speech Coalition

535 U.S. 234 (2002)

FACTS

The Child Pornography Prevention Act of 1996 (CPPA) expands the federal prohibition on child pornography to include not only pornographic images made using actual children, 18 U. S. C. §2256(8)(A), but also "any visual depiction, including any photograph, film, video, picture, or computer or computer-generated image or picture" that "is, or appears to be, of a minor engaging in sexually explicit conduct," §2256(8)(B), and any sexually explicit image that is "advertised, promoted, presented, described, or distributed in such a manner that conveys the impression" it depicts "a minor engaging in sexually explicit conduct," §2256(8)(D). Thus, §2256(8)(B) bans a range of sexually explicit images, sometimes called "virtual child pornography," that appear to depict minors but were produced by means other than using real children, such as through the use of youthful-looking adults or computer-imaging technology. Section 2256(8)(D) is aimed at preventing the production or distribution of pornographic material pandered as child pornography. Fearing that the CPPA threatened their activities, respondents, an adult-entertainment trade association and others, filed this suit alleging that the "appears to be" and "conveys the impression" provisions are overbroad and vague, chilling production of works protected by the First Amendment. The District Court disagreed and granted the Government summary judgment, but the Ninth Circuit reversed. Generally, pornography can be banned only if it is obscene under *Miller* v. *California*, but pornography depicting actual children can be proscribed whether or not the images are obscene because of the State's interest in protecting the children exploited by the production process, *New York* v. *Ferber*, and in prosecuting those who promote such sexual exploitation. The Ninth Circuit held the CPPA invalid on its face, finding it to be substantially overbroad because it bans materials that are neither obscene under *Miller* nor produced by the exploitation of real children as in *Ferber*.

I

Is the CPPA, which expands the federal prohibition on child pornography to include "any visual depiction, including any photograph, film, video, picture, or computer or computer-generated image or picture" that "is, or appears to be, of a minor engaging in sexually explicit conduct ..." constitutional?

R

The CPPA is unconstitutional because it extends to images that are not obscene under the *Miller* standard, which requires the Government to prove that the work in question, taken as a whole, appeals to the prurient interest, is patently offensive in light of community standards, and lacks serious literary, artistic, political, or scientific value.

A

The prohibitions of §§2256(8)(B) and 2256(8)(D) are overbroad and unconstitutional. Section 2256(8)(B) covers materials beyond the categories recognized in *Ferber* and *Miller,* and the reasons the Government offers in support of limiting the freedom of speech have no justification in this Court's precedents or First Amendment law. The CPPA is inconsistent with *Miller.* It extends to images that are not obscene under the *Miller* standard, which requires the Government to prove that the work in question, taken as a whole, appeals to the prurient interest, is patently offensive in light of community standards, and lacks serious literary, artistic, political, or scientific value. Materials need not appeal to the prurient interest under the CPPA, which proscribes any depiction of sexually explicit activity, no matter how it is presented. It is not necessary, moreover, that the image be patently offensive. Pictures of what appear to be 17-year-olds engaging in sexually explicit activity do not in every case contravene community standards. The CPPA also prohibits speech having serious redeeming value, proscribing the visual depiction of an idea--that of teenagers engaging in sexual activity--that is a fact of modern society and has been a theme in art and literature for centuries. A number of acclaimed movies, filmed without any child actors, explore themes within the wide sweep of the statute's prohibitions. If those movies contain a single graphic depiction of sexual activity within the statutory definition, their possessor would be subject to severe punishment without inquiry into the literary value of the work. This is inconsistent with an essential First Amendment rule: A work's artistic merit does not depend on the presence of a single explicit scene. Under *Miller*, redeeming value is judged by considering the work as a whole. Where the scene is part of the narrative, the work itself does not for this reason become obscene, even though the scene in isolation might be offensive. The CPPA cannot be read to prohibit obscenity, because it lacks the required link between its prohibitions and the affront to community standards prohibited by the obscenity definition. The CPPA finds no support in *Ferber*. The Court rejects the Government's argument that speech prohibited by the CPPA is virtually indistinguishable from material that may be banned under *Ferber*. That case upheld a prohibition on the distribution and sale of child pornography, as well as its production, because the acts were "intrinsically related" to the sexual abuse of children in two ways. First, as a permanent record of a child's abuse, the continued circulation itself would harm the child who had participated. Second, because the traffic in child pornography was an economic motive for its production, the State had an interest in closing the distribution network. Under either rationale, the speech had what the Court in effect held was a proximate link to the crime from which it came. In contrast to the speech in *Ferber*, speech that is itself the record of sexual abuse, the CPPA prohibits speech that records no crime and creates no victims by its production. Virtual child pornography is not "intrinsically related" to the sexual abuse of children. While the Government asserts that the images can lead to actual instances of child abuse, the causal link is contingent and indirect. The harm does not necessarily follow from the speech, but depends upon some unquantified potential for subsequent criminal acts. Where a defendant engages in the "commercial exploitation" of erotica solely for the sake of prurient appeal, the context created may be relevant to evaluating whether the materials are obscene. Section 2256(8)(D), however, prohibits a substantial amount of speech that falls outside *Ginzburg*'s rationale. Proscribed material is tainted and unlawful in the hands of all who receive it, though they bear no responsibility for how it was marketed, sold, or described. The statute, furthermore, does not require that the context be part of an effort at "commercial exploitation." Thus, the CPPA does more than prohibit pandering. It bans possession of material pandered as child pornography by someone earlier in the distribution chain, as well as a sexually explicit film that contains no youthful actors but has been packaged to suggest a prohibited movie. Possession is a crime even when the possessor knows the movie was mislabeled. The First Amendment requires a more precise restriction. In light of the foregoing, respondents' contention that §§2256(8)(B) and 2256(8)(D) are void for vagueness need not be addressed.

C

Affirmed.

Young v. American Mini Theatres Inc.

427 U.S. 50 (1976)

FACTS

Respondent operators of two adult motion picture theaters brought this action against petitioner city officials for injunctive relief and a declaratory judgment of unconstitutionality regarding two 1972 Detroit zoning ordinances that amended an "Anti-Skid Row Ordinance" adopted 10 years earlier. The 1972 ordinances provide that an adult theater may not (apart from a special waiver) be located within 1,000 feet of any two other "regulated uses" or within 500 feet of a residential area. The term "regulated uses" applies to 10 different kinds of establishments in addition to adult theaters, including adult book stores, cabarets, bars, taxi dance halls, and hotels. If the theater is used to present "material distinguished or characterized by an emphasis on matter depicting . . . `Specified Sexual Activities' or `Specified Anatomical Areas'" it is an "adult" establishment. The District Court upheld the ordinances, and granted petitioners' motion for summary judgment. The Court of Appeals reversed, holding that the ordinances constituted a prior restraint on constitutionally protected communication and violated equal protection. Respondents, in addition to asserting the correctness of that court's ruling with respect to those constitutional issues, contend that the ordinances are void for vagueness. While not attacking the specificity of the definitions of sexual activities or anatomical areas, respondents maintain (1) that they cannot determine how much of the described activity may be permissible before an exhibition is "characterized by an emphasis" on such matter, and (2) that the ordinances do not specify adequate procedures or standards for obtaining a waiver of the 1,000-foot restriction.

I Is a zoning ordnance to disperse pornographic businesses, constitutional?

R The government may, consistent with the Constitution, restrict pornographic businesses via zoning laws.

A The ordinances as applied to these respondents do not violate the Due Process Clause of the Fourteenth Amendment on the ground of vagueness. Neither of the asserted elements of vagueness has affected these respondents, both of which propose to offer adult fare on a regular basis and allege no ground for claiming or anticipating any waiver of the 1,000-foot restriction. The ordinances will have no demonstrably significant effect on the exhibition of films protected by the First Amendment. To the extent that any area of doubt exists as to the amount of sexually explicit activity that may be portrayed before material can be said to be "characterized by an emphasis" on such matter, there is no reason why the ordinances are not "readily subject to a narrowing construction by the state courts." This would therefore be an inappropriate case to apply the principle urged by respondents that they be permitted to challenge the ordinances, not because their own rights of free expression are violated, but because of the assumption that the ordinances' very existence may cause others not before the court to refrain from constitutionally protected speech or expression. The ordinances are not invalid under the First Amendment as prior restraints on protected communication because of the licensing or zoning requirements. Though adult films may be exhibited commercially only in licensed theaters, that is also true of all films. That the place where films may be exhibited is regulated does not violate free expression, the city's interest in planning and regulating the use of property for commercial purposes being clearly adequate to support the location restriction.

C

Reversed.

City of Erie v. Pap's A.M.

529 U.S. 277 (2000)

FACTS

Erie, Pennsylvania, enacted an ordinance making it a summary offense to knowingly or intentionally appear in public in a "state of nudity." Respondent Pap's A. M. (hereinafter Pap's), a Pennsylvania corporation, operated "Kandyland," an Erie establishment featuring totally nude erotic dancing by women. To comply with the ordinance, these dancers had to wear, at a minimum, "pasties" and a "G-string." Pap's filed suit against Erie and city officials seeking declaratory relief and a permanent injunction against the ordinance's enforcement. The Court of Common Pleas struck down the ordinance as unconstitutional, but the Commonwealth Court reversed. The Pennsylvania Supreme Court in turn reversed, finding that the ordinance's public nudity sections violated Pap's right to freedom of expression as protected by the First and Fourteenth Amendments. The Pennsylvania court held that nude dancing is expressive conduct entitled to some quantum of protection under the First Amendment, a view that the court noted was endorsed by eight Members of this Court in *Barnes* v. *Glen Theatre, Inc.* The Pennsylvania court explained that, although one stated purpose of the ordinance was to combat negative secondary effects, there was also an unmentioned purpose to "impact negatively on the erotic message of the dance." Accordingly, the Pennsylvania court concluded that the ordinance was related to the suppression of expression. Because the ordinance was not content neutral, it was subject to strict scrutiny. The court held that the ordinance failed the narrow tailoring requirement of strict scrutiny. After this Court granted certiorari, Pap's filed a motion to dismiss the case as moot, noting that Kandyland no longer operated as a nude dancing club, and that Pap's did not operate such a club at any other location. The U.S. Supreme Court denied the motion.

I

Does the ordinance's public nudity sections violate Pap's right to freedom of expression as protected by the First and Fourteenth Amendments?

R

Government restrictions on public nudity such as Erie's ordinance should be evaluated under the framework set forth in *United States* v. *O'Brien*, for content-neutral restrictions on symbolic speech.

A

Government restrictions on public nudity such as Erie's ordinance should be evaluated under the framework set forth in *United States* v. *O'Brien*, for content-neutral restrictions on symbolic speech. Although being "in a state of nudity" is not an inherently expressive condition, nude dancing of the type at issue here is expressive conduct that falls within the outer ambit of the First Amendment's protection. What level of scrutiny applies is determined by whether the ordinance is related to the suppression of expression. If the governmental purpose in enacting the ordinance is unrelated to such suppression, the ordinance need only satisfy the "less stringent," intermediate *O'Brien* standard. If the governmental interest is related to the expression's content, however, the ordinance falls outside *O'Brien* and must be justified under the more demanding, strict scrutiny standard. The ordinance here, like the statute in *Barnes*, is on its face a general prohibition on public nudity. By its terms, it regulates conduct alone. It does not target nudity that contains an erotic message; rather, it bans all public nudity, regardless of whether that nudity is accompanied by expressive activity. Although Pap's contends that the ordinance is related to the suppression of expression because its preamble suggests that its actual purpose is to prohibit erotic dancing of the type performed at Kandyland that is not how the Pennsylvania Supreme Court interpreted that language. Rather, the Pennsylvania Supreme Court construed the preamble to mean that one purpose of the ordinance was to combat negative secondary effects. That is, the ordinance is aimed at combating crime and other negative secondary effects caused by the presence of adult entertainment establishments like Kandyland and not at suppressing the erotic message conveyed by this type of nude dancing. Moreover, this Court will not strike down an otherwise constitutional statute on the basis of an alleged illicit motive. Even if Erie's public nudity ban has some minimal effect on the erotic message by muting that portion of the expression that occurs when the last stitch is dropped, the dancers at Kandyland and other such establishments are free to perform wearing pasties and G-strings. Any effect on the overall expression is therefore *de minimis*. Thus, Erie's ordinance is valid if it satisfies the *O'Brien* test. Here, Erie's ordinance satisfies *O'Brien*'s four-factor test. First, the ordinance is within Erie's constitutional power to enact because the city's efforts to protect public health and safety are clearly within its police powers. Second, the ordinance furthers the important government interests of regulating conduct through a public nudity ban and of combating the harmful secondary effects associated with nude dancing. The evidentiary standard described in *Renton* controls here, and Erie meets that standard. In any event, the ordinance's preamble also relies on the city council's express findings that "certain lewd, immoral activities carried on in public places for profit are highly detrimental to the public health, safety and welfare . . ." The council members, familiar with commercial downtown Erie, are the individuals who would likely have had first-hand knowledge of what took place at and around nude dancing establishments there, and can make particularized, expert judgments about the resulting harmful secondary effects. The fact that this sort of leeway is appropriate in this case, which involves a content-neutral restriction that regulates conduct, says nothing whatsoever about its appropriateness in a case involving actual regulation of First Amendment expression. Also, although requiring dancers to wear pasties and G-strings may not greatly reduce these secondary effects, *O'Brien* requires only that the regulation further the interest in combating such effects. The ordinance also satisfies *O'Brien*'s third factor, that the government interest is unrelated to the suppression of free expression, as discussed *supra*. The fourth *O'Brien* factor--that the restriction is no greater than is essential to the furtherance of the government interest--is satisfied as well. The ordinance regulates conduct, and any incidental impact on the expressive element of nude dancing is *de minimis*. The pasties and G-string requirement is a minimal restriction in furtherance of the asserted government interests, and the restriction leaves ample capacity to convey the dancer's erotic message.

C

The judgment is reversed, and the case is remanded.

Stanley v. Georgia

394 U.S. 557 (1969)

FACTS

Under authority of a warrant to search appellant's home for evidence of his alleged bookmaking activities, officers found some films in his bedroom. The films were projected and deemed to be obscene. Appellant was arrested for their possession. He was thereafter indicted, tried, and convicted for "knowingly hav[ing] possession of . . . obscene matter" in violation of a Georgia law. The Georgia Supreme Court affirmed, holding it "not essential to an indictment charging one with possession of obscene matter that it be alleged that such possession was `with intent to sell, expose or circulate the same.'" Appellant contends that the Georgia obscenity statute is unconstitutional insofar as it punishes mere private possession of obscene matter. Georgia, relying on *Roth v. United States*, argues the statute's validity on the ground that "obscenity is not within the area of constitutionally protected speech or press."

I

Can a state ban the possession of obscene materials?

R

The state cannot criminalize the private possession of obscene materials.

A

The First Amendment as made applicable to the States by the Fourteenth prohibits making mere private possession of obscene material a crime. Neither *Roth*, nor subsequent decisions of the Court were made in the context of a statute punishing mere private possession of obscene material, but involved governmental power to prohibit or regulate certain public actions respecting obscene matter. The Constitution protects the right to receive information and ideas, regardless of their social worth, and to be generally free from governmental intrusions into one's privacy and control of one's thoughts. The State may not prohibit mere possession of obscene matter on the ground that it may lead to antisocial conduct, Roth, supra, distinguished, or proscribe such possession on the ground that it is a necessary incident to a statutory scheme prohibiting distribution.

C

Reversed and remanded.

Cohen v. California

403 U.S. 15 (1971)

FACTS

On April 26, 1968, the defendant-appellant Paul Robert Cohen was observed in the Los Angeles County Courthouse in the corridor outside of division 20 of the municipal court wearing a jacket bearing the words `Fuck the Draft' which were plainly visible. There were women and children present in the corridor. The defendant was arrested. The defendant testified that he wore the jacket knowing that the words were on the jacket as a means of informing the public of the depth of his feelings against the Vietnam War and the draft. The defendant did not engage in, nor threaten to engage in, nor did anyone as the result of his conduct in fact commit or threaten to commit any act of violence. The defendant did not make any loud or unusual noise, nor was there any evidence that he uttered any sound prior to his arrest. Cohen was convicted in the Los Angeles Municipal Court of violating that part of California Penal Code 415 which prohibits "maliciously and willfully disturbing the peace or quiet of any neighborhood or person . . . by . . . offensive conduct . . . ." He was given 30 days' imprisonment. In affirming the conviction the Court of Appeal held that "offensive conduct" means "behavior which has a tendency to provoke others to acts of violence or to in turn disturb the peace," and that the State had proved this element because, on the facts of this case, "it was certainly reasonably foreseeable that such conduct might cause others to rise up to commit a violent act against the person of the defendant or attempt to forceably remove his jacket." The California Supreme Court declined review by a divided vote. The case then went before the U.S. Supreme Court.

I

Can states constitutionally suppress speech that contains offensive words or phrases simply because these words can disturb the peace?

R

The states cannot constitutionally restrict speech on the ground that words or phrases are, in of themselves and without more, patently offensive; however, when they are likely to incite lawlessness and violence, the government may impose restrictions.

A

The conviction quite clearly rests upon the asserted offensiveness of the words Cohen used to convey his message to the public. The only "conduct" which the State sought to punish is the fact of communication. Thus, we deal here with a conviction resting solely upon "speech," not upon any separately identifiable conduct which allegedly was intended by Cohen to be perceived by others as expressive of particular views but which, on its face, does not necessarily convey any message and hence arguably could be regulated without effectively repressing Cohen's ability to express himself. Further, the State certainly lacks power to punish Cohen for the underlying content of the message the inscription conveyed. At least so long as there is no showing of an intent to incite disobedience to or disruption of the draft, Cohen could not, consistently with the First and Fourteenth Amendments, be punished for asserting the evident position on the inutility or immorality of the draft his jacket reflected. Appellant's conviction, then, rests squarely upon his exercise of the "freedom of speech" protected from arbitrary governmental interference by the Constitution and can be justified, if at all, only as a valid regulation of the manner in which he exercised that freedom, not as a permissible prohibition on the substantive message it conveys. This does not end the inquiry, of course, for the First and Fourteenth Amendments have never been thought to give absolute protection to every individual to speak whenever or wherever he pleases. First, there is nothing in the statute that says that this speech, acceptable elsewhere, is not allowed in a courthouse. Second there is no rule of law that states that the government can, without more, restrict this type of speech. Third, the words on Cohen's jacket were not fighting words in that they were directed to one particular person or group to people; and there was no intent on the part of Cohen to provoke anyone to act. Fourth, the fact that there might have been disinclined listeners in the courthouse does not permit the state to restrict Cohen's speech; people in public places risk confronting speech that they might find offensive. Finally, and in the same vein, we cannot indulge the simplistic assumption that one can forbid particular words without also running a substantial risk of suppressing ideas in the process. Indeed, governments might soon seize upon the censorship of particular words as a convenient guise for banning the expression of unpopular views. We have been able, as noted above, to discern little social benefit that might result from running the risk of opening the door to such grave results. It is, in sum, our judgment that, absent a more particularized and compelling reason for its actions, the State may not, consistently with the First and Fourteenth Amendments, make the simple public display here involved of this single four-letter expletive a criminal offense. Because that is the only arguably sustainable rationale for the conviction here at issue, the judgment below must be reversed.

C The judgment below must be reversed.

FCC v. Pacifica Foundation

438 U.S. 726 (1978)

FACTS

A radio station of Defendant-respondent Pacifica Foundation (hereinafter respondent) made an afternoon broadcast of a satiric monologue, entitled "Filthy Words," which listed and repeated a variety of colloquial uses of "words you couldn't say on the public airwaves." A father who heard the broadcast while driving with his young son complained to the Federal Communications Commission (FCC), which, after forwarding the complaint for comment to and receiving a response from respondent, issued a declaratory order granting the complaint. While not imposing formal sanctions, the FCC stated that the order would be "associated with the station's license file, and in the event subsequent complaints are received, the Commission will then decide whether it should utilize any of the available sanctions it has been granted by Congress." In its memorandum opinion, the FCC stated that it intended to "clarify the standards which will be utilized in considering" the growing number of complaints about indecent radio broadcasts, and it advanced several reasons for treating that type of speech differently from other forms of expression. The FCC found a power to regulate indecent broadcasting in 18 U.S.C. 1464 (1976 ed.), which forbids the use of "any obscene, indecent, or profane language by means of radio communications." The FCC characterized the language of the monologue as "patently offensive," though not necessarily obscene, and expressed the opinion that it should be regulated by principles analogous to the law of nuisance where the "law generally speaks to channeling behavior rather than actually prohibiting it." The FCC found that certain words in the monologue depicted sexual and excretory activities in a particularly offensive manner, noted that they were broadcast in the early afternoon "when children are undoubtedly in the audience," and concluded that the language as broadcast was indecent and prohibited by 1464. A three-judge panel of the Court of Appeals reversed, one judge concluding that the FCC's action was invalid either on the ground that the order constituted censorship, which was expressly forbidden by 326 of the Communications Act of 1934, or on the ground that the FCC's opinion was the functional equivalent of [438 U.S. 726, 727] a rule, and as such was "overbroad." Another judge, who felt that 326's censorship provision did not apply to broadcasts forbidden by 1464, concluded that 1464, construed narrowly as it has to be, covers only language that is obscene or otherwise unprotected by the First Amendment. The third judge, dissenting, concluded that the FCC had correctly condemned the daytime broadcast as indecent. Respondent contends that the broadcast was not indecent within the meaning of the statute because of the absence of prurient appeal.

I Can the government constitutionally limit the public broadcast of indecent language without violating the First Amendment?

R Indecent words that are broadcasted can, in certain situations (where the message can be [accessed] heard by children, for example), be limited by the government without violating the First Amendment.

FCC v. Pacifica Foundation

438 U.S. 726 (1978)

A The FCC's order was an adjudication under 5 U.S.C. 554 (e), the character of which was not changed by the general statements in the memorandum opinion; nor did the FCC's action constitute rulemaking or the promulgation of regulations. Hence, the Court's review must focus on the FCC's determination that the monologue was indecent as broadcast. Section 326 does not limit the FCC's authority to sanction licensees who engage in obscene, indecent, or profane broadcasting. Though the censorship ban precludes editing proposed broadcasts in advance, the ban does not deny the FCC the power to review the content of completed broadcasts. The FCC was warranted in concluding that indecent language within the meaning of 1464 was used in the challenged broadcast. The words "obscene, indecent, or profane" are in the disjunctive, implying that each has a separate meaning. Though prurient appeal is an element of "obscene," it is not an element of "indecent," which merely refers to noncomformance with accepted standards of morality. Contrary to respondent's argument, this Court in *Hamling v. United States* has not foreclosed a reading of 1464 that authorizes a proscription of "indecent" language that is not obscene, for the statute involved in that case, unlike 1464, focused upon the prurient, and dealt primarily with printed matter in sealed envelopes mailed from one individual to another, whereas 1464 deals with the content of public broadcasts. Of all forms of communication, broadcasting has the most limited First Amendment protection. Among the reasons for specially treating indecent broadcasting is the uniquely pervasive presence that medium of expression occupies in the lives of our people. Broadcasts extend into the privacy of the home and it is impossible completely to avoid those that are patently offensive. Broadcasting, moreover, is uniquely accessible to children. MR. JUSTICE STEVENS, joined by THE CHIEF JUSTICE, and MR. JUSTICE REHNQUIST, concluded that the FCC's authority to proscribe this particular broadcast is not invalidated by the possibility that its construction of the statute may deter certain hypothetically protected broadcasts containing patently offensive references to sexual and excretory activities. The First Amendment does not prohibit all governmental regulation that depends on the content of speech. The content of respondent's broadcast, which was "vulgar," "offensive," and "shocking," is not entitled to absolute constitutional protection in all contexts; it is therefore necessary to evaluate the FCC's action in light of the context of that broadcast. MR. JUSTICE POWELL, joined by MR. JUSTICE BLACKMUN, concluded that the FCC's holding does not violate the First Amendment, though, being of the view that Members of this Court are not free generally to decide on the basis of its content which speech protected by the First Amendment is most valuable and therefore deserving of First Amendment protection, and which is less "valuable" and hence less deserving of protection.

C The judgment is reversed.

Sable Communications of California v. FCC

492 U.S. 115 (1989)

FACTS

Section 223(b) of the Communications Act of 1934, as amended, bans indecent as well as obscene interstate commercial telephone messages commonly known as "dial-a-porn." Under its predecessor provision - which sought to restrict minors' access to dial-a-porn - the Federal Communications Commission (FCC), after lengthy court proceedings, had promulgated regulations laying out means by which dial-a-porn sponsors could screen out underaged callers. Sable Communications of California, which offers sexually oriented prerecorded telephone messages to callers both in and outside the Los Angeles metropolitan area, brought suit in the District Court, claiming that 223(b)'s obscenity and indecency provisions were unconstitutional, chiefly under the First and Fourteenth Amendments, and seeking an injunction enjoining the FCC and the Justice Department from initiating any criminal investigation or prosecution, civil action, or administrative proceeding under the statute and a declaratory judgment. The court denied Sable's request for a preliminary injunction against enforcement of the ban on obscene telephone messages, rejecting the argument that the statute was unconstitutional because it created a national standard of obscenity. However, it issued the injunction with regard to the indecent speech provision, holding that the provision was overbroad and unconstitutional because it was not narrowly drawn to achieve the legitimate state interest of protecting children from exposure to indecent dial-a-porn messages.

I May the government ban indecent phone messages?

R The government may ban indecent phone messages only if by doing so it is promoting a "compelling" governmental interest[s] by using the least restrictive means possible.

A Section 223(b) does not unconstitutionally prohibit the interstate transmission of obscene commercial telephone messages. The protection of the First Amendment does not extend to obscene speech. In addition, 223(b) does not contravene the "contemporary community standards" requirement of *Miller v. California*, since it no more establishes a "national standard" of obscenity than do federal statutes prohibiting the mailing of obscene materials or the broadcasting of obscene messages. There is no constitutional barrier under Miller to prohibiting communications that are obscene in some communities under local standards even though they are not obscene in others. Sable, which has the burden of complying with the prohibition, is free to tailor its messages, on a selective basis to the communities it chooses to serve. Section 223(b)'s ban on indecent telephone messages violates the First Amendment since the statute's denial of adult access to such messages far exceeds that which is necessary to serve the compelling interest of preventing minors from being exposed to the messages. *FCC v. Pacifica Foundation*, an emphatically narrow ruling giving the FCC power to regulate an indecent radio broadcast, is readily distinguishable from these cases. *Pacifica*, which did not involve a total ban on broadcasting indecent material, relied on the "unique" attributes of broadcasting, which can intrude on the privacy of the home without prior warning of content and which is uniquely accessible to children. In contrast, the dial-it medium requires the listener to take affirmative steps to receive the communications. The Government's argument that nothing less than a total ban could prevent children from gaining access to the messages and that this Court should defer to Congress' conclusions and factual findings to that effect is unpersuasive. There is no evidence to show that children would have evaded the rules that the FCC, after prolonged proceedings, had determined would keep the messages out of their reach. Moreover, deference to Congress' legislative findings cannot limit judicial inquiry where First Amendment rights are at stake. Here, the congressional record contains no legislative findings that would justify a conclusion that there are no constitutionally acceptable less restrictive means to achieve the Government's interest in protecting minors.

C

Affirmed.

Reno v. American Civil Liberties Union

521 U.S. 844 (1997)

FACTS

Two provisions of the Communications Decency Act of 1996 (CDA or Act) seek to protect minors from harmful material on the Internet, an international network of interconnected computers that enables millions of people to communicate with one another in "cyberspace" and to access vast amounts of information from around the world. Title 47 U. S. C. A. §223(a)(1)(B)(ii) (Supp. 1997) criminalizes the "knowing" transmission of "obscene or indecent" messages to any recipient under 18 years of age. Section 223(d) prohibits the "knowin[g]" sending or displaying to a person under 18 of any message "that, in context, depicts or describes, in terms patently offensive as measured by contemporary community standards, sexual or excretory activities or organs." Affirmative defenses are provided for those who take "good faith, . . . effective . . . actions" to restrict access by minors to the prohibited communications, §223(e)(5)(A), and those who restrict such access by requiring certain designated forms of age proof, such as a verified credit card or an adult identification number, §223(e)(5)(B). A number of plaintiffs filed suit challenging the constitutionality of §§223(a)(1) and 223(d). After making extensive findings of fact, a three judge District Court convened pursuant to the Act entered a preliminary injunction against enforcement of both challenged provisions. The court's judgment enjoins the Government from enforcing §223(a)(1)(B)'s prohibitions insofar as they relate to "indecent" communications, but expressly preserves the Government's right to investigate and prosecute the obscenity or child pornography activities prohibited therein. The injunction against enforcement of §223(d) is unqualified because that section contains no separate reference to obscenity or child pornography. The Government appealed to the U.S. Supreme Court under the Act's special review provisions, arguing that the District Court erred in holding that the CDA violated both the First Amendment because it is overbroad and the Fifth Amendment because it is vague.

I Without offending the First Amendment, can the government restrict the posting of indecent or offensive messages and images on the Internet?

R The government may regulate access to indecent and sexually explicit content; however, such laws must be narrowly tailored, specific and not overbroad and written in a way that the constitutional rights of adults to access the same material will not be violated.

A The CDA's "indecent transmission" and "patently offensive display" provisions abridge "the freedom of speech" protected by the First Amendment. Although the CDA's vagueness is relevant to the First Amendment overbreadth inquiry, the judgment should be affirmed without reaching the Fifth Amendment issue. A close look at the precedents relied on by the Government - *Ginsberg v. New York; FCC v. Pacifica Foundation*; and *Renton v. Playtime Theatres, Inc.* - raises, rather than relieves, doubts about the CDA's constitutionality. The CDA differs from the various laws and orders upheld in those cases in many ways, including that it does not allow parents to consent to their children's use of restricted materials; is not limited to commercial transactions; fails to provide any definition of "indecent" and omits any requirement that "patently offensive" material lack socially redeeming value; neither limits its broad categorical prohibitions to particular times nor bases them on an evaluation by an agency familiar with the medium's unique characteristics; is punitive; applies to a medium that, unlike radio, receives full First Amendment protection; and cannot be properly analyzed as a form of time, place, and manner regulation because it is a content based blanket restriction on speech. These precedents, then, do not require the Court to uphold the CDA and are fully consistent with the application of the most stringent review of its provisions. The special factors recognized in some of the Court's cases as justifying regulation of the broadcast media-- the history of extensive government regulation of broadcasting; the scarcity of available frequencies at its inception; and its "invasive" nature - are not present in cyberspace. Thus, these cases provide no basis for qualifying the level of First Amendment scrutiny that should be applied to the Internet. Regardless of whether the CDA is so vague that it violates the Fifth Amendment, the many ambiguities concerning the scope of its coverage render it problematic for First Amendment purposes. For instance, its use of the undefined terms "indecent" and "patently offensive" will provoke uncertainty among speakers about how the two standards relate to each other and just what they mean. The vagueness of such a content based regulation coupled with its increased deterrent effect as a criminal statute raise special First Amendment concerns because of its obvious chilling effect on free speech. Contrary to the Government's argument, the CDA is not saved from vagueness by the fact that its "patently offensive" standard repeats the second part of the three prong obscenity test set forth in *Miller v. California*. The second *Miller* prong reduces the inherent vagueness of its own "patently offensive" term by requiring that the proscribed material be "specifically defined by the applicable state law." In addition, the CDA applies only to "sexual conduct," whereas, the CDA prohibition extends also to "excretory activities" and "organs" of both a sexual and excretory nature. Each of *Miller's* other two prongs also critically limits the uncertain sweep of the obscenity definition. Just because a definition including three limitations is not vague, it does not follow that one of those limitations, standing alone, is not vague. The CDA's vagueness undermines the likelihood that it has been carefully tailored to the congressional goal of protecting minors from potentially harmful materials. The CDA lacks the precision that the First Amendment requires when a statute regulates the content of speech. Although the Government has an interest in protecting children from potentially harmful materials the CDA pursues that interest by suppressing a large amount of speech that adults have a constitutional right to send and receive. Its breadth is wholly unprecedented. The CDA's burden on adult speech is unacceptable if less restrictive alternatives would be at least as effective in achieving the Act's legitimate purposes. The Government has not proved otherwise. On the other hand, the District Court found that currently available user based software suggests that a reasonably effective method by which parents can prevent their children from accessing material which the parents believe is inappropriate will soon be widely available. Moreover, the arguments in this Court referred to possible alternatives such as requiring that indecent material be "tagged" to facilitate parental control, making exceptions for messages with artistic or educational value, providing some tolerance for parental choice, and regulating some portions of the Internet differently than others. Particularly in the light of the absence of any detailed congressional findings, or even hearings addressing the CDA's special problems, the Court is persuaded that the CDA is not narrowly tailored. The Government's three additional arguments for sustaining the CDA's affirmative prohibitions are rejected. First, the contention that the Act is constitutional because it leaves open ample "alternative channels" of communication is unpersuasive because the CDA regulates speech on the basis of its content, so that a "time, place, and manner" analysis is inapplicable. Second, the assertion that the CDA's "knowledge" and "specific person" requirements significantly restrict its permissible application to communications to persons the sender knows to be under 18 is untenable, given that most Internet forums are open to all comers and that even the strongest reading of the "specific person" requirement would confer broad powers of censorship, in the form of a "heckler's veto," upon any opponent of indecent speech. Finally, there is no textual support for the submission that material having scientific, educational, or other redeeming social value will necessarily fall outside the CDA's prohibitions. The §223(e)(5) defenses do not constitute the sort of "narrow tailoring" that would save the CDA. The Government's argument that transmitters may take protective "good faith actio[n]" by "tagging" their indecent communications in a way that would indicate their contents, thus permitting recipients to block their reception with appropriate software, is illusory, given the requirement that such action be "effective": The proposed screening software does not currently exist, but, even if it did, there would be no way of knowing whether a potential recipient would actually block the encoded material. The Government also failed to prove that §223(b)(5)'s verification defense would significantly reduce the CDA's heavy burden on adult speech. Although such verification is actually being used by some commercial providers of sexually explicit material, the District Court's findings indicate that it is not economically feasible for most noncommercial speakers. The Government's argument that this Court should preserve the CDA's constitutionality by honoring its severability clause, §608, and by construing nonseverable terms narrowly, is acceptable in only one respect. Because obscene speech may be banned totally, see §223(a)'s restriction of "obscene" material enjoys a textual manifestation separate from that for "indecent" material, the Court can sever the term "or indecent" from the statute, leaving the rest of §223(a) standing. The Government's argument that its "significant" interest in fostering the Internet's growth provides an independent basis for upholding the CDA's constitutionality is singularly unpersuasive. The dramatic expansion of this new forum contradicts the factual basis underlying this contention: that the unregulated availability of "indecent" and "patently offensive" material is driving people away from the Internet.

C

Judgment affirmed

Ashcroft v. American Civil Liberties Union

124 S.Ct. 2783 (2004)

FACTS

To protect minors from exposure to sexually explicit materials on the Internet, Congress enacted the Child Online Protection Act (COPA), 47 U. S. C. §231, which, among other things, imposes a $50,000 fine and 6 months in prison for the knowing posting, for "commercial purposes," of World Wide Web content that is "harmful to minors," but provides an affirmative defense to commercial Web speakers who restrict access to prohibited materials by "requiring use of a credit card" or "any other reasonable measures that are feasible under available technology," §231(c)(1). COPA was enacted in response to *Reno* v. *American Civil Liberties Union*, in which this Court held that the Communications Decency Act of 1996, Congress' first attempt to make the Internet safe for minors by criminalizing certain Internet speech, was unconstitutional because it was not narrowly tailored to serve a compelling governmental interest and because less restrictive alternatives were available. Respondents, Web speakers and others concerned with protecting the freedom of speech, filed suit for a preliminary injunction against COPA's enforcement. After considering testimony presented by both respondents and the Government, the District Court granted the preliminary injunction, concluding that respondents were likely to prevail on their argument that there were less restrictive alternatives to COPA, particularly blocking or filtering technology. The Third Circuit affirmed on different grounds, but this Court reversed, *Ashcroft* v. *American Civil Liberties Union*. On remand, the Third Circuit again affirmed, concluding, *inter alia*, that COPA was not the least restrictive means available for the Government to serve the interest of preventing minors from using the Internet to gain access to harmful materials.

I

Is the enforcement of COPA, which, among other things, imposes a $50,000 fine and 6 months in prison for the knowing posting, for "commercial purposes," of World Wide Web content that is "harmful to minors," constitutional?

R

COPA should be enjoined because the statute likely violates the First Amendment.

A

The Third Circuit was correct to affirm the District Court's ruling that enforcement of COPA should be enjoined because the statute likely violates the First Amendment. The District Court did not abuse its discretion when it entered the preliminary injunction. The abuse-of-discretion standard applies on review of such an injunction. Because 28 U. S. C. §1254(1)'s grant of appellate jurisdiction does not give this Court license to depart from an established review standard, the injunction must be upheld and the case remanded for trial on the merits if the underlying constitutional question is close. There is therefore no need to consider the broader constructions of the statute adopted by the Court of Appeals. The District Court concentrated primarily on the argument that there are plausible, less restrictive alternatives to COPA. When plaintiffs challenge a content-based speech restriction, the Government has the burden to prove that the proposed alternatives will not be as effective as the challenged statute. The purpose of the test is to ensure that speech is restricted no further than is necessary to accomplish Congress' goal. The District Court's conclusion that respondents were likely to prevail was not an abuse of discretion, because, on the record, the Government has not met its burden. Most importantly, respondents propose that blocking and filtering software is a less restrictive alternative, and the Government had not shown it would be likely to disprove that contention at trial. Filters impose selective restrictions on speech at the receiving end, not universal restrictions at the source. Under a filtering regime, childless adults may gain access to speech they have a right to see without having to identify themselves or provide their credit card information. Even adults with children may obtain access to the same speech on the same terms simply by turning off the filter on their home computers. Promoting filter use does not condemn as criminal any category of speech, and so the potential chilling effect is eliminated, or at least much diminished. Filters, moreover, may well be more effective than COPA. First, the record demonstrates that a filter can prevent minors from seeing all pornography, not just pornography posted to the Web from America. That COPA does not prevent minors from accessing foreign harmful materials alone makes it possible that filtering software might be more effective in serving Congress' goals. COPA's effectiveness is likely to diminish even further if it is upheld, because providers of the materials covered by the statute simply can move their operations overseas. In addition, the District Court found that verification systems may be subject to evasion and circumvention, *e.g.*, by minors who have their own credit cards. Finally, filters also may be more effective because they can be applied to all forms of Internet communication, including e-mail, not just the World Wide Web. Although filtering software is not a perfect solution because it may block some materials not harmful to minors and fail to catch some that are, the Government has not satisfied its burden to introduce specific evidence proving that filters are less effective. The argument that filtering software is not an available alternative because Congress may not require its use carries little weight, since Congress may act to encourage such use by giving strong incentives to schools and libraries and by promoting the development of filters by industry and their use by parents. The reasoning of *Playboy Entertainment Group*, and the holdings and force of this Court's precedents, compel the Court to affirm the preliminary injunction here. To do otherwise would be to do less than the First Amendment commands. Important practical reasons also support letting the injunction stand pending a full trial on the merits. First, the potential harms from reversal outweigh those of leaving the injunction in place by mistake. Extraordinary harm and a serious chill upon protected speech may result where, as here, a prosecution is a likely possibility but only an affirmative defense is available, so that speakers may self-censor rather than risk the perils of trial. Second, there are substantial factual disputes remaining in the case, including a serious gap in the evidence as to the filtering software's effectiveness. By allowing the preliminary injunction to stand and remanding for trial, the Court requires the Government to shoulder its full constitutional burden of proof respecting the less restrictive alternative argument, rather than excuse it from doing so. Third, the factual record does not reflect current technological reality - a serious flaw in any case involving the Internet, which evolves at a rapid pace. It is reasonable to assume that technological developments important to the

C

Affirmed and remanded.

Virginia State Board of Pharmacy v. Virginia Citizens Consumer Council 425 U.S. 748 (1976)

FACTS

Plaintiff-appellees, as consumers of prescription drugs, brought suit against the Virginia State Board of Pharmacy and its individual members, defendant-appellants herein, challenging the validity under the First and Fourteenth Amendments of a Virginia statute declaring it unprofessional conduct for a licensed pharmacist to advertise the prices of prescription drugs. A three-judge District Court declared the statute void and enjoined appellants from enforcing it.

I Can the government regulate commercial speech by way of a statute that declares it unprofessional for licensed pharmacist to advertise the prices of prescription drugs?

R Commercial speech is not completely outside the reach of the First Amendment – the statute is therefore invalid.

A Any First Amendment protection enjoyed by advertisers seeking to disseminate prescription drug price information is also enjoyed, and thus may be asserted, by appellees as recipients of such information. "Commercial speech" is not wholly outside the protection of the First and Fourteenth Amendments, and the Virginia statute is therefore invalid. That the advertiser's interest in a commercial advertisement is purely economic does not disqualify him from protection under the First and Fourteenth Amendments. Both the individual consumer and society in general may have strong interests in the free flow of commercial information. The ban on advertising prescription drug prices cannot be justified on the basis of the State's interest in maintaining the professionalism of its licensed pharmacists; the State is free to require whatever professional standards it wishes of its pharmacists, and may subsidize them or protect them from competition in other ways, but it may not do so by keeping the public in ignorance of the lawful terms that competing pharmacists are offering. Whatever may be the bounds of time, place, and manner restrictions on commercial speech, they are plainly exceeded by the Virginia statute, which singles out speech of a particular content and seeks to prevent its dissemination completely. No claim is made that the prohibited prescription drug advertisements are false, misleading, or propose illegal transactions, and a State may not suppress the dissemination of concededly truthful information about entirely lawful activity, fearful of that information's effect upon its disseminators and its recipients.

C Affirmed.

Bolger v. Youngs Drug Products Corp.

463 U.S. 60 (1983)

FACTS

Title 39 U.S.C. 3001(e)(2) prohibits the mailing of unsolicited advertisements for contraceptives. When appellee manufacturer of contraceptives proposed to mail to the public unsolicited advertisements including informational pamphlets promoting its products but also discussing venereal disease and family planning, the Postal Service notified appellee that the proposed mailings would violate 3001(e)(2). Appellee then brought an action for declaratory and injunctive relief in Federal District Court, which held that the statute, as applied to the proposed mailings, violated the First Amendment.

I

Can the government regulate informational advertising as "commercial speech?"

R

The government can regulate informational advertising as "commercial speech" which is defined a communication which does no more than propose a commercial traction or is an advertisement AND references a specific product[s] and is mailed for economic motivations.

A

As applied to appellee's proposed mailings, 3001(e)(2) is unconstitutional. The mailings, which are concededly advertisements, refer to specific products, and are economically motivated, constitute commercial speech notwithstanding the fact that they contain discussions of important public issues such as the prevention of venereal disease and family planning. Advertising for contraceptives not only implicates "substantial individual and societal interests" in the free flow of commercial information, but also relates to activity that is protected from unwarranted governmental interference. Thus, appellee's proposed commercial speech is clearly protected by the First Amendment. Neither of the interests asserted by appellants - that 3001(e)(2) shields recipients of mail from materials that they are likely to find offensive and aids parents' efforts to control the manner in which their children become informed about birth control - is sufficient to justify the sweeping prohibition on the mailing of unsolicited contraceptive advertisements. The fact that protected speech may be offensive to some persons does not justify its suppression, and, in any event, recipients of objectionable mailings can avoid further offensiveness simply by averting their eyes or disposing of the mailings in a trash can. While the second asserted interest is substantial, 3001(e)(2) as a means of effectuating this interest fails to withstand scrutiny. The statute's marginal degree of protection afforded those parents who desire to keep their children from confronting such mailings is improperly achieved by purging all mailboxes of unsolicited material that is entirely suitable for adults. Section 3001(e)(2) is also defective because it denies parents truthful information bearing on their ability to discuss birth control and to make informed decisions in this area.

C

Reversed.

Central Hudson Gas v. Public Service Comm'n.

447 U.S. 557 (1980)

FACTS

In December 1973, the New York Public Service Commission (the "Commission") ordered electric utilities in New York State to cease all advertising that "promotes the use of electricity." The order was based on the Commission's finding that "the interconnected utility system in New York State does not have sufficient fuel stocks or sources of supply to continue furnishing all customer demands for the 1973-1974 winter." Three years later, when the fuel shortage had eased, the Commission requested comments from the public on its proposal to continue the ban on promotional advertising. Central Hudson Gas & Electric Corp., the plaintiff-appellant in this case, opposed the ban on First Amendment grounds. After reviewing the public comments, the Commission extended the prohibition in a Policy Statement issued on February 25, 1977. The Policy Statement divided advertising expenses "into two broad categories: promotional - advertising intended to stimulate the purchase of utility services - and institutional and informational, a broad category inclusive of all advertising not clearly intended to promote sales." The Commission declared all promotional advertising contrary to the national policy of conserving energy. It acknowledged that the ban is not a perfect vehicle for conserving energy. The Commission's order explicitly permitted "informational" advertising designed to encourage "shifts of consumption" from peak demand times to periods of low electricity demand. Appellant challenged the order in state court, arguing that the Commission had restrained commercial speech in violation of the First and Fourteenth Amendments. The Commission's order was upheld by the trial court and at the intermediate appellate level. The New York Court of Appeals affirmed. It found little value to advertising in "the noncompetitive market in which electric corporations operate." Since consumers "have no choice regarding the source of their electric power," the court denied that "promotional advertising of electricity might contribute to society's interest in `informed and reliable' economic decisionmaking." The court also observed that by encouraging consumption, promotional advertising would only exacerbate the current energy situation. The court concluded that the governmental interest in the prohibition outweighed the limited constitutional value of the commercial speech at issue. The U.S. Supreme Court noted probable jurisdiction.

I Does a regulation of the Public Service Commission of the state of New York violate the First and Fourteenth Amendments because it completely bans promotional advertising (commercial speech) by an electrical utility?

R Restrictions on commercial speech will be upheld if they serve a substantial governmental interest, directly advance the governmental interest asserted, and do so in the most limited way possible.

A A regulation of Defendant-appellee New York Public Service Commission which completely bans an electric utility from advertising to promote the use of electricity violates the First and Fourteenth Amendments. Although the Constitution accords a lesser protection to commercial speech than to other constitutionally guaranteed expression, nevertheless the First Amendment protects commercial speech from unwarranted governmental regulation. For commercial speech to come within the First Amendment, it at least must concern lawful activity and not be misleading. Next, it must be determined whether the asserted governmental interest to be served by the restriction on commercial speech is substantial. If both inquires yield positive answers, it must then be decided whether the regulation directly advances the governmental interest asserted, and whether it is not more extensive than is necessary to serve that interest. In this case, it is not claimed that the expression at issue is either inaccurate or unlawful activity; nor is appellant electrical utility's promotional advertising unprotected commercial speech merely because appellant holds a monopoly over the sale of electricity in its service area. Since monopoly over the supply of a product provides no protection from competition with substitutes for that product, advertising by utilities is just as valuable to consumers as advertising by unregulated firms, and there is no indication that appellant's decision to advertise was not based on the belief that consumers were interested in the advertising. The State's interest in energy conservation is clearly substantial and is directly advanced by appellee's regulations. The State's further interest in preventing inequities in appellant's rates - based on the assertion that successful promotion of consumption in "off-peak" periods would create extra costs that would, because of appellant's rate structure, be borne by all consumers through higher overall rates - is also substantial. The latter interest does not, however, provide a constitutionally adequate reason for restricting protected speech because the link between the advertising prohibition and appellant's rate structure is, at most, tenuous. Appellee's regulation, which reaches all promotional advertising regardless of the impact of the touted service on overall energy use, is more extensive than necessary to further the State's interest in energy conservation which, as important as it is, cannot justify suppressing information about electric devices or services that would cause no net increase in total energy use. In addition, no showing has been made that a more limited restriction on the content of promotional advertising would not serve adequately the State's interests.

C Reversed.

Friedman v. Rogers

440 U.S. 1 (1979)

FACTS

Section 5.13 (d) of the Texas Optometry Act prohibits the practice of optometry under a trade name and 2.02 requires that four of the six members of the Texas Optometry Board, which regulates the practice of optometry in the State, be members of the Texas Optometric Association (TOA), a professional organization of optometrists. Rogers, a Board member but ineligible for membership in TOA because of noncompliance with the code of ethics required for membership, brought an action challenging the constitutionality of these provisions. A three-judge District Court held that 2.02 is related reasonably to the State's purpose of ensuring enforcement of the Act and therefore constitutional under the Equal Protection Clause of the Fourteenth Amendment, but that 5.13 (d) is an unconstitutional restriction of the "free flow of commercial information" under the First Amendment.

I

Can a state ban the use of trade names?

R

A state may ban the use of trade names.

A

Section 5.13 (d) is constitutional. The use of a trade name in connection with optometrical practice conveys no information about the price and nature of the services offered by an optometrist until it acquires meaning over a period of time by associations formed in the minds of the public between the name and some standard of price or quality. Because these ill-defined associations of trade names with price and quality information can be manipulated by the users of trade names, there is a significant possibility that trade names will be used to mislead the public. The State's interest in protecting the public from such deceptive and misleading use of optometrical trade names is substantial and well demonstrated in this case, and the prohibition against the use of trade names is constitutionally permissible regulation in furtherance of this interest. Rather than stifling commercial speech, such prohibition ensures that information regarding optometrical services will be communicated more fully and accurately to consumers than it had been in the past. Section 2.02 is also constitutional. The history of the Texas Optometry Act shows that such provision is related reasonably to the State's legitimate purpose of securing a regulatory board that will administer the Act faithfully. While Rogers has a constitutional right to a fair and impartial hearing in any disciplinary proceeding conducted against him by the Texas Optometry Board, his challenge to the fairness of the Board does not arise from any disciplinary proceeding against him.

C

Affirmed in part and reversed and remanded in part.

Linmark Assoc. v. Township of Willingboro

431 U.S. 85 (1977)

FACTS

A township ordinance prohibiting the posting of real estate "For Sale" and "Sold" signs for the purpose of stemming what the township perceived as the flight of white homeowners from a racially integrated community held to violate the First Amendment.

I

Can a local government ban "house for sale" signs to prevent panic selling?

R

A local government cannot restrict commercial communications unless those communications are false.

A

The ordinance cannot be sustained on the ground that it restricts only one method of communication while leaving ample alternative communication channels open. The alternatives (primarily newspaper advertising and listing with real estate agents, which involve more cost and less autonomy than signs, are less likely to reach persons not deliberately seeking sales information, and may be less effective) are far from satisfactory. And the ordinance is not genuinely concerned with the place (front lawns) or the manner (signs) of the speech, but rather proscribes particular types of signs based on their content because the township fears their "primary" effect - that they will cause those receiving the information to act upon it. Moreover, despite the importance of achieving the asserted goal of promoting stable, integrated housing, the ordinance cannot be upheld on the ground that it promotes an important governmental objective, since it does not appear that the ordinance was needed to achieve that objective and, in any event, the First Amendment disables the township from achieving that objective by restricting the free flow of truthful commercial information.

C

Reversed.

44 Liquormart Inc. v. Rhode Island

517 U.S. 484 (1996)

FACTS

Plaintiff-petitioners, a licensed Rhode Island liquor retailer, 44 Liquormart Inc. and a licensed Massachusetts liquor retailer patronized by Rhode Island residents, filed this action seeking a declaratory judgment that Rhode Island laws banning the advertisement of retail liquor prices except at the place of sale violate the First Amendment. In concluding that the ban was unconstitutional because it did not directly advance the State's (defendant-respondent) asserted interest in the promotion of temperance and was more extensive than necessary to serve that interest, the District Court reasoned that the party seeking to uphold a restriction on commercial speech carries the burden of justifying it and that the Twenty-first Amendment did not shift or diminish that burden. In reversing, the Court of Appeals found "inherent merit" in the State's submission that competitive price advertising would ultimately increase sales, and agreed with it that the Twenty-first Amendment gave its advertising ban an added presumption of validity.

I

Can the government outright restrict non-misleading commercial speech to achieve a goal which it could alternately achieve in a way which does not restrict free speech?

R

When the means to achieve the government's goal involves a more burdensome approach which does not restrict free speech, the state should utilize that approach rather than restrict non-misleading commercial speech when the objective is the same.

A

The Twenty-first Amendment cannot save Rhode Island's price advertising ban because that Amendment does not qualify the First Amendment's prohibition against laws abridging the freedom of speech. Although the Twenty-first Amendment - which repealed Prohibition and gave the States the power to prohibit commerce in, or the use of, alcoholic beverages - limits the dormant Commerce Clause's effect on a State's regulatory power over the delivery or use of liquor within its borders, the Amendment does not license the States to ignore their obligations under other constitutional provisions. Because the First Amendment must be included among those other provisions, the Twenty-first Amendment does not shield the advertising ban from constitutional scrutiny. Because Rhode Island has failed to carry its heavy burden of justifying its complete ban on price advertising, that ban is invalid. Rhode Island's ban on advertisements that provide the public with accurate information about retail liquor prices is an unconstitutional abridgment of the freedom of speech. Although the First Amendment protects the dissemination of truthful and non-misleading commercial messages about lawful products and services in order to ensure that consumers receive accurate information, the special nature of commercial speech, including its "greater objectivity" and "greater hardiness," authorizes the State to regulate potentially deceptive or overreaching advertising more freely than other forms of protected speech. However, regulations that entirely suppress commercial speech in order to pursue a policy not related to consumer protection must be reviewed with "special care," and such blanket bans should not be approved unless the speech itself was flawed in some way, either because it was deceptive or related to unlawful activity. A review of the case law reveals that commercial speech regulations are not all subject to a similar form of constitutional review simply because they target a similar category of expression. When a State regulates commercial messages to protect consumers from misleading, deceptive, or aggressive sales practices, or requires the disclosure of beneficial consumer information, the regulation's purpose is consistent with the reasons for according constitutional protection to commercial speech and therefore justifies less than strict review. However, where a State entirely prohibits the dissemination of truthful, nonmisleading commercial messages for reasons unrelated to the preservation of a fair bargaining process, there is far less reason to depart from the rigorous review that the First Amendment generally demands. The special dangers that attend such complete bans - including, most obviously, the fact that they all but foreclose alternative channels of communication - present sound reasons that justify more careful review. Because Rhode Island's advertising ban constitutes a blanket prohibition against truthful, nonmisleading speech about a lawful product, and serves an end unrelated to consumer protection, it must be reviewed with "special care" under *Central Hudson.* It cannot survive that review because it does not satisfy even the less than strict standard that generally applies in commercial speech cases under *Central Hudson.* First, the advertising ban does not directly advance the State's substantial interest in promoting temperance. Because a commercial speech regulation may not be sustained if it provides only ineffective or remote support for the government's purpose, the State bears the burden of showing not merely that its regulation will advance its interest, but also that it will do so "to a material degree." In this case, therefore, the State must show that the ban will significantly reduce alcohol consumption, but has presented no evidence to suggest a significant reduction. Second, the ban is more extensive than necessary to serve its stated interest, since alternative forms of regulation that would not involve any speech restrictions - e.g., the maintenance of higher prices either by direct regulation or by increased taxation, the rationing of per capita purchases, or the use of educational campaigns focused on drinking problems - would be more likely to achieve the goal of promoting temperance. Thus, the State has failed to establish the requisite "reasonable fit" between its regulation and its goal. The State's arguments in support of its claim that it merely exercised appropriate "legislative judgment" in determining that a price advertising ban would best promote temperance - i.e., 1) that because expert opinions as to the effectiveness of the ban "go both ways," the Court of Appeals correctly concluded that the ban constituted a "reasonable choice" by the legislature; 2) that precedent requires that particular deference be accorded that legislative choice because the State could, if it chose, ban the sale of alcoholic beverages outright; and 3) that deference is appropriate because alcoholic beverages are so-called "vice" products - must be rejected. Last Term we held that a federal law abridging a brewer's right to provide the public with accurate information about the alcoholic content of malt beverages is unconstitutional. We now hold that Rhode Island's statutory prohibition against advertisements that provide the public with accurate information about retail prices of alcoholic beverages is also invalid. Our holding rests on the conclusion that such an advertising ban is an abridgment of speech protected by the First Amendment and that it is not shielded from constitutional scrutiny by the 21st Amendment.

C We hold that Rhode Island's statutory prohibition against advertisements that provide the public with accurate information about retail prices of alcoholic beverages is invalid.

Lorillard Tobacco Co. v. Reilly

533 U.S. 525 (2001)

FACTS

After the Attorney General of Massachusetts (Attorney General) promulgated comprehensive regulations governing the advertising and sale of cigarettes, smokeless tobacco, and cigars, petitioners, a group of tobacco manufacturers and retailers, filed this suit asserting, among other things, the Supremacy Clause claim that the cigarette advertising regulations are pre-empted by the Federal Cigarette Labeling and Advertising Act (FCLAA), which prescribes mandatory health warnings for cigarette packaging and advertising, 15 U. S. C. §1333, and pre-empts similar state regulations, §1334(b); and a claim that the regulations violate the First and Fourteenth Amendments to the Federal Constitution. In large measure, the District Court upheld the regulations. Among its rulings, the court held that restrictions on the location of advertising were not pre-empted by the FCLAA, and that neither the regulations prohibiting outdoor advertising within 1,000 feet of a school or playground nor the sales practices regulations restricting the location and distribution of tobacco products violated the First Amendment. The court ruled, however, that the point-of-sale advertising regulations requiring that indoor advertising be placed no lower than five feet from the floor were invalid because the Attorney General had not provided sufficient justification for that restriction. The First Circuit affirmed the District Court's rulings that the cigarette advertising regulations are not pre-empted by the FCLAA and that the outdoor advertising regulations and the sales practices regulations do not violate the First Amendment under *Central Hudson Gas & Elec. Corp.* v. *Public Serv. Comm'n of N. Y.*, but reversed the lower court's invalidation of the point-of-sale advertising regulations, concluding that the Attorney General is better suited than courts to determine what restrictions are necessary.

I

Under the Supremacy Clause, are cigarette advertising regulations pre-empted by the Federal Cigarette Labeling and Advertising Act (FCLAA), which prescribes mandatory health warnings for cigarette packaging and advertising and pre-empts similar state regulations? Are the outdoor advertising regulations and the sales practices regulations violative of the First Amendment?

R

The FCLAA pre-empts Massachusetts' regulations governing outdoor and point-of-sale cigarette advertising.

A

The FCLAA pre-empts Massachusetts' regulations governing outdoor and point-of-sale cigarette advertising. The FCLAA's pre-emption provision, §1334, prohibits (a) requiring cigarette packages to bear any "statement relating to smoking and health, other than the statement required by" §1333, and (b) any "requirement or prohibition based on smoking and health ... imposed under state law with respect to the advertising or promotion of any cigarettes the packages of which are labeled in conformity with" §1333. The Court's analysis begins with the statute's language. The statute's interpretation is aided by considering the predecessor pre-emption provision and the context in which the current language was adopted. The original provision simply prohibited any "statement relating to smoking and health ... in the advertising of any cigarettes the packages of which are labeled in conformity with the

[Act's] provisions." Without question, the current pre-emption provision's plain language is much broader. Rather than preventing only "statements," the amended provision reaches all "requirement[s] or prohibition[s] ... imposed under State law." And, although the former statute reached only statements "in the advertising," the current provision governs "with respect to the advertising or promotion" of cigarettes. At the same time that Congress expanded the pre-emption provision with respect to the States, it enacted a provision prohibiting cigarette advertising in electronic media altogether. Congress pre-empted state cigarette advertising regulations like the Attorney General's because they would upset federal legislative choices to require specific warnings and to impose the ban on cigarette advertising in electronic media in order to address concerns about smoking and health. In holding that the FCLAA does not nullify the Massachusetts regulations, the First Circuit concentrated on whether they are "with respect to" advertising and promotion, concluding that the FCLAA only pre-empts regulations of the content of cigarette advertising. The court also reasoned that the regulations are a form of zoning, a traditional area of state power, and, therefore, a presumption against pre-emption applied. This Court rejects the notion that the regulations are not "with respect to" cigarette advertising and promotion. There is no question about an indirect relationship between the Massachusetts regulations and cigarette advertising: The regulations expressly target such advertising. The Attorney General's argument that the regulations are not "based on smoking and health" since they do not involve health-related content, but instead target youth exposure to cigarette advertising, is unpersuasive because, at bottom, the youth exposure concern is intertwined with the smoking and health concern. The FCLAA's pre-emption provision does not restrict States' and localities' ability to enact generally applicable zoning restrictions on the location and size of advertisements that apply to cigarettes on equal terms with other products or to regulate conduct as it relates to the sale or use of cigarettes, as by prohibiting cigarette sales to minors, as well as common inchoate offenses that attach to criminal conduct, such as solicitation, conspiracy, and attempt. Because the issue was not decided below, the Court declines to reach the smokeless tobacco petitioners' argument that, if the outdoor and point-of-sale advertising regulations for cigarettes are pre-empted, then the same regulations for smokeless tobacco must be invalidated because they cannot be severed from the cigarette provisions. Massachusetts' outdoor and point-of-sale advertising regulations relating to smokeless tobacco and cigars violate the First Amendment, but the sales practices regulations relating to all three tobacco products are constitutional. Under *Central Hudson's* four-part test for analyzing regulations of commercial speech, the Court must determine (1) whether the expression is protected by the First Amendment, (2) whether the asserted governmental interest is substantial, (3) whether the regulation directly advances the governmental interest asserted, and (4) whether it is not more extensive than is necessary to serve that interest. Only the last two steps are at issue here. The Attorney General has assumed for summary judgment purposes that the First Amendment protects the speech of petitioners, none of whom contests the importance of the State's interest in preventing the use of tobacco by minors. The third step of *Central Hudson* requires that the government demonstrate that the harms it recites are real and that its restriction will in fact alleviate them to a material degree. The fourth step of *Central Hudson* requires a reasonable fit between the legislature's ends and the means chosen to accomplish those ends, a means narrowly tailored to achieve the desired objective. The outdoor advertising regulations prohibiting smokeless tobacco or cigar advertising within 1,000 feet of a school or playground violate the First Amendment. Those regulations satisfy *Central Hudson*'s third step by directly advancing the governmental interest asserted to justify them. The Court's detailed review of the record reveals that the Attorney General has provided ample documentation of the problem with underage use of smokeless tobacco and cigars. In addition, the Court disagrees with petitioners' claim that there is no evidence that preventing targeted advertising campaigns and limiting youth exposure to advertising will decrease underage use of those products. On the record below and in the posture of summary judgment, it cannot be concluded that the Attorney General's decision to regulate smokeless tobacco and cigar advertising in an effort to combat the use of tobacco products by minors was based on mere "speculation and conjecture." *Edenfield*. Whatever the strength of the Attorney General's evidence to justify the outdoor advertising regulations, however, the regulations do not satisfy *Central Hudson's* fourth step. Their broad sweep indicates that the Attorney General did not "carefully calculat[e] the costs and benefits associated with the burden on speech imposed," *Cincinnati* v. *Discovery Network, Inc*. The record indicates that the regulations prohibit advertising in a substantial portion of Massachusetts' major metropolitan areas; in some areas, they would constitute nearly a complete ban on the communication of truthful information. The governmental interest in preventing underage tobacco use is substantial, and even compelling, but it is no less true that the sale and use of tobacco products by adults is a legal activity. A speech regulation cannot unduly impinge on the speaker's ability to propose a commercial transaction and the adult listener's opportunity to obtain information about products. The Attorney General has failed to show that the regulations at issue are not more extensive than necessary. The regulations prohibiting indoor, point-of-sale advertising of smokeless tobacco and cigars lower than 5 feet from the floor of a retail establishment located within 1,000 feet of a school or playground fail both the third and fourth steps of the *Central Hudson* analysis. The 5-foot rule does not seem to advance the goals of preventing minors from using tobacco products and curbing demand for that activity by limiting youth exposure to advertising. Not all children are less than 5 feet tall, and those who are can look up and take in their surroundings. Nor can the blanket height restriction be construed as a mere regulation of communicative action under *United States* v. *O'Brien,* since it is not unrelated to expression, but attempts to regulate directly the communicative impact of indoor advertising. Moreover, the restriction does not constitute a reasonable fit with the goal of targeting tobacco advertising that entices children. Although the First Circuit decided that the restriction's burden on speech is very limited, there is no *de minimis* exception for a speech restriction that lacks sufficient tailoring or justification. The Court declines to address the cigar petitioners' First Amendment challenge to a regulation prohibiting sampling or promotional giveaways of cigars and little cigars. That claim was not sufficiently briefed and argued before this Court.

C

Affirmed in part, reversed in part, and remanded.

New York Times v. Sullivan

376 U.S. 254 (1964)

FACTS

Plaintiff-respondent Sullivan, a police chief and elected official in Montgomery, Alabama, brought suit in a state court alleging that he had been libeled by an advertisement in corporate petitioner's newspaper, The New York Times, the text of which appeared over the names of the four individual petitioners and many others. The advertisement included statements, some of which were false, about police action allegedly directed against students who participated in a civil rights demonstration and against a leader of the civil rights movement; respondent claimed the statements referred to him because his duties included supervision of the police department. The trial judge instructed the jury that such statements were "libelous per se," legal injury being implied without proof of actual damages, and that for the purpose of compensatory damages malice was presumed, so that such damages could be awarded against petitioners if the statements were found to have been published by them and to have related to respondent. As to punitive damages, the judge instructed that mere negligence was not evidence of actual malice and would not justify an award of punitive damages; he refused to instruct that actual intent to harm or recklessness had to be found before punitive damages could be awarded, or that a verdict for respondent should differentiate between compensatory and punitive damages. The jury found for respondent and the State Supreme Court affirmed. Sullivan was awarded a judgment for $500,000 despite offering no proof that he suffered any pecuniary loss, and the New York Times appealed the judgment.

I

Can a public official recover damages from a newspaper publication or a member of the public when the latter group criticizes the actions of the former?

R

A public official may not recover damages for deformation relating to his official conduct unless he proves that the statement was made with actual malice (knowledge that the statement was false or made with reckless disregard of its truth).

A

A State cannot, under the First and 14th Amendments, award damages to a public official for defamatory falsehood relating to his official conduct unless he proves "actual malice;" that is, that the statement was made with knowledge of its falsity or with reckless disregard of whether it was true or false. Application by state courts of a rule of law, whether statutory or not, to award a judgment in a civil action, is "state action" under the 14th Amendment. Expression does not lose constitutional protection to which it would otherwise be entitled because it appears in the form of a paid advertisement. Factual error, content defamatory of official reputation, or both, are insufficient to warrant an award of damages for false statements unless "actual malice" - knowledge that statements are false or in reckless disregard of the truth - is alleged and proved. State court judgment entered upon a general verdict which does not differentiate between punitive damages, as to which under state law actual malice must be proved, and general damages, as to which it is "presumed," precludes any determination as to the basis of the verdict and requires reversal, where presumption of malice is inconsistent with federal constitutional requirements. The evidence was constitutionally insufficient to support the judgment for respondent, since it failed to support a finding that the statements were made with actual malice or that they related to respondent.

C

Reversed and remanded.

Gertz v. Welch

418 U.S. 323 (1974)

FACTS

A Chicago policeman named Nuccio was convicted of murder. The victim's family retained petitioner, a reputable attorney, to represent them in civil litigation against Nuccio. An article appearing in respondent's magazine alleged that Nuccio's murder trial was part of a Communist conspiracy to discredit the local police, and it falsely stated that petitioner had arranged Nuccio's "frame-up," implied that petitioner had a criminal record, and labeled him a "Communist-fronter." Petitioner brought this diversity libel action against respondent. After the jury returned a verdict for petitioner, the District Court decided that the standard enunciated in *New York Times Co. v. Sullivan* which bars media liability for defamation of a public official absent proof that the defamatory statements were published with knowledge of their falsity or in reckless disregard of the truth, should apply to this suit. The court concluded that that standard protects media discussion of a public issue without regard to whether the person defamed is a public official as in *Sullivan*, or a public figure, as in *Curtis Publishing Co. v. Butts*. The court found that petitioner had failed to prove knowledge of falsity or reckless disregard for the truth and therefore entered judgment n.o.v. for respondent. The Court of Appeals affirmed.

I

Can non-public plaintiffs recover for negligent or reckless deformation?

R

A state may enact laws to allow non-public plaintiffs to recover for negligent or reckless deformation upon proof of any level of fault; however, it cannot permit presumed damages or punitive damages without proof of "knowing" falsity or reckless disregard for the truth.

A

A publisher or broadcaster of defamatory falsehoods about an individual who is neither a public official nor a public figure may not claim the New York Times protection against liability for defamation on the ground that the defamatory statements concern an issue of public or general interest. Because private individuals characteristically have less effective opportunities for rebuttal than do public officials and public figures, they are more vulnerable to injury from defamation. Because they have not voluntarily exposed themselves to increased risk of injury from defamatory falsehoods, they are also more deserving of recovery. The state interest in compensating injury to the reputation of private individuals is therefore greater than for public officials and public figures. To extend the New York Times standard to media defamation of private persons whenever an issue of general or public interest is involved would abridge to an unacceptable degree the legitimate state interest in compensating private individuals for injury to reputation and would occasion the additional difficulty of forcing courts to decide on an ad hoc basis which publications and broadcasts address issues of general or public interest and which do not. So long as they do not impose liability without fault, the States may define for themselves the appropriate standard of liability for a publisher or broadcaster of defamatory falsehood which injures a private individual and whose substance makes substantial danger to reputation apparent. The States, however, may not permit recovery of presumed or punitive damages when liability is not based on knowledge of falsity or reckless disregard for the truth, and the private defamation plaintiff who establishes liability under a less demanding standard than the New York Times test may recover compensation only for actual injury. Petitioner was neither a public official nor a public figure. Neither petitioner's past service on certain city committees nor his appearance as an attorney at the coroner's inquest into the death of the murder victim made him a public official. Petitioner was also not a public figure. Absent clear evidence of general fame or notoriety in the community and pervasive involvement in ordering the affairs of society, an individual should not be deemed a public figure for all aspects of his life. Rather, the public-figure question should be determined by reference to the individual's participation in the particular controversy giving rise to the defamation. Petitioner's role in the Nuccio affair did not make him a public figure.

C

Reversed and remanded.

Dunn & Bradstreet v. Greenmoss Builders

472 U.S. 749 (1985)

FACTS

Petitioner, a credit reporting agency, sent a report to five subscribers indicating that respondent construction contractor had filed a voluntary petition for bankruptcy. The report was false and grossly misrepresented respondent's assets and liabilities. Thereafter, petitioner issued a corrective notice, but respondent still brought a defamation action in Vermont state court, alleging that the false report had injured its reputation and seeking damages. After trial, the jury returned a verdict in respondent's favor and awarded both compensatory or presumed damages and punitive damages. But the trial court believed that *Gertz v. Robert Welch, Inc.*, controlled, and granted petitioner's motion for a new trial on the ground that the instructions to the jury permitted it to award damages on a lesser showing than "actual malice." The Vermont Supreme Court reversed, holding that *Gertz* was inapplicable to non-media defamation actions.

I May a deformation plaintiff recover presumed and punitive damages for inaccurate credit reporting?

R Deformation laws allow plaintiffs to recover presumed and/or punitive damages without proving actual malice for defamatory speech not involving "matters of public concern."

A The fact that the jury instructions in question referred to "malice," "lack of good faith," and "actual malice," did not require the jury to find "actual malice," as respondent contends, where the instructions failed to define any of these terms. Consequently, the trial court correctly concluded that the instructions did not satisfy *Gertz*. Permitting recovery of presumed and punitive damages in defamation cases absent a showing of "actual malice" does not violate the First Amendment when the defamatory statements do not involve matters of public concern. In light of the reduced constitutional value of speech on matters of purely private concern, as opposed to speech on matters of public concern, the state interest in compensating private individuals for injury to their reputation adequately supports awards of presumed and punitive damages - even absent a showing of "actual malice." *Gertz* does not apply to this case. Petitioner's credit report concerned no public issue but was speech solely in the individual interest of the speaker and its specific business audience. This particular interest warranted no special protection when it was wholly false and damaging to the victim's business reputation. Moreover, since the credit report was made available to only five subscribers, who, under the subscription agreement, could not disseminate it further, it cannot be said that the report involved any strong interest in the free flow of commercial information.

C Judgment affirmed.

Hustler Magazine v. Farwell

485 U.S. 46 (1988)

FACTS

Respondent, a nationally known minister and commentator on politics and public affairs, filed a diversity action in Federal District Court against petitioners, a nationally circulated magazine and its publisher, to recover damages for, *inter alia*, libel and intentional infliction of emotional distress arising from the publication of an advertisement "parody" which, among other things, portrayed respondent as having engaged in a drunken incestuous rendezvous with his mother in an outhouse. The jury found against respondent on the libel claim, specifically finding that the parody could not "reasonably be understood as describing actual facts . . . or events," but ruled in his favor on the emotional distress claim, stating that he should be awarded compensatory and punitive damages. The Court of Appeals affirmed, rejecting petitioners' contention that the "actual malice" standard of *New York Times Co. v. Sullivan* must be met before respondent can recover for emotional distress.

I

May a public figure recover compensatory and punitive damages for intentional infliction of emotional distress?

R

A public figure cannot recover compensatory and punitive damages for intentional infliction of emotional distress from defamatory publications unless he proves (1) it contained false statements of fact and (2) it was made with actual malice.

A

In order to protect the free flow of ideas and opinions on matters of public interest and concern, the First and Fourteenth Amendments prohibit public figures and public officials from recovering damages for the tort of intentional infliction of emotional distress by reason of the publication of a caricature such as the ad parody at issue without showing in addition that the publication contains a false statement of fact which was made with "actual malice," i. e., with knowledge that the statement was false or with reckless disregard as to whether or not it was true. The State's interest in protecting public figures from emotional distress is not sufficient to deny First Amendment protection to speech that is patently offensive and is intended to inflict emotional injury when that speech could not reasonably have been interpreted as stating actual facts about the public figure involved. Here, respondent is clearly a "public figure" for First Amendment purposes, and the lower courts' finding that the ad parody was not reasonably believable must be accepted. "Outrageousness" in the area of political and social discourse has an inherent subjectiveness about it which would allow a jury to impose liability on the basis of the jurors' tastes or views, or perhaps on the basis of their dislike of a particular expression, and cannot, consistently with the First Amendment, form a basis for the award of damages for the instant conduct.

C

Reversed.

Cox Broadcasting Corp. v. Cohn

420 U.S. 469 (1975)

FACTS

Appellant reporter, an employee of a television station owned by Defendant-appellant Cox Broadcasting Company, broadcast a deceased rape victim's name during a news report of a rape case which he had obtained from the indictments, which were public records available for inspection. The victim's father, Plaintiff-appellee Cohn, brought a damages action against appellants in reliance on a Georgia statute making it a misdemeanor to broadcast a rape victim's name, claiming that his right to privacy had been invaded by the broadcast of his daughter's name. The trial court, rejecting appellants' claims that the broadcast was privileged under the First and Fourteenth Amendments, held that the Georgia statute gave a civil remedy to those injured by its violation and granted summary judgment for appellee. On appeal, the Georgia Supreme Court initially held that, while the trial court erred in construing the Georgia statute to extend a cause of action for invasion of privacy, the complaint stated a cause of action for common-law invasion of privacy, and that the First and Fourteenth Amendments did not, as a matter of law, require judgment for appellants. On a motion for rehearing appellants contended that a rape victim's name was a matter of public interest and hence could be published with impunity, but the Supreme Court denied the motion on the ground that the statute declared a state policy that a rape victim's name was not a matter of public concern, and sustained the statute as a legitimate limitation on the First Amendment's freedom of expression.

I

Can a state extend a cause of action for invasion of privacy for the publication of a deceased rape victim's name which made part of the public record in connection with the prosecution of the criminal case?

R

The State may not, consistently with the First and Fourteenth Amendments, impose sanctions on the accurate publication of a rape victim's name obtained from judicial records that are maintained in connection with a public prosecution and that themselves are open to public inspection.

A

This Court has jurisdiction over the appeal under 28 U.S.C. 1257(2). The constitutionality of the Georgia statute was "drawn in question" within the meaning of 1257(2), since, when the Georgia Supreme Court relied upon it as a declaration of state public policy, the statute was drawn in question in a manner directly bearing upon the merits of the action, and the decision upholding its constitutional validity invokes this Court's appellate jurisdiction. The Georgia Supreme Court's decision is a "final judgment or decree" within the meaning of 1257. It was plainly final on the federal issue of whether the broadcasts were privileged under the First and Fourteenth Amendments and is not subject to further review in the state courts; and appellants would be liable for damages if the elements of the state cause of action were proved. Moreover, since the litigation could be terminated by this Court's decision on the merits and a failure to decide the free speech question now will leave the Georgia press operating in the shadow of civil and criminal sanctions of a rule of law and statute whose constitutionality is in serious doubt, this Court's reaching the merits comports with its past pragmatic approach in determining finality. The State may not, consistently with the First and Fourteenth Amendments, impose sanctions on the accurate publication of a rape victim's name obtained from judicial records that are maintained in connection with a public prosecution and that themselves are open to public inspection. Here, under circumstances where appellant reporter based his televised report upon notes taken during court proceedings and obtained the rape victim's name from official court documents open to public inspection, the protection of freedom of the press provided by the First and Fourteenth Amendments bars Georgia from making appellants' broadcast the basis of civil liability in a cause of action for invasion of privacy that penalizes pure expression - the content of a publication. The commission of a crime, prosecutions resulting therefrom, and judicial proceedings arising from the prosecutions are events of legitimate concern to the public and consequently fall within the press' responsibility to report the operations of government. The interests of privacy fade when the information involved already appears on public record, especially when viewed in terms of the First and Fourteenth Amendments and in light of the public interest in a vigorous press.

C

Reversed.

Florida Star v. B.J.F.

491 U.S. 524 (1989)

FACTS

Appellant, The Florida Star, is a newspaper which publishes a "Police Reports" section containing brief articles describing local criminal incidents under police investigation. After appellee B. J. F. reported to the Sheriff's Department (Department) that she had been robbed and sexually assaulted, the Department prepared a report, which identified B. J. F. by her full name, and placed it in the Department's pressroom. The Department does not restrict access to the room or to the reports available there. A Star reporter-trainee sent to the pressroom copied the police report verbatim, including B.J.F.'s full name. Consequently, her name was included in a "Police Reports" story in the paper, in violation of the Star's internal policy. Florida Stat. 794.03 makes it unlawful to "print, publish, or broadcast . . . in any instrument of mass communication" the name of the victim of a sexual offense. B. J. F. filed suit in a Florida court alleging, inter alia, that the Star had negligently violated 794.03. The trial court denied the Star's motion to dismiss, which claimed, among other things, that imposing civil sanctions on the newspaper pursuant to 794.03 violated the First Amendment. However, it granted B.J.F.'s motion for a directed verdict on the issue of negligence, finding the Star per se negligent based on its violation of 794.03. The jury then awarded B. J. F. both compensatory and punitive damages. The verdict was upheld on appeal.

I

May a newspaper be found liable for publishing lawfully-obtained information that was truthful?

R

A newspaper may not be found liable for publishing lawfully-obtained information that was truthful absent a need to further a state interest that was "of the highest order."

A

Imposing damages on the Star for publishing B.J.F.'s name violates the First Amendment. The sensitivity and significance of the interests presented in clashes between First Amendment and privacy rights counsels the Court to rely on limited principles that sweep no more broadly than the appropriate context of the instant case, rather than to accept invitations to hold broadly that truthful publication may never be punished consistent with the First Amendment or that publication of a rape victim's name never enjoys constitutional protection. One such principle is that "if a newspaper lawfully obtains truthful information about a matter of public significance then state officials may not constitutionally punish publication of the information, absent a need to further a state interest of the highest order." Applied to the instant case, the Daily Mail principle commands reversal. The Star "lawfully obtain[ed] truthful information." The actual news article was accurate, and the Star lawfully obtained B.J.F.'s name from the government. The fact that state officials are not required to disclose such reports or that the Sheriff's Department apparently failed to fulfill its 794.03 obligation not to cause or allow B.J.F.'s name to be published does not make it unlawful for the Star to have received the information, and Florida has taken no steps to proscribe such receipt. The government has ample means to safeguard the information that are less drastic than punishing truthful publication. Furthermore, it is clear that the news article generally, as opposed to the specific identity contained in it, involved "a matter of public significance": the commission, and investigation, of a violent crime that had been reported to authorities. Imposing liability on the Star does not serve "a need to further a state interest of the highest order." Although the interests in protecting the privacy and safety of sexual assault victims and in encouraging them to report offenses without fear of exposure are highly significant, imposing liability on the Star in this case is too precipitous a means of advancing those interests. Since the Star obtained the information because the Sheriff's Department failed to abide by 794.03's policy, the imposition of damages can hardly be said to be a narrowly tailored means of safeguarding anonymity. Self-censorship is especially likely to result from imposition of liability when a newspaper gains access to the information from a government news release. Moreover, the negligence per se standard adopted by the courts below does not permit case-by-case findings that the disclosure was one a reasonable person would find offensive and does not have a scienter requirement of any kind. In addition, 794.03's facial under-inclusiveness - which prohibits publication only by an "instrument of mass communication" and does not prohibit the spread of victims' names by other means - raises serious doubts about whether Florida is serving the interests specified by B. J. F. A State must demonstrate its commitment to the extraordinary measure of punishing truthful publication in the name of privacy by applying its prohibition evenhandedly to both the smalltime disseminator and the media giant.

C

Reversed.

Bartnicki v. Vopper

532 U.S. 514 (2001)

FACTS

During contentious collective-bargaining negotiations between a union representing teachers at a Pennsylvania high school and the local school board, an unidentified person intercepted and recorded a cell phone conversation between the chief union negotiator and the union president (hereinafter petitioners). After the parties accepted a nonbinding arbitration proposal generally favorable to the teachers, respondent Vopper, a radio commentator, played a tape of the intercepted conversation on his public affairs talk show in connection with news reports about the settlement. Petitioners filed this damages suit under both federal and state wiretapping laws, alleging, among other things, that their conversation had been surreptitiously intercepted by an unknown person; that respondent Yocum, the head of a local organization opposed to the union's demands, had obtained the tape and intentionally disclosed it to media representatives; and that they had repeatedly published the conversation even though they knew or had reason to know that it had been illegally intercepted. In ruling on cross-motions for summary judgment, the District Court concluded that, under the statutory language, an individual violates the federal Act by intentionally disclosing the contents of an electronic communication when he or she knows or has reason to know that the information was obtained through an illegal interception, even if the individual was not involved in that interception; found that the question whether the interception was intentional raised a genuine issue of material fact; and rejected respondents' defense that they were protected by the First Amendment even if the disclosures violated the statutes, finding that the statutes were content-neutral laws of general applicability containing no indicia of prior restraint or the chilling of free speech. The Third Circuit accepted an interlocutory appeal, and the United States, also a petitioner, intervened to defend the federal Act's constitutionality. Applying intermediate scrutiny, the court found the statutes invalid because they deterred significantly more speech than necessary to protect the private interests at stake, and remanded the case with instructions to enter summary judgment for respondents.

I

Are the interceptions of wire, electronic, and oral communications (i.e. wire taps) and there subsequent publication protected by the First Amendment even if the disclosures violated certain state statutes?

R

There is no violation of the First Amendment if those accused played no part in the illegal interception, their access to the information was obtained lawfully, and if the conversations dealt with a matter of public concern.

A

The First Amendment protects the disclosures made by respondents in this suit. Title III of the Omnibus Crime Control and Safe Streets Act of 1968, as amended, generally prohibits the interception of wire, electronic, and oral communications. Title 18 U. S. C. §2511(1)(a) applies to the person who willfully intercepts such communications and subsection (c) to any person who, knowing or having reason to know that the communication was obtained through an illegal interception, willfully discloses its contents. Because of this suit's procedural posture, the Court accepts that the interception was unlawful and that respondents had reason to know that. Accordingly, the disclosures violated the statutes. In answering the remaining question whether the statutes' application in such circumstances violates the First Amendment, the Court accepts respondents' submissions that they played no part in the illegal interception, that their access to the information was obtained lawfully, and that the conversations dealt with a matter of public concern. Section 2511(1)(c) is a content-neutral law of general applicability. The statute's purpose is to protect the privacy of wire, electronic, and oral communications, and it singles out such communications by virtue of the fact that they were illegally intercepted--by virtue of the source rather than the subject matter. On the other hand, the prohibition against disclosures is fairly characterized as a regulation of speech. In *New York Times Co.* v. *United States,* this Court upheld the press' right to publish information of great public concern obtained from documents stolen by a third party. In so doing, this Court focused on the stolen documents' character and the consequences of public disclosure, not on the fact that the documents were stolen. It also left open the question whether, in cases where information has been acquired unlawfully by a newspaper or by a source, government may punish not only the unlawful acquisition, but also the ensuing publication. The issue here is a narrower version of that question: Where the publisher has lawfully obtained information from a source who obtained it unlawfully, may the government punish the ensuing publication based on the defect in a chain? The Court's refusal to construe the issue more broadly is consistent with its repeated refusal to answer categorically whether the publication of truthful information may ever be punished consistent with the First Amendment. Accordingly, the Court considers whether, given the facts here, the interests served by §2511(1)(c) justify its restrictions on speech. The first interest identified by the Government--removing an incentive for parties to intercept private conversations--does not justify applying §2511(1)(c) to an otherwise innocent disclosure of public information. The normal method of deterring unlawful conduct is to punish the person engaging in it. It would be remarkable to hold that speech by a law-abiding possessor of information can be suppressed in order to deter conduct by a non-law-abiding third party. In virtually all §2511(1)(a), (c), or (d) violations, the interceptor's identity has been known. There is no evidence that Congress thought that the prohibition against disclosures would deter illegal interceptions, and no evidence to support the assumption that the prohibition reduces the number of such interceptions. The Government's second interest--minimizing the harm to persons whose conversations have been illegally intercepted--is considerably stronger. Privacy of communication is an important interest. However, in this suit, privacy concerns give way when balanced against the interest in publishing matters of public importance. One of the costs associated with participation in public affairs is an attendant loss of privacy. The profound national commitment to the principle that debate on public issues should be uninhibited, robust, and wide open supported this Court's holding in *New York Times Co.* v. *Sullivan,* that neither factual error nor defamatory content, nor a combination of the two, sufficed to remove the First Amendment shield from criticism of official conduct. Parallel reasoning requires the conclusion that a stranger's illegal conduct does not suffice to remove the First Amendment shield from speech about a matter of public concern.

C

The judgment is affirmed.

United States v. O'Brien

391 U.S. 367 (1968)

FACTS

Defendant O'Brien burned his Selective Service registration certificate before a sizable crowd in order to influence others to adopt his antiwar beliefs. He was indicted, tried, and convicted for violating 50 U.S.C. App. 462 (b), a part of the Universal Military Training and Service Act, subdivision (3) of which applies to any person "who forges, alters, knowingly destroys, knowingly mutilates, or in any manner changes any such certificate . . .," the words italicized herein having been added by amendment in 1965. The District Court rejected O'Brien's argument that the amendment was unconstitutional because it was enacted to abridge free speech and served no legitimate legislative purpose. The Court of Appeals held the 1965 Amendment unconstitutional under the First Amendment as singling out for special treatment persons engaged in protests, on the ground that conduct under the 1965 Amendment was already punishable since a Selective Service System regulation required registrants to keep their registration certificates in their "personal possession at all times," 32 CFR 1617.1, and willful violation of regulations promulgated under the Act was made criminal by 50 U.S.C. App. 462 (b) (6). The court, however, upheld O'Brien's conviction under 462 (b) (6), which in its view made violation of the non-possession regulation a lesser included offense of the crime defined by the 1965 Amendment. The United States (plaintiff) appealed.

I Can the government constitutionally place restrictions on symbolic ["nonspeech"] speech?

R A governmental can regulate symbolic "nonspeech" if 1) it is within the constitutional power of the government to promulgate it, 2) it furthers a substantial or important governmental interest unrelated to the suppression of free expression, and 3) the incidental restriction on alleged First Amendment freedoms is no greater than is essential to the furtherance of that interest.

A The 1965 Amendment to 50 U.S.C. App. 462 (b) (3) is constitutional as applied in this case. The 1965 Amendment plainly does not abridge free speech on its face. When "speech" and "nonspeech" elements are combined in the same course of conduct, a sufficiently important governmental interest in regulating the nonspeech element can justify incidental limitations on First Amendment freedoms. A governmental regulation is sufficiently justified if it is within the constitutional power of the Government and furthers an important or substantial governmental interest unrelated to the suppression of free expression, and if the incidental restriction on alleged First Amendment freedom is no greater than is essential to that interest. The 1965 Amendment meets all these requirements. The 1965 Amendment came within Congress' "broad and sweeping" power to raise and support armies and make all laws necessary to that end. The registration certificate serves purposes in addition to initial notification, e.g., it proves that the described individual has registered for the draft; facilitates communication between registrants and local boards; and provides a reminder that the registrant must notify his local board of changes in address or status. The regulatory scheme involving the certificates includes clearly valid prohibitions against alteration, forgery, or similar deceptive misuse. The pre-existence of the nonpossession regulation does not negate Congress' clear interest in providing alternative statutory avenues of prosecution to assure its interest in preventing destruction of the Selective Service certificates. The governmental interests protected by the 1965 Amendment and the nonpossession regulation, though overlapping, are not identical. The 1965 Amendment is a narrow and precisely drawn provision which specifically protects the Government's substantial interest in an efficient and easily administered system for raising armies. O'Brien was convicted only for the willful frustration of that governmental interest. The noncommunicative impact of his conduct for which he was convicted makes his case readily distinguishable from *Stromberg v. California*. The 1965 Amendment is constitutional as enacted. Congress' purpose in enacting the law affords no basis for declaring an otherwise constitutional statute invalid.

C Vacated; judgment and sentence of District Court reinstated

Texas v. Johnson

491 U.S. 397 (1989)

FACTS

During the 1984 Republican National Convention in Dallas, Texas, Defendant-respondent Johnson participated in a political demonstration to protest the policies of the Reagan administration and some Dallas-based corporations. After a march through the city streets, Johnson burned an American flag while protesters chanted. No one was physically injured or threatened with injury, although several witnesses were seriously offended by the flag burning. Johnson was convicted of desecration of a venerated object in violation of a Texas statute, and a State Court of Appeals affirmed. However, the Texas Court of Criminal Appeals reversed, holding that the State, consistent with the First Amendment, could not punish Johnson for burning the flag in these circumstances. The court first found that Johnson's burning of the flag was expressive conduct protected by the First Amendment. The court concluded that the State could not criminally sanction flag desecration in order to preserve the flag as a symbol of national unity. It also held that the statute did not meet the State's goal of preventing breaches of the peace, since it was not drawn narrowly enough to encompass only those flag burnings that would likely result in a serious disturbance, and since the flag burning in this case did not threaten such a reaction. Further, it stressed that another Texas statute prohibited breaches of the peace and could be used to prevent disturbances without punishing this flag desecration. The State of Texas (plaintiff) appealed to the Supreme Court.

I

Is flag burning a type of expressive conduct protected by the First Amendment?

R

When the government's interest in restricting speech is content-based [based on a desire to suppress the ideas or viewpoints expressed by the speech] a strict scrutiny standard of review [is the interest necessary to achieve a compelling state interest?] must be applied.

A

Johnson's conviction for flag desecration is inconsistent with the First Amendment. Under the circumstances, Johnson's burning of the flag constituted expressive conduct, permitting him to invoke the First Amendment. The State conceded that the conduct was expressive. Occurring as it did at the end of a demonstration coinciding with the Republican National Convention, the expressive, overtly political nature of the conduct was both intentional and overwhelmingly apparent. Texas has not asserted an interest in support of Johnson's conviction that is unrelated to the suppression of expression and would therefore permit application of the test set forth in *United States v. O'Brien*, whereby an important governmental interest in regulating nonspeech can justify incidental limitations on First Amendment freedoms when speech and nonspeech elements are combined in the same course of conduct. An interest in preventing breaches of the peace is not implicated on this record. Expression may not be prohibited on the basis that an audience that takes serious offense to the expression may disturb the peace, since the government cannot assume that every expression of a provocative idea will incite a riot but must look to the actual circumstances surrounding the expression. Johnson's expression of dissatisfaction with the Federal Government's policies also does not fall within the class of "fighting words" likely to be seen as a direct personal insult or an invitation to exchange fisticuffs. This Court's holding does not forbid a State to prevent "imminent lawless action" and, in fact, Texas has a law specifically prohibiting breaches of the peace. Texas' interest in preserving the flag as a symbol of nationhood and national unity is related to expression in this case and, thus, falls outside the *O'Brien* test. The latter interest does not justify Johnson's conviction. The restriction on Johnson's political expression is content based, since the Texas statute is not aimed at protecting the physical integrity of the flag in all circumstances, but is designed to protect it from intentional and knowing abuse that causes serious offense to others. It is therefore subject to "the most exacting scrutiny." The government may not prohibit the verbal or nonverbal expression of an idea merely because society finds the idea offensive or disagreeable, even where our flag is involved. Nor may a State foster its own view of the flag by prohibiting expressive conduct relating to it, since the government may not permit designated symbols to be used to communicate a limited set of messages. Moreover, this Court will not create an exception to these principles protected by the First Amendment for the American flag alone.

C

Affirmed

Buckley v. Valeo

424 U.S. 1 (1976)

FACTS

The Federal Election Campaign Act of 1971 (Act): (a) limits political contributions to candidates for federal elective office by an individual or a group to $1,000 and by a political committee to $5,000 to any single candidate per election, with an overall annual limitation of $25,000 by an individual contributor; (b) limits expenditures by individuals or groups "relative to a clearly identified candidate" to $1,000 per candidate per election, and by a candidate from his personal or family funds to various specified annual amounts depending upon the federal office sought, and restricts overall general election and primary campaign expenditures by candidates to various specified amounts, again depending upon the federal office sought; (c) requires political committees to keep detailed records of contributions and expenditures, including the name and address of each individual contributing in excess of $10, and his occupation and principal place of business if his contribution exceeds $100, and to file quarterly reports with the Federal Election Commission disclosing the source of every contribution exceeding $100 and the recipient and purpose of every expenditure over $100, and also requires every individual or group, other than a candidate or political committee, making contributions or expenditures exceeding $100 "other than by contribution to a political committee or candidate" to file a statement with the Commission; and (d) creates the eight-member Commission as the administering agency with recordkeeping, disclosure, and investigatory functions and extensive rulemaking, adjudicatory, and enforcement powers, and consisting of two members appointed by the President pro tempore of the Senate, two by the Speaker of the House, and two by the President (all subject to confirmation by both Houses of Congress), and the Secretary of the Senate and the Clerk of the House as ex officio nonvoting members. Subtitle H of the Internal Revenue Code of 1954 (IRC), as amended in 1974, provides for public financing of Presidential nominating conventions and general election and primary campaigns from general revenues and allocates such funding to conventions and general election campaigns by establishing three categories: (1) "major" parties (those whose candidate received 25% or more of the vote in the most recent election), which receive full funding, (2) "minor" parties (those whose candidate received at least 5% but less than 25% of the votes at the last election), which receive only a percentage of the funds to which the major parties are entitled; and (3) "new" parties (all other parties), which are limited to receipt of post-election funds or are not entitled to any funds if their candidate receives less than 5% of the vote. A primary candidate for the Presidential nomination by a political party who receives more than $5,000 from private sources (counting only the first $250 of each contribution) in each of at least 20 States is eligible for matching public funds. Appellants (various federal officeholders and candidates, supporting political organizations, and others) brought suit against appellees (the Secretary of the Senate, Clerk of the House, Comptroller General, Attorney General, and the Commission) seeking declaratory and injective relief against the above statutory provisions on various constitutional grounds. The Court of Appeals, on certified questions from the District Court, upheld all but one of the statutory provisions. A three-judge District Court upheld the constitutionality of Subtitle H.

I

Are the Act's contribution provisions and expenditure provisions violative of the First Amendment?

Buckley v. Valeo

424 U.S. 1 (1976)

R The Act's contribution provisions are constitutional, but the expenditure provisions violate the First Amendment because the expenditures are so closely related to and necessary for political expression as to fall under the First Amendment protection of free expression.

A This litigation presents an Art. III "case or controversy," since the complaint discloses that at least some of the appellants have a sufficient "personal stake" in a determination of the constitutional validity of each of the challenged provisions to present "a real and substantial controversy admitting of specific relief through a decree of a conclusive character, as distinguished from an opinion advising what the law would be upon a hypothetical state of facts." The Act's contribution provisions are constitutional, but the expenditure provisions violate the First Amendment. The contribution provisions, along with those covering disclosure, are appropriate legislative weapons against the reality or appearance of improper influence stemming from the dependence of candidates on large campaign contributions, and the ceilings imposed accordingly serve the basic governmental interest in safeguarding the integrity of the electoral process without directly impinging upon the rights of individual citizens and candidates to engage in political debate and discussion. The First Amendment requires the invalidation of the Act's independent expenditure ceiling, its limitation on a candidate's expenditures from his own personal funds, and its ceilings on overall campaign expenditures, since those provisions place substantial and direct restrictions on the ability of candidates, citizens, and associations to engage in protected political expression, restrictions that the First Amendment cannot tolerate. The Act's disclosure and recordkeeping provisions are constitutional. The general disclosure provisions, which serve substantial governmental interests in informing the electorate and preventing the corruption of the political process, are not overbroad insofar as they apply to contributions to minor parties and independent candidates. No blanket exemption for minor parties is warranted since such parties in order to prove injury as a result of application to them of the disclosure provisions need show only a reasonable probability that the compelled disclosure of a party's contributors' names will subject them to threats, harassment, or reprisals in violation of their First Amendment associational rights. The provision for disclosure by those who make independent contributions and expenditures, as narrowly construed to apply only (1) when they make contributions earmarked for political purposes or authorized or requested by a candidate or his agent to some person other than a candidate or political committee and (2) when they make an expenditure for a communication that expressly advocates the election or defeat of a clearly identified candidate is not unconstitutionally vague and does not constitute a prior restraint but is a reasonable and minimally restrictive method of furthering First Amendment values by public exposure of the federal election system. The extension of the recordkeeping provisions to contributions as small as those just above $10 and the disclosure provisions to contributions above $100 is not on this record overbroad since it cannot be said to be unrelated to the informational and enforcement goals of the legislation. Subtitle H of the IRC is constitutional. Subtitle H is not invalid under the General Welfare Clause but, as a means to reform the electoral process, was clearly a choice within the power granted to Congress by the Clause to decide which expenditures will promote the general welfare, nor does Subtitle H violate the First Amendment. Rather than abridging, restricting, or censoring speech, it represents an effort to use public money to facilitate and enlarge public discussion and participation in the electoral process. Subtitle H, being less burdensome than ballot-access regulations and having been enacted in furtherance of vital governmental interests in relieving major-party candidates from the rigors of soliciting private contributions, in not funding candidates who lack significant public support, and in eliminating reliance on large private contributions for funding of conventions and campaigns, does not invidiously discriminate against minor and new parties in violation of the Due Process Clause of the Fifth Amendment. Invalidation of the spending-limit provisions of the Act does not render Subtitle H unconstitutional, but the Subtitle is severable from such provisions and is not dependent upon the existence of a generally applicable expenditure limit. The Commission's composition as to all but its investigative and informative powers violates Art. II, 2, cl. 2. With respect to the Commission's powers, all of which are ripe for review, to enforce the Act, including primary responsibility for bringing civil actions against violators, to make rules for carrying out the Act, to temporarily disqualify federal candidates for failing to file required reports, and to authorize convention expenditures in excess of the specified limits, the provisions of the Act vesting such powers in the Commission and the prescribed method of appointment of members of the Commission to the extent that a majority of the voting members are appointed by the President pro tempore of the Senate and the Speaker of the House, violate the Appointments Clause, which provides in pertinent part that the President shall nominate, and with the Senate's advice and consent appoint, all "Officers of the United States," whose appointments are not otherwise provided for, but that Congress may vest the appointment of such inferior officers, as it deems proper, in the President alone, in the courts, or in the heads of departments. Hence (though the Commission's past acts are accorded de facto validity and a stay is granted permitting it to function under the Act for not more than 30 days), the Commission, as presently constituted, may not because of that Clause exercise such powers, which can be exercised only by "Officers of the United States" appointed in conformity with the Appointments Clause, although it may exercise such investigative and informative powers as are in the same category as those powers that Congress might delegate to one of its own committees.

C

Affirmed in part and reversed in part.

Nixon v. Shrink Missouri Government Inc.

528 U.S. 377 (2000)

FACTS

Respondents Shrink Missouri Government PAC, a political action committee, and Zev David Fredman, a candidate for the 1998 Republican nomination for Missouri state auditor, filed suit, alleging that a Missouri statute imposing limits ranging from $275 to $1,075 on contributions to candidates for state office violated their First and Fourteenth Amendment rights. Shrink Missouri gave Fredman $1,025 in 1997, and $50 in 1998, and represented that, without the statutory limitation, it would contribute more. Fredman alleged he could campaign effectively only with more generous contributions than the statute allowed. On cross-motions for summary judgment, the District Court sustained the statute. Applying *Buckley* v. *Valeo,* the court found adequate support for the law in the proposition that large contributions raise suspicions of influence peddling tending to undermine citizens' confidence in government integrity. The court rejected respondents' contention that inflation since *Buckley*'s approval of a federal $1,000 restriction meant that the state limit of $1,075 for a statewide office could not be constitutional today. In reversing, the Eighth Circuit found that *Buckley* had articulated and applied a strict scrutiny standard of review, and held that Missouri had to demonstrate that it had a compelling interest and that the contribution limits at issue were narrowly drawn to serve that interest. Treating Missouri's claim of a compelling interest in avoiding the corruption or the perception of corruption caused by candidates' acceptance of large campaign contributions as insufficient by itself to satisfy strict scrutiny, the court required demonstrable evidence that genuine problems resulted from contributions in amounts greater than the statutory limits. It ruled that the State's evidence was inadequate for this purpose.

I

May a state impose campaign contribution limits?

R

A state may impose campaign contribution limits which do not make contributions pointless.

A

Buckley is authority for comparable state limits on contributions to state political candidates, and those limits need not be pegged to the precise dollar amounts approved in *Buckley.* The *Buckley* Court held, *inter alia,* that a Federal Election Campaign Act provision placing a $1,000 annual ceiling on independent expenditures linked to specific candidates for federal office infringed speech and association guarantees of the First Amendment and the Equal Protection Clause of the Fourteenth, but upheld other provisions limiting contributions by individuals to any single candidate to $1,000 per election. In addressing the speech claim, the *Buckley* Court explicitly rejected both intermediate scrutiny for communicative action, and the similar standard applicable to merely time, place, and manner restrictions, and instead referred generally to "the exacting scrutiny required by the First Amendment." The Court then drew a line between expenditures and contributions, treating expenditure restrictions as direct restraints on speech, but saying, in effect, that limiting contributions left communication significantly unimpaired. The Court flagged a similar difference between the impacts of expenditure and contribution limits on association rights and later made that distinction explicit. Thus, under *Buckley* 's standard of scrutiny, a contribution limit involving significant interference with associational rights could survive if the Government demonstrated that regulating contributions was a means "closely drawn" to match a "sufficiently important interest," though the dollar amount of the limit need not be "fine tun[ed]." While *Buckley* did not attempt to parse distinctions between the speech and associational standards of scrutiny for contribution limits, the Court made clear that such restrictions bore more heavily on associational rights than on speech rights, and thus proceeded on the understanding that a contribution limitation surviving a claim of associational abridgement would survive a speech challenge as well. The Court found the prevention of corruption and the appearance of corruption to be a constitutionally sufficient justification for the contribution limits at issue. In defending its statute, Missouri espouses those same interests of preventing corruption and the appearance of it. Even without *Buckley*, there would be no serious question about the legitimacy of these interests, which underlie bribery and anti-gratuity statutes. Rather, respondents take the State to task for failing to justify the invocation of those interests with empirical evidence of actually corrupt practices or of a perception among Missouri voters that unrestricted contributions must have been exerting a covertly corrosive influence. The state statute is not void, however, for want of evidence. There is no support for respondents' various arguments that the Missouri limitations are so different in kind from those sustained in *Buckley* as to raise essentially a new issue about the adequacy of the Missouri statute's tailoring to serve its purposes. Here, as in *Buckley,* there is no indication that those limits have had any dramatic adverse effect on the funding of campaigns and political associations, and thus there is no showing that the limitations prevented candidates from amassing the resources necessary for effective advocacy. Indeed, the District Court found that since the Missouri limits became effective, candidates for state office have been able to raise funds sufficient to run effective campaigns, and that candidates are still able to amass impressive campaign war chests. The plausibility of these conclusions is buttressed by petitioners' evidence that in the last election before the contributions became effective, 97.62% of all contributors to candidates for state auditor made contributions of $2,000 or less. Even assuming that the contribution limits affected respondent Fredman's ability to wage a competitive campaign, a showing of one affected individual does not point up a system of suppressed political advocacy that would be unconstitutional under *Buckley*.

C Reversed and remanded.

First National Bank of Boston v. Bellotti

435 U.S. 765 (1978)

FACTS

Appellants, national banking associations and business corporations, wanted to spend money to publicize their views opposing a referendum proposal to amend the Massachusetts Constitution to authorize the legislature to enact a graduated personal income tax. They brought this action challenging the constitutionality of a Massachusetts criminal statute that prohibited them and other specified business corporations from making contributions or expenditures "for the purpose of . . . influencing or affecting the vote on any question submitted to the voters, other than one materially affecting any of the property, business or assets of the corporation." The statute specified that "[n]o question submitted to the voters solely concerning the taxation of the income, property or transactions of individuals shall be deemed materially to affect the property, business or assets of the corporation." On April 26, 1976, the case was submitted to a single Justice of the Supreme Judicial Court of Massachusetts on an expedited basis and upon agreed facts. Judgment was reserved and the case was referred to the full court. On September 22, 1976, the court directed entry of a judgment for appellee and issued its opinion upholding the constitutionality of the statute after the referendum, at which the proposal was rejected.

I

May a state deny corporations the right to advocate their views publicly?

R

A state cannot deny corporations the right to advocate their views publicly.

A

The case is not rendered moot by the fact that the 1976 referendum has been held and the proposal for a constitutional amendment defeated. The 18-month interval between legislative authorization of placement of the proposal on the ballot and its submission to the voters was too short for appellants to obtain complete judicial review, and likely would be too short in any future challenge to the statute; and in view of the number of times that such a proposal has been submitted to the electorate, there is reasonable expectation that appellants again will be subjected to the threat of prosecution under the statute. The portion of the Massachusetts statute at issue violates the First Amendment as made applicable to the States by the Fourteenth. The expression proposed by appellants, namely, the expression of views on an issue of public importance, is at the heart of the First Amendment's concern. There is no support in the First or Fourteenth Amendment, or in this Court's decisions, for the proposition that such speech loses the protection otherwise afforded it by the First Amendment simply because its source is a corporation that cannot prove, to a court's satisfaction, a material effect on its business. Although appellee suggests that this Court's decisions generally have extended First Amendment rights only to corporations in the business of communications or which foster the self-expression of individuals, those decisions were not based on the rationale that the challenged communication materially affected the company's business. They were based, at least in part, on the Amendment's protection of public discussion and the dissemination of information and ideas. Similarly, commercial speech is accorded some constitutional protection not so much because it pertains to the seller's business as because it furthers the societal interest in the "free flow of commercial information," *Virginia State Bd. of Pharmacy v. Virginia Citizens Consumer Council.* The asserted justifications for the challenged statute cannot survive the exacting scrutiny required when the legislative prohibition is directed at speech itself and speech on a public issue. This statute cannot be justified by the State's asserted interest in sustaining the active role of the individual citizen in the electoral process and preventing diminution of his confidence in government. Even if it were permissible to silence one segment of society upon a sufficient showing of imminent danger, there has been no showing that the relative voice of corporations has been overwhelming or even significant in influencing referenda in Massachusetts, or that there has been any threat to the confidence of the citizenry in government. And the risk of corruption perceived in this Court's decisions involving candidate elections is not present in a popular vote on a public issue. Nor can the statute be justified on the asserted ground that it protects the rights of shareholders whose views differ from those expressed by management on behalf of the corporation. The statute is both under-inclusive and over-inclusive in serving this purpose, and therefore could not be sustained even if the purpose itself were deemed compelling.

C

Reversed.

Hague v. Committee for Industrial Organization

307 U.S. 496 (1939)

FACTS

The respondents, who are individual citizens and unincorporated labor organizations composed of such citizens and a membership corporation, brought suit in the United States District Court against the petitioners, the Mayor, the Director of Public Safety, and the Chief of Police of Jersey City, New Jersey, and the Board of Commissioners, the governing body of the city. The bill alleges that acting under a city ordinance forbidding the leasing of any hall, without a permit from the Chief of Police, for a public meeting at which a speaker shall advocate obstruction of the Government of the United States or a state, or a change of government by other than lawful means, the petitioners, and their subordinates, have denied respondents the right to hold lawful meetings in Jersey City on the ground that they are Communists or Communist organizations; that pursuant to an unlawful plan, the petitioners have caused the eviction from the municipality of persons they considered undesirable because of their labor organization activities, and have announced that they will continue so to do. It further alleges that acting under an ordinance which forbids any person to 'distribute or cause to be distributed or strewn about any street or public place any newspapers, paper, periodical, book magazine, circular, card or pamphlet', the petitioners have discriminated against the respondents by prohibiting and interfering with distribution of leaflets and pamphlets by the respondents while permitting others to distribute similar printed matter; that pursuant to a plan and conspiracy to deny the respondents their Constitutional rights as citizens of the United States, the petitioners have caused respondents, and those acting with them, to be arrested for distributing printed matter in the streets, and have caused them, and their associates, to be carried beyond the limits of the city or to remote places therein, and have compelled them to board ferry boats destined for New York; have, with violence and force, interfered with the distribution of pamphlets discussing the rights of citizens under the National Labor Relations Act; have unlawfully searched persons coming into the city and seized printed matter in their possession; have arrested and prosecuted respondents for attempting to distribute such printed matter; and have threatened that if respondents attempt to hold public meetings in the city to discuss rights afforded by the National Labor Relations Act, they would be arrested; and unless restrained, the petitioners will continue in their unlawful conduct. After trial upon the merits the District Court entered findings of fact and conclusions of law and a decree in favor of respondents. The Circuit Court of Appeals concurred in the findings of fact; held the District Court had jurisdiction; modified the decree in respect of one of its provisions, and, as modified, affirmed it.

I

May a city ordinance give discretion to officials to prevent speech and assembly in public streets and parks?

R

The government must allow public places to be used for speech but could regulate access only to maintain order.

Hague v. Committee for Industrial Organization

307 U.S. 496 (1939)

A Although it has been held that the Fourteenth Amendment created no rights in citizens of the United States, but merely secured existing rights against state abridgment, it is clear that the right peaceably to assemble and to discuss these topics, and to communicate respecting them, whether orally or in writing, is a privilege inherent in citizenship of the United States which the Amendment protects. In *United States v. Cruikshank*, the court said: 'The right of the people peaceably to assemble for the purpose of petitioning Congress for a redress of grievances, or for anything else connected with the powers or the duties of the National Government, is an attribute of national citizenship and, as such, under the protection of and guaranteed by, the United States. The very idea of a government, republican in form, implies a right on the part of its citizens to meet peaceably for consultation in respect to public affairs and to petition for a redress of grievances. If it had been alleged in these counts that the object of the defendants was to prevent a meeting for such a purpose, the case would have been within the statute, and within the scope of the sovereignty of the United States.' We think the court below was right in holding the ordinance quoted in Note 1 void upon its face. It does not make comfort or convenience in the use of streets or parks the standard of official action. It enables the Director of Safety to refuse a permit on his mere opinion that such refusal will prevent 'riots, disturbances or disorderly assemblage.' It can thus, as the record discloses, be made the instrument of arbitrary suppression of free expression of views on national affairs for the prohibition of all speaking will undoubtedly 'prevent' such eventualities. But uncontrolled official suppression of the privilege cannot be made a substitute for the duty to maintain order in connection with the exercise of the right. Although the court below held the ordinance void, the decree enjoins the petitioners as to the manner in which they shall administer it. There is an initial command that the petitioners shall not place 'any previous restraint' upon the respondents in respect of holding meetings provided they apply for a permit as required by the ordinance. This is followed by an enumeration of the conditions under which a permit may be granted or denied. We think this is wrong. As the ordinance is void, the respondents are entitled to a decree so declaring and an injunction against its enforcement by the petitioners. They are free to hold meetings without a permit and without regard to the terms of the void ordinance. The courts cannot rewrite the ordinance, as the decree, in effect, does. The bill should be dismissed as to all save the individual plaintiffs, and Section B, paragraphs 2, 3 and 4, of the decree should be modified as indicated. In other respects the decree should be affirmed.

C Affirmed; the ordinance is void.

Schneider v. New Jersey

308 U.S. 147 (1939)

FACTS

The appellant was charged in the Municipal Court with a violation of Sec. 28.01 which provides that 'No person shall distribute any hand-bill to or among pedestrians along or upon any street, sidewalk or park, or to passengers on any street car, or throw, place or attach any hand-bill in, to or upon any automobile or other vehicle.' Upon his trial it was proved that he distributed handbills to pedestrians on a public sidewalk and had more than three hundred in his possession for that purpose. Judgment of conviction was entered and sentence imposed. The Superior Court of Los Angeles County affirmed the judgment. The handbill which the appellant was distributing bore a notice of a meeting to be held under the auspices of 'Friends Lincoln Brigade' at which speakers would discuss the war in Spain.

I

May a municipality ban pamphleteering to prevent littering?

R

Although a municipality may enact regulations in the interest of the public safety, health, welfare or convenience, these may not abridge the individual liberties secured by the Constitution to those who wish to speak, write, print or circulate information or opinion.

A

Municipal authorities, as trustees for the public, have the duty to keep their communities' streets open and available for movement of people and property, the primary purpose to which the streets are dedicated. So long as legislation to this end does not abridge the constitutional liberty of one rightfully upon the street to impart information through speech or the distribution of literature, it may lawfully regulate the conduct of those using the streets. For example, a person could not exercise this liberty by taking his stand in the middle of a crowded street, contrary to traffic regulations, and maintain his position to the stoppage of all traffic; a group of distributors could not insist upon a constitutional right to form a cordon across the street and to allow no pedestrian to pass who did not accept a tendered leaflet; nor does the guarantee of freedom of speech or of the press deprive a municipality of power to enact regulations against throwing literature broadcast in the streets. Prohibition of such conduct would not abridge the constitutional liberty since such activity bears no necessary relationship to the freedom to speak, write, print or distribute information or opinion.

C

Reversed and remanded.

Perry Education Assn. v. Perry Local Educators' Assn.

460 U.S. 37 (1983)

FACTS

Under a collective-bargaining agreement between the Board of Education of Perry Township, Ind., and Perry Education Association (PEA) as the exclusive bargaining representative for the School District's teachers, PEA was granted access to the interschool mail system and teacher mail-boxes in the Perry Township schools. The bargaining agreement also provided that access rights to the mail facilities were not available to any rival union, such as Perry Local Educators' Association (PLEA). PLEA and two of its members filed suit in Federal District Court against PEA and individual members of the School Board, contending that PEA's preferential access to the internal mail system violated the First Amendment and the Equal Protection Clause of the Fourteenth Amendment. The court entered summary judgment for the defendants, but the Court of Appeals reversed.

I

Can a school board let its interschool mail system be used by one union while, at the same time, denying its use to a rival union?

R

The differential access provided the rival union does not constitute impermissible content discrimination in violation of the Equal Protection Clause.

A

The appeal is not proper under 28 U.S.C. 1254(2), which grants this Court appellate jurisdiction over federal court of appeals' decisions holding a state statute repugnant to the Federal Constitution. Here, only certain provisions of the collective-bargaining agreement, not the Indiana statute authorizing such agreements, were held to be constitutionally invalid, and the bargaining agreement cannot be considered to be in essence a legislative act. However, regarding the jurisdictional statement as a petition for a writ of certiorari, certiorari is granted because the constitutional issues presented are important and the decision below conflicts with the judgments of other federal and state courts. The First Amendment is not violated by the preferential access to the interschool mail system granted to PEA. With respect to public property that is not by tradition or government designation a forum for public communication, a State may reserve the use of the property for its intended purposes, communicative or otherwise, as long as a regulation on speech is reasonable and not an effort to suppress expression merely because public officials oppose the speaker's view. The school mail facilities were not a "limited public forum" merely because the system had been opened for periodic use by [460 U.S. 37, 38] civic and church organizations, or because PLEA was allowed to use the school mail facilities on an equal footing with PEA prior to PEA's certification as the teachers' exclusive bargaining representative. The differential access provided PEA and PLEA is reasonable because it is wholly consistent with the School District's legitimate interest in preserving the property for the use to which it was lawfully dedicated. Use of school mail facilities enables PEA to perform effectively its statutory obligations as exclusive representative of all Perry Township teachers. Conversely, PLEA does not have any official responsibility in connection with the School District and need not be entitled to the same rights of access to school mailboxes. The reasonableness of the limitations on PLEA's access to the school mail system is also supported by the substantial alternative channels that remain open for union-teacher communication to take place. Moreover, under Indiana law, PLEA is assured of equal access to all modes of communication while a representation election is in progress. The differential access provided the rival union does not constitute impermissible content discrimination in violation of the Equal Protection Clause. Since the grant of exclusive access to PEA does not burden a fundamental right of PLEA, the School District's policy need only rationally further a legitimate state purpose. That purpose is clearly found in the special responsibilities of an exclusive bargaining representative.

C Appeal dismissed and certiorari granted; 652 F.2d 1286, reversed.

Police Dept. of the City of Chicago v. Mosley

408 U.S. 92 (1972)

FACTS

The suit was brought by Earl Mosley, a federal postal employee, who for seven months prior to the enactment of the ordinance had frequently picketed Jones Commercial High School in Chicago. During school hours and usually by himself, Mosley would walk the public sidewalk adjoining the school, carrying a sign that read: "Jones High School practices black discrimination. Jones High School has a black quota." His lonely crusade was always peaceful, orderly, and quiet, and was conceded to be so by the city of Chicago. On March 26, 1968, Chapter 193-1 (i) was passed, to become effective on April 5. This ordinance provided that: "A person commits disorderly conduct when he knowingly (i) Pickets or demonstrates on a public way within 150 feet of any primary or secondary school building while the school is in session and one-half hour before the school is in session and one-half hour after the school session has been concluded, provided that this subsection does not prohibit the peaceful picketing of any school involved in a labor dispute . . ." Seeing a newspaper announcement of the new ordinance, Mosley contacted the Chicago Police Department to find out how the ordinance would affect him; he was told that, if his picketing continued, he would be arrested. On April 4, the day before the ordinance became effective, Mosley ended his picketing next to the school. Thereafter, he brought this action in the United States District Court for the Northern District of Illinois, seeking declaratory and injunctive relief, pursuant to 28 U.S.C. 2201 and 42 U.S.C. 1983. He alleged a violation of constitutional rights in that (1) the statute punished activity protected by the First Amendment; and (2) by exempting only peaceful labor picketing from its general prohibition against picketing, the statute denied him equal protection of the law in violation of the First and Fourteenth Amendments. After a hearing, the District Court granted a directed verdict dismissing the complaint. The Seventh Circuit reversed, holding that because the ordinance prohibited even peaceful picketing next to a school, it was overbroad and therefore "patently unconstitutional on its face." The U.S. Supreme Court granted certiorari

I When an ordinance distinguishes labor picketing from any other type of picketing, and punishes the latter while allowing the former, is it violative of the Equal Protection Clause of the 14th Amendment?

R An ordinance, law or statute may not discriminate between different protesters based on the content of their message without violating the Equal Protection Clause.

A The City of Chicago exempts peaceful labor picketing from its general prohibition on picketing next to a school. The question we consider here is whether this selective exclusion from a public place is permitted. Our answer is "No." Because Chicago treats some picketing differently from others, we analyze this ordinance in terms of the Equal Protection Clause of the Fourteenth Amendment. Of course, the equal protection claim in this case is closely intertwined with First Amendment interests; the Chicago ordinance affects picketing, which is expressive conduct; moreover, it does so by classifications formulated in terms of the subject of the picketing. As in all equal protection cases, however, the crucial question is whether there is an appropriate governmental interest suitably furthered by the differential treatment. The central problem with Chicago's ordinance is that it describes permissible picketing in terms of its subject matter. Peaceful picketing on the subject of a school's labor-management dispute is permitted, but all other peaceful picketing is prohibited. The operative distinction is the message on a picket sign. But, above all else, the First Amendment means that government has no power to restrict expression because of its message, its ideas, its subject matter, or its content. The Equal Protection Clause requires that statutes affecting First Amendment interests be narrowly tailored to their legitimate objectives. Chicago may not vindicate its interest in preventing disruption by the wholesale exclusion of picketing on all but one preferred subject. Given what Chicago tolerates from labor picketing, the excesses of some non-labor picketing may not be controlled by a broad ordinance prohibiting both peaceful and violent picketing. Such excesses "can be controlled by narrowly drawn statutes," *Saia v. New York* [focusing on the abuses and dealing even-handedly with picketing regardless of subject matter]. Chicago's ordinance imposes a selective restriction on expressive conduct far "greater than is essential to the furtherance of [a substantial governmental] interest," *United States v. O'Brien*. Far from being tailored to a substantial governmental interest, the discrimination among pickets is based on the content of their expression. Therefore, under the Equal Protection Clause, it may not stand.

C Affirmed.

Hill v. Colorado

530 U.S. 703 (2000)

FACTS

Colorado Rev. Stat. §18-9-122(3) makes it unlawful for any person within 100 feet of a health care facility's entrance to "knowingly approach" within 8 feet of another person, without that person's consent, in order to pass "a leaflet or handbill to, displa[y] a sign to, or engag[e] in oral protest, education, or counseling with [that] person ... ." Claiming that the statute was facially invalid, petitioners sought to enjoin its enforcement in state court. In dismissing the complaint, the District Judge held that the statute imposed content-neutral time, place, and manner restrictions narrowly tailored to serve a significant government interest under *Ward* v. *Rock Against Racism,* in that Colorado had not "adopted a regulation of speech because of disagreement with the message it conveys." The State Court of Appeals affirmed, and the State Supreme Court denied review. This Court vacated that judgment in light of its holding in *Schenck* v. *Pro-Choice Network of Western N. Y.,* that an injunctive provision creating a speech-free floating buffer zone with a 15-foot radius violated the First Amendment. On remand, the Court of Appeals reinstated its judgment, and the State Supreme Court affirmed, distinguishing *Schenck,* concluding that the statute was narrowly drawn to further a significant government interest, rejecting petitioners' overbreadth challenge, and concluding that ample alternative channels of communication remained open to petitioners.

I

Can a state law ban people from approaching patients entering medical facilities?

R

A state law can ban people from approaching patients entering medical facilities as long as it is a valid, content-neutral, "time, place and manner" restriction.

A

Section 18-9-122(3)'s restrictions on speech-related conduct are constitutional. Section 18-9-122(3) passes the *Ward* content-neutrality test for three independent reasons. First, it is a regulation of places where some speech may occur, not a "regulation of speech." Second, it was not adopted because of disagreement with the message of any speech. Most importantly, the State Supreme Court unequivocally held that the restrictions apply to all demonstrators, regardless of viewpoint, and the statute makes no reference to the content of speech. Third, the State's interests are unrelated to the content of the demonstrators' speech. Petitioners contend that insofar as the statute applies to persons who "knowingly approach" within eight feet of another to engage in "oral protest, education, or counseling," it is "content-based" under *Carey* v. *Brown,* because it requires examination of the content of a speaker's comments. This Court, however, has never held that it is improper to look at a statement's content in order to determine whether a rule of law applies to a course of conduct. Here, it is unlikely that there would often be any need to know exactly what words were spoken in order to determine whether sidewalk counselors are engaging in oral protest, education, or counseling rather than social or random conversation. The statute is easily distinguishable from the one in *Carey*, which prohibited all picketing except for picketing of a place of employment in a labor dispute, thereby according preferential treatment to expression concerning one particular subject. In contrast, §18-19-122(3) merely places a minor place restriction on an extremely broad category of communications with unwilling listeners. Section 18-9-122(3) is also a valid time, place, and manner regulation under *Ward,* for it is "narrowly tailored" to serve the State's significant and legitimate governmental interests and it leaves open ample alternative communication channels. When a content-neutral regulation does not entirely foreclose any means of communication, it may satisfy the tailoring requirement even though it is not the least restrictive or least intrusive means of serving the statutory goal. The 8-foot zone should not have any adverse impact on the readers' ability to read demonstrators' signs. That distance can make it more difficult for a speaker to be heard, but there is no limit on the number of speakers or the noise level. Nor does the statute suffer from the failings of the "floating buffer zone" rejected in *Schenck.* The zone here allows the speaker to communicate at a "normal conversational distance," and to remain in one place while other individuals pass within eight feet. And the "knowing" requirement protects speakers who thought they were at the proscribed distance from inadvertently violating the statute. Whether the 8-foot interval is the best possible accommodation of the competing interests, deference must be accorded to the Colorado Legislature's judgment. The burden on the distribution of handbills is more serious, but the statute does not prevent a leafletter from simply standing near the path of oncoming pedestrians and proffering the material, which pedestrians can accept or decline. Section 18-9-122(3) is not overbroad. First, the argument that coverage is broader than the specific concern that led to the statute's enactment does not identify a constitutional defect. It is precisely because the state legislature made a general policy choice that the statute is assessed under *Ward* rather than a stricter standard. Second, the argument that the statute bans virtually the universe of protected expression is based on a misreading of the statute and an incorrect understanding of the overbreadth doctrine. The statute does not ban any forms of communication, but regulates the places where communications may occur; and petitioners have not, as the doctrine requires, persuaded the Court that the statute's impact on the conduct of other speakers will differ from its impact on their own sidewalk counseling. Nor is §18-9-122(3) unconstitutionally vague, either because it fails to provide people with ordinary intelligence a reasonable opportunity to understand what it says or because it authorizes or encourages arbitrary and discriminatory enforcement. The first concern is ameliorated by §18-9-122(3)'s scienter requirement. It is unlikely that anyone would not understand the common words used in the statute, and hypothetical situations not before the Court will not support a facial attack on a statute that is surely valid in the vast majority of its intended applications. The Court is likewise unpersuaded that inadequate direction is given to law enforcement authorities. Indeed, one of §18-9-122(3)'s virtues is the specificity of the definitions of the zones. Finally, §18-9-122(3)'s consent requirement does not impose a prior restraint on speech. This argument was rejected in both *Schenck* and *Madsen.* Furthermore, "prior restraint" concerns relate to restrictions imposed by official censorship, but the regulations here only apply if the pedestrian does not consent to the approach.

C

Affirmed.

Ward v. Rock Against Racism

491 U.S. 781 (1989)

FACTS

Respondent Rock Against Racism (RAR), furnishing its own sound equipment and technicians, has sponsored yearly programs of rock music at the Naumberg Acoustic Bandshell in New York City's Central Park. The city received numerous complaints about excessive noise at RAR's concerts from users of the nearby Sheep Meadow, an area designated by the city for passive recreation, from other users of the park, and from residents of areas adjacent to the park. Moreover, when the city shut off the power after RAR ignored repeated requests to lower the volume at one of its concerts, the audience became abusive and disruptive. The city also experienced problems at bandshell events put on by other sponsors, who, due to their use of inadequate sound equipment or sound technicians unskilled at mixing sound for the bandshell area, were unable to provide sufficient amplification levels, resulting in disappointed or unruly audiences. Rejecting various other solutions to the excessive noise and inadequate amplification problems, the city adopted a Use Guideline for the bandshell which specified that the city would furnish high quality sound equipment and retain an independent, experienced sound technician for all performances. After the city implemented this guideline, RAR amended a pre-existing District Court complaint against the city to seek damages and a declaratory judgment striking down the guideline as facially invalid under the First Amendment. The court upheld the guideline, finding, inter alia, that performers who had used the city's sound system and technician had been uniformly pleased; that, although the city's technician ultimately controlled both sound volume and mix, the city's practice was to give the sponsor autonomy as to mix and to confer with him before turning the volume down; and that the city's amplification system was sufficient for RAR's needs. Applying this Court's three-part test for judging the constitutionality of governmental regulation of the time, place, and manner of protected speech, the court found the guideline valid. The Court of Appeals reversed on the ground that such regulations' method and extent must be the least intrusive upon the freedom of expression as is reasonably necessary to achieve the regulations purpose, finding that there were various less restrictive means by which the city could control excessive volume without also intruding on RAR's ability to control sound mix.

I Must the government use the least restrictive methods when imposing "time, place and manner" restrictions?

R The government need not use the least restrictive methods when imposing "time, place and manner" restrictions as long as they are sufficiently "narrowly tailored" and are more effective than no regulation at all.

A The city's sound-amplification guideline is valid under the First Amendment as a reasonable regulation of the place and manner of protected speech. The guideline is content neutral, since it is justified without reference to the content of the regulated speech. The city's principal justification - the desire to control noise in order to retain the sedate character of the Sheep Meadow and other areas of the park and to avoid intrusion into residential areas - has nothing to do with content. The city's other justification, its interest in ensuring sound quality, does not render the guideline content based as an attempt to impose subjective standards of acceptable sound mix on performers, since the city has expressly disavowed any such intent and requires its technician to defer to the sponsor's wishes as to mix. On the record below, the city's sound quality concern extends only to the clearly content-neutral goals of ensuring adequate amplification and avoiding volume problems associated with inadequate mix. There is no merit to RAR's argument that the guideline is nonetheless invalid on its face because it places unbridled discretion in the hands of city enforcement officials. Even granting the doubtful proposition that this claim falls within the narrow class of permissible facial challenges to allegedly unconstrained grants of regulatory authority, the claim nevertheless fails, since the guideline's own terms in effect forbid officials purposely to select an inadequate system or to vary sound quality or volume based on the performer's message. Moreover, the city has applied a narrowing construction to the guideline by requiring officials to defer to sponsors on sound quality and confer with them as to volume problems, and by mandating that amplification be sufficient for the sound to reach all concert ground listeners. The guideline is narrowly tailored to serve significant governmental interests. That the city has a substantial interest in protecting citizens from unwelcome and excessive noise, even in a traditional public forum such as the park, cannot be doubted. Moreover, it has a substantial interest in ensuring the sufficiency of sound amplification at bandshell events in order to allow citizens to enjoy the benefits of the park, in light of the evidence that inadequate amplification had resulted in the inability of some audiences to hear performances. The Court of Appeals erred in requiring the city to prove that the guideline was the least intrusive means of furthering these legitimate interests, since a "less-restrictive-alternative analysis" has never been - and is here, again, specifically rejected as - a part of the inquiry into the validity of a time, place, or manner regulation. The requirement of narrow tailoring is satisfied so long as the regulation promotes a substantial governmental interest that would be achieved less effectively absent the regulation, and the means chosen are not substantially broader than necessary to achieve that interest. If these standards are met, courts should defer to the government's reasonable determination. Here, the city's substantial interest in limiting sound volume is served in a direct and effective way by the requirement that its technician control the mixing board. Absent this requirement, the city's interest would have been served less well, as is evidenced by the excessive noise complaints generated by RAR's past concerts. The city also could reasonably have determined that, overall, its interest in ensuring that sound amplification was sufficient to reach all concert ground listeners would be served less effectively without the guideline than with it, since, by providing competent technicians and adequate equipment, the city eliminated inadequate amplification problems that plagued some performers in the past.

C

Reversed.

Adderley v. Florida

385 U.S. 39 (1966)

FACTS

Petitioners, 32 students, were members of a group of about 200 who on a nonpublic jail driveway, which they blocked, and on adjacent county jail premises had, by singing, clapping, and dancing, demonstrated against their schoolmates' arrest and perhaps against segregation in the jail and elsewhere. The sheriff, the jail's custodian, advised them that they were trespassing on county property and would have to leave or be arrested. The 107 demonstrators refusing to depart were thereafter arrested and convicted under a Florida trespass statute for "trespass with a malicious and mischievous intent." Petitioners contend that their convictions, affirmed by the Florida Circuit Court and the District Court of Appeal, deprived them of their "rights of free speech, assembly, petition, due process of law and equal protection of the laws" under the Fourteenth Amendment.

I

Is a protest on jailhouse property protected by the First Amendment barring a conviction for trespass?

R

A protest on jailhouse property, which is non-public property, is not protected by the First Amendment such that the protesters can be convicted for trespass.

A

The Florida trespass statute, here applied to a demonstration on the premises of a jail, which is built for security purposes and is not open to the public, is aimed at conduct of a limited kind and is not unconstitutionally vague as were the common-law, breach-of-the-peace statutes invalidated in *Edwards v. South Carolina*, and *Cox v. Louisiana*. Petitioners seem to argue that the Florida trespass law is void for vagueness because it requires a trespass to be "with a malicious and mischievous intent . . . ." But these words do not broaden the scope of trespass so as to make it cover a multitude of types of conduct as does the common-law breach-of-the-peace charge. On the contrary, these words narrow the scope of the offense. The use of these terms in the statute, instead of contributing to uncertainty and misunderstanding, actually makes its meaning more understandable and clear. Next, petitioners in this Court invoke the doctrine of abatement announced by this *Court in Hamm v. City of Rock Hill.* But that holding was that the Civil Rights Act of 1964, 78 Stat. 241, which made it unlawful for places of public accommodation to deny service to any person because of race, effected an abatement of prosecutions of persons for seeking such services that arose prior to the passage of the Act. But this case in no way involves prosecution of petitioners for seeking service in establishments covered by the Act. It involves only an alleged trespass on jail grounds - a trespass which can be prosecuted regardless of the fact that it is the means of protesting segregation of establishments covered by the Act.

C

Affirmed.

Greer v. Spock

424 U.S. 828 (1976)

FACTS

Fort Dix, a federal military reservation devoted primarily to basic training for newly inducted Army personnel, and over which the Government exercises exclusive jurisdiction, permits free civilian access to certain unrestricted areas. However, post regulations ban speeches and demonstrations of a partisan political nature and also prohibit the distribution of literature without prior approval. Pursuant to these regulations the commanding officer of Fort Dix rejected the request of respondent candidates for President and Vice President to distribute campaign literature and hold a political meeting on the post, and the other respondents, who had been evicted on several occasions for distributing literature not previously approved, were barred from re-entering the post. Respondents brought suit to enjoin enforcement of these regulations on the ground that they violated the First and Fifth Amendments. The District Court issued an injunction prohibiting the military authorities from interfering with the making of political speeches or the distribution of leaflets in areas of Fort Dix open to the general public, and the Court of Appeals affirmed.

I

Can the government forbid political speech at army training facilities?

R

Military bases are considered non-public forums such that the government may restrict speech there.

A

The regulations are not constitutionally invalid on their face. Since under the Constitution it is the basic function of a military installation like Fort Dix to train soldiers, not to provide a public forum, and since, as a necessary concomitant to this basic function, a commanding officer has the historically unquestioned power to exclude civilians from the area of his command, any notion that federal military installations, like municipal streets and parks, have traditionally served as a place for free public assembly and communication of thoughts by private citizens is false, and therefore respondents had no generalized constitutional right to make political speeches or distribute leaflets at Fort Dix. Nor were the regulations unconstitutionally applied under the circumstances of this case. As to the regulation banning political speeches and demonstrations, there is no claim that the military authorities discriminated in any way among candidates based upon the candidates' supposed political views; on the contrary it appears that Fort Dix has a policy, objectively and evenhandedly applied, of keeping official military activities there wholly free of entanglement with any partisan political campaigns, a policy that the post was constitutionally free to pursue.

C

Reversed.

Lehman v. City of Shaker Heights

418 U.S. 298 (1974)

FACTS

Petitioner, a candidate for state office, who was refused available advertising space on vehicles of a city transit system, brought this suit challenging the constitutionality of the municipal policy on which the refusal was based of not permitting political advertising but allowing other types of public transit advertising. Specifically, when petitioner applied for space, he was informed that, although space was then available, the management agreement with the city did not permit political advertising. The system, however, accepted ads from cigarette companies, banks, savings and loan associations, liquor companies, retail and service establishments, churches, and civic and public-service oriented groups. There was uncontradicted testimony at the trial that during the 26 years of public operation, the Shaker Heights system, pursuant to city council action, had not accepted or permitted any political or public issue advertising on its vehicles. When petitioner did not succeed in his effort to have his copy accepted, he sought declaratory and injunctive relief in the state courts of Ohio without success. The Supreme Court of Ohio concluded that "the constitutionally protected right of free speech with respect to forums for oral speech, or the dissemination of literature on a city's streets, does not extend to commercial or political advertising on rapid transit vehicles." There was no equal protection violation, the court said, because, "as a class, all candidates for political office are treated alike under the Shaker Heights Rapid Transit System's commercial advertising policy." The U.S. Supreme Court granted certiorari.

I

Can political advertising be banned on the city owned transit system by the local government?

R

When the government is involved in a commercial venture, such as the ownership and operation of a city transit system, it may prohibit advertising by political candidates for public office.

A

It is urged that the car cards here constitute a public forum protected by the First Amendment, and that there is a guarantee of nondiscriminatory access to such publicly owned and controlled areas of communication "regardless of the primary purpose for which the area is dedicated." We disagree. In *Packer Corp. v. Utah*, Mr. Justice Brandeis, in speaking for a unanimous Court, recognized that "there is a difference which justifies the classification between display advertising and that in periodicals or newspapers." In *Packer* the Court upheld a Utah statute that made it a misdemeanor to advertise cigarettes on "any bill board, street car sign, street car, placard,'" but exempted dealers' signs on their places of business and cigarette advertising "`in any newspaper, magazine, or periodical." The Court found no equal protection violation. It reasoned that viewers of billboards and streetcar signs had no "choice or volition" to observe such advertising and had the message "thrust upon them by all the arts and devices that skill can produce. . . . The radio can be turned off, but not so the billboard or street car placard." The streetcar audience is a captive audience. It is there as a matter of necessity, not of choice. In such situations, "the legislature may recognize degrees of evil and adapt its legislation accordingly." These situations are different from the traditional settings where First Amendment values inalterably prevail. Although American constitutional jurisprudence, in the light of the First Amendment, has been jealous to preserve access to public places for purposes of free speech, the nature of the forum and the conflicting interests involved have remained important in determining the degree of protection afforded by the Amendment to the speech in question. Here, we have no open spaces, no meeting hall, park, street corner, or other public thoroughfare. Instead, the city is engaged in commerce. It must provide rapid, convenient, pleasant, and inexpensive service to the commuters of Shaker Heights. The car card space, although incidental to the provision of public transportation, is a part of the commercial venture. In much the same way that a newspaper or periodical, or even a radio or television station, need not accept every proffer of advertising from the general public, a city transit system has discretion to develop and make reasonable choices concerning the type of advertising that may be displayed in its vehicles. In making these choices, this Court has held that a public utility "will be sustained in its protection of activities in public places when those activities do not interfere with the general public convenience, comfort and safety." *Public Utilities Comm'n v. Pollak.* Because state action exists, however, the policies and practices governing access to the transit system's advertising space must not be arbitrary, capricious, or invidious. Here, the city has decided that "[p]urveyors of goods and services saleable in commerce may purchase advertising space on an equal basis, whether they be house builders or butchers." This decision is little different from deciding to impose a 10¢, 25¢, or 35¢ fare, or from changing schedules or the location of bus stops. Revenue earned from long-term commercial advertising could be jeopardized by a requirement that short-term candidacy or issue-oriented advertisements be displayed on car cards. Users would be subjected to the blare of political propaganda. There could be lurking doubts about favoritism, and sticky administrative problems might arise in parceling out limited space to eager politicians. In these circumstances, the managerial decision to limit car card space to innocuous and less controversial commercial and service oriented advertising does not rise to the dignity of a First Amendment violation. Were we to hold to the contrary, display cases in public hospitals, libraries, office buildings, military compounds, and other public facilities immediately would become Hyde Parks open to every would-be pamphleteer and politician. This the Constitution does not require. No First Amendment forum is here to be found. The city consciously has limited access to its transit system advertising space in order to minimize chances of abuse, the appearance of favoritism, and the risk of imposing upon a captive audience. These are reasonable legislative objectives advanced by the city in a proprietary capacity. In these circumstances, there is no First or Fourteenth Amendment violation.

C

Judgment of the Supreme Court of Ohio is affirmed.

United States v. Kokinda

497 U.S. 720 (1990)

FACTS

Respondents, members of a political advocacy group, set up a table on a sidewalk near the entrance to a United States Post Office to solicit contributions, sell books and subscriptions to the organization's newspaper, and distribute literature on a variety of political issues. The sidewalk is the sole means by which customers may travel from the parking lot to the post office building and lies entirely on Postal Service property. When respondents refused to leave the premises, they were arrested and subsequently convicted by a Federal Magistrate of violating, *inter alia*, 39 CFR 232.1(h)(1), which prohibits solicitation on postal premises. The District Court affirmed the convictions. It rejected respondents' argument that 232.1(h)(1) violated the First Amendment, holding that the postal sidewalk was not a public forum and that the ban on solicitation is reasonable. The Court of Appeals reversed. Finding that the sidewalk is a public forum and analyzing the regulation as a time, place, and manner restriction, it determined that the Government has no significant interest in banning solicitation and that the regulation is not narrowly tailored to accomplish the asserted governmental interest.

I May the government regulate free speech on the sidewalks outside government property?

R Speech restrictions are valid if "reasonable" and if the sidewalk outside the government installation was constructed only to permit access, as opposed to facilitating the public's convenience.

A The regulation, as applied, does not violate the First Amendment. Although solicitation is a recognized form of speech protected by the First Amendment, the Government may regulate such activity on its property to an extent determined by the nature of the relevant forum. Speech activity on governmental property that has been traditionally open to the public for expressive activity or has been expressly dedicated by the Government to speech activity is subject to strict scrutiny. However, where the property is not a traditional public forum and the Government has not dedicated its property to First Amendment activity, such regulation is examined only for reasonableness. Section 232.1(h)(1) must be analyzed under the standards applicable to nonpublic forum: it must be reasonable and "not an effort to suppress expression merely because public officials oppose the speaker's view." The postal sidewalk is not a traditional public forum. The fact that the sidewalk resembles the municipal sidewalk across the parking lot from the post office is irrelevant to forum analysis. The sidewalk was constructed solely to provide for the passage of individuals engaged in postal business, not as a public passageway. Nor has the Postal Service expressly dedicated its sidewalk to any expressive activity. Postal property has only been dedicated to the posting of public notices on designated bulletin boards. A practice of allowing individuals and groups to leaflet, speak, and picket on postal premises and a regulation prohibiting disruptive conduct do not add up to such dedication. Even conceding that the forum has been dedicated to some First Amendment uses, and thus is not a purely nonpublic forum, regulation of the reserved nonpublic uses would still require application of the reasonableness test. It is reasonable for the Postal Service to prohibit solicitation where it has determined that the intrusion creates significant interference with Congress' mandate to ensure the most effective and efficient distribution of the mails. The categorical ban is based on the Service's long, real-world experience with solicitation, which has shown that, because of continual demands from a wide variety of groups, administering a program of permits and approvals had distracted postal facility managers from their primary jobs. Whether or not the Service permits other forms of speech, it is not unreasonable for it to prohibit solicitation on the ground that it inherently disrupts business by impeding the normal flow of traffic. Confrontation by a person asking for money disrupts passage and is more intrusive and intimidating than an encounter with a person giving out information. Even if more narrowly tailored regulations could be promulgated, the Service is only required to promulgate reasonable regulations, not the most reasonable or the only reasonable regulation possible. Clearly, the regulation does not discriminate on the basis of content or viewpoint. The Service's concern about losing customers because of the potentially unpleasant situation created by solicitation per se does not reveal an effort to discourage one viewpoint and advance another.

C Reversed.

International Society for Krishna Consciousness v. Lee
505 U.S. 672 (1992)

FACTS

The Port Authority of New York and New Jersey, which owns and operates three major airports in the New York City area and controls certain terminal areas at the airports (hereinafter terminals), adopted a regulation forbidding, inter alia, the repetitive solicitation of money within the terminals. However, solicitation is permitted on the sidewalks outside the terminal buildings. Petitioner International Society for Krishna Consciousness, Inc. (ISKCON), a not-for-profit religious corporation whose members, among other things, solicit funds in public places to support their movement, brought suit seeking declaratory and injunctive relief under 42 U.S.C. 1983, alleging that the regulation deprived its members of their First Amendment rights. The District Court granted ISKCON summary judgment, concluding that the terminals were public forums, and that the regulation banning solicitation failed because it was not narrowly tailored to support a compelling state interest. The Court of Appeals reversed as here relevant. It determined that the terminals are not public forums, and found that the ban on solicitation was reasonable.

I

Can an airport ban solicitations?

R

Airports may ban solicitations as they are no considered public forums.

A

An airport terminal operated by a public authority is a non-public forum, and thus a ban on solicitation need only satisfy a reasonableness standard. The extent to which the Port Authority can restrict expressive activity on its property depends on the nature of the forum. Regulation of traditional public forums or designated a public forum survives only if it is narrowly drawn to achieve a compelling state interest, but limitations on expressive activity conducted on any other government-owned property need only be reasonable to survive. Neither by tradition nor purpose can the terminals be described as public forum. Airports have not historically been made available for speech activity. Given the lateness with which the modern air terminal has made its appearance, it hardly qualifies as a property that has "immemorially . . . time out of mind" been held in the public trust and used for the purposes of expressive activity. Nor have airport operators opened terminals to such activities, as evidenced by the operators' frequent and continuing litigation in this area. That speech activities may have historically occurred at "transportation nodes" such as rail and bus stations, wharves, and Ellis Island is not relevant. Many of these sites traditionally have had private ownership. In addition, equating airports with other transportation centers would not take into account differences among the various facilities that may affect the extent to which such facilities can accommodate expressive activity. It is unsurprising to find differences among the facilities. The Port Authority, other airport builders and managers, and the Federal Government all share the view that terminals are dedicated to the facilitation of efficient air travel, not the solicitation of contributions. The Port

Authority's ban on solicitation is reasonable. Solicitation may have a disruptive effect on business by slowing the path of both those who must decide whether to contribute and those who must alter their paths to avoid the solicitation. In addition, a solicitor may cause duress by targeting the most vulnerable persons or commit fraud by concealing his affiliation or shortchanging purchasers. The fact that the targets are likely to be on a tight schedule, and thus are unlikely to stop and complain to authorities, compounds the problem. The Port Authority has determined that it can best achieve its legitimate interest in monitoring solicitation activity to assure that travelers are not interfered with unduly by limiting solicitation to the sidewalk areas outside the terminals. That area is frequented by an overwhelming percentage of airport users, making ISKCON access to the general public quite complete. Moreover, it would be odd to conclude that the regulation is unreasonable when the Port Authority has otherwise assured access to a universally traveled area. While the inconvenience caused by ISKCON may seem small, the Port Authority could reasonably worry that the incremental effects of having one group and then another seek such access could prove quite disruptive.

C

Affirmed in part.

Arkansas Educational Television Comm. v. Forbes

523 U.S. 666 (1998)

FACTS

Petitioner Arkansas Educational Television Commission (AETC), a state-owned public television broadcaster, sponsored a debate between the major party candidates for the 1992 election in Arkansas' Third Congressional District. When AETC denied the request of respondent Forbes, an independent candidate with little popular support, for permission to participate in the debate, Forbes filed this suit, claiming, inter alia , that he was entitled to participate under the First Amendment. The jury made express findings that Forbes' exclusion had not been influenced by political pressure or disagreement with his views. The District Court entered judgment for AETC. The Eighth Circuit reversed, holding that the debate was a public forum to which all ballot-qualified candidates had a presumptive right of access. Applying strict scrutiny, the court determined that AETC's assessment of Forbes' "political viability" was neither a compelling nor a narrowly tailored reason for excluding him.

I

Can a television station deny access to some candidates for public office with respect to publicly-televised debates?

R

The public generally has no right of access to state-owned TV and publicly-televised debates are considered non-public forums such that a TV station may deny access to some candidates with respect to them.

A

AETC's exclusion of Forbes from the debate was consistent with the First Amendment. Unlike most other public television programs, candidate debates are subject to scrutiny under this Court's public forum doctrine. Having first arisen in the context of streets and parks, the doctrine should not be extended in a mechanical way to the different context of television broadcasting. Broad rights of access for outside speakers would be antithetical, as a general rule, to the editorial discretion that broadcasters must exercise to fulfill their journalistic purpose and statutory obligations. For two reasons, however, candidate debates present the narrow exception to the rule. First, unlike AETC's other broadcasts, the debate was by design a forum for candidates' political speech. Consistent with the long tradition of such debates, AETC's implicit representation was that the views expressed were those of the candidates, not its own. The debate's very purpose was to allow the expression of those views with minimal intrusion by the broadcaster. Second, candidate debates are of exceptional significance in the electoral process. Deliberation on candidates' positions and qualifications is integral to our system of government, and electoral speech may have its most profound and widespread impact when it is disseminated through televised debates. Thus, the special characteristics of candidate debates support the conclusion that the AETC debate was a forum of some type. The question of what type must be answered by reference to this Court's public forum precedents. For the Court's purposes, it will suffice to employ the categories of speech fora already established in the case law. The Court has identified three types of forums: the traditional public forum, the public forum created by government designation, and the nonpublic forum. Traditional public forums are defined by the objective characteristics of the property, such as whether, "by long tradition or by government fiat," the property has been "devoted to assembly and debate." The government can exclude a speaker from a traditional public forum only when the exclusion is necessary to serve a compelling state interest and is narrowly drawn to achieve that interest. Designated public forums are created by purposeful governmental action opening a nontraditional public forum for expressive use by the general public or by a particular class of speakers. If the government excludes a speaker who falls within the class to which such a forum is made generally available, its action is subject to strict scrutiny. Property that is not a traditional public forum or a designated public forum is either a nonpublic forum or not a forum at all. Access to a nonpublic forum can be restricted if the restrictions are reasonable and are not an effort to suppress expression merely because public officials oppose the speaker's views. The AETC debate was a nonpublic forum. The parties agree that it was not a traditional public forum, and it was not a designated public forum under this Court's precedents. Those cases demonstrate, inter alia, that the government does not create a designated public forum when it does no more than reserve eligibility for access to a forum to a particular class of speakers, whose members must then, as individuals, "obtain permission" to use it. Contrary to the Eighth Circuit's assertion, AETC did not make its debate generally available to candidates for the congressional seat at issue. Instead, it reserved eligibility for participation to candidates for that seat (as opposed to some other seat), and then made candidate-by-candidate determinations as to which of the eligible candidates would participate in the debate. Such "selective access," unsupported by evidence of a purposeful designation for public use, does not create a public forum, but indicates that the debate was a nonpublic forum. AETC's decision to exclude Forbes was a reasonable, viewpoint-neutral exercise of journalistic discretion consistent with the First Amendment. The record demonstrates beyond dispute that Forbes was excluded not because of his viewpoint, but because he had not generated appreciable public interest. There is no serious argument that AETC did not act in good faith in this case.

C

Reversed.

Parker v. Levy

417 U.S. 733 (1974)

FACTS

Article 90 (2) of the Uniform Code of Military Justice (Code) provides for punishment of any person subject to the Code who "willfully disobeys a lawful command of his superior commissioned officer"; Art. 133 punishes a commissioned officer for "conduct unbecoming an officer and a gentleman"; and Art. 134 (the general article) punishes any person subject to the Code for, *inter alia*, "all disorders and neglects to the prejudice of good order and discipline in the armed forces," though not specifically mentioned in the Code. Appellee, an Army physician assigned to a hospital, was convicted by a general court-martial of violating Art. 90 (2) for disobeying the hospital commandant's order to establish a training program for Special Forces aide men, and of violating Arts. 133 and 134 for making public statements urging Negro enlisted men to refuse to obey orders to go to Vietnam and referring to Special Forces personnel as "liars and thieves," "killers of peasants," and "murderers of women and children." After his conviction was sustained within the military and he exhausted this avenue of relief, appellee sought habeas corpus relief in the District Court, challenging his conviction on the ground that both Art. 133 and Art. 134 are "void for vagueness" under the Due Process Clause of the Fifth Amendment and overbroad in violation of the First Amendment. The District Court denied relief, but the Court of Appeals reversed, holding that Arts. 133 and 134 are void for vagueness, that while appellee's conduct fell within an example of Art. 134 violations contained in the Manual for Courts-Martial, the possibility that the articles would be applied to others' future conduct as to which there was insufficient warning, or which was within the area of protected First Amendment expression, was enough to give appellee standing to challenge both articles on their face, and that the joint consideration of the Art. 90 charges gave rise to a "reasonable possibility" that appellee's right to a fair trial was prejudiced, so that a new trial was required.

I Are the Uniform Code of Military Justice's speech restrictions overbroad?

R The Uniform Code of Military Justice's speech restrictions are not overbroad because the First Amendment offers military personnel less protection than it affords civilians.

A Articles 133 and 134 are not unconstitutionally vague under the Due Process Clause of the Fifth Amendment. Each article has been construed by the United States Court of Military Appeals or by other military authorities, such as the Manual for Courts-Martial, so as to limit its scope, thus narrowing the very broad reach of the literal language of the articles, and at the same time supplying considerable specificity by way of examples of the conduct that they cover. The articles are not subject to being condemned for specifying no standard of conduct at all, but are of the type of statutes which "by their terms or as authoritatively construed apply without question to certain activities, but whose application to other behavior is uncertain," *Smith v. Goguen*. Because of the factors differentiating military from civilian society, Congress is permitted to legislate with greater breadth and flexibility when prescribing rules for the former than when prescribing rules for the latter, and the proper standard of review for a vagueness challenge to Code articles is the standard that applies to criminal statutes regulating economic affairs, and that standard was met here, since appellee could have had no reasonable doubt that his statements urging Negro enlisted men not to go to Vietnam if ordered to do so was both "unbecoming an officer and gentleman" and "to the prejudice of good order and discipline in the armed forces," in violation of Arts. 133 and 134, respectively. Nor are Arts. 133 and 134 facially invalid because of overbreadth. Doctrines of First Amendment overbreadth asserted in support of challenges to imprecise language like that contained in Arts. 133 and 134 are not exempt from the operation of the principles that while military personnel are not excluded from First Amendment protection, the fundamental necessity for obedience, and the consequent necessity for discipline, may render permissible within the military that which would be constitutionally impermissible outside it. There is a wide range of conduct to which Arts. 133 and 134 may be applied without infringing the First Amendment, and while there may be marginal applications in which First Amendment values would be infringed, this is insufficient to invalidate either article at appellee's behest. His conduct in publicly urging enlisted personnel to refuse to obey orders which might send them into combat was unprotected under the most expansive notions of the First Amendment, and Arts. 133 and 134 may constitutionally prohibit that conduct, and a sufficiently large number of similar or related types of conduct so as to preclude their invalidation for overbreadth. Appellee's contention that even if Arts. 133 and 134 are constitutional, his conviction under Art. 90 should be invalidated because to carry out the hospital commandant's order would have constituted participation in a war crime and because the commandant gave the order, knowing it would be disobeyed, for the sole purpose of increasing appellee's punishment, is not of constitutional significance and is beyond the scope of review, since such defenses were resolved against appellee on a factual basis by the court-martial that convicted him.

C Reversed.

Thornburgh v. Abbott

490 U.S. 401 (1989)

FACTS

Federal Bureau of Prisons regulations generally permit prisoners to receive publications from the "outside," but authorize wardens, pursuant to specified criteria, to reject an incoming publication if it is found "to be detrimental to the security, good order, or discipline of the institution or if it might facilitate criminal activity." Wardens may not reject a publication "solely because its content is religious, philosophical, political, social[,] sexual, or . . . unpopular or repugnant," or establish an excluded list of publications, but must review each issue of a subscription separately. Respondents, a class of inmates and certain publishers, filed suit in the District Court, claiming that the regulations, both on their face and as applied to 46 specifically excluded publications, violated their First Amendment rights under the standard set forth in *Procunier v. Martinez*. The District Court refrained from adopting the Martinez standard in favor of an approach more deferential to the judgment of prison authorities, and upheld the regulations without addressing the propriety of the 46 exclusions. The Court of Appeals, however, utilized the Martinez standard, found the regulations wanting, and remanded the case for an individualized determination on the constitutionality of the 46 exclusions.

I

May prison regulations allow wardens to bar publications which threaten the prison's security or discipline?

R

Restrictions on prison speech is valid if (1) the government's objective is legitimate; (2) neutral; and (3) the regulations are "rationally related" to that objective.

A

Regulations such as those at issue that affect the sending of publications to prisoners must be analyzed under the standard set forth in *Turner v. Safley*, and are therefore "valid if [they are] reasonably related to legitimate penological interests." Prison officials are due considerable deference in regulating the delicate balance between prison order and security and the legitimate demands of "outsiders" who seek to enter the prison environment. The less deferential standard of Martinez - whereby prison regulations authorizing mail censorship must be "generally necessary" to protect one or more legitimate governmental interests - is limited to regulations concerning outgoing personal correspondence from prisoners, regulations which are not centrally concerned with the maintenance of prison order and security. Moreover, *Martinez* is overruled to the extent that it might support the drawing of a categorical distinction between incoming correspondence from prisoners (to which *Turner* applied its reasonableness standard) and incoming correspondence from non-prisoners. The regulations at issue are facially valid under the *Turner* standard. Their underlying objective of protecting prison security is undoubtedly legitimate and is neutral with regard to the content of the expression regulated. Also, the broad discretion the regulations accord wardens is rationally related to security interests. Furthermore, alternative means of expression remain open to the inmates, since the regulations permit a broad range of publications to be sent, received, and read, even though specific publications are prohibited. Moreover, respondents have established no alternative to the regulations that would accommodate prisoners' constitutional rights at a *de minimis* cost to valid penological interests. The case is remanded for an examination of the validity of the regulations as applied to any of the 46 publications introduced at trial as to which there remains a live controversy.

C The judgment is vacated, and the case is remanded.

Shaw v. Murphy

532 U.S. 223 (2001)

FACTS

While respondent Murphy was incarcerated in state prison, he learned that a fellow inmate had been charged with assaulting a correctional officer. Murphy decided to assist the inmate with his defense and sent him a letter, which was intercepted in accordance with prison policy. Based on the letter's content, the prison sanctioned Murphy for violating prison rules prohibiting insolence and interfering with due process hearings. Murphy then sought declaratory and injunctive relief under 42 U. S. C. §1983, alleging that the disciplinary action violated, *inter alia,* his First Amendment rights, including the right to provide legal assistance to other inmates. In granting petitioners summary judgment, the District Court applied the decision in *Turner* v. *Safley,* - that a prison regulation impinging on inmates' constitutional rights is valid if it is reasonably related to legitimate penological interests - and found a valid, rational connection between the inmate correspondence policy and the objectives of prison order, security, and inmate rehabilitation. The Ninth Circuit reversed, finding that inmates have a First Amendment right to give legal assistance to other inmates and that this right affected the *Turner* analysis.

I Do inmates possess a special First Amendment right to provide legal assistance to fellow inmates that enhances the protections otherwise available under *Turner*?

R Inmates do not possess a special First Amendment right to provide legal assistance to fellow inmates that enhances the protections otherwise available under *Turner*.

A Inmates do not possess a special First Amendment right to provide legal assistance to fellow inmates that enhances the protections otherwise available under *Turner*. Prisoners' constitutional rights are more limited in scope than the constitutional rights held by individuals in society at large. For instance, some First Amendment rights are simply inconsistent with the corrections system's "legitimate penological objectives," *Pell* v. *Procunier,* and thus this Court has sustained restrictions on, *e.g.,* inmate-to-inmate written correspondence. Moreover, because courts are ill equipped to deal with the complex and intractable problems of prisons, *Procunier* v. *Martinez,* this Court has generally deferred to prison officials' judgment in upholding such regulations against constitutional challenge. *Turner* reflects this understanding, setting a unitary, deferential standard for reviewing prisoners' claims that does not permit an increase in the constitutional protection whenever a prisoner's communication includes legal advice. To increase the constitutional protection based upon a communication's content first requires an assessment of that content's value. But the *Turner* test simply does not accommodate valuations of content. On the contrary, it concerns only the relationship between the asserted penological interests and the prison regulation. Moreover, prison officials are to remain the primary arbiters of the problems that arise in prison management. Seeking to avoid unnecessarily perpetuating federal courts' involvement in prison administration affairs, the Court rejects an alteration of the *Turner* analysis that would entail additional federal-court oversight. Even if this Court were to consider giving special protection to particular kinds of speech based on content, it would not do so for speech that includes legal advice. Augmenting First Amendment protection for such advice would undermine prison officials' ability to address the complex and intractable problems of prison administration. The legal text could be an excuse for making clearly inappropriate comments, which may circulate among prisoners despite prison measures to screen individual inmates or officers from the remarks. To prevail on remand on the question whether the prison regulations, as applied to Murphy, are reasonably related to legitimate penological interests, he must overcome the presumption that the prison officials acted within their broad discretion.

C Reversed and remanded.

Tinker v. Des Moines Independent Community School District 393 U.S. 503 (1969)

FACTS

Petitioners, three public school pupils in Des Moines, Iowa, were suspended from school for wearing black armbands to protest the Government's policy in Vietnam. They sought nominal damages and an injunction against a regulation that the respondents had promulgated banning the wearing of armbands. The District Court dismissed the complaint on the ground that the regulation was within the Board's power, despite the absence of any finding of substantial interference with the conduct of school activities. The Court of Appeals, sitting en banc, affirmed by an equally divided court.

I

Can a public school suspend students for wearing expressive symbols?

R

Public schools cannot restrict students' expression unless is "materially and substantially interferes" with suitable school discipline.

A

In wearing armbands, the petitioners were quiet and passive. They were not disruptive and did not impinge upon the rights of others. In these circumstances, their conduct was within the protection of the Free Speech Clause of the First Amendment and the Due Process Clause of the Fourteenth. First Amendment rights are available to teachers and students, subject to application in light of the special characteristics of the school environment. A prohibition against expression of opinion, without any evidence that the rule is necessary to avoid substantial interference with school discipline or the rights of others, is not permissible under the First and Fourteenth Amendments.

C

Reversed and remanded.

Bethel School District No. 403 v. Fraser

478 U.S. 675 (1986)

FACTS

Respondent public high school student (hereafter respondent) delivered a speech nominating a fellow student for a student elective office at a voluntary assembly that was held during school hours as part of a school-sponsored educational program in self-government, and that was attended by approximately 600 students, many of whom were 14-year-olds. During the entire speech, respondent referred to his candidate in terms of an elaborate, graphic, and explicit sexual metaphor. Some of the students at the assembly hooted and yelled during the speech, some mimicked the sexual activities alluded to in the speech, and others appeared to be bewildered and embarrassed. Prior to delivering the speech, respondent discussed it with several teachers, two of whom advised him that it was inappropriate and should not be given. The morning after the assembly, the Assistant Principal called respondent into her office and notified him that the school considered his speech to have been a violation of the school's "disruptive-conduct rule," which prohibited conduct that substantially interfered with the educational process, including the use of obscene, profane language or gestures. Respondent was given copies of teacher reports of his conduct, and was given a chance to explain his conduct. After he admitted that he deliberately used sexual innuendo in the speech, he was informed that he would be suspended for three days, and that his name would be removed from the list of candidates for graduation speaker at the school's commencement exercises. Review of the disciplinary action through petitioner School District's grievance procedures resulted in affirmance of the discipline, but respondent was allowed to return to school after serving only two days of his suspension. Respondent, by his father (also a respondent) as guardian *ad litem*, then filed suit in Federal District Court, alleging a violation of his First Amendment right to freedom of speech and seeking injunctive relief and damages under 42 U.S.C. 1983. The court held that the school's sanctions violated the First Amendment, that the school's disruptive-conduct rule was unconstitutionally vague and overbroad, and that the removal of respondent's name from the graduation speaker's list violated the Due Process Clause of the Fourteenth Amendment. The court awarded respondent monetary relief and enjoined the School District from preventing him from speaking at the commencement ceremonies. The Court of Appeals affirmed.

I

Can a school sanction a student's vulgar speech?

R

A school may sanction a student's vulgar speech.

A

The First Amendment did not prevent the School District from disciplining respondent for giving the offensively lewd and indecent speech at the assembly. Under the First Amendment, the use of an offensive form of expression may not be prohibited to adults making what the speaker considers a political point, but it does not follow that the same latitude must be permitted to children in a public school. It is a highly appropriate function of public school education to prohibit the use of vulgar and offensive terms in public discourse. Nothing in the Constitution prohibits the states from insisting that certain modes of expression are inappropriate and subject to sanctions. The inculcation of these values is truly the work of the school, and the determination of what manner of speech is inappropriate properly rests with the school board. First Amendment jurisprudence recognizes an interest in protecting minors from exposure to vulgar and offensive spoken language, as well as limitations on the otherwise absolute interest of the speaker in reaching an unlimited audience where the speech is sexually explicit and the audience may include children. Petitioner School District acted entirely within its permissible authority in imposing sanctions upon respondent in response to his offensively lewd and indecent speech, which had no claim to First Amendment protection. There is no merit to respondent's contention that the circumstances of his suspension violated due process because he had no way of knowing that the delivery of the speech would subject him to disciplinary sanctions. Given the school's need to be able to impose disciplinary sanctions for a wide range of unanticipated conduct disruptive of the educational process, the school disciplinary rules need not be as detailed as a criminal code which imposes criminal sanctions. The school disciplinary rule proscribing "obscene" language and the pre-speech admonitions of teachers gave adequate warning to respondent that his lewd speech could subject him to sanctions.

C

Reversed.

Hazelwood School District v. Kuhlmeier

484 U.S. 260 (1988)

FACTS

Respondents, former high school students who were staff members of the school's newspaper, filed suit in Federal District Court against petitioners, the school district and school officials, alleging that respondents' First Amendment rights were violated by the deletion from a certain issue of the paper of two pages that included an article describing school students' experiences with pregnancy and another article discussing the impact of divorce on students at the school. The newspaper was written and edited by a journalism class, as part of the school's curriculum. Pursuant to the school's practice, the teacher in charge of the paper submitted page proofs to the school's principal, who objected to the pregnancy story because the pregnant students, although not named, might be identified from the text, and because he believed that the article's references to sexual activity and birth control were inappropriate for some of the younger students. The principal objected to the divorce article because the page proofs he was furnished identified by name (deleted by the teacher from the final version) a student who complained of her father's conduct, and the principal believed that the student's parents should have been given an opportunity to respond to the remarks or to consent to their publication. Believing that there was no time to make necessary changes in the articles if the paper was to be issued before the end of the school year, the principal directed that the pages on which they appeared be withheld from publication even though other, unobjectionable articles were included on such pages. The District Court held that no First Amendment violation had occurred. The Court of Appeals reversed.

I

Can a school censor a student's writings in a school-funded publication?

R

A school may censor a student's writings in a school-funded publication if their actions are (1) reasonably related (2) to a "legitimate pedagogical concern."

A

Respondents' First Amendment rights were not violated. First Amendment rights of students in the public schools are not automatically coextensive with the rights of adults in other settings, and must be applied in light of the special characteristics of the school environment. A school need not tolerate student speech that is inconsistent with its basic educational mission, even though the government could not censor similar speech outside the school. The school newspaper here cannot be characterized as a forum for public expression. School facilities may be deemed to be public forums only if school authorities have by policy or by practice opened the facilities for indiscriminate use by the general public, or by some segment of the public, such as student organizations. If the facilities have instead been reserved for other intended purposes, communicative or otherwise, then no public forum has been created, and school officials may impose reasonable restrictions on the speech of students, teachers, and other members of the school community. The school officials in this case did not deviate from their policy that the newspaper's production was to be part of the educational curriculum and a regular classroom activity under the journalism teacher's control as to almost every aspect of publication. The officials did not evince any intent to open the paper's pages to indiscriminate use by its student reporters and editors, or by the student body generally. Accordingly, school officials were entitled to regulate the paper's contents in any reasonable manner. The standard for determining when a school may punish student expression that happens to occur on school premises is not the standard for determining when a school may refuse to lend its name and resources to the dissemination of student expression. Educators do not offend the First Amendment by exercising editorial control over the style and content of student speech in school-sponsored expressive activities so long as their actions are reasonably related to legitimate pedagogical concerns. The school principal acted reasonably in this case in requiring the deletion of the pregnancy article, the divorce article, and the other articles that were to appear on the same pages of the newspaper.

C Reversed.

NAACP v. Alabama

357 U.S. 449 (1958)

FACTS

Plaintiff-petitioner NAACP is a nonprofit membership corporation organized under the laws of New York for the purpose of advancing the welfare of Negroes. It operates through chartered affiliates which are independent unincorporated associations, with membership therein equivalent to membership in petitioner. It had local affiliates in Alabama and opened an office of its own there without complying with an Alabama statute which, with some exceptions, requires a foreign corporation to qualify before doing business in the State by filing its corporate charter and designating a place of business and an agent to receive service of process. Alleging that petitioner's activities were causing irreparable injury to the citizens of the State for which criminal prosecution and civil actions at law afforded no adequate relief, the State (Defendant-respondent) brought an equity suit in a state court to enjoin petitioner from conducting further activities in, and to oust it from, the State. The court issued an *ex parte* order restraining petitioner from engaging in further activities in the State and from taking any steps to qualify to do business there. Petitioner moved to dissolve the restraining order, and the court, on the State's motion, ordered the production of many of petitioner's records, including its membership lists. After some delay, petitioner produced substantially all the data called for except its membership lists. It was adjudged in contempt and fined $100,000 for failure to produce the lists. The State Supreme Court denied certiorari to review the contempt judgment, and the U.S. Supreme Court granted certiorari.

I

Is the state's interest in acquiring the names of members of an association sufficiently compelling to justify an invasion of the right of association?

R

Unless it is necessary to achieve a compelling state interest [strict scrutiny standard], an invasion of the fundamental right of free association will be found unconstitutional.

A

Denial of relief by the State Supreme Court did not rest on an adequate state ground, and this Court has jurisdiction to entertain petitioner's federal claims. Petitioner has a right to assert on behalf of its members a claim that they are entitled under the Federal Constitution to be protected from being compelled by the State to disclose their affiliation with the Association. Immunity from state scrutiny of petitioner's membership lists is here so related to the right of petitioner's members to pursue their lawful private interests privately and to associate freely with others in doing so as to come within the protection of the Fourteenth Amendment. The State has failed to show a controlling justification for the deterrent effect on the free enjoyment of the right to associate which disclosure of petitioner's membership lists is likely to have. Accordingly, the judgment of civil contempt and the fine which resulted from petitioner's refusal to produce its membership lists must fall. Freedom to engage in association for the advancement of beliefs and ideas is an inseparable aspect of the "liberty" assured by the Due Process Clause of the Fourteenth Amendment. In the circumstances of this case, compelled disclosure of petitioner's membership lists is likely to constitute an effective restraint on its members' freedom of association. Whatever interest the State may have in obtaining the names of petitioner's ordinary members, it has not been shown to be sufficient to overcome petitioner's constitutional objections to the production order. The question whether the state court's temporary restraining order preventing petitioner from soliciting support in the State violates the Fourteenth Amendment is not properly before this Court, since the merits of the controversy have not been passed upon by the state courts.

C Reversed and cause remanded.

Board of Regents of the University of Wisconsin v. Southworth 529 U.S. 217 (2000)

FACTS

Petitioner, Board of Regents of the University of Wisconsin System (hereinafter University), requires students at the University's Madison campus to pay a segregated activity fee. The fee supports various campus services and extracurricular student activities. In the University's view, such fees enhance students' educational experience by promoting extracurricular activities, stimulating advocacy and debate on diverse points of view, enabling participation in campus administrative activity, and providing opportunities to develop social skills, all consistent with the University's broad educational mission. Registered student organizations (RSO's) engaging in a number of diverse expressive activities are eligible to receive a portion of the fees, which are administered by the student government subject to the University's approval. The parties have stipulated that the process for reviewing and approving RSO applications for funding is administered in a viewpoint-neutral fashion. RSO's may also obtain funding through a student referendum. Respondents, present and former Madison campus students, filed suit against the University, alleging, *inter alia,* that the fee violates their First Amendment rights, and that the University must grant them the choice not to fund RSO's that engage in political and ideological expression offensive to their personal beliefs. In granting respondents summary judgment, the Federal District Court declared the fee program invalid under *Abood* v. *Detroit Bd. of Ed.* and *Keller* v. *State Bar of Cal.,* and enjoined the University from using the fees to fund any RSO engaging in political or ideological speech. Agreeing with the District Court that this Court's compelled speech precedents control, the Seventh Circuit concluded that the program was not germane to the University's mission, did not further a vital University policy, and imposed too great a burden on respondents' free speech rights. It added that protecting those rights was of heightened concern following *Rosenberger* v. *Rector and Visitors of Univ. of Va.,* because if the University could not discriminate in distributing the funds, students could not be compelled to fund organizations engaging in political and ideological speech. It extended the District Court's order and enjoined the University from requiring students to pay that portion of the fee used to fund RSO's engaged in political or ideological expression.

I May a public university to charge its students an activity fee used to fund a program to facilitate extracurricular student speech?

R The First Amendment permits a public university to charge its students an activity fee used to fund a program to facilitate extracurricular student speech, provided that the program is viewpoint neutral.

A The First Amendment permits a public university to charge its students an activity fee used to fund a program to facilitate extracurricular student speech, provided that the program is viewpoint neutral. The University exacts the fee at issue for the sole purpose of facilitating the free and open exchange of ideas by, and among, its students. Objecting students, however, may insist upon certain safeguards with respect to the expressive activities they are required to support. The Court's public forum cases are instructive here by close analogy. Because the complaining students must pay fees to subsidize speech they find objectionable, even offensive, the rights acknowledged in *Abood* and *Keller* are implicated. In those cases, this Court held that a required service fee paid by nonunion employees to a union and fees paid by lawyers who were required to join a state bar association could be used to fund speech germane to those organizations' purposes but not to fund the organizations' own political expression. While these precedents identify the protesting students' interests, their germane speech standard is unworkable in the context of student speech at a university and gives insufficient protection both to the objecting students and to the University program itself. Even in the union context, this Court has encountered difficulties in deciding what is germane and what is not. The standard becomes all the more unmanageable in the public university setting, particularly where, as here, the State undertakes to stimulate the whole universe of speech and ideas. To insist upon asking what speech is germane would be contrary to the very goal the University seeks to pursue. The vast extent of permitted expression also underscores the high potential for intrusion on the objecting students' First Amendment rights, for it is all but inevitable that the fees will subsidize speech that some students find objectionable or offensive. A university is free to protect those rights by allowing an optional or refund system, but such a system is not a constitutional requirement. If a university determines that its mission is well served if students have the means to engage in dynamic discussion on a broad range of issues, it may impose a mandatory fee to sustain such dialogue. It must provide some protection to its students' First Amendment interests, however. The proper measure, and the principal standard of protection for objecting students, is the requirement of viewpoint neutrality in the allocation of funding support. This obligation was given substance in *Rosenberger* v. *Rector and Visitors of Univ. of Va.,* which concerned a student's right to use an extracurricular speech program already in place. The instant case considers the antecedent question whether a public university may require students to pay a fee which creates the mechanism for the extracurricular speech in the first instance. The University may sustain the extracurricular dimensions of its programs by using mandatory student fees with viewpoint neutrality as the operational principle. There is symmetry then in the holding here and in *Rosenberger.* Because the parties have stipulated that the University's program respects the principle of viewpoint neutrality, the program in its basic structure must be found consistent with the First Amendment. This decision makes no distinction between campus and off-campus activities; and it ought not be taken to imply that when the University, its agents, employees, or faculty speak, they are subject to the First Amendment analysis which controls in this case. While not well developed on the present record, the referendum aspect of the University's program appears to permit RSO funding or defunding by majority vote of the student body. To the extent the referendum substitutes majority determinations for viewpoint neutrality it would undermine the constitutional protection the program requires.

C

Reversed and remanded.

Roberts v. United States Jaycees

468 U.S. 609 (1984)

FACTS

Appellee United States Jaycees is a nonprofit national membership corporation whose objective, as stated in its bylaws, is to pursue such educational and charitable purposes as will promote and foster the growth and development of young men's civic organizations. The bylaws establish several classes of membership, including individual regular and associate members and local chapters. Regular membership is limited to young men between the ages of 18 and 35, while associate membership is available to persons ineligible for regular membership, principally women and older men. An associate member may not vote or hold local or national office. Two local chapters in Minnesota have been violating the bylaws for several years by admitting women as regular members, and, as a result, have had a number of sanctions imposed on them by appellee, including denying their members eligibility for state or national office. When these chapters were notified by appellee that revocation of their charters was to be considered, members of both chapters filed discrimination charges with the Minnesota Department of Human Rights, alleging that the exclusion of women from full membership violated the Minnesota Human Rights Act (Act), which makes it "an unfair discriminatory practice . . . [t]o deny any person the full and equal enjoyment of the goods, services, facilities, privileges, advantages, and accommodations of a place of public accommodation because of race, color, creed, religion, disability, national origin or sex." Before a hearing took place on the state charges, appellee brought suit against appellant state officials to prevent enforcement of the Act, alleging that, by requiring appellee to accept women as regular members, application of the Act would violate the male members' constitutional rights of free speech and association. Ultimately, a state hearing officer decided against appellee, and the District Court certified to the Minnesota Supreme Court the question whether appellee is "a place of public accommodation" within the meaning of the Act. That court answered the question in the affirmative, and, in the course of its holding, suggested that, unlike appellee, the Kiwanis Club might be sufficiently "private" to be outside the Act's scope. Appellee then amended its federal complaint to claim [468 U.S. 609, 610] that the Minnesota Supreme Court's interpretation of the Act rendered it unconstitutionally vague and overbroad. After trial, the District Court entered judgment in appellant's favor. The Court of Appeals reversed, holding that application of the Act to appellee's membership policies would produce a "direct and substantial" interference with appellee's freedom of association guaranteed by the First Amendment, and, in the alternative, that the Act was vague as construed and applied and hence unconstitutional under the Due Process Clause of the Fourteenth Amendment.

I

May a state force private associations to stop discriminating in admitting members?

R

The government may force expressive associations to admit other members non-discriminatorily if the regulation serves a compelling governmental interest which is unrelated to suppressing ideas that cannot be achieved through significantly less restrictive means.

Roberts v. United States Jaycees

468 U.S. 609 (1984)

A Application of the Act to appellee to compel it to accept women as regular members does not abridge either the male members' freedom of intimate association or their freedom of expressive association. Several features of appellee's organization place it outside the category of highly personal relationships entitled to constitutional protection against unjustified interference by the State. Local chapters are neither small nor selective, no criteria being employed for judging applicants for membership. Moreover, many of the activities central to the formation and maintenance of the association of members with one another involve the participation of strangers to that relationship, numerous nonmembers of both genders regularly participating in a substantial portion of the activities. Accordingly, local chapters lack the distinctive characteristics that might afford constitutional protection to their members' decision to exclude women. Minnesota's compelling interest in eradicating discrimination against its female citizens, an interest unrelated to the suppression of expression, justifies the impact that application of the Act to appellee may have on its male members' freedom of expressive association. By prohibiting gender discrimination in places of public accommodation, the Act protects the State's citizenry from a number of serious social and personal harms. Assuring women equal access to the goods, privileges, and advantages of a place of public accommodation clearly furthers compelling state interests. In applying the Act to appellee, the State has advanced those interests through the least restrictive means of achieving its ends. There is no basis in the record for concluding that admission of women as full voting members will impede appellee's ability to engage in its constitutionally protected civic, charitable, lobbying, fundraising, and other activities or to disseminate its preferred views. In any event, even if enforcement of the Act causes some incidental abridgment of appellee's protected speech, that effect is not greater than necessary to accomplish the State's legitimate purposes. The Act is not unconstitutionally vague and overbroad. The due process concerns of the void-for-vagueness doctrine are not seriously implicated by the Act, either on its face or as construed in this case. The Minnesota Supreme Court's construction of the Act by use of objective criteria typically employed in determining the applicability of antidiscrimination statutes to the membership policies of assertedly private clubs, ensures that the Act's reach is readily ascertainable. The contrast that court drew between appellee and the Kiwanis Club also disposes of appellee's contention that the Act is unconstitutionally overbroad. That court's articulated willingness to adopt limiting constructions that would exclude private groups from the Act's reach, together with the commonly used and sufficiently precise standards it employed to determine that appellee is not such a group, establishes that the Act, as construed, does not create an unacceptable risk of application to a substantial amount of protected conduct.

C Reversed.

Hurley v. Irish-American Gay, Lesbian & Bisexual Group of Boston 515 U.S. 557 (1995)

FACTS

Petitioner South Boston Allied War Veterans Council, an unincorporated association of individuals elected from various veterans groups, was authorized by the city of Boston to organize and conduct the St. Patrick's Day-Evacuation Day Parade. The Council refused a place in the 1993 event to respondent GLIB, an organization formed for the purpose of marching in the parade in order to express its members' pride in their Irish heritage as openly gay, lesbian, and bisexual individuals, to show that there are such individuals in the community, and to support the like men and women who sought to march in the New York St. Patrick's Day parade. GLIB and some of its members filed this suit in state court, alleging that the denial of their application to march violated, inter alia, a state law prohibiting discrimination on account of sexual orientation in places of public accommodation. In finding such a violation and ordering the Council to include GLIB in the parade, the trial court, among other things, concluded that the parade had no common theme other than the involvement of the participants, and that, given the Council's lack of selectivity in choosing parade participants and its failure to circumscribe the marchers' messages, the parade lacked any expressive purpose, such that GLIB's inclusion therein would not violate the Council's First Amendment rights. The Supreme Judicial Court of Massachusetts affirmed.

I Can a state anti-discrimination law require private parade organizers to admit certain groups?

R State anti-discrimination laws cannot require private parade organizers to admit certain groups if by doing so the parade's message would be changed.

A The state courts' application of the Massachusetts public accommodations law to require private citizens who organize a parade to include among the marchers a group imparting a message that the organizers do not wish to convey violates the First Amendment. Confronted with the state courts' conclusion that the factual characteristics of petitioners' activity place it within the realm of non-expressive conduct, this Court has a constitutional duty to conduct an independent examination of the record as a whole, without deference to those courts, to assure that their judgment does not constitute a forbidden intrusion on the field of free expression. The selection of contingents to make a parade is entitled to First Amendment protection. Parades such as petitioners' are a form of protected expression because they include marchers who are making some sort of collective point, not just to each other but to bystanders along the way. Moreover, such protection is not limited to a parade's banners and songs, but extends to symbolic acts. Although the Council has been rather lenient in admitting participants to its parade, a private speaker does not forfeit constitutional protection simply by combining multifarious voices, by failing to edit their themes to isolate a specific message as the exclusive subject matter of the speech, or by failing to generate, as an original matter, each item featured in the communication. Thus, petitioners are entitled to protection under the First Amendment. GLIB's participation as a unit in the parade was equally expressive, since the organization was formed to celebrate its members' sexual identities and for related purposes. The Massachusetts law does not, as a general matter, violate the First or Fourteenth Amendments. Its provisions are well within a legislature's power to enact when it has reason to believe that a given group is being discriminated against. And the statute does not, on its face, target speech or discriminate on the basis of its content. The state court's application, however, had the effect of declaring the sponsors' speech itself to be the public accommodation. Since every participating parade unit affects the message conveyed by the private organizers, the state courts' peculiar application of the Massachusetts law essentially forced the Council to alter the parade's expressive content and thereby violated the fundamental First Amendment rule that a speaker has the autonomy to choose the content of his own message and, conversely, to decide what not to say. Petitioners' claim to the benefit of this principle is sound, since the Council selects the expressive units of the parade from potential participants and clearly decided to exclude a message it Page III did not like from the communication it chose to make, and that is enough to invoke its right as a private speaker to shape its expression by speaking on one subject while remaining silent on another, free from state interference. The constitutional violation is not saved by *Turner Broadcasting System, Inc. v. FCC*. The Council is a speaker in its own right; a parade does not consist of individual, unrelated segments that happen to be transmitted together for individual selection by members of the audience; and there is no assertion here that some speakers will be destroyed in the absence of the Massachusetts law. Nor has any other legitimate interest been identified in support of applying that law in the way done by the state courts to expressive activity like the parade.

C

Reversed and remanded.

Boy Scouts of America v. Dale

530 U.S. 640 (2000)

FACTS

Petitioners are the Boy Scouts of America and its Monmouth Council (collectively, Boy Scouts). The Boy Scouts is a private, not-for-profit organization engaged in instilling its system of values in young people. It asserts that homosexual conduct is inconsistent with those values. Respondent Dale is an adult whose position as assistant scoutmaster of a New Jersey troop was revoked when the Boy Scouts learned that he is an avowed homosexual and gay rights activist. He filed suit in the New Jersey Superior Court, alleging, *inter alia*, that the Boy Scouts had violated the state statute prohibiting discrimination on the basis of sexual orientation in places of public accommodation. That court's Chancery Division granted summary judgment for the Boy Scouts, but its Appellate Division reversed in pertinent part and remanded. The State Supreme Court affirmed, holding, *inter alia*, that the Boy Scouts violated the State's public accommodations law by revoking Dale's membership based on his avowed homosexuality. Among other rulings, the court held that application of that law did not violate the Boy Scouts' First Amendment right of expressive association because Dale's inclusion would not significantly affect members' ability to carry out their purposes; determined that New Jersey has a compelling interest in eliminating the destructive consequences of discrimination from society, and that its public accommodations law abridges no more speech than is necessary to accomplish its purpose; and distinguished *Hurley* v. *Irish-American Gay, Lesbian and Bisexual Group of Boston, Inc.*, on the ground that Dale's reinstatement did not compel the Boy Scouts to express any message.

I

May the Boy Scouts expel gay Scout leaders?

R

"Expressive associations" need not accept members whose presence significantly impacts their ability to advocate their viewpoint.

A

Applying New Jersey's public accommodations law to require the Boy Scouts to admit Dale violates the Boy Scouts' First Amendment right of expressive association. Government actions that unconstitutionally burden that right may take many forms, one of which is intrusion into a group's internal affairs by forcing it to accept a member it does not desire. Such forced membership is unconstitutional if the person's presence affects in a significant way the group's ability to advocate public or private viewpoints. However, the freedom of expressive association is not absolute; it can be overridden by regulations adopted to serve compelling state interests, unrelated to the suppression of ideas that cannot be achieved through means significantly less restrictive of associational freedoms. To determine whether a group is protected, this Court must determine whether the group engages in "expressive association." The record clearly reveals that the Boy Scouts does so when its adult leaders inculcate its youth members with its value system. See *id.,* at 636. Thus, the Court must determine whether the forced inclusion of Dale would significantly affect the Boy Scouts' ability to advocate public or private viewpoints. The

Court first must inquire, to a limited extent, into the nature of the Boy Scouts' viewpoints. The Boy Scouts asserts that homosexual conduct is inconsistent with the values embodied in the Scout Oath and Law, particularly those represented by the terms "morally straight" and "clean," and that the organization does not want to promote homosexual conduct as a legitimate form of behavior. The Court gives deference to the Boy Scouts' assertions regarding the nature of its expression. The Court then inquires whether Dale's presence as an assistant scoutmaster would significantly burden the expression of those viewpoints. Dale, by his own admission, is one of a group of gay Scouts who have become community leaders and are open and honest about their sexual orientation. His presence as an assistant scoutmaster would interfere with the Scouts' choice not to propound a point of view contrary to its beliefs. This Court disagrees with the New Jersey Supreme Court's determination that the Boy Scouts' ability to disseminate its message would not be significantly affected by the forced inclusion of Dale. First, contrary to the state court's view, an association need not associate for the purpose of disseminating a certain message in order to be protected, but must merely engage in expressive activity that could be impaired. Second, even if the Boy Scouts discourages Scout leaders from disseminating views on sexual issues, its method of expression is protected. Third, the First Amendment does not require that every member of a group agree on every issue in order for the group's policy to be "expressive association." Given that the Boy Scouts' expression would be burdened, the Court must inquire whether the application of New Jersey's public accommodations law here runs afoul the Scouts' freedom of expressive association, and concludes that it does. Such a law is within a State's power to enact when the legislature has reason to believe that a given group is the target of discrimination and the law does not violate the First Amendment. See, *e.g., id.,* at 572. The Court rejects Dale's contention that the intermediate standard of review enunciated in *United States* v. *O'Brien,* should be applied here to evaluate the competing interests of the Boy Scouts and the State. Rather, the Court applies an analysis similar to the traditional First Amendment analysis it applied in *Hurley*. A state requirement that the Boy Scouts retain Dale would significantly burden the organization's right to oppose or disfavor homosexual conduct. The state interests embodied in New Jersey's public accommodations law do not justify such a severe intrusion on the freedom of expressive association. In so ruling, the Court is not guided by its view of whether the Boy Scouts' teachings with respect to homosexual conduct are right or wrong; public or judicial disapproval of an organization's expression does not justify the State's effort to compel the organization to accept members in derogation of the organization's expressive message. While the law may promote all sorts of conduct in place of harmful behavior, it may not interfere with speech for no better reason than promoting an approved message or discouraging a disfavored one, however enlightened either purpose may seem.

C Reversed and remanded.

Minneapolis Star & Tribune Co. v. Minnesota Commissioner of Revenue

460 U.S. 575 (1983)

FACTS

While exempting periodic publications from its general sales and use tax, the State of Minnesota in 1967 through its Commissioner of Revenue (defendant-appellee) imposed a "use tax" on the cost of paper and ink products consumed in the production of such a publication, but exempts the first $100,000 worth of paper and ink consumed in any calendar year. Plaintiff-appellant newspaper publisher, the Minneapolis Star & Tribune Company, brought an action seeking a refund of the ink and paper use taxes it had paid during certain years, contending that the tax violates the guarantee of the freedom of the press in the First Amendment. The Minnesota Supreme Court upheld the tax.

I

Can the state, by way of a special use tax, single out one class of business (newspapers) for deferential treatment?

R

A tax that singles out a class of business for special treatment is presumptively unconstitutional as violative of First Amendment rights and will be held invalid unless the state can show a counterbalancing interest of compelling importance that it cannot achieve without differential taxation.

A

The tax in question violates the First Amendment. There is no legislative history, and no indication, apart from the structure of the tax itself, of any impermissible or censorial motive on the part of the Minnesota Legislature in enacting the tax. But by creating the special use tax, which is without parallel in the State's tax scheme, Minnesota has singled out the press for special treatment. When a State so singles out the press, the political constraints that prevent a legislature from imposing crippling taxes of general applicability are weakened, and the threat of burdensome taxes becomes acute. That threat can operate as effectively as a censor to check critical comment by the press, thus undercutting the basic assumption of our political system that the press will often serve as an important restraint on government. Moreover, differential treatment, unless justified by some special characteristic of the press, suggests that the goal of the regulation is not unrelated to suppression of expression, and such goal is presumptively unconstitutional. Differential treatment of the press, then, places such a burden on the interests protected by the First Amendment that such treatment cannot be countenanced unless the State asserts a counterbalancing interest of compelling importance that it cannot achieve without differential taxation. Minnesota has offered no adequate justification for the special treatment of newspapers. Its interest in raising revenue, standing alone, cannot justify such treatment, for the alternative means of taxing businesses generally is clearly available. And the State has offered no explanation of why it chose to use a substitute for the sales tax rather than the sales tax itself. A rule that would automatically allow the State to single out the press for a different method of taxation as long as the effective burden is no different from that on other taxpayers or, as Minnesota asserts here, is lighter than that on other businesses, is to be avoided. The possibility of error inherent in such a rule poses too great a threat to concerns at the heart of the First Amendment.

Minneapolis Star & Tribune Co. v. Minnesota Commissioner of Revenue 460 U.S. 575 (1983)

Minnesota's ink and paper tax violates the First Amendment not only because it singles out the press, but also because it targets a small group of newspapers. The effect of the $100,000 exemption is that only a handful of publishers in the State pay any tax at all, and even fewer pay any significant amount of tax. To recognize a power in the State not only to single out the press but also to tailor the tax so that it singles out a few members of the press presents such a potential for abuse that no interest suggested by Minnesota can justify the scheme.

C

Reversed.

Cohen v. Cowles Media Co.

501 U.S. 663 (1991)

FACTS

During the 1982 Minnesota gubernatorial race, petitioner Cohen, who was associated with one party's campaign, gave court records concerning another party's candidate for Lieutenant Governor to respondent publishers' newspapers after receiving a promise of confidentiality from their reporters. Nonetheless, the papers identified him in their stories, and he was fired from his job. He filed suit against respondents in state court, alleging, among other things, a breach of contract. The court rejected respondents' argument that the First Amendment barred the suit, and a jury awarded him, inter alia, compensatory damages. The State Court of Appeals affirmed, but the State Supreme Court reversed, holding that a contract cause of action was inappropriate. It then went on to address the question whether Cohen could recover under state law on a promissory estoppel theory, even though that issue was never tried to a jury, nor briefed nor argued by the parties, concluding that enforcement under such a theory would violate respondents' First Amendment rights.

I

Can the media be sued for promissory estoppel [when a person makes a false statement to another and the listener relies on what was told to him/her in good faith and to his/her disadvantage] for revealing confidential sources?

R

The level of First Amendment scrutiny is set no higher when applied to the media.

A

This Court has jurisdiction. Respondents' contention that the case should be dismissed because the promissory estoppel theory was not argued or presented in the courts below and because the State Supreme Court's decision rests entirely on a state law interpretation is rejected. It is irrelevant to this Court's jurisdiction whether a party raised below and argued a federal law issue that the state supreme court actually considered and decided. Moreover, the Minnesota Supreme Court made clear that its holding rested on federal law, and respondents have defended against this suit all along by arguing that the First Amendment barred the enforcement of the reporters' promises. The First Amendment does not bar a promissory estoppel cause of action against respondents. Such a cause of action, although private, involves state action within the meaning of the Fourteenth Amendment, and therefore triggers the First Amendment's protections, since promissory estoppel is a state law doctrine creating legal obligations never explicitly assumed by the parties that are enforceable through the Minnesota courts' official power. However, the doctrine is a law of general applicability that does not target or single out the press, but rather is applicable to all Minnesota citizens' daily transactions. Thus, the First Amendment does not require that its enforcement against the press be subject to stricter scrutiny than would be applied to enforcement against others, even if the payment is characterized as compensatory damages. Nor does that Amendment grant the press protection from any law which in any fashion or to any degree limits or restricts its right to report truthful information. Moreover, Cohen sought damages for a breach of promise that caused him to lose his job and lowered his earning capacity, and did not attempt to use a promissory estoppel cause of action to avoid the strict requirements for establishing a libel or defamation claim. Any resulting inhibition on truthful reporting is no more than the incidental, and constitutionally insignificant, consequence of applying to the press a generally applicable law requiring them to keep certain promises. Cohen's request that his compensatory damages award be reinstated is rejected. The issues whether his verdict should be upheld on the ground that a promissory estoppel claim had been established under state law and whether the State Constitution may be construed to shield the press from an action such as this one are matters for the State Supreme Court to address and resolve in the first instance.

Reversed and remanded.

Branzburg v. Hayes

408 U.S. 665 (1972)

FACTS

The writ of certiorari brings before the U.S. Supreme Court two judgments of the Kentucky Court of Appeals, both involving petitioner Branzburg, a staff reporter for the Courier-Journal, a daily newspaper published in Louisville, Kentucky. On November 15, 1969, the Courier-Journal carried a story under petitioner's by-line describing in detail his observations of two young residents of Jefferson County synthesizing hashish from marijuana, an activity which, they asserted, earned them about $5,000 in three weeks. The article included a photograph of a pair of hands working above a laboratory table on which was a substance identified by the caption as hashish. The article stated that petitioner had promised not to reveal the identity of the two hashish makers. Petitioner was shortly subpoenaed by the Jefferson County grand jury; he appeared, but refused to identify the individuals he had seen possessing marihuana or the persons he had seen making hashish from marihuana. A state trial court judge ordered petitioner to answer these questions and rejected his contention that the Kentucky reporters' privilege statute, Ky. Rev. Stat. 421.100 (1962), the First Amendment of the United States Constitution, or 1, 2, and 8 of the Kentucky Constitution authorized his refusal to answer. Petitioner then sought prohibition and mandamus in the Kentucky Court of Appeals on the same grounds, but the Court of Appeals denied the petition. It held that petitioner had abandoned his First Amendment argument in a supplemental memorandum he had filed and tacitly rejected his argument based on the Kentucky Constitution. It also construed Ky. Rev. Stat. 421.100 as affording a newsman the privilege of refusing to divulge the identity of an informant who supplied him with information, but held that the statute did not permit a reporter to refuse to testify about events he had observed personally, including the identities of those persons he had observed.

The second case involving petitioner Branzburg arose out of his later story published on January 10, 1971, which described in detail the use of drugs in Frankfort, Kentucky. The article reported that in order to provide a comprehensive survey of the "drug scene" in Frankfort, petitioner had "spent two weeks interviewing several dozen drug users in the capital city" and had seen some of them smoking marihuana. A number of conversations with and observations of several unnamed drug users were recounted. Subpoenaed to appear before a Franklin County grand jury "to testify in the matter of violation of statutes concerning use and sale of drugs," petitioner Branzburg moved to quash the summons; the motion was denied, although an order was issued protecting Branzburg from revealing "confidential associations, sources or information" but requiring that he "answer any questions which concern or pertain to any criminal act, the commission of which was actually observed by [him]." Prior to the time he was slated to appear before the grand jury, petitioner sought mandamus and prohibition from the Kentucky Court of Appeals, arguing that if he were forced to go before the grand jury or to answer questions regarding the identity of informants or disclose information given to him in confidence, his effectiveness as a reporter would be greatly damaged. The Court of Appeals once again denied the requested writs and rejected petitioner's claim of a First Amendment privilege. It characterized petitioner's fear that his ability to obtain news would be destroyed as "so tenuous that it does not, in the opinion of this court, present an issue of abridgment of the freedom of the press within the meaning of that term as used in the Constitution of the United States." Petitioner sought a writ of certiorari to review both judgments of the Kentucky Court of Appeals, and the U.S. Supreme Court granted the writ.

I

Does requiring newsmen to appear and testify before state or federal grand juries abridge the freedom of speech and press guaranteed by the First Amendment?

R

The First Amendment does not protect news reporters from the obligation to testify before a grand jury; First Amendment rights may be curtailed when justified by a public interest that is "compelling" or "paramount," such as the prosecution of crimes.

A

Requiring newsmen to appear and testify before state or federal grand juries does not abridge the freedom of speech and press guaranteed by the First Amendment. The First Amendment does not relieve a newspaper reporter of the obligation that all citizens have to respond to a grand jury subpoena and answer questions relevant to a criminal investigation, and therefore the Amendment does not afford him a constitutional testimonial privilege for an agreement he makes to conceal facts relevant to a grand jury's investigation of a crime or to conceal the criminal conduct of his source or evidence thereof. Even if we accept as fact that a number of informants not implicated in criminal activity will nevertheless refuse to talk to newsmen for fear of being identified in an investigation, we still cannot accept that the public interest in news about crime must take precedence over the public interest in stopping and prosecuting crimes reported to the press by informants. This is because the requirement that the state's interest must be compelling to justify a burden on First Amendment rights is satisfied here. It is so ordered.

C

See above.

Red Lion Broadcasting Co. v. FCC

395 U.S. 367 (1969)

FACTS

The Federal Communications Commission (FCC) has for many years imposed on broadcasters a "fairness doctrine," requiring that public issues be presented by broadcasters and that each side of those issues be given fair coverage. Accordingly, the FCC declared that Petitioner Red Lion Broadcasting Co. had failed to meet its obligation under the fairness doctrine when it carried a program which constituted a personal attack on one Cook, and ordered it to send a transcript of the broadcast to Cook and provide reply time, whether or not Cook would pay for it. The Court of Appeals upheld the FCC's position. After the commencement of the Red Lion litigation the FCC began a rule-making proceeding to make the personal attack aspect of the fairness doctrine more precise and more readily enforceable, and to specify its rules relating to political editorials. The U.S. Supreme Court granted certiorari.

I Does the FCC's "fairness doctrine," requiring that public issues be presented by broadcasters and that each side of those issues be given fair coverage, impinge upon a broadcaster's freedom of speech and press in violation of the First Amendment?

R The FCC's "fairness doctrine," requiring that public issues be presented by broadcasters and that each side of those issues be given fair coverage, does not impinge upon a broadcaster's freedom of speech and press in violation of the First Amendment.

A The history of the fairness doctrine and of related legislation shows that the FCC's action in the Red Lion case did not exceed its authority, and that in adopting the new regulations the FCC was implementing congressional policy. The fairness doctrine began shortly after the Federal Radio Commission was established to allocate frequencies among competing applicant in the public interest, and insofar as there is an affirmative obligation of the broadcaster to see that both sides are presented, the personal attack doctrine and regulations do not differ from the fairness doctrine. The FCC's statutory mandate to see that broadcasters operate in the public interest and Congress' reaffirmation, in the 1959 amendment to 315 of the Communications Act, of the FCC's view that the fairness doctrine inhered in the public interest standard, support the conclusion that the doctrine and its component personal attack and political editorializing regulations are a legitimate exercise of congressionally delegated authority. The fairness doctrine and its specific manifestations in the personal attack and political editorial rules do not violate the First Amendment. The First Amendment is relevant to public broadcasting, but it is the right of the viewing and listening public, and not the right of the broadcasters, which is paramount. The First Amendment does not protect private censorship by broadcasters who are licensed by the Government to use a scarce resource which is denied to others. The danger that licensees will eliminate coverage of controversial issues as a result of the personal attack and political editorial rules is at best speculative, and, in any event, the FCC has authority to guard against this danger. There was nothing vague about the FCC's specific ruling in the Red Lion case. It is not necessary to decide every aspect of the fairness doctrine to decide these cases. Problems involving more extreme applications or more difficult constitutional questions will be dealt with if and when they arise. It has not been shown that the scarcity of broadcast frequencies, which impelled governmental regulation, is entirely a thing of the past, as new uses for the frequency spectrum have kept pace with improved technology and more efficient utilization of that spectrum.

C

Affirmed.

Miami Herald v. Tornillo

418 U.S. 241 (1974)

FACTS

After appellant newspaper had refused to print appellee's replies to editorials critical of appellee's candidacy for state office, appellee brought suit in Florida Circuit Court seeking injunctive and declaratory relief and damages, based on Florida's "right of reply" statute that grants a political candidate a right to equal space to answer criticism and attacks on his record by a newspaper, and making it a misdemeanor for the newspaper to fail to comply. The Circuit Court held the statute unconstitutional as infringing on the freedom of the press and dismissed the action. The Florida Supreme Court reversed, holding that the statute did not violate constitutional guarantees and that civil remedies, including damages, were available, and remanded to the trial court for further proceedings.

I

Can the government require newspapers to give criticized people a "right of access?"

R

The government cannot require newspapers to grant a "right of reply."

A

The Florida Supreme Court's judgment is "final" under 28 U.S.C. 1257, and thus is ripe for review by this Court. The statute violates the First Amendment's guarantee of a free press. Governmental compulsion on a newspaper to publish that which "reason" tells it should not be published is unconstitutional. The statute operates as a command by a State in the same sense as a statute or regulation forbidding appellant to publish specified matter. The statute exacts a penalty on the basis of the content of a newspaper by imposing additional printing, composing, and materials costs and by taking up space that could be devoted to other material the newspaper may have preferred to print. Even if a newspaper would face no additional costs to comply with the statute and would not be forced to forgo publication of news or opinion by the inclusion of a reply, the statute still fails to clear the First Amendment's barriers because of its intrusion into the function of editors in choosing what material goes into a newspaper and in deciding on the size and content of the paper and the treatment of public issues and officials.

C

Reversed.

Richmond Newspapers v. Virginia

448 U.S. 555 (1980)

FACTS

At the commencement of a fourth trial on a murder charge (the defendant's conviction after the first trial having been reversed on appeal, and two subsequent retrials having ended in mistrials), the Virginia trial court granted defense counsel's motion that the trial be closed to the public without any objections having been made by the prosecutor or by appellants, a newspaper and two of its reporters who were present in the courtroom, defense counsel having stated that he did not "want any information being shuffled back and forth when we have a recess as to . . . who testified to what." Later that same day, however, the trial judge granted appellants' request for a hearing on a motion to vacate the closure order, and appellants' counsel contended that constitutional considerations mandated that before ordering closure the court should first decide that the defendant's rights could be protected in no other way. But the trial judge denied the motion, saying that if he felt that the defendant's rights were infringed in any way and others' rights were not overridden he was inclined to order closure, and ordered the trial to continue "with the press and public excluded." The next day, the court granted defendant's motion to strike the prosecution's evidence, excused the jury, and found the defendant not guilty. Thereafter, the court granted appellants' motion to intervene in the case, and the Virginia Supreme Court dismissed their mandamus and prohibition petitions and, finding no reversible error, denied their petition for appeal from the closure order.

I

Is the right to attend a criminal trial by the public and press guaranteed by the Constitution?

R

The right to attend a criminal trial by the public and press is implicitly guaranteed by the Constitution.

A

The Court concluded that the right of the public and press to attend criminal trials is guaranteed under the First and Fourteenth Amendments. Absent an overriding interest articulated in findings, the trial of a criminal case must be open to the public. The historical evidence of the evolution of the criminal trial in Anglo-American justice demonstrates conclusively that at the time this Nation's organic laws were adopted, criminal trials both here and in England had long been presumptively open, thus giving assurance that the proceedings were conducted fairly to all concerned and discouraging perjury, the misconduct of participants, or decisions based on secret bias or partiality. In addition, the significant community therapeutic value of public trials was recognized: when a shocking crime occurs, a community reaction of outrage and public protest often follows, and thereafter the open processes of justice serve an important prophylactic purpose, providing an outlet for community concern, hostility, and emotion. To work effectively, it is important that society's criminal process "satisfy the appearance of justice," *Offutt v. United States*, which can best be provided by allowing people to observe such process. From this unbroken, uncontradicted history, supported by reasons as valid today as in centuries past, it must be concluded that a presumption of openness inheres in the very nature of a criminal trial under this Nation's system of justice. The freedoms of speech, press, and assembly, expressly guaranteed by the First Amendment, share a common core purpose of assuring freedom of communication on matters relating to the functioning of government. In guaranteeing freedoms such as those of speech and press, the First Amendment can be read as protecting the right of everyone to attend trials so as to give meaning to those explicit guarantees; the First Amendment right to receive information and ideas means, in the context of trials, that the guarantees of speech and press, standing alone, prohibit government from summarily closing courtroom doors which had long been open to the public at the time the First Amendment was adopted. Moreover, the right of assembly is also relevant, having been regarded not only as an independent right but also as a catalyst to augment the free exercise of the other First Amendment rights with which it was deliberately linked by the draftsmen. A trial courtroom is a public place where the people generally - and representatives of the media - have a right to be present, and where their presence historically has been thought to enhance the integrity and quality of what takes place. Even though the Constitution contains no provision which by its terms guarantees to the public the right to attend criminal trials, various fundamental rights, not expressly guaranteed, have been recognized as indispensable to the enjoyment of enumerated rights. The right to attend criminal trials is implicit in the guarantees of the First Amendment: without the freedom to attend such trials, which people have exercised for centuries, important aspects of freedom of speech and of the press could be eviscerated. With respect to the closure order in this case, despite the fact that this was the accused's fourth trial, the trial judge made no findings to support closure: no inquiry was made as to whether alternative solutions would have met the need to ensure fairness: there was no recognition of any right under the Constitution for the public or press to attend the trial: and there was no suggestion that any problems with witnesses could not have been dealt with by exclusion from the courtroom or sequestration during the trial, or that sequestration of the jurors would not have guarded against their being subjected to any improper information.

C

Reversed.

Pell v. Procunier

417 U.S. 817 (1973)

FACTS

Four California prison inmates and three professional journalists brought this suit in the District Court challenging the constitutionality of a regulation, 415.071, of the California Department of Corrections Manual, which provides that "[p]ress and other media interviews with specific individual inmates will not be permitted." That provision was promulgated following a violent prison episode that the correction authorities attributed at least in part to the former policy of free face-to-face prisoner-press interviews, which had resulted in a relatively small number of inmates gaining disproportionate notoriety and influence among their fellow inmates. The District Court granted the inmate appellees' motion for summary judgment, holding that 415.071, insofar as it prohibited inmates from having face-to-face communication with journalists unconstitutionally infringed the inmates' First and Fourteenth Amendment freedoms. The court granted a motion to dismiss with respect to the claims of the media appellants, holding that their rights were not infringed, in view of their otherwise available rights to enter state institutions and interview inmates at random and the even broader access afforded prisoners by the court's ruling with respect to the inmate appellees. The prison officials (in No. 73-754) and the journalists (in No. 73-918) have appealed.

I

Do reporters have a First Amendment right to gain access to prisons and interview inmates?

R

Reporters do not have any First Amendment right to gain access to prisons and interview inmates beyond those rights granted to the general public.

A

In light of the alternative channels of communication that are open to the inmate appellees, 415.071 does not constitute a violation of their rights of free speech. A prison inmate retains those First Amendment rights that are not inconsistent with his status as prisoner or with the legitimate penological objectives of the corrections system, and here the restrictions on inmates' free speech rights must be balanced against the State's legitimate interest in confining prisoners to deter crime, to protect society by quarantining criminal offenders for a period during which rehabilitative procedures can be applied, and to maintain the internal security of penal institutions. Alternative means of communication remain open to the inmates; they can correspond by mail with persons (including media representatives); they have rights of visitation with family, clergy, attorneys, and friends of prior acquaintance; and they have unrestricted opportunity to communicate with the press or public through their prison visitors. "[T]he First Amendment does not guarantee the press a constitutional right of special access to information not available to the public generally," *Branzburg v. Hayes.*

C

Vacated and remanded.

Houchins v. KQED

438 U.S. 1 (1978)

FACTS

After respondent broadcasting company, KQED, had been refused permission to inspect and take photographs at a portion (Little Greystone) of a county jail where a prisoner's suicide reportedly had occurred and where conditions were assertedly responsible for prisoners' problems, respondents brought this action under 42 U.S.C. 1983 against petitioner, who supervised the jail, claiming deprivation of their First Amendment rights. Thereafter petitioner announced a program of regular monthly tours open to the public, including media reporters, of parts of the jail (but not including Little Greystone). Cameras or tape recorders were not allowed on the tours, nor were interviews with inmates. Persons, including members of the media, who knew a prisoner at the jail could visit him. The District Court preliminarily enjoined petitioner from denying KQED news personnel and responsible news media representatives reasonable access to the jail, including Little Greystone, and from preventing their using photographic or sound equipment or from conducting inmate interviews. The Court of Appeals affirmed. Held: The judgment is reversed and the case is remanded.

I

Does the First Amendment require jails to allow reporters to enter with recording equipment?

R

The First Amendment does not grant the press any special right to enter a prison with recording equipment.

A

Neither the First Amendment nor the Fourteenth Amendment provides a right of access to government information or sources of information within the government's control. The news media have no constitutional right of access to the county jail, over and above that of other persons, to interview inmates and make sound recordings, films, and photographs for publication and broadcasting by newspapers, radio, and television. The public importance of conditions in penal facilities and the media's role of providing information afford no basis for reading into the Constitution a right of the public or the media to enter those institutions, gather information, and take pictures for broadcast purposes. The First Amendment does not guarantee a right of access to sources of information within government control. *Grosjean v. American Press*, *Mills v. Alabama*, and other cases relied upon by respondents, concerned the freedom of the press to communicate information already obtained, but neither *Grosjean* nor *Mills* indicated that the Constitution compels the government to provide the press with information. Whether the government should open penal institutions in the manner sought by respondents is a matter for legislative, not judicial, resolution.

C

Reversed and remanded.

United States v. Seeger

380 U.S. 163 (1965)

FACTS

Together with No. 51, *United States v. Jakobson*, on certiorari to the same court, and No. 29, *Peter v. United States*, on certiorari to the United States Court of Appeals for the Ninth Circuit. These three cases involve the exemption claims under 6(j) of the Universal Military Training and Service Act of conscientious objectors who did not belong to an orthodox religious sect. Section 6(j) excepts from combatant service in the armed forces those who are conscientiously opposed to participation in war by reason of their "religious training and belief," i.e., belief in an individual's relation to a Supreme Being involving duties beyond a human relationship but not essentially political, sociological, or philosophical views or a merely personal moral code. In all the cases convictions were obtained in the District Courts for refusal to submit to induction in the armed forces; in Nos. 50 and 51 the Court of Appeals reversed and in No. 29 the conviction was affirmed.

I

Does Section 6(j), which excepts from combatant service in the armed forces those who are conscientiously opposed to participation in war by reason of their "religious training and belief," i.e., belief in an individual's relation to a Supreme Being involving duties beyond a human relationship but not essentially political, sociological, or philosophical views or a merely personal moral code, preclude conviction for refusing to submit to induction into the armed forces (the Draft)?

R

Under the broad construction applicable to 6(j) the applications involved in these cases, none of which was based on merely personal moral codes, qualified for exemption.

A

The test of religious belief within the meaning of the exemption in 6(j) is whether it is a sincere and meaningful belief occupying in the life of its possessor a place parallel to that filled by the God of those admittedly qualified for the exemption. The exemption does not cover those who oppose war from a merely personal moral code nor those who decide that war is wrong on the basis of essentially political, sociological or economic considerations rather than religious belief. There is no issue here of atheistic beliefs and accordingly the decision does not deal with that question. This test accords with long-established legislative policy of equal treatment for those whose objection to military service is based on religious beliefs. Local boards and courts are to decide whether the objector's beliefs are sincerely held and whether they are, in his own scheme of things, religious: they are not to require proof of the religious doctrines nor are they to reject beliefs because they are not comprehensible. Under the broad construction applicable to 6(j) the applications involved in these cases, none of which was based on merely personal moral codes, qualified for exemption.

C

326 F.2d 846 and 325 F.2d 409, affirmed; 324 F.2d 173, reversed.

United States v. Ballard

322 U.S. 78 (1944)

FACTS

The indictment contained twelve counts, one of which charged a conspiracy to defraud. The first count set forth all of the eighteen representations. Each of the other counts incorporated and re-alleged all of them and added no additional ones. There was a demurrer and a motion to quash each of which asserted among other things that the indictment attacked the religious beliefs of respondents and sought to restrict the free exercise of their religion in violation of the Constitution of the United States. These motions were denied by the District Court. Early in the trial, however, objections were raised to the admission of certain evidence concerning respondents' religious beliefs. The court conferred with counsel in absence of the jury and with the acquiescence of counsel for the United States and for respondents confined the issues on this phase of the case to the question of the good faith of respondents. At the request of counsel for both sides the court advised the jury of that action. The District Court reiterated that admonition in the charge to the jury and made it abundantly clear. Counsel for the defense acquiesced in this treatment of the matter, made no objection to it during the trial, and indeed treated it without protest as the law of the case throughout the proceedings prior to the verdict. Respondents did not change their position before the District Court after verdict and contend that the truth or verity of their religious doctrines or beliefs should have been submitted to the jury. In their motion for new trial they did contend, however, that the withdrawal of these issues from the jury was error because it was in effect an amendment of the indictment. That was also one of their specifications of errors on appeal. And other errors urged on appeal included the overruling of the demurrer to the indictment and the motion to quash, and the disallowance of proof of the truth of respondents' religious doctrines or beliefs. The Circuit Court of Appeals reversed the judgment of conviction and granted a new trial, one judge dissenting. In its view the restriction of the issue in question to that of good faith was error. Its reason was that the scheme to defraud alleged in the indictment was that respondents made the eighteen alleged false representations; and that to prove that defendants devised the scheme described in the indictment 'it was necessary to prove that they schemed to make some, at least, of the (eighteen) representations ... and that some, at least, of the representations which they schemed to make were false.' One judge thought that the ruling of the District Court was also error because it was 'as prejudicial to the issue of honest belief as to the issue of purposeful misrepresentation.' The case comes before the U.S. Supreme Court on a petition for a writ of certiorari which was granted.

I May jury consider questions concerning the truth or falsity of religious beliefs?

R Finders of fact may only determine if a religious belief is sincere, but may not determine whether the beliefs themselves are true or false.

United States v. Ballard

322 U.S. 78 (1944)

A

The United States contends that the District Court withdrew from the jury's consideration only the truth or falsity of those representations which related to religious concepts or beliefs and that there were representations charged in the indictment which fell within a different category. The argument is that this latter group of representations was submitted to the jury, that they were adequate to constitute an offense under the Act, and that they were supported by the requisite evidence. It is thus sought to bring the case within the rule of *Hall v. United States*, which held that where an indictment contained 'all the necessary averments to constitute an offense created by the statute', a conviction would not be set aside because a 'totally immaterial fact' was averred but not proved. We do not stop to ascertain the relevancy of that rule to this case, for we are of the view that all of the representations charged in the indictment which related at least in part to the religious doctrines or beliefs of respondents were withheld from the jury. The trial judge did not differentiate them. A careful reading of the whole charge leads us to agree with the Circuit Court of Appeals on this phase of the case that the only issue submitted to the jury was the question as stated by the District Court, of respondents' 'belief in their representations and promises.' The United States contends that respondents acquiesced in the withdrawal from the jury of the truth of their religious doctrines or beliefs and that their consent bars them from insisting on a different course once that one turned out to be unsuccessful. The real objection of respondents is not that the truth of their religious doctrines or beliefs should have been submitted to the jury. Their demurrer and motion to quash made clear their position that that issue should be withheld from the jury on the basis of the First Amendment. Moreover, their position at all times was and still is that the court should have gone the whole way and withheld from the jury both that issue and the issue of their good faith. Their demurrer and motion to quash asked for dismissal of the entire indictment. Their argument that the truth of their religious doctrines or beliefs should have gone to the jury when the question of their good faith was submitted was and is merely an alternative argument. They never forsook their position that the indictment should have been dismissed and that none of it was good. Moreover, respondents' motion for new trial challenged the propriety of the action of the District Court in withdrawing from the jury the issue of the truth of their religious doctrines or beliefs without also withdrawing the question of their good faith. Respondents maintain that the reversal of the judgment of conviction was justified on other distinct grounds. The Circuit Court of Appeals did not reach those questions. Respondents may, of course, urge them here in support of the judgment of the Circuit Court of Appeals. But since attention was centered on the issues which we have discussed, the remaining questions were not fully presented to this Court either in the briefs or oral argument. In view of these circumstances we deem it more appropriate to remand the cause to the Circuit Court of Appeals so that it may pass on the questions reserved. If any questions of importance survive and are presented here, we will then have the benefit of the views of the Circuit Court of Appeals. The judgment is reversed and the cause is remanded to the Circuit Court of Appeals for further proceedings in conformity to this opinion.

C

Reversed.

Employment Div. Dept. of Human Resources v. Smith

494 U.S. 872 (1990)

FACTS

Oregon law prohibits the possession of peyote, a hallucinogen. Respondents Smith and Black were fired by a private drug rehabilitation organization because they ingested peyote, a hallucinogenic drug, for sacramental purposes at a ceremony of their Native American Church. Their applications for unemployment compensation were denied by the State of Oregon under a state law disqualifying employees discharged for work-related "misconduct." Holding that the denials violated respondents' First Amendment free exercise rights, the State Court of Appeals reversed. The State Supreme Court affirmed, but the U.S. Supreme Court vacated the judgment and remanded for a determination whether sacramental peyote use is proscribed by the State's controlled substance law, which makes it a felony to knowingly or intentionally possess the drug. Pending that determination, the U.S. Supreme Court refused to decide whether such use is protected by the Constitution. On remand, the State Supreme Court held that sacramental peyote use violated, and was not excepted from, the state-law prohibition, but concluded that that prohibition was invalid under the Free Exercise Clause.

I May the state deny benefits (unemployment compensation) to persons who violate a criminal statute the justification of which was for religious purposes?

R The Free Exercise Clause will not be violated when the state imposes restrictions or prohibitions which are generally applicable and religiously neutral, even if such laws burden a particular religion or religious practice, they need not be justified by a compelling governmental interest.

A The Free Exercise Clause permits the State to prohibit sacramental peyote use and thus to deny unemployment benefits to persons discharged for such use. Although a State would be "prohibiting the free exercise [of religion]" in violation of the Clause if it sought to ban the performance of (or abstention from) physical acts solely because of their religious motivation, the Clause does not relieve an individual of the obligation to comply with a law that incidentally forbids (or requires) the performance of an act that his religious belief requires (or forbids) if the law is not specifically directed to religious practice and is otherwise constitutional as applied to those who engage in the specified act for nonreligious reasons. The only decisions in which this Court has held that the First Amendment bars application of a neutral, generally applicable law to religiously motivated action are distinguished on the ground that they involved not the Free Exercise Clause alone, but that Clause in conjunction with other constitutional protections. Respondents' claim for a religious exemption from the Oregon law cannot be evaluated under the balancing test set forth in the line of cases following *Sherbert v. Verner*, whereby governmental actions that substantially burden a religious practice must be justified by a "compelling governmental interest." That test was developed in a context - unemployment compensation eligibility rules - that lent itself to individualized governmental assessment of the reasons for the relevant conduct. The test is inapplicable to an across-the-board criminal prohibition on a particular form of conduct. A holding to the contrary would create an extraordinary right to ignore generally applicable laws that are not supported by "compelling governmental interest" on the basis of religious belief. Nor could such a right be limited to situations in which the conduct prohibited is "central" to the individual's religion, since that would enmesh judges in an impermissible inquiry into the centrality of particular beliefs or practices to a faith. Thus, although it is constitutionally permissible to exempt sacramental peyote use from the operation of drug laws, it is not constitutionally required.

C

Reversed.

Sherbert v. Verner

374 U.S. 398 (1963)

FACTS

Plaintiff-appellant Sherbert, a member of the Seventh-Day Adventist Church, was discharged by her South Carolina employer because she would not work on Saturday, the Sabbath Day of her faith. She was unable to obtain other employment because she would not work on Saturday, and she filed a claim for unemployment compensation benefits under the South Carolina Unemployment Compensation Act, which provides that a claimant is ineligible for benefits if he has failed, without good cause, to accept available suitable work when offered him. The State Commission denied appellant's application on the ground that she would not accept suitable work when offered, and its action was sustained by the State Supreme Court.

I Does a State's disqualification of an employee for unemployment compensation benefits, solely because of her refusal to accept employment in which she would have to work on Saturday contrary to her religious belief, impose an unconstitutional burden on the free exercise of her religion?

R Disqualification of an employee for unemployment compensation benefits, solely because of her refusal to accept employment in which she would have to work on Saturday contrary to her religious belief, imposes an unconstitutional burden on the free exercise of her religion.

A As so applied, the South Carolina statute abridged appellant's right to the free exercise of her religion, in violation of the First Amendment, made applicable to the states by the Fourteenth Amendment. Disqualification of appellant for unemployment compensation benefits, solely because of her refusal to accept employment in which she would have to work on Saturday contrary to her religious belief, imposes an unconstitutional burden on the free exercise of her religion. There is no compelling state interest enforced in the eligibility provisions of the South Carolina statute which justifies the substantial infringement of appellant's right to religious freedom under the First Amendment. This decision does not foster the "establishment" of the Seventh-Day Adventist religion in South Carolina contrary to the First Amendment.

C Reversed.

Church of the Lukumi Babalu Aye v. City of Hialeah

508 U.S. 520 (1993)

FACTS

Petitioner church and its congregants practice the Santeria religion, which employs animal sacrifice as one of its principal forms of devotion. The animals are killed by cutting their carotid arteries, and are cooked and eaten following all Santeria rituals except healing and death rites. After the church leased land in respondent city and announced plans to establish a house of worship and other facilities there, the city council held an emergency public session and passed, among other enactments Resolution 87-66, which noted city residents' "concern" over religious practices inconsistent with public morals, peace, or safety, and declared the city's "commitment" to prohibiting such practices; Ordinance 87-40, which incorporates the Florida animal cruelty laws and broadly punishes "[w]hoever . . . unnecessarily or cruelly . . . kills any animal," and has been interpreted to reach killings for religious reasons; Ordinance 87-52, which defines "sacrifice" as "to unnecessarily kill . . . an animal in a . . . ritual . . . not for the primary purpose of food consumption," and prohibits the "possess[ion], sacrifice, or slaughter" of an animal if it is killed in "any type of ritual" and there is an intent to use it for food, but exempts "any licensed [food] establishment" if the killing is otherwise permitted by law; Ordinance 87-71, which prohibits the sacrifice of animals, and defines "sacrifice" in the same manner as Ordinance 87-52; and Ordinance 87-72 which defines "slaughter" as "the killing of animals for food" and prohibits slaughter outside of areas zoned for slaughterhouses, but includes an exemption for "small numbers of hogs and/or cattle" when exempted by state law. Petitioners filed this suit under 42 U.S.C. 1983, alleging violations of their rights under the Free Exercise Clause of the First Amendment. Although acknowledging that the foregoing ordinances are not religiously neutral, the District Court ruled for the city, concluding, among other things, that compelling governmental interests in preventing public health risks and cruelty to animals fully justified the absolute prohibition on ritual sacrifice accomplished by the ordinances, and that an exception to that prohibition for religious conduct would unduly interfere with fulfillment of the governmental interest, because any more narrow restrictions would be unenforceable as a result of the Santeria religion's secret nature. The Court of Appeals affirmed.

I

May laws which burden the practice of a religion always be justified by a compelling governmental interest in order to be held constitutional?

R

Under the Free Exercise Clause, a law that burdens religious practice need not be justified by a compelling governmental interest if it is neutral and of general applicability; however, where such a law is not neutral or not of general application, it must undergo the most rigorous of scrutiny: it must be justified by a compelling governmental interest, and must be narrowly tailored to advance that interest.

A

Under the Free Exercise Clause, a law that burdens religious practice need not be justified by a compelling governmental interest if it is neutral and of general applicability. However, where such a law is not neutral or not of general application, it must undergo the most rigorous of scrutiny: it must be justified by a compelling governmental interest, and must be narrowly tailored to advance that interest. Neutrality and general applicability are interrelated, and failure to satisfy one requirement is a likely indication that the other has not been satisfied. The ordinances' texts and operation demonstrate that they are not neutral, but have as their object the suppression of Santeria's central element: animal sacrifice. That this religious exercise has been targeted is evidenced by Resolution 87-66's statements of "concern" and "commitment," and by the use of the words "sacrifice" and "ritual" in Ordinances 87-40, 87-52, and 87-71. Moreover, the latter ordinances' various prohibitions, definitions, and exemptions demonstrate that they were "gerrymandered" with care to proscribe religious killings of animals by Santeria church members but to exclude almost all other animal killings. They also suppress much more religious conduct than is necessary to achieve their stated ends. The legitimate governmental interests in protecting the public health and preventing cruelty to animals could be addressed by restrictions stopping far short of a flat prohibition of all Santeria sacrificial practice, such as general regulations on the disposal of organic garbage or on methods of slaughter. Although 87-72 appears to apply to substantial nonreligious conduct and not to be overbroad, it must also be invalidated because it functions in tandem with the other ordinances to suppress Santeria religious worship. Each of the ordinances pursues the city's governmental interests only against conduct motivated by religious belief, and thereby violates the requirement that laws burdening religious practice must be of general applicability. Ordinances 87-40, 87-52, and 87-71 are substantially underinclusive with regard to the city's interest in preventing cruelty to animals, since they are drafted with care to forbid few animal killings but those occasioned by religious sacrifice, while many types of animal deaths or kills for nonreligious reasons are either not prohibited or approved by express provision. The city's assertions that it is "self-evident" that killing for food is "important," that the eradication of insects and pests is "obviously justified" and that euthanasia of excess animals "makes sense" do not explain why religion alone must bear the burden of the ordinances. These ordinances are also substantially underinclusive with regard to the city's public health interests in preventing the disposal of animal carcasses in open public places and the consumption of uninspected meat, since neither interest is pursued by respondent with regard to conduct that is not motivated by religious conviction. Ordinance 87-72 is underinclusive on its face, since it does not regulate nonreligious slaughter for food in like manner, and respondent has not explained why the commercial slaughter of "small numbers" of cattle and hogs does not implicate its professed desire to prevent cruelty to animals and preserve the public health. The ordinances cannot withstand the strict scrutiny that is required. They are not narrowly tailored to accomplish the asserted governmental interests. All four are overbroad or underinclusive in substantial respects because those interests could be achieved by narrower ordinances that burdened religion to a far lesser degree. Moreover, where, as here, government restricts only conduct protected by the First Amendment and fails to enact feasible measures to restrict other conduct producing substantial harm or alleged harm of the same sort, the governmental interests given in justification of the restriction cannot be regarded as compelling.

C

Judgment reversed.

Locke v. Davey

124 S.Ct. 1307 (2004)

FACTS

Washington State established its Promise Scholarship Program to assist academically gifted students with postsecondary education expenses. In accordance with the State Constitution, students may not use such a scholarship to pursue a devotional theology degree. Plainitff-respondent Davey was awarded a Promise Scholarship and chose to attend Northwest College, a private, church-affiliated institution that is eligible under the program. When he enrolled, Davey chose a double major in pastoral ministries and business management/administration. It is undisputed that the pastoral ministries degree is devotional. After learning that he could not use his scholarship to pursue that degree, Davey brought this action under 42 U. S. C. §1983 for an injunction and damages, arguing that the denial of his scholarship violated, *inter alia*, the First Amendment's Free Exercise and Establishment Clauses. The District Court rejected Davey's constitutional claims and granted the State summary judgment. The Ninth Circuit reversed, concluding that, because the State had singled out religion for unfavorable treatment, its exclusion of theology majors had to be narrowly tailored to achieve a compelling state interest under *Church of Lukumi Babalu Aye, Inc.* v. *Hialeah*. Finding that the State's anti-establishment concerns were not compelling, the court declared the program unconstitutional.

I Does the State of Washington's exclusion of the pursuit of a devotional theology degree from its otherwise-inclusive scholarship aid program violate the Free Exercise Clause?

R A state does not violate the Free Exercise Clause by refusing to fund a student pursuing a degree in devotional theology.

A Washington's exclusion of the pursuit of a devotional theology degree from its otherwise-inclusive scholarship aid program does not violate the Free Exercise Clause. This case involves the "play in the joints" between the Establishment and Free Exercise Clauses. That is, it concerns state action that is permitted by the former but not required by the latter. The Court rejects Davey's contention that, under *Lukumi, supra,* the program is presumptively unconstitutional because it is not facially neutral with respect to religion. To accept this claim would extend the *Lukumi* line of cases well beyond not only their facts but their reasoning. Here, the State's disfavor of religion (if it can be called that) is of a far milder kind than in *Lukumi,* where the ordinance criminalized the ritualistic animal sacrifices of the Santeria religion. Washington's program imposes neither criminal nor civil sanctions on any type of religious service or rite. It neither denies to ministers the right to participate in community political affairs nor requires students to choose between their religious beliefs and receiving a government benefit. The State has merely chosen not to fund a distinct category of instruction. Even though the differently worded Washington Constitution draws a more stringent line than does the Federal Constitution, the interest it seeks to further is scarcely novel. In fact, there are few areas in which a State's antiestablishment interests come more into play. Since this country's founding, there have been popular uprisings against procuring taxpayer funds to support church leaders, which was one of the hallmarks of an "established" religion. Most States that sought to avoid such an establishment around the time of the founding placed in their constitutions formal prohibitions against using tax funds to support the ministry. That early state constitutions saw no problem in explicitly excluding *only* the ministry from receiving state dollars reinforces the conclusion that religious instruction is of a different ilk from other professions. Moreover, the entirety of the Promise Scholarship Program goes a long way toward including religion in its benefits, since it permits students to attend pervasively religious schools so long as they are accredited, and students are still eligible to take devotional theology courses under the program's current guidelines. Nothing in the Washington Constitution's history or text or in the program's operation suggests animus towards religion. Given the historic and substantial state interest at issue, it cannot be concluded that the denial of funding for vocational religious instruction alone is inherently constitutionally suspect. Without a presumption of unconstitutionality, Davey's claim must fail. The State's interest in not funding the pursuit of devotional degrees is substantial, and the exclusion of such funding places a relatively minor burden on Promise Scholars. If any room exists between the two Religion Clauses, it must be here.

C

Reversed.

County of Allegheny v. American Civil Liberties Union

492 U.S. 573 (1989)

FACTS

This litigation concerns the constitutionality of two recurring holiday displays located on public property in downtown Pittsburgh. The first, a creche depicting the Christian Nativity scene, was placed on the Grand Staircase of the Allegheny County Courthouse, which is the "main," "most beautiful," and "most public" part of the courthouse. The creche was donated by the Holy Name Society, a Roman Catholic group, and bore a sign to that effect. Its manager had at its crest an angel bearing a banner proclaiming "Gloria in Excelsis Deo," meaning "Glory to God in the Highest." The second of the holiday displays in question was an 18-foot Chanukah menorah or candelabrum, which was placed just outside the City-County Building next to the city's 45-foot decorated Christmas tree. At the foot of the tree was a sign bearing the mayor's name and containing text declaring the city's "salute to liberty." The menorah is owned by Chabad, a Jewish group, but is stored, erected, and removed each year by the city. Respondents, the Greater Pittsburgh Chapter of the American Civil Liberties Union and seven local residents, filed suit seeking permanently to enjoin the county from displaying the creche and the city from displaying the menorah on the ground that the displays violated the Establishment Clause of the First Amendment, made applicable to state governments by the Fourteenth Amendment. The District Court denied relief, relying on *Lynch v. Donnelly*, which held that a city's inclusion of a creche in its annual Christmas display in a private park did not violate the Establishment Clause. The Court of Appeals reversed, distinguishing Lynch v. Donnelly, and holding that the creche and the menorah in the present case must be understood as an impermissible governmental endorsement of *Christianity and Judaism under Lemon v. Kurtzman.*

I In a determination whether the government's use of an object with religious significance violates the Establishment Clause, must the point of view of the viewers be considered [whether the viewers fairly understood the purpose of the display]?

R A government act will be found unconstitutional under the Establishment Clause if viewers of the act understood it to be endorsing religion or the act actually did endorse religion.

A Under *Lemon v. Kurtzman*, a "practice which touches upon religion, if it is to be permissible under the Establishment Clause," must not, inter alia, "advance [or] inhibit religion in its principal or primary effect." Although, in refining the definition of governmental action that unconstitutionally "advances" religion, the Court's subsequent decisions have variously spoken in terms of "endorsement," "favoritism," "preference," or "promotion," the essential principle remains the same: The Clause, at the very least, prohibits government from appearing to take a position on questions of religious belief or from "making adherence to a religion relevant in any way to a person's standing in the political community." When viewed in its overall context, the creche display violates the Establishment Clause. The creche angel's words endorse a patently Christian message: Glory to God for the birth of Jesus Christ. Moreover, in contrast to Lynch, nothing in the creche's setting detracts from that message. Although the government may acknowledge Christmas as a cultural phenomenon, it may not observe it as a Christian holy day by suggesting that people praise God for the birth of Jesus. JUSTICE KENNEDY'S reasons for permitting the creche on the Grand Staircase and his condemnation of the Court's reasons for deciding otherwise are unpersuasive. History cannot legitimate practices like the creche display that demonstrate the government's allegiance to a particular sect or creed. The question whether a particular practice would constitute governmental proselytization is much the same as the endorsement inquiry, except to the extent the proselytization test requires an "obvious" allegiance between the government and the favored sect. This Court's decisions, however, impose no such burden on demonstrating that the government has favored a particular sect or creed, but, to the contrary, have required strict scrutiny of practices suggesting a denominational preference. The Constitution mandates that the government remain secular, rather than affiliating itself with religious beliefs or institutions, precisely in order to avoid discriminating against citizens on the basis of their religious faiths. Thus, the claim that prohibiting government from celebrating Christmas as a religious holiday discriminates against Christians in favor of non-adherents must fail, since it contradicts the fundamental premise of the Establishment Clause itself. In contrast, confining the government's own Christmas celebration to the holiday's secular aspects does not favor the religious beliefs of non-Christians over those of Christians, but simply permits the government to acknowledge the holiday without expressing an impermissible allegiance to Christian beliefs.

C

The judgment is affirmed in part and reversed in part, and the cases are remanded.

Larson v. Valente

456 U.S. 228 (1982)

FACTS

A section (309.515, subd. 1(b)) of Minnesota's charitable solicitations Act provides that only those religious organizations that receive more than half of their total contributions from members or affiliated organizations are exempt from the registration and reporting requirements of the Act. The individual appellees, claiming to be followers of the tenets of appellee Unification Church (later joined as a plaintiff) brought suit in Federal District Court seeking a declaration that the statute on its face and as applied to them violated, inter alia, the Establishment Clause of the First Amendment, and also seeking injunctive relief. After obtaining a preliminary injunction, appellees moved for summary judgment. Upon finding that the "overbreadth" doctrine gave appellees standing to challenge the statute, the Magistrate to whom the action had been transferred held that the application of the statute to religious organizations violated the Establishment Clause, and therefore recommended declaratory and permanent injunctive relief. The District Court, accepting this recommendation, entered summary judgment for appellees. The Court of Appeals affirmed on both the standing issue and on the merits. But the court, disagreeing with the District Court's conclusion that appellees and others should enjoy the religious-organization exemption from the Act merely by claiming to be such organizations, held that proof of religious-organization status was required in order to gain the exemption, and left the question of appellees' status "open . . . for further development." Accordingly, the court vacated the District Court's judgment and remanded for entry of a modified injunction and further proceedings.

I

In order to be upheld under the Establishment Clause, must a government act or regulation that discriminates among religious groups be justified by a compelling interest and narrowly tailored to serve that interest?

R

In order to be upheld under the Establishment Clause, a government act or regulation that discriminates among religious groups must be justified by a compelling interest and narrowly tailored to serve that interest.

A

Appellees have Art. III standing to raise their Establishment Clause claims. The State attempted to use 309.515, subd. 1(b)'s fifty per cent rule to compel the Unification Church to register and report under the Act. The fact that the fifty per cent rule only applies to religious organizations compels the conclusion that, at least for purposes of this suit challenging that application, appellee Unification Church is a religious organization within the meaning of the Act. The controversy between the parties is not rendered any less concrete by the fact that appellants, in the course of this litigation, have changed their position to contend that the Unification Church is not a religious organization within the meaning of the Act and that therefore it would not be entitled to an exemption under 309.515, subd. 1(b) even if the 50% rule were declared unconstitutional. This is so because the threatened application of 309.515, subd. 1(b), and its fifty per cent rule to appellees amounts to a distinct and palpable injury to them, in that it disables them from soliciting contributions in Minnesota unless they comply with the registration and reporting requirements of the

Act. Moreover, there is a causal connection between the claimed injury and the challenged conduct. The fact that appellees have not yet shown an entitlement to a permanent injunction barring the State from subjecting them to the Act's registration and reporting requirements does not detract from the palpability of the particular and discrete injury caused to appellees. Section 309.515, subd. 1(b), in setting up precisely the sort of official denominational preference forbidden by the First Amendment, violates the Establishment Clause. Since the challenged statute grants denominational preferences, it must be treated as suspect, and strict scrutiny must be applied in adjudging its constitutionality. Assuming, arguendo, that appellants' asserted interest in preventing fraudulent solicitations is a "compelling" interest, appellants have nevertheless failed to demonstrate that 309.515, subd. 1(b)'s fifty per cent rule is "closely fitted" to that interest. Appellants' argument to the contrary is based on three premises: (1) that members of a religious organization can and will exercise supervision and control over the solicitation activities of the organization when membership contributions exceed fifty per cent; (2) that membership control, assuming its existence, is an adequate safeguard against abusive solicitations of the public; and (3) that the need for public disclosure rises in proportion with the percentage of nonmember contributions. There is no substantial support in the record for any of these premises. Where the principal effect of 309.515, subd. 1(b)'s fifty per cent rule is to impose the Act's registration and reporting requirements on some religious organizations but not on others, the "risk of politicizing religion" inhering in the statute is obvious.

C Affirmed.

Lemon v. Kurtzman

403 U.S. 602 (1971)

FACTS

Rhode Island's 1969 Salary Supplement Act provides for a 15% salary supplement to be paid to teachers in nonpublic schools at which the average per-pupil expenditure on secular education is below the average in public schools. Eligible teachers must teach only courses offered in the public schools, using only materials used in the public schools, and must agree not to teach courses in religion. A three-judge court found that about 25% of the State's elementary students attended nonpublic schools, about 95% of whom attended Roman Catholic affiliated schools, and that to date about 250 teachers at Roman Catholic schools are the sole beneficiaries under the Act. The court found that the parochial school system was "an integral part of the religious mission of the Catholic Church," and held that the Act fostered "excessive entanglement" between government and religion, thus violating the Establishment Clause. Pennsylvania's Nonpublic Elementary and Secondary Education Act, passed in 1968, authorizes the state Superintendent of Public Instruction to "purchase" certain "secular educational services" from nonpublic schools, directly reimbursing those schools solely for teachers' salaries, textbooks, and instructional materials. Reimbursement is restricted to courses in specific secular subjects, the textbooks and materials must be approved by the Superintendent, and no payment is to be made for any course containing "any subject matter expressing religious teaching, or the morals or forms of worship of any sect." Contracts were made with schools that have more than 20% of all the students in the State, most of which were affiliated with the Roman Catholic Church. The complaint challenging the constitutionality of the Act alleged that the church-affiliated schools are controlled by religious organizations, have the purpose of propagating and promoting a particular religious faith, and conduct their operations to fulfill that purpose. A three-judge court granted the State's motion to dismiss the complaint for failure to state a claim for relief, finding no violation of the Establishment or Free Exercise Clause.

I

Will a state program that provides financial assistance to private schools and church-related entities violate the First Amendment's Establishment Clause?

R

A non discriminatorily regulation must (1) have a secular purpose; (2) have a secular principle effect; and (3) not foster excessive government entanglement with religion, in order to be found constitutional.

A

Both statutes are unconstitutional under the Religion Clauses of the First Amendment, as the cumulative impact of the entire relationship arising under the statutes involves excessive entanglement between government and religion. The entanglement in the Rhode Island program arises because of the religious activity and purpose of the church-affiliated schools, especially with respect to children of impressionable age in the primary grades, and the dangers that a teacher under religious control and discipline poses to the separation of religious from purely secular aspects of elementary education in such schools. These factors require continuing state surveillance to ensure that the statutory restrictions are obeyed and the First Amendment otherwise respected. Furthermore, under the Act the government must inspect school records to determine what part of the expenditures is attributable to secular education as opposed to religious activity, in the event a nonpublic school's expenditures per pupil exceed the comparable figures for public schools. The entanglement in the Pennsylvania program also arises from the restrictions and surveillance necessary to ensure that teachers play a strictly non-ideological role and the state supervision of nonpublic school accounting procedures required to establish the cost of secular as distinguished from religious education. In addition, the Pennsylvania statute has the further defect of providing continuing financial aid directly to the church-related schools. Historically governmental control and surveillance measures tend to follow cash grant programs, and here the government's post-audit power to inspect the financial records of church-related schools creates an intimate and continuing relationship between church and state. Political division along religious lines was one of the evils at which the First Amendment aimed, and in these programs, where successive and probably permanent annual appropriations that benefit relatively few religious groups are involved, political fragmentation and divisiveness on religious lines are likely to be intensified. Unlike the tax exemption for places of religious worship, upheld in *Walz v. Tax Commission*, which was based on a practice of 200 years, these innovative programs have self-perpetuating and self-expanding propensities which provide a warning signal against entanglement between government and religion.

C No. 89, 310 F. Supp. 35, reversed and remanded; Nos. 569 and 570, 316 F. Supp. 112, affirmed.

Rosenberger v. Rector & Visitors of the U. of Virginia

515 U.S. 819 (1995)

FACTS

Respondent University of Virginia, a state instrumentality, authorizes payments from its Student Activities Fund (SAF) to outside contractors for the printing costs of a variety of publications issued by student groups called "Contracted Independent Organizations" (CIOs). The SAF receives its money from mandatory student fees and is designed to support a broad range of extracurricular student activities related to the University's educational purpose. CIOs must include in their dealings with third parties and in all written materials a disclaimer stating that they are independent of the University and that the University is not responsible for them. The University withheld authorization for payments to a printer on behalf of petitioners' CIO, Wide Awake Productions (WAP), solely because its student newspaper, Wide Awake: A Christian Perspective at the University of Virginia, "primarily promotes or manifests a particular belie[f] in or about a deity or an ultimate reality," as prohibited by the University's SAF Guidelines. Petitioners filed this suit under 42 U.S.C. 1983, alleging, *inter alia*, that the refusal to authorize payment violated their First Amendment right to freedom of speech. After the District Court granted summary judgment for the University, the Fourth Circuit affirmed, holding that the University's invocation of viewpoint discrimination to deny third-party payment violated the Speech Clause, but concluding that the discrimination was justified by the necessity of complying with the Establishment Clause.

I

Is the refusal to authorize payment [from its Student Activities Fund (SAF) to outside contractors for the printing costs of a variety of publications issued by student groups] a violation of petitioners' First Amendment right to freedom of speech?

R

The Guideline invoked to deny SAF support, both in its terms and in its application to these petitioners, is a denial of their right of free speech.

A

The Guideline violates the principles governing speech in limited public forums, which apply to the SAF under, e.g., *Perry Ed. Assn. v. Perry Local Educators' Assn.* In determining whether a State is acting within its power to preserve the limits it has set for such a forum so that the exclusion of a class of speech there is legitimate, this Court has observed a distinction between, on the one hand, content discrimination - i.e., discrimination against speech because of its subject matter - which may be permissible if it preserves the limited forum's purposes, and, on the other hand, viewpoint discrimination i.e., discrimination because of the speaker's specific motivating ideology, opinion, or perspective - which is presumed impermissible when directed against speech otherwise within the forum's limitations. The most recent and most apposite case in this area is *Lamb's Chapel v. Center Moriches Union Free School Dist.*, in which the Court held that permitting school property to be used for the presentation of all views on an issue except those dealing with it from a religious standpoint constitutes prohibited viewpoint discrimination. Here, as in that case, the State's actions are properly interpreted as unconstitutional viewpoint discrimination rather than permissible line-drawing based on content: By the very terms of the SAF prohibition, the University does not exclude religion as a subject matter, but selects for disfavored treatment those student journalistic efforts with religious editorial viewpoints. The University's attempt to escape the consequences of *Lamb's Chapel* by urging that this case involves the provision of funds rather than access to facilities is unavailing. Although it may regulate the content of expression when it is the speaker or when it enlists private entities to convey its own message, the University may not discriminate based on the viewpoint of private persons whose speech it subsidizes. Its argument that the scarcity of public money may justify otherwise impermissible viewpoint discrimination among private speakers is simply wrong. Vital First Amendment speech principles are at stake here. There is no suggestion that the University created its program to advance religion or aid a religious cause. The SAF's purpose is to open a forum for speech and to support various student enterprises, including the publication of newspapers, in recognition of the diversity and creativity of student life. The SAF Guidelines have a separate classification for, and do not make third-party payments on behalf of, "religious organizations," and WAP did not seek a subsidy because of its Christian editorial viewpoint; it sought funding under the Guidielines as a "student . . . communications . . . grou[p]." Neutrality is also apparent in the fact that the University has taken pains to disassociate itself from the private speech involved in this case. The program's neutrality distinguishes the student fees here from a tax levied for the direct support of a church or group of churches, which would violate the Establishment Clause. This case is not controlled by the principle that special Establishment Clause dangers exist where the government makes direct money payments to sectarian institutions, since it is undisputed that no public funds flow directly into WAP's coffers under the program at issue. A public university does not violate the Establishment Clause when it grants access to its facilities on a religion-neutral basis to a wide spectrum of student groups, even if some of those groups would use the facilities for devotional exercises. This is so even where the upkeep, maintenance, and repair of those facilities is paid out of a student activities fund to which students are required to contribute. There is no difference in logic or principle, and certainly no difference of constitutional significance, between using such funds to operate a facility to which students have access, and paying a third-party contractor to operate the facility on its behalf. That is all Page IV that is involved here: The University provides printing services to a broad spectrum of student newspapers. Were the contrary view to become law, the University could only avoid a constitutional violation by scrutinizing the content of student speech, lest it contain too great a religious message. Such censorship would be far more inconsistent with the Establishment Clause's dictates than would governmental provision of secular printing services on a religion-blind basis.

C

Reversed.

Santa Fe Independent School District v. Doe

530 U.S. 290 (2000)

FACTS

Prior to 1995, a student elected as Santa Fe High School's student council chaplain delivered a prayer over the public address system before each home varsity football game. Respondents, Mormon and Catholic students or alumni and their mothers, filed a suit challenging this practice and others under the Establishment Clause of the First Amendment. While the suit was pending, petitioner school district (District) adopted a different policy, which authorizes two student elections, the first to determine whether "invocations" should be delivered at games, and the second to select the spokesperson to deliver them. After the students held elections authorizing such prayers and selecting a spokesperson, the District Court entered an order modifying the policy to permit only nonsectarian, non-proselytizing prayer. The Fifth Circuit held that, even as modified by the District Court, the football prayer policy was invalid.

I

Does a policy permitting student-led, student-initiated prayer at football games violate the Establishment Clause?

R

Allowing invocations at a high school football game will violate the Establishment Clause because it constitutes excessive entanglement of government and religion.

A

The District's policy permitting student-led, student-initiated prayer at football games violates the Establishment Clause. The Court's analysis is guided by the principles endorsed in *Lee* v. *Weisman*. There, in concluding that a prayer delivered by a rabbi at a graduation ceremony violated the Establishment Clause, the Court held that, at a minimum, the Constitution guarantees that government may not coerce anyone to support or participate in religion or its exercise, or otherwise act in a way that establishes a state religion or religious faith, or tends to do so. The District argues unpersuasively that these principles are inapplicable because the policy's messages are private student speech, not public speech. The delivery of a message such as the invocation here - on school property, at school-sponsored events, over the school's public address system, by a speaker representing the student body, under the supervision of school faculty, and pursuant to a school policy that explicitly and implicitly encourages public prayer - is not properly characterized as "private" speech. Through its election scheme, the District has established a governmental mechanism that turns the school into a forum for religious debate and empowers the student body majority to subject students of minority views to constitutionally improper messages. The award of that power alone is not acceptable. For the foregoing reasons, the policy is invalid on its face.

C

Affirmed.

Engel v. Vitale

370 U.S. 421 (1962)

FACTS

The respondent Board of Education of Union Free School District No. 9, New Hyde Park, New York, acting in its official capacity under state law, directed the School District's principal to cause a prayer to be said aloud by each class in the presence of a teacher at the beginning of each school day. Shortly after the practice of reciting the Regents' prayer was adopted by the School District, the parents of ten pupils brought this action in a New York State Court insisting that use of this official prayer in the public schools was contrary to the beliefs, religions, or religious practices of both themselves and their children. Among other things, these parents challenged the constitutionality of both the state law authorizing the School District to direct the use of prayer in public schools and the School District's regulation ordering the recitation of this particular prayer on the ground that these actions of official governmental agencies violate the Establishment Clause. The New York Court of Appeals, over the some dissent, sustained an order of the lower state courts which had upheld the power of New York to use the Regents' prayer as a part of the daily procedures of its public schools so long as the schools did not compel any pupil to join in the prayer over his or his parents' objection.

I Is a state order directing a school's principle, under its official capacity, to cause prayer to be said aloud by each class in the presence of a teacher violative of the First Amendment?

R State officials may not compose an official state prayer and require that it be recited in the public schools of the State at the beginning of each school day even if the prayer is denominationally neutral and pupils who wish to do so may remain silent or be excused from the room during the recitation.

A Because of the prohibition of the First Amendment against the enactment of any law "respecting an establishment of religion," which is made applicable to the States by the Fourteenth Amendment, state officials may not compose an official state prayer and require that it be recited in the public schools of the State at the beginning of each school day - even if the prayer is denominationally neutral and pupils who wish to do so may remain silent or be excused from the room while the prayer is being recited. We think that by using its public school system to encourage recitation of the Regents' prayer, the State of New York has adopted a practice wholly inconsistent with the Establishment Clause. There can, of course, be no doubt that New York's program of daily classroom invocation of God's blessings as prescribed in the Regents' prayer is a religious activity. It is a solemn avowal of divine faith and supplication for the blessings of the Almighty. The nature of such a prayer has always been religious, none of the respondents has denied this and the trial court expressly so found. The judgment of the Court of Appeals of New York is reversed and the cause remanded for further proceedings not inconsistent with this opinion.

C Reversed and remanded.

Lee v. Weisman

505 U.S. 577 (1992)

FACTS

Principals of public middle and high schools in Providence, Rhode Island, are permitted to invite members of the clergy to give invocations and benedictions at their schools' graduation ceremonies. Petitioner Lee, a middle school principal, invited a rabbi to offer such prayers at the graduation ceremony for Deborah Weisman's class, gave the rabbi a pamphlet containing guidelines for the composition of public prayers at civic ceremonies, and advised him that the prayers should be nonsectarian. Shortly before the ceremony, the District Court denied the motion of respondent Weisman, Deborah's father, for a temporary restraining order to prohibit school officials from including the prayers in the ceremony. Deborah and her family attended the ceremony, and the prayers were recited. Subsequently, Weisman sought a permanent injunction barring Lee and other petitioners, various Providence public school officials, from inviting clergy to deliver invocations and benedictions at future graduations. It appears likely that such prayers will be conducted at Deborah's high school graduation. The District Court enjoined petitioners from continuing the practice at issue on the ground that it violated the Establishment Clause of the First Amendment. The Court of Appeals affirmed.

I Does the incorporation of religious subject matter in an official public school function violate the Establishment Clause?

R The incorporation of religious subject matter in an official public school function will violate the Establishment Clause of the First Amendment.

A Including clergy who offer prayers as part of an official public school graduation ceremony is forbidden by the Establishment Clause. This Court need not revisit the questions of the definition and scope of the principles governing the extent of permitted accommodation by the State for its citizens' religious beliefs and practices, for the controlling precedents as they relate to prayer and religious exercise in primary and secondary public schools compel the holding here. Thus, the Court will not reconsider its decision in *Lemon v. Kurtzman*. The principle that government may accommodate the free exercise of religion does not supersede the fundamental limitations imposed by the Establishment Clause, which guarantees, at a minimum, that a government may not coerce anyone to support or participate in religion or its exercise, or otherwise act in a way which "establishes a [state] religion or religious faith, or tends to do so." State officials here direct the performance of a formal religious exercise at secondary schools' promotional and graduation ceremonies. Lee's decision that prayers should be given and his selection of the religious participant are choices attributable to the State. Moreover, through the pamphlet and his advice that the prayers be nonsectarian, he directed and controlled the prayers' content. That the directions may have been given in a good-faith attempt to make the prayers acceptable to most persons does not resolve the dilemma caused by the school's involvement, since the government may not establish an official or civic religion as a means of avoiding the establishment of a religion with more specific creeds. The Establishment Clause was inspired by the lesson that in the hands of government what might begin as a tolerant expression of religious views may end in a policy to indoctrinate and coerce. Prayer exercises in elementary and secondary schools carry a particular risk of indirect coercion. The school district's supervision and control of a high school graduation ceremony places subtle and indirect public and peer pressure on attending students to stand as a group or maintain respectful silence during the invocation and benediction. A reasonable dissenter of high school age could believe that standing or remaining silent signified her own participation in, or approval of, the group exercise, rather than her respect for it. And the State may not place the student dissenter in the dilemma of participating or protesting. Since adolescents are often susceptible to peer pressure, especially in matters of social convention, the State may no more use social pressure to enforce orthodoxy than it may use direct means. The embarrassment and intrusion of the religious exercise cannot be refuted by arguing that the prayers are of a *de minimis* character, since that is an affront to the rabbi and those for whom the prayers have meaning, and since any intrusion was both real and a violation of the objectors' rights. Petitioners' argument that the option of not attending the ceremony excuses any inducement or coercion in the ceremony itself is rejected. In this society, high school graduation is one of life's most significant occasions, and a student is not free to absent herself from the exercise in any real sense of the term "voluntary." Also not dispositive is the contention that prayers are an essential part of these ceremonies because, for many persons, the occasion would lack meaning without the recognition that human achievements cannot be understood apart from their spiritual essence. This position fails to acknowledge that what for many was a spiritual imperative was for the Weismans religious conformance compelled by the State. It also gives insufficient recognition to the real conflict of conscience faced by a student who would have to choose whether to miss graduation or conform to the state-sponsored practice in an environment where the risk of compulsion is especially high. Inherent differences between the public school system and a session of a state legislature distinguish this case from *Marsh v. Chambers*, which condoned a prayer exercise. The atmosphere at a state legislature's opening, where adults are free to enter and leave with little comment and for any number of reasons, cannot compare with the constraining potential of the one school event most important for the student to attend.

C

Affirmed.

Mitchell v. Helms

530 U.S. 793 (2000)

FACTS

Chapter 2 of the Education Consolidation and Improvement Act of 1981 channels federal funds via state educational agencies (SEA's) to local educational agencies (LEA's), which in turn lend educational materials and equipment, such as library and media materials and computer software and hardware, to public and private elementary and secondary schools to implement "secular, neutral, and non-ideological" programs. The enrollment of each participating school determines the amount of Chapter 2 aid that it receives. In an average year, about 30% of Chapter 2 funds spent in Jefferson Parish, Louisiana, are allocated for private schools, most of which are Catholic or otherwise religiously affiliated. Respondents filed suit alleging, among other things, that Chapter 2, as applied in the parish, violated the First Amendment's Establishment Clause. Agreeing, the Chief Judge of the District Court held, under *Lemon* v. *Kurtzman,* that Chapter 2 had the primary effect of advancing religion because the materials and equipment loaned to the Catholic schools were direct aid and the schools were pervasively sectarian. He relied primarily on *Meek* v. *Pittenger* and *Wolman* v. *Walter,* in which programs providing many of the same sorts of materials and equipment as does Chapter 2 were struck down, even though programs providing for the loan of public school textbooks to religious schools were upheld. After the judge issued an order permanently excluding pervasively sectarian schools in the parish from receiving any Chapter 2 materials or equipment, he retired. Another judge then reversed that order, upholding Chapter 2 under, *inter alia, Zobrest* v. *Catalina Foothills School Dist.,* in which a public school district was allowed to provide a sign-language interpreter to a deaf student at a Catholic high school as part of a federal program for the disabled. While respondents' appeal was pending, this Court decided *Agostini* v. *Felton,* approving a program under Title I of the Elementary and Secondary Education Act of 1965 that provided public employees to teach remedial classes at religious and other private schools. Concluding that *Agostini* had neither directly overruled *Meek* and *Wolman* nor rejected their distinction between textbooks and other in-kind aid, the Fifth Circuit relied on those two cases to invalidate Chapter 2.

I Does a federal program, whose funds are used to loan educational material and equipment to public and private schools, including religious schools, violative of the Establishment Clause?

R A federal student aid funding program will not violate the Establishment Clause if (1) it does not result in religious indoctrination by the government; (2) define its recipients by religion; and (3) cannot be viewed as an endorsement of religion.

A Chapter 2, as applied in Jefferson Parish, is not a law respecting an establishment of religion simply because many of the private schools receiving Chapter 2 aid in the parish are religiously affiliated. In modifying the *Lemon* test - which asked whether a statute (1) has a secular purpose, (2) has a primary effect of advancing or inhibiting religion, or (3) creates an excessive entanglement between government and religion - *Agostini* examined only the first and second of those factors, recasting the entanglement inquiry as simply one criterion relevant to determining a statute's effect. The Court also acknowledged that its cases had pared somewhat the factors that could justify a finding of excessive entanglement. It then set out three primary criteria for determining a statute's effect: Government aid has the effect of advancing religion if it (1) results in governmental indoctrination, (2) defines its recipients by reference to religion, or (3) creates an excessive entanglement. In this case, the inquiry under *Agostini*'s purpose and effect test is a narrow one. Because the District Court's holding that Chapter 2 has a secular purpose is not challenged, only Chapter 2's effect need be considered. Further, in determining that effect, only the first two *Agostini* criteria need be considered, because the District Court's holding that Chapter 2 does not create an excessive entanglement is not challenged. Whether governmental aid to religious schools results in religious indoctrination ultimately depends on whether any indoctrination that occurs could reasonably be attributed to governmental action. As a way of assuring neutrality, the Court has repeatedly considered whether any governmental aid to a religious institution results from the genuinely independent and private choices of individual parents. *Agostini*'s second primary criterion - whether an aid program defines its recipients by reference to religion -is closely related to the first. It looks to the same facts as the neutrality inquiry, but uses those facts to answer a somewhat different question - whether the criteria for allocating the aid create a financial incentive to undertake religious indoctrination. Such an incentive is not present where the aid is allocated on the basis of neutral, secular criteria that neither favor nor disfavor religion, and is made available to both religious and secular beneficiaries on a nondiscriminatory basis. Two rules offered by respondents to govern the determination whether Chapter 2 has the effect of advancing religion are rejected. Respondents' chief argument - that direct, non-incidental aid to religious schools is always impermissible - is inconsistent with this Court's more recent cases. The purpose of the direct/indirect distinction is to present "subsidization" of religion, and the Court's more recent cases address this concern through the principle of private choice, as incorporated in the first *Agostini* criterion (*i.e.*, whether any indoctrination could be attributed to the government). Respondents' second argument - that provision to religious schools of aid that is divertible to religious use is always impermissible - is also inconsistent with the Court's more recent cases, particularly *Zobrest*, and *Witters* and is also unworkable. *Meek* and *Wolman,* on which respondents appear to rely for their divertibility rule, offer little, if any, support for their rule. The issue is not divertibility but whether the aid itself has an impermissible content. Where the aid would be suitable for use in a public school, it is also suitable for use in any private school. To the extent that *Meek* and *Wolman* conflict with the foregoing analysis, they are overruled.

C

Judgment reversed.